Lecture Notes in Computer Science 16368

The series Lecture Notes in Computer Science (LNCS), including its subseries Lecture Notes in Artificial Intelligence (LNAI) and Lecture Notes in Bioinformatics (LNBI), has established itself as a medium for the publication of new developments in computer science and information technology research, teaching, and education.

LNCS enjoys close cooperation with the computer science R & D community, the series counts many renowned academics among its volume editors and paper authors, and collaborates with prestigious societies. Its mission is to serve this international community by providing an invaluable service, mainly focused on the publication of conference and workshop proceedings and postproceedings. LNCS commenced publication in 1973.

Irfan Awan · Muhammad Younas ·
Yanchun Zhang · Mahmoud Barhamgi ·
Hua Wang
Editors

Web Information Systems Engineering – WISE 2025

26th International Conference, Marrakech, Morocco, December 15–17, 2025
Proceedings, Part II

Editors
Irfan Awan
University of Bradford
Bradford, UK

Muhammad Younas
Oxford Brookes University
Oxford, UK

Yanchun Zhang
Zhejiang Normal University
Jinhua, China

Mahmoud Barhamgi
Qatar University
Doha, Qatar

Hua Wang
Victoria University
Melbourne, VIC, Australia

ISSN 0302-9743 ISSN 1611-3349 (electronic)
Lecture Notes in Computer Science
ISBN 978-981-95-7250-2 ISBN 978-981-95-7251-9 (eBook)
https://doi.org/10.1007/978-981-95-7251-9

This Springer imprint is published by the registered company Springer Nature Singapore Pte Ltd.
The registered company address is: 152 Beach Road, #21-01/04 Gateway East, Singapore 189721, Singapore

Preface

Welcome to the 26th International Conference on Web Information Systems Engineering (WISE 2025). It is a great privilege to present the proceedings of WISE 2025, which was held in the historic city of Marrakech. Marrakech is a former imperial city and is still one of the economic and intellectual centres in Morocco. Historically, Morocco was one of the most intellectual centres in the world. The University of Al-Qarawiyyin was the first university in the history of humanity and still exists in the city of Fez. It was founded by an Arab lady, Fatima Al-Fihri, between 857 and 859.

WISE has been successfully running for more than two decades, and it has established itself as one of the top-tier conferences in the area of the World Wide Web. Research on the Web is highly dynamic and has continuously evolved since its invention in the late 1990s. Developments in the Web are driven by technological advances in both hardware and software, continuously opening up new directions and opportunities in various domains, including education, business, science, the public sector, and governmental organisations.

The WISE 2025 program committee put together an exciting technical program that brought together effective solutions, methods, and models that contribute to addressing critical research and development problems in the Web. The research papers covered interesting and timely work on state-of-the-art topics such as web applications and services, AI, machine learning, recommender systems, large language models, deep learning, networking, knowledge graphs, sentiment analysis, information retrieval, usability, HCI, and data management. In addition, the papers presented work on practical applications in supply chains, healthcare, finance, education, and social media, among others.

This year, the conference received 140 papers from authors from different countries. The review followed a single-blind review process. Each paper was reviewed by at least three reviewers. Based on the review, a total of 54 regular papers and 22 short papers were accepted for the final technical program. The acceptance rate was 38% for the regular submissions. The papers are presented in two proceedings volumes.

We sincerely appreciate the support of the international and local organising committee members in organising the conference. We extend our gratitude to the technical program committee members for providing constructive feedback to the authors. We are also thankful to all the authors for submitting quality papers to the conference. We truly appreciate the support of the Program Co-Chairs, Publication Co-Chairs, Publicity Co-Chairs, Workshop Co-Chairs, Web Chair, DEI Chair, and Local Organising Co-Chairs for their help and support throughout the conference. We sincerely thank the members of the senior program committee for their continuous support for the WISE conference series.

We are greatly indebted to our distinguished keynote speakers, Jie Lu (University of Technology Sydney), Yannis Ioannidis, (University of Athens), and Mounir Ghogho,

(University Mohammed VI Polytechnic) for delivering engaging and thought-provoking keynote talks.

Alongside the leading conference, WISE 2025 also featured international workshops, special topics, a PhD symposium, and a Demo and Poster track. The workshops included the International Workshop on LLM-Driven Agents (LLMA 2025) and the 7th International Symposium on Advanced Web and Mobile Applications (AWMA 2025). We greatly appreciate the efforts and contributions of the organising and program committee members of the international workshops, special topics, PhD symposium, and the Demo and Poster track. The papers accepted for these events will be published in a separate volume as the WISE 2025 Workshops series.

December 2025

Irfan Awan
Muhammad Younas
Yanchun Zhang
Mahmoud Barhamgi
Hua Wang

Organization

General Co-chairs

Yanchun Zhang	Zhejiang Normal University, China
Muhammad Younas	Oxford Brookes University, UK
Hua Wang	Victoria University, Australia

Program Co-chairs

Mahmoud Barhamgi	Qatar University, Qatar
Xin Wang	Tianjin University, China
Joe Tekli	Lebanese American University, Lebanon

Senior Program Committee

Qing Li	Hong Kong Polytechnic University, China
Xiaohua Jia	City University of Hong Kong, China
Elisa Bertino	Purdue University, USA
XiaoFang Zhou	Hong Kong University of Science and Technology, China

Local Organizing Co-chairs

Youssef Iraqi	University Mohammed VI Polytechnic, Morocco
Ismail Berrada	University Mohammed VI Polytechnic, Morocco
Loubna Mekouar	University Mohammed VI Polytechnic, Morocco
Jamal Bentahar	Khalifa University, UAE

Finance Co-chairs

Irfan Awan	University of Bradford, UK
Anitta P. Namanya	Broad Institute of MIT & Harvard, USA

Academia/Industry Relationships Chair

Hamad Al-Mohannadi	MoD, Qatar

Publication Chair

Irfan Awan	University of Bradford, UK

Workshops Co-chairs

Salima Benbernou	Université Paris Cité, France
Allel Hadjali	ENSMA, Poitiers, France

DEI Chair

Jinli Cao	La Trobe University, Australia

Publicity Co-chairs

Attila Kertesz	University of Szeged, Hungary
Ji Zhang	University of Southern Queensland, Australia
Meriyem Chergui	Hassan II University Casablanca, Morocco
Bohan Li	Nanjing University of Aeronautics and Astronautics, China

Web Chair

Fatima Zahrah	University of Bradford, UK

Program Committee

Abdelhak Belhi	Joaan Bin Jassim Academy for Defence Studies, Qatar
Abdelhak-Djamel Seriai	University of Montpellier, France
Abyayananda Maiti	Indian Institute of Technology Patna, India

Adam Wójtowicz	Poznań University of Economics and Business, Poland
Afonso Delerue Arriaga	University of Luxembourg, Luxembourg
Alessandro Campi	Politecnico di Milano, Italy
Alessandro Tundo	TU Wien, Austria
Alexander Knapp	Universität Augsburg, Germany
Alexandra Cristea	Durham University, UK
Alfredo Cuzzocrea	University of Calabria, Italy
Allel Hadjali	LIAS/ENSMA, France
Amirhossein Ghaffari	Oulu University, Finland
Andrés Rodríguez	Universidad Nacional de La Plata, Argentina
Aneesh Krishna	Curtin University, Australia
Aniello Castiglione	University of Salerno, Italy
Arash Mahboubi	Charles Sturt University, Australia
Armin Haller	Australian National University, Australia
Ashkan Sami	Edinburgh Napier University, UK
Aydin Abadi	Newcastle University, UK
Ayman El Hajjar	University of Westminster, UK
Azadeh Ghari Neiat	Deakin University, Australia
Barbara Catania	University of Genoa, Italy
Bin Cao	Zhejiang University of Technology, China
Boris Sedlak	TU Wien, Austria
Boualem Benatallah	University of New South Wales, Australia
Bernd Amann	Sorbonne Université, France
Bo Dang	San Francisco Bay University, USA
Bo Tang	Southern University of Science and Technology, China
Catarina Ferreira da Silva	Iscte, University Institute of Lisbon, Portugal
Catuscia Palamidessi	Inria, France
Cédric Eichler	INSA Val de Loire, France
Chaima Ben Rabah	AI Innovation Lab Weill Cornell Medicine, Qatar
Chamikara M. Arachchige	CSIRO, Australia
Chadni Islam	Queensland University of Technology, Australia
Chao Tong	Beihang University, China
Chaogang Tang	China University of Mining and Technology, China
Chen Wang	Huazhong University of Science & Technology, China
Chouki Tibermacine	University of Montpellier, France
Cindy Chen	University of Massachusetts Lowell, USA
Cinzia Cappiello	Politecnico di Milano, Italy
Conggai Li	CSIRO's Data61, Australia

Cynthia Marcelino	TU Wien, Austria
Damiano Distante	University of Rome Unitelma Sapienza, Italy
Dan Lin	Vanderbilt University, USA
Daniela Grigori	Université Paris-Dauphine PSL, France
Dario Colazzo	Université Paris-Dauphine PSL, France
Devis Bianchini	University of Brescia, Italy
Dimitri Theodoratos	New Jersey Institute of Technology, USA
Dimitris Kotzinos	CY Cergy Paris University, France
Dickson K. W. Chiu	University of Hong Kong, China
Dimitris Plexousakis	Institute of Computer Science, FORTH, Greece
Dimitrios Katsaros	University of Thessaly, Greece
Erisa Karafili	University of Southampton, UK
Esma Aïmeur	University of Montreal, Canada
Eleanna Kafeza	Technology Innovation Institute, UAE
Elio Masciari	University of Naples Federico II, Italy
Epaminondas Kapetanios	University of Hertfordshire, UK
Faheem Ullah	University of Adelaide, Australia
Fouzi Harrag	Ferhat Abbas Sétif1 University, Algeria
Flavius Frasincar	Erasmus University Rotterdam, Netherlands
Florence Sèdes	University of Toulouse, France
Francisco Jose D. Mayo	University of Seville, Spain
Francesco Marchiori	University of Padua, Italy
Gang Wang	Northeastern University, China
Garrison Gao	CSIRO's Data61, Australia
Gefei Zhang	Hochschule für Technik und Wirtschaft Berlin, Germany
George Papastefanatos	ATHENA Research Center, Greece
Georgia Kapitsaki	University of Cyprus, Cyprus
Georgios Kambourakis	University of the Aegean, Greece
Gorrab Abir	National School of Computer Science, Tunisia
Guanfeng Liu	Macquarie University, Australia
Guy-Vincent Jourdan	University of Ottawa, Canada
Hajer Baazaoui	CY Cergy Paris University, France
Haobing Liu	Ocean University of China, China
Hanchen Wang	University of Technology Sydney, Australia
Harsha Vasudev	University of Padua, Italy
Hassan Mehmood	Oulu University, Finland
Hayato Yamana	Waseda University, Japan
Heiko Schuldt	University of Basel, Switzerland
Hong-Tri Nguyen	Aalto University, Finland
Hossein Shirazi	San Diego State University, USA
Hongzhi Wang	Harbin Institute of Technology, China

Hong Va Leong	Hong Kong Polytechnic University, China
Huizi Yu	Amazon Science, USA
Imen Megdiche	University of Toulouse, France
Ismail Badache	Aix-Marseille Université, France
Jarogniew Rykowski	Poznań University of Economics, Poland
Jayamine Alupotha	University of Bern, Switzerland
Javier Luis Canovas Izquierdo	Universitat Oberta de Catalunya, Spain
Ji Zhang	University of Southern Queensland, Australia
Jiafan Wang	CSIRO's Data61, Australia
Jiaxin Li	University of Padua, Italy
Jide Edu	University of Strathclyde, UK
Jiefu Song	IRIT – Université Toulouse Capitole, France
Jinli Cao	La Trobe University, Australia
Jiujing Zhang	University of New South Wales, Australia
Joe Tekli	Lebanese American University, Lebanon
Jose Ignacio Panach Navarrete	Universitat de València, Spain
José María de Fuentes	Universidad Carlos III de Madrid, Spain
Junhu Wang	Griffith University, Australia
Julián Grigera	Universidad Nacional de La Plata, Argentina
Jürgen Ziegler	University of Duisburg-Essen, Germany
Kewen Liao	Australian Catholic University, Australia
Khouloud Boukadi	University of Sfax, Tunisia
Ladjel Bellatreche	LIAS/ENSMA, France
Laurent Bobelin	INSA Centre Val de Loire, France
Leong Hou U.	University of Macau, China
Liang Yuan	Swinburne University, Australia
Liu Peng	Singapore Management University, Singapore
Lizhen Wang	Yunnan University, China
Lizhou Fan	Harvard Medical School, USA
Lokesh Jain	Delhi Technological University, India
Lotenna Nwana	University of Arkansas at Little Rock, USA
Lucia Cascone	Università degli Studi di Salerno, Italy
Luciano Baresi	Politecnico di Milano, Italy
Manolis Gergatsoulis	Ionian University, Greece
Malik Khalfallah	Airbus, France
Marco Anisetti	Università degli Studi di Milano, Italy
Marco Winckler	Université Côte d'Azur, France
Marco Minici	University of Pisa, Italy
Marco Aiello	University of Stuttgart, Germany
Maria Malek	CY Cergy Paris University, France
Marinette Savonnet	University of Burgundy, France
Maristella Matera	Politecnico di Milano, Italy

Markel Vigo	University of Manchester, UK
Martin Weise	TU Wien, Austria
Maumita Bhattacharya	Charles Sturt University, Australia
Maurizio Leotta	Università di Genova, Italy
Michael Bewong	Charles Sturt University, Australia
Mingming Li	University of Chinese Academy of Sciences, China
Mitsunori Ogihara	University of Miami, USA
Mohamed Reda Bouadjenek	Deakin University, Australia
Mohamed Sellami	Télécom SudParis, France
Mohamed-Amine Baazizi	Sorbonne Université, France
Mourad Khayati	University of Fribourg, Switzerland
Muhammad Ali	Anglia Ruskin University, UK
Murali Mani	University of Michigan-Flint, USA
Mehmet Dalkilic	Indiana University, USA
Nathalie Moreno	Universidad de Málaga, Spain
Nawal Guermouche	INSA de Toulouse, France
Nicolas Anciaux	Inria, France
Nicola Zannone	Eindhoven University of Technology, Netherlands
Nora Faci	Université Lyon 1, France
Osama Almurshed	Cardiff University, UK
Peiquan Jin	University of Science and Technology of China, China
Peter Rønne	University of Luxembourg, Luxembourg
Qi Luo	University of New South Wales, Australia
Qiang Zhu	University of Michigan – Dearborn, USA
Qiang Ma	Kyoto University, Japan
Rafiqul Islam	Charles Sturt University, Australia
Romain Bourqui	University of Bordeaux, France
Roberto Metere	University of York, UK
Sajib Mistry	Curtin University, Australia
Saeid Hosseini	Sohar University, Oman
Sanjay Chaudhary	Ahmedabad University, India
Santiago Melia	Universidad de Alicante, Spain
Sandeep Kumar	Indian Institute of Technology Roorkee, India
Schahram Dustdar	Vienna University of Technology, Austria
Sebastian Link	University of Auckland, New Zealand
Sergio Ilarri	University of Zaragoza, Spain
Shaoyi Yin	University of Toulouse, France
Sharif Abuadbba	CSIRO's Data61, Australia
Shiting Wen	Zhejiang University, China
Shigang Liu	CSIRO's Data61, Australia

Silviu Maniu	Université Paris-Saclay, France
Slim Kallel	University of Sfax, Tunisia
Stefan Tai	TU Berlin, Germany
Stefano Cirillo	Università degli Studi di Salerno, Italy
Sven Groppe	University of Lübeck, Germany
Stéphane Jean	University of Poitiers, France
Syed Atif Moqurrab	University of Southampton, UK
Tanzima Hashem	Bangladesh University of Engineering & Technology, Bangladesh
Thomas Richter	Rhein-Waal University of Applied Sciences, Germany
Tomas Vitvar	Czech Technical University, Czech Republic
Tommaso Bianchi	University of Padua, Italy
Tooba Aamir	CSIRO's Data61, Australia
Toshiyuki Amagasa	University of Tsukuba, Japan
Tsz Nam-Chan	Shenzhen University, China
Venkata M. V. Gunturi	University of Hull, UK
Verena Kantere	University of Ottawa, Canada
Vianney Perchet	ENSAE & Criteo AI Lab, France
Victor Casamayor Pujol	TU Wien, Austria
Vitaliy Yakovyna	University of Warmia and Mazury in Olsztyn, Poland
Vincent Oria	New Jersey Institute of Technology, USA
Wafa Ben Slama Souei	University of Sousse, Tunisia
Wei Shen	Nankai University, China
Wenjie Zhang	University of New South Wales, Australia
Werner Retschitzegger	Johannes Kepler University Linz, Austria
Wieland Schwinger	Johannes Kepler University Linz, Austria
Xiang Lian	Kent State University, USA
Xiangmin Zhou	RMIT University, Australia
Xiaoyi Liu	Arizona State University, USA
Xiaohui Tao	University of Southern Queensland, Australia
Xiangyang Gou	Peking University, China
Xiaoye Miao	Zhejiang University, China
Xin Cao	University of New South Wales, Australia
Xun Yi	RMIT University, Australia
Xuhong Zhang	Indiana University, USA
Yain-Whar Si	University of Macau, China
Yicheng Feng	Chinese University of Hong Kong, China
Yixiang Fang	Chinese University of Hong Kong, China
Yiyi Tao	Peking University, China
Yijie Weng	University of Maryland, College Park, USA

Yilei Zhao	Zhejiang University, China
Yongfeng Ge	Victoria University, Australia
Yonghong Yu	Nanjing University of Posts and Telecommunications, China
Young-Gab Kim	Sejong University, South Korea
Yuting Wang	University of Michigan, USA
Zhao Li	Zhejiang University, China
Zhigao Zheng	Wuhan University, China
Zhisheng Huang	Vrije Universiteit Amsterdam, Netherlands
Zhizhong Wu	University of California, Berkeley, USA
Zichao Li	University of Waterloo, Canada
Nikolaos Polatidis	University of Brighton, UK

Contents

Route Optimisation and Networks

Large Language Models II

Knowledge Graphs II

Information Retrieval and Keywords

Graph Models and Methods

Human-Centred Applications and Services

Distributed Data and Code Generation

Recommender Systems II

A Multi-modal Short-Video Recommendation Method for Enhancing User Behaviors Based on Graph Contrastive Learning

Xingting Wen[1], Baojun Tian[1,3](✉), Jiandong Fang[2,3], Tiantian Liu[1], and Wangwang Zhang[2]

[1] College of Intelligent Science and Technology, Inner Mongolia University of Technology, Hohhot 010080, China
ngdtbj@126.com, 20231800134@imut.edu.cn

[2] College of Information Engineering, Inner Mongolia University of Technology, Hohhot 010080, China
fangjd@imut.edu.cn, 20221800111@imut.edu.cn

[3] Inner Mongolia Key Laboratory of Intelligent Perception and System Engineering, Hohhot 010080, China

Abstract. Although existing short video recommendation methods have explored user-video interaction behaviors, they still suffer from data sparsity and weak supervision signals due to the scarcity of single or partial multi-behavior data (e.g., views, likes, and favorites). Furthermore, heterogeneous noise across behavior types, particularly the significantly higher noise ratio in "view" interactions, severely degrades the accuracy of multi-behavior short video recommendation systems. Therefore, we propose MBGCL, a multi-modal short-video recommendation method for enhancing user behaviors based on graph contrastive learning, to address these limitations. Firstly, the various modal data (text, image, and video) of short videos are dynamically fused to obtain more accurate short video representations. Secondly, the self-supervised contrastive learning method is introduced to learn the features of nodes from the perspective of behaviors, solving the problems of data scarcity and weak supervision signals. Finally, to reduce the problem caused by behavior noise, the behavior subgraph enhanced contrastive learning is introduced to counteract the negative transfer effect of behavior noise on the recommendation results. Through a large number of experiments on three public datasets (TikTok, KuaiRand, and MicroLens-100K), it is proved that our proposed model significantly outperforms the baseline models.

Keywords: Short-video recommendation · Multi-modal fusion · Multi-behavior enhancement · Self-supervised contrastive learning

I. Awan et al. (Eds.): WISE 2025, LNCS 16368, pp. 3–16, 2026.
https://doi.org/10.1007/978-981-95-7251-9_1

1 Introduction

In short video recommendations, some studies have explored user-item multi-behavior interactions, but the contextual behaviors in user-short video interactions may lead to data sparsity due to their complexity [4,9]. Meanwhile, key multi-modal information is often overlooked, resulting in significant deviations in the learned representations, which ultimately leads to insufficiently accurate understanding of user interests [12]. Our solution to this issue is an interaction bipartite graph that integrates multi-modal features of short videos with multi-behavior characteristics of users. By introducing self-supervised contrastive learning in behavioral subgraphs, our method enables cross-behavior contrastive learning of node features from inter-behavior perspectives, mitigating over-reliance on single interaction signals and effectively resolving data sparsity challenges in short video recommendations.

While existing studies [17] predominantly rely on multi-behavior self-supervised learning to augment data volume, they often neglect the inherent behavioral noise introduced by such methods. We design an intra-behavior self-supervised learning framework that amplifies behavioral impacts through interaction pattern refinement within individual behavior sequences, thereby mitigating noise propagation while preserving authentic user preference signals.

In this paper, we propose MBGCL, a multi-modal short video recommendation method for enhancing user behaviors based on graph contrastive learning. Specifically, this paper first extracts textual, audio, and visual features of short videos along with users' behavioral features (browsing, liking, and bookmarking) to construct a user-video interaction graph. From behavioral perspectives, we apply contrastive learning to three behavioral subgraphs (browsing, liking, bookmarking) to derive node representations. For the browsing subgraph with higher noise ratios, we implement edge dropout augmentation during contrastive learning to counteract the negative transfer effects caused by heterogeneous noise distributions across behaviors. Finally, a rating prediction module leverages the refined representations to generate more accurate recommendations.

The main contributions of this paper lie in the following aspects:

(1) Constructs a heterogeneous interaction bipartite graph that integrates short videos' textual, audio, and visual features with users' behavioral characteristics (browsing, liking, and bookmarking). Through contrastive learning applied from inter-behavior perspectives across three behavioral subgraphs, we effectively address the data sparsity challenge in short video recommendations by learning robust node representations.

(2) To address the noise challenges inherent in users' multi-behavior interactions, this work proposes a novel framework that applies edge dropout augmentation to the noise-intensive browsing subgraph to generate two augmented views, while conducting cross-subgraph contrastive learning among the three behavioral subgraphs (browsing, liking, bookmarking). This dual mechanism effectively counteracts the negative transfer effects caused by heterogeneous noise distributions across behaviors, systematically mitigating noise propagation while preserving discriminative behavioral signals.

(3) Evaluated on three public benchmarks, our proposed MBGCL model showcases significant outperformance against leading baselines in the domain of multi-modal short-video recommendation.

2 Related Work

2.1 Short-Video Recommendation System Based on Self-supervised Contrastive Learning

Introducing self-supervised contrastive learning into video recommendation is a popular research direction [15]. The CMI model [6] enhances the user's historical interaction sequence through random sampling, but the multi-modal information of short-videos has not been fully utilized. However, multi-modal information is very important in accurately capturing user interests in actual recommendations. Zhao et al. [19] proposed a model named CLAS Rec for short video recommendation. Leveraging contrastive learning to reduce intrinsic noise in interaction embeddings, they employed dual contrastive encoders to synchronize the representations of semantically equivalent sequence pairs. The MMGCL model [14] generates negative samples by using modal edge discarding and modal masking enhancement techniques as well as perturbation strategies. However, it does not utilize other self-supervised information. We address the data sparsity issue in short video recommendations by constructing an interaction bipartite graph that fuses multi-modal features from short videos with multi-behavior features from users, and introducing self-supervised contrastive learning on behavioral subgraphs to enhance representation learning.

2.2 Multi-behavioral Recommendation System

So far, work in multi-behavior recommendation has predominantly centered on capturing the complex semantic relationships between various user interaction types [3,7,11]. The SINE model [8] improves short video recommendation performance by constructing a sub-interest sequence encoder to identify dominant sub-interests through positive and negative feedback, then integrating these sub-interests via a fusion prediction layer. Pan et al. [10] designed a multi-objective prediction component that explicitly models the interdependencies and distinctions between various goals in short-video recommendation, and developed a feedback-aware encoding module to precisely capture user behavioral preferences while incorporating contextual influences. Wu et al. [13] developed a multi-task learning model that integrates multiple user behavior-related tasks to uncover the latent relationships between diverse behaviors. To address the high noise ratio inherent in multi-behavior interactions, we propose a self-supervised intra-behavior learning framework that amplifies the discriminative signals of user behaviors while suppressing noise. This is achieved by leveraging contrastive learning to model intrinsic dependencies within behavioral sequences, thereby enhancing robustness against noisy interactions.

3 Methodology

3.1 Problem Statement

The MBGCL model leverages both multi-modal short video data and diverse user interactions to infer users' holistic preferences for recommendation. The user set and the short video set are respectively denoted as $\mathcal{U}(\mathrm{u} \in \mathcal{U})$ and $\mathcal{V}(v \in \mathcal{V})$, where $|\mathcal{U}|$ and $|\mathcal{V}|$ respectively represent the number of users and the number of short videos. The bipartite graph $\mathcal{G}$ based on the interaction between users and short videos contains three types of nodes: user node $\mathcal{U}$, short video node $\mathcal{V}$, and various types of edges, where edge set ε represents their different interactions. In a multi-behavior scenario with k types of interaction behaviors, the entire bipartite graph $\mathcal{G}$ can be divided into k behavior subgraphs $\{\mathcal{G}_1, \mathcal{G}_2, \ldots, \mathcal{G}_\mathrm{k}\}$ based on the differences in interaction behavior types. To reflect multi-behavior interaction data, a tensor $\mathrm{X} \epsilon \mathbf{R}^{|u| \times |\nu| \times \mathrm{K}}$ is defined here. If the individual element $\mathrm{x}_{\mathrm{u,v}}^{\mathrm{k}} \epsilon \mathrm{X}$ approaches 1, it indicates that user u interacts with item v under behavior k; otherwise, it approaches 0. In this article, project representatives are used as short videos, so projects and short videos are not distinguished.

Input: User multi-behavior interaction sequences and target short video multi-modal information.

Output: Use the objective function to predict the probability of users clicking on the target short video.

3.2 Overall Framework

This section presents the architecture of MBGCL, a graph contrastive learning-based method for multi-modal short-video recommendation that enhances user behavior modeling. It mainly consists of four parts: multi-modal feature fusion, multi-behavior self-supervised contrast module, behavior subgraph enhancement module, and rating prediction module. An overview of the MBGCL model's architecture is presented in Fig. 1.

3.3 Multi-modal Feature Fusion Module

Previously, a paper published by Zhang et al. [16] from our research group at the WISE 2024 Conference has already investigated the core points discussed in this section. Unlike the conventional practice of randomly initializing user and video embedding, in this study, we first complete the initialization operation by means of an embedding fusion layer, which fuses the corresponding multi-modal features of each. According to the specific types of different modal features, we adopted various methods to carry out the pre-training work of modal features in a targeted manner. For the image and text content of the video, this study directly adopts the currently most outstanding model (Bert Pre-Training of Image Transformers - 3, BEiT-3) [1] to accurately capture the features contained in different modalities. For audio data, we first use the FFmpeg tool to separate the audio tracks, and then extract audio features with the VGGish model [18]. After the

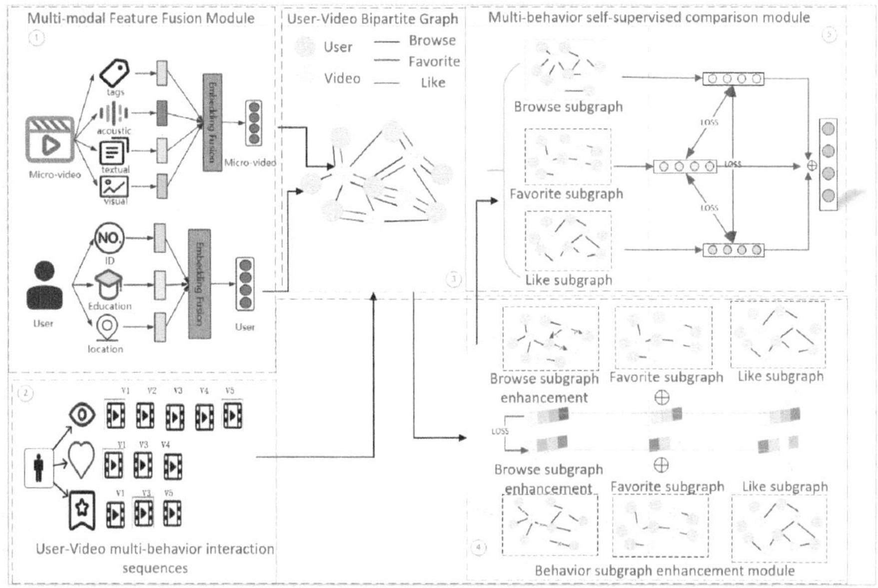

Fig. 1. MBGCL Framework Diagram

above series of operations, each feature of the short video will be mapped into the form of a low-dimensional vector. On this basis, we obtain the corresponding user or video embeddings by connecting and integrating various attribute features. The fused embedding of the short-video nodes is generated by a fully connected neural network:

$$X_v = W_v A_v + b \tag{1}$$

where W_V is the weight matrix in the fully connected neural network. Through the fully connected neural network, the text, image and audio features of short videos are weighted and concatenated, and the overall feature vector of the short video is finally obtained, denoted as X_ν.

The characteristics of users include three types: user ID, location, and educational background. Moreover, the fusion process of these three user features X_u is similar to that of the short video features X_v. In summary, the multi-modal feature fusion module provides robust data support for achieving precise personalized short video recommendations.

3.4 Multi-behavior Self-supervised Contrast Module

Considering the implicit relationships among different behaviors, this paper adopts the vanilla attention mechanism to effectively model the cross-behavior dependencies.

The embedding representation of user u under K behaviors is denoted as $\mathrm{e_u} \in \mathbf{R}^{\mathrm{K}\times \mathrm{d}}$, and then $\mathrm{a_{u,k}} \in \mathbf{R}^{\mathrm{K}}$ is calculated to represent the coefficient of the dependency relationship among the k different behaviors of user u.

$$a_{u,K} = softmax\left(\left(W_2^k\right)^T tanh\left(\left(e_u W_1^k\right)^T\right)\right) \quad (2)$$

Among them, $W_1^k \in \mathbf{R}^{d \times d'}$ and $W_2^k \in \mathbf{R}^{d'}$ are two parameters based on specific behaviors, and d' is the size of the output dimension. Therefore, the enhanced embedding representation of user u under k different behaviors can be calculated as:

$$\dot{e}_{u,k} = a_{u,K} e_u \quad (3)$$

The formula for calculating the embedding of all layers using mean pooling is as follows:

$$e_{u,K} = \frac{1}{L}\sum_{i=0}^{L-1} \dot{e}_{u,K}^{i} \quad (4)$$

where L is the number of embedding layers.

Single behavioral interaction suffers from the problem of data sparsity. This paper considers multiple behavioral supervision signals to effectively alleviate the impact of overly sparse interaction behavioral supervision signals. Meanwhile, to handle the noise caused by an excessive number of behavioral types, this paper adopts selective contrastive learning to transfer knowledge among multiple interaction behaviors, effectively dealing with the interference brought by multiple behaviors. The multi-behavior self-supervised contrast module is shown in the Fig. 2.

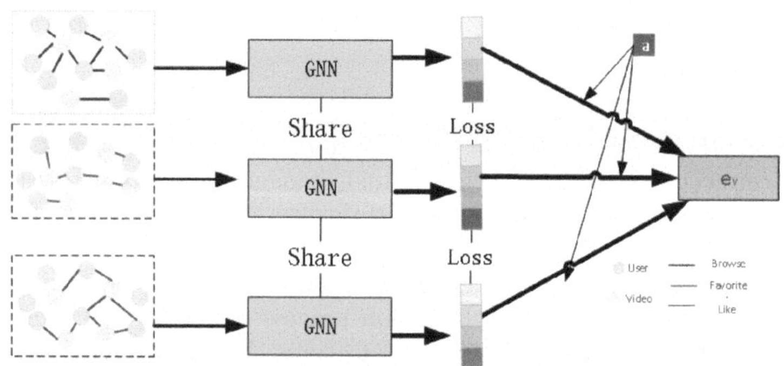

Fig. 2. Multi-behavior self-supervised graphs contrastive learning modules

Specifically, this paper conducts contrastive learning on the semantics of the behavioral subgraphs of two different behaviors, $k_o, k_p \epsilon k = \{1, 2, \ldots, K-1\}, k_o \neq k_p$. The common practice is to consider different views of the same node as positive pairs $\{(e_{u,k_o}, e_{u,k_p}) | u \epsilon \mathcal{U}\}$.

However, in such recommendation systems that involve various interaction behaviors, similar objects usually share certain commonalities, such as users having similar preferences or items having similar attributes. When constructing negative pairs using traditional methods, highly similar nodes may be introduced, which can reduce feature discrimination and affect model convergence. This results in the loss of genuine semantic information, thereby undermining the objective of contrastive learning. Therefore, to address this issue, this project utilizes the Swing algorithm [5] to identify potential false negatives by calculating similarity scores and filter them out when comparing positive and negative sample pairs, thereby eliminating their influence. In this way, relevant semantic information can be more accurately discovered and utilized. More specifically, the similarity score between two users in subgraph $\mathcal{G}_{\mathrm{k}}(\mathrm{k}\epsilon\{1,2,\ldots,\mathrm{K}\})$ is calculated using the Swing algorithm as follows:

$$\mathrm{S}_{\mathcal{G}_{\mathrm{k}}}(\mathrm{u}_1,\mathrm{u}_2)=\sum_{\mathrm{i}\in\mathrm{N}_{\mathrm{u}_1,\mathrm{k}}\cap\mathrm{N}_{\mathrm{u}_2,\mathrm{k}}}\ \sum_{\mathrm{j}\in\mathrm{N}_{\mathrm{u}_1,\mathrm{k}}\cap\mathrm{N}_{\mathrm{u}_2,\mathrm{k}}}\frac{1}{\alpha+|\mathrm{N}_{\mathrm{i},\mathrm{k}}\cap\mathrm{N}_{\mathrm{j},\mathrm{k}}|} \tag{5}$$

where, α is the smoothing coefficient, and $\mathcal{N}_{\mathrm{u}_1,\mathrm{k}}$ is the neighbor set of u_1 under the k-behavior. The final similarity score $\mathrm{S}(\mathrm{u}_1,\mathrm{u}_2)$ is the average of the scores in each subgraph, $\mathrm{S}_{\mathcal{G}_{\mathrm{k}}}(\mathrm{u}_1,\mathrm{u}_2)$.

Then, here the false negative of u is defined as the users with the top n similarity scores, $\mathrm{FN}(\mathrm{u})=\{\mathrm{u}|\mathrm{S}(\mathrm{u}_1,\mathrm{u}_2)\epsilon\ \mathrm{top}(\mathrm{S}(\mathrm{u}),\mathrm{N})\}$. Therefore, the contrastive loss for eliminating the specific false negative behavior k_0 and k_p is defined as:

$$\mathcal{L}_{\mathrm{ssl}_1,\mathrm{user}}^{\mathrm{k}_0,\mathrm{k}_p}=\sum_{\mathrm{u}_1\in\mathcal{U}}-\log\frac{\exp\left(\phi\left(\mathrm{e}_{\mathrm{u}_1,\mathrm{k}_0},\ \mathrm{e}_{\mathrm{u}_1,\mathrm{k}_p}\right)/\tau\right)}{\sum_{\mathrm{u}_2\in\mathcal{U}/\mathrm{FN}(\mathrm{u})}\exp\left(\phi\left(\mathrm{e}_{\mathrm{u}_1,\mathrm{k}_0},\ \mathrm{e}_{\mathrm{u}_2,\mathrm{k}_p}\right)/\tau\right)} \tag{6}$$

Therefore, the final contrastive loss between behaviors is half the sum of all the differences, that is:

$$\mathcal{L}_1=\frac{1}{2}\sum_{\mathrm{k}_o,\mathrm{k}_p\epsilon\mathrm{k},\ \mathrm{k}_o\neq\mathrm{k}_p}\mathcal{L}_{\mathrm{ssl}_1}^{\mathrm{k}_o,\mathrm{k}_p} \tag{7}$$

3.5 Behavior Subgraph Enhancement Module

Given that the proportion of noise is relatively high under certain types of (browsing) behaviors, more noise will be implicitly transferred to the feature learning process, leading to significant deviations in the representation and the loss of the intrinsic semantic association between the user and the behavior. Therefore, this paper constructs a behavior subgraph enhancement module, which utilizes a self-supervised contrastive learning method to generate structural enhancement views of the browsing behavior subgraph, as shown in the Fig. 3. In this way, the internal supervision signal of the behavior itself can be strengthened and highlighted to counteract the negative transfer effect of its noise distribution on learning.

Specifically, edge dropout is utilized to augment the graph data, generating two enhanced views $\mathcal{G}_{\mathrm{k}}^1$ and $\mathcal{G}_{\mathrm{k}}^2$ from the browsing behavior subgraph, that is:

$$\mathcal{G}_{\mathrm{k}}^1=(\mathcal{V}_{\mathrm{k}},\mathcal{M}_1\odot\mathcal{E}_{\mathrm{k}}),\mathcal{G}_{\mathrm{k}}^2=(\mathcal{V}_{\mathrm{k}},\mathcal{M}_2\odot\mathcal{E}_{\mathrm{k}}) \tag{8}$$

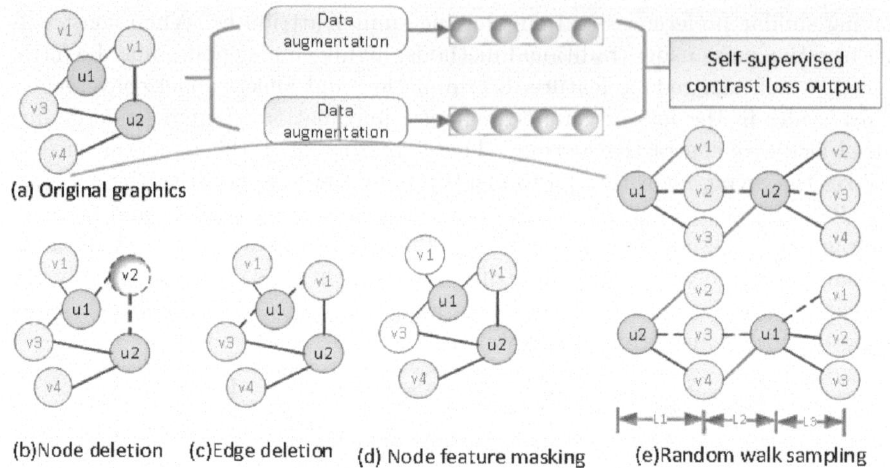

Fig. 3. Behavioral subgraph enhancement network module

Among them, M_1 and $\mathcal{M}_2 \epsilon \{0,1\}^{|\mathcal{E}_\mathrm{K}|}$ are two random masking vectors, which control the retained edge sets with the same dropout ratio ρ. After encoding the two enhanced views together with other behavioral subgraphs respectively, the node representations $\mathrm{e}^1_{\mathrm{u,k}}$ and $\mathrm{e}^2_{\mathrm{u,k}}$ of the enhanced views are obtained. Similar to before, then compare the two views of positive pair $\{(\mathrm{e}^1_{\mathrm{u,k}}, \mathrm{e}^2_{\mathrm{u,k}}) | \mathrm{u} \epsilon \mathcal{U}\}$ and negative pair $\left\{\left(\mathrm{e}^1_{\mathrm{u}_1,\mathrm{k}}, \mathrm{e}^2_{\mathrm{u}_2,\mathrm{k}}\right) | \mathrm{u}_1, \mathrm{u}_2 \epsilon \mathcal{U},\ \mathrm{u}_1 \neq \mathrm{u}_2\right\}$ at the node scale. The optimization objective is calculated through the InfoNCE function as follows:

$$\mathcal{L}_{\mathrm{ssl}_2,\mathrm{u}} = \sum_{\mathrm{u}_1 \in \mathcal{U}} -\log \frac{\exp\left(\phi(\mathrm{e}^1_{\mathrm{u}_1,\mathrm{K}}, \mathrm{e}^2_{\mathrm{u}_1,\mathrm{K}})/\tau\right)}{\sum_{\mathrm{u}_2 \in \mathcal{U}} \exp\left(\phi(\mathrm{e}^1_{\mathrm{u}_1,\mathrm{K}}, \mathrm{e}^2_{\mathrm{u}_2,\mathrm{K}})/\tau\right)} \tag{9}$$

Similarly, by combining the loss on the project side, the final objective function of the enhanced behavior subgraph is:

$$\mathcal{L}_2 = \mathcal{L}_{\mathrm{ssl}_2,\mathrm{u}} + \mathcal{L}_{\mathrm{ssl}_2,\mathrm{v}} \tag{10}$$

3.6 Loss Function

To optimize the model's prediction accuracy, we enhance the recommendation performance through a customized self-supervised contrastive learning task. The ultimate learning objective is the combination of the main supervised task loss and the SSL task loss, defined as:

$$\mathcal{L}^u_{rec} = -\alpha((y \log \hat{y}) + (1-y)\log(1-\hat{y})) + \beta\mathcal{L}_1 + \gamma\mathcal{L}_2 + \|\theta\|^2_2 \tag{11}$$

Here, λ represents the regularization term used to avoid overfitting, θ is the model's trainable weights, and α, β and γ are hyperparameters that balance the two parts of the loss function, used to control the intensity of the corresponding self-supervised contrastive learning tasks.

4 Experiments

4.1 Experimental Setting

Datasets. To evaluate our model, we conducted experiments on three public datasets: TikTok[1], KuaiRand[2], and MicroLens-100K[3]. Table 1 summarizes the characteristics of these datasets. To extract features, we used the pre-trained Beit model to obtain visual features from key frames and extract text features from descriptions. For acoustic information, we utilized FFmpeg to separate audio tracks and employed the VGGish model to learn acoustic deep features.

Table 1. Characteristics of the dataset

DataSet	Users	Item	Interaction	density	Behavior Type
KuaiRand	22611	329510	1664305	99.98%	Browse, like, favorite
TikTok	36656	76085	726065	99.99%	Browse, like, favorite
MicroLens-100K	100000	19738	719405	99.96%	Browse, like, favorite

Baselines. To evaluate the effectiveness of our model, we compare the model proposed in this paper with the following baselines: short video recommendation methods: D2Co [18], HHFAN [2]; short video recommendation methods based on contrastive learning: MMGCL [19], CMI [15], SINE [8].

Evaluation Metrics. The Area Under the Curve (AUC) is employed as the key evaluation metric to quantify the degree of separability. Additionally, in the short video prediction scenario, there are many multi-modal features of short videos and the behaviors of different users in browsing, liking, and collecting short videos are rather complex. To evaluate the performance of each model, we also use other evaluation metrics, including NDCG@K, P@K, and R@K. It is worth noting that larger AUC, NDCG@K, P@K, and R@K indicate better recommendation performance.

Parameter Settings. In the hyperparameter setting section, we applied grid search to find the best hyperparameters and selected the ones that performed best on the validation data. We used Xavier initialization to initialize the parameters. LeakyReLU was used as the activation function, and the model was optimized with Adam. For training, we used the Adam optimizer. We searched for the learning rate in 0.0001, 0.0005, 0.001, 0.005, 0.01, the batch size in 128, 256, 512, and the regularization coefficient in 0, 0.00001, 0.0001, 0.001, 0.01, 0.1.

[1] https://www.kaggle.com/datasets/yasaminjafarian/tiktokdataset.

[2] https://www.kuaishou.com/activity/.

[3] https://github.com/westlake-repl/MicroLens.

4.2 Overall Performance

As shown in Table 2, On all datasets, our model MBGCL consistently outperforms all baseline methods, demonstrating varying degrees of improvement across three evaluation metrics.

Table 2. Comparison of model performance

Dataset	Metrics	Model						%Improve
		D2Co	HHFAN	MMGCL	CMI	SINE	MBGCL	
KualRand	AUC	0.6530	<u>0.7644</u>	0.6545	0.6454	0.6362	**0.7893**	2.49%
	NDCG	0.5300	0.5323	0.5203	0.5624	<u>0.6196</u>	**0.6279**	0.83%
	R@10	0.3129	<u>0.4671</u>	0.3468	0.2723	0.2836	**0.4699**	0.28%
Tiktok	AUC	0.5560	<u>0.7001</u>	0.6065	0.6589	0.6609	**0.7207**	2.06%
	NDCG	0.5362	0.4697	0.4681	0.5371	<u>0.6253</u>	**0.6388**	1.35%
	R@10	0.3001	<u>0.4384</u>	0.2067	0.3838	0.3652	**0.4502**	1.18%
MicroLens-1	AUC	0.6560	0.7001	0.6925	<u>0.7033</u>	0.6565	**0.7364**	3.31%
	NDCG	0.5700	0.4595	0.3725	0.6284	<u>0.6752</u>	**0.6909**	1.57%
	R@10	0.3036	0.4279	<u>0.4943</u>	0.3256	0.3834	**0.5168**	2.25%

Through the analysis of the experimental results, three main reasons were identified: (1) The incorporation of multi-modal data enriches short video features, enables comprehensive feature mining, strengthens feature representation, and ultimately enhances recommendation performance. (2) By introducing a multi-behavior self-supervised graph contrastive learning module, this approach effectively addresses the sparsity issue of interaction behavior supervision signals.(3) By introducing a behavior subgraph enhancement module, this method effectively mitigates the interaction noise issue in user behaviors. Furthermore, it has been observed that some multi-behavior models underperform compared to single-behavior models on certain metrics. The primary reasons for this outcome may be their inability to effectively distinguish between different behavior types and the noisy interactions introduced by incorporating multiple behaviors. Through comparative experiments with baseline models, it is demonstrated that semantic contrast across multiple behaviors (e.g., clicks, likes, shares) provides richer supervision signals. Furthermore, multi-behavior subgraph contrast (e.g., likes vs. favorites) captures the intrinsic nature of user interests more effectively than single-modal view contrast.

4.3 Sensitivity Analysis of Model Parameters

The size of the ranking position K:

Figures 4, 5, and 6 illustrate the performance of the Top-K recommendation list across the three datasets, with the ranking threshold K varying from

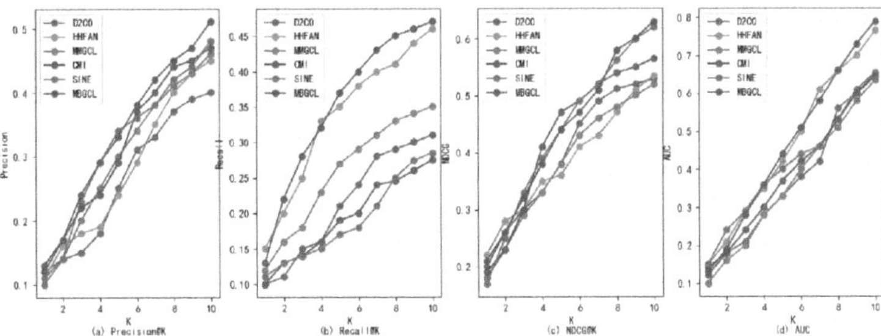

Fig. 4. Assessment of Top-K recommendation performance under settings where K varies from 1 to 10 on the KuaiRand dataset, $trainingrate = 0.8$

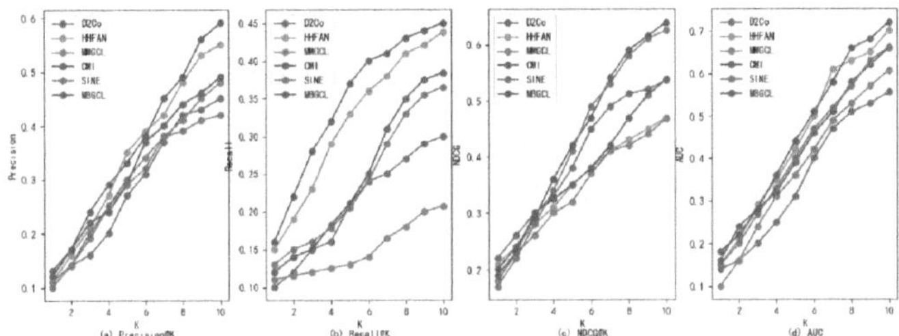

Fig. 5. Assessment of Top-K recommendation performance under settings where K varies from 1 to 10 on the Tiktok dataset, $trainingrate = 0.8$

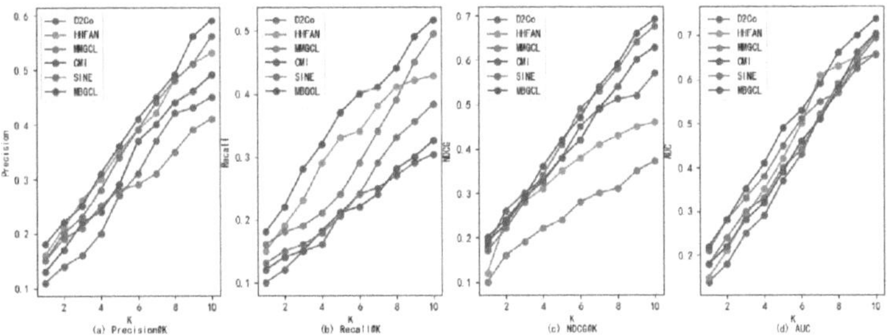

Fig. 6. Assessment of Top-K recommendation performance under settings where K varies from 1 to 10 on the MicroLens-100K dataset, $trainingrate = 0.8$

1 to 10. It can be seen that MBGCL consistently outperforms other methods across all ranking positions, underscoring the importance of modeling heterogeneous information—including diverse node types and relational structures—and demonstrating our model's enhanced representation learning capacity. Furthermore, compared to baseline methods, MBGCL exhibits more stable performance gains as K increases, indicating greater robustness in short-video recommendation. For clearer visualization, K is set to 10 in the presented results.

4.4 Ablation Experiment

The ablation study comprises the following variants: MBGCL/a: without introducing the multi-behavior self-supervised contrastive learning module; MBGCL/b: without introducing the behavior subgraph enhancement module; MBGCL/v: post-fusing multi-modal features and user behavior features (the method adopted in this paper belongs to the pre-fusion category).

Table 3. Performance comparison of ablation experiments

Data metrics	KuaiRand		TikTok		MicroLens - 100K	
	P@10	R@10	P@10	R@10	P@10	R@10
MBGCL/a	0.455	0.406	0.543	0.401	0.534	0.481
MBGCL/b	0.486	0.431	0.552	0.426	0.565	0.496
MBGCL/v	0.503	0.446	0.567	0.439	0.576	0.503
Ours	**0.516**	**0.469**	**0.583**	**0.450**	**0.593**	**0.517**

From Table 3, it can be observed that the self-attention mechanism has a strong ability to capture the latent dependencies across behaviors. Removing any part of the self-supervised contrastive learning will affect the experimental results. Specifically, the performance gap between MBGCL and MBGCL/a demonstrates the effectiveness of the multi-behavior self-supervised contrastive learning module in alleviating the data sparsity of the target behavior. The performance improvements achieved by the behavior subgraph enhancement module further validate the importance of addressing noisy interactions in multi-behavior data. Through MBGCL/v, it can be found that there is consistency between multi-modal and user behaviors in the recommendation process. Separately mining interests from multimodality and user multi-behaviors separates the consistency between user behaviors and item features, resulting in a decline in recommendation performance on both Precision and Recall metrics.

In conclusion, through the analysis of the ablation experiment results, it can be concluded that on the three public short video datasets, both the multi-modal information of short videos and the multi-behavior data of users are enriching the features of short videos. Merging them at the beginning of modeling will achieve better results. Secondly, there is a data sparsity problem in users' multiple interaction behaviors. When introducing multi-behavior, we not only need to perform data augmentation but also remove the noise inherent in the behaviors themselves.

5 Conclusion

In this paper, we introduced a novel multi-modal short video recommendation method for enhancing user behaviors based on graph contrastive learning

(MBGCL). This method optimizes the sparsity and noise issues of the behavior supervision signals in the existing short-video recommendation systems. Experimental results on three public short video datasets rigorously validate the effectiveness and robustness of our approach. In the future, we expect to establish a more stable position for self-supervised contrastive learning in recommendation tasks, fully exploiting the potential of self-supervised contrastive learning to address the long-tail problem.

Acknowledgments. This study was funded by the Natural Science Foundation of Inner Mongolia Autonomous Region, China (grant 2023LHMS06008) and the Science and Technology Plan Project of Inner Mongolia Autonomous Region, China (grant 2025KYPT0088).

Disclosure of Interests. The authors have no competing interests to declare that are relevant to the content of this article.

References

1. Bao, H., Dong, L., Piao, S., Wei, F.: Beit: Bert pre-training of image transformers. arXiv preprint arXiv:2106.08254 (2021)
2. Cai, D., Qian, S., Fang, Q., Xu, C.: Heterogeneous hierarchical feature aggregation network for personalized micro-video recommendation. IEEE Trans. Multimedia **24**, 805–818 (2021)
3. Chen, X., Li, Z., Pan, W., Ming, Z.: A survey on multi-behavior sequential recommendation. arXiv preprint arXiv:2308.15701 (2023)
4. Gu, P., Hu, H., Xu, G.: Modeling multi-behavior sequence via hypergru contrastive network for micro-video recommendation. Knowl.-Based Syst. **295**, 111841 (2024)
5. Huynh, T., Kornblith, S., Walter, M.R., Maire, M., Khademi, M.: Boosting contrastive self-supervised learning with false negative cancellation. In: Proceedings of the IEEE/CVF Winter Conference on Applications of Computer Vision, pp. 2785–2795 (2022)
6. Li, B., Jin, B., Song, J., Yu, Y., Zheng, Y., Zhou, W.: Improving micro-video recommendation via contrastive multiple interests. In: Proceedings of the 45th International ACM SIGIR Conference on Research and Development in Information Retrieval, pp. 2377–2381 (2022)
7. Liu, H., et al.: Modeling multi-aspect preferences and intents for multi-behavioral sequential recommendation. Knowl.-Based Syst. **280**, 111013 (2023)
8. Liu, K., Wang, J., Zhang, X.: Debiased momentum contrastive learning for multimodal video similarity measures. Neurocomputing **563**, 126938 (2024)
9. Liu, Y., Rao, Q., Pan, W., Ming, Z.: Variational collective graph autoencoder for multi-behavior recommendation. In: 2023 IEEE International Conference on Data Mining (ICDM), pp. 438–447. IEEE (2023)
10. Pan, Y., et al.: Learning and optimization of implicit negative feedback for industrial short-video recommender system. In: Proceedings of the 32nd ACM International Conference on Information and Knowledge Management, pp. 4787–4793 (2023)
11. Wang, F., Zhou, Y.: Personalized multi-behavior sequential recommendation with temporal-aware contrastive learning and self-attention. In: 2024 IEEE Smart World Congress (SWC), pp. 1554–1561. IEEE (2024)

12. Wei, W., Huang, C., Xia, L., Zhang, C.: Multi-modal self-supervised learning for recommendation. In: Proceedings of the ACM Web Conference 2023, pp. 790–800 (2023)
13. Wu, Y., Fu, R., Xing, T., Yu, Z., Yin, F.: A user behavior-aware multi-task learning model for enhanced short video recommendation. Neurocomputing **617**, 129076 (2025)
14. Yi, Z., Wang, X., Ounis, I., Macdonald, C.: Multi-modal graph contrastive learning for micro-video recommendation. In: Proceedings of the 45th International ACM SIGIR Conference on Research and Development in Information Retrieval, pp. 1807–1811 (2022)
15. Yu, L., Hu, J., Du, Q., Niu, X.: Mvideorec: micro video recommendations through modality decomposition and contrastive learning. ACM Trans. Inf. Syst. (2025)
16. Zhang, W., Tian, B., Wang, T., Yuan, L., Jiang, M.: Research on micro-videos recommendation method integrating multimodal data and user multi-behavior. In: International Conference on Web Information Systems Engineering, pp. 3–16. Springer (2024)
17. Zhang, Z., Zhang, J., Chen, J., Huang, Y., Huang, X.: Self-supervised enhancement method for multi-behavior session-based recommendation. IEEE Access (2024)
18. Zhao, H., Zhang, L., Xu, J., Cai, G., Dong, Z., Wen, J.R.: Uncovering user interest from biased and noised watch time in video recommendation. In: Proceedings of the 17th ACM Conference on Recommender Systems, pp. 528–539 (2023)
19. Zhao, R., Jin, B., Yu, Y., Li, B.: Denoising sequence embeddings via contrastive learning for micro-video recommendation. In: 2022 IEEE Smartworld, Ubiquitous Intelligence & Computing, Scalable Computing & Communications, Digital Twin, Privacy Computing, Metaverse, Autonomous & Trusted Vehicles (SmartWorld/UIC/ScalCom/DigitalTwin/PriComp/Meta), pp. 929–936. IEEE (2022)

Enhancing Multi-behavior Sequential Recommendation via Transformer-Based Cross-Layer Contrastive Learning

Lichang Zhao[1], Baojun Tian[1,3](✉), Tengjiao Wang[2], Jiandong Fang[2,3], and Pengyu Chen[1]

[1] College of Intelligent Science and Technology, Inner Mongolia University of Technology, Hohhot 010080, China
ngdtbj@126.com

[2] College of Information Engineering, Inner Mongolia University of Technology, Hohhot 010080, China
fangjd@imut.edu.cn

[3] Inner Mongolia Key Laboratory of Intelligent Perception and System Engineering, Hohhot 010080, China

Abstract. Multi-behavior sequential recommendation methods have surpassed the limitations of single-behavior sequence modeling by capturing diverse user interactions. However, existing approaches often rely on shallow, static feature extraction across behavior types, overlooking the rich dynamic semantics embedded in user interaction sequences. Furthermore, traditional data augmentation strategies are susceptible to random noise during auxiliary view construction, resulting in semantic incompleteness and representation sensitivity. To address these limitations, we propose A Multi-behavior Sequential Recommendation Framework with Transformer and Cross-layer Contrastive Learning (MST-CCL). Specifically, we first construct a heterogeneous item-behavior graph using users' multi-type interactions and contextual information. Next, we encode this graph via a graph attention network, where cross-layer contrastive learning simultaneously enforces noise robustness and semantic consistency alignment. Finally, a self-attention mechanism is employed to adaptively fuse users' temporal dynamics with multi-behavioral item relationships. Experimental results demonstrate that MST-CCL significantly outperforms state-of-the-art baselines on the Taobao and IJCAI datasets. Notably, our method achieves substantial improvements in Hit Rate (HR@10), with gains of +2.60% on Taobao and +2.10% on IJCAI, validating the effectiveness of cross-behavior signal mining and multi-view semantic alignment via contrastive learning.

Keywords: Sequential recommendation · Cross-layer contrastive learning · Multi-behavior · Transformer

I. Awan et al. (Eds.): WISE 2025, LNCS 16368, pp. 17–27, 2026.
https://doi.org/10.1007/978-981-95-7251-9_2

1 Introduction

Multi-behavior sequential recommendation systems leverage Transformer-based architectures (e.g., SGFormer [3]) to model user interaction sequences and address data sparsity. However, they often process behavior data in a simplistic way, missing dynamic semantic signals. Additionally, they suffer from noise effects, such as random clicks and node dropout strategies used in SimGCL [6].

Graph contrastive learning (GCL) improves semantic representations through multi-view contrastive tasks. For example, SGL [20] and SimGCL [6] enhance robustness with node dropout, DCCF [10] decouples user intentions for better feature extraction, SSGCL [11] uses dual-view contrast, SG-CLR [22] refines consistency, and DFGCL [7] boosts embedding diversity via feature fusion.

We propose a novel recommendation framework that combines a multi-scale temporal Transformer with contrastive learning. The temporal Transformer models time gaps between behaviors, enabling dynamic preference representation, while a hierarchical multi-view contrastive module refines item preference representations. Finally, a prediction layer generates accurate recommendations.

An earlier version of this work was presented at WISE 2024 [12]. Key enhancements in this version include: A hierarchical multi-view cross-layer contrastive model that integrates cross-layer and global contrastive strategies to improve semantic representations and reduce noise. The introduction of multi-relational edges in heterogeneous graphs, explicitly encoding item attribute similarities and spatiotemporal correlations, offering improvements over GAT-based models.

The main contributions are:

(1) A hierarchical cross-layer contrastive module that performs intra- and inter-layer semantic comparisons, achieving hierarchical aggregation and overcoming node-level contrastive learning limitations.
(2) A global multi-view contrastive module that separates noise (e.g., misclicks, structural dropout) and emphasizes stable associations, enhancing robustness in noisy settings.
(3) Extensive experiments on public datasets demonstrate superior performance compared to state-of-the-art methods.

2 Related Work

2.1 Multi-behavior Sequential Recommendation

Multi-behavior sequential recommendation improves user preference modeling by integrating various user interaction behaviors. MBSPRec [1] alleviates data sparsity by incorporating multi-behavior sequential patterns. MBHT [18] uses a user-behavior hypergraph to reveal high-order dependencies, and HEC-GCN [19] enhances multi-behavior modeling with a consistency alignment strategy. MLP-based models like MLP4Rec [5] improve efficiency and representation. To address these, we propose a cross-modal Transformer framework enhanced by multi-behavior temporal signals, incorporating dynamic intensity awareness and cross-behavior dependency modeling for better dynamic semantic representation.

2.2 Contrastive Learning for Recommendation

Contrastive learning has become an effective self-supervised approach to tackle data sparsity in recommendation systems by enhancing representation discriminability through data augmentation and mutual information maximization. Existing methods can be divided into two main directions: data augmentation-based contrastive learning and knowledge-aware contrastive learning. In the former, SubGCL [17] uses adaptive noise-resistant augmentation, DuoRec [9] applies model-level augmentation to prevent representation degradation, and MCLRec [8] leverages meta-learning for adaptive augmentation. ContrastVAE [13] combines multiple augmentation types, MC-CRS [21] utilizes knowledge graphs to improve semantic representation learning. However, these approaches often focus on single-level representations and struggle with capturing dynamic semantics and handling noise sensitivity in augmented views. This work introduces a multi-view cross-layer contrastive learning framework to address these issues, improving semantic representation and noise robustness.

3 Methodology

3.1 Problem Statement

Multi-behavior Interaction Sequence in sequential recommendation, let $u_i \in U$ denote a user ($|U| = I$) and $v_j \in V$ an item ($|V| = J$). For each user u_i, we define a multi-behavior interaction sequence:

$$S_i = [(v_{i,1}, t_{i,1}, b_{i,1}), \ldots, (v_{i,M}, t_{i,M}, b_{i,M})],$$

where $t_{i,m}$ is the interaction timestamp and $b_{i,m}$ denotes the behavior type (e.g., view, favorite, cart, or purchase). The sequence is ordered chronologically with length $M = |S_i|$.

We treat one behavior (e.g., purchase) as the target behavior to predict, and others as auxiliary signals to assist preference learning. The goal is to predict the next item $v_{i,M+1}$ the user is likely to interact with under the target behavior.

Input: A user u_i's multi-behavior interaction sequence S_i.
Output: A function that predicts the target item $v_{i,M+1}$ for user u_i.

3.2 Overall Framework

In this section, we introduce MST-CCL, a multi-behavior sequential recommendation model consisting of three components. The architecture of MST-CCL is shown in Fig. 1. First, the Multi-Scale Temporal Transformer (MSTT) models temporal dependencies among multi-behavior interactions, distinguishing users' short-term and long-term behavioral patterns. Second, the Multi-view Fusion with Cross-layer Contrastive Learning (MFCCL) captures semantic differences within individual behaviors and complementary signals across behaviors via a cross-layer contrastive mechanism and a global contrastive objective. Finally, the Prediction Layer integrates the sequential features and contrastive representations from multiple layers for accurate preference inference and recommendation.

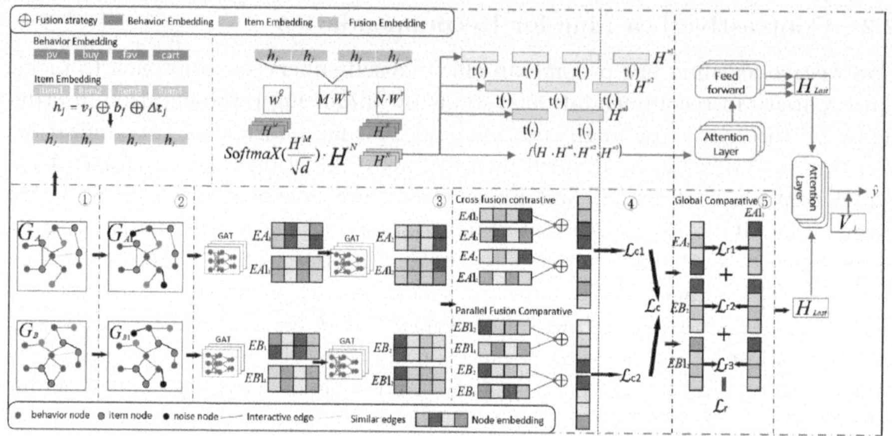

Fig. 1. Framework Diagram of MST-CCL Model.

3.3 Multi-view Heterogeneous Graph Construction

This paper proposes a dual-view heterogeneous graph framework that models user behaviors and item attributes. The Behavioral Similarity Graph captures interaction patterns, while the Attribute-Associated Graph encodes semantic relations based on category and temporal overlap. Item similarity is computed based on category and purchase time, with the overall similarity defined as a weighted sum of these factors. The model dynamically links items based on user behavior similarity, improving recommendation accuracy and diversity. A global temporal similarity score is computed by averaging item-pair weights per user and establishing item-item connections based on a similarity threshold.

3.4 View Augmentation

Random Edge Dropout. This work enhances the model by applying structural perturbation to the graph through random edge dropout, which reduces over-reliance on specific edges and improves training efficiency. The node representation update with dropout and residual connections is formulated as:

$$V_{i,l}^{(v)} = \sigma\left(\rho\left(\tilde{A}_{i,:}\right) \cdot E_{l-1}^{(v)}\right) + V_{i,l-1}^{(v)} \tag{1}$$

Here, $\rho(\cdot)$ denotes the edge dropping operation, and the residual connection preserves the original node information across layers.

Random Noise Injection. We apply uniform noise to the original representations as a data augmentation technique to regularize the embedding space and enhance representation consistency. The noise is added to the aggregated output at the l-th layer, and the process is described by the following equation:

$$e_j^{(v)} = \sum_{l=0}^{L} \mathrm{ReLU}\left(Z_{j,l}^{(v)} \cdot \alpha \cdot \frac{\Delta_v^l}{\max(\|\Delta_v^l\|_{p,\epsilon})} + e_{j,l-1}^{\prime(v)}\right) \tag{2}$$

Here, $Z_{j,l}^{(v)}$ is the input embedding at the l-th layer, Δ_v^l represents the noise vector, α is a learnable noise scaling parameter, and $e_{j,l-1}^{\prime(v)}$ denotes the previous layer's output. This formulation captures multi-level representations and incorporates residual connections for feature propagation.

3.5 Hierarchical Multi-view Fusion with Cross-Layer Contrastive Learning

To fully capture the shared hidden information across embeddings from different layers in multiple views, as well as to exploit the unique characteristics of neighborhood aggregation and view-specific augmentations, this paper employs a multi-view cross-layer approach. By leveraging hierarchical feature complementarity and deep fusion of multi-view representations, the method utilizes contrastive learning to effectively integrate embeddings across layers and views.

Multi-view Cross-Layer Contrastive Learning. Existing contrastive learning methods in sequential recommendation often overlook the hierarchical semantics captured by multi-layer GAT, limiting representation expressiveness. We propose a multi-view cross-layer contrastive learning framework that integrates representations across layers and views, enhancing semantic fusion.

We introduce view augmentation through edge dropout and noise injection, constructing behavior- and attribute-aware views. Cross-layer contrastive learning enforces consistency and captures complementary signals, improving robustness.

The InfoNCE loss is computed for embeddings $(Z1_{i,1}^{(u)} + Z2_{i,2}^{(u)})$ and $(Z2_{i,1}^{(u)} + Z1_{i,2}^{(u)})$ from cross-layer fusion, as shown in Eq. (3):

$$\mathcal{L}_{c1}^{(u)} = \sum_{i=0}^{l} -\log_a \frac{\exp\left(\frac{s\left(f_{\text{cross}}\left(Z1_{i,1}^{(u)}+Z2_{i,2}^{(u)}\right), f_{\text{cross}}\left(Z2_{i,1}^{(u)}+Z1_{i,2}^{(u)}\right)\right)}{\tau}\right)}{\sum_{l',v\in B}\exp\left(\frac{s\left(f_{\text{cross}}\left(Z1_{i,1}^{(u)}+Z2_{i,2}^{(u)}\right), f_{\text{cross}}\left(Z2_{i,1}^{(v)}+Z1_{i,2}^{(v)}\right)\right)}{\tau}\right)} \tag{3}$$

Parallel contrastive fusion at the same layer is used for embeddings $(Z_2^{(u)} + Z_1^{(u)})$ and $(Z_1^{(u)} + Z_2^{(u)})$, as shown in Eq. (4):

$$\mathcal{L}_{c2}^{(u)} = \sum_{i=0}^{l} -\log_a \frac{\exp\left(\frac{s\left(f_{\text{parallel}}\left(z1_{i,1}^{(u)}+z2_{i,1}^{(u)}\right), f_{\text{parallel}}\left(z1_{i,2}^{(u)}+z2_{i,2}^{(u)}\right)\right)}{\tau}\right)}{\sum_{i',v\in B}\exp\left(\frac{s\left(f_{\text{parallel}}\left(z1_{i,1}^{(u)}+z2_{i,1}^{(u)}\right), f_{\text{parallel}}\left(z1_{i,2}^{(v)}+z2_{i,2}^{(v)}\right)\right)}{\tau}\right)} \tag{4}$$

The total loss is the weighted sum of the cross-layer and parallel contrastive losses, as defined in Eq. (5):

$$\mathcal{L}_{\text{total}} = \mathcal{L}_{c1}^{(u)} + \mathcal{L}_{c2}^{(u)} \tag{5}$$

Global Multi-view Contrastive Learning. items are connected via different relational views. To enhance these views, the previous section introduced graph data augmentation techniques to generate diverse global views. Since each view carries distinct supervision signals, performing contrastive learning on item nodes across views helps the model better capture semantic differences and mitigate noise interference.

The original item-behavior graph is used as the primary target view G_A, while the augmented views generated through data augmentation serve as auxiliary target views G_B, where B is the number of auxiliary views. Each auxiliary view G_k, $k \in \{1, \ldots, B\}$ is individually contrasted with the primary view. Let h_i^K and h_j^K denote the representations of node i in the primary view and the k-th auxiliary view, respectively. The contrastive loss between these representations is calculated using the InfoNCE loss, as defined in Eq. (6).

$$\mathcal{L}_{(G_A,G_k)} = -\log_a \frac{\exp\left(\frac{s(\mathrm{h}_i^K,\mathrm{h}_j^k)}{\tau}\right)}{\sum_{j \in V} \exp\left(\frac{s(\mathrm{h}_i^K,\mathrm{h}_j^k)}{\tau}\right)} \tag{6}$$

Here, $s(\cdot)$ denotes cosine similarity, and h_i^K and h_j^K represent the embeddings of node i in the primary and the k-th auxiliary view, respectively.

The total loss is then obtained by summing the contrastive losses over all auxiliary views, as shown in Eq. (7).

$$\mathcal{L}_{total_2} = \sum_{k=1}^{B} \mathcal{L}_{(G_A,G_k)} \tag{7}$$

3.6 Prediction Layer

The model estimates the probability that the i-th item in the sequence corresponds to item v_j, as defined in Eq. (8):

$$y_{i,j} = r_i^T v_j \tag{8}$$

Here, v_j represents the feature embedding of item V_j, and $y_{i,j}$ is computed as the dot product between the representation r_i of the item at position iii and the embeddings v_j of all candidate items.

Finally, candidate items are ranked by their predicted scores $y_{i,j}$, with the top item selected as the recommendation. To enhance accuracy, the final training objective integrates contrastive loss from the representation module with the primary supervised loss, as defined in Eq. (9).

$$Loss = \sum_{i,j \in V} -\log\left(\frac{\exp(y_{i,j})}{\sum_{k \in V}\exp(y_{i,k})}\right) + \lambda(\mathcal{L}_{total_1} + \mathcal{L}_{total_2}) \tag{9}$$

4 Experimental Evaluation and Analysis

4.1 Datasets and Evaluation Metrics

We evaluate the proposed method on two public benchmark datasets: Taobao[1] and IJCAI[2]. The Taobao dataset, sourced from a widely used e-commerce platform, contains four user behavior types (View, Favorite, Cart, Buy). The IJCAI dataset, released by the IJCAI Challenge, shares identical behavior types with Taobao, where View denotes clicking to view items, Favorite represents adding items to favorites, Cart indicates adding items to shopping carts, and Buy refers to purchasing items (Table 1).

Table 1. Statistical Information of Experimental Datasets

Datasets	Users	Items	Interactions	Behavior Types	Average Length
Taobao	147,894	99,037	7,658,926	View, Favorite, Add to Cart, Purchase	48.23
IJCAI	423,423	874,328	36,222,123	View, Favorite, Add to Cart, Purchase	78.58

Evaluation and Parameter Settings. Experiments use a leave-one-out strategy, where the last purchase is the test sample, the penultimate one is for validation, and the remaining data is for training. Model performance is evaluated using Hit Rate (HR@N) and NDCG@N, with $N = \{5, 10\}$, where higher values indicate better performance.All models are implemented in PyTorch, trained for 20 epochs with five runs for stability. The batch size and learning rate are selected from {32, 64, 128, 256, 512} and {0.0001, 0.0005, 0.001, 0.005, 0.01}, with optimal values of 128 and 0.001, respectively. The user interaction sequence length is capped at 200, and the number of propagation layers in the graph neural network is set to 2.

4.2 Overall Performances

Table 2 presents the performance metrics of seven methods on two public benchmark datasets. The best and second-best results are highlighted in bold and underlined, respectively.

[1] https://tianchi.aliyun.com/dataset/dataDetail?dataId=649.

[2] https://tianchi.aliyun.com/dataset/42.

Baselines. Recent studies in multi-behavior recommendation have explored graph structures, contrastive learning, and multi-view modeling. LightGCN [2] simplifies GCN by removing feature transformation and activation to focus on neighborhood aggregation. SGL [15] applies graph data augmentation and contrastive learning to enhance node representation. MMCLR [9] introduces contrastive objectives in sequential and graph views to capture shared user preferences. CML [14] models behavior heterogeneity via inter-behavior contrastive learning and a meta-network. MB-GCN [4] encodes semantic relations through behavior-aware edge construction. MB-GMN [16] utilizes meta-learning to model behavior heterogeneity and cross-type dependencies. MBHT [18] employs a hypergraph-enhanced multi-scale Transformer to capture hierarchical and cross-behavior dependencies.

Table 2. Statistical Information of Experimental Datasets

Dataset	Taobao				IJCAI			
Method	HR@5	NDCG@5	HR@10	NDCG@10	HR@5	NDCG@5	HR@10	NDCG@10
LightGCN	0.191	0.157	0.243	0.186	0.198	0.183	0.264	0.244
MB-GCN	0.283	0.207	0.372	0.233	0.312	0.209	0.389	0.254
SGL	0.193	0.143	0.255	0.192	0.226	0.171	0.363	0.251
MMCLR	0.253	0.154	0.372	0.236	0.294	0.236	0.464	0.335
MBHT	0.423	0.364	0.505	0.392	0.446	0.371	0.533	0.407
MB-MSTI	<u>0.485</u>	<u>0.403</u>	<u>0.564</u>	<u>0.429</u>	<u>0.517</u>	<u>0.421</u>	<u>0.587</u>	<u>0.443</u>
CML	0.301	0.273	0.388	0.324	0.395	0.289	0.525	0.369
MB-GMN	0.341	0.216	0.472	0.302	0.391	0.317	0.461	0.374
MST-CCL	**0.511**	**0.414**	**0.577**	**0.444**	**0.539**	**0.437**	**0.601**	**0.467**
%Improve	2.60%	1.10%	1.30%	1.50%	2.10%	1.60%	1.40%	2.40%

Table 2 shows that MST-CCL consistently outperforms all baselines on two public datasets across four metrics, validating its effectiveness. The gains mainly stem from the MFCCL module, which leverages dual heterogeneous graphs and cross-layer/view contrastive learning to enhance item representations.

Multi-behavioral models also outperform traditional sequential and GNN-based methods. Among contrastive baselines, CML and MMCLR surpass SGL, highlighting the advantage of multi-view contrastive learning.

4.3 Model Parameter Sensitivity Analysis

To identify an optimal learning rate, the model is trained with values from 0.0001, 0.0005, 0.001, 0.005, 0.01. As shown in Fig. 2, a learning rate of 0.001 achieves the best performance on both the Taobao and IJCAI datasets, and is thus adopted for all experiments.

4.4 Ablation Experiment

To validate the effectiveness of the MFCCL module in the MST-CCL framework, we conduct ablation studies on two public datasets using three variants: MF/UI replaces the user-similarity-based heterogeneous graph with a standard item-behavior graph; MF/CT removes contextual similarities (category and time); MF/KL eliminates cross-layer contrastive learning. As shown in Table 3, MF/KL performs the worst, highlighting the importance of cross-layer contrastive learning in capturing multi-level semantics. MF/UI and MF/CT also degrade performance, demonstrating the value of incorporating user behavior and contextual attributes in heterogeneous graph construction.

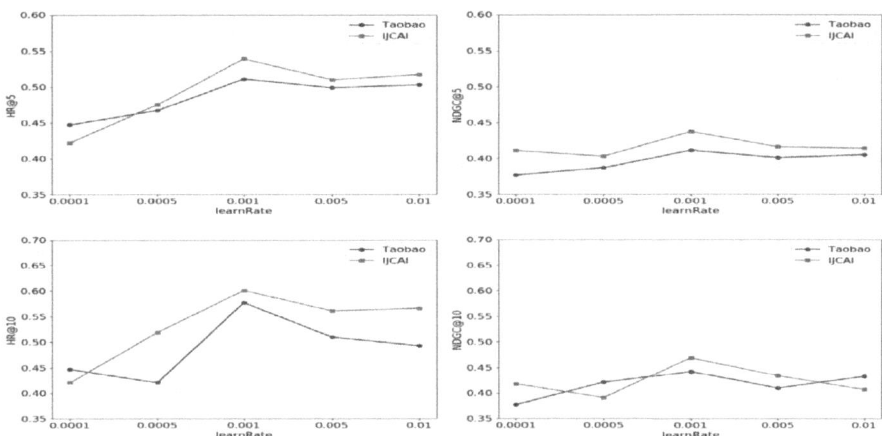

Fig. 2. Learning Rate Analysis Schematic Diagram

Table 3. Performance of the Ablation Experiment Model

Dataset	Taobao				IJCAI			
Method	HR@N		NDCG@N		HR@N		NDCG@N	
	5	10	5	10	5	10	5	10
MF/CT	0.477	0.506	0.368	0.374	0.475	0.537	0.382	0.413
MF/KL	0.455	0.472	0.356	0.367	0.471	0.545	0.379	0.397
Our	0.511	0.577	0.414	0.444	0.539	0.601	0.437	0.467

Overall, the results confirm the complementary roles of dual-view heterogeneous graph modeling and cross-layer contrastive learning in enhancing representation quality.

5 Conclusion

We propose MST-CCL, a hierarchical multi-view contrastive learning model for multi-behavior sequential recommendation. By leveraging a heterogeneous graph and contrastive learning, MST-CCL improves item representations, achieving 1.1%–2.6% gains on key metrics across Taobao and IJCAI datasets. Future work points toward multi-source integration, multimodal interpretability, real-time adaptation, and enhanced privacy.

Acknowledgments. This study was funded by the Natural Science Foundation of Inner Mongolia Autonomous Region, China (grant 2023LHMS06008) and the Science and Technology Plan Project of Inner Mongolia Autonomous Region, China (grant 2025KYPT0088).

Disclosure of Interests. The authors have no competing interests to declare that are relevant to the content of this article.

References

1. Bandreddy, S., Ezeife, C., Gidado, A.: Mining historical multi-behavior sequential patterns for e-commerce recommendation. In: International Conference on Information Integration and Web Intelligence, pp. 55–74. Springer (2025)
2. He, X., Deng, K., Wang, X., Li, Y., Zhang, Y., Wang, M.: Lightgcn: simplifying and powering graph convolution network for recommendation. In: Proceedings of the 43rd International ACM SIGIR Conference on Research and Development in Information Retrieval, pp. 639–648 (2020)
3. He, Z., et al.: A survey on user behavior modeling in recommender systems. arXiv preprint arXiv:2302.11087 (2023)
4. Jin, B., Gao, C., He, X., Jin, D., Li, Y.: Multi-behavior recommendation with graph convolutional networks. In: Proceedings of the 43rd International ACM SIGIR Conference on Research and Development in Information Retrieval, pp. 659–668 (2020)
5. Li, M., Zhao, X., Lyu, C., Zhao, M., Wu, R., Guo, R.: Mlp4rec: a pure MLP architecture for sequential recommendations. arXiv preprint arXiv:2204.11510 (2022)
6. Liu, C., Yu, C., Gui, N., Yu, Z., Deng, S.: Simgcl: graph contrastive learning by finding homophily in heterophily. Knowl. Inf. Syst. **66**(3), 2089–2114 (2024)
7. Liu, Y.S., et al.: Data augmentation and feature fusion to improve graph contrastive learning for recommender systems. In: 2024 International Conference on Wavelet Analysis and Pattern Recognition (ICWAPR), pp. 1–6. IEEE (2024)
8. Qin, X., et al.: Meta-optimized contrastive learning for sequential recommendation. In: Proceedings of the 46th International ACM SIGIR Conference on Research and Development in Information Retrieval, pp. 89–98 (2023)
9. Qiu, R., Huang, Z., Yin, H., Wang, Z.: Contrastive learning for representation degeneration problem in sequential recommendation. In: Proceedings of the Fifteenth ACM International Conference on Web Search and Data Mining, pp. 813–823 (2022)
10. Ren, X., Xia, L., Zhao, J., Yin, D., Huang, C.: Disentangled contrastive collaborative filtering. In: Proceedings of the 46th International ACM SIGIR Conference on Research and Development in Information Retrieval, pp. 1137–1146 (2023)

11. Tu, L., Meng, S., Liu, X., Liu, G., Beheshti, A., Zhang, X.: Semantic similarity-based graph contrastive learning for recommender system. In: International Conference on Web Information Systems Engineering, pp. 17–31. Springer (2024)
12. Wang, T., Tian, B., Zhang, W., Yuan, L., Jiang, M.: The research of sequence recommendation method based on heterogeneous enhanced transformer with multi-behavior data. In: International Conference on Web Information Systems Engineering, pp. 148–163. Springer (2024)
13. Wang, Y., Zhang, H., Liu, Z., Yang, L., Yu, P.S.: Contrastvae: contrastive variational autoencoder for sequential recommendation. In: Proceedings of the 31st ACM International Conference on Information & Knowledge Management, pp. 2056–2066 (2022)
14. Wei, W., Huang, C., Xia, L., Xu, Y., Zhao, J., Yin, D.: Contrastive meta learning with behavior multiplicity for recommendation. In: Proceedings of the Fifteenth ACM International Conference on Web Search and Data Mining, pp. 1120–1128 (2022)
15. Wu, J., et al.: Self-supervised graph learning for recommendation. In: Proceedings of the 44th International ACM SIGIR Conference on Research and Development in Information Retrieval, pp. 726–735 (2021)
16. Xia, L., Xu, Y., Huang, C., Dai, P., Bo, L.: Graph meta network for multi-behavior recommendation. In: Proceedings of the 44th International ACM SIGIR Conference on Research and Development in Information Retrieval, pp. 757–766 (2021)
17. Yang, Y., Guan, S., Wen, X.: Enhancing robustness in implicit feedback recommender systems with subgraph contrastive learning. Inf. Process. Manag. **62**(1), 103962 (2025)
18. Yang, Y., Huang, C., Xia, L., Liang, Y., Yu, Y., Li, C.: Multi-behavior hypergraph-enhanced transformer for sequential recommendation. In: Proceedings of the 28th ACM SIGKDD Conference on Knowledge Discovery and Data Mining, pp. 2263–2274 (2022)
19. Yin, Y., et al.: HEC-GCN: hypergraph enhanced cascading graph convolution network for multi-behavior recommendation. arXiv preprint arXiv:2412.14476 (2024)
20. Yu, J., Yin, H., Xia, X., Chen, T., Cui, L., Nguyen, Q.V.H.: Are graph augmentations necessary? In: Proceedings of the 45th International ACM SIGIR Conference on Research and Development in Information Retrieval, pp. 1294–1303. ACM (2022)
21. Yuan, W., Yang, C., Qu, L., Ye, G., Nguyen, Q.V.H., Yin, H.: Robust federated contrastive recommender system against targeted model poisoning attack. SCIENCE CHINA Inf. Sci. **68**(4), 1–16 (2025)
22. Zhang, Y., Zhu, J., Zhang, Y., Zhu, Y., Zhou, J., Xie, Y.: Social-aware graph contrastive learning for recommender systems. Appl. Soft Comput. **158**, 111558 (2024)

Meta-User2Vec: Recommendations Based on Embeddings for Users and Products Using Meta-data

Daan G. H. Wassenberg[1], Flavius Frasincar[1], and Tarmo Robal[2(✉)]

[1] Erasmus University Rotterdam, Burgemeester Oudlaan 50, 3062 PA Rotterdam, The Netherlands
456231dw@student.eur.nl, frasincar@ese.eur.nl

[2] Tallinn University of Technology, Ehitajate tee 5, 19086 Tallinn, Estonia
tarmo.robal@taltech.ee

Abstract. A good recommender system can enhance sales both offline and on the Web, while lowering maintenance and labour costs. Recent research shows that hybrid recommender systems, built on memory-based and knowledge-based techniques, deliver good results. Hybrid recommender systems leverage strong predicting power both for existing users as well as for new users, making these methods useful for a wide range of applications. In this paper, we use a Natural Language Processing (NLP) embedding technique word2vec in the context of sequential sales data, incorporating meta-data from multiple sources. We extend the Meta-Prod2vec method with jointly trained embeddings for users and related meta-data. The embeddings are made on a unique dataset representing sequential sales and website behaviour data in multiple European countries. The embeddings and features are concatenated and fed to a Neural Network (NN) to model consumers' behaviour. The proposed Meta-User2vec method, which advantages from both product and user meta-data, outperforms existing methods Meta-Prod2vec and user2vec.

Keywords: Product Recommendation · word2vec · Hybrid Recommender System

1 Introduction

Consumer behaviour has been an interest of research for decades. The prediction of consumer behaviour includes recommender systems (RS), often designed to provide personal recommendations, e.g., news [4,12], suitable products in e-shop environments [24], but could bring high value also to business-to-business (B2B) operations, where the data used for predictions is of high volume, covering several regions or countries, customer sales history, Web shop tracking data, etc. Automated prediction systems would improve accuracy, save time and money, uncover hidden patterns, and enable frequent reruns (e.g., daily). Artificial Intelligence (AI) techniques can help to leverage large amounts of data, representing users as low-dimensional real-valued vectors, called embeddings [14], to be

I. Awan et al. (Eds.): WISE 2025, LNCS 16368, pp. 28–38, 2026.
https://doi.org/10.1007/978-981-95-7251-9_3

trained on purchase history and views of product pages. Similar to the Natural Language Processing (NLP) method *word2vec* [15,16], representations for products and users can be made as product2vec or user2vec, where similar products or users are expected to also be close to each other in the embedding space [10]. The embeddings for products are trained by using the products that are bought together or just before/after as context words. Closely related products or users can thus be defined as frequently appearing together in shopping baskets. This is a Collaborative Filtering (CF) technique, where the user-item interactions in historic data are leveraged. CF is known for very high predicting power. Still, as it only leverages historic data, CF suffers from a cold start problem [17,29], and thus does not perform well for new customers or products for which historic data does not exist yet. This is in contrast to Content-Based (CB) methods that use extensive meta-data for products and/or users to make recommendations.

In this paper, we focus on predicting the behaviour of existing and potential new users, where the users of interest are businesses in the catering industry (e.g., bars, restaurants, hotels), and propose a hybrid Meta-User2vec method combining CF and CB models to enhance product representations and solve an industry problem. We use a unique dataset from a global consumer goods company specialised in the catering industry. The aim of prediction is to identify the next most likely purchased product and use it for personalized targeting, e.g., via sales visits, Web shop recommendations, or email campaigns, and through this boost sales, and reduce costs to meet sales targets. In the hybrid approach, user embeddings are designed using both CF and CB, trained separately, and concatenated afterwards. For the CF technique, user embeddings can be trained alongside product embeddings based on the sequential product or page view data, capturing the global context of the user. Conversely, the CB representations of products can be made by using product-specific data (e.g., ingredients, nutrients), and of user features (e.g., geographic location, business type).

The proposed Meta-User2vec combines the jointly trained product and user embeddings with the product characteristics by adding CB embeddings for users as well as for products. The CB user embeddings are trained using features from various open-source data platforms and Google Places to capture features for the area around the user (e.g., population, population age, number of facilities, urbanisation level). Thus, the final model is based on four things – CF and CB for both products and users – and combines the high predictive power of CF with enhanced meta data for products and users. This also solves the cold start problem, enabling to target new users with high potential. To the best of our knowledge, this combination of a hybrid model for both users and products, has not been used in literature before. The research question that we answer is: *Does a hybrid method combining CB and CF methods for both products and users provide enhanced product recommendations compared to non-hybrid variants?*

The rest of this paper is organized as follows. Section 2 discusses the related work, Sect. 3 the used data, Sect. 4 explains the methodology and Sect. 5 provides its evaluation. Last, Sect. 6 draws conclusions.

2 Related Work

Research on RS is divided in CB methods, which use extensive data on products (e.g., category, ingredients, price), or consumers (e.g., age, income, brand loyalty), and CF methods that employ user-item or item-item interactions (e.g., views, clicks, purchases) and do not require domain knowledge. Yet, CF methods suffer from cold-start problem, which CB methods avoid.

NLP embedding techniques, such as word2vec [15,16] and its variants [10, 21,23], provide low-dimensional embeddings [14,19] for sequential data in CF. A simple way to reveal the meaning of text in NLP, and make it readable for algorithms is one-hot encoding [11]. However, this technique is incapable to learn semantic relationships, which can be captured with word embeddings [19]. These embeddings can be trained on a large corpus of data resulting in closely related embeddings for terms that are semantically close (e.g., synonyms). Widely used word embedding techniques are word2vec [15,16], GloVe [21], and FastText [3]. Doc2vec [13] extends word2vec by enabling to capture entire document into a single vector. ELMo [22] and BERT [7] are the recent embedding methods used for NLP but as they focus on word embeddings and do not adapt well to other sequential data, such as sales data of interest in this research, we exclude them. The use of word2vec extends beyond NLP, e.g., recommending Tumblr blogs [27], predicting venues [20], recommending top N products [18], improving purchase prediction [9], or recommendations in e-commerce [10,28]. Item2vec [1] is based on word2vec Skip-Gram and Negative Sampling for item-based CF RS. Grbovic et al. [10] proposed the first product RS based on word2vec – product2vec, which analysed the co-occurrences of products in shopping baskets, and [23] extended this with a user2vec, where the model predicts the most probable product based on embeddings for both product and user, showing the potential the inclusion of additional product or user characteristics holds, which we also want to explore.

Hybrid RS combine the predicting power of CF and extend this with additional CB data, solving the cold start problem [5,25]. Combining CF methods product2vec and user2vec with CB could advance the results and prevent the cold start problem, as domain-specific data is added. Djuric et al. [8] extended [10] by adding meta-data. The proposed model is more like doc2vec [13], where embeddings for documents are learned together with embeddings for words, and a layer of user information is added. Meta-prod2vec hybrid method [28] trains low dimensional embeddings for items based on local product co-occurrence information on product sequences and adds meta-data for products (i.e., the characteristics of products) for recommendations. In [17], also a Meta-User2vec approach is proposed with a focus on complete cold-start problem, where users and items with unknown history are modelled based on meta-data. In comparison, we focus at improvement gained by inclusion of meta-data.

In hybrid methods [8,28], product characteristics are added to enhance the CF techniques with a CB part. Our proposed Meta-User2Vec uses trained embeddings for products and users together with user and product-specific features as a combined input.

3 Data

We use a unique dataset from a fast-moving consumer goods company in the catering industry, and combine several sources of data as follows. For products and user on CF, we use sales data (shopping baskets of products) and website tracking data (product pages visited) as features. These are extended with CB input data on users (customer type, location, population age, urbanisation level, number of businesses close by), and on products (ingredients, nutrients, brand, recipe links) to predict the propensity to buy or the affinity to click. We used proprietary data as we are not aware of an existing open dataset combining such data. Due to its sensitivity, this multi-faceted data cannot be made public.

For testing, the last 3 shopping baskets are selected, leaving all other earlier purchases as training data. From this training data, the last 2 shopping baskets are taken for validation during the training of the methods. Overall, the split into train:validation:test is 75%:11%:14%. The sales and website data is filtered to remove users (46%) who have less than 10 distinct shopping baskets or who have bought less than 10 distinct products, as this data provides little value.

The sequential sales and website tracking data offer strong predictive power for user behaviour, as they contain user actions, i.e., purchases or clicks on product pages. The sales data comprises 5% Direct Sales Data (DSD) via the website known directly for all purchases on a temporal granular level, and 95% Secondary Sales Data (SSD) provided by retailers, not always available on a granular level. The data covers 85 million data points (Table 1) on sales of consumer goods to consumers in catering industry since 2015. The SSD sales data contains product ID, buyer ID, time-frame, and at times price and quantity. As there is no unique consumer ID over all retailers, consumers in the data are matched using fuzzy match on address and name. The more detailed DSD data includes user-specific features like page views, clicks, source of user (e.g., ads), with website tracking data (e.g., viewed pages, time spent on website, etc.) collected with Google Analytics. This sales and online data is used to build product- and user-specific features. For users, this includes the number of products, shopping baskets, brands, categories, and re-orders over the past 30, 60, and 90 days; for products, counts of users, orders, and re-orders over the same periods. For online data, clicks are used instead of purchases.

For the CB part, the product data consists of product characteristics (e.g., ingredients), and for users open-source data from Open Street maps, Worldpop.org, and the European Eurostat database, providing demographic data and points of interest (POI) for areas. In addition, Google Places data (not open-source and costly to extract) is used for detailed information on POIs in the catering industry (e.g., restaurants, bars, schools, hospitals, hotels) via the Google API.

The training data is of high volume and the models computationally intensive, so they are run on Amazon cloud using distributed computing with Apache Spark, where a driver allocates jobs across multiple workers. The implementation is written in PySpark.

Table 1. Descriptive statistics for sales and online data.

		AT	BE	FR	DE	NL
Sales data	# Sold products ($*10^6$)	4.3	3.1	1.0	4.0	1.2
	# Shopping baskets ($*10^5$)	4.4	3.5	0.6	3.5	1.2
	# Unique users ($*10^4$)	1.3	1.2	0.8	1.1	0.5
	# Unique products ($*10^2$)	6.0	4.0	3.6	7.2	4.2
	$\#_{max}$ Baskets per consumer ($*10^2$)	3.8	3.8	2.0	3.6	3.1
Online data	# Visited pages ($*10^6$)	4.1	9.5	3.6	12.0	6.2
	# Online sessions ($*10^5$)	4.0	8.6	4.0	13.0	8.3
	# Unique users ($*10^3$)	1.7	4.0	2.1	4.0	4.0
	# Unique products ($*10^2$)	6.0	4.1	3.6	7.2	4.6
	$\#_{max}$ Online sessions per consumer ($*10^3$)	1.3	1.3	2.9	2.8	2.0

4 Methodology

We use word2vec to learn product, basket, and user representations, then apply a NN to train product and user embeddings combined with their specific features. For word2vec, two model architectures exist [15,16]: Continuous Bag-Of-Words (CBOW), predicting a word from its context, and Skip-Gram (SG), predicting context from a given word. The model is trained using a Negative-Sampling (NS) technique, as computationally less heavy objective function for optimisation. We compare the performance of SG against CBOW, and NS against hierarchical softmax. These hyperparameters, along with embedding size and learning rate α, are optimised using hit rate in a masked product task.

As we adapt word2vec and doc2vec to products and users, we refer to these as product2vec and user2vec. Product2vec models sequences of products viewed or bought together. While for words the exact order matters, with products presence in a shopping basket is important and the order may be random. Like word2vec, the model maximizes products frequently bought together and minimizes those rarely bought, resulting in real-valued feature vectors. Product vectors are trained using SG and NS, where SG predicts context products in the shopping basket using the target product (Fig. 1a). With CBOW, the input and output are turned around (Fig. 1b), and the embeddings are trained by predicting the target products by the context products. Sales and website data yield two separate embeddings: products from sequential sales and product pages from website tracking data. As with text, embeddings close in space are semantically related – here meaning products are frequently bought/viewed together.

For CF embedding for users, product2vec is extended like doc2vec extends word2vec [13]: for each basket of sales or page visits a $user_{id}$ is added (Fig. 1) and included in SG or CBOW training, allowing product and user representations to influence each other. User identifier is added to all orders, capturing all user information in one representation, and trained jointly with product embeddings. Like prod2vec, user2vec also learns product vectors, which remain largely similar.

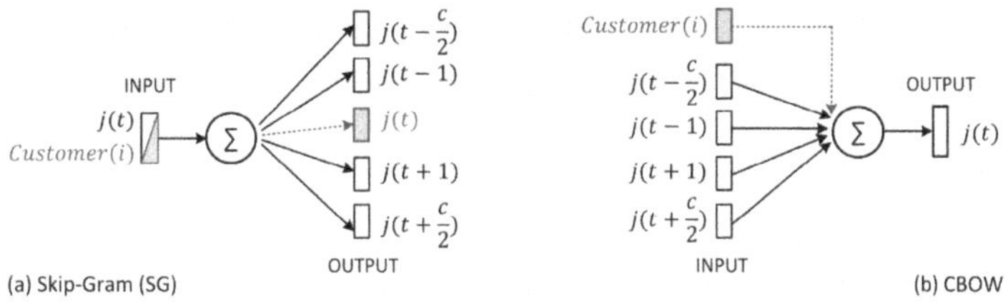

Fig. 1. Possible architectures to train embeddings for product2vec (in black), with products j instead of words, $j(t)$ the target product, Σ the hidden layer of the NN used in the word2vec methodology, and c shopping basket size. In blue are indicated changes when adding $user_{id}$ for product embedding training (doc2vec like approach) for user2vec; with the input for SG being $Customer(i)$ instead of $j(t)$.

As the connection between users and products is of interest, both the user and product embeddings are trained jointly with the user2vec model.

The CF method used for product and consumer representations is prone to cold start. To solve this, we combine CF with CB, and add for both products and users CB features (e.g., the no. of restaurants in the neighbourhood for users, or nutrients for products). Following the methodology for CF, real-valued embedding vectors can be established for products and users for CB, which can already be used to make simple product recommendations. To advance these models, all CF and CB features and representations can be concatenated into a joint input layer. For the proposed Meta-User2vec model, the input features are concatenated and fed into a NN (Fig. 2) to model consumers' behaviour. The dimensions for the CB features and the features calculated from the historic sales data are equal to the number of features. The dimensionality of the CF embeddings are equal to the embedding size (optimal at 15). Following the methodology of [29], we apply Rectified Linear Unit (ReLU) with three layers, where we use 64, 32,

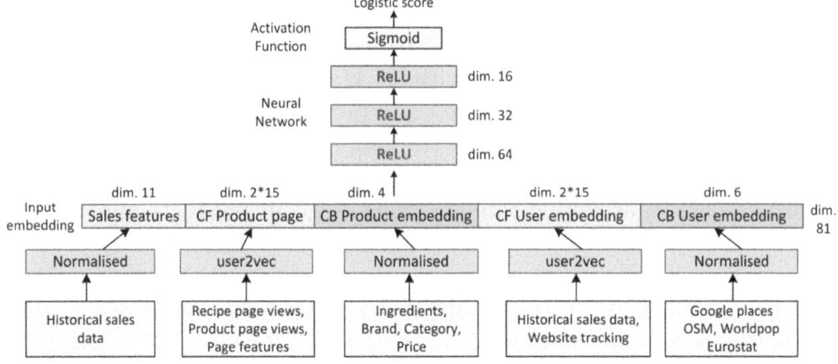

Fig. 2. An overview of the proposed NN with a concatenated embedding as input.

and 16 as the dimensions of the hidden layers. As the aim is to predict a logistic class model, a Sigmoid activation layer is chosen as the final layer.

5 Results

5.1 Evaluation Models and Measures

The trained product and user embeddings can be used directly to recommend products, or as NN input. As [28], we compare these methods against BestOf (ranks products by sales frequency globally as BestOf-global, or per user as BestOf-user), and CoCounts (builds a co-occurrence matrix of products appearing together in baskets and combines it with each user's purchase history to recommend products frequently bought with their past purchases). The logistic baseline model is a GLM with a logit link function. To predict the propensity to buy a product, a logit model is trained per product and product-page, with the dependent variable being 1 if the product is bought and 0 if not. We test the proposed recommendation methods by comparing predicted products with actual purchases in the test data. For the NN approach and logit model, each product-user combination is fed into the model, and per user products with the highest probabilistic scores are compared to the actual purchases of the user in the test data. For the BestOf method, the actual bought products are compared to the most bought products in the training period. For the CoCounts method, the most co-occurring products in the whole training data with the earlier bought products are the products to recommend for the current user. We compare the predicting power of the methods using standard RS metrics [10,28–30]: Hit Rate @k ($HR@k$), Mean Average Precision @k ($MAP@k$), and Normalized Discounted Cumulative Gain @k ($NDCG@k$), evaluating these at $k = 5$ recommended products, considering the basket size. For all the measures, values are calculated per user and averaged over all users.

For training data, the representations for users and products based on sales and online data are jointly trained with user2vec with embeddings randomly initialised and trained over multiple epochs with either a SG or CBOW technique. Further, several doc2vec model hyperparameters affect the quality of the resulting embeddings, which we evaluate with $MAP@k$ in a product masking task, where a product is hidden in each basket and prediction is correct if it appears in the top 5 results. For the doc2vec, the training used 10 epochs with a minimum product count of 10 to filter rare items. The SG/CBOW window size was set to the largest basket, assuming random order (i.e., all products in a basket are considered to be neighbouring), with smaller baskets padded. The considered hyperparameters along with the search space are: the initial learning rate $\alpha \in (0.01, 0.015, \ldots, 0.095, 0.1)$, the number of negative values used $neg\_val \in \{0, 5, 10, 15, 20\}$, the method used for training $SG\_CBOW \in \{\text{SG}, \text{CBOW}\}$, and the embedding size $emb\_size \in \{10, 15, 25, 50, 100, 150, 250, 300\}$.

With neg_val=0, model training uses hierarchical softmax instead of NS. Since training doc2vec and computing cosine similarities for $MAP@k$ are costly, testing all 1520 combinations is infeasible; and hyperparameter tuning on sales data from all countries is done with Hyperopt [2], and the average of $MAP@k$ with $k = 5$ is used for final selection. Embeddings trained with $\alpha = 0.025$, $neg\_val = 5$, $emb\_size = 15$, and a CBOW model yield the best performance.

5.2 Model Evaluation

We analyse the discussed methods for two categories: All products, and with Top 10% products removed (Table 2), and report averaged results over countries for the benchmark models CoCounts, BestOf-global, BestOf-user, and GLM, followed by the proposed Meta-User2vec model, Prod2vec as a part of the Meta-Prod2vec model, which is part of the Meta-User2vec model along with User2vec.

For the analysis with **all the products**, the measures show similar results, though $MAP@k$ and $NDCG@k$ provide more insight into the quality of the recommendation quality. The benchmark CoCounts outperforms BestOf-global, aligning with [28]. This is expected as BestOf-global recommends the same products to each user, whereas CoCounts personalizes recommendations using the products bought by the user in the training data. BestOf-user outperforms all models, due to the nature of the sales and online behaviour data – the data consists of users often buying a small number of unique products repeatedly (96.6% of the shopping baskets in the test data contain one of the top five products).

In Prod2vec, the weighted average of product embeddings is compared across all products, while User2vec uses jointly trained user and product embeddings, and is superior. As a memory-based CF method, User2vec emphasizes reorders, giving more weight to previously bought products. Comparing the hybrid models Meta-Prod2vec and Meta-User2vec with the pure CF variants, we see adding CB data leads to a significant improvement. This confirms that adding CB meta-data to CF, making it a hybrid model, improves RS performance, aligning with the original Meta-Prod2vec [28]. Using meta-data for both users and products boosts performance, although this is already visible between Prod2vec and User2vec.

We repeat the analysis **without popular products**, as it might be useful to introduce users to less known products, e.g., during a campaign, and remove the n most popular products from the data set as in [6,26], focusing on the products in the longer tail. The top 10% most popular products per sales of a country are removed, in average 50 products being removed across the 5 countries. The BestOf-user method (Table 2) outperforms the other methods once again. The BestOf-global model performs worse, likely because the products are bought by less users in the test data than those recommended in the earlier setup. CoCounts and GLM show significant improvement after removal of popular products, suggesting these models perform better with fewer unique user-item and item-item co-occurrences. Comparing the proposed Meta-User2vec and its components, we see all methods to perform better after removing the most popular products. The improved performance of Meta-User2vec after removing popular products is a promising result and suggests it is good at predicting longer-tail products. Still, we need to consider that there are in general less products and, hence, the ratio of good products versus wrong products becomes larger.

Table 2. Measures scores for different recommender systems with and without the most popular products, scores are averaged over countries.

	All products			Without popular products		
	HR@5	MAP@5	NDCG@5	HR@5	MAP@5	NDCG@5
CoCounts	73.69	26.85	28.73	80.94	33.56	34.57
BestOf-global	50.17	13.54	13.22	30.04	7.17	6.99
BestOf-user	**96.63**	**65.51**	**68.05**	**96.22**	**63.32**	**66.12**
GLM model	59.89	22.11	21.28	63.35	24.18	23.67
Prod2vec	40.12	13.21	12.84	43.12	15.60	15.57
User2vec	76.38	30.67	31.42	79.68	32.99	33.74
Meta-Prod2vec	52.11	21.34	20.33	55.19	24.18	23.35
Meta-User2vec	**87.30**	**35.63**	**35.33**	**87.85**	**36.10**	**35.93**

6 Conclusion

Good recommender systems drive marketing value from 'frequently bought with' banners to personalized campaigns, saving costs and boosting sales. In this paper, we proposed a recommendation method that combines the strengths of collaborative filtering (CF) and content-based (CB) approaches into a hybrid model, to create comprehensive embeddings for products and users using sales data and available meta-data. In particular, we applied the word2vec method to sequential sales data, referred to as prod2vec [10]. As word2vec extends to doc2vec, prod2vec extends to user2vec, where embeddings for products and users are jointly trained. Adding metadata yields to the hybrid method called Meta-Prod2vec [28]. We extended this to Meta-User2vec by including user metadata and training user2vec embeddings jointly with product embeddings, combining elements of prior RS methods [23,28,29]. We tested the model on a unique data set from five European countries, consisting of CF and CB part.

The proposed Meta-User2vec model outperforms Meta-Prod2vec and User2vec. Yet, a direct prediction of a user's most bought products performs best, likely due to many reorders in the data. Removing the top-n most popular products, as in [6,26], improves Meta-User2vec inprediction measures, suggesting potential for further research.

A limitation is that this research used a single, yet unique, proprietary data set. Future work should test additional datasets, though open-source data with insightful meta-data for both users and products is scarce.

Disclosure of Interests. The authors have no competing interests to declare that are relevant to the content of this article.

References

1. Barkan, O., Koenigstein, N.: Item2vec: neural item embedding for collaborative filtering. In: 2016 IEEE 26th International Workshop on Machine Learning for Signal Processing (MLSP), pp. 1–6 (2016). https://doi.org/10.1109/MLSP.2016.7738886
2. Bergstra, J., Komer, B., Eliasmith, C., Yamins, D., Cox, D.D.: Hyperopt: a python library for model selection and hyperparameter optimization. In: Python in Science Conference (SCIPY 2013), vol. 12, no. 1, p. 014008 (2013)
3. Bojanowski, P., Grave, E., Joulin, A., Mikolov, T.: Enriching word vectors with subword information. Trans. Assoc. Comput. Linguist. **5**, 135–146 (2017)
4. Brocken, E., et al.: Bing-CF-IDF+: a semantics-driven news recommender system. In: Giorgini, P., Weber, B. (eds.) Advanced Information Systems Engineering, pp. 32–47. Springer, Cham (2019)
5. Burke, R.: Hybrid recommender systems: survey and experiments. User Model. User-Adap. Inter. **12**(4), 331–370 (2002)
6. Cremonesi, P., Koren, Y., Turrin, R.: Performance of recommender algorithms on top-n recommendation tasks. In: Proceedings of the Fourth ACM Conference on Recommender Systems, pp. 39–46. ACM (2010)
7. Devlin, J., Chang, M.W., Lee, K., Toutanova, K.: BERT: pre-training of deep bidirectional transformers for language understanding. In: The 2019 Conference of the North American Chapter of the Association for Computational Linguistics: Human Language Technologies (NAAC-HLT 2019), pp. 4171–4186 (2019)
8. Djuric, N., Wu, H., Radosavljevic, V., Grbovic, M., Bhamidipati, N.: Hierarchical neural language models for joint representation of streaming documents and their content. In: 24th International Conference on World Wide Web (WWW 2015), pp. 248–255. Association for Computing Machinery (ACM) (2015)
9. Esmeli, R., Bader-El-Den, M., Abdullahi, H.: Using word2vec recommendation for improved purchase prediction. In: 2020 International Joint Conference on Neural Networks (IJCNN), pp. 1–8 (2020). https://doi.org/10.1109/IJCNN48605.2020.9206871
10. Grbovic, M., et al.: E-commerce in your inbox: product recommendations at scale. In: 21th ACM SIGKDD International Conference on Knowledge Discovery and Data Mining (KDD 2015), pp. 1809–1818 (2015)
11. Hackeling, G.: Mastering Machine Learning with Scikit-learn. Packt Publishing, Birmingham (2017)
12. van Huijsduijnen, L.H., et al.: Bing-CSF-IDF+: a semantics-driven recommender system for news. In: New Trends in Databases and Information Systems, pp. 143–153. Springer, Cham (2020)
13. Le, Q., Mikolov, T.: Distributed representations of sentences and documents. In: International Conference on Machine Learning (ICML 2014), pp. 1188–1196. JMLR.org (2014)
14. Li, Y., Xu, L., Tian, F., Jiang, L., Zhong, X., Chen, E.: Word embedding revisited: a new representation learning and explicit matrix factorization perspective. In: Proceedings of the 24th International Conference on Artificial Intelligence, IJCAI 2015, pp. 3650–3656. AAAI Press (2015)
15. Mikolov, T., Chen, K., Corrado, G., Dean, J.: Efficient estimation of word representations in vector space. In: Bengio, Y., LeCun, Y. (eds.) 1st International Conference on Learning Representations, (ICLR) 2013, Scottsdale, Arizona, USA, 2–4 May 2013, Workshop Track Proceedings (2013)

16. Mikolov, T., Sutskever, I., Chen, K., Corrado, G., Dean, J.: Distributed representations of words and phrases and their compositionality. In: Proceedings of the 26th International Conference on Neural Information Processing Systems - Volume 2, NIPS 2013, pp. 3111–3119. Curran Associates Inc., Red Hook, NY, USA (2013)
17. Misztal-Radecka, J., Indurkhya, B., Smywiński-Pohl, A.: Meta-user2vec model for addressing the user and item cold-start problem in recommender systems. User Model. User-Adap. Inter. **31**(2), 261–286 (2021). https://doi.org/10.1007/s11257-020-09282-4
18. Musto, C., Semeraro, G., de Gemmis, M., Lops, P.: Learning word embeddings from wikipedia for content-based recommender systems. In: Advances in Information Retrieval, pp. 729–734. Springer, Cham (2016)
19. Naseem, U., Razzak, I., Khan, S.K., Prasad, M.: A comprehensive survey on word representation models: from classical to state-of-the-art word representation language models. Trans. Asian Low-Resour. Lang. Inf. Process. **20**(5), 1–35 (2020)
20. Ozsoy, M.G.: From word embeddings to item recommendation. CoRR abs/1601.01356 (2016). http://arxiv.org/abs/1601.01356
21. Pennington, J., Socher, R., Manning, C.D.: Glove: global vectors for word representation. In: Conference on Empirical Methods in Natural Language Processing (EMNLP 2014), pp. 1532–1543 (2014)
22. Peters, M.E., et al.: Deep contextualized word representations. In: Conference of the North American Chapter of the Association for Computational Linguistics: Human Language Technologies (NAAC-HLT 2018), pp. 2227–2237 (2018)
23. Piciu, L., Damian, A., Tapus, N., Simion-Constantinescu, A., Dumitrescu, B.: Deep recommender engine based on efficient product embeddings neural pipeline. In: 2018 17th RoEduNet Conference: Networking in Education and Research (RoEduNet 2018), pp. 1–6. IEEE (2018)
24. Poppink, B., Frasincar, F., Robal, T.: An experimental study on re-ranking web shop search results using semantic segmentation of user profiles. Electron. Commer. Res. Appl. **62**, 101310 (2023). https://doi.org/10.1016/j.elerap.2023.101310
25. Quadrana, M., Cremonesi, P., Jannach, D.: Sequence-aware recommender systems. ACM Comput. Surv. **51**(4) (2018)
26. Rossum, B.V., Frasincar, F.: Augmenting LOD-based recommender systems using graph centrality measures. In: International Conference on Web Engineering (ICWE 2019), pp. 19–31. Springer (2019)
27. Shin, D., Cetintas, S., Lee, K.: Recommending tumblr blogs to follow with inductive matrix completion. In: CEUR Workshop Proceedings, vol. 1247 (2014)
28. Vasile, F., Smirnova, E., Conneau, A.: Meta-prod2vec: product embeddings using side-information for recommendation. In: 10th ACM Conference on Recommender Systems (ACM), pp. 225–232. ACM (2016)
29. Wu, C., Yan, M.: Session-aware information embedding for e-commerce product recommendation. In: ACM on Conference on Information and Knowledge Management (CIKM 2017), pp. 2379–2382. ACM (2017)
30. Yu, F., Liu, Q., Wu, S., Wang, L., Tan, T.: A dynamic recurrent model for next basket recommendation. In: 39th International ACM SIGIR Conference on Research and Development in Information Retrieval (SIGIR 2016), pp. 729–732. ACM (2016)

Semantic-Guided Data Augmentation and Filtering for Sequential Recommendation

Zitong Zhu, Meixiu Long, and Jiahai Wang(✉)

School of Computer Science and Engineering, Sun Yat-sen University, Guangzhou, People's Republic of China
{zhuzt5,longmx7}@mail2.sysu.edu.cn, wangjiah@mail.sysu.edu.cn

Abstract. Data augmentation is widely employed in sequential recommendation to mitigate data sparsity issues without requiring additional supervised labels. This process generally consists of two stages: augmented data construction and augmented data filtering. Although existing methods have investigated various effective strategies for both stages, they still encounter two primary limitations: (1) limited semantic diversity during the augmented data construction stage, and (2) inefficient filtering mechanisms during the augmented data filtering stage. To address these limitations and achieve more effective data augmentation, this paper proposes **S**emantic-guided **D**ata **A**ugmentation and Filtering for Sequential **Rec**ommendation (**SDARec**), which leverages semantic information of items to guide both the construction and filtering of augmented data. In the augmented data construction stage, dataset retrieval augmentation and sequence retrieval augmentation strategies are designed to construct semantically controllable and diverse augmented data. In the augmented data filtering stage, a large language model is employed to evaluate and filter the augmented data through a chain-of-thought prompting approach, eliminating the need for expert knowledge or complex heuristic designs. SDARec performs augmentation at the dataset level without requiring model training, making it highly generalizable and adaptable to various conventional recommendation models. Extensive experiments on three public datasets demonstrate the effectiveness of SDARec. Source code is available at https://github.com/zzzzzdev/SDARec.

Keywords: Recommender System · Sequential Recommendation · Data Augmentation

1 Introduction

Sequential Recommendation (SR) aims to predict the next item a user will interact with based on their historical behavior. In practical applications, user interaction data is often highly sparse, leading to suboptimal recommendation

I. Awan et al. (Eds.): WISE 2025, LNCS 16368, pp. 39–53, 2026.
https://doi.org/10.1007/978-981-95-7251-9_4

performance [19]. To address this challenge, extensive research has been conducted to alleviate data sparsity issues [21]. Among these methods, data augmentation has emerged as a key research direction due to its ability to enhance model performance without requiring additional supervised labels [5]. Typically, data augmentation in sequential recommendation involves two critical stages [17]: (1) augmented data construction stage, which aims to construct augmented data through heuristic-based methods [15,21,31], model-based methods [4,16,20,22,32], or large language model-based methods [3,18,28,29]; and (2) augmented data filtering stage, which aims to evaluate and filter the augmented data. Both augmented data construction and filtering stages are essential for constructing high-quality augmented data [17].

Although existing data augmentation methods have demonstrated their success in both stages, they still face several key limitations.

- **Limited semantic diversity during the augmented data construction stage**. Existing methods for augmented data construction are mainly classified into heuristic-based and model-based approaches [5]. Heuristic-based methods [15,21,31] construct augmented data by applying heuristic or random operations to modify the original sequences. These approaches often result in uncontrollable semantic shifts due to the limited consideration of sequence contextual information [20,22]. To address this problem, model-based methods [4,16,32] train predictors or discriminators on the original dataset to generate augmented data while preserving contextual coherence. However, since these methods are solely trained on the original dataset, the generated augmented data inevitably inherit the collaborative filtering patterns and data sparsity issues present in the original dataset. As a result, they fail to explore new collaborative filtering patterns beyond the dataset's inherent constraints, thereby limiting the diversity of the augmented data and reducing its effectiveness in alleviating data sparsity in downstream sequential recommendation tasks.
- **Inefficient filtering mechanisms during the augmented data filtering stage**. Efficient evaluation and filtering mechanisms for augmented data remain underexplored in sequential recommendation [5]. LLM4DSR [28] introduces an uncertainty estimation module to identify high-quality replacements in augmented sequences, while LLM4IDRec [3] designs filtering rules based on prior knowledge to select high-quality augmented data. Although these approaches are effective, they rely on expert knowledge and complex model designs, which are inefficient and less adaptable to different datasets.

To overcome these two limitations and enhance data augmentation and filtering for sequential recommendation, this paper proposes **S**emantic-guided **D**ata **A**ugmentation and Filtering for Sequential **Rec**ommendation (**SDARec**), which leverages semantic information of items to guide both the construction and filtering of augmented data. **To address the first limitation**, we explore the intrinsic relationship between semantic and collaborative filtering spaces in the augmented data construction stage, and design Dataset Retrieval Augmentation (DRA) and Sequence Retrieval Augmentation (SRA) strategies to construct semantically controllable and diverse augmented data. These two strategies leverage semantic space information to construct augmented data in collaborative filtering space, effectively breaking collaborative filtering constraints in original dataset and improving the diversity of the augmented data. **To address the second limitation**, we develop an efficient and effective filtering mechanism leveraging large language models (LLMs) in the augmented data filtering stage. By employing a chain-of-thought prompting strategy, LLMs perform zero-shot evaluation and filtering without requiring expert knowledge or complex model designs, ensuring robust generalization and adaptability. Notably, SDARec operates entirely at the dataset level, without requiring additional training, contributing to high efficiency, strong generalization, and independence from specific recommendation models.

Our main contributions are summarized as follows:

- The limitations of existing data augmentation methods in semantic diversity and filtering mechanisms are addressed, more effectively alleviating the data sparsity issue in SR.
- A semantic-guided data augmentation and filtering method named SDARec is proposed. In the construction stage, SDARec constructs semantically controllable and diverse augmented data by leveraging semantic information. In the filtering stage, SDARec employs a generalizable and adaptive mechanism to evaluate augmented data using LLMs.
- Extensive experiments are conducted on three public datasets, demonstrating that SDARec effectively overcomes critical limitations of existing data augmentation in SR.

2 Related Work

2.1 Data Augmentation for SR

Data augmentation is widely applied in sequential recommendation to address data sparsity issue. It typically involves two key stages: augmented data construction and augmented data filtering [5,17].

In the augmented data construction stage, existing methods can be categorized into two main types: heuristic-based data augmentation and model-based data augmentation [5]. Heuristic-based data augmentation (e.g., CL4SRec [31], CoSeRec [15], ICSRec [21]) modify the original sequence using random or heuristic operations. These methods often suffer from semantic uncontrollability, as they fail to fully consider contextual dependencies within sequences [20]. To address this issue, model-based data augmentation methods train predictors or discriminators on the original dataset, thereby fully considering contextual information during the construction of augmented data. For example, ASReP [16] first trains a generator on the original dataset and then generates pseudo-prior items for each original sequence to construct augmented data. Similarly, DR4SR [32] trains a generator on the original dataset and subsequently regenerates a more informative augmented dataset through the trained generator. Different from these methods that rely solely on collaborative filtering space for data augmentation, SDARec leverages the intrinsic relationship between semantic space and collaborative filtering space to enhance data augmentation. By incorporating semantic similarity constraints, SDARec ensures semantic controllability while breaking collaborative filtering constraints in original dataset, thereby increasing the diversity of augmented data.

In the augmented data filtering stage, only a few studies have proposed evaluation methods for augmented data in SR. For example, LLM4DSR [28] introduces an uncertainty estimation module to filter high-quality noise-replacement items within augmented sequences, while LLM4IDRec [3] employs heuristic rules to select high-quality augmented data. Additionally, DEALRec [13] presents a scoring function to assess data quality and perform filtering. Different from these approaches that rely on expert knowledge or complex model designs, SDARec explores the application of LLMs for evaluating and filtering augmented data. By effectively leveraging world knowledge and reasoning capabilities of LLMs, SDARec eliminates the need for expert knowledge and complex model designs, ensuring high efficiency and robust generalization.

2.2 Large Language Model for SR

Recently, numerous pioneering studies have explored the effective application of LLMs in recommendation systems, which can be broadly categorized into two approaches: "LLM as Recommender" and "LLM-enhanced Recommender." [26] The "LLM as Recommender" approach directly utilizes LLMs for prediction or ranking in recommendation tasks, employing techniques such as instruction fine-tuning [3], knowledge distillation [25], and model architecture modifications [34]. In contrast, the "LLM-enhanced Recommender" approach employs LLMs as auxiliaries to conventional recommendation models by generating informative textual data or encoding auxiliary information [26]. Additionally, recent studies have also explored the effectiveness of LLMs in addressing cold-start and data sparsity issues (e.g., Llama4Rec [18]). However, the integration of LLMs into recommendation systems is still evolving, requiring further exploration of effective integration strategies [12]. To this end, SDARec investigates the application of LLMs in evaluating and filtering augmented data, offering insights into their novel application in SR.

3 Methodology

3.1 Task Formulation and Framework Overview

User and item sets are denoted as $\mathcal{U}$ and $\mathcal{V}$, respectively. $\mathcal{S}$ represents all users' interaction sequences arranged in chronological order. $|\mathcal{U}|$, $|\mathcal{V}|$, and $|\mathcal{S}|$ indicate the number of samples in each set. Given a user $u_i \in \mathcal{U}, 1 \leq i \leq |\mathcal{U}|$, the user's interaction sequence is $s_i = \{v_1, v_2, v_3, \ldots, v_n\} \in \mathcal{S}$, where $v_j \in \mathcal{V}$ represents the item interacted with at timestamp j. Sequential recommendation aims to predict the next item, denoted as v_{n+1}, that a user is most likely to interact

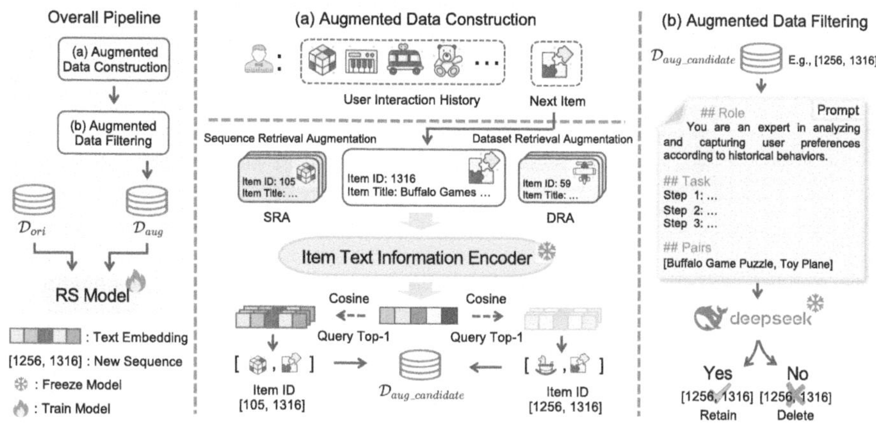

Fig. 1. SDARec consists of two stages: (a) Augmented Data Construction, which involves Dataset Retrieval Augmentation (DRA) and Sequence Retrieval Augmentation (SRA) strategies for constructing candidate augmented data, and (b) Augmented Data Filtering, where a Chain-of-Thought prompt instructs LLMs to evaluate and filter the candidate augmented data, producing the final augmented dataset $\mathcal{D}_{\text{aug}}$. The original dataset $\mathcal{D}_{\text{ori}}$, and the augmented dataset $\mathcal{D}_{\text{aug}}$, are then combined to train downstream sequential recommendation models.

with at timestamp $n+1$, based on the user's historical interaction sequence s_i. It can be formulated as:

$$\arg\max_{v_k \in \mathcal{V}} P(v_{n+1} = v_k \mid s_i). \tag{1}$$

Figure 1 presents an overview framework of SDARec, which leverages semantic information of items to guide both the construction and filtering of augmented data. In the augmented data construction stage (Sect. 3.2), SDARec employs Dataset Retrieval Augmentation (DRA) and Sequence Retrieval Augmentation (SRA) strategies to construct semantically controllable and diverse candidate augmented data. To enhance data quality, the augmented data filtering stage (Sect. 3.3) employs LLMs to evaluate and filter the candidate data. The final augmented dataset is then combined with the original dataset to train various conventional recommendation models (Sect. 3.4).

3.2 Augmented Data Construction

Current data augmentation methods in SR face limitations in semantic controllability and diversity. On the one hand, heuristic-based augmentation [31] suffer from semantic uncontrollability due to their neglect of sequence contextual information, often resulting in semantic deviations between the augmented and original data [21,22]. On the other hand, model-based augmentation [3,16,32] exhibits limited semantic diversity, as they primarily depend on the collaborative filtering information from the original dataset. This reliance restricts augmented

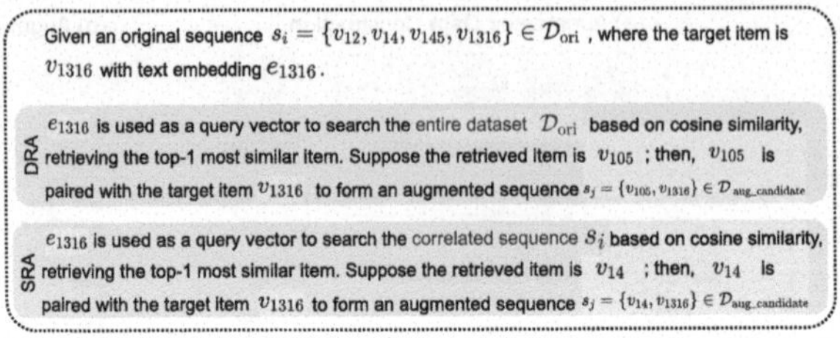

Given an original sequence $s_i = \{v_{12}, v_{14}, v_{145}, v_{1316}\} \in \mathcal{D}_{\text{ori}}$, where the target item is v_{1316} with text embedding e_{1316}.

DRA: e_{1316} is used as a query vector to search the entire dataset $\mathcal{D}_{\text{ori}}$ based on cosine similarity, retrieving the top-1 most similar item. Suppose the retrieved item is v_{105}; then, v_{105} is paired with the target item v_{1316} to form an augmented sequence $s_j = \{v_{105}, v_{1316}\} \in \mathcal{D}_{\text{aug\_candidate}}$

SRA: e_{1316} is used as a query vector to search the correlated sequence S_i based on cosine similarity, retrieving the top-1 most similar item. Suppose the retrieved item is v_{14}; then, v_{14} is paired with the target item v_{1316} to form an augmented sequence $s_j = \{v_{14}, v_{1316}\} \in \mathcal{D}_{\text{aug\_candidate}}$

Fig. 2. The examples of DRA and SRA strategies. The differences are highlighted.

data to existing user-item interaction patterns, hindering the exploration of novel behaviors beyond the dataset's scope [17]. Motivated by the above analysis, two perspectives need to be considered to construct higher-quality augmented data: (1) incorporating auxiliary information from domains beyond collaborative filtering, and (2) integrating sequence contextual information during the data augmentation process.

Regarding the auxiliary information from domains beyond collaborative filtering, rich and dense textual information is readily available, which starkly contrasts with the sparse nature of the collaborative filtering space. Numerous studies have attempted to improve traditional recommendation models by incorporating textual semantic information [11]. However, these works often overlook the intrinsic relationship between the semantic space and the collaborative filtering space, resulting in an underutilization of semantic information [33]. Moreover, AlphaRec [23] proposes that a linear mapping can transform items from the semantic space into the collaborative filtering space, suggesting that textual data has the potential to enrich collaborative filtering information. Inspired by these findings, we attempt to leverage semantic information from the text space to guide the construction of augmented data in the collaborative filtering space.

Specifically, dataset retrieval augmentation and sequence retrieval augmentation strategies are designed to construct semantically controllable and diverse augmented data. To construct augmented sequential data using these strategies, a text encoder (e.g., BERT [6], BGE [2], and Jina [24]) is first employed to encode the textual information of all items (e.g., title, brand, and category) and obtain their corresponding semantic embeddings. Subsequently, these retrieval augmentation strategies are applied to each user behavior sequence s_i in the original dataset $\mathcal{D}_{\text{ori}}$ to construct augmented sequence data.

- **Dataset Retrieval Augmentation (DRA).** The core idea of the DRA strategy is to construct augmented data using the semantic embedding of the target item e_{target}. By computing the cosine similarity between e_{target} and the embeddings of other items, the highest-ranked (i.e., top-1) item is retrieved from the entire dataset. This retrieved item is then paired with the target item to form an augmented sequence of length $n = 2$. The generated augmented data is subsequently evaluated and filtered during the augmented data filtering stage. Figure 2 illustrates an example of DRA strategy.

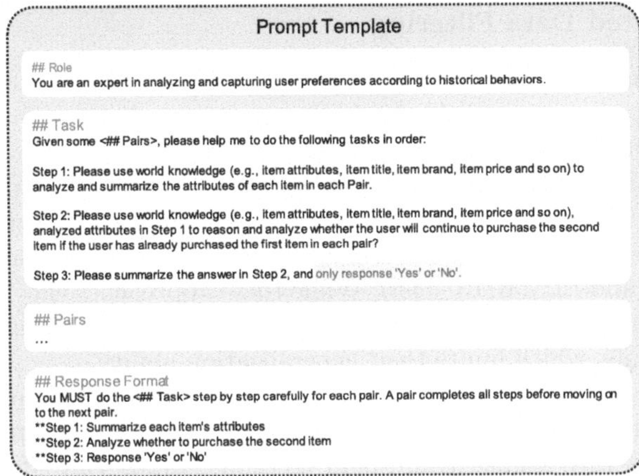

Fig. 3. The Chain-of-Thought prompt for filtering augmented data.

– **Sequence Retrieval Augmentation (SRA).** Unlike previous studies that rely solely on collaborative filtering information, DRA uses semantic information to construct augmented sequence data, enhancing semantic diversity. However, DRA does not incorporate contextual information within sequences, which risks semantic uncontrollability [5]. To address this limitation, SRA incorporates sequence context into the augmentation process. Instead of retrieving from the entire dataset, SRA narrows the retrieval scope to sequences related to the target item. An illustrative example of the SRA strategy is presented in Fig. 2.

To balance resource costs with model performance, the proposed DRA and SRA strategies retrieve only the top-1 item with the highest semantic similarity, rather than considering additional top-k items ($k = 2,3,4,5,...$). This design is guided by two key considerations. Firstly, not all augmented sequences generated by DRA and SRA are beneficial for downstream recommendation tasks. Retrieving top-k items may introduce more noise than useful information, thereby degrading the quality of the augmented data and increasing the training cost of downstream models. Secondly, since sequential recommendation tasks are highly sensitive to the order of items in a sequence [19], restricting retrieval to only the top-1 item helps mitigate order sensitivity issues. When only the top-1 item is selected, the order of the two items in the augmented sequence can be interchanged without affecting the recommendation task. For example, for an augmented sequence $\{v_a, v_b\} \in \mathcal{D}_{\text{aug\_candidate}}$, representing it as either $\{v_a, v_b\}$ or $\{v_b, v_a\}$ yields the same cross-entropy loss during optimization, ensuring that the learning process for the downstream task remains unaffected.

3.3 Augmented Data Filtering

Once the augmented data is constructed, a candidate set of augmented sequences, $\mathcal{D}_{\text{aug\_candidate}}$, is obtained. However, not all augmented sequences generated by the DRA and SRA strategies are beneficial for downstream recommendation tasks [17]. Therefore, it is essential to develop an effective filtering mechanism to ensure the quality of the augmented data. Previous studies have proposed various methods for evaluating and filtering augmented data (e.g., LLM4DSR [28] and LLM4IDRec [3]). While these approaches effectively filtering high-quality augmented data, they often rely on expert knowledge or complex rule-based designs, which limits their generalization ability.

Recently, LLMs have demonstrated remarkable performance in complex reasoning tasks, highlighting their extensive world knowledge and powerful inference capabilities [27]. Unlike traditional methods, LLMs can effectively tackle diverse tasks without relying on expert knowledge or manually crafted rules [12]. Additionally, LLMs generate responses within a dense semantic space, which offers richer and more meaningful semantic information compared to the sparse collaborative filtering space. Motivated by these insights, we investigate the potential of LLMs for evaluating and filtering augmented data. Specifically, we design a Chain-of-Thought (CoT) [30] prompting template to guide LLMs through a structured reasoning process, enabling a comprehensive analysis of the augmented sequence. By utilizing LLM APIs (e.g., Llama [8], Qwen [1], and DeepSeek [14]), we harness the zero-shot reasoning capabilities of LLMs to effectively evaluate and filter augmented data. As illustrated in Fig. 3, the proposed prompting template consists of three key steps:

- Step 1: LLMs analyze item attributes by leveraging their pre-trained and post-trained knowledge.
- Step 2: LLMs evaluate the relationship between two items in the augmented sequence and estimate likelihood of their co-occurrence in user interactions.
- Step 3: Based on the preceding analyses, LLMs decide whether to retain or discard the augmented sequence.

The entire process can be formally expressed as follows:

$$s_m = \{v_{1256}, v_{1316}\} \in \mathcal{D}_{\text{aug\_candidate}}, \tag{2}$$

$$p_m = \text{Prompt}(s_m), \tag{3}$$

$$\text{Answer} = \text{LLMs}(p_m), \tag{4}$$

where s_m represents a candidate augmented sequence generated during the augmented data construction stage, p_m is the corresponding prompt, and the final output *Answer* is either "Yes" or "No," indicating whether the augmented sequence is retained.

Unlike standard prompting templates that directly generate answers, the CoT prompting template guides LLMs through a step-by-step analysis of item attributes and their relationships before generating a response. This structured reasoning process improves the zero-shot recommendation capabilities of LLMs, allowing them to efficiently process item-related information without the need for task-specific fine-tuning [3]. As a result, SDARec achieves strong recommendation performance while significantly reducing both time and computational costs.

3.4 RS Model Training

After the augmented data filtering stage, the final augmented dataset, $\mathcal{D}_{\text{aug}}$, is obtained. This dataset consists of high-quality augmented data constructed with the guidance of dense and rich semantic information, supplementing the sparse original dataset. $\mathcal{D}_{\text{aug}}$ is then combined with the original dataset $\mathcal{D}_{\text{ori}}$ to form the final training dataset, represented as $\mathcal{D}_{\text{ori + aug}}$. The resulting dataset is used to train downstream recommendation models.

3.5 Characteristics of SDARec

The characteristics of SDARec are as follows.

Firstly, existing data augmentation methods in sequential recommendation suffer from limitations in semantic controllability and diversity (e.g., CL4SRec [31], ICSRec [21], CaDiRec [4], and DR4SR [32]). Moreover, most approaches do not fully capture the intrinsic relationship between the semantic space and the collaborative filtering space, leading to suboptimal utilization of semantic information (e.g., Recformer [11]). In contrast, SDARec effectively leverages the linear mapping between these spaces to guide augmented data construction. The proposed dataset retrieval augmentation and sequence retrieval augmentation strategies construct semantically controllable and diverse augmented data while offering advantages such as high efficiency, no training requirements, and dataset independence.

Secondly, few studies have focused on the evaluation and filtering of augmented data. Unlike previous methods that depend on expert knowledge and complex model designs, SDARec utilizes LLMs to evaluate and filter augmented data based on semantic information. Through a simple CoT prompting design, SDARec achieves effective zero-shot evaluation without requiring training, expert knowledge, or complex model designs, providing an efficient and adaptable solution for augmented data evaluation.

4 Experiment

4.1 Experimental Settings

Datasets. We collect three publicly available Amazon subcategory datasets: ***Sports, Toys, and Clothing***[1]. We keep "5-core" interactions for users and items. User interaction histories are sorted chronologically, with a maximum sequence length of 50. The processed dataset statistics are summarized in Table 1.

[1] https://cseweb.ucsd.edu/~jmcauley/datasets.html.

Table 1. The statistics of experimented datasets.

Dataset	#Users	#Items	Avg.Length	#Actions	Sparsity
Sports	35598	18357	8.3	296337	99.95%
Toys	19412	11924	8.6	167597	99.93%
Clothing	39387	23033	7.1	278677	99.97%

Evaluation Metrics. We split our datasets into training, validation, and test sets using a "leave one out" strategy. We evaluate all items in the dataset without negative sampling. The evaluation metrics used in our experiments are top-k Hit Ratio (HR@k) and top-k Normalized Discounted Cumulative Gain (NDCG@k), with k set to $\{10, 20\}$. Note that the validation and test sets do not include newly constructed augmented data.

Baselines. Our SDARec is a plug-and-play component. To assess its adaptability and effectiveness across various sequence recommendation models, we select several representative models as backbones: (1) **Vanilla SR models**: GRU4Rec [9] and SASRec [10]. (2) **Diffusion models for SR**: T-DiffRec [7]. (3) **Contrastive learning for SR**: CL4SRec [31] and DuoRec [22]. The comparison baselines are as follows.

- **None**: This setting indicates that no data augmentation methods are used, and the models are trained solely on the original dataset.
- $*_{\text{text}}$: To evaluate the performance differences in incorporating semantic information, we follow previous methods [11] to construct variant models where item ID embeddings are enriched with text embeddings, formulated as "$\text{Emb} = \text{Emb}_{\text{ID}} + \text{Emb}_{\text{text}}$". The variant models are then trained on the original dataset. Notably, T-DiffRec does not have a T-DiffRec$_{\text{text}}$ variant, as it does not include ID embeddings.
- **LLM4IDRec** [3]: A state-of-the-art data augmentation method that fine-tunes LLMs on the original dataset and employs the fine-tuned LLMs to generate augmented interactions.

Implementation Details. All backbone model reproductions and hyperparameter settings are based on the RecBole framework[2]. LLM4IDRec [3] is reproduced using the code provided by the original author. Due to space constraints, our source code is available at https://github.com/zzzzzdev/SDARec.

4.2 Overall Performance

According to the results in Table 2, several observations can be made as follows.

Firstly, significant performance differences are observed across the five backbone models when trained solely on the original dataset. This validates the

[2] https://github.com/RUCAIBox/RecBole.

Table 2. Performance comparisons of various methods across five backbones. The best and second-best results are bolded and underlined. Improvements over baselines are statistically significant with $p \leq 0.01$.

BackBone	Datasets	Toys				Sports				Clothing			
	Method	HR@10	HR@20	NDCG@10	NDCG@20	HR@10	HR@20	NDCG@10	NDCG@20	HR@10	HR@20	NDCG@10	NDCG@20
GRU4Rec	None	0.0517	0.0755	0.0303	0.0363	0.0364	0.0546	0.0191	0.0237	0.0132	0.0220	0.0070	0.0092
	GRU4Rec$_{text}$	0.0588	0.0842	0.0346	0.0410	0.0361	0.0577	0.0194	0.0248	0.0201	0.0324	0.0101	0.0132
	LLMIDRec	0.0565	0.0861	0.0326	0.0400	0.0413	0.0605	0.0217	0.0281	0.0154	0.0275	0.0087	0.0119
	SDARec	**0.0711**	**0.1001**	**0.0401**	**0.0474**	**0.0431**	**0.0649**	**0.0231**	**0.0285**	**0.0222**	**0.0364**	**0.0115**	**0.0151**
SASRec	None	0.0881	0.1189	0.0439	0.0516	0.0478	0.0701	0.0224	0.0281	0.0263	0.0395	0.0121	0.0154
	SASRec$_{text}$	0.0890	0.1223	0.0475	0.0559	0.0468	0.0703	0.0244	0.0304	0.0294	0.0439	0.0146	0.0182
	LLM4IDRec	0.0987	0.1297	0.0487	0.0557	0.0542	0.0770	0.0240	0.0307	0.0294	0.0478	0.0144	0.0188
	SDARec	**0.1161**	**0.1558**	**0.0603**	**0.0703**	**0.0612**	**0.0878**	**0.0304**	**0.0371**	**0.0469**	**0.0658**	**0.0224**	**0.0271**
T-DiffRec	None	0.0651	0.0874	0.0384	0.0441	0.0405	0.0560	0.0235	0.0274	0.0234	0.0329	0.0133	0.0157
	LLM4IDRec	**0.0659**	**0.0894**	0.0389	0.0455	**0.0429**	**0.0579**	0.0247	0.0282	0.0252	0.0352	0.0141	0.0164
	SDARec	0.0634	0.0891	**0.0395**	**0.0466**	0.0414	0.0572	**0.0259**	**0.0303**	**0.0267**	**0.0371**	**0.0154**	**0.0182**
CL4SRec	None	0.0620	0.0843	0.0309	0.0365	0.0337	0.0540	0.0175	0.0226	0.0199	0.0305	0.0095	0.0122
	CL4SRec$_{text}$	0.0605	0.0840	0.0305	0.0365	0.0340	0.0534	0.0175	0.0223	0.0204	0.0338	0.0105	0.0138
	LLM4IDRec	0.0724	0.0964	0.0338	0.0424	0.0391	0.0613	0.0201	0.0249	0.0229	0.0348	0.0106	0.0142
	SDARec	**0.0997**	**0.1342**	**0.0512**	**0.0599**	**0.0505**	**0.0740**	**0.0261**	**0.0320**	**0.0440**	**0.0610**	**0.0207**	**0.0249**
DuoRec	None	0.0926	0.1266	0.0474	0.0559	0.0470	0.0689	0.0242	0.0297	0.0303	0.0441	0.0145	0.0180
	DuoRec$_{text}$	0.0961	0.1320	0.0497	0.0588	0.0475	0.0698	0.0253	0.0309	0.0310	0.0451	0.0149	0.0184
	LLM4IDRec	0.1053	0.1460	0.0518	0.0656	0.0549	0.0766	0.0282	0.0334	0.0364	0.0496	0.0166	0.0208
	SDARec	**0.1138**	**0.1552**	**0.0595**	**0.0700**	**0.0599**	**0.0850**	**0.0315**	**0.0378**	**0.0411**	**0.0607**	**0.0210**	**0.0260**

rationale for evaluating various data augmentation methods on these models, ensuring that the evaluation results are both applicable and representative.

Secondly, comparing the $*_{\text{text}}$ variant of each backbone model reveals that incorporating textual information significantly improves performance, particularly in highly sparse datasets (e.g., Clothing). However, SDARec outperforms these $*_{\text{text}}$ variants, suggesting that the traditional "$\text{Emb}_{\text{ID}} + \text{Emb}_{\text{text}}$" approach does not effectively utilize semantic information. This further supports the motivation for using semantic information to guide the construction of augmented data.

Thirdly, LLM4IDRec achieves a notable performance boost by leveraging fine-tuned LLMs, demonstrating the strong potential of LLMs in data augmentation. However, LLM4IDRec underperforms compared to SDARec. This because LLM4IDRec relies solely on the existing collaborative filtering information in the dataset, whereas SDARec effectively utilizes dense semantic information to enhance the sparse collaborative filtering space.

Finally, SDARec consistently outperforms all baselines across all evaluation metrics and datasets. This superior performance can be attributed to two main factors: (1) SDARec explicitly explores the linear relationship between the semantic space and the collaborative filtering space when constructing augmented data. By using semantic information to guide data construction, two retrieval augmentation strategies construct semantically controllable and diverse augmented data; and (2) SDARec utilizes LLMs for the evaluation and filtering of augmented data, effectively obtaining high-quality data without the need for expert knowledge or complex model designs.

Table 3. Ablation study with important designs.

	SASRec														
	Toys					Sports					Clothing				
Models	None	w/o DRA	w/o SRA	w/o LLM	**SDARec**	None	w/o DRA	w/o SRA	w/o LLM	**SDARec**	None	w/o DRA	w/o SRA	w/o LLM	**SDARec**
HR@10	0.0881	0.1075	0.1011	0.1113	**0.1161**	0.0478	0.0575	0.0524	0.0591	**0.0612**	0.0263	0.0357	0.0374	0.0459	**0.0469**
HR@20	0.1189	0.1459	0.1378	0.1538	**0.1558**	0.0701	0.0810	0.0763	0.0847	**0.0878**	0.0395	0.0523	0.0535	0.0651	**0.0658**
NDCG@10	0.0439	0.0550	0.0494	0.0560	**0.0603**	0.0224	0.0280	0.0251	0.0295	**0.0304**	0.0121	0.0169	0.0176	0.0219	**0.0224**
NDCG@20	0.0516	0.0647	0.0587	0.0667	**0.0703**	0.0281	0.0339	0.0311	0.0359	**0.0371**	0.0154	0.0211	0.0217	0.0268	**0.0271**
	DuoRec														
	Toys					Sports					Clothing				
Models	None	w/o DRA	w/o SRA	w/o LLM	**SDARec**	None	w/o DRA	w/o SRA	w/o LLM	**SDARec**	None	w/o DRA	w/o SRA	w/o LLM	**SDARec**
HR@10	0.0924	0.1065	0.1058	0.1096	**0.1138**	0.0478	0.0558	0.0519	0.0536	**0.0599**	0.0303	0.0377	0.0418	**0.0441**	0.0411
HR@20	0.1263	0.1460	0.1413	0.1513	**0.1552**	0.0710	0.0808	0.0752	0.0782	**0.0850**	0.0441	0.0534	0.0587	**0.0631**	0.0607
NDCG@10	0.0472	0.0556	0.0534	0.0561	**0.0595**	0.0245	0.0297	0.0268	0.0286	**0.0315**	0.0145	0.0189	0.0202	**0.0212**	0.0210
NDCG@20	0.0558	0.0655	0.0624	0.0666	**0.0700**	0.0303	0.0361	0.0327	0.0348	**0.0378**	0.0180	0.0228	0.0245	0.0260	**0.0260**

4.3 Ablation Study

To verify the effectiveness of each design in SDARec, we conduct experiments on two backbone models: SASRec [10] and DuoRec [22]. Three variant models are made as follows: (1) **w/o DRA**: removes dataset retrieval augmentation strategy; (2) **w/o SRA**: removes sequence retrieval augmentation strategy; (3) **w/o LLM**: removes the augmented data filtering stage. The ablation results are shown in the Table 3.

The effectiveness of dataset retrieval augmentation and sequence retrieval augmentation strategies can be evaluated by comparing the performance of **w/o DRA**, **w/o SRA**, and SDARec. In recommendation scenarios, items with similar semantic descriptions often belong to the same category and are frequently purchased together. However, their occurrence frequencies may vary in real-world datasets, which affects the quality of item ID embeddings and recall probabilities, potentially hindering recommendation performance [22]. The proposed DRA and SRA strategies address these issues by augmenting sequential data, enabling models to capture collaborative filtering similarities between semantically similar items and ultimately improving recommendation performance.

When the augmented data filtering stage is removed, the performance of **w/o LLM** significantly drops, indicating that LLMs are essential for evaluating and filtering high-quality augmented data. This is due to the extensive world knowledge and reasoning capabilities of LLMs, which allow them to assess and retain high-quality augmented data in the semantic space. However, in the case of the Clothing dataset and the DuoRec backbone, **w/o LLM** outperforms SDARec. This may be attributed to the higher sparsity of Clothing dataset compared to Toys and Sports datasets, which reduces need for high-quality augmented data.

4.4 Long-Tail Problem Analysis

Sequential recommendation has long been challenged by the long-tail problem [19]. To evaluate SDARec's ability to address this issue, we categorized interaction sequence lengths into three groups: "<10", "[10, 40]", and ">40", representing different levels of sparsity. As shown in Fig. 4, SDARec performs well across all groups with varying sparsity levels. Notably, SDARec demonstrates

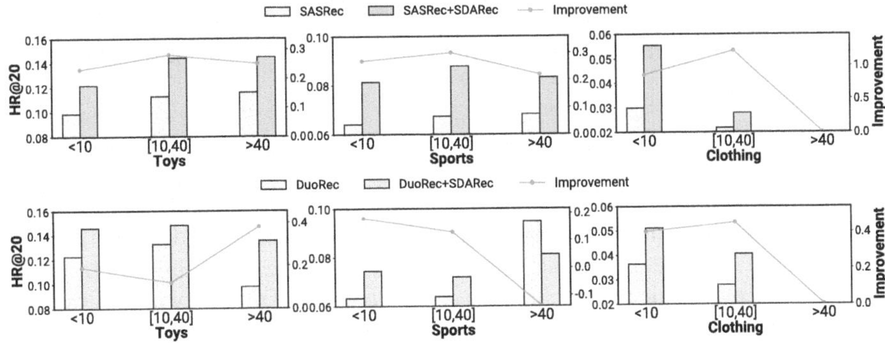

Fig. 4. The performance of SDARec on different groups with different sparsity levels. The backbone models are SASRec (Upper) and DuoRec (Bottom). The bar graph shows HR@20 performance, while the line chart illustrates the relative performance improvement before and after data augmentation with SDARec.

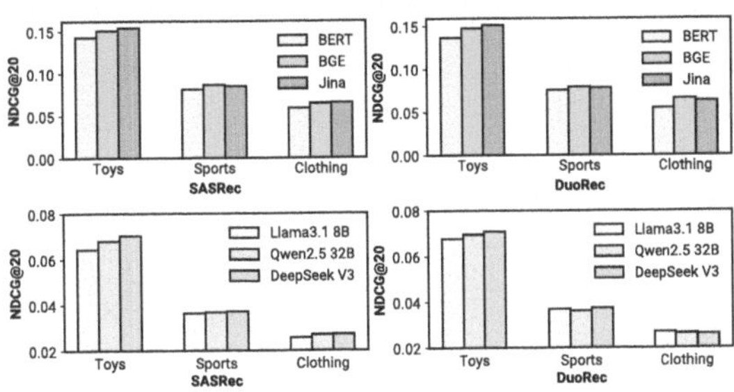

Fig. 5. The performance of various text encoders (Upper) and LLMs (Bottom).

a significantly higher improvement ratio in groups where the backbone models perform poorly (e.g., SASRec in the "[10, 40]" group of the Clothing dataset and DuoRec in the ">40" group of the Toys dataset). These results highlight SDARecn's effectiveness in tackling the long-tail problem.

4.5 Advanced Analysis

Impact of different text encoders. To assess the impact of different text encoders, we consider three options: BERT [6], BGE [2], and Jina [24]. As shown in Fig. 5, both BGE and Jina significantly outperform BERT, as they are more advanced text encoders. This indicates that more sophisticated text encoders generate higher-quality semantic embeddings, which in turn enhance the construction of high-quality augmented data.

Impact of different LLMs. To assess the impact of different LLMs, we consider three options: Llama3.1 8B [8], Qwen2.5 32B [1], and DeepSeek V3 [14]. As shown in Fig. 5, DeepSeek V3 outperforms the other models, owing to its superior world knowledge and reasoning capabilities. This indicates that more powerful LLMs are more effective at filtering and retaining high-quality augmented data.

5 Conclusion

This paper addresses two key limitations of current data augmentation methods in SR: (1) limited semantic diversity during the augmented data construction stage, and (2) inefficient filtering mechanisms during the augmented data filtering stage. To overcome these challenges, we propose SDARec, which leverages semantic information of items to guide both the construction and filtering of augmented data. In the augmented data construction stage, dataset retrieval augmentation and sequence retrieval augmentation strategies are introduced to generate semantically controllable and diverse augmented data. In the augmented data filtering stage, LLMs are used to evaluate and filter high-quality augmented data without the need for expert knowledge or complex model designs. Extensive experiments demonstrate the effectiveness of each component and the state-of-the-art performance of SDARec.

References

1. Bai, J., et al.: Qwen technical report. arXiv preprint arXiv:2309.16609 (2023)
2. Chen, J., Xiao, S., Zhang, P., Luo, K., Lian, D., Liu, Z.: BGE M3-embedding: multi-lingual, multi-functionality, multi-granularity text embeddings through self-knowledge distillation. arXiv preprint arXiv:2402.03216 (2024)
3. Chen, L., et al.: Enhancing ID-based recommendation with large language models. ACM TOIS (2024)
4. Cui, Z., Wu, H., He, B., Cheng, J., Ma, C.: Diffusion-based contrastive learning for sequential recommendation. arXiv preprint arXiv:2405.09369 (2024)
5. Dang, Y., et al.: Data augmentation for sequential recommendation: a survey. arXiv preprint arXiv:2409.13545 (2024)
6. Devlin, J., Chang, M., Lee, K., Toutanova, K.: BERT: pre-training of deep bidirectional transformers for language understanding. In: NAACL, pp. 4171–4186 (2019)
7. Du, H., Yuan, H., Huang, Z., Zhao, P., Zhou, X.: Sequential recommendation with diffusion models. arXiv preprint arXiv:2304.04541 (2023)
8. Dubey, A., et al.: The llama 3 herd of models. arXiv preprint arXiv:2407.21783 (2024)
9. Hidasi, B., Karatzoglou, A.: Recurrent neural networks with top-k gains for session-based recommendations. In: CIKM, pp. 843–852 (2018)
10. Kang, W., McAuley, J.J.: Self-attentive sequential recommendation. In: ICDM, pp. 197–206 (2018)
11. Li, J., et al.: Text is all you need: learning language representations for sequential recommendation. In: KDD, pp. 1258–1267 (2023)
12. Lin, J., et al.: How can recommender systems benefit from large language models: a survey. ACM TOIS **43**(2), 1–47 (2025)
13. Lin, X., et al.: Data-efficient fine-tuning for LLM-based recommendation. In: SIGIR, pp. 365–374 (2024)

14. Liu, A., et al.: Deepseek-v3 technical report. arXiv preprint arXiv:2412.19437 (2024)
15. Liu, Z., Chen, Y., Li, J., Yu, P.S., McAuley, J., Xiong, C.: Contrastive self-supervised sequential recommendation with robust augmentation. arXiv preprint arXiv:2108.06479 (2021)
16. Liu, Z., Fan, Z., Wang, Y., Yu, P.S.: Augmenting sequential recommendation with pseudo-prior items via reversely pre-training transformer. In: SIGIR, pp. 1608–1612 (2021)
17. Long, L., et al.: On LLMs-driven synthetic data generation, curation, and evaluation: a survey. arXiv preprint arXiv:2406.15126 (2024)
18. Luo, S., et al.: Integrating large language models into recommendation via mutual augmentation and adaptive aggregation. arXiv preprint arXiv:2401.13870 (2024)
19. Pan, L., Pan, W., Wei, M., Yin, H., Ming, Z.: A survey on sequential recommendation. arXiv preprint arXiv:2412.12770 (2024)
20. Qin, X., et al.: Meta-optimized contrastive learning for sequential recommendation. In: SIGIR, pp. 89–98 (2023)
21. Qin, X., Yuan, H., Zhao, P., Liu, G., Zhuang, F., Sheng, V.S.: Intent contrastive learning with cross subsequences for sequential recommendation. In: WSDM, pp. 548–556 (2024)
22. Qiu, R., Huang, Z., Yin, H., Wang, Z.: Contrastive learning for representation degeneration problem in sequential recommendation. In: WSDM, pp. 813–823 (2022)
23. Sheng, L., Zhang, A., Zhang, Y., Chen, Y., Wang, X., Chua, T.S.: Language representations can be what recommenders need: findings and potentials. arXiv preprint arXiv:2407.05441 (2024)
24. Sturua, S., et al.: Jina-embeddings-v3: multilingual embeddings with task lora. arXiv preprint arXiv:2409.10173 (2024)
25. Sun, G., Zhang, H.: Delrec: distilling sequential pattern to enhance LLM-based recommendation. arXiv preprint arXiv:2406.11156 (2024)
26. Sun, Z., et al.: Large language models enhanced collaborative filtering. In: CIKM, pp. 2178–2188 (2024)
27. Tang, Z., Zhang, X., Wang, B., Wei, F.: Mathscale: scaling instruction tuning for mathematical reasoning. arXiv preprint arXiv:2403.02884 (2024)
28. Wang, B., et al.: Llm4dsr: leveraing large language model for denoising sequential recommendation. arXiv preprint arXiv:2408.08208 (2024)
29. Wang, J., Lu, H., Caverlee, J., Chi, E.H., Chen, M.: Large language models as data augmenters for cold-start item recommendation. In: WWW, pp. 726–729 (2024)
30. Wei, J., et al.: Chain-of-thought prompting elicits reasoning in large language models. In: NeurIPS, pp. 24824–24837 (2022)
31. Xie, X., et al.: Contrastive learning for sequential recommendation. In: ICDE, pp. 1259–1273 (2022)
32. Yin, M., et al.: Dataset regeneration for sequential recommendation. In: KDD, pp. 3954–3965 (2024)
33. Zhang, X., Xu, B., Li, C., Zhou, Y., Li, L., Lin, H.: Side information-driven session-based recommendation: a survey. arXiv preprint arXiv:2402.17129 (2024)
34. Zhang, Y., Bao, K., Yan, M., Wang, W., Feng, F., He, X.: Text-like encoding of collaborative information in large language models for recommendation. arXiv preprint arXiv:2406.03210 (2024)

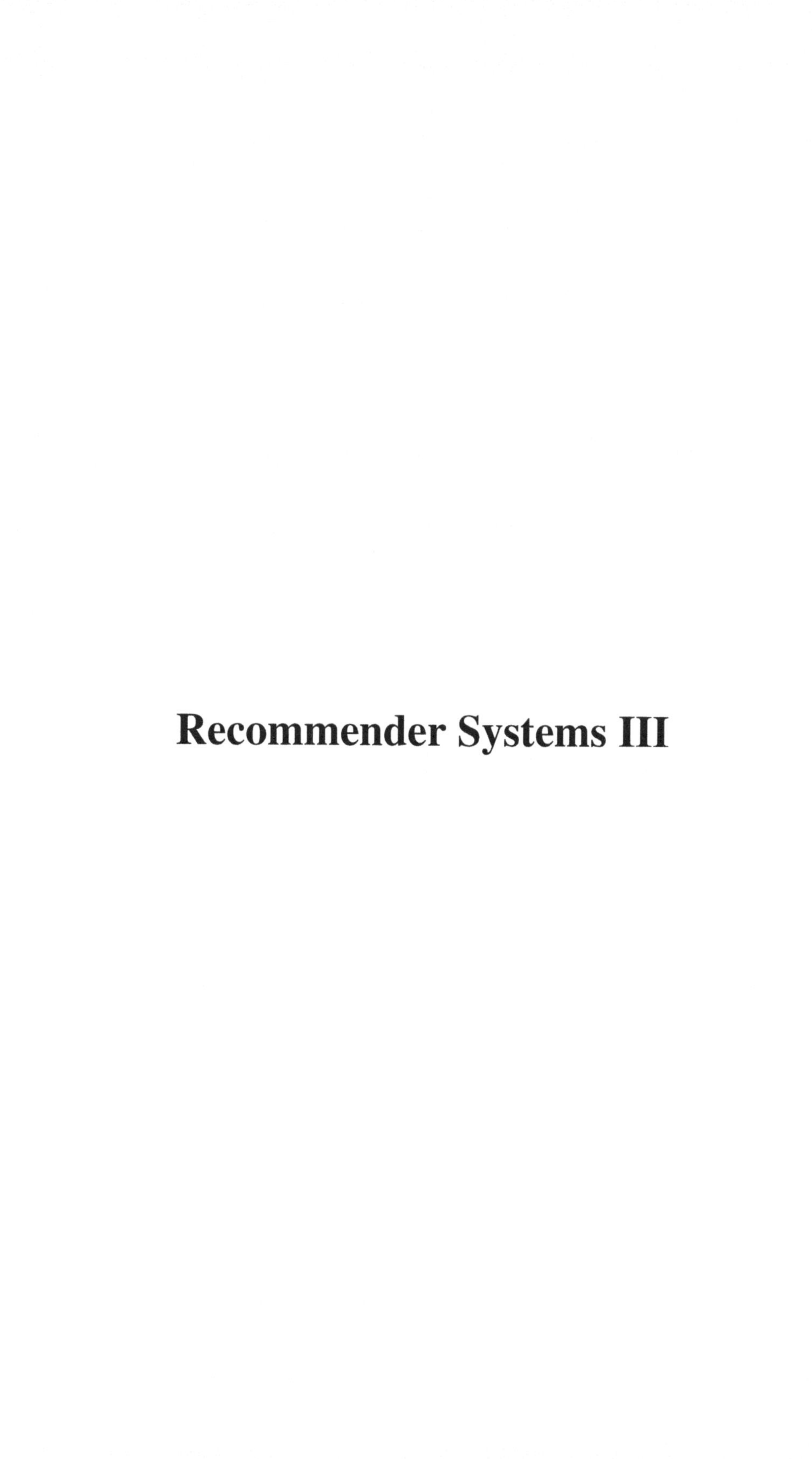

Recommender Systems III

GACS: Graph Contrastive Learning with Augmented Collaborative Signals for Recommendation

Haibo Liu[1], Lianjie Yu[1(✉)], Wenlong Zheng[1], Yunlong Zhou[1], Jinglian Liu[2], and ShiYong Fan[1]

[1] School of Cyber Security and Computer, Hebei University, Baoding, China
lianjieyu806@gmail.com

[2] School of Computer Science and Engineering, Suzhou University of Technology, Suzhou, China

Abstract. Graph Contrastive Learning (GCL) is a self-supervised learning paradigm that extracts features from unlabeled data by comparing similarities and differences between views and has shown great potential in graph-based recommender systems. Most GCL-based recommender models construct distinguishable contrast views through graph perturbation that makes embeddings uniformly distributed, which alleviates the over-smoothing problem. However, the perturbation obscures the collaborative signals between entities, which reduces the representation ability of the model. Additionally, current GCL-based recommender models utilize invariant weights to optimize contrastive learning, recommendation, and other tasks, which cannot adapt to the dynamic changes of tasks during the training phase. To address these issues, we propose a **G**raph contrastive learning model with **A**ugmented **C**ollaborative **S**ignals for recommendation (GACS). GACS constructs the differentiation enhancement view by adding noise to the embeddings and the collaborative signals augmentation view by leveraging implicit relationships between entities. Both views are used for contrastive learning to mitigate the over-smoothing problem and enhance the representation ability. Furthermore, GACS employs learnable weights to optimize tasks dynamically and improves the robustness through parameter limitations. Extensive experiments demonstrate the effectiveness and rationality of our model. The source code of our model is available at https://github.com/CoderYu233/GACS.

Keywords: Graph Contrastive Learning · Collaborative Signals · Contrastive Learning View Construction · Recommender System

1 Introduction

The collaborative signals are utilized to reveal these latent relationships (i.e., the implicit similarity between entities) in user-item interactions, and Graph Convolutional Network (GCN) is employed to extract these signals in graph-based recommendation [1,2]. Specifically, GCN constructs a user-item bipartite graph

I. Awan et al. (Eds.): WISE 2025, LNCS 16368, pp. 57–71, 2026.
https://doi.org/10.1007/978-981-95-7251-9_5

through user-item interactions and utilizes the graph for embedding propagation to explicitly encode the collaborative signals into the embeddings [3]. GCN employs a supervised learning paradigm that relies on labeled data (i.e., explicit interaction data) for model training, but these labeled data are sparse [4,5]. Furthermore, as embedding propagates, node features tend to converge to the same value (i.e., the same location in space), leading to the over-smoothing problem.

To address these problems, numerous studies have adopted Graph Contrastive Learning (GCL) to recommender systems [6–8]. GCL utilizes GCN to construct views and captures patterns in graph structures by contrasting sample pairs in different views [9,10]. GCL can extract the generalized knowledge contained in the raw data to provide effective information for the main task, and this is consistent with recommender systems alleviating the sparsity. Additionally, GCL constructs highly differentiated views to extract discriminative sample pairs and prevent features from converging to the same value by comparing sample pairs to increase the distinction between different entities. Although GCL has achieved commendable results, there are still several problems as follows.

Reduction of Representation Ability. In order to generate discriminative sample pairs and improve the distinguishing ability of GCL-based recommender models, current research attempts to construct differentiated views by perturbing the graph [9,11], which can effectively mitigate the over-smoothing problems [10,12]. As illustrated in Fig. 1, $\boldsymbol{e}_u$ represents the user embedding, $\boldsymbol{e}_{i+}$ and $\boldsymbol{e}_{i-}$ represent the embedding of items that the user has engaged with and has not engaged with. $\boldsymbol{e}^{'}$ and $\boldsymbol{e}^{''}$ represent the distribution of embeddings that may appear after adding the perturbation. In Fig. 1(b) it can be seen that the moderate perturbations preserve most of the information of the original embedding, but its embedding distribution changes are very limited and not uniformly distributed in space. In Fig. 1(c) excessive perturbations make the embedding widely distributed in the space, but blur the relationship between entities which destroys the collaborative signals. In addition, the recommendation model is trained by calculating the similarity between $\boldsymbol{e}_u$ and $\boldsymbol{e}_{i+}$, as well as the similarity between $\boldsymbol{e}_u$ and $\boldsymbol{e}_{i-}$. The perturbation disturbs their similarity, causing the model to learn distorted features, and impairing its representation ability.

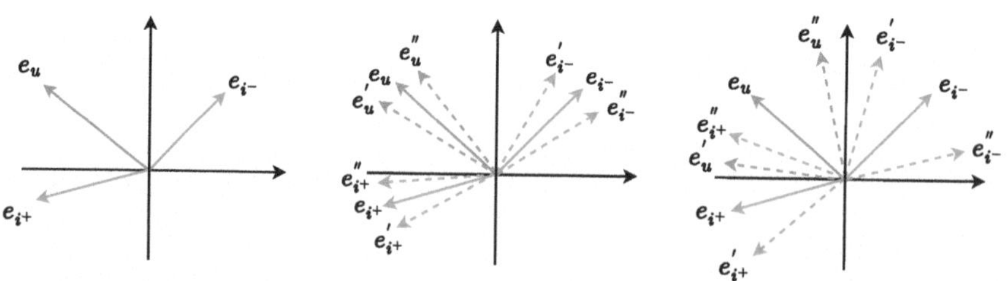

(a) No perturbations (b) Moderate perturbations (c) Excessive perturbations

Fig. 1. The effect of perturbation of different strengths on embedding.

Invariant Weights for Tasks Optimization. The GCL-based recommendations include the main task of recommendation and auxiliary tasks of contrastive learning and regularization [9,13]. Most of them employ invariant weights paradigm [10,12]. However, these invariant weights cannot adapt to the variations in recommendation scenarios, resulting in a lack of dynamic adaptability to the changes in data distribution. Previous works [14] adapted models by measuring differences between tasks, and others proposed new modeling techniques with parameter additions to handle task variations in the training phase [15,16]. Although these methods add parameters to accommodate the difference in tasks, the lack of restrictions on these parameters makes the model overfit the training data, negatively impacting its generalizability and robustness.

To deal with these issues, we propose a **G**raph contrastive learning model with **A**ugmented **C**ollaborative **S**ignals for recommendation (GACS), which contains three main modules. (1) Multi-view generation module: To mitigate the over-smoothing and improve the representation ability, the model constructs two distinct views for contrastive learning. The first view is the collaborative signals augmentation view. Existing models capture collaborative signals through explicit user-item interactions while ignoring implicit user-user and item-item relationships. These implicit relationships reveal higher-order relationships between entities, which can enhance collaborative signals to aid the model in capturing complex relationships between entities, thereby improving its representation ability. Some studies pre-train models to capture implicit relationships and augment collaborative signals [1,4], but their quality depends on pre-trained model performance, causing instability. GACS directly derives these relationships from explicit interactions for more stable signals. The second view is the differentiation enhancement view. Inspired by the graph data perturbation models [10–12], noise is added to the graph to learn evenly distributed embeddings, which alleviates the over-smoothing problem. (2) Contrastive learning module: Contrastive learning is performed on the collaborative signals augmentation view and the differentiation enhancement view, which is used to capture the features of both views. (3) Tasks optimization module: Motivated by UW loss [15], learnable task weights are utilized to optimize the tasks dynamically. To minimize the impact of the parameters and improve the robustness, we optimize UW loss by limiting the task weights and parameters. Our contributions include:

- We propose a new multi-view generation module that constructs the differentiation enhancement view and the collaborative signals augmentation view to mitigate the over-smoothing problem and improve the representation ability of the GCL-based recommender model.
- We innovatively incorporate the tasks optimization module into the GCL-based recommender model to adapt to the dynamic changes of tasks during the training phase and limit the parameter variations to enhance the robustness of the model.
- We conduct extensive experiments on six datasets to prove the superiority of GACS and analyze its rationality in depth.

2 Related Work

2.1 Graph Convolutional Networks for Recommendation

GCN, with its ability to learn from non-Euclidean structures, is suitable for capturing graph-structured relationships. NGCF [3] combines GCN and collaborative filtering to enhance embedding quality through feature transformations, neighborhood aggregation, and nonlinear activation. LightGCN [2] simplifies the nonlinear activation module of GCN to improve the calculation speed. GraphDA [1] enhances and denoises the adjacency matrix by using a pre-trained GCN model. Despite the commendable performance of GCN, it relies heavily on supervised signals extracted from the sparse user-item interactions. Furthermore, GCN leads to the homogenization of node feature information (i.e., over-smoothing problem) when aggregating information.

2.2 Graph Contrastive Learning for Recommendation

GCL is a self-supervised method designed to alleviate the data sparsity problem by extracting features from unlabeled data [17]. Additionally, GCL can learn common features between similar examples and distinguish differences between non-similar examples, which prevents their feature values from converging to the same value and mitigates the over-smoothing problem [12]. SGL [9] first combines GCL with recommender systems, proposing three data enhancement methods by perturbing the graph: node discarding, edge discarding, and random wandering. Many studies attempt to generate views by perturbing the graph data. XSimGCL [12] and SimGCL [10] create noise views by introducing controlled random noise to the node embeddings during the message passing process. DIVGCL [18] employs Gaussian noise-augmented GCL for recommendation. These perturbation methods of adding noise can construct highly discriminative views that help the model improve its distinguishability. However, these perturbation information distort the embedding, reducing the representation ability.

3 Methodology

We describe our proposed framework GACS in detail in this section. GACS consists of three modules: (1) Multi-view generation module: Noise is added during the aggregation process to generate the differentiation enhancement view, which is used to amplify the differences between entities to alleviate the over-smoothing problem. Implicit relationships between users (or items) are utilized to enhance collaborative signals and build the collaborative signals augmentation view, which improves the representation ability. (2) Contrastive learning module: Contrastive learning is applied to capture features from the collaborative signals augmentation view and the differentiation enhancement view. (3) Tasks optimization module: Learnable parameters are employed to adjust the weights. The framework of GACS is shown in Fig. 2.

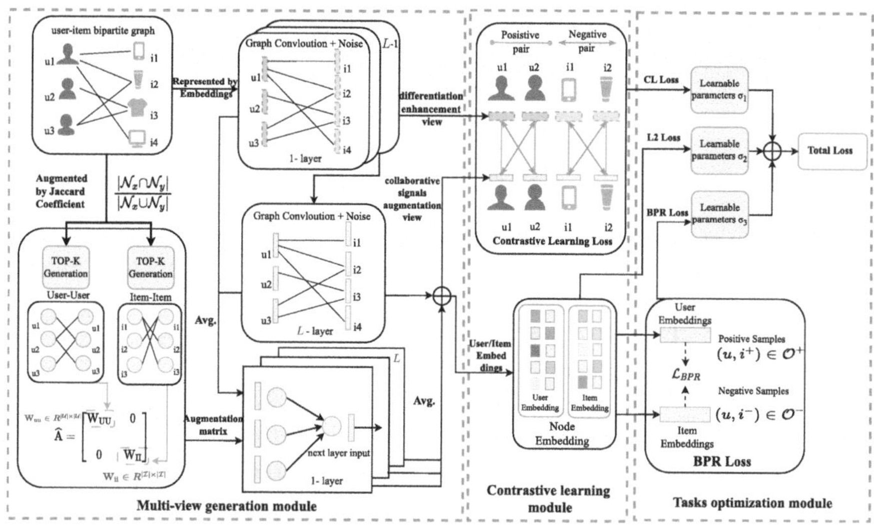

Fig. 2. Overall framework of the GACS.

3.1 Multi-view Generation Module

Differentiation Enhancement View: Inspired by XSimGCL [12], uniform noise is added to the aggregation process, which is formulated as:

$$\mathbf{E}_{ns}^{(l)} = \varepsilon \cdot \rho + \mathbf{AGG}(\mathbf{E}_{ns}^{(l-1)}, \mathrm{A}) \tag{1}$$

ρ represents the uniform noise and ϵ is used to adjust the strength of the uniform noise on the original embedding. $\mathbf{E}_{ns}^{(l)}$ represents the embedding of the user and item in the (l)-layer after adding noise. The number of the layer is controlled by hyperparameters L. $\mathbf{E}_{ns}^{(0)}$ is the node embeddings to be learned. The $(L-1)$-layer embedding $\mathbf{E}_{ns}^{(L-1)}$ is used as the differentiation enhancement view $\mathbf{E}_{NS}$. $\mathrm{A} = \begin{bmatrix} 0 & \mathrm{R} \\ \mathrm{R}^\top & 0 \end{bmatrix}$ represents the adjacency matrix, where R is the user-item interaction matrix. The aggregation function **AGG** utilizes GCN to aggregate embedding, which is specified as follows:

$$\begin{aligned} e_u^{(l)} &= \sum_{i \in \mathcal{N}_u} \frac{1}{\sqrt{|\mathcal{N}_u|}\sqrt{|\mathcal{N}_i|}} e_i^{(l-1)} \\ e_i^{(l)} &= \sum_{u \in \mathcal{N}_i} \frac{1}{\sqrt{|\mathcal{N}_i|}\sqrt{|\mathcal{N}_u|}} e_u^{(l-1)} \end{aligned} \tag{2}$$

$\mathcal{N}_i$ and $\mathcal{N}_u$ represent the set of neighbors of i and u. $\frac{1}{\sqrt{|\mathcal{N}_u|}\sqrt{|\mathcal{N}_i|}}$ is the normalization factor. $e_i^{(l-1)}$ and $e_u^{(l-1)}$ denote the item and user embeddings in the $(l-1)$-layer. $e_i^{(l)}$ and $e_u^{(l)}$ are the item and user embeddings in the (l)-layer.

Collaborative Signals Augmentation View: The Jaccard coefficient enhances the original collaborative signals by calculating the similarity between users (or items) x and y, which is formulated as follows:

$$sim_{x,y} = \frac{|\mathcal{N}_x \cap \mathcal{N}_y|}{|\mathcal{N}_x \cup \mathcal{N}_y|} \tag{3}$$

$\mathcal{N}_x$ and $\mathcal{N}_y$ are the set of neighbors of x and y. $sim_{x,y}$ represents similarity between x and y. The specific treatment of the Jaccard coefficients is as follows:

$$\widehat{A}_{x,y} = \begin{cases} \frac{1}{k} & \text{if } sim_{x,y} \text{ is the } k^{th} \text{ largest value for node } x \\ 0 & \text{others} \end{cases} \tag{4}$$

$\widehat{A}_{x,y}$ is set to $\frac{1}{k}$ if $sim_{x,y}$ is the kth largest value, where $k \in [1, K]$. $\widehat{A}_{x,y}$ is assigned to 0 if $sim_{x,y}$ is not among the top-K largest values. Finally, the augmented matrix $\widehat{\mathrm{A}} = \begin{bmatrix} \mathrm{W_{UU}} & 0 \\ 0 & \mathrm{W_{II}} \end{bmatrix}$ is obtained, where $\mathrm{W_{UU}}$ is the user-user behavior relationships augmentation matrix and $\mathrm{W_{II}}$ is the item-item semantic relationships augmentation matrix. The hyperparameter K_{user} and K_{item} control the top-K values for each user and item.

$\widehat{\mathrm{A}}$ is used to generate the collaborative signals augmentation view with the following formula:

$$\begin{aligned} \mathbf{E}_{aug}^{(0)} &= \frac{1}{L}\sum_{l=1}^{L}(\mathbf{E}_{ns}^{(l)}) \\ \mathbf{E}_{aug}^{(l)} &= \widehat{\mathrm{A}}\mathbf{E}_{aug}^{(l-1)} \end{aligned} \tag{5}$$

$\mathbf{E}_{aug}^{(0)}$ represents the initial embedding, which is obtained through the mean embedding of $\mathbf{E}_{ns}^{(l)}$. The initial embedding $\mathbf{E}_{aug}^{(0)}$ helps nodes retain specific information and prevents them from converging to the same values in the process of encoding the implicit relationships. $\mathbf{E}_{aug}^{(l)}$ and $\mathbf{E}_{aug}^{(l-1)}$ represent the augmented embeddings of the (l)-layer and $(l-1)$-layer. GACS encodes implicit relationships between entities into embeddings by matrix multiplication. The collaborative signals augmentation view $\mathbf{E}_{AG}$ generation formula is as follows:

$$\mathbf{E}_{AG} = \mathbf{E}_{aug}^{(0)} + \eta \cdot \frac{1}{L}\sum_{l=1}^{L}(\mathbf{E}_{aug}^{(l)}) \tag{6}$$

$\mathbf{E}_{AG}$ is obtained by summing the mean embedding of the $\mathbf{E}_{aug}^{(l)}$ and the initial augmented embedding $\mathbf{E}_{aug}^{(0)}$. The parameter η controls the intensity of mean embedding of the $\mathbf{E}_{aug}^{(l)}$. GACS captures complex relationships between nodes through embedding summation to improve the model representation ability.

3.2 Contrastive Learning Module

As illustrated in Fig. 2, the collaborative signals augmentation view $\mathbf{E}_{AG}$ and the differentiation enhancement view $\mathbf{E}_{NS}$ are utilized as inputs for contrastive learning to assist the model in capturing the features of both views, which is formulated as follows:

$$\mathcal{L}_{cl} = \sum_{x \in \mathcal{B}} -\log \frac{\exp\left(\frac{\boldsymbol{e}_{AG}^{x\top} \boldsymbol{e}_{NS}^{x}}{\tau}\right)}{\sum_{y \in \mathcal{B}} \exp\left(\frac{\boldsymbol{e}_{AG}^{x\top} \boldsymbol{e}_{NS}^{y}}{\tau}\right)} \tag{7}$$

$\mathcal{B}$ represents a mini-batch, where x and y are the users(or items) in $\mathcal{B}$. $\boldsymbol{e}_{AG}$ and $\boldsymbol{e}_{NS}$ are the user(or item) embeddings from $\mathbf{E}_{AG}$ and $\mathbf{E}_{NS}$. τ is the temperature coefficient, which controls the strength of differentiation between the samples. $\boldsymbol{e}_{AG}^{x}$ and $\boldsymbol{e}_{NS}^{x}$ are the same node in different views, which are the positive samples. $\boldsymbol{e}_{AG}^{x}$ and $\boldsymbol{e}_{NS}^{y}$ denote the different nodes in different views, which are the negative samples. Contrastive learning encourages consistency in positive samples and minimizes similarity in negative samples.

3.3 Tasks Optimization Module

As presented in Fig. 2, BPR loss is used to evaluate the recommendation performance of the model, which is defined as follows:

$$\mathcal{L}_{\mathrm{BPR}} = -\sum_{(u,i) \in \mathcal{B}} \log\left(\varphi(\boldsymbol{e}_u^{\top} \boldsymbol{e}_{i^+} - \boldsymbol{e}_u^{\top} \boldsymbol{e}_{i^-})\right) \tag{8}$$

$\boldsymbol{e}_u$ represents a user embedding. $\boldsymbol{e}_{i^+}$ denotes an item embedding that the user u has engaged with, where $\boldsymbol{e}_{i^+} \in \mathcal{O}^+$. $\boldsymbol{e}_{i^-}$ is an item embedding that the user u has not engaged with, where $\boldsymbol{e}_{i^-} \in \mathcal{O}^-$. $\boldsymbol{e}_u$, $\boldsymbol{e}_{i^+}$ and $\boldsymbol{e}_{i^-}$ are all from $\mathbf{E}_{AG}$. φ denotes an activation function. $\mathcal{B}$ represents a mini-batch. Inspired by the UW loss [15], the learnable parameter is utilized to balance the loss of each task, and the total loss formula is defined as follows:

$$\mathcal{L} = \frac{\lambda}{2\sigma_1^2}\mathcal{L}_{cl} + \frac{\gamma}{2\sigma_2^2}\|\Theta\|_2 + \frac{1}{2\sigma_3^2}\mathcal{L}_{BPR} + \log \sigma_1\sigma_2\sigma_3 \tag{9}$$

$\mathcal{L}$ is the total loss, which consists of contrastive learning task loss $\mathcal{L}_{cl}$, L2 loss $\|\Theta\|_2$, and recommendation task BRP loss $\mathcal{L}_{BPR}$. Θ represents all the learnable parameters. We set the initial weight of the main task BPR to 1 and use $\lambda(\lambda<1)$ and $\gamma(\gamma<1)$ to control the initial weights of the auxiliary tasks $\mathcal{L}_{cl}$ and $\|\Theta\|_2$. The initialization of weights helps to identify the main tasks and capture key features in the data. σ_i is defined as a learnable parameter used to dynamically adjust the weights of each loss, where σ_1, σ_2 and σ_3 control the weights of $\mathcal{L}_{cl}$, $\|\Theta\|_2$ and $\mathcal{L}_{BPR}$, respectively. Before learning the task loss weights, GACS limits the tuning range of the learnable parameter σ_i, which constrains the impact of additional parameters on the model and improves the robustness. Finally, GACS utilizes the total loss $\mathcal{L}$ to optimize the model.

4 Experiments

To verify the superiority and effectiveness of the GACS, we perform extensive experiments to answer the following research questions:

- RQ1: How does GACS perform on different datasets?
- RQ2: How does GACS against the over-smooth and improve the representation ability?
- RQ3: How does parameter limitation contribute to the tasks optimization module?
- RQ4: How do the various components and hyperparmeters impact GACS?

4.1 Experimental Settings

Datasets and Evaluation Protocols. We conducted experiments on six datasets: Beauty, Sports, Toys, Home, and Tools from the Amazon review datasets[1] and Yelp dataset from SimGCL [10][2]. The statistics of these datasets are presented in Table 1. We arranged each user interaction in chronological order, using the last interaction for testing and the penultimate interaction for validation. Recall@K and Normalized Discounted Cumulative Gain (NDCG)@K are used as evaluation metrics, where $K = \{1, 5, 10\}$.

Table 1. Statistics of the experimented datasets.

Dataset	User	Item	Density	Interactions	Avg/len
Beauty	22,363	12,101	0.073%	198,502	8.87
Sports	35,598	18,357	0.045%	296,337	8.32
Toys	19,412	11,924	0.072%	167,597	8.63
Home	66,519	28,327	0.029%	551,682	8.29
Tools	16,638	10,217	0.079%	134,476	8.10
Yelp	19,539	21,266	0.108%	450,884	23.08

Baseline Methods. Twelve SOTA models can be divided into three categories, namely Graph-based models: MF [19], LightGCN [2], DirectAU [20], Turbo-CF [21], Data Augmentation (DA)-based models: SelfCF [22], BUIR [23], GraphDA [1], and Graph Contrastive Learning (GCL)-based models: SimGCL [10], XSimGCL [12], AdaGCL [13], SGL [9], AUPlus [24].

[1] https://jmcauley.ucsd.edu/data/amazon/.

[2] https://github.com/Coder-Yu/QRec.

Hyperparameter Settings. To ensure fair comparisons, we adjusted the hyperparameters of all baselines within the ranges suggested in the original papers. For all methods, the L2 regularization coefficient is used as 0.0001 and the learning rate is set as 0.001. We search for K_{user} and K_{item} in $\{1, 3, 5, 7, 9\}$, and η in $\{0.001, 0.01, 0.1, 1\}$. We also search for λ in $\{0.01, 0.1, 0.2, 0.5\}$, and ϵ in $\{0.01, 0.05, 0.1, 0.5, 1\}$. τ is fixed at 0.15 for all GCL-based models and L is fixed at 2 for all GCN-based models.

Table 2. Performance comparison. R and N represent Recall and NDCG. Bold and underlined numbers are denoted as the best and second-best results, respectively.

Type		Graph-based models				DA-based models			GCL-based models					Ours	
Dataset	Metric	MF	Turbo-CF	LightGCN	DirectAU	SelfCF	BUIR	GraphDA	SGL	SimGCL	AdaGCL	XSimGCL	AUPlus	GACS	Improv.
Beauty	R@1	0.0059	0.0055	0.0072	0.0075	0.0055	0.0060	0.0082	0.0063	0.0074	0.0068	0.0070	0.0074	**0.0084**	2.4%
	R@5	0.0259	0.0222	0.0303	0.0313	0.0264	0.0268	0.0312	0.0282	0.0313	0.0299	0.0313	0.0305	**0.0339**	8.3%
	N@5	0.0158	0.0136	0.0186	0.0195	0.0158	0.0161	0.0197	0.0171	0.0192	0.0182	0.0190	0.0188	**0.0211**	7.1%
	R@10	0.0435	0.0381	0.0504	0.0512	0.0450	0.0467	0.0514	0.0495	0.0515	0.0509	0.0522	0.0517	**0.0550**	5.3%
	N@10	0.0215	0.0187	0.0251	0.0258	0.0217	0.0225	0.0264	0.0239	0.0257	0.0249	0.0258	0.0261	**0.0279**	5.6%
Tools	R@1	0.0058	0.0063	0.0071	0.0066	0.0067	0.0071	0.0066	0.0076	0.0076	0.0073	0.0071	0.0074	**0.0078**	2.6%
	R@5	0.0182	0.0216	0.0235	0.0218	0.0227	0.0229	0.0230	0.0229	0.0242	0.0231	0.0246	0.0242	**0.0260**	5.6%
	N@5	0.0121	0.0139	0.0152	0.0141	0.0147	0.0151	0.0150	0.0154	0.0158	0.0151	0.0162	0.0159	**0.0171**	5.5%
	R@10	0.0270	0.0320	0.0358	0.0372	0.0363	0.0364	0.0373	0.0372	0.0381	0.0355	0.0382	0.0376	**0.0403**	5.4%
	N@10	0.0149	0.0172	0.0192	0.0191	0.0192	0.0195	0.0205	0.0199	0.0202	0.0191	0.0206	0.0203	**0.0216**	4.8%
Toys	R@1	0.0079	0.0061	0.0073	0.0079	0.0059	0.0068	0.0084	0.0071	0.0073	0.0072	0.0078	0.0070	**0.0091**	8.3%
	R@5	0.0293	0.0222	0.0312	0.0321	0.0241	0.0285	0.0327	0.0316	0.0321	0.0324	0.0322	0.0317	**0.0344**	5.1%
	N@5	0.0188	0.0143	0.0194	0.0204	0.0152	0.0178	0.0208	0.0197	0.0199	0.0200	0.0203	0.0196	**0.0223**	7.2%
	R@10	0.0449	0.0348	0.0499	0.0514	0.0412	0.0456	0.0549	0.0501	0.0511	0.0516	0.0509	0.0516	**0.0563**	2.5%
	N@10	0.0238	0.0183	0.0254	0.0265	0.0207	0.0233	0.0289	0.0256	0.0260	0.0262	0.0264	0.0260	**0.0291**	0.6%
Sports	R@1	0.0048	0.0037	0.0044	0.0058	0.0039	0.0049	0.0059	0.0046	0.0060	0.0050	0.0057	0.0057	**0.0065**	14.0%
	R@5	0.0166	0.0143	0.0177	0.0194	0.0155	0.0191	0.0216	0.0181	0.0213	0.0189	0.0214	0.0213	**0.0228**	6.5%
	N@5	0.0107	0.0091	0.0110	0.0126	0.0097	0.0119	0.0136	0.0113	0.0138	0.0119	0.0137	0.0136	**0.0146**	6.5%
	R@10	0.0278	0.0253	0.0301	0.0334	0.0293	0.0337	0.0346	0.0307	0.0349	0.0330	0.0351	0.0345	**0.0372**	5.9%
	N@10	0.0143	0.0126	0.0150	0.0171	0.0141	0.0166	0.0177	0.0153	0.0181	0.0164	0.0181	0.0178	**0.0192**	6.0%
Home	R@1	0.0025	0.0020	0.0030	0.0026	0.0020	0.0021	0.0030	0.0028	0.0022	0.0020	0.0031	0.0031	**0.0037**	19.3%
	R@5	0.0081	0.0078	0.0102	0.0100	0.0079	0.0092	0.0104	0.0108	0.0113	0.0092	0.0121	0.0120	**0.0138**	14.0%
	N@5	0.0053	0.0049	0.0066	0.0063	0.0049	0.0057	0.0067	0.0069	0.0070	0.0056	0.0076	0.0075	**0.0088**	15.7%
	R@10	0.0126	0.0129	0.0152	0.0162	0.0136	0.0142	0.0172	0.0176	0.0178	0.0153	0.0187	0.0191	**0.0205**	7.3%
	N@10	0.0067	0.0065	0.0081	0.0083	0.0067	0.0073	0.0088	0.0088	0.0091	0.0076	0.0097	0.0098	**0.0110**	10.9%
Yelp	R@1	0.0025	0.0031	0.0034	0.0033	0.0013	0.0020	0.0031	0.0046	0.0036	0.0049	0.0050	0.0049	**0.0057**	14.0%
	R@5	0.0124	0.0163	0.0176	0.0145	0.0086	0.0112	0.0153	0.0216	0.0181	0.0218	0.0192	0.0199	**0.0238**	9.1%
	N@5	0.0073	0.0095	0.0103	0.0088	0.0049	0.0064	0.0091	0.0131	0.0108	0.0134	0.0121	0.0123	**0.0153**	14.1%
	R@10	0.0254	0.0304	0.0309	0.0247	0.0173	0.0232	0.0291	0.0356	0.0300	0.0388	0.0342	0.0330	**0.0409**	5.4%
	N@10	0.0115	0.0141	0.0145	0.0120	0.0077	0.0102	0.0135	0.0176	0.0146	0.0188	0.0169	0.0165	**0.0208**	10.6%

4.2 Performance Validation (RQ1)

As demonstrated in Table 2, GACS outperforms the other three types. Graph-based models are inferior to GCL-based models due to their reliance on sparse supervised data for capturing user preferences. GCL-based models excel on the Tools, Home, and Yelp datasets because they can extract self-supervised signals from unlabeled data. However, GCL-based models overlook implicit relationships between entities and employ invariant task weights, limiting adaptability during the training phase. Among the DA-based models, GraphDA performs the best, and its collaborative signals augmentation helps the model learn more generalized features. Nevertheless, the augmented signals of GraphDA depend on a pre-trained GCN model, which suffers from the over-smoothing problem, leading to embedding distortion. In contrast, our proposed GACS outperforms other baseline models. This is because GACS utilizes Jaccard coefficients to generate implicit relationships between entities, which helps the model capture higher-order connectivity between entities, and uses a tasks optimization module to allow the model to adapt to the changes in the data distribution. The comprehensive experimental results demonstrate the superiority of GACS.

4.3 Againsting Over-Smooth and Improving Representation Ability (RQ2)

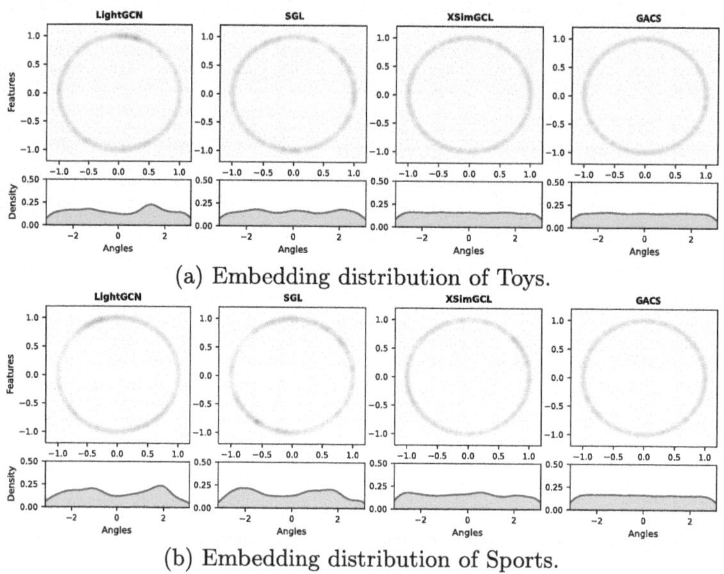

(a) Embedding distribution of Toys.

(b) Embedding distribution of Sports.

Fig. 3. Embedding distribution for different datasets.

Againsting Over-Smooth. To study the embedding distribution of GACS, T-SNE [25] is used to map the learned embeddings (2000 randomly selected nodes per dataset) to 2-D vectors on the unit hypersphere S^1 (A darker color means more nodes at that position) and Gaussian kernel density estimation on angles (i.e., arctan2 (y, x) for each point, where ((x,y) $\in S^1$). XSimGCL and SGL are selected as comparative models to observe the embedding distribution of GCL-based models. Additionally, LightGCN [2] is selected to observe the effects of the over-smoothing problem on embedding distribution.

As shown in Fig. 3, LightGCN is characterized by a high degree of aggregation, manifested in the uneven color distribution of arcs and irregular angular curves. This is because LightGCN employs a GCN structure, and as the number of iterations increases, the features tend to converge to the same value. Compared with LightGCN, the embedding distribution of SGL is more uniform. SGL reduces the links between nodes by discarding nodes and edges, helping to alleviate the over-smoothing problem. XSimGCL has a uniform embedding distribution due to its method of adding noise, which helps the view contain more distinguishable nodes while protecting the graph structure. GACS has a uniform arc color distribution and smooth angular curves. It utilizes noise and implicit relationships to generate more diverse pairs of samples, which helps the model distinguish different nodes by comparing the differences and similarities of these samples. A more uniform distribution maintains the intrinsic features of the nodes and improves generalization.

Improving Representation Ability. As shown in Fig. 4, users are grouped according to their interaction numbers into four categories: ≤3, (3,7], (7,20), and ≥20. SGL and XSimGCL are selected as comparative models to study the effects of graph perturbation on predictive accuracy.

As illustrated in Fig. 4, SGL does not match the performance of XSimGCL in the first three subgroups but performs well in the active users (i.e., number of interactions ≥ 20) subgroup. This is because active users aggregate a lot of noise, and SGL reduces the impact of noise by discarding nodes and edges. XSimGCL performs well in the inactive user (i.e., number of interactions ≤ 3) subgroup. This is due to the fact that the method of dropping nodes and edges in SGL can exacerbate the sparsity problem for inactive users, while XSimGCL better preserves the information of nodes and edges. XSimGCL enhances generalization by adding noise to prevent inactive users from overfitting limited interactions. However active users aggregate more noise to destroy collaborative signals. GACS outperforms the other models in all subgroups. It utilizes implicit relationships to construct collaborative signals enhancement views and contrastive learning with the differentiation enhancement view, which makes active users have uniform embedding distribution while retaining more collaborative signals and mitigating the effects of noise.

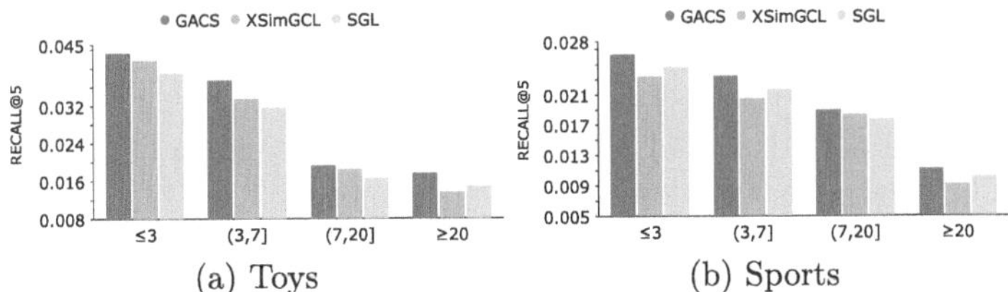

(a) Toys (b) Sports

Fig. 4. Performance comparison of different user groups.

4.4 Contribution of Parameter Limitation (RQ3)

To investigate the contribution of loss weight parameter limitation (LWL) and learnable parameter limitation (LPL) to the tasks optimization module, we performed ablation experiments. The ablation of LWL and LPL is achieved by removing all loss weight limits and learnable parameter limits, respectively.

As shown in Table 3, removing any of the parameter limitations reduces the performance of the model. The overall performance drops obviously when there is no LWL and LPL. This is because removing the parameter limitation causes the model to overfit the training data distribution. Removing the LWL also affects the performance. This is attributed to the fact that the main task of the model is recommendation, and the L2 and CL losses are used as auxiliary tasks to enhance recommendation performance. Without limitation on auxiliary tasks, the model is unable to recognize the main task, making it difficult to capture the key features and patterns in the data. Additionally, without LPL, the model becomes overly sensitive to input data changes, leading to large fluctuations in prediction results. GACS effectively improves the robustness and generalization by limiting the parameters.

Table 3. Impact of different designs of tasks optimization component on model performance on all datasets.

LWL	LPL	Beauty		Tools		Home		Sports		Toys		Yelp	
		R@5	N@5	R@5	N@5	R@5	N@5	R@5	N@5	R@5	N@5	R@5	N@5
✓	✓	**0.0339**	**0.0211**	**0.0260**	**0.0171**	**0.0138**	**0.0088**	**0.0228**	**0.0146**	**0.0344**	**0.0223**	**0.0238**	**0.0153**
×	×	0.0291	0.0181	0.0132	0.0093	0.0118	0.0078	0.0217	0.0141	0.0319	0.0201	0.0209	0.0130
×	✓	0.0322	0.0202	0.0145	0.0099	0.0129	0.0085	0.0212	0.0136	0.0334	0.0211	0.0228	0.0146
✓	×	0.0317	0.0198	0.0132	0.0095	0.0119	0.0080	0.0218	0.0139	0.0332	0.0207	0.0222	0.0139

4.5 Ablation Test (RQ4)

Ablation Test. In this section, we conduct ablation experiments on the Collaborative Signals Augmentation component (CSA), Differentiation Enhancement component (DE), and Tasks Optimization component (TO). The experiments are categorized into the following groups:

w/o CSA: The augmented embedding is removed.

w/o DE: No noise is added when aggregating embedding.

w/o TO: Learnable task loss weights are removed.

As shown in Table 4, deleting any component negatively impacts performance. Notably, removing the DE significantly decreases performance. With no noise added, the model lacks diverse sample pairs and is prone to overfitting the training data, and the nodes in the view tend to converge to the same value during aggregation, affected by the over-smoothing problem. Without the CSA, the model cannot capture implicit relationships and is susceptible to noise, which damages the collaborative signals and weakens the representation ability. Additionally, without the TO, the model cannot capture the relationship between tasks, affecting its dynamic adaptability. GACS uses learnable parameters to adjust the weights, effectively improving the generalization performance.

Table 4. Ablation study of GACS, we report R@5, N@5 on all datasets.

	Beauty		Tools		Home		Sports		Toys		Yelp	
	R@5	N@5	R@5	N@5	R@5	N@5	R@5	N@5	R@5	N@5	R@5	N@5
GACS	**0.0339**	**0.0211**	**0.0260**	**0.0171**	**0.0138**	**0.0088**	**0.0228**	**0.0146**	**0.0344**	**0.0223**	**0.0238**	**0.0153**
w/o CSA	0.0291	0.0181	0.0254	0.0162	0.0101	0.0064	0.0205	0.0130	0.0314	0.0198	0.0192	0.0121
w/o DE	0.0070	0.0049	0.0246	0.0161	0.0039	0.0025	0.0028	0.0020	0.0108	0.0073	0.0003	0.0005
w/o TO	0.0322	0.0207	0.0244	0.0159	0.0133	0.0085	0.0216	0.0137	0.0337	0.0204	0.0220	0.0138

Hyperparmeter Analysis (RQ4). We visualize the effect of the mean augmented embedding strength parameter η and the contrastive learning task weight parameter λ on the performance of GACS.

In Fig. 5(a), the model performs best on all datasets when η is 0.1. However, as η increases, the performance of GACS decreases dramatically. This suggests that appropriate collaborative signals augmentation helps the model capture implicit connections between entities. Conversely, excessive signal strength reduces the generalization of the model. Most GCL-based models are very sensitive to λ [9,10,12]. In Fig. 5(b), it can be seen that the performance of GACS fluctuates slightly under the influence of different λ. This is because GACS utilizes learnable parameters to dynamically adjust the weights of the tasks, and the model achieves superior performance even if it is not the best λ, which effectively improves the robustness of the model.

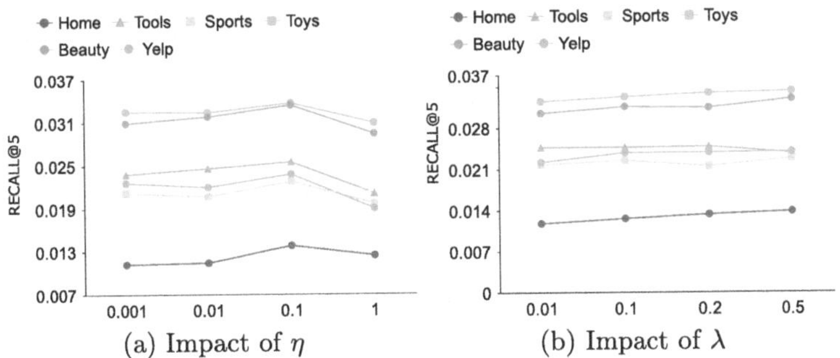

Fig. 5. The influence of η, λ and ϵ on all datasets.

5 Conclusion

In this paper, we propose a **G**raph contrastive learning model with **A**ugmented **C**ollaborative **S**ignals for recommendation (GACS). To alleviate the over-smoothing problem and improve the representation ability, GACS constructs the differentiation enhancement view and the collaborative signals augmentation view that aid the model in differentiating nodes and capturing implicit relationships between nodes. Additionally, the model incorporates tasks optimization module to enhance dynamic adaptability and generalization performance. Extensive experiments on six real-world datasets demonstrate that GACS is an efficient and superior recommendation model.

Acknowledgements. This research was funded by the Research Found for Talented Scholars of Hebei University (No. 521100221088).

References

1. Fan, Z., Xu, K., Dong, Z., Peng, H., Zhang, J., Yu, P.S.: Graph collaborative signals denoising and augmentation for recommendation. In: Proceedings of the 46th International ACM SIGIR Conference on Research and Development in Information Retrieval, pp. 2037–2041 (2023)
2. He, X., Deng, K., Wang, X., Li, Y., Zhang, Y., Wang, M.: Lightgcn: simplifying and powering graph convolution network for recommendation. In: Proceedings of the 43rd International ACM SIGIR Conference on Research and Development in Information Retrieval, pp. 639–648 (2020)
3. Wang, X., He, X., Wang, M., Feng, F., Chua, T.S.: Neural graph collaborative filtering. In: Proceedings of the 42nd International ACM SIGIR Conference on Research and Development in Information Retrieval, pp. 165–174 (2019)
4. Hao, B., Zhang, J., Yin, H., Li, C., Chen, H.: Pre-training graph neural networks for cold-start users and items representation. In: Proceedings of the 14th ACM International Conference on Web Search and Data Mining, pp. 265–273 (2021)
5. Bayer, I., He, X., Kanagal, B., Rendle, S.: A generic coordinate descent framework for learning from implicit feedback. In: Proceedings of the 26th International Conference on World Wide Web, pp. 1341–1350 (2017)
6. Xia, X., Yin, H., Yu, J., Wang, Q., Cui, L., Zhang, X.: Self-supervised hypergraph convolutional networks for session-based recommendation. In: Proceedings of the AAAI Conference on Artificial Intelligence, vol. 35, pp. 4503–4511 (2021)
7. Yang, Y., Huang, C., Xia, L., Li, C.: Knowledge graph contrastive learning for recommendation. In: Proceedings of the 45th International ACM SIGIR Conference on Research and Development in Information Retrieval, pp. 1434–1443 (2022)
8. Yu, J., Yin, H., Gao, M., Xia, X., Zhang, X., Viet Hung, N.Q.: Socially-aware self-supervised tri-training for recommendation. In: Proceedings of the 27th ACM SIGKDD Conference on Knowledge Discovery & Data Mining, pp. 2084–2092 (2021)
9. Wu, J., et al.: Self-supervised graph learning for recommendation. In: Proceedings of the 44th International ACM SIGIR Conference on Research and Development in Information Retrieval, pp. 726–735 (2021)

10. Yu, J., Yin, H., Xia, X., Chen, T., Cui, L., Nguyen, Q.V.H.: Are graph augmentations necessary? Simple graph contrastive learning for recommendation. In: Proceedings of the 45th International ACM SIGIR Conference on Research and Development in Information Retrieval, pp. 1294–1303 (2022)
11. Ye, H., Li, X., Yao, Y., Tong, H.: Towards robust neural graph collaborative filtering via structure denoising and embedding perturbation. ACM Trans. Inf. Syst. **41**(3), 1–28 (2023)
12. Yu, J., Xia, X., Chen, T., Cui, L., Hung, N.Q.V., Yin, H.: Xsimgcl: towards extremely simple graph contrastive learning for recommendation. IEEE Trans. Knowl. Data Eng. (2023)
13. Jiang, Y., Huang, C., Huang, L.: Adaptive graph contrastive learning for recommendation. In: Proceedings of the 29th ACM SIGKDD Conference on Knowledge Discovery and Data Mining, pp. 4252–4261 (2023)
14. Baxter, J.: A model of inductive bias learning. J. Artif. Intell. Res. **12**, 149–198 (2000)
15. Kendall, A., Gal, Y., Cipolla, R.: Multi-task learning using uncertainty to weigh losses for scene geometry and semantics. In: Proceedings of the IEEE Conference on Computer Vision and Pattern Recognition, pp. 7482–7491 (2018)
16. Yang, Y., Hospedales, T.M.: Deep multi-task representation learning: a tensor factorisation approach. In: International Conference on Learning Representations (2017)
17. Yu, J., Gao, M., Li, J., Yin, H., Liu, H.: Adaptive implicit friends identification over heterogeneous network for social recommendation. In: Proceedings of the 27th ACM International Conference on Information and Knowledge Management, pp. 357–366 (2018)
18. Gong, W., et al.: Divgcl: a graph contrastive learning model for diverse recommendation. In: Proceedings of the AAAI Conference on Artificial Intelligence, vol. 39, pp. 16853–16861 (2025)
19. Koren, Y., Bell, R., Volinsky, C.: Matrix factorization techniques for recommender systems. Computer **42**(8), 30–37 (2009)
20. Wang, C., et al.: Towards representation alignment and uniformity in collaborative filtering. In: Proceedings of the 28th ACM SIGKDD Conference on Knowledge Discovery and Data Mining, pp. 1816–1825 (2022)
21. Park, J.D., Shin, Y.M., Shin, W.Y.: Turbo-CF: matrix decomposition-free graph filtering for fast recommendation. arXiv preprint arXiv:2404.14243 (2024)
22. Zhou, X., Sun, A., Liu, Y., Zhang, J., Miao, C.: SelfCF: a simple framework for self-supervised collaborative filtering. ACM Trans. Recommender Syst. **1**(2), 1–25 (2023)
23. Lee, D., Kang, S., Ju, H., Park, C., Yu, H.: Bootstrapping user and item representations for one-class collaborative filtering. In: Proceedings of the 44th International ACM SIGIR Conference on Research and Development in Information Retrieval, pp. 317–326 (2021)
24. Ouyang, Z., Zhang, C., Hou, S., Zhang, C., Ye, Y.: How to improve representation alignment and uniformity in graph-based collaborative filtering? In: International AAAI Conference on Web and Social Media (2024)
25. Van der Maaten, L., Hinton, G.: Visualizing data using t-SNE. J. Mach. Learn. Res. **9**(11) (2008)

ReGeS: Reciprocal Retrieval–Generation Synergy for Conversational Recommender Systems

Dayu Yang(✉) and Hui Fang

University of Delaware, Newark, DE 19702, USA
{dayu,hfang}@udel.edu

Abstract. Connecting conversation with external domain knowledge is vital for conversational recommender systems (CRS) to correctly understand user preferences. However, existing solutions either require domain-specific engineering, which limits flexibility, or rely solely on large language models, which increases the risk of hallucination. While Retrieval-Augmented Generation (RAG) holds promise, its naive use in CRS is hindered by noisy dialogues that weaken retrieval and by overlooked nuances among similar items. We propose **ReGeS**, a reciprocal **Re**trieval–**Ge**neration **S**ynergy framework that unifies generation-augmented retrieval to distill informative user intent from conversations and retrieval-augmented generation to differentiate subtle item features. This synergy obviates the need for extra annotations, reduces hallucinations, and simplifies continuous updates. Experiments on multiple CRS benchmarks show that ReGeS achieves state-of-the-art performance in recommendation accuracy, demonstrating the effectiveness of reciprocal synergy for knowledge-intensive CRS tasks. Our code is publicly available at the link: https://github.com/dayuyang1999/ReGeS.

Keywords: Conversational Recommender System · Large Language Model · Information Retrieval System

1 Introduction

Traditional Recommender Systems (RS) rely on implicit signals—such as clicks and ratings—to generate item suggestions [11], but struggle when user interests shift or require nuanced clarifications. By contrast, Conversational Recommender Systems (CRS) employ multi-turn dialogues to iteratively refine user preferences [30], yet they must decode subtle, colloquial intents and map them onto structured item data, a task necessitating considerable domain expertise [4]. To incorporate such knowledge, two main approaches have emerged. Representation-based methods inject domain-specific features into the pipeline [21,30] but require intricate engineering and lack cross-domain flexibility. In contrast, Large Language Models (LLMs) serve as universal knowledge sources [3,7,28]; however, they must be continuously updated to accommodate new items and are prone to hallucinations, limiting their reliability in fast-evolving domains [10,27].

I. Awan et al. (Eds.): WISE 2025, LNCS 16368, pp. 72–87, 2026.
https://doi.org/10.1007/978-981-95-7251-9_6

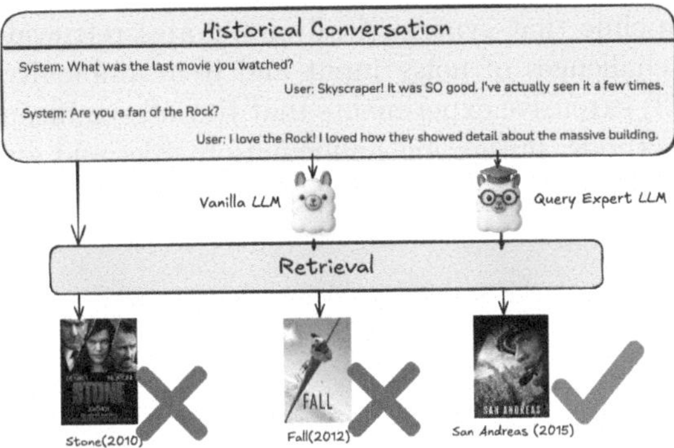

Fig. 1. Given historical conversation in CRS, both directly using historical conversation and prompting vanilla LLMs fall short in retrieval.

RAG has proven highly effective in knowledge-intensive NLP tasks by grounding outputs in external knowledge sources [14,22,24]. Given its strong capacity to inject factual information into conversational exchanges, one might expect RAG to be extensively studied in conversational recommendation systems (CRS). Surprisingly, it remains underexplored in this domain. Our initial attempts at applying RAG to CRS reveal two major hurdles (See experiment in Sect. 3.5): 1) *noisy, lengthy conversation transcripts* impair retrieval effectiveness, and it cannot be easily solved by simply prompting LLMs as illustrated in Fig. 1. 2) *suboptimal item generation* when confronted with multiple similar candidates, as LLMs struggle to differentiate subtle features.

Addressing the challenges of nosiy input and fine-grained item differentiation in isolation would be expensive, typically requiring extensive manual labeling [26]. Specifically, training a model to denoise raw conversation transcripts is usually costly because it demands additional, annotated labels [8]. In contrast, when coupled with a generative component, the LLM can leverage the ground-truth item to identify and extract the most salient concepts connecting the conversation to the desired recommendation, thereby generating high-quality supervision without human annotations.

Furthermore, LLMs often fail to distinguish subtle differences among similar retrieved items. Addressing this via hard negative training requires an effective retrieval stage capable of identifying these crucial near-miss examples. Initial poor retrieval performance thus obstructs effective generator training. This motivates a synergistic approach.

We propose **ReGeS**, a domain-agnostic framework that synergizes retrieval and generation for CRS. ReGeS introduces: 1) **generation-augmented retrieval**, where a trained LLM performs as the query expert to produce concise, preference-focused queries for a retrieve by leveraging the generated pseudo guiding signal. 2) **retrieval-augmented item generation**, where retrieved candidates train the LLM to discern subtle item distinctions. Our contributions are: 1) the first RAG-based CRS framework integrating grounded knowledge retrieval;

2) a reciprocal pipeline that synergistically integrates retrieval and generation to overcome the challenges of noisy input and item ambiguity without costly annotations; and 3) extensive experiments that ReGeS significantly outperforms state-of-the-art methods, mitigating hallucination risks and avoiding laborious domain-specific engineering.

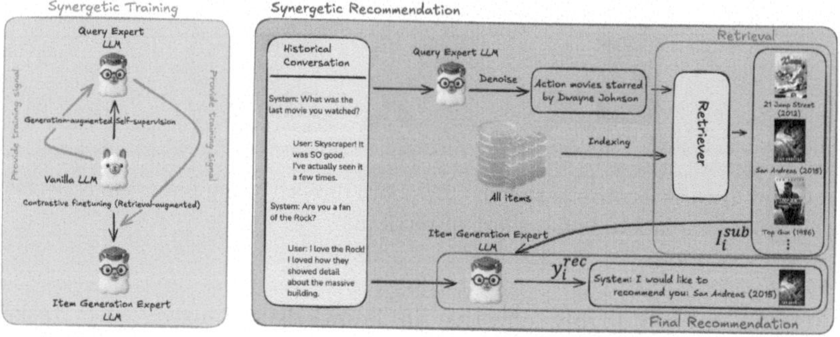

Fig. 2. Overview of the ReGeS framework, illustrating the reciprocal synergy. Left (Training): Generation guides Query Expert LLM_{QR} training, while Retrieval provides training signals for Item Generation Expert LLM_G training. Right (Inference): The trained components collaborate to produce the recommendation.

2 Methodology

In this section, we introduce the methodological detail of ReGeS. Section 2.1 provides an overview of how these two components collaborate, followed by a formal problem definition in Sect. 2.2. We then present two core modules: *Generation-augmented Retrieval* (Sect. 2.3) and *Retrieval-augmented Generation* (Sect. 2.4). This bidirectional flow—where generation refines retrieval and retrieval sharpens generation—ensures final recommendations are both contextually grounded and factually accurate.

2.1 Overview

Figure 2 illustrates the reciprocal interplay of retrieval and generation in ReGeS. At the retrieval stage, a *query expert LLM* first condenses a user–system dialogue history $\mathcal{H}_i$ into a concise, preference-aware query $\hat{q}_i$. By leveraging grounded user-system interaction to generate pseudo supervision signal as self-supervision, query expert LLM learns which aspects of $\mathcal{H}_i$ matter for retrieval, alleviating the challenge of noisy and lengthy conversations. During generation, the predicted informative query $\hat{q}_i$ is used by a retriever R to select candidate items $\mathcal{I}_i^{\text{sub}}$. Given $\mathcal{H}_i$ and these retrieval results (including closely-related "hard negatives"), a contrastively trained generator G pinpoints the most suitable recommendation $y_i^{\text{rec}} \in \mathcal{I}_i^{\text{sub}}$.

2.2 Problem Statement

The problem of CRS can be expressed as learning a mapping between the i-th user-system interaction history $\mathcal{H}_i$ and the ground-truth item y_i, given the candidate set $\mathcal{I}$:

$$y_i^{\text{rec}} = CRS(\mathcal{H}_i; \mathcal{I}),$$

where y_i^{rec} is the recommended (predicted) item that should ideally be the same as y_i. $\mathcal{I} = \{i_1, i_2, \ldots, i_M\}$ is the set of all possible items that are agnostic to users. Typically, a Retrieval-Augmented Generation paradigm that decomposes the process into two steps:

$$\mathcal{I}_i^{\text{sub}} = R(\mathcal{H}_i, \mathcal{I}),$$

$$y_i^{\text{rec}} = G(\mathcal{H}_i, \mathcal{I}_i^{\text{sub}}),$$

where R retrieves a relevant candidate set, and G generates the final recommendation. Despite this formulation's appeal, two obstacles hinder CRS effectiveness: (1) noisy conversational input complicates retrieval, and (2) hard-to-distinguish item candidates challenge generation. In what follows, we describe how ReGeS solves both issues by leveraging a circular flow of information between retrieval and generation.

2.3 Generation-Augmented Retrieval

To improve retrieval performance under noisy input, we introduce a *generation-augmented query expert LLM*, as shown in Fig. 3, that learns to produce a concise, information-rich query $\hat{q}_i$ from the conversation history $\mathcal{H}_i$. This module is built in a self-supervised manner, alleviating the need for costly human annotations.

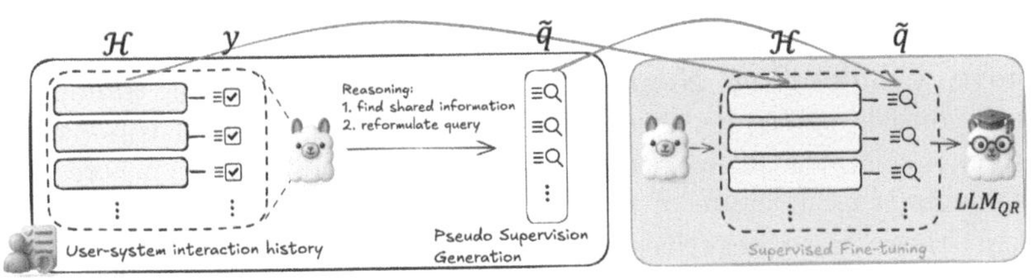

Fig. 3. Process of building generation-augmented query expert LLM_{QR} via generative self-supervision.

Generative Self-supervision via Ground-Truth Guidance. Given a training instance with conversation and its ground-truth recommended item $(\mathcal{H}_i, y_i)$, we first prompt a LLM to produce an informative query $\tilde{q}_i$:

$$\tilde{q}_i = \text{LLM}(\mathcal{H}_i, y_i).$$

Because y_i is provided, the LLM focuses on the essential features in $\mathcal{H}_i$ that justify why y_i is recommended, thus generating $\tilde{q}_i$ as a pseudo-labeled query without manual annotations.

Next, we fine-tune a second LLM instance, denoted LLM_{QR}, to reproduce $\tilde{q}_i$ *without* access to y_i. Formally, we minimize the cross-entropy loss:

$$\mathcal{L}_{\text{QR}} = \sum_{i=1}^{N} \mathcal{L}_{\text{CE}}\Big(\text{LLM}_{\text{QR}}(\mathcal{H}_i), \tilde{q}_i\Big),$$

over the training set. At inference time, LLM_{QR} transforms $\mathcal{H}_i$ into a compact query $\hat{q}_i = \text{LLM}_{\text{QR}}(\mathcal{H}_i)$ capturing the most salient user preferences.

Refined Retrieval. The refined query $\hat{q}_i$ serves as input to the retriever R, which selects a subset of relevant items:

$$\mathcal{I}_i^{\text{sub}} = R(\hat{q}_i, \mathcal{I}).$$

By disentangling user intents from extraneous chatter, LLM_{QR} substantially boosts retrieval accuracy. Moreover, LLM_{QR} itself is *generation-augmented*—it relies on knowledge gleaned from the final item y_i, harnessing generation to improve retrieval.

2.4 Retrieval-Augmented Generation

With $\mathcal{I}_i^{\text{sub}}$ now distilled to the most relevant candidates, the next step is to generate the final recommendation y_i^{rec}. A pure text-generation approach could overlook subtle differences among items, leading to hallucinated or incorrect picks, especially when multiple items in $\mathcal{I}_i^{\text{sub}}$ are nearly interchangeable. ReGeS avoids this pitfall by feeding the retrieved candidates back into the generation process in a contrastive manner, ensuring the generator can pinpoint the precise match.

Retrieve Challenging Negatives with LLM_{QR}. During training, each instance consists of $\mathcal{H}_i$, its ground-truth item y_i, and a set of top-k retrieved items $\{c_{i_1}, \ldots, c_{i_k}\}$ utilizing LLM_{QR} that is previously built, where none of the elements is y_i. Because of the improved retrieval performance brought by LLM_{QR}, these "hard negatives" will share strong relevance signals with $\mathcal{H}_i$, they elevate challenges the Item Generation Expert LLM_Q to distinguish subtle nuances. Let $\mathcal{S}_i$ be the item set we fed into LLM during training, i.e.,

$$\mathcal{S}_i = \{\, y_i,\, c_{i_1},\, \ldots,\, c_{i_k} \},$$

$|\mathcal{S}_i| = k + 1$ for all training instances. The model sees $\mathcal{H}_i, \mathcal{S}_i$, and a prompt specifying that only y_i is correct.

Contrastive Fine-Tuning. We then fine-tune an LLM-based generator LLM_G to maximize the likelihood of selecting y_i. Formally, we encourage

$$P\big(\text{text}(y_i) \mid \mathcal{H}_i, \mathcal{S}_i\big) \;>\; P\big(\text{text}(c_{i_k}) \mid \mathcal{H}_i, \mathcal{S}_i\big),$$

for all c_{i_k}. We implement this using a standard cross-entropy loss, maximizing the probability assigned to the ground-truth item y_i within the context of the candidate set S_i. By confronting LLM with multiple lookalike items, it acquires a fine-grained capability to identify the correct candidate.

Final Recommendation. At inference time, LLM_G receives both $\mathcal{H}_i$ and the retrieved subset $\mathcal{I}_i^{\text{sub}}$. Because the generator has learned to discriminate items using hard negatives, it selects the true best item $y_i^{\text{rec}} \in \mathcal{I}_i^{\text{sub}}$ with higher fidelity. Consequently, retrieval is *generation-augmented*, and generation is *retrieval-augmented*, creating a bidirectional synergy that overcomes the pitfalls of either component in isolation (Fig. 4).

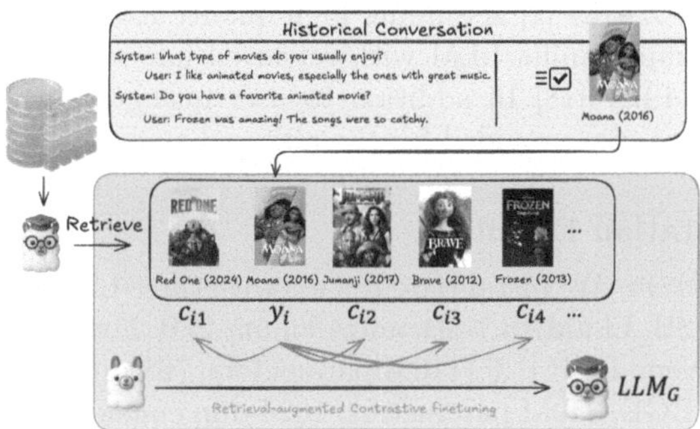

Fig. 4. Retrieval-augmented Contrastive fine-tuning for building Item Generation Expert LLM_G.

3 Experiments

In this section, we first introduce the benchmark datasets, the baselines and experimental settings in Sect. 3.1, Sect. 3.2 and Sect. 3.3 respectively. We then present the overall results in Sect. 3.4, show ablation studies in Sect. 3.5, and conduct additional analyses, including chain-of-thought generation in Sect. 3.6.

3.1 Datasets

Consistent with most previous CRS studies [1,3,15,21,30], we conduct experiments on two widely-used CRS datasets, **ReDial** [15] and **INSPIRED** [6]. ReDial contains 10,006 training and 1,342 test dialogs, focusing on movie recommendations. While relatively large, each conversation tends to be shorter, offering limited explicit preference cues. INSPIRED contains 801 training and 198 validation/test dialogs with richer preference interactions. Both datasets provide ground-truth recommended movies for each conversation, which we treat as the target item(s). Following prior work [21,29], we apply the same preprocessing pipelines and focus on the *recommendation* turn in each dialogue.

3.2 Baselines

We compare our proposed **ReGeS** with three categories of conversational recommendation methods:

Traditional Representation-Based Methods. *KBRD* [1] integrates DBpedia knowledge for semantic enhancement, while *KGSF* [30] leverages both DBpedia and ConceptNet for enriched reasoning. *UniCRS* [21] encodes item meta-information in prompt embeddings for unified modeling of user–item interactions. **LLM-Based Methods (LLM-CRS).** *GPT-3.5-turbo* and *GPT-4* are closed-source LLMs, while *Vicuna-13B* is open-source. Each generates recommendations by analyzing the conversation history without explicit retrieval-based updates. **RAG Methods directly borrow from Recommender System (RAG-RS).** *RARS* [2] Assuming high-quality user query is provided for Retreiver and prompt vanilla LLM with retrieved information to generate recommendations. *RAMO* [18] In addition to user query, relevant document for mentioned items are also provided for the retrieval stage.

3.3 Implementation Details

Models and Retrievers. We instantiate ReGeS with three Large Language Models (LLMs): Gemma-2B, LLaMA3.1-8B, and Gemma-27B. For retrieval, we evaluate three dense retrievers: DPR [13] (110M parameters, 768-dim embeddings), BGE-large-1.5-en [23] (BGE, 340M parameters, 1024-dim embeddings), and OpenAI's text-embedding-3-large (3074-dim embeddings). The retriever provides the top-50 candidates ($k = 50$) for generation; Sect. 3.7 analyzes k's impact.

ReGeS Training Protocol. We detail the fine-tuning procedures for the two core LLM components of ReGeS:

1) Generation-Augmented query expert (LLM_{QR}*)*: the LLM is fine-tuned using the pseudo-queries generated via self-supervision (Sect. 2.3). For Gemma-2B and Llama3.1-8B, we train for one epoch with a batch size of 2. For the larger Gemma-27B model, we use a batch size of 1 for one epoch. We employ the AdamW optimizer with learning rates of 1e-4 for the 2B/8B models and 2e-5 for the 27B model. A linear learning rate warmup schedule is used over the first 10% of training steps.

2) Retrieval-Augmented Item Generation Expert (LLM_G*)*: The item generation LLM is fine-tuned using a contrastive objective with hard negatives supplied by the retriever (Sect. 2.4). One epoch with a batch size of 2 (2B/8B) or 1 (27B). The AdamW optimizer is used with learning rates of 1e-4 (2B/8B) and 5e-5 (27B), again with a 10% warmup phase.

Technical Specifications. To manage computational resources effectively, we set the maximum input sequence length to 4096 tokens, truncating longer sequences. We utilize Low-Rank Adaptation (LoRA) with rank $r = 8$ and scaling factor $\alpha = 32$, applied only to the query and value projection matrices within the self-attention mechanism of the LLMs. During inference for item generation, we set the decoding temperature to 0.1 to promote deterministic and reproducible outputs. All experiments were conducted on a single NVIDIA H100 80GB GPU.

Baseline Implementations. For baseline comparisons, we implemented UniCRS [21], KGSF [30], and KBRD [1] using their publicly available code and recommended hyperparameters. For LLM-based baselines (GPT-3.5-turbo, GPT-4, Vicuna-13B), we followed the experimental setups and prompts described in prior work [7,9]. As code for RAMO [18] and RARS [2] was not available, we re-implemented their core methodologies using DPR and Llama3.1-8B for a fair comparison within our experimental setup.

Evaluation Metric. Our primary evaluation metric is the Recommendation Success Rate (Rec Success Rate in Table 1), equivalent to Recall@1 or Hit@1, focusing on the accuracy of the final item recommendation. We deliberately omit traditional natural language generation metrics (e.g., BLEU, ROUGE, DIST). While historically relevant for assessing the fluency challenges of earlier CRS models [1,21,30], these metrics offer diminishing returns for evaluating modern LLMs, which consistently produce high-quality, coherent text [5,17]. Such n-gram based metrics are often saturated and fail to capture the semantic correctness or relevance of the recommendation itself [20,25]. Therefore, focusing on Rec Success Rate provides a more direct and meaningful assessment of the core recommendation task in contemporary CRS.[1]

3.4 Overall Performance

Table 1. Recommendation success rate on the two datasets. Bold indicates the best overall result. The dagger (†) marks the ReGeS (Small) setting; statistical significance tests (paired McNemar's Test, $p < 0.01$) confirm that even this weakest ReGeS configuration significantly outperforms the strongest baselines from each category (UniCRS, GPT-4, RARS) on both datasets.

Method			ReDial	INSPIRED
Representation-CRS			Rec Success Rate	
	KBRD		0.027	0.036
	KGSF		0.030	0.051
	UniCRS		0.049	0.041[1]
LLM-CRS				
	GPT-3.5		0.041	0.047
	GPT-4		0.043	0.062
	Vicuna-13B		0.031	0.067
RAG-RS				
	RAMO		0.017	0.039
	RARS		0.041	0.059
ReGeS				
Computational Budget	Retriever	Generation		
Small	DPR	2B	0.054†	0.108†
Middle	BGE	8B	0.084	0.196
Large	OpenAI	27B	0.083	0.137
Best (CoT)	OpenAI	8B	**0.094**	**0.218**

[1] Value obtained through reproduction using authors' published code and recommended hyperparameters. Original reported value was 0.094, but multiple independent reproductions achieved 0.041.

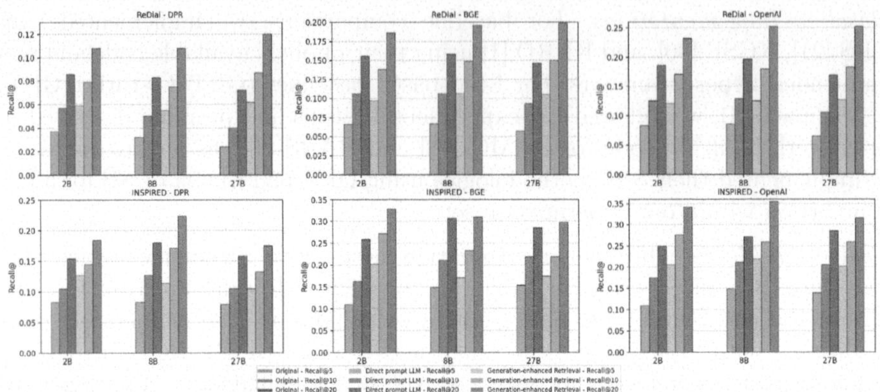

Fig. 5. Retrieval performance comparison between our method (Green) and other baseline methods across different queries and retrievers on both datasets. Note that the scales of y-axis may be different. (Color figure online)

Table 1 presents the recommendation performance of our proposed method, ReGeS, compared to the baseline methods. We showcase three Retriever-LLM combinations in the table, each representing different levels of computational budget. Notably, performance does not always improve with larger retrievers and LLMs. This may be due to the fact that the Llama3.1 models are newer and more efficient than the older Gemma models. We also highlight the best overall performance of ReGeS, achieved when using Chain-of-Thought (CoT) item generation, the text-embedding-large-3 retriever, and Llama3.1-8B. By default, CoT is not used.

Compared to traditional graph-based methods like KBRD and KGSF, ReGeS directly retrieves and filters item knowledge from a broader pool, obviating the need for separate graph modules. ReGeS also outperforms purely LLM-based systems (GPT-3.5-turbo, GPT-4, and Vicuna-13B), highlighting the value of retrieval-augmentation in handling domain-specific updates and reducing hallucinations. Moreover, compared to existing **RAG-RS** methods (RAMO, RARS), our approach substantially boosts accuracy, underscoring the importance of *reciprocal* synergy, as we will discuss in the next subsection.

3.5 Effect of Reciprocal Synergy

We now examine how ReGeS's two core components: Generation-Augmented Retrieval (G-augmented R) and Retrieval-Augmented Generation (R-augmented G) address their respective challenges and merge into a synergetic framework.

Generation-Augmented Retrieval. Figure 5 illustrates how each query denoising method impacts retrieval performance on INSPIRED. We highlight three key observations:

1) Query Quality Is Crucial. When using the unprocessed *Original* conversation as the query, all retrievers underperform markedly. For instance, with the DPR retriever, the Recall@5 is only 0.035, meaning just 3.5% of the top five retrieved items include the ground-truth recommendation.

2) Direct Prompt Alleviates Some Noise. Prompting a vanilla LLM to produce a shorter query helps increase retrieval metrics compared to *Original.* However, *Direct Prompt* still falls short when crucial details are inadvertently omitted, emphasizing the importance of a careful query refinement.

3) G-Augmented R Achieves Consistently Superior Results. Our approach substantially outperforms the other two strategies. On average, Recall@20 improves by 47% over *Original* and 26% over *Direct Prompt*, while Recall@5 sees gains of 81% and 60%. This improvement arises because the self-refinement process systematically identifies the key attributes linking the conversation to the ground-truth item, rather than preserving noise.

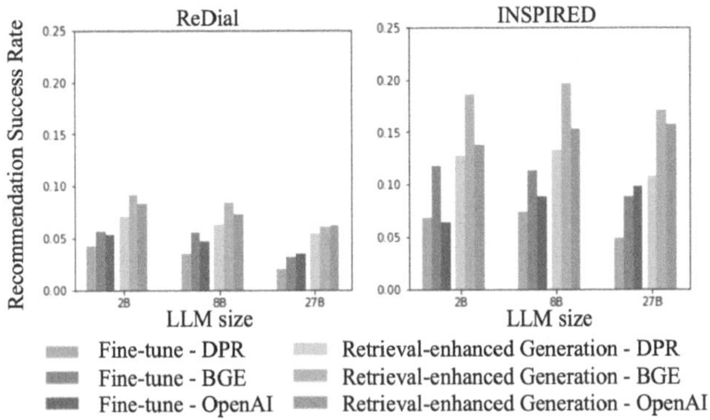

Fig. 6. Item recommendation performance comparison between our method (Orange) and baseline methods (Blue) across various RAG settings. (Color figure online)

Retrieval-Augmented Generation. Figure 6 compares the item recommendation success rate of our proposed R-augmented G method with the baseline method "fine-tune", which fine-tunes the LLM without incorporating hard negatives obtained from the retriever into the training data. On average, incorporating hard negatives boosts recommendation success rate by **79%** on ReDial and **85%** on INSPIRED. This underlines the importance of bridging the distribution gap between training data (where random negatives might not resemble real-world distractors) and actual inference data (where retrieval returns plausible, similar candidates). R-augmented G mitigates hallucination and confusion, thereby reducing errors in the final recommendation step.

3.6 Additional Analyses

This section shows how two obstacles hinder RAG-CRS effectiveness and how G-augmented R and R-augmented G overcome them.

Generation-Augmented Retrieval: Improving Query Quality. We hypothesize that G-augmented R will yield queries that are both semantically closer to user-preferred items and more aligned with human annotaions. To test this, we conduct two primary analyses: 1) measuring how queries from different methods compared in the latent space to ground-truth items, and 2) evaluating textual similarity against human-annotated queries.

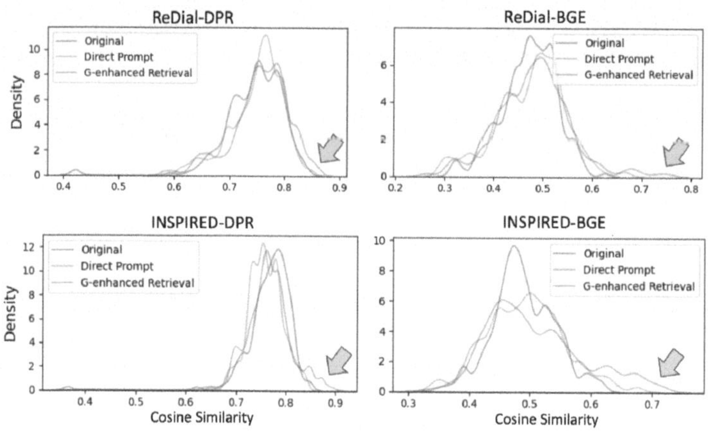

Fig. 7. Comparison of query vs. ground-truth cosine similarity distribution (higher is better, Ours is green). (Color figure online)

1) Latent Space Alignment. We analyze the *cosine similarity* distribution between queries and ground-truth items. Because the retrieval module only shows top-ranked items to the generator, queries with higher cosine similarity to the ground-truth item are more likely to yield correct recommendations. We evaluate three query sets: (i) those generated by the LLM_{QR} in G-augmented R, (ii) the original conversation text, and (iii) queries from directly prompting a vanilla LLM (without self-refinement).

Figure 7 compares the distributions across these three approaches using both DPR and BGE encoders. We observe that G-augmented R yields significantly more queries with higher cosine similarity (note the heavier right tail). This indicates that our self-refinement process produces queries more akin to ground-truth item embeddings—an essential step for retrieving highly relevant candidates.

2) Textual Similarity with Expert-Annotated Queries. We assessed how closely our queries match linguistic expert annotations by randomly sampling 200 data points from the ReDial and INSPIRED datasets. An expert linguistics annotator received the full conversation context and ground-truth user-preferred item, then wrote a concise query reflecting the user's needs.

Table 2. Comparison of BLEU and ROUGE scores across different queries.

Metric	Raw	Direct Prompt	G-augmented R
BLEU-1	0.0505	0.0423	**0.0527**
BLEU-2	0.0155	0.0086	**0.0184**
BLEU-3	0.0050	0.0016	**0.0067**
ROUGE-1	0.1334	0.1122	**0.1742**
ROUGE-2	0.0182	0.0244	**0.0448**
ROUGE-L	0.1157	0.0998	**0.1529**

We computed BLEU and ROUGE scores to compare our query outputs with these human annotations. As reported in Table 2, G-augmented R demonstrates higher BLEU and ROUGE scores than both the *raw conversation* text (Raw) and *direct LLM prompting.* The improvement underscores the effectiveness of our generative self-refining approach in capturing the salient details of user intent without discarding critical contextual information—thereby closely mirroring the way humans reformulate queries.

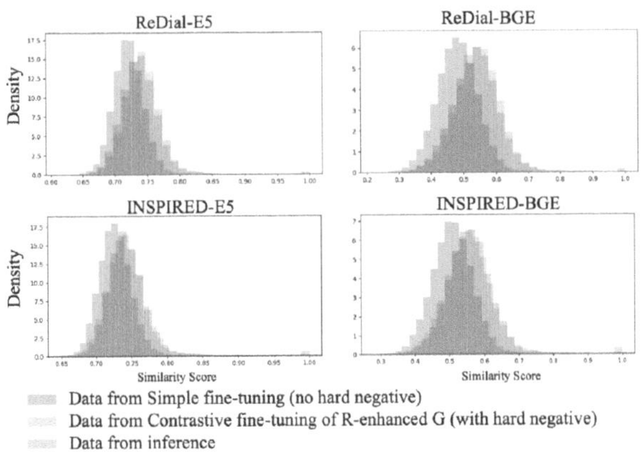

Fig. 8. Distribution of LLM's input during training and inference.

Retrieval-Augmented Generation: Enhance Accuracy on Item Recommendation. As shown in Fig. 8, we project the training inputs and inference inputs into a shared embedding space (e.g., using E5 [19] or BGE [23]). For the random-negative baseline (blue distribution), there is a significant discrepancy between the embeddings of training data and inference data. Conversely, when hard negatives (orange distribution) are used, the alignment between training and inference distributions improves considerably. This alignment explains our observed performance gains: the system trained with hard negatives achieves a higher recommendation success rate because better discrimination between similar items.

Figure 8 shows how both training and inference inputs are projected into the same embedding space (e.g., using E5 [19] or BGE [23]). Under the random-negative baseline (blue distribution), there is a pronounced mismatch between the two sets of embeddings. In contrast, using hard negatives (orange distribution) more closely aligns training and inference embeddings. This closer alignment underpins the performance improvements: models trained with hard negatives achieve higher recommendation success rates because they better discriminate among closely related items (Table 3).

Table 3. Comparison of Average Hallucination Ratio.

	Model Size	Avg Hallu. Ratio
ReGeS (Middle)	8B	**0.13%**
LLM-CRS[a]	~20B (GPT3.5)	4.49%
	~200B (GPT4)	5.14%

[a] Halluciation Ratios of LLM-CRS are directly obtained from [7].

We also compare the hallucination ratio of ReGeS (Middle Computation Setup) with LLM-CRS baselines [7,9]. By implementing ReGeS, the hallucination ratio is dramatically decreases from around 5% in existing LLM-based CRS to under 0.13%.

Overall, R-augmented G directly addresses the second challenge raised in our introduction—namely, how to refine item generation to handle similar or confusing item candidates. By ensuring the LLM's training data closely matches its real-world usage scenario, we reduce hallucinations and bolster recommendation accuracy.

3.7 Discussion

Impact of the Number of Retrieved Candidates. The number of candidates passed from retriever to generator presents a trade-off: more candidates increase the odds of including the ground-truth item (coverage) but complicate the generation task by introducing more distractors. To analyze this, we measure **Overall Success Rate** (end-to-end performance) and **Item Generation**

Success Rate (generator's accuracy when the correct item is guaranteed to be in the candidate set).

Table 4. Performance under different final-list sizes. *Overall Rec Success Rate* measures the end-to-end system accuracy, including retrieval errors. *Item Generation Success Rate* measures how well the generation stage picks the correct item *when it is guaranteed to be in the final list.*

ReDial				
Num Candidates	Model Size	Retriever	Overall Rec Success Rate	Item Generation Success
50	2B	DPR	**0.1078**	0.2108
50	8B	BGE	**0.1961**	0.2451
10	2B	DPR	0.0420	0.5549
10	8B	BGE	0.0593	0.5886
INSPIRED				
Num Candidates	Model Size	Retriever	Overall Rec Success Rate	Item Generation Success
50	2B	DPR	0.0543	0.1948
50	8B	BGE	0.0835	0.1894
10	2B	DPR	**0.0784**	0.3873
10	8B	BGE	**0.0846**	0.4314

As shown in Table 4, the optimal number of candidates is dataset-dependent, hinging on the system's bottleneck. On **ReDial**, where shorter dialogues create less precise queries, performance is **retrieval-bottlenecked**; thus, a larger candidate set ($k = 50$) is superior, as the benefit of higher coverage outweighs the increased difficulty for the generator. Conversely, on **INSPIRED**, richer dialogues make the system **generation-bottlenecked**, where a smaller set ($k = 10$) yields better performance by simplifying the generator's discrimination task. For our main experiments, we default to $k = 50$, a choice that favors maximizing retrieval coverage and aligns with the strength of our Retrieval-Augmented Generation module, which is specifically designed to disambiguate fine-grained differences among many similar items.

4 Related Work

Conversational Recommender Systems (CRS) aim to overcome the limitations of traditional, static recommendation by using multi-turn dialogues to capture nuanced user preferences [4,30]. Early approaches relied on domain-specific knowledge graphs, which require significant engineering and struggle to adapt to subtle linguistic cues [1,21,30]. While Large Language Models (LLMs) offer a more flexible alternative, they suffer from two critical flaws: their knowledge is static, preventing them from recommending new items, and they are prone to hallucination [7,12]. Retrieval-Augmented Generation (RAG) has emerged as a potent solution to these problems by grounding LLMs in external, up-to-date knowledge [14,22]. Although explored in traditional RS [2,16,18], its application to the unique challenges of conversational settings remains underdeveloped.

Existing RAG frameworks for RS are ill-equipped for the distinct challenges of CRS. They do not account for the noisy, multi-turn nature of conversational queries, nor do they address the problem of fine-grained item ambiguity, where a generator must distinguish between multiple highly similar retrieved candidates. Our work, **ReGeS**, introduces the first RAG-based framework tailored for CRS by establishing a *reciprocal synergy*: generation augments retrieval to distill user intent from noisy dialogues, while retrieval augments generation to sharpen the model's ability to differentiate between similar items. This approach offers a flexible, up-to-date, and hallucination-resistant solution for conversational recommendation.

5 Conclusion

We introduced ReGeS, a unified framework that leverages reciprocal synergy between retrieval and generation for conversational recommendation. By self-supervised query refinement and contrastive fine-tuning with hard negatives, ReGeS transforms noisy dialogues into concise retrieval queries and sharpens item selection, eliminating manual annotations and reducing hallucinations by over 30×. Extensive experiments on ReDial and INSPIRED confirm ReGeS's superior accuracy and robustness. We hope ReGeS catalyzes further RAG innovations in real-world conversational recommendation.

References

1. Chen, Q., et al.: Towards knowledge-based recommender dialog system. arXiv preprint arXiv:1908.05391 (2019)
2. Di Palma, D.: Retrieval-augmented recommender system: enhancing recommender systems with large language models. In: Proceedings of the 17th ACM Conference on Recommender Systems, pp. 1369–1373 (2023)
3. Feng, Y., et al.: A large language model enhanced conversational recommender system. arXiv preprint arXiv:2308.06212 (2023)
4. Gao, C., et al.: Advances and challenges in conversational recommender systems: a survey. AI Open **2**, 100–126 (2021)
5. Gao, M., et al.: LLM-based NLG evaluation: current status and challenges. arXiv preprint arXiv:2402.01383 (2024)
6. Hayati, S.A., et al.: Inspired: toward sociable recommendation dialog systems. arXiv preprint arXiv:2009.14306 (2020)
7. He, Z., et al.: Large language models as zero-shot conversational recommenders. In: Proceedings of the 32nd ACM International Conference on Information and Knowledge Management, pp. 720–730 (2023)
8. Hirsch, S., et al.: Query reformulation in E-commerce search. In: SIGIR, pp. 1319–1328 (2020)
9. Hou, Y., et al.: Large language models are zero-shot rankers for recommender systems. In: European Conference on Information Retrieval, pp. 364–381. Springer (2024)

10. Huang, L., et al.: A survey on hallucination in large language models: principles, taxonomy, challenges, and open questions. ACM Trans. Inf. Syst. (2024)
11. Jannach, D., et al.: A survey on conversational recommender systems. ACM Comput. Surv. (CSUR) **54**(5), 1–36 (2021)
12. Ji, Z., et al.: Towards mitigating LLM hallucination via self reflection. In: EMNLP Findings 2023, pp. 1827–1843 (2023)
13. Karpukhin, V., et al.: Dense passage retrieval for open-domain question answering. arXiv preprint arXiv:2004.04906 (2020)
14. Lewis, P., et al.: Retrieval-augmented generation for knowledge-intensive NLP tasks. Adv. Neural. Inf. Process. Syst. **33**, 9459–9474 (2020)
15. Li, R., et al.: Towards deep conversational recommendations. In: Advances in Neural Information Processing Systems, vol. 31 (2018)
16. Ma, Y., et al.: Simple but Efficient: A Multi-Scenario Nearline Retrieval Framework for Recommendation on Taobao. arXiv preprint arXiv:2408.00247 (2024)
17. Mendonça, J., Lavie, A., Trancoso, I.: On the Benchmarking of LLMs for Open-Domain Dialogue Evaluation. arXiv preprint arXiv:2407.03841 (2024)
18. Rao, J., Lin, J.: RAMO: Retrieval-Augmented Generation for Enhancing MOOCs Recommendations. arXiv preprint arXiv:2407.04925 (2024)
19. Wang, L., et al.: Text Embeddings by Weakly-Supervised Contrastive Pre-training. arXiv preprint arXiv:2212.03533 (2022)
20. Wang, X., et al.: Rethinking the evaluation for conversational recommendation in the era of large language models. arXiv preprint arXiv:2305.13112 (2023)
21. Wang, X., et al.: Towards unified conversational recommender systems via knowledge-enhanced prompt learning. In: KDD, pp. 1929–1937 (2022)
22. Wu, S., et al.: Retrieval-Augmented Generation for Natural Language Processing: A Survey. arXiv preprint arXiv:2407.13193 (2024)
23. Xiao, S., et al.: C-Pack: Packaged Resources To Advance General Chinese Embedding. arXiv:2309.07597 (2023)
24. Xu, Z., et al.: Retrieval-augmented generation with knowledge graphs for customer service question answering. In: Proceedings of the 47th International ACM SIGIR Conference on Research and Development in Information Retrieval, pp. 2905–2909 (2024)
25. Yang, D., Chen, F., Fang, H.: Behavior alignment: a new perspective of evaluating LLM-based conversational recommendation systems. In: Proceedings of the 47th International ACM SIGIR Conference on Research and Development in Information Retrieval, pp. 2286–2290 (2024)
26. Yang, D., Zhang, Y., Fang, H.: Zero-shot query reformulation for conversational search. In: Proceedings of the 2023 ACM SIGIR International Conference on Theory of Information Retrieval, pp. 257–263 (2023)
27. Ye, H., et al.: Cognitive mirage: a review of hallucinations in large language models. arXiv preprint arXiv:2309.06794 (2023)
28. Zhang, G.: User-centric conversational recommendation: adapting the need of user with large language models. In: Proceedings of the 17th ACM Conference on Recommender Systems, pp. 1349–1354 (2023)
29. Zhou, K., et al.: CRSLab: An Open-Source Toolkit for Conversational Recommender System. arXiv preprint arXiv:2101.00939 (2021)
30. Zhou, K., et al.: Improving conversational recommender systems via knowledge graph based semantic fusion. In: KDD, pp. 1006–1014 (2020)

Ontology-Enhanced RAG Architecture for Sensory-Aware Food Recommendation

Ada Bagozi(✉), Devis Bianchini, Paola Magrino, Michele Melchiori, Stefano Picchi, and Anisa Rula

University of Brescia, Brescia, Italy
{ada.bagozi,devis.bianchini,paola.magrino,michele.melchiori, stefano.picchi,anisa.rula}@unibs.it

Abstract. Food recommender systems must integrate heterogeneous, multi-level knowledge, including nutritional, environmental, and sensory aspects. However, sensory perception, despite its key role in user satisfaction, remains underinvestigated. In this work, we propose a web-based food advisory architecture that includes a Sensory Analysis Ontology, aligned with ISO standards, and embedded within a modular Retrieval-Augmented Generation (RAG) pipeline. Our main contribution is the design and engineering of a web-based system that combines symbolic and sub-symbolic components to enable: (i) ontology-driven semantic indexing of food-related data, (ii) query rewriting using domain-aligned vocabulary, and (iii) a hybrid retrieval layer combining dense vector search with Text-to-SQL over structured sensory databases. This design enables recommendations that match user's taste preferences based on certified panelists evaluations. Experimental evaluation, performed using a benchmark of real-world, multi-domain queries across nutrition, sustainability, and sensory domains, shows that full integration of ontological knowledge across indexing, retrieval, and generation phases improves response quality, achieving up to +34.6% in actionability, +20.1% in relevance and +26.0% in completeness compared to the baseline.

Keywords: Sensory Analysis · Sustainable Food Recommendation · Multi-perspective Ontologies · Large Language Models · Text-to-SQL

1 Introduction

Supporting consumers in making autonomous food choices that are sustainable, nutritionally balanced, and aligned with personal preferences is a multifaceted challenge [15]. Compared to recommender systems in other domains, food recommendation presents a unique complexity: choices are influenced not only by objective constraints, such as health conditions (e.g., diabetes or allergies), dietary restrictions, or sustainability goals (e.g., low carbon footprint), but also by highly subjective factors, including individual taste preferences and sensory perceptions. Sensory analysis, the scientific discipline that evaluates products through human senses (sight, smell, taste, touch, hearing), plays a key role in

I. Awan et al. (Eds.): WISE 2025, LNCS 16368, pp. 88–103, 2026.
https://doi.org/10.1007/978-981-95-7251-9_7

shaping food satisfaction and acceptance. Yet, despite its relevance, sensory perception remains largely underinvestigated in AI-based food advisory systems. As shown in [3], sensory descriptors like `firmness`, `astringency`, or `visual appeal` are difficult to model using purely statistical or textual approaches. These descriptors are typically gathered via standardized protocols, such as those outlined in ISO 20613:2019, involving trained panelists and certified evaluation procedures. Including sensory analysis benefits both consumers and food producers: consumers receive suggestions aligned with their taste preferences, while producers gain insights into user expectations, which can inform product development and refinement. This work evolves our previous study on ontology-aided food recommendation [2], which introduced a modular ontology to enrich LLM context for nutrition- and sustainability-aware guidance, applied it to condition LLM prompts over largely unstructured data (without a RAG pipeline), and validated the approach in a small-scale user study. In contrast, here we propose a web-based food advisory architecture that embeds a Sensory Analysis Ontology, aligned with ISO standards, within a modular Retrieval-Augmented Generation (RAG) pipeline that combines symbolic and sub-symbolic components. Concretely, the ontology informs (i) ontology-driven semantic indexing of food-related data, (ii) query rewriting with domain-aligned vocabulary, and (iii) a hybrid retriever that pairs dense vector search with Text-to-SQL over certified sensory databases. This enables LLMs to reason over structured sensory knowledge (e.g., `crispiness`, `bitterness`, `visual appeal`) and to generate context-aware, taste-aligned responses based on panelists' certified evaluations, bridging subjective user language and formalized knowledge. The system supports real-world, multi-domain queries across nutrition, sustainability, and sensory aspects, such as: *"What sweet and crunchy products match the dietary profile of Elizabeth Gonzalez?"* and *"What are some sustainable alternatives that match Elizabeth Gonzalez's taste preferences for the meat category?"*. The system supports role-aware, web-based interactions tailored to both consumers and expert users. We demonstrate how the integration of ontology modeling, hybrid retrieval techniques, and modular architecture enhances performances, as evidenced by our experimental evaluation using a benchmark of real-world, multi-domain queries across nutrition, sustainability, and sensory domains.

The remainder of the paper is structured as follows: Sect. 2 discusses the motivating scenario and underlying challenges, Sect. 3 describes the ontological and database foundations, Sect. 4 presents the design of the modular RAG architecture, Sect. 5 presents experimental results, Sect. 6 reviews related work, and finally, Sect. 7 concludes and outlines future work.

2 Context and Motivations

Consider *Elizabeth Gonzalez*, 37, with type 2 diabetes and lactose intolerance, who enjoys Mediterranean cuisine and avoids slimy textures, asking for food suggestions; her choices balance health constraints, taste preferences, and calorie limits, and her queries span nutrition, sustainability, and sensory perception.

On the other hand, *Laura Odels* is a sensory panel leader, in charge of evaluating product quality through rigorous sensory sessions. She supervises a "Honey Panel" tasting session and requires support to establish which descriptors to use, which best tasters to select for this panel, and how to monitor tasters' performances. Despite their different roles, both Elizabeth and Laura rely on the same underlying knowledge infrastructure, which integrates semantically heterogeneous data. Nutritional and sustainability information is typically structured and quantitative, whereas sensory descriptors are subjective and context dependent, requiring nuanced interpretation. Terms like `crispy` or `not rubbery` express preferences that are difficult to interpret through statistical means alone. Even in expert settings governed by ISO standards (e.g., 20613:2019), semantic drift can occur: for instance, the `grainy` descriptor may vary in meaning across food categories. To ensure consistency and relevance, food advisory systems must bridge informal consumers' language and formal experts' protocols through robust semantic grounding and knowledge representation. These scenarios highlight the need for a system capable of handling diverse, semantically rich queries, while maintaining alignment with domain standards. In Elizabeth's case, this involves integrating dietary constraints with structured sensory profiles to surface preference-aligned suggestions. Laura, by contrast, requires analytical access to certified evaluation records, such as monitoring a taster's efficiency index over time. To address these issues, our architecture integrates a modular ontology across multiple retrieval and generation stages. Dense vector search supports open-ended natural language queries, while Text-to-SQL components enable precise access to relational databases hosting certified sensory analysis results. This hybrid infrastructure enables consistent reasoning across users' roles and data modalities. Grounding retrieval in formal ontologies and rewriting queries with domain-aligned vocabulary bridges the gap between informal language and certified food knowledge. This is particularly crucial for high-stakes scenarios such as health-constrained diets or certified product evaluation.

2.1 Approach Overview

Figure 1 outlines the conceptual foundations of our approach. The model comprises five interrelated layers that support the integration of heterogeneous food-related data, the formalization of domain knowledge, and the delivery of semantically grounded interactions tailored to distinct user goals. At the base lies the `food supply chain (FSC)`, where actors such as producers, processors, retailers, and certification authorities generate data that describe different facets of food items, including origin, processing steps, traceability, and certification status. This layer encodes transformations across the food lifecycle. Building on this, the `data storage` layer harmonizes diverse information sources, such as ingredient declarations, nutritional tables, environmental impact scores, and sensory profiles, collected across the supply chain. Structured and unstructured content is preprocessed into semantically annotated units. These units comprise collected data and embeddings generated from data chunks, with LLM-produced, ontology-guided descriptions. Domain knowledge is modeled through a modu-

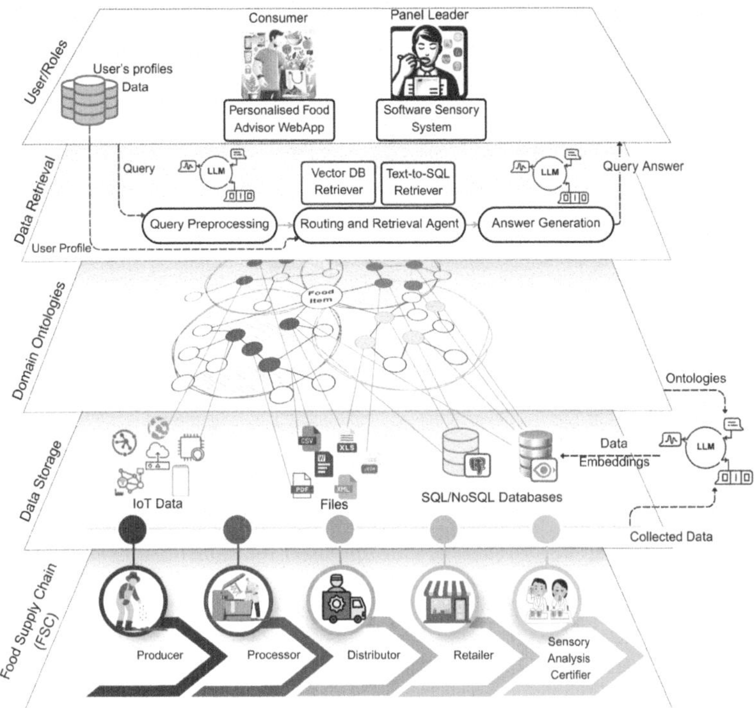

Fig. 1. Overview of the Ontology Driven Food Advisory with LLMs approach.

lar ontology suite that covers nutrition, sustainability, and a newly introduced Sensory Analysis Ontology. This layer supports the interpretation of vague/-subjective user's expressions, such as `not rubbery`, by mapping them to structured concepts and constraints defined under standardized evaluation protocols. The data retrieval layer supports a hybrid retrieval mechanism that pairs dense vector search over semantically tagged content with **Text-to-SQL** on databases containing certified sensory evaluations, handling both flexible preferences and strict constraints. Finally, the interaction layer supports different roles. Consumers submit natural language queries, which are rewritten using domain-aligned vocabulary and contextualized with profile data. Expert users, such as panel leaders, access structured queries and analytics functionalities through the Software Sensory System. By aligning structured domain semantics with hybrid retrieval and role-aware interaction patterns, the system supports targeted access to heterogeneous food knowledge. Rather than offering generic suggestions, it adapts its outputs to the informational context and task-specific needs of each user role.

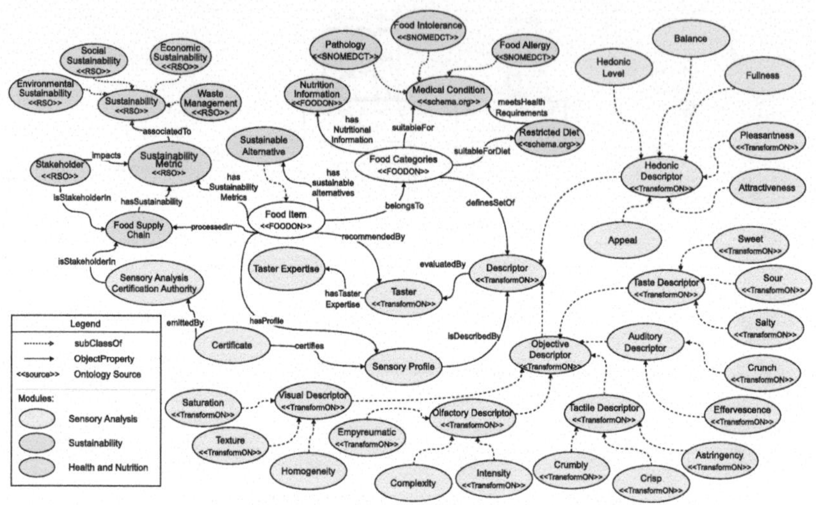

Fig. 2. Ontological concepts and relationships.

3 Ontological and Database Foundations

3.1 FoCOSA Modular Ontology

We engineered the modular ontology, named FoCOSA (Food Consumer-Oriented Sustainability-Aware)[1], following the Linked Open Terms (LOT) methodology [12], adopting a reuse-first strategy that reuses terms from published vocabularies and ontologies. FoCOSA is presented in Fig. 2 and is structured around three interlinked domains: `Nutrition`, `Sustainability`, and `Sensory Analysis`. Each module captures specific facets of food characterization and user's requirements, enabling semantic alignment across heterogeneous data.

The **Nutrition** module builds upon existing vocabularies such as `FOODON` and `SNOMED CT` to model nutrient composition, dietary suitability, and medical restrictions. It links food items with health-related conditions (e.g., diabetes, lactose intolerance) and dietary regimes (e.g., low-carb, vegan).

The **Sustainability** module is aligned with the Recipe Sustainability Ontology (RSO) and models environmental, economic, and social impacts across the food supply chain, including stakeholders' roles and sustainability metrics. For both modules, additional modeling details are discussed in a previous work [2].

The **Sensory Analysis** module, introduced in this work, formalizes subjective descriptors, structured evaluation processes, including the actors involved, the descriptive dimensions used and the connection to food items. By extending the TransformON[2] ontology, this module enables structured and certifiable modeling of sensory evaluations. It supports traceability of sensory quality by linking certified descriptors to food items and their production and

[1] https://dbwis.gitlab.io/focosa/WISE_2025.

[2] https://agroportal.lirmm.fr/ontologies/TRANSFORMON.

distribution stages within the supply chain. At its core is the `Taster` concept, representing individuals performing tastings. Each taster may have a `Taster Expertise` that evaluates their efficiency, supporting the trustworthiness of the sensory analysis results. Sensory characteristics of `Food Items` are described through the `Descriptor` concept, which is further specialized into multiple sub-concepts to capture the full spectrum of sensory experience. These include `Visual Descriptors` (e.g., Saturation, Texture, Homogeneity), `Olfactory Descriptors` (e.g., Empyreumatic, Complexity, Intensity), `Taste Descriptors` (e.g., Sweet, Sour, Salty), `Tactile Descriptors` (e.g., Crumbly, Crisp, Astringency), and `Auditory Descriptors` (e.g., Crunch, Effervescence). In addition, descriptors are semantically classified as `Objective Descriptors` or `Hedonic Descriptors`, the latter reflecting affective responses such as `Pleasantness`, `Attractiveness`, `Balance`, `Fullness` and `Appeal`. Descriptors are aggregated into a Sensory Profile, representing the multidimensional sensory characteristics of a food product. The `Sensory Profile` is directly associated with the `Food Item`, enabling the ontology to describe how individual foods are perceived in sensory evaluations. Each `Food Item` is also linked to a broader `Food Category`, providing a taxonomic structure that supports comparative analysis across similar products and facilitates the identification of sensory patterns relevant to consumer's preferences. These profiles are evaluated by tasters and formally certified by a `Sensory Analysis Certification Authority`. Certifications are modeled with the `Certificate` concept, attesting sensory qualities and compliance with defined standards. The `Sensory Analysis Certification Authority` can be involved at different stages of the `Food Supply Chain` to assess how sensory attributes are developed, modified and preserved during production, processing and distribution, thereby enabling traceability of sensory quality throughout the chain. This ontology lets the system compute semantic similarity between food items and consumers' preferences, by matching descriptors against their profile and constraints. It guarantees interoperability with expert knowledge, for instance when retrieving panel judgments or evaluating tasters' performance in a standardized setting. This forms a semantic bridge between expert-centric data and consumer-centric preferences, yielding a powerful knowledge base for context-aware food recommendations.

The ontology modules align with structured relational databases used in the hybrid retrieval infrastructure of the system. Specifically, certified sensory evaluations are stored in a dedicated sensory analysis database, while consumers' preferences and profiles are maintained in a separate database. Below we present simplified versions of the corresponding schemas (Figs. 3 and 4), which are leveraged by the Text-to-SQL component for symbolic access (see Sect. 4).

3.2 Consumer Profile Database Schema

Figure 3 presents the relational schema that models the consumer's profile within our architecture. The central entity, `Consumer`, is connected to multiple dimensions reflecting lifestyle, preferences, health status, and purchasing behavior. The `ConsumerLifestyleData` entity captures qualitative information such as

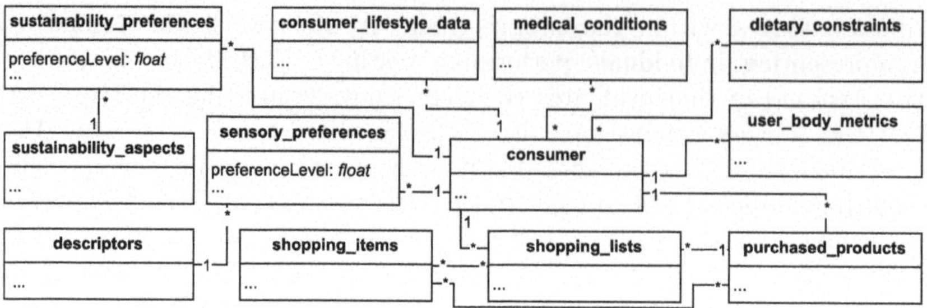

Fig. 3. Relational schema of the consumers' profile database.

physical activity level, smoking habits, and alcohol consumption, providing an essential context for recommendations. In parallel, the `UserBodyMetrics` entity records quantitative physiological measurements over time, including weight, height, hydration, and body composition indicators, crucial for continuous health monitoring and personalized dietary guidance. The model also incorporates consumer-specific constraints and priorities through the `DietaryConstraints`, `MedicalConditions` and `SustainabilityPreferences` entities. These represent both strict requirements (e.g., gluten intolerance, adherence to a vegan diet) and preference-driven goals (e.g., favoring locally sourced or organic products). To enable fine-grained personalization at the sensory level, `Consumer` is connected to `SensoryPreferences`, which specifies a `preferenceLevel` for particular `Descriptors`, encoding subjective taste and texture inclinations, such as preferences for `crunchy` or an aversion to `rubbery`. These preferences can be derived from the user's past purchase history, allowing the system to adapt dynamically to individual sensory profiles. Similarly, each `Consumer` is linked to `SustainabilityPreferences`, which capture a `preferenceLevel` for specific `SustainabilityAspects`, such as `energy use`. On the behavioral side, the schema models consumers' engagement with food products through `ShoppingLists`, which represent sets of items the user intends to purchase or evaluate. Each list contains multiple `ShoppingItems`, corresponding to specific food products and enriched with contextual attributes such as price, brand, or promotional status at the time of listing. In contrast, the `PurchasedProducts` entity logs the user's actual buying history, enabling retrospective analysis of consumption behavior. This separation supports a flexible representation of both planned and realized actions, facilitating context-aware recommendations that reflect intent, availability, and confirmed choices.

3.3 Sensory Analysis Database Schema

Figure 4 shows the relational schema supporting certification-oriented sensory data management. The process is structured around `PanelSessions`, which represent formal evaluation events configured via `PanelConfigurations`. Each session involves a set of `PanelSamples`, drawn from certified `Products` and linked

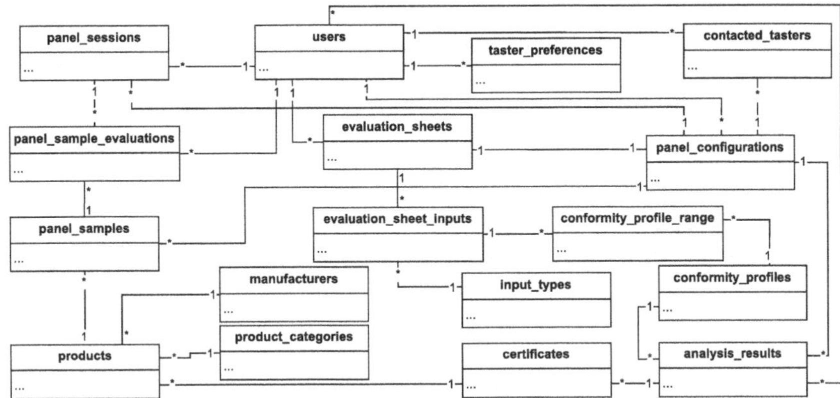

Fig. 4. Relational schema of the sensory analysis database.

to corresponding `Manufacturers` and `ProductCategories`, ensuring traceability and standardization. Tasters are invited to participate to a `PanelSession` through `ContactedTasters`, during the `PanelConfigurations` phase. The `TasterPreferences` entity supports the panel configuration phase by capturing sensory inclinations of tasters or domain expertise, which can be used to select the most appropriate tasters for specific product categories or evaluation protocols. On the date of the organized panel session, the tasters participate by evaluating the assigned samples using structured `EvaluationSheets`. Each sheet consists of multiple `EvaluationSheetInputs`, which are semantically defined through the `InputTypes` entity (e.g., intensity scale, hedonic score, binary judgment), supporting protocol customization and reproducibility. During the session, tasters generate `PanelSampleEvaluations`, which associate tasters, inputs, and samples with raw evaluation data. These evaluations are enriched by optional `TasterPreferences`, capturing individual hedonic inclinations that can be analyzed separately or excluded from conformity assessments. All data collected are processed into aggregated metrics stored in the `AnalysisResults` entity. These results are systematically compared against predefined `ConformityProfiles`, which encode expected descriptor ranges via the `ConformityProfileRange` entity. This comparison allows the system to verify compliance and issue sensory quality certifications, recorded in the `Certificates` table. The schema ensures methodological rigor, auditability, and semantic transparency, reflecting ISO 20613:2019 principles for sensory methods.

4 Multi-source RAG Architecture

Figure 5 illustrates the proposed ontology-enhanced RAG architecture, where the RAG pipeline is implemented using LlamaIndex[3] and consists of three main macro-phases: (a) **indexing**, ingesting data from external sources, applying

[3] https://www.llamaindex.ai/.

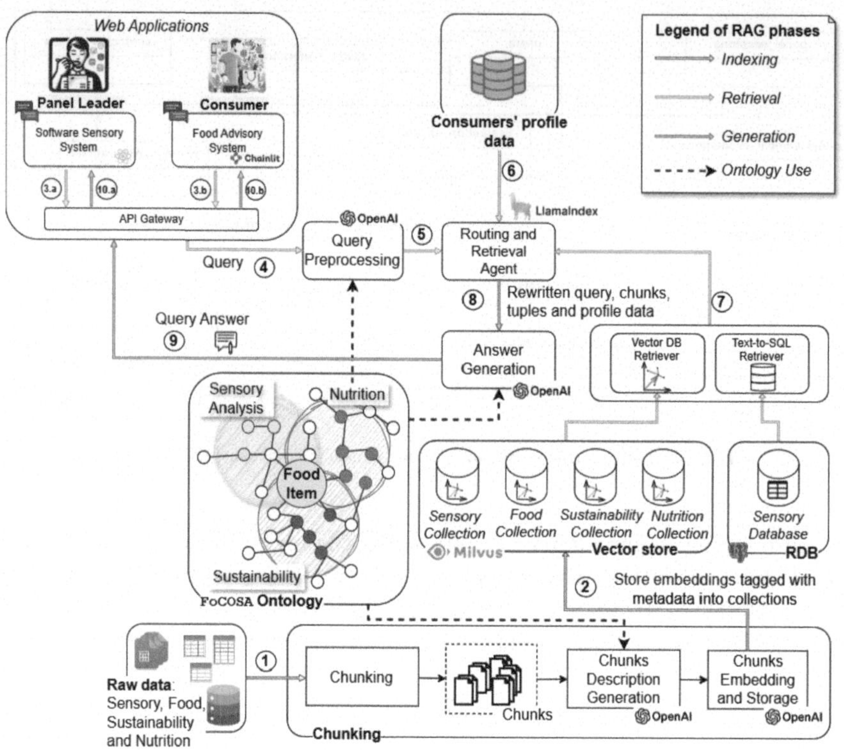

Fig. 5. Proposed ontology-enhanced RAG architecture of the food advisory system. In the figure, three dashed arrows highlight the steps of RAG where the ontology has been employed.

chunking and then indexing the chunks as dense numeric vectors (*embeddings*) in a vector database; (b) **retrieval**, using the user's query to select tools that fetch relevant information; (c) **generation**, where a prompt combining the user's query, retrieved context, and structured data is processed by an LLM to generate a response. We compose specialized components for indexing, retrieval, and generation, enabling direct search over heterogeneous sources (dense vectors and Text-to-SQL). *A pivotal innovation in our proposed RAG framework is the employment of the ontology across all the three RAG macro-phases.* This integration enables us to examine how incorporating domain-specific knowledge at different stages of the RAG architecture influences contextual understanding, precision, and clarity in the generated answer. We outline each RAG phase below, using circled numbers (e.g., ①) to reference the steps shown in Fig. 5.

Indexing Phase. In this phase raw structured and unstructured data, such as sensory analysis results, product/ingredient descriptions, food nutritional values, and sustainability data (e.g., production impacts), are transformed into a format optimized for retrieval. To handle large datasets, data is segmented into *chunks* to maintain a balance between preserving contextual integrity and excluding irrelevant content (①). The *Chunks Description Generation* component uses OpenAI's `gpt-4o-mini` model and the modular ontology to generate semantically aligned chunk descriptions. Then, the *Chunks Embedding and Storage* component (②) encodes descriptions into dense vectors using an embedding model, tags them and stores them in the Milvus[4] vector database. It assigns each embedding to the appropriate collection based on the ontology module, so that they align with the modular structure of the ontology and they are optimally organized for downstream RAG phases. For clarity, indexing refers to the global vector store of reusable domain knowledge. We therefore do not embed user-specific profile instances; these remain in the relational store and are applied at retrieval/generation time via Text-to-SQL, preserving privacy and avoiding leakage while enabling personalization.

Retrieval Phase. In the retrieval phase, the system selects the most relevant sources, based on the user's query. Both the Panel Leader and the Consumer use the system through their respective web front-ends. The former interacts through an interface built in React and integrated within the *Software Sensory System* (3.a), a suite of tools that supports the entire sensory analysis process [3]. The latter uses the *Food Advisory System*, a system developed using Chainlit[5] Conversational AI front-end (3.b). Both users enter the query into their respective interfaces, which interact with the *API Gateway*. User's query is first rewritten through an LLM-based preprocessing step by the *Query Preprocessing* component (④), using the *FoCOSA* ontology to produce a version of the query semantically aligned with the domain knowledge. This refined query aligns better with the strategy used to organize indexed data according to the ontology, with the aim of improving retrieval accuracy. After refinement, the rewritten query is forwarded to the *Routing and Retrieval Agent* component (⑤), which leverages different *tools*[6] to access the most contextually relevant information to answer the user's query (⑦). Specifically, three tasks are performed by this component: (T1) the query is encoded using the embedding model and a cosine similarity score is computed between this vector and the embeddings stored in the vector store, to retrieve the top-k relevant chunks. This method helps preventing the so-called *long-context issue*, which may lead the LLM to focus on less relevant chunks in the generation phase or exceed its token limit. (T2) the user query is translated into a SQL query for the PostgreSQL database leveraging the LLM and the NLSQLRetriever[7] from LlamaIndex, which provides the LLM with a clear and concise description of the database schema, listing the columns and types of each table, and including foreign key constraints, crucial for generating complex queries. (T3) User-specific dietary restrictions and sustainability goals are retrieved from the users' profiles data (⑥).

[4] https://milvus.io.
[5] https://docs.chainlit.io/get-started/overview.
[6] https://docs.llamaindex.ai/en/stable/module_guides/deploying/agents/tools/.
[7] https://docs.llamaindex.ai/en/stable/examples/index_structs/struct_indices/SQLIndexDemo/#part-4-text-to-sql-retriever.

Table 1. Sensory domain questions from consumer and panel leader perspectives.

	Competency Question	Domain
Q1	Which products match the characteristics of being sweet and crunchy while considering the dietary preferences of Elizabeth Gonzalez?	Consumer, Sensory, Nutrition
Q2	What are some sustainable alternatives that match the taste preferences of Elizabeth Gonzalez for meat food category?	Consumer, Sensory, Sustainability
Q3	What are some products with a sensory profile similar to pig meat that have lower total emissions?	Sensory, Sustainability
Q4	What are some healthier products that Elizabeth Gonzalez might like considering her taste preferences?	Consumer, Sensory, Nutrition
Q5	Which descriptors were used in the Honey Panel?	Panel Leader, Sensory
Q6	How many tasters participated in the Honey Panel?	Panel Leader, Sensory
Q7	How has taster G079 improved over time based on their effectiveness?	Panel Leader, Sensory
Q8	In the analysis of which food product did the taster G079 achieve the highest effectiveness?	Panel Leader, Sensory
Q9	Provide a ranking of the most well-rated biscuits based on their hedonic index	Panel Leader, Sensory

Generation Phase. The final phase of our RAG framework leverages `gpt-4o-mini` from OpenAI to generate an answer (e.g., a food advice) to the user's query by exploiting the inference capabilities of the LLM upon the data retrieved from the previous RAG phase. The prompt, which contains placeholders, instructs the LLM to generate an appropriate response. These placeholders are filled by the *Answer Generation* component using data from the *Routing and Retrieval Agent* (⑧), including retrieved data from databases, the rewritten query (from ⑤) and the user's profile data (from ⑥). The *Answer Generation* component invokes the LLM with the aforementioned prompt, which instructs the LLM to produce an output answer semantically aligned with the ontology ⑨. During generation, the prompt constrains the LLM to (i) use the ontology as a structural guide, following approved descriptors, entity relationships, and schema-level semantics, and (ii) ground any sensory claims directly in the provided data ensuring that the generated output is semantically aligned with the domain model. Finally, the answer is forwarded to the *API Gateway*, which returns it to the web application front-end that issued the query ((10.a), (10.b)).

Note that, at runtime, FoCOSA is loaded from the OWL artifact; upon a new release, its concepts and relations are immediately available to the *Retrieval* and *Generation* phases. Conversely, when the ontology is updated, the *Indexing* phase must be rerun to regenerate embeddings for ontology-tagged chunks. Finally, to support reproducibility, we release code, prompt templates, evaluation datasets and a quick-start guide in our GitLab repository[8].

[8] https://gitlab.com/dbwis/food-rag-system/-/tree/WISE_2025.

Table 2. Metrics for Assessing Response Quality

2.7 Relevance	Does the answer directly address the question?
Clarity	Is the response clear, coherent, and easy to understand?
Completeness	Does the answer cover all important aspects of the question?
Fluency	Is the language used in the response grammatically correct and natural?
Consistency	Is the response logically consistent with no contradictions?
Actionability	Does the response provide actionable advices (i.e., practical, useful, and feasible to follow in real life)
Minimization of Hallucinations (MoH)	Does the LLM fabricate facts or suggest unsupported claims, which cannot be inferred from the provided context?
Data Utilization Effectiveness (DUE)	How effectively the response leverages the available data to provide an informed and comprehensive response?

5 Experiments

We evaluate the system's performance using both consumer and expert-level queries. Nine competency questions have been used (Table 1), reflecting real-world use cases. All questions concern sensory aspects; some of them are additionally aimed at suggesting products for improving nutrition habits (Q1, Q4) and promoting sustainable choices (Q2, Q3). The experiments were conducted using data from various sources (see Footnote 8), including publicly available datasets and generated datasets designed to capture different aspects of consumer's behavior. Our evaluation compares five configurations: (i) *Baseline (CMT1)* - ontology was not used; (ii) *Ontology-Enhanced Indexing (CMT2)* - the ontology is used solely in the prompt for generating chunk descriptions; (iii) *Ontology-Enhanced Retrieval (CMT3)* - queries were rewritten using the LLM and the ontology concepts to improve retrieval; (iv) *Ontology-Enhanced Response (CMT4)* - responses leveraged the ontology for more accurate answers; (v) *Full-Ontology (CMT5)* - the ontology was integrated in all RAG phases. We evaluated responses on eight dimensions including relevance, actionability, fluency, Minimization of Hallucinations (MoH) and Data Utilization Effectiveness (DUE) (Table 2), using the LLM-as-a-Judge approach [18], adopting OpenAI's `gpt-4o-mini`.

Figure 6(a) reports the main evaluation across all metrics, with scores from 1 (low) to 5 (high), and shows that full integration (CMT5) consistently outperforms all other configurations, achieving the highest scores in Relevance (4.67), Actionability (3.89), and Fluency (4.67). This configuration also obtains the highest average score overall (4.20) as shown in Fig. 6(b). Ontology-enhanced chunk descriptions (CMT2) also lead to notable gains, with respect to the

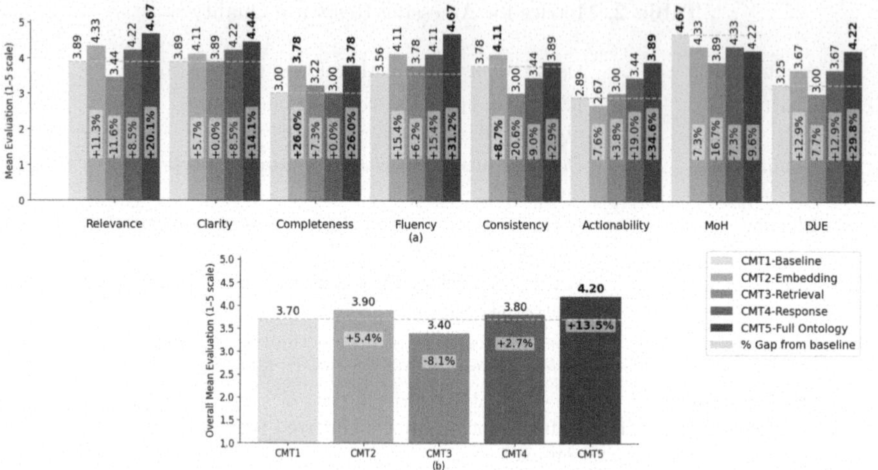

Fig. 6. (a) Average metric scores across configurations (see Table 2 for metrics definitions); (b) average scores for each ontology integration configuration.

baseline (CMT1), in terms of Relevance (+11.3%) and Completeness (+26%). Response generation benefits from symbolic grounding in CMT4, improving Fluency (+15.4%) and Clarity (+8.5). These partial enhancements demonstrate the modular utility of the ontology. However, query rewriting alone (CMT3) underperforms across most metrics, scoring even below the baseline in average terms (−8.1%). While modest gains appear in Actionability and Completeness, this configuration degrades Relevance, DUE, and MoH. These findings suggest that query rewriting alone is insufficient without end-to-end ontology alignment during indexing and generation. Lack of semantic alignment harms retrieval and factual grounding. Although MoH scores remain high across all configurations, the baseline keeps hallucinations low by refusing uncertain answers, at the cost of actionability and DUE. In contrast, ontology-enhanced configurations provide more informative and actionable responses while preserving hallucination control, as shown by consistently strong MoH and improved DUE scores. Further work should target additional hallucination reduction.

Overall, the results confirm that full end-to-end integration of ontological knowledge offers the most coherent, useful, and factually reliable outputs. Partial integration yields uneven benefits, and retrieval-only alignment may introduce semantic inconsistency that hinders overall performance.

6 Related Work

LLMs improve recommendation accuracy and contextual relevance in recommender systems. Ontologies improve data integration and interoperability, with frameworks such as the OBO Foundry[9] promoting shared vocabularies [7].

[9] https://obofoundry.org/.

Authors in [1] show that ontologies can improve LLM performance in question answering tasks, motivating our integration of domain knowledge into food guidance. OG-RAG [16] leverages ontologies for indexing domain data as a hypergraph to enhance retrieval, though it does not incorporate them in generation. Only a few recent approaches have explored injecting factual ontological knowledge into LLM fine-tuning [4,14]. Nonetheless, existing food knowledge systems often fail to meet nuanced consumers' needs, including personalized preferences, sustainability values, health constraints, and complex dietary profiles. LLMs offer new opportunities for food advising by interpreting natural language queries and adapting to emotional and situational user contexts. FoodGPT [13] applies incremental pre-training and integrates a knowledge graph to reduce hallucinations, enhancing reliability. Despite their potential, LLM-based food recommendations face challenges, particularly regarding the depth needed to handle complex health conditions, emphasizing the necessity for expert oversight [6,10]. Sensory analysis, despite its key role for food acceptance, remains difficult to encode computationally. Traditional AI approaches rely on ML models to process data from trained panels, sensors, or vision systems [9]. Advances such as electronic noses and tongues have improved the reproducibility and objectivity of sensory assessments [5]. Initial efforts to incorporate LLMs into sensory reasoning include Digital Sommelier (DS) [11], which uses conversational interfaces to support wine-tasting sessions. Authors in [8] further integrate LLMs with RAG and role-based frameworks to explore flavor profiles through scientific document synthesis. In parallel, the TransformON/PO2 framework [17] introduces an ontology that represents food transformation processes and sensory characteristics in line with FAIR principles, enabling semantic annotation and retrieval of product-level sensory data. While these threads demonstrate progress, they have not yet converged. Our work proposes an ontology-enhanced RAG architecture that unifies nutrition, sustainability, and sensory ontologies. It uses structured descriptors across indexing, retrieval, and generation to align personalized guidance with standardized sensory semantics and improve explainability. We release evaluation results and datasets to support future research comparisons.

7 Conclusions and Future Work

This work presented a web-based food advisory system that integrates a Sensory Analysis Ontology, embedded within a modular RAG pipeline, for improving personalized and role-aware recommendations, reasoning over hedonic and descriptive food properties. Experimental results show that integrating ontological knowledge throughout the RAG pipeline improves the actionability, relevance, and factual grounding of system outputs, both for consumers and expert users. Future efforts will extend the evaluation beyond the current set of queries and will combine the LLM-as-a-Judge with domain-expert assessment (including inter-annotator agreement) to better assess the semantic precision of sensory descriptors. Future work will also include enhanced sensory reasoning (e.g., multi-item comparisons, descriptor co-occurrence) and users' feedback to dynamically refine both recommendations and ontological structures, based on evolving preferences and standards, and to further minimize hallucinations in recommended results.

References

1. Allemang, D., Sequeda, J.: Increasing the accuracy of LLM question-answering systems with ontologies. In: ISWC 2024. 23rd International Semantic Web Conference, Baltimore, MD, USA, 11–15 November 2024, pp. 324–339. Springer, Heidelberg (2024)
2. Bagozi, A., Bianchini, D., Melchiori, M., Rula, A.: Enhancing LLMs contextual knowledge with ontologies for personalised food recommendation. In: Barhamgi, M., Wang, H., Wang, X. (eds.) Web Information Systems Engineering - WISE 2024, pp. 273–283. Springer, Singapore (2025)
3. Bagozi, A., Bianchini, D., et al.: Food certification through collaborative sensory analysis methods and tools. In: CEUR Workshop Proceedings, vol. 3741, pp. 392–400. CEUR-WS (2024)
4. Baldazzi, T., Bellomarini, L., Ceri, S., Colombo, A., Gentili, A., Sallinger, E.: Fine-tuning large enterprise language models via ontological reasoning. In: Fensel, A., Ozaki, A., Roman, D., Soylu, A. (eds.) Rules and Reasoning, pp. 86–94. Springer, Cham (2023)
5. Cui, Z., et al.: Artificial intelligence and food flavor: How AI models are shaping the future and revolutionary technologies for flavor food development. Compreh. Rev. Food Sci. Food Saf. **24**(1), e70068 (2025)
6. Dergaa, I., et al.: Evaluating the applicability and appropriateness of ChatGPT as a source for tailored nutrition advice: a multi-scenario study. New Asian J. Med. **2**(1), 1–16 (2024)
7. Dooley, D.M., et al.: OBO foundry food ontology interconnectivity. Semant. Web **15**(4), 1239–1258 (2024)
8. Huang, T., et al.: FoodPuzzle: toward developing large language model agents as autonomous flavor scientists. In: Proceedings of the 31st ACM SIGKDD Conference on Knowledge Discovery and Data Mining, vol. 2, p. 5493–5504. Association for Computing Machinery, New York (2025)
9. Nunes, C.A., Ribeiro, M.N., de Carvalho, T.C., Ferreira, D.D., de Oliveira, L.L., Pinheiro, A.C.: Artificial intelligence in sensory and consumer studies of food products. Curr. Opin. Food Sci. **50**, 101002 (2023)
10. Papastratis, I., Stergioulas, A., Konstantinidis, D., Daras, P., Dimitropoulos, K.: Can ChatGPT provide appropriate meal plans for NCD patients? Nutrition **121**, 112291 (2024)
11. Parra, M.O., Favela, J., Castro, L.A.: A digital sommelier to enhance multisensory wine tasting. In: Proceedings of the 2024 ACM International Conference on Interactive Media Experiences Workshops, pp. 7–10 (2024)
12. Poveda-Villalón, M., Fernández-Izquierdo, A., Fernández-López, M., García-Castro, R.: LOT: an industrial oriented ontology engineering framework. Eng. Appl. Artif. Intell. **111**, 104755 (2022)
13. Qi, Z., Yu, Y., Tu, M., Tan, J., Huang, Y.: FoodGPT: a large language model in food testing domain with incremental pre-training and knowledge graph prompt (2023). https://arxiv.org/abs/2308.10173
14. Ronzano, F., Nanavati, J.: Towards ontology-enhanced representation learning for large language models (2024). https://arxiv.org/abs/2405.20527

15. Sedrakyan, G., Gavai, A., van Hillegersberg, J.: Design implications towards human-centric semantic recommenders for sustainable food consumption. In: Sales, T.P., Araújo, J., Borbinha, J., Guizzardi, G. (eds.) Advances in Conceptual Modeling (ER2023) Workshops, Lisbon, Portugal, vol. 14319, pp. 312–328 (2023)
16. Sharma, K., Kumar, P., Li, Y.: OG-RAG: ontology-grounded retrieval-augmented generation for large language models (2024). https://arxiv.org/abs/2412.15235
17. Weber, M., et al.: PO2/TransformON, an ontology for data integration on food, feed, bioproducts and biowaste engineering. NPJ Sci. Food **7**(1) (2023)
18. Zheng, L., et al.: Judging LLM-as-a-judge with mt-bench and chatbot arena. In: Proceedings of the 37th International Conference on Neural Information Processing Systems. Curran Associates Inc., Red Hook (2023)

LSA: A Long-Short-Term Aspect Interest Transformer for Aspect-Based Recommendation

Le Liu[1], Junrui Liu[2](✉), Yunhan Gao[1], Ziheng Wang[1], and Tong Li[3]

[1] Beijing-Dublin International College, Beijing University of Technology, Beijing, China
{le.liu,gaoyunhan,wangziheng}@emails.bjut.edu.cn

[2] Beijing Institute of Graphic Communication, Beijing, China
liujunrui@bigc.edu.cn

[3] College of Computer Science, Beijing University of Technology, Beijing, China
litong@bjut.edu.cn

Abstract. Aspect-based recommendation methods extract aspect terms from reviews, such as price, to model fine-grained user preferences on items, making them a critical approach in personalized recommender systems. Existing methods utilize graphs to represent the relationships among users, items, and aspect terms, modeling user preferences based on graph neural networks. However, they overlook the dynamic nature of user interests - users may temporarily focus on aspects they previously paid little attention to - making it difficult to assign accurate weights to aspect terms for each user-item interaction. In this paper, we propose a long-short-term aspect interest Transformer (LSA) for aspect-based recommendation, which effectively captures the dynamic nature of user preferences by integrating both long-term and short-term aspect interests. Specifically, the short-term interests model the temporal changes in the importance of recently interacted aspect terms, while the long-term interests consider global behavioral patterns, including aspects that users have not interacted with recently. Finally, LSA combines long- and short-term interests to evaluate the importance of aspects within the union of user and item aspect neighbors, therefore accurately assigns aspect weights for each user-item interaction. Experiments conducted on four real-world datasets demonstrate that LSA improves MSE by 2.55% on average over the best baseline.

Keywords: Recommender Systems · Aspect-based Recommendation · Long-term Interest Modeling · Short-term Interest Modeling

1 Introduction

Aspect-based recommendation methods effectively learn the fine-grained user preferences and have attracted significant attention [4,15,19]. Existing approaches primarily employ two paradigms: CNN-based and GNN-based methods. CNN-based methods [5,8] leverage CNN to extract aspect features from

I. Awan et al. (Eds.): WISE 2025, LNCS 16368, pp. 104–115, 2026.
https://doi.org/10.1007/978-981-95-7251-9_8

reviews. In contrast, recent graph-based methods [11,13] explicitly model user-item-aspect relations using graph structures to better capture contextual and sentiment-aware representations.

However, existing methods only focus on modeling static user preferences from historical reviews and overlook the dynamic nature of user interests. Users may temporarily focus on aspects they previously paid little attention to, which makes themn difficult to assign accurate weights to aspect terms for each user-item interaction [1,11,14]. For example, a user expresses consistent interest in aspect terms, such as "sound quality" and "build quality" in history reviews, showing a long-term preference for high-performance audio equipment. The user then often mentioned "portability" in recent product reviews, suggesting a short-term interest in "portability" due to a possible upcoming trip. Long-term interests represent the stable interests of users, while short-term interests are the preferences of users recently.

In this paper, we propose a Long-Short-term Aspect interest Transformer (LSA) for aspect-based recommendation, which effectively captures the dynamic nature of user preferences by integrating both long-term and short-term aspect interests. Specifically, to capture users' transient needs, we propose a time-aware Transformer that models temporal changes in the importance of recently interacted aspect terms. Furthermore, LSA models the long-term interests by considering global behavioral patterns, including aspects that users have not interacted with recently. Those two interests are integrated through a gated fusion mechanism. To generate a personalized prediction, we introduce an interest-aware aspect term aggregation method, which uses user preferences to justify the importance of aspect terms, over the union of user- and item-specific aspect terms. The resulting aspect representation is concatenated with user and item embeddings and passed into a factorization machine for final scoring.

The main contributions of this paper are summarized as follows: (1) We propose a Long-Short-term Aspect Interest Transformer (LSA) for aspect-based recommendation, which models the evolution of user interests through considering long- and short-term of interests. (2) We design a dual aspect selection method to capture users' long-term and short-term interests effectively at the aspect granularity. (3) We introduce an interest-aware aspect term aggregation mechanism to align user preferences with item attributes for personalized prediction. (4) Extensive experiments conducted on four real-world datasets demonstrate that LSA improves MSE by an average of 2.55% over the best baseline.

2 Related Work

In this section, we review previous work relevant to our work, including Aspect-Based Recommendation and Modeling Long- and Short-Term User Interests.

2.1 Aspect-Based Recommendation

Aspect-based recommender systems leverage fine-grained information from user reviews (i.e. aspect–sentiment pairs) to provide more personalized recommendations. Early works start to explore the sentiment of each aspects in user review instead of serving as a single source to explore the user's preference on different aspects [15,19]. Building on this idea, researchers have proposed models to extract aspect terms from reviews and incorporate them into recommendation algorithms. For example, ANR [4] applies attention-based neural networks to identify aspect-level semantics and employs co-attention to capture asymmetric importance of aspects between users and items. Subsequent works integrate sentiment reasoning into aspect modeling. ARPM [6] incorporates social signals for preference modeling, while CARP [7] introduces logic-unit based capsule reasoning for fine-grained aspect-sentiment understanding. SENGR [17] integrates sentiment-aware review attention and graph-based user-item-user modeling to enhance rating prediction. Most recently, APH [11] models the aspect performance of items using a sentiment-aware hypergraph neural network, introducing a novel aspect hypergraph to aggregate conflicting user sentiments for fine-grained recommendation.

2.2 Modeling Long and Short-Term User Interests

Users' preferences are not static. Traditional models mainly consider long and short-term user interests at the item level. PLASTIC [21] proposes an adversarial framework that fuses long-term matrix-factorization profiles with short-term RNN session dynamics. Yu et al. [20] model short-term intent with an LSTM equipped with time- and content-aware controllers, then adaptively fuse it—via attention—with an attentive long-term preference vector. Most recently, LS-TGNN [14] leverages a temporal graph neural network and self-supervised contrastive learning to disentangle and model users' evolving long- and short-term interests, significantly enhancing session-based recommendation performance.

3 Methodology

To model the dynamic nature of user interests at the aspect level, this paper proposes LSA for aspect-based recommendation, with its architecture illustrated in Fig. 1. Specifically, LSA (1) extracts aspect terms from reviews and constructs a *user–item–aspect graph*; (2) captures long-term preferences by a graph Transformer; (3) captures short-term preferences by forming time-ordered aspect sequences within temporal window; and (4) fuses the two views through a long–short attention mechanism to aggregate aspect terms. Finally, we describe the final prediction layer.

3.1 Aspect Graph

We initially extract aspect terms from reviews to construct the aspect graph. Following existing methods [9,11], we choose a rule-based unsupervised method, which considers three dependency relations to extract aspect terms: *amod*, *dobj* and *nsubj+acomp*. After extracting aspect-sentiment from each review, we construct user-item-aspect graph, where nodes represent users, items, and aspect

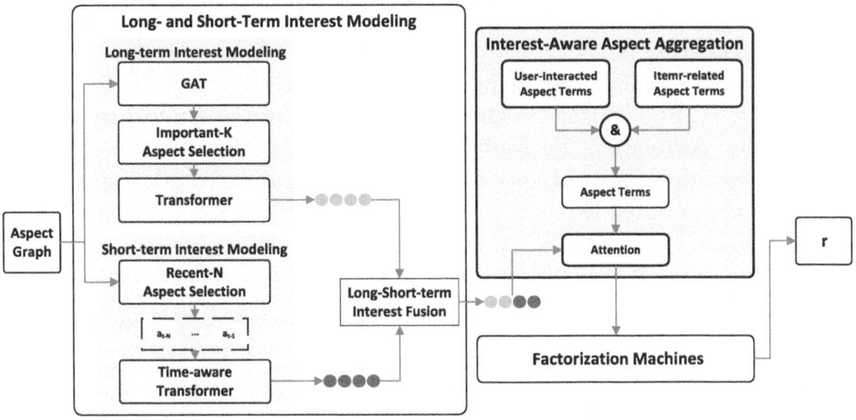

Fig. 1. Architecture of LSA.

terms. Edges are created between nodes based on review interactions, and edge weights reflect either aspect frequency or user-item rating. In addition, the interaction timestamps are also recorded to support time-aware modeling.

3.2 Long and Short-Term Interest Modeling

Users' interests are shaped by both stable long-term behavior and transient short-term needs. Thus, LSA models short-term interests using a time-aware Transformer that encodes the most recent N aspect terms within a T-day window, and long-term interests via a graph Transformer over the user-item-aspect graph with an important-K aspect selection strategy to filter out irrelevant or temporary aspects

Modeling Long-Term Interest. Users' long-term interests reflect stable preferences formed over extended periods, but existing GNN-based methods overlook future-relevant aspects by only aggregating interacted aspect nodes. To address this, we employ a graph Transformer that leverages self-attention to capture both global and local structural dependencies in the user-item-aspect graph, while an Important-K Aspect Selection method filters out noisy aspects by retaining only the most representative ones based on interaction frequency and rating preferences, ensuring more efficient and focused long-term interest modeling.

First, **Edge Weight Encoding** quantifies the frequency of interactions between users/items and aspects, under the assumption that higher interaction frequency typically signals stronger and more stable preferences. The interaction score is computed as:

$$s_{u,a}^{\mathrm{edge}} = \sigma\left(\exp\left(\frac{w_{u,a}}{100}\right)\right) \tag{1}$$

where $w_{u,a}$ represents the frequency of interactions between user u and aspect a, and $\sigma(\cdot)$ denotes a sigmoid function for normalization. The denominator 100 is an empirically chosen scaling factor to prevent the exponential term from becoming excessively large.

In addition to interaction frequency, users' interest in certain aspects can often be inferred from ratings. Thus, **Rating Preference Encoding** incorporates semantic correlations derived from user ratings, reflecting user sentiment and perceived importance of specific aspects. The rating-based semantic relevance score is computed as:

$$s_{u,a}^{\text{pre}} = f(\mathbf{W}_1 \mathbf{y}_u, \mathbf{e}_a), \tag{2}$$

where $\mathbf{y}_u$ is rating preference embedding of user u, $\mathbf{W}_1$ is a learnable transformation matrix, and $\mathbf{e}_a$ represents the embedding of aspect a obtained from the graph encoder. The function $f(\cdot)$ denotes a similarity function that measures the correlation between the transformed user embedding and the aspect embedding.

By summing these two encoding scores, we derive a comprehensive relevance score for user u to rank entire aspects:

$$s_{u,a} = s_{u,a}^{\text{edge}} + s_{u,a}^{\text{pre}}. \tag{3}$$

The user node is then added to the beginning of this sequence, forming the input sequence for the Transformer for modeling long-term interest as $\mathcal{A}_u^l = [\mathbf{e}_u, \mathbf{e}_{a_1}, \ldots, \mathbf{e}_{a_K}]$.

In practice, we enhance the Transformer by replacing its self-attention mechanism with GATv2 [2]. After the encoding of the Transformer, we obtain the user's long-term interest representation, denoted as $\hat{\mathbf{e}}_u^l$. This representation encapsulates both structural insights and semantic preferences, precisely capturing the user's stable and enduring aspect interests.

Modeling Short-Term Interest. Users' interests evolve over time, and recent interactions reveal their short-term preferences—for instance, a guitarist's reviews may shift from beginner-focused features to performance-level aspects over a year. To capture this dynamic behavior, we propose a Recent-N Aspect Selection method that selects the most recent N aspect terms from a user's history, highlighting their current short-term interests.

Formally, given a sequence of user interactions, each associated with aspect terms and timestamps, we first define the user's interaction history as $H_u = \{(a_i, t_i) | t_i < t_{\text{curr}}, 1 \leq i \leq n\}$, where a_i denotes an interacted aspect term, and t_i is the timestamp of interaction. From this historical set, we filter and retain valid interactions within a specified temporal window, ensuring temporal relevance. Next, we sort the valid interactions in descending order by timestamp and select the most recent N aspect to form a short-term sequence, thereby emphasizing the recency of the interactions and their direct relevance to current preferences. We then concatenate the user node with the embeddings of these recent aspects, constructing an ordered sequence $\mathcal{A}_u^s = [\mathbf{e}_u, \mathbf{e}_{a_1^{(t)}}, \ldots, \mathbf{e}_{a_N^{(t)}}]$ as input to the Transformer encoder.

After processing with the Transformer encoder, the embedding corresponding to the user node (i.e., the first token in the sequence) is extracted as the user's refined short-term interest representation, denoted as $\hat{e}_u^s$.

Gated Long-Short-Term Interest Fusion. This layer attempts to combine both long- and short-term interest via a gate-residual mechanism. Firstly, it projects long-term and short-term representations into a shared latent space:

$$\mathbf{e}_u^{l'} = \mathbf{W}_l\,\hat{\mathbf{e}}_u^l, \quad \mathbf{e}_u^{s'} = \mathbf{W}_s\,\hat{\mathbf{e}}_u^s, \tag{4}$$

where $\mathbf{W}_l, \mathbf{W}_s \in \mathbb{R}^{d\times d}$ are learnable linear projections. Next, a gated neural network dynamically balances contributions from long-term and short-term embeddings:

$$\mathbf{g}_u = \sigma\Big(\mathbf{W}_g\left[\,\mathbf{e}_u^{l'} \,\|\, \mathbf{e}_u^{s'}\,\right] + \mathbf{b}_g\Big), \tag{5}$$

$$\mathbf{e}_u = \mathbf{g}_u \odot \mathbf{e}_u^{l'} + (1 - \mathbf{g}_u) \odot \mathbf{e}_u^{s'} + \mathbf{e}_u^{l'}. \tag{6}$$

where $\sigma(\cdot)$ denotes the sigmoid activation function, and $\odot$ represents multiplication.

Finally, we concatenate the non-linear transformation of the user embedding $\mathbf{y}_u$ after passing it through an MLP layer with the aspect-aware aggregation representation to generate the final representation of the user u as follows,

$$\mathbf{p}_u = \text{ReLU}(\mathbf{y}_u\mathbf{W}_3 + \mathbf{b}) \oplus \mathbf{e}_u. \tag{7}$$

Similarly, we can get the representation of the item i as $\mathbf{q}_i$.

3.3 Interest-Aware Aspect Term Aggregation

Aspect terms influence user preferences and item features differently, but existing methods often predict ratings using only user and item representations. To capture both known and novel influences, we construct the aspect term set as the union of user and item aspects, allowing the model to consider previously unobserved aspects that may affect the interaction. Formally, for user-item pair (u, i), we define the candidate aspect set as:

$$\mathcal{A}_{u,i} = \mathcal{A}_u \cup \mathcal{A}_i \tag{8}$$

where $\mathcal{A}_u$ and $\mathcal{A}_i$ denote the aspect terms extracted from the user's historical reviews and from the candidate item's associated aspects, respectively.

To model the unequal contribution of different aspect terms in a given interaction, we adopt an attention-based aggregation mechanism considered on the user-item context. Firstly, the information of the user and the item is combined together by a fusion layer:

$$\mathbf{f}_{ui} = \text{ReLU}(\mathbf{W}_f \cdot [\mathbf{p}_u \oplus \mathbf{q}_i] + \mathbf{b}_f) \tag{9}$$

where $\mathbf{p}_u$ is the fused user interest vector, $\mathbf{q}_i$ is the item representation, and $\mathbf{W}_f$, $\mathbf{b}_f$ are learnable parameters. The fused representation $\mathbf{f}_{ui}$ captures the contextual interaction signal.

We then use this fused vector as a query to attend over the candidate aspect terms in $\mathcal{A}_{u,i}$. Each aspect term $a_k \in \mathcal{A}_{u,i}$ has been embedded as $\mathbf{e}_{a_k} \in \mathbb{R}^d$, and is projected into key–value pairs using learnable transformations. The user–item fusion representation $\mathbf{f}_{ui}$ is projected into query space to capture interaction-specific context:

$$\mathbf{q}_{ui} = \mathbf{W}_q \mathbf{f}_{ui}, \quad \mathbf{k}_k = \mathbf{W}_K \mathbf{e}_{a_k}, \quad \mathbf{v}_k = \mathbf{W}_V \mathbf{e}_{a_k} \tag{10}$$

Finally, the final aspect representation is obtained by aggregating different aspect terms according to their attention scores.

$$\mathbf{h}_a = \sum_{k=1}^{|\mathcal{A}_{u,i}|} \frac{\exp(\mathbf{q}_{ui}^\top \mathbf{k}_k)}{\sum_{j=1}^{|\mathcal{A}_{u,i}|} \exp(\mathbf{q}_{ui}^\top \mathbf{k}_j)} \cdot \mathbf{v}_k \tag{11}$$

3.4 Prediction

This section adopts an Factorization Machines (FM) layer to predict final scores [16]. It captures higher-order interactions between users, items, and aspects. Specifically, we concatenate the user, item, and aspect representation:

$$\mathbf{x} = \mathbf{p}_u \oplus \mathbf{q}_i \oplus \lambda \cdot \mathbf{h}_a \tag{12}$$

The prediction score $\hat{r}_{ui}$ is computed as follows

$$\hat{r}_{ui} = b_0 + b_u + b_i + \mathbf{x}\mathbf{w}^\top + \sum_{i=1}^{d'} \sum_{j=i+1}^{d'} < \mathbf{v}_i, \mathbf{v}_j > \mathbf{x}_i \mathbf{x}_j, \tag{13}$$

where b_0, b_u, and b_i are the global, user, and item biases, respectively. $\mathbf{w} \in \mathbb{R}^{1\times d'}$ is the coefficient vector of the linear term. $\langle \mathbf{v}_i, \mathbf{v}_j \rangle$ denotes the inner product of the latent vectors associated with the i-th and j-th feature dimensions. x_i is the value of the i−th dimension of x. The overall objective is to minimize the Mean Squared Error (MSE) between predicted and true ratings over the training set.

4 Experiment

In this section, we complete experiments to identify the performance of the proposed method. We first describe the experiment setup, then show the comparison results with diverse baselines, and finally explore the effect of model components.

4.1 Experimental Setup

Dataset. Experiments are done on the Amazon review datasets[1], which have been widely used in recommendation research. Following existing works [13], we use 4 core subsets: Musical Instrument, Office Product, Beauty, and Video Games (respectively represented by Music, Office, Beauty, and Games).

Baseline Methods. We compared our method with the following SOTA baselines: review-based method includes DeepCoNN [22], NARRE [3], CARL [18], DAML [10], DSRLN [12]; and a graph-based method RGNN [13].

Evaluation Metrics. To evaluate the performance of our method, we adopt three metrics, i.e., Mean Square Error (MSE), Mean Absolute Error (MAE) and Normalized Discounted Cumulative Gain (NDCG) [13,18,22]. These metrics are commonly used in existing recommendation studies, and we follow this practice to ensure fair comparability with prior work. For each experiment, we randomly choose 20% of the user-item review pairs (denoted by D_{test}) for evaluating the model performance in the testing phase, and the remaining 80% of the review pairs (denoted by D_{train}) are used in the training phase.

4.2 Performance Comparison

Table 1 summarizes the performance comparison between our proposed method and several baselines across four datasets. The best results are highlighted in boldface, and the second-best are underlined. LSA achieves the lowest MSE on every dataset, with relative improvements over the strongest baseline ranging from 0.41% (Games) to 5.52% (Music) – an average MSE gain of about 2.55%. In terms of MAE, LSA also demonstrates strong performance on most datasets, particularly Music, Office, and Games. On Beauty, while DSRLN slightly outperforms LSA, the overall performance remains competitive. For NDCG@10(N@10), LSA achieves the best performance on three datasets: Music, Office, and Beauty. However, on the Games dataset, LSA shows slightly lower results compared to DAML and DSRLN. One contributing factor could be the model's frequency-based long-term aspect selection, which might emphasize common aspect terms while under-representing niche user preferences. Furthermore, we does not optimize for ranking objectives, it may be result poor performance on top-k recommendation metrics lisk N@10. Overall, LSA consistently delivers robust improvements across diverse datasets and metrics, affirming the effectiveness of integrating fine-grained aspect terms with long- and short-term user preference modeling.

[1] http://jmcauley.ucsd.edu/data/amazon/.

Table 1. Comparison results. **Bold** values indicate the best performance, and underlined values indicate the second best.

Model	Music			Office			Beauty			Games		
	MSE	MAE	N@10	MSE	MAE	N@10	MSE	MAE	N@10	MSE	MAE	N@10
DCN	0.7909	0.7590	0.977	0.7315	0.7113	0.973	1.2210	0.9209	0.966	1.1234	0.8750	0.971
NARRE	0.7688	0.6950	0.978	0.7266	0.6812	0.976	1.1997	0.9228	0.971	1.1120	0.7990	0.968
CARL	0.7632	0.6771	0.980	0.7193	0.6477	0.978	1.2250	0.8809	0.966	1.1308	0.7980	0.969
DAML	0.7401	0.6512	0.982	0.7164	0.6122	0.978	1.2175	0.9192	0.967	1.1086	0.7880	**0.979**
DSRLN	0.7538	0.6207	0.781	0.7131	0.6210	0.974	1.1951	**0.8105**	0.967	1.1205	0.7713	**0.979**
RGNN	0.7319	0.6019	0.982	0.7125	0.6231	0.983	1.1885	0.9303	0.973	1.0996	0.7864	0.976
LSA	**0.6915**	**0.5800**	**0.986**	**0.6897**	**0.6099**	**0.985**	**1.1760**	0.8119	**0.974**	**1.0950**	**0.7799**	0.977

4.3 Ablation Study

This experiment develops some variants by removing aspect attnetion, fusion, short-term and long-term layers to verify their contribution for LSA. The result of ablation experiments is shown in Table 2. LSA outperforms all variants, demonstrating that each module contributes positively to performance. A user has mentioned multiple aspects, but not all are equally relevant to a specific interaction. Therefore, we design an interest-aware aspect aggregation layer that attends to informative aspects based on user-item context. If we replace the gated fusion with a simple average, it will limit the model's ability to adaptively weigh long- and short-term interests, resulting in poor performance.

Overall, this ablation experiment confirms the effectiveness and complementary contributions of the aspect-aware attention mechanism, gated fusion strategy, and distinct long- and short-term interest encoders in our method.

Table 2. MSE results of ablation study.

Model Variant	Music	Office	Beauty	Games
LSA	**0.6915**	**0.6897**	**1.1760**	**1.0950**
w/o Aspect Attention	0.7030	0.7018	1.1762	1.0966
w/o Fusion	0.7034	0.6942	1.2059	1.1390
w/o Short Term	0.6993	0.6956	1.2065	1.1381
w/o Long Term	0.6932	0.6948	1.2063	1.1393

4.4 Parameter Sensitivity Analysis

In this section, we conduct a sensitivity analysis on three key hyperparameters: the number of long-term aspects (K), the number of recent aspects (N), varying each while fixing the others. For space limitation, we show the experiment results of the Music dataset with fixed batch size = 16 and num layers = 2 when analyzing K and N. On the Music dataset, we observe that increasing K generally improves performance, with the best MSE at $K = 80$, likely due to richer user preference coverage. For N, the optimal value is 20, suggesting that a moderate temporal window best captures short-term intent (Fig. 2).

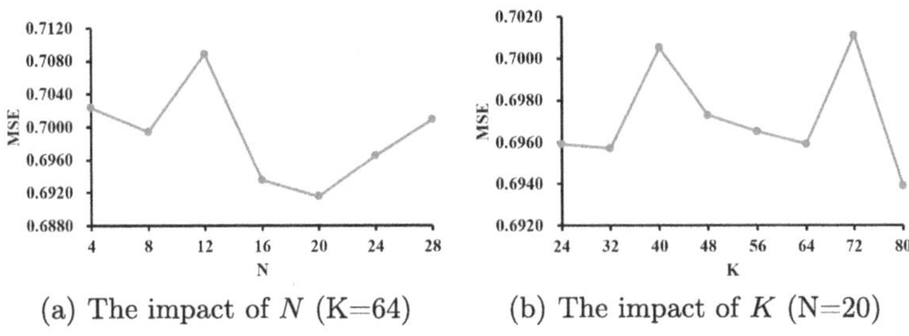

(a) The impact of N (K=64)　(b) The impact of K (N=20)

Fig. 2. MSE under different values of K and N on the Music dataset.

5 Conclusion

Existing aspect-based recommendation methods use GNN to model relationships among users, items, and aspect terms, which only focus on modeling static user preferences and overlook the dynamic nature of user interests In this paper, we propose a long-short-term aspect interest Transformer for aspect-based recommendation, which considers long- and short-term user interests on aspect terms to learn the dynamic nature of user preferences on them. Experiments on four real-world datasets demonstrate the effectiveness of LSA. In future work, we plan to explore sentiment-aware aspect modeling to enhance the representation, aiming for more personalized and interpretable recommendations.

Acknowledgments. This work was supported by the Beijing University of Technology Education and Teaching Research Project (No. ER2024KCA01), the open project of Key Laboratory Ministry of Industry and Information Technology (No. ZCQP2024000337), the open project of IoT Standards and Application Key Laboratory of the Ministry of Industry and Information Technology (No. 202407), and the National Training Program of Innovation and Entrepreneurship for Undergraduates of China (Beijing University of Technology) under Grant No. GJDC2024018383.

References

1. Bauman, K., Liu, B., Tuzhilin, A.: Aspect based recommendations: recommending items with the most valuable aspects based on user reviews. In: Proceedings of the 23rd ACM SIGKDD, pp. 717–725. ACM (2017)
2. Brody, S., Alon, U., Yahav, E.: How attentive are graph attention networks? In: ICLR 2022, Virtual Event, 25–29 April 2022. OpenReview.net (2022)
3. Chen, C., Zhang, M., Liu, Y., Ma, S.: Neural attentional rating regression with review-level explanations. In: Proceedings of the WWW 2018, WWW 2018, pp. 1583–1592 (2018)
4. Chin, J.Y., Zhao, K., Joty, S.R., Cong, G.: ANR: aspect-based neural recommender. In: Proceedings of the 27th ACM CIKM, pp. 147–156. ACM (2018)
5. Jose, G.J.A., Mastan, M., Al-Nuaimy, L.A.H.: Aspect based hotel recommendation system using dilated multichannel CNN and BiGRU with hyperbolic linear unit. Int. J. Mach. Learn. Cybern. **15**(11), 4867–4886 (2024)
6. Lai, C., Hsu, C.: Rating prediction based on combination of review mining and user preference analysis. Inf. Syst. **99**, 101742 (2021)
7. Li, C., Quan, C., Peng, L., Qi, Y., Deng, Y., Wu, L.: A capsule network for recommendation and explaining what you like and dislike. In: Proceedings of the 42nd International ACM, SIGIR, pp. 275–284. ACM (2019)
8. Li, W., Xu, B.: Aspect-based recommendation model for fashion merchandising. In: DMEC, pp. 243–250 (2021)
9. Li, Z., Cheng, W., Kshetramade, R., Houser, J., Chen, H., Wang, W.: Recommend for a reason: Unlocking the power of unsupervised aspect-sentiment co-extraction. In: EMNLP 2021, pp. 763–778. Association for Computational Linguistics (2021)
10. Liu, D., Li, J., Du, B., Chang, J., Gao, R.: DAML: dual attention mutual learning between ratings and reviews for item recommendation. In: Proceedings of the 25th ACM SIGKDD, KDD 2019, pp. 344–352 (2019)
11. Liu, J., Li, T., Wu, D., Tang, Z., Fang, Y., Yang, Z.: An aspect performance-aware hypergraph neural network for review-based recommendation. In: Proceedings of the Eighteenth ACM WSDM, pp. 503–511. ACM (2025)
12. Liu, T., Lou, S., Liao, J., Feng, H.: Dynamic and static representation learning network for recommendation. IEEE TNNLS **35**(1), 831–841 (2024)
13. Liu, Y., Yang, S., Zhang, Y., Miao, C., Nie, Z., Zhang, J.: Learning hierarchical review graph representations for recommendation. IEEE Trans. Knowl. Data Eng. **35**(1), 658–671 (2023)
14. Ou, Z., Zhang, X., Zhu, Y., Lyu, S., Liu, J., Ao, T.: LS-TGNN: long and short-term temporal graph neural network for session-based recommendation. In: AAAI, pp. 12426–12434. AAAI Press (2025)
15. Qiu, L., Gao, S., Cheng, W., Guo, J.: Aspect-based latent factor model by integrating ratings and reviews for recommender system. Knowl. Based Syst. **110**, 233–243 (2016)
16. Rendle, S.: Factorization machines. In: 2010 IEEE International Conference on Data Mining, pp. 995–1000. IEEE
17. Shi, L., et al.: SENGR: sentiment-enhanced neural graph recommender. Inf. Sci. **589**, 655–669 (2022)
18. Wu, L., Quan, C., Li, C., Wang, Q., Zheng, B., Luo, X.: A context-aware user-item representation learning for item recommendation. ACM Trans. Inf. Syst. **37**(2) (2019)

19. Yang, C., Yu, X., Liu, Y., Nie, Y., Wang, Y.: Collaborative filtering with weighted opinion aspects. Neurocomputing **210**, 185–196 (2016)
20. Yu, Z., Lian, J., Mahmoody, A., Liu, G., Xie, X.: Adaptive user modeling with long and short-term preferences for personalized recommendation. In: Proceedings of the Twenty-Eighth IJCAI, pp. 4213–4219. ijcai.org (2019)
21. Zhao, W., Wang, B., Ye, J., Gao, Y., Yang, M., Chen, X.: PLASTIC: prioritize long and short-term information in top-n recommendation using adversarial training. In: Proceedings of the Twenty-Seventh IJCAI, pp. 3676–3682. ijcai.org (2018)
22. Zheng, L., Noroozi, V., Yu, P.S.: Joint deep modeling of users and items using reviews for recommendation. In: WSDM 2017, pp. 425–434 (2017)

Route Optimisation and Networks

A Comparative Study on Sub-route Merging Ways for Clustering Assisted Ant Colony Optimization to Solve Large-Scale Traveling Salesman Problem

Zhongheng Jiang[1], Qiang Yang[1(✉)], Danting Duan[2], Zhen-Yu Lu[1], and Jun Zhang[2,3,4,5]

[1] Nanjing University of Information Science and Technology, Nanjing, China
mmmyq@126.com

[2] ERICA, Hanyang University, Seoul, South Korea

[3] Nankai University, Tianjin, China

[4] Zhejiang Normal University, Jinhua, China

[5] Chaoyang University of Technology, Taichung, Taiwan

Abstract. Large-Scale Traveling Salesman Problem (TSP) has remained as a significantly challenging task for swarm intelligent optimization algorithms to solve due to their low effectiveness and efficiency in face of a huge number of cities. Clustering-Assisted Ant Colony Optimization (CA-ACO) has been considered as a promising way to solve large-scale TSP. It divides the cities into a number of clusters by using clustering algorithms and then optimizes the sub-route for each cluster of cities. Finally, it gets the optimal route of the entire TSP by merging all sub-routes. In this way, CA-ACO reduces the time and space complexity significantly and thus could solve large-scale TSP with high efficiency. Particularly, in CA-ACO, how to merge sub-routes makes significant influence on the quality of the complete route of the large-scale TSP. However, few studies have investigated such influence of sub-route merging ways. To fill this gap, this paper provides an in-depth investigation on the impact of different merging methods on the performance of CA-ACO in solving large-scale TSP. To this end, this paper develops six different merging methods, that is, sequential merging, pairwise merging, max-first merging, min-first merging, hierarchical merging, and probabilistic merging. Then, this paper embeds these merging methods into CA-ACO with five classical ACOs, namely Ant System (AS), Elitist AS (EAS), Rank-based AS (RAS), Max-Min AS (MMAS), and Ant Colony System (ACS) to solve large-scale TSP. Experiments conducted on six large-scale TSP instances with different numbers of clusters have demonstrated that the sequential merging method is the most effective one for CA-ACO to address large-scale TSP.

Keywords: Large-Scale Traveling Salesman Problem · Ant Colony Optimization · Clustering · Route Optimization · Combinatorial Optimization

I. Awan et al. (Eds.): WISE 2025, LNCS 16368, pp. 119–134, 2026.
https://doi.org/10.1007/978-981-95-7251-9_9

1 Introduction

Traveling Salesman Problem (TSP) is a well-known route optimization problem [1, 2]. Given a set of cities, its goal is to find the shortest Hamilton loop, such that all cities are visited and each city is exactly visited only once except for the starting city. In the literature, TSP has been widely researched and extended to a lot of variants to simulate real-world applications, like multiple travelling salesmen problems (MTSP) [3–5] and vehicle routing problems (VRP) [6–8].

In the literature, evolutionary algorithms (EAs) [9–12] have been widely used to solve TSP effectively. Among them, Ant Colony Optimization (ACO) [13, 14] is the most widely used EA to solve TSP. Specifically, ACO mainly iterates an ant colony of ants to build routes generation by generation based on a gradually updated pheromone matrix. There are two major steps in ACO, namely route construction and pheromone update. With respect to these two steps, researchers have developed various novel techniques [15–17] to improve the performance of ACO in addressing TSP. Besides, thanks to the great success of ACO in solving TSP, it has been widely employed to solve other various route optimization problems [18–22] and other NP-hard optimization problems in the real-world applications [23–26].

Though ACO shows quite good performance in solving TSP, its effectiveness deteriorates rapidly in face of large-scale TSP, especially when the number of cities becomes very huge (10^4 or more). This is because on the one hand, the solution space of large-scale TSP enlarges exponentially as the number of cities increases [27] on the other hand, the time complexity of ACO also increases quickly as the number of cities increases [28]. Particularly, in the route construction, since it requires calculating the probabilities of all candidate cities, ACO takes O(n^2) (where n is the number of cities) to construct one complete route. Besides, in the pheromone update process, ACO takes O(n^2) space to store this matrix and takes O(n^2) to update this matrix. As a consequence, when the number of cities is huge, traditional ACO becomes infeasible to solve large-scale TSP [29].

To adapt ACO to solve large-scale TSP effectively, researchers have proposed Clustering-Assisted Ant Colony Optimization (CA-ACO) [30] by combining clustering algorithms and ACO together. Specifically, the main working principle of CA-ACO is to divide the huge number of cities into a number of clusters with each cluster containing only a small number of cities and then optimize the route of each cluster separately by ACO. Particularly, the overall flowchart of CA-ACO is shown in Fig. 1. This figure indicates that CA-ACO consists of four major steps, namely the clustering, the intra-cluster optimization, the inter-cluster optimization, and the sub-route merging [31].

Among the four major processes in CA-ACO, one crucial step is the sub-route merging step, which merges all sub-routes to get the complete route of the large-scale TSP. After the sub-route optimization, the merging step directly determines the quality of the final route of the large-scale TSP. However, in the literature, few studies pay attention to the influence of the sub-route merging methods on the performance of CA-ACO.

To fill this gap, this paper provides an in-depth investigation on the influence of the sub-route merging methods on the effectiveness of CA-ACO in solving large-scale TSP. To this end, this paper first develops six different sub-route merging methods, that is, sequential merging, pairwise merging, max-first merging, min-first merging, hierarchical merging, and probabilistic merging, to cooperate with CA-ACO. Besides, to address the high time and space complexity of ACO in optimizing sub-routes of all clusters, this paper further proposes a nearest neighbor-based candidate rule for ACO to determine the candidate cities for ants to select, such that ants could construct sub-routes efficiently for clusters. Further, the paper devises an edge destroy-and-rebuilding operator based on the nearest neighbors of cities to further refine the solution to the large-scale TSP.

By embedding the above techniques into five classical ACOs, namely Ant System (AS) [32], Elitist AS (EAS) [32], Rank-based AS (RAS) [33], Max-Min AS (MMAS) [34] and Ant Colony System (ACS) [35], we conduct experiments on six ArtTSP instances (https://www.math.uwaterloo.ca/tsp/data/art/index.html) by using the k-mean clustering algorithm configured with different numbers of clusters.

2 CA-ACO

As shown in Fig. 1, CA-ACO has four core processes, that is clustering cities into clusters, finding the optimal sub-routes of all clusters and the optimal merging sequence to merge all clusters, merging all sub-routes to get the complete route, and performing local search to refine the quality of the final route.

In the clustering process, different clustering algorithms can be used to divide the large-scale cities into clusters consisting a small number of cities. For instance, Yu et al. [26] employed the K-means clustering algorithm, Liao et al. [30] utilized the density peak clustering (DPC) algorithm, and Tan et al. [36] combined the K-medoids clustering algorithm with DPC, to separate cities into clusters. In our precious study [37], we have compared different clustering algorithms with respect to their influence on the performance of CA-ACO. Based on the comparison results, we use the K-means clustering algorithm in this paper to divide cities into clusters.

In the sub-route optimization process of the separated intra-clusters and the inter-cluster, ACO is widely used to find the optimal sub-routes of all clusters [30, 36]. Besides, local search methods, like 2-opt, are also usually employed to further improve the quality of the optimized sub-routes. Along with the sub-route optimization of all clusters, the merging sequence optimization for merging all sub-routes is also executed by using ACO. During this optimization, the centroids of all clusters are used as the virtual cities. It deserves attention that since all clusters are separate, the sub-route optimization of all inter-clusters and even the merging sequence optimization of intra-clusters can be executed in parallel for high efficiency. As for the termination of each sub-route optimization by ACO, we set it as when the optimal sub-route remains unimproved for 500 consecutive generations.

In the sub-route merging process, all sub-routes are merged according to the optimized merging sequence based on the centroids of all clusters. However, how to merge these sub-routes based on the merging sequence usually has crucial influence on the quality of the final complete route. Some researchers have proposed some methods to merge sub-routes. For instance, Liao et al. [30] proposed a node reorganization strategy based on the shortest cross-cluster boundaries, Tan et al. [36] designed an entrance/exit connection mechanism to merge neighbor sub-routes, and Yu et al. [26] adopted a nearest node docking method to merge adjacent sub-routes.

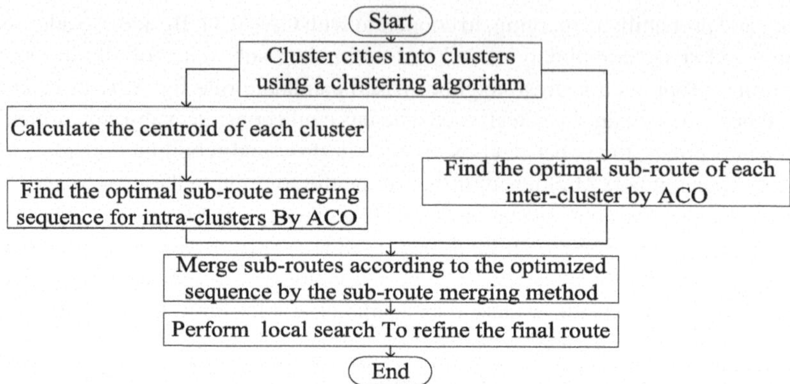

Fig. 1. General flowchart of CA-ACO.

After all sub-routes are merged to form the complete route of the large-scale TSP, local search is usually executed on the final complete route to further improve its quality. Most existing studies used the k-opt operator [30] or the simulated annealing operator [26, 36] to refine the final route. However, it is usually too time-consuming or too low-efficient to get better complete routes. To address this problem, this paper devises an edge destroy-and-rebuilding local search method to effectively and efficiently refine the quality of the final complete route, which is to be described in Sect. 4.

Among the above four major processes of CA-ACO, very few studies have paid attention to the sub-route merging process. Though sub-routes are merged according to the optimized merging sequence based on the centroids of clusters, which sub-routes are merged first may have effect on the connecting of sub-routes and then have influence on the quality of the complete route. To investigate the influence of the sub-route merging ways on the quality of CA-ACO, this paper develops six different merging methods, which are elucidated in the following.

3 Sub-route Merging Methods

Before elucidating the devised six sub-route merging methods, we first give the procedure of merging two sub-routes, which is presented in Algorithm 1.

Specifically, for two sub-routes ***A*** and ***B***, we try to check every edge in ***A*** and ***B*** to find the optimal connection between the two sub-routes, so as to get the minimal route length of the merged route. Given that one edge in ***A*** is (*a1*, *a2*) and one edge in ***B*** is (*b1*, *b2*), we first break these two edges and then connect the two endpoints in the two edges to merge these two sub-routes. Since each edge has two endpoints, there are two different connections, namely a1 is connected with *b1* while *a2* is connected with *b2*, and *a1* is connected with *b2*, while *a2* is connected with *b1*. Then, we respectively compute the lengths of the merged routes after the two connections. Subsequently, we compare these two merged routes with the best one. If they are better than the maintained best route, we update the best route. After checking all edges in ***A*** and ***B***, we finally output the best merged route.

Algorithm 1: Two Sub-routes Merging

Input: ***Sub-route A, Sub-route B***.

```
min_cost = inf;
Merged_path = null;
For each edge (a_1, a_2) in A do
    For each edge (b_1, b_2) in B do
        cost_1=(A.length-dis(a_1, a_2)) + (B.length-dis(b_1, b_2)) + dis(a_2, b_1) + dis(b_2, a_1);
        path_1=A[a_2: a_1] + B[b_2: b_1];
        cost_2=(A.length-dis(a_1, a_2)) + (B.length-dis(b_1, b_2)) + dis(a_2, b_2) + dis(b_1, a_1);
        path_2=A[a_2: a_1] + reverse(B[b_2: b_1]);
        If cost_1 < min_cost then
            min_cost = cost_1;
            Merged_path = path_1;
        End If
        If cost_2 < min_cost then
            min_cost = cost_2;
            Merged_path = path_2;
        End If
    End For
End For
```

Output: *Merged_path*.

The above sub-route merging process only involves two adjacent sub-routes. However, in the optimized merging sequence of all clusters, we need to merge all sub-routes one by one. Since Algorithm 1 is to find the optimal merged route of two adjacent sub-routes, how to select two adjacent sub-routes to merge first usually has effect on the quality of the final complete route. This paper just takes deep investigation on such influence of selecting two adjacent sub-routes to merge first. To this end, this paper designs six sub-route merging methods, namely the sequential merging method (SMM), the pairwise merging method (PMM), the max-first merging method (MMM), the min-first merging method (NMM), the hierarchical merging method (HMM), and the probabilistic merging method (PrMM). The visual processes of these merging methods are shown in Fig. 2, while their detailed elucidations are presented in the following:

3.1 Sequential Merging Method (SMM)

This method just merges all sub-routes according to the optimized merging sequence from one starting sub-route to the last one. As for the starting sub-route, it just randomly selects one from all sub-routes. Subsequently, it continuously executes Algorithm 1 from the starting sub-route to the last one to merge all sub-routes.

Figure 2(a) shows an example process of SMM. Given four sub-routes (***C1***, ***C2***, ***C3***, and ***C4***) of four clusters, SMM randomly selects one sub-route as the starting sub-route. Provided that the selected starting sub-route is ***C1***, SMM first merges sub-routes ***C1*** and ***C2*** to get a merged route. Then, it further merges the merged route with ***C3*** to get a new larger merged route. Finally, it merges the new merged route with ***C4*** to get the complete route of the large-scale TSP.

3.2 Pairwise Merging Method (PMM)

This method separates the optimized merging sequence into pairs and then merges the two sub-routes in each pair. Subsequently, the merged routes are further separated into pairs and then the two merged routes in each pair are merged into a larger route. This process continues until a final complete route is obtained.

Figure 2(b) displays an example process of PMM. In the first step, the optimized merging sequence is separated into two pairs, namely (***C2***, ***C3***) and (***C1***, ***C4***). Then, in the second step, sub-routes ***C2*** and ***C3*** are merged to form a new sub-route. Next, in the third step, sub-routes ***C1*** and ***C4*** are merged into a new sub-route. Subsequently, in the fourth step, the two new sub-routes are merged to get a complete route.

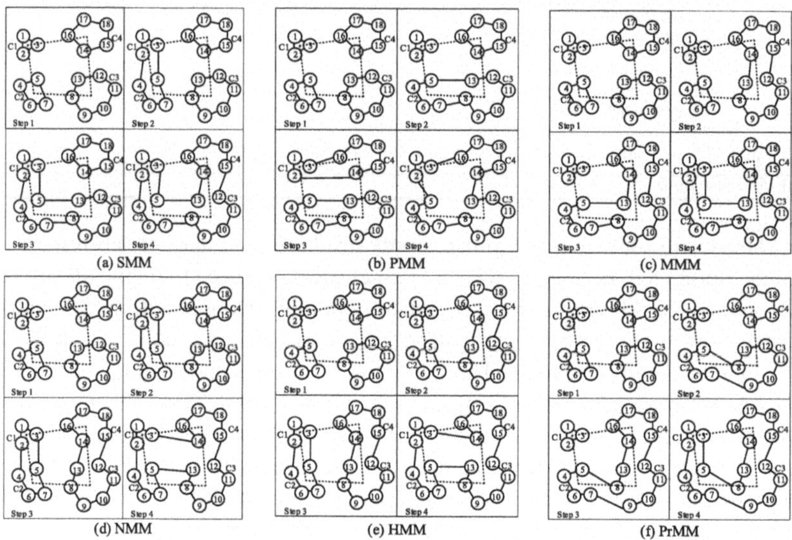

Fig. 2. Visual processes of different sub-route merging methods

3.3 Max-First Merging Method (MMM)

This method always chooses the sub-route with the largest number of cities from all sub-routes as the first sub-route to merge. Then, it chooses the adjacent sub-route with a larger number of cities from its two adjacent ones in the optimized merging sequence as the second sub-route to merge. Subsequently, the two selected sub-routes are merged to form a new sub-route. Next, it continues to execute the above process until all sub-routes are merged to get the final complete route.

Figure 2(c) exhibits an example process of MMM. In the first step, it selects the sub-route consisting of the most cities, namely ***C3***, as the first sub-route. Then, it finds the two adjacent sub-routes of ***C3***, namely ***C4*** and ***C2***. Subsequently, it selects ***C4*** as the second sub-route to merge because ***C4*** has more cities than ***C2***. Next, it merges ***C3*** and ***C4*** to form a new sub-route. In the next round of merging, since the new sub-route contains the most cities, it acts as the first sub-route. Then, ***C2*** is selected as the second sub-route to merge because it has more cities than ***C1***. Therefore, ***C2*** and the new sub-route are merged to form another bigger sub-route. At last, ***C1*** and the new sub-route are merged to get the complete route.

3.4 Min-First Merging Method (NMM)

This method is just the opposite of MMM. That is, it always selects the sub-route with the fewest cities as the first sub-route to merge. Then, from its two adjacent sub-routes in the optimized merging sequence, it chooses the one with fewer cities as the second sub-route to merge. Then, these two selected sub-routes are merged to form a new sub-route. The above sub-route selection and merging processes continue until all sub-routes are merged to get a complete route.

Figure 2(d) shows an example process of NMM. In the first step, sub-route ***C1*** is selected because it has the fewest cities. Then, sub-routes ***C2*** and ***C4***, which are adjacent to ***C1*** are compared and then ***C2*** is selected because it has fewer cities. Subsequently, ***C1*** and ***C2*** are merged to form a new sub-route. Subsequently, in the next round of merging, sub-routes ***C3*** and ***C4*** are selected and then merged to form a new sub-route because ***C4*** has the fewest cities and ***C3*** is the adjacent sub-route of ***C4*** and has much fewer cities than the other adjacent sub-route of ***C4***. At last, the two merged sub-routes are left and thus they are merged to form a complete route.

3.5 Hierarchical Merging Method (HMM)

This method merges sub-routes hierarchically. Specifically, it first sorts all sub-routes according to the number of cities they contain. Then, in this hierarchy, HMM merges sub-routes from the one with the largest number of cities. In particular, in the first step, the sub-route with the most cities is picked and then it is merged with the one of its two adjacent sub-routes with more cities. Next, the merged sub-route is put into the next hierarchy. Then, HMM finds the sub-route with the most cities from the remaining ones and merges it with the one of its two adjacent sub-routes with more cities. This process continues until all sub-routes in this hierarchy are merged. If only one sub-route in this hierarchy is not merged, it is directly put into the next hierarchy. Subsequently, HMM merges the merged sub-route in the next hierarchy in the same way. This hierarchical merging process continues until a complete route is formed.

Figure 2(e) displays an example process of HMM. In the first hierarchy, all sub-routes are sorted in the order of the number of cities they have. Thus, we get (***C3***, ***C4***, ***C2***, ***C1***). Then, ***C3*** is merged with ***C4***, and ***C2*** is merged with ***C1***. Therefore, two new sub-routes are obtained and they are put into the next hierarchy. Subsequently, the above merging process continues until a complete route is formed.

3.6 Probabilistic Merging Method (PrMM)

This method assigns each edge in the optimized merging sequence a probability based on the number of cities in the two sub-routes connected by the edge. Then, it uses the roulette wheel selection (RWS) to pick one edge and then merges the connected two sub-routes. Once two sub-routes are merged, the merged sub-route is inserted into the merging sequence and then the probabilities on all edges are re-calculated. This process continues until all sub-routes are merged to form a complete route.

Figure 2(f) gives an example process of PrMM. Specifically, in the first step, we calculate the probabilities of all edges in the optimized merging sequence, namely (***C1***,

C2), (***C2***, ***C3***), (***C3***, ***C4***), (***C4***, ***C1***). Their probabilities are 7/36, 10/36, 11/36, and 8/36, respectively. Then, RWS is employed to select one edge. In this example, edge (***C2***, ***C3***) is selected. Therefore, sub-routes ***C2*** and ***C3*** are first merged to form a new sub-route, which we denote as ***C23***. Then, the probabilities of the edges (***C1***, ***C23***), (***C23***, ***C4***), and (***C4***, ***C1***) are re-calculated, which are 13/36, 15/36, and 8/36, respectively. Next, in this example, edge (***C23***, ***C4***) is selected by RWS. Therefore, sub-routes ***C23*** and ***C4*** are merged to form a new sub-route. At last, since there are only two sub-routes left, they are merged to form a complete route.

4 Nearest Neighbor-Based Candidate City Selection and Edge Destroy-and-Rebuilding Local Search

4.1 Nearest Neighbor-Based Candidate City Selection

Although a large-scale TSP instance with a huge number of cities is divided into clusters by the clustering algorithm, some clusters may still contain a large number of cities. As a consequence, ACO is still of low effectiveness and efficiency in finding the optimal sub-routes of these clusters. To solve this issue, this paper further devises a nearest neighbor-based candidate city selection strategy to assist ants to select the next city to visit for ACO.

Specifically, one ant in ACO selects the next city to visit during the route construction according to the following rule:

$$j = \begin{cases} j^* & rand(0,1) > q_0 \\ \arg\max_{k \in \boldsymbol{J}} (\tau_{i,k})^{\alpha} \cdot (\eta_{i,k})^{\beta} & otherwise \end{cases} \tag{1}$$

$$p_j = \frac{(\tau_{i,j})^{\alpha} \cdot (\eta_{i,j})^{\beta}}{\sum_{k \in \boldsymbol{J}} (\tau_{i,k})^{\alpha} \cdot (\eta_{i,k})^{\beta}} \tag{2}$$

where α and β are the constant factors in charge of the influence of the pheromone and the heuristic information, respectively, j^* represents the selected city by the route wheel selection strategy with the selection probability of each candidate computed by Eq. (2), $\boldsymbol{J}$ is the set of candidate cities, $\tau_{i,j}$ and $\eta_{i,j}$ are the pheromone and heuristic information on edge (i, j), respectively.

In Eq. (1), the candidate city set $\boldsymbol{J}$ in traditional ACO usually contains all those cities that have not been visited by this ant. This is suitable for small-scale TSP with a small number of cities. However, in face of large-scale TSP, it becomes less effective and efficient because of the too large candidate city set. To address this issue, this paper only selects several nearest neighbors of the last visited city from the remaining unvisited cities as the candidates for the ant to select. The number of the nearest neighbors is called the nearest neighbor size and is denoted as *NS*. In this paper, we set *NS* as 32.

With this strategy, the candidate city set only contains *NS* cities for each ant to select during the sub-route construction for each cluster. In this way, the selection process becomes much more effective and efficient. Here, it should be mentioned that the nearest neighbors are utilized because in the large-scale TSP, it is highly impossible that in the optimal sub-route, two cities with large distance are connected. On the contrary, close cities are likely connected in the optimal route.

4.2 Edge Destroy-and-Rebuilding Local Search

After all sub-routes are merged to form a complete route, this route is usually of low quality due to that the sub-route merging process merges sub-routes one by one and thus the obtained new sub-routes after one-by-one merging are usually locally optimal. As a consequence, the complete route is also likely locally optimal. To further refine the quality of the final route, this paper devises an edge destroy-and-rebuilding local search method.

Specifically, this method temporarily removes a city and then attempts to insert it back into the route by finding the optimal position, which leads to the largest reduction of the route length. If the route length cannot be shortened by attempting all possible positions, the position of this city is not changed. This process continues until no further improvement is achieved.

To improve efficiency, this paper introduces two improvements:

1) **Limiting the insertion range:** The removed cities are inserted back into the route only around their neighboring cities. That is, each removed city tries to connect with its nearest neighbors. In this way, a lot of meaningless insertions could be avoided. This is very beneficial for accelerating the local search process.
2) **Maintaining a candidate queue:** During the local search, a queue of cities to be removed is maintained. Initially, the queue contains all cities. Every time a city is removed from the queue for an attempt. If this attempt successfully improves the route, the city, its predecessor and successor in the original route, and its predecessor and successor in the new route are all added into the queue. In this way, the local search only focuses on promising cities for improvement. This significantly reduces ineffective searches and thus is beneficial for improving efficiency.

Figure 3 shows an example of the devised local search. In this example, city 2 is first removed from its original location and then is inserted between cities 4 and 5. Because this attempt reduces the route length, the change of city 2 is retained.

By embedding the above two techniques into CA-ACO, we deem that the effectiveness and efficiency of CA-ACO in solving large-scale TSP could be further improved.

5 Experiments

5.1 Experimental Setup

This paper investigates the influence of the six merging methods on CA-ACO by conducting experiments on six ArtTSP instances, which can be downloaded from https://www.math.uwaterloo.ca/tsp/data/art/index.html. All these six instances contain a huge number of cities with the magnitude 10^5. Figure 4 shows the visual plots of these six ArtTSP instances.

For comprehensive investigation, this paper instantiates CA-ACO with the five classic ACO variants, namely AS [32], EAS [32], RAS [33], MMAS [34], and ACS [35]. All the parameters of the five ACOs are set as the classical ones in the original papers, which are listed in Table 1. As for the city clustering, this paper employs the k-mean clustering algorithm to divide cities into clusters. For comprehensive evaluation, we set three different numbers of clusters, namely 100, 500, and 1000.

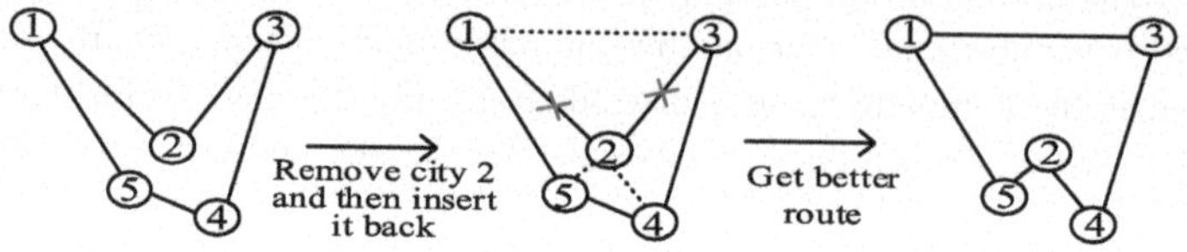

Fig. 3. Visual process of the edge destroy-and-rebuilding local search strategy

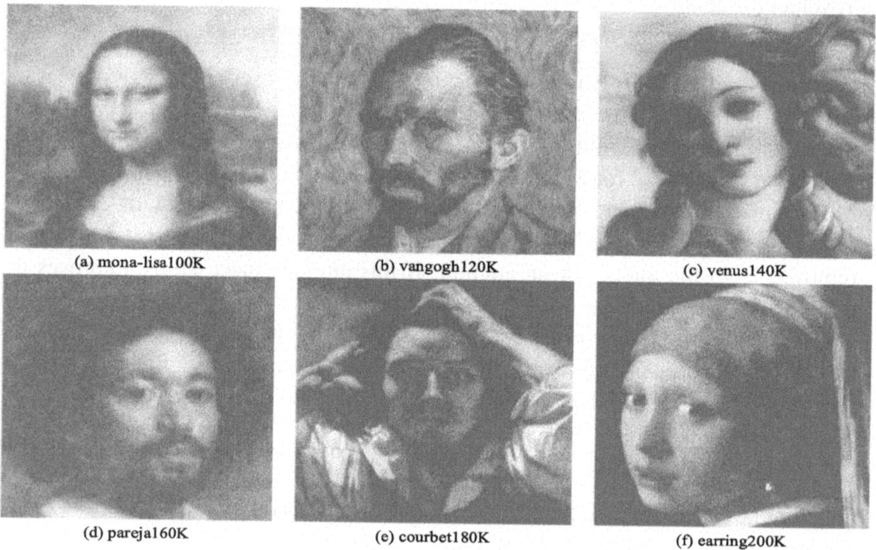

Fig. 4. Visualization of the six ArtTSP instances

To evaluate the performance of CA-ACO, we utilize the following measurement:

$$error = \frac{fit(\boldsymbol{R}^{best}) - fit(\boldsymbol{R}^{optimial})}{fit(\boldsymbol{R}^{optimial})} \times 100\% \tag{3}$$

where $fit(\boldsymbol{R}^{best})$ is the length of the best route found by CA-ACO in one run, $fit(\boldsymbol{R}^{optimial})$ is the length of the already known optimal route, which can be found in the previous website, and *error* is the relative difference between the found optimal route and the true optimal one.

In the experiments, each algorithm is executed independently 10 times. Then, the minimal value, the maximal value, the mean value, and the standard deviation value over the 10 independent results are reported for comparisons. For statistical tests, we perform the Friedman test at the significant level of $\alpha = 0.05$ to get two average ranking values, namely the local ranking and the global ranking. The former is the ranking value of each sub-route merging method under one same ACO algorithm (AS, EAS, RAS, MMAS, and ACS), while the latter is the ranking value of each sub-route merging method under all the five ACOs.

5.2 Experimental Results and Analysis

Table 2 shows the experimental results of the six merging methods under the five ACO variants. In this table, the smallest value of each indicator under one same ACO is bolded, while that under all the five ACOs is shaded. From this table, we get the following conclusions:

Table 1. Parameter settings of the five ACOs

Parameter	AS	EAS	RAS	MMAS	ACS
NP	50	50	50	50	10
α	1	1	1	1	1
β	2	2	2	2	2
ρ	0.1	0.1	0.1	0.02	0.1

1) With respect to the local ranking, it is found that under the five ACOs, SMM consistently achieves the smallest ranking value. Besides, its ranking value is significantly smaller than the other five merging methods. This proves that SMM is the best merging method for CA-ACO to solve large-scale TSP.
2) Regarding the global ranking, it is found that the combination between SMM and ACS gains the smallest ranking value. Besides, such a value is noticeably smaller than those of the other combinations between the six merging methods and the five ACOs. This just demonstrates that ACS with SMM is the most promising for solving large-scale TSP. This actually is not strange because ACS is able to find much higher-quality sub-routes for all clusters than the other four ACOs.
3) It is interesting to find that with the number of clusters increasing, the performance of CA-ACO under the five ACOs and the six sub-route merging methods becomes better and better. This indicates that to solve large-scale TSP, a properly large number of clusters should be given to CA-ACO to divide cities into smaller clusters, such that ACO could find the optimal sub-route of each smaller cluster.
4) Further, it is also interesting to find that on the one hand, the difference between the maximal result and the minimal result of CA-ACO under each ACO and each merging method on each ArtTSP instance with each number of clusters among the 10 independent results is not so large; on the other hand, the associated standard deviation value over the 10 independent results is also very small. This reveals that CA-ACO solves large-scale TSP very stably.

Table 2. Experimental results of the five CA-ACOs with the six merging methods.

Instances	k	Indicators	AS SMM	AS PMM	AS MMM	AS NMM	AS HMM	AS PrMM	EAS SMM	EAS PMM	EAS MMM	EAS NMM	EAS HMM	EAS PrMM	RAS SMM	RAS PMM	RAS MMM
mona-lisa 100K	100	mean	**3.346**	5.707	5.708	5.712	5.715	5.702	**3.327**	5.654	5.655	5.666	5.619	5.654	**3.425**	5.876	5.865
		max	**3.381**	5.753	5.775	5.784	5.767	5.736	**3.349**	5.703	5.721	5.716	5.660	5.723	**3.449**	5.900	5.878
		min	**3.316**	5.670	5.679	5.664	5.668	5.638	**3.309**	5.605	5.606	5.606	5.574	5.599	**3.398**	5.857	5.843
		std	**0.020**	0.024	0.029	0.032	0.029	0.027	**0.015**	0.031	0.032	0.034	0.024	0.034	0.018	0.014	**0.011**
	500	mean	**2.956**	4.541	4.455	4.522	4.459	4.517	**2.917**	4.445	4.380	4.454	4.388	4.438	**3.046**	4.693	4.651
		max	**2.978**	4.595	4.470	4.572	4.480	4.554	**2.945**	4.486	4.394	4.476	4.409	4.459	**3.078**	4.735	4.680
		min	**2.930**	4.506	4.446	4.483	4.435	4.444	**2.887**	4.418	4.367	4.433	4.359	4.416	**3.018**	4.676	4.628
		std	0.015	0.024	**0.008**	0.023	0.012	0.030	0.016	0.021	**0.009**	0.013	0.015	0.013	0.020	0.017	0.020
	1000	mean	**2.680**	3.860	3.737	3.856	3.743	3.836	**2.641**	3.760	3.652	3.775	3.654	3.755	**2.722**	3.920	3.799
		max	**2.709**	3.888	3.762	3.880	3.759	3.878	**2.657**	3.782	3.666	3.796	3.685	3.776	**2.750**	3.964	3.830
		min	**2.655**	3.815	3.714	3.827	3.729	3.808	**2.630**	3.741	3.636	3.742	3.609	3.724	**2.692**	3.860	3.739
		std	0.014	0.021	0.014	0.016	**0.008**	0.022	**0.007**	0.014	0.011	0.018	0.019	0.017	0.015	0.029	0.026
vangogh 120K	100	mean	**3.502**	5.967	5.975	5.973	5.984	5.979	**3.479**	5.917	5.885	5.921	5.913	5.902	**3.572**	6.141	6.126
		max	**3.545**	6.022	6.028	5.998	6.058	6.015	**3.502**	5.970	5.962	5.977	5.962	5.946	**3.597**	6.172	6.154
		min	**3.459**	5.914	5.916	5.935	5.934	5.944	**3.453**	5.873	5.810	5.863	5.859	5.874	**3.546**	6.109	6.098
		std	0.026	0.035	0.038	**0.018**	0.030	0.023	**0.015**	0.033	0.044	0.032	0.032	0.023	0.016	0.019	0.016
	500	mean	**3.151**	4.883	4.828	4.886	4.826	4.874	**3.122**	4.812	4.763	4.812	4.748	4.805	**3.260**	5.094	5.045
		max	**3.178**	4.916	4.849	4.924	4.850	4.903	**3.138**	4.844	4.798	4.851	4.767	4.834	**3.289**	5.125	5.057
		min	**3.132**	4.854	4.794	4.846	4.807	4.852	**3.104**	4.767	4.728	4.778	4.725	4.771	**3.236**	5.061	5.029
		std	0.015	0.022	**0.014**	0.021	0.014	0.015	**0.011**	0.022	0.024	0.020	0.014	0.022	0.018	0.020	**0.007**
	1000	mean	**2.888**	4.203	4.094	4.203	4.101	4.187	**2.846**	4.112	4.023	4.113	4.014	4.101	**2.933**	4.323	4.232
		max	**2.907**	4.239	4.113	4.235	4.144	4.222	**2.871**	4.164	4.040	4.150	4.036	4.142	**2.947**	4.367	4.267
		min	**2.863**	4.175	4.080	4.171	4.073	4.146	**2.831**	4.098	4.005	4.074	3.996	4.072	**2.916**	4.281	4.207
		std	0.012	0.018	**0.008**	0.019	0.019	0.023	0.012	0.018	0.012	0.023	**0.011**	0.023	**0.011**	0.024	0.018
venus 140K	100	mean	**3.406**	5.837	5.835	5.848	5.832	5.856	**3.390**	5.785	5.793	5.799	5.798	5.787	**3.465**	5.994	5.988
		max	**3.444**	5.907	5.886	5.886	5.874	5.901	**3.410**	5.840	5.840	5.830	5.848	5.836	**3.480**	6.014	6.007
		min	**3.376**	5.781	5.780	5.786	5.795	5.823	**3.369**	5.728	5.735	5.761	5.753	5.741	**3.444**	5.948	5.979
		std	**0.025**	0.039	0.030	0.031	0.025	0.026	**0.012**	0.036	0.036	0.022	0.030	0.029	0.011	0.018	**0.009**
	500	mean	**3.108**	4.876	4.817	4.856	4.811	4.864	**3.074**	4.794	4.737	4.791	4.749	4.781	**3.192**	5.061	5.006
		max	**3.129**	4.903	4.845	4.887	4.845	4.885	**3.086**	4.844	4.760	4.835	4.759	4.810	**3.221**	5.088	5.036
		min	**3.082**	4.841	4.791	4.828	4.775	4.833	**3.052**	4.768	4.688	4.768	4.732	4.747	**3.174**	5.037	4.978
		std	0.014	0.020	0.017	0.017	0.019	**0.013**	0.010	0.027	0.022	0.021	**0.008**	0.021	**0.013**	0.015	0.016
	1000	mean	**2.848**	4.212	4.122	4.214	4.131	4.190	**2.800**	4.127	4.036	4.121	4.036	4.116	**2.905**	4.344	4.239
		max	**2.861**	4.242	4.139	4.258	4.172	4.210	**2.822**	4.139	4.060	4.141	4.053	4.145	**2.922**	4.367	4.260
		min	**2.837**	4.176	4.109	4.178	4.098	4.154	**2.780**	4.104	4.021	4.083	4.016	4.095	**2.884**	4.310	4.208
		std	**0.008**	0.017	0.008	0.024	0.020	0.017	0.015	**0.009**	0.012	0.016	0.013	0.015	**0.011**	0.018	0.017
pareja 160K	100	mean	**3.588**	6.168	6.182	6.153	6.177	6.183	**3.565**	6.140	6.109	6.131	6.100	6.135	**3.656**	6.340	6.321
		max	**3.603**	6.217	6.252	6.202	6.223	6.233	**3.607**	6.186	6.162	6.217	6.151	6.197	**3.690**	6.362	6.349
		min	**3.573**	6.102	6.148	6.102	6.111	6.147	**3.535**	6.087	6.043	6.066	5.977	6.080	**3.621**	6.326	6.262
		std	**0.008**	0.035	0.030	0.034	0.031	0.025	**0.023**	0.035	0.040	0.047	0.054	0.035	0.021	**0.012**	0.023
	500	mean	**3.293**	5.228	5.173	5.220	5.194	5.217	**3.259**	5.156	5.112	5.154	5.106	5.154	**3.389**	5.456	5.406
		max	**3.312**	5.281	5.215	5.233	5.208	5.237	**3.278**	5.195	5.134	5.194	5.122	5.188	**3.417**	5.472	5.426
		min	**3.280**	5.200	5.131	5.197	5.173	5.194	**3.241**	5.117	5.081	5.127	5.085	5.128	**3.371**	5.443	5.378
		std	0.011	0.024	0.021	0.010	**0.009**	0.014	0.012	0.026	0.016	0.021	**0.011**	0.021	0.012	**0.009**	0.016
	1000	mean	**3.048**	4.585	4.507	4.586	4.500	4.573	**3.013**	4.504	4.419	4.503	4.420	4.486	**3.139**	4.763	4.679
		max	**3.073**	4.606	4.518	4.630	4.531	4.593	**3.035**	4.539	4.437	4.521	4.432	4.535	**3.157**	4.787	4.715
		min	**3.021**	4.548	4.490	4.563	4.476	4.546	**2.981**	4.478	4.396	4.485	4.408	4.455	**3.123**	4.736	4.655
		std	0.014	0.019	**0.008**	0.021	0.015	0.012	0.014	0.019	0.012	0.014	**0.008**	0.024	0.011	0.017	0.016
courbet 180K	100	mean	**3.757**	6.413	6.426	6.425	6.428	6.431	**3.732**	6.373	6.351	6.382	6.362	6.356	**3.814**	6.592	6.588
		max	**3.790**	6.481	6.489	6.485	6.468	6.491	**3.784**	6.433	6.400	6.437	6.429	6.402	**3.845**	6.611	6.621
		min	**3.713**	6.333	6.363	6.351	6.375	6.395	**3.687**	6.334	6.306	6.280	6.315	6.302	**3.787**	6.564	6.566
		std	**0.021**	0.039	0.039	0.034	0.033	0.026	0.030	0.029	0.029	0.054	0.036	**0.028**	0.016	0.015	0.017
	500	mean	**3.469**	5.537	5.480	5.535	5.483	5.512	**3.440**	5.455	5.413	5.455	5.404	5.454	**3.572**	5.761	5.704
		max	**3.493**	5.585	5.504	5.563	5.505	5.536	**3.454**	5.479	5.428	5.489	5.428	5.484	**3.598**	5.790	5.727
		min	**3.446**	5.505	5.455	5.496	5.461	5.493	**3.421**	5.426	5.401	5.420	5.376	5.428	**3.529**	5.740	5.686
		std	0.014	0.024	0.017	0.023	**0.012**	0.013	**0.009**	0.017	0.010	0.023	0.014	0.017	0.021	0.017	**0.012**
	1000	mean	**3.234**	4.889	4.809	4.876	4.815	4.873	**3.186**	4.799	4.725	4.803	4.718	4.791	**3.322**	5.092	5.004
		max	**3.246**	4.920	4.831	4.904	4.852	4.903	**3.216**	4.825	4.744	4.830	4.748	4.828	**3.342**	5.147	5.017
		min	**3.212**	4.862	4.783	4.849	4.800	4.846	**3.167**	4.778	4.708	4.776	4.698	4.732	**3.304**	5.055	4.975
		std	**0.010**	0.017	0.013	0.013	0.014	0.016	0.015	0.015	**0.011**	0.017	0.013	0.028	**0.011**	0.027	0.012
earring 200K	100	mean	**4.017**	6.858	6.837	6.858	6.841	6.851	**3.989**	6.813	6.790	6.819	6.778	6.794	**4.085**	7.020	7.017
		max	**4.048**	6.943	6.904	6.988	6.891	6.897	**4.013**	6.864	6.864	6.887	6.855	6.852	**4.122**	7.041	7.035
		min	**3.969**	6.809	6.743	6.797	6.809	6.802	**3.951**	6.762	6.712	6.773	6.650	6.705	**4.041**	6.991	6.990
		std	**0.025**	0.045	0.041	0.049	0.029	0.034	**0.016**	0.036	0.053	0.034	0.068	0.041	0.023	0.017	0.012
	500	mean	**3.723**	5.929	5.888	5.934	5.891	5.921	**3.685**	5.848	5.818	5.846	5.818	5.838	**3.826**	6.200	6.156
		max	**3.754**	5.965	5.923	5.959	5.921	5.964	**3.703**	5.876	5.841	5.883	5.848	5.866	**3.836**	6.221	6.172
		min	**3.698**	5.889	5.850	5.912	5.852	5.887	**3.662**	5.810	5.786	5.821	5.786	5.814	**3.812**	6.179	6.142
		std	**0.014**	0.023	0.025	0.018	0.019	0.024	**0.014**	0.020	0.017	0.018	0.020	0.016	**0.008**	0.013	0.010
	1000	mean	**3.473**	5.298	5.223	5.311	5.224	5.302	**3.427**	5.208	5.126	5.204	5.126	5.195	**3.576**	5.521	5.441
		max	**3.514**	5.319	5.248	5.336	5.239	5.319	**3.456**	5.261	5.165	5.227	5.148	5.219	**3.605**	5.547	5.464
		min	**3.453**	5.274	5.207	5.278	5.207	5.285	**3.398**	5.175	5.102	5.189	5.104	5.165	**3.534**	5.475	5.415
		std	0.016	0.018	0.011	0.016	0.010	**0.010**	0.014	0.023	0.018	**0.012**	0.015	0.016	0.019	0.022	0.015
Local Ranking			**1.278**	4.903	3.056	4.625	3.083	4.056	**1.264**	4.861	3.000	4.958	2.847	4.056	**1.514**	4.583	2.583
Global Ranking			9.236	20.528	16.333	19.500	16.667	18.458	8.139	16.514	13.556	16.639	13.042	15.500	10.097	22.972	19.722

(continued)

Table 2. (*continued*)

Instances	k	Indicators	RAS			MMAS						ACS					
			NMM	HMM	PrMM	SMM	PMM	MMM	NMM	HMM	PrMM	SMM	PMM	MMM	NMM	HMM	PrMM
mona-lisa 100K	100	mean	5.891	5.873	5.880	**3.429**	5.892	5.875	5.895	5.878	5.879	1.930	2.541	2.545	2.526	2.535	2.537
		max	5.912	5.889	5.903	**3.465**	5.925	5.901	5.923	5.898	5.899	1.989	2.613	2.625	2.594	2.623	2.585
		min	5.875	5.843	5.861	**3.396**	5.862	5.846	5.869	5.858	5.857	1.896	2.494	2.477	2.460	2.430	2.419
		std	0.012	0.015	0.015	0.020	0.015	0.015	0.020	0.014	**0.012**	**0.026**	0.034	0.048	0.039	0.049	0.048
	500	mean	4.709	4.644	4.703	**3.087**	4.814	4.752	4.821	4.747	4.803	1.558	1.881	1.843	1.884	1.844	1.885
		max	4.752	4.677	4.722	**3.099**	4.862	4.771	4.857	4.764	4.851	1.576	1.900	1.863	1.910	1.857	1.902
		min	4.650	4.613	4.686	**3.069**	4.779	4.740	4.795	4.716	4.752	1.543	1.869	1.830	1.866	1.832	1.856
		std	0.030	0.020	**0.013**	0.011	0.022	**0.010**	0.020	0.014	0.027	0.010	0.009	0.012	0.015	**0.009**	0.012
	1000	mean	3.930	3.808	3.918	**2.838**	4.128	4.014	4.135	4.011	4.113	1.723	2.135	2.056	2.145	2.056	2.126
		max	3.970	3.838	3.939	**2.876**	4.164	4.040	4.173	4.023	4.145	1.731	2.148	2.071	2.177	2.069	2.136
		min	3.871	3.782	3.894	**2.806**	4.098	3.989	4.112	3.992	4.091	1.711	2.124	2.046	2.125	2.045	2.116
		std	0.027	0.017	**0.013**	0.018	0.019	0.014	0.019	**0.009**	0.016	0.005	0.006	0.008	0.016	0.009	0.006
vangogh 120K	100	mean	6.139	6.146	6.138	**3.568**	6.144	6.133	6.136	6.141	6.139	2.094	2.851	2.817	2.830	2.828	2.840
		max	6.161	6.170	6.163	**3.588**	6.157	6.161	6.158	6.173	6.159	2.149	2.927	2.867	2.977	2.918	2.932
		min	6.118	6.122	6.105	**3.545**	6.124	6.092	6.120	6.111	6.121	2.046	2.778	2.766	2.740	2.708	2.740
		std	**0.012**	0.015	0.017	0.013	0.011	0.018	0.011	0.020	0.012	**0.028**	0.043	0.029	0.065	0.054	0.051
	500	mean	5.089	5.030	5.099	**3.279**	5.155	5.110	5.171	5.119	5.165	1.597	1.908	1.883	1.899	1.881	1.908
		max	5.117	5.058	5.142	**3.297**	5.185	5.121	5.205	5.136	5.212	1.621	1.922	1.910	1.905	1.902	1.920
		min	5.059	5.004	5.054	**3.263**	5.112	5.086	5.140	5.090	5.139	1.574	1.897	1.858	1.884	1.860	1.895
		std	0.020	0.016	0.025	**0.010**	0.019	0.011	0.019	0.014	0.018	0.013	0.008	0.014	0.006	0.014	0.007
	1000	mean	4.327	4.218	4.309	**3.033**	4.496	4.399	4.506	4.398	4.483	1.700	2.094	2.034	2.099	2.033	2.092
		max	4.358	4.243	4.329	**3.054**	4.511	4.422	4.537	4.419	4.505	1.716	2.108	2.045	2.116	2.041	2.110
		min	4.288	4.192	4.265	**3.001**	4.481	4.384	4.480	4.386	4.458	1.683	2.083	2.023	2.086	2.024	2.077
		std	0.024	0.015	0.020	0.017	**0.009**	0.012	0.015	0.009	0.013	0.010	0.009	0.007	0.008	0.005	0.010
venus 140K	100	mean	5.989	5.986	5.995	**3.471**	5.997	5.970	5.996	5.992	5.986	2.172	3.045	3.021	3.037	3.043	3.039
		max	6.004	6.019	6.022	**3.494**	6.020	5.998	6.032	6.022	6.003	2.207	3.131	3.089	3.099	3.088	3.127
		min	5.968	5.948	5.982	**3.455**	5.965	5.938	5.976	5.963	5.960	2.147	2.987	2.953	2.976	2.918	2.993
		std	0.012	0.019	0.012	0.014	0.015	0.017	0.015	0.017	**0.013**	**0.017**	0.038	0.039	0.045	0.051	0.037
	500	mean	5.049	5.008	5.055	**3.224**	5.125	5.069	5.142	5.071	5.119	1.595	1.918	1.893	1.916	1.888	1.912
		max	5.067	5.055	5.110	**3.250**	5.154	5.105	5.173	5.096	5.145	1.607	1.944	1.919	1.941	1.915	1.925
		min	5.005	4.982	5.005	**3.208**	5.102	5.039	5.114	5.048	5.089	1.574	1.892	1.881	1.896	1.853	1.901
		std	0.019	0.020	0.026	**0.013**	0.017	0.018	0.021	0.014	0.018	0.010	0.014	0.010	0.013	0.019	**0.008**
	1000	mean	4.345	4.245	4.330	**2.992**	4.492	4.410	4.495	4.399	4.484	1.652	2.024	1.969	2.022	1.971	2.017
		max	4.370	4.272	4.362	**3.004**	4.513	4.439	4.518	4.428	4.506	1.666	2.040	1.980	2.038	1.984	2.034
		min	4.326	4.215	4.281	**2.974**	4.466	4.387	4.473	4.376	4.459	1.636	2.012	1.959	2.006	1.960	2.001
		std	0.016	0.016	0.023	**0.011**	0.016	0.016	0.015	0.015	0.013	0.010	0.009	0.007	0.010	0.007	0.009
pareja 160K	100	mean	6.333	6.336	6.339	**3.657**	6.327	6.330	6.334	6.323	6.323	2.329	3.346	3.338	3.355	3.327	3.315
		max	6.378	6.357	6.363	**3.687**	6.350	6.359	6.353	6.340	6.341	2.352	3.394	3.423	3.443	3.389	3.371
		min	6.303	6.312	6.323	**3.633**	6.304	6.312	6.311	6.290	6.307	2.293	3.273	3.274	3.297	3.261	3.230
		std	0.023	0.012	0.013	0.016	0.012	0.013	0.012	0.015	**0.010**	**0.019**	0.036	0.041	0.064	0.043	0.041
	500	mean	5.449	5.409	5.447	**3.423**	5.507	5.458	5.513	5.462	5.487	1.630	1.953	1.938	1.954	1.942	1.951
		max	5.474	5.430	5.474	**3.442**	5.552	5.480	5.544	5.478	5.509	1.642	1.973	1.954	1.964	1.971	1.971
		min	5.421	5.379	5.425	**3.408**	5.474	5.442	5.485	5.444	5.452	1.613	1.940	1.926	1.943	1.923	1.937
		std	0.015	0.017	0.016	**0.010**	0.023	0.013	0.019	0.011	0.015	0.010	0.011	0.009	0.008	0.014	0.011
	1000	mean	4.765	4.695	4.761	**3.203**	4.900	4.815	4.890	4.813	4.889	1.659	2.015	1.975	2.016	1.972	2.012
		max	4.785	4.716	4.785	**3.219**	4.918	4.833	4.911	4.843	4.913	1.673	2.032	1.986	2.033	1.984	2.022
		min	4.754	4.676	4.735	**3.186**	4.882	4.794	4.865	4.798	4.869	1.647	1.997	1.964	2.002	1.961	1.994
		std	**0.009**	0.013	0.012	**0.010**	0.010	0.012	0.013	0.011	0.015	0.007	0.009	0.006	0.010	0.008	0.008
courbet 180K	100	mean	6.600	6.594	6.588	**3.813**	6.580	6.575	6.584	6.568	6.576	2.486	3.589	3.595	3.596	3.601	3.560
		max	6.618	6.630	6.618	**3.838**	6.610	6.601	6.612	6.587	6.594	2.509	3.671	3.649	3.634	3.700	3.605
		min	6.579	6.570	6.567	**3.788**	6.565	6.563	6.567	6.551	6.560	2.457	3.522	3.525	3.555	3.522	3.474
		std	**0.010**	0.016	0.014	0.015	0.012	0.013	0.015	0.009	0.011	**0.016**	0.044	0.038	0.027	0.051	0.041
	500	mean	5.762	5.718	5.758	**3.591**	5.814	5.766	5.809	5.768	5.800	1.756	2.122	2.092	2.117	2.087	2.112
		max	5.788	5.747	5.798	**3.625**	5.839	5.787	5.841	5.783	5.834	1.778	2.143	2.102	2.137	2.108	2.144
		min	5.744	5.688	5.732	**3.561**	5.794	5.744	5.779	5.750	5.780	1.742	2.109	2.072	2.104	2.070	2.089
		std	0.014	0.016	0.019	0.021	0.016	0.014	0.021	**0.011**	0.015	0.011	0.010	0.008	0.010	0.012	0.015
	1000	mean	5.082	5.005	5.074	**3.378**	5.222	5.126	5.207	5.120	5.204	1.738	2.115	2.071	2.117	2.075	2.110
		max	5.110	5.028	5.112	**3.390**	5.249	5.147	5.230	5.144	5.226	1.751	2.138	2.080	2.133	2.083	2.125
		min	5.061	4.992	5.044	**3.369**	5.203	5.111	5.189	5.109	5.168	1.726	2.097	2.063	2.102	2.062	2.101
		std	0.015	0.013	0.023	**0.006**	0.014	0.010	0.013	0.010	0.017	0.008	0.011	0.006	0.010	0.006	0.007
earring 200K	100	mean	7.049	7.021	7.035	**4.087**	7.021	7.008	7.015	7.023	7.020	2.697	3.911	3.908	3.901	3.909	3.909
		max	7.069	7.036	7.064	**4.132**	7.040	7.036	7.037	7.047	7.038	2.739	3.992	3.971	3.972	4.012	3.987
		min	7.035	7.004	7.012	**4.063**	7.002	6.983	6.992	7.006	6.998	2.643	3.811	3.836	3.832	3.780	3.825
		std	0.010	0.010	0.017	0.018	0.012	0.015	0.017	**0.012**	0.013	**0.027**	0.047	0.041	0.041	0.065	0.044
	500	mean	6.200	6.149	6.199	**3.862**	6.238	6.200	6.238	6.202	6.231	1.869	2.252	2.230	2.251	2.229	2.251
		max	6.221	6.192	6.226	**3.882**	6.265	6.218	6.263	6.226	6.247	1.881	2.269	2.251	2.267	2.250	2.274
		min	6.176	6.129	6.166	**3.833**	6.217	6.177	6.215	6.155	6.210	1.863	2.239	2.205	2.240	2.209	2.227
		std	0.015	0.018	0.018	0.014	0.014	**0.012**	0.016	0.019	0.012	0.005	0.010	0.012	0.008	0.012	0.016
	1000	mean	5.532	5.443	5.525	**3.632**	5.649	5.566	5.646	5.567	5.636	1.850	2.243	2.209	2.253	2.209	2.246
		max	5.557	5.465	5.543	**3.647**	5.669	5.579	5.677	5.581	5.687	1.872	2.266	2.219	2.269	2.225	2.261
		min	5.506	5.424	5.510	**3.608**	5.630	5.549	5.631	5.551	5.604	1.838	2.229	2.193	2.237	2.192	2.232
		std	0.013	0.012	**0.012**	0.012	0.012	0.010	0.013	**0.010**	0.025	0.009	0.011	0.007	0.009	0.008	0.009
Local Ranking			4.611	3.264	4.417	**1.556**	4.806	2.875	5.056	2.861	3.847	**1.389**	4.722	3.000	4.653	3.208	4.028
Global Ranking			22.847	21.125	23.000	10.139	24.764	21.583	25.292	21.764	23.694	2.764	7.014	5.000	6.889	5.708	6.444

In summary, the above experimental results have proved that CA-ACO under the five ACOs and the six sub-route merging methods could solve large-scale TSP very effectively. Particularly, among the six sub-route merging methods, SMM performs the best under all the five ACOs, and among the five ACOs, ACS performs the best under all the six sub-route merging methods. Consequently, CA-ACO with ACS and SMM achieves the best results in solving large-scale TSP.

6 Conclusion

This study investigates the influence of sub-route merging methods on the performance of CA-ACO in solving large-scale TSP. For this purpose, this paper has developed six different sub-route merging methods from different perspectives, that is, the sequential merging method (SMM), the pairwise merging method (PMM), the max-first merging method (MMM), the min-first merging method (NMM), the hierarchical merging method (HMM), and the probabilistic merging method (PrMM). Particularly, to further reduce the time consumption of ACO in optimizing sub-routes of all clusters, this paper has devised a nearest neighbor-based candidate city selection rule to determine candidate cities for ants in ACO to construct sub-routes efficiently. Besides, this paper has also designed an edge destroy-rebuilding local search method to refine the quality of the final complete routes.

By embedding the six sub-route merging methods into CA-ACO with the k-mean clustering algorithm and the five classical ACOs, namely AS, EAS, RAS, MMAS, and ACS, we have conducted extensive experiments on six ArtTSP instances with a huge number of cities (with magnitude of 10^5). The experimental results have demonstrated that among the six merging methods, SMM is the most effective one in cooperating with CA-ACO under the five ACOs to solve large-scale TSP. Besides, among the five ACOs, ACS is the most effective one in collaborating with CA-ACO under the six sub-route merging methods to solve large-scale TSP. By combining ACS with SMM, CA-ACO solves large-scale TSP very effectively and efficiently.

Acknowledgments. This work was supported in part by the National Natural Science Foundation of China under Grant 62576172, in part by the National Research Foundation of Korea under Grant RS-2025-00555463, in part by the Tianjin Top Scientist Studio Project under Grant 24JRRCRC00030, and in part by the Tianjin Belt and Road Joint Laboratory under Grant 24PTLYHZ00250.

Disclosure of Interests. The authors have no competing interests to declare that are relevant to the content of this article.

References

1. Liu, C., et al.: Deep reinforcement learning combined with transformer to solve the traveling salesman problem. J. Supercomput. **81** (2025)
2. Bo, Z.Y., et al.: Evolutionary algorithm with cross-generation environmental selection for traveling salesman problem. In: Proceedings of the Genetic and Evolutionary Computation Conference Companion, pp. 635–638, (2024)
3. Shi, X.L., et al.: A distributed ant colony system with pheromone transfer for multiagent traveling salesmen problem. IEEE Trans. Evol. Comput. 1 (2025)
4. Bo, Z.-Y., et al.: A benchmark test suite for multiple traveling salesmen problem with pivot cities. In: International Conference on Web Information Systems Engineering, pp. 145–157 (2024)
5. Bai, H.-L., et al.: Destination-oriented route construction for ant colony optimization to solve minmax multiple travelling salesmen problems. In: Proceedings of the Genetic and Evolutionary Computation Conference Companion, pp. 199–202 (2025)

6. Nie, Z.H., et al.: Ant colony optimization for electric vehicle routing problem with capacity and charging time constraints. In: IEEE International Conference on Systems, Man, and Cybernetics, pp. 480–485 (2022)
7. Jia, Y.H., Mei, Y., Zhang, M.: A Bilevel ant colony optimization algorithm for capacitated electric vehicle routing problem. IEEE Trans. Cybern. **52**, 10855–10868 (2022)
8. Jia, Y.H., Mei, Y., Zhang, M.: Confidence-based ant colony optimization for capacitated electric vehicle routing problem with comparison of different encoding schemes. IEEE Trans. Evol. Comput. **26**, 1394–1408 (2022)
9. Lei, Z.Y., Hao, J.K.: An effective memetic algorithm for the close-enough traveling salesman problem. Appl. Soft Comput. **153** (2024)
10. Panwar, K., Deep, K.: Discrete grey wolf optimizer for symmetric travelling salesman problem. Appl. Soft Comput. **105**, 107298 (2021)
11. Dou, X.A., et al.: A comparative study on crossover operators of genetic algorithm for traveling salesman problem. In: International Conference on Advanced Computational Intelligence, pp. 1–8 (2023)
12. Bao, C., et al.: A comparative study on population-based evolutionary algorithms for multiple traveling salesmen problem with visiting constraints. In: IEEE Symposium Series on Computational Intelligence, pp. 01–08 (2021)
13. Stodola, P., Nohel, J.: Adaptive ant colony optimization with node clustering for the multidepot vehicle routing problem. IEEE Trans. Evol. Comput. **27**, 1866–1880 (2023)
14. Su, H.B., et al.: Sonar echo beam optimization based on ant colony algorithm. J. Nonlinear Convex Anal. **25**, 1381–1390 (2024)
15. Wang, B., et al.: Adaptive ant selection for pheromone update in ant colony optimization. In: IEEE International Conference on Systems, Man, and Cybernetics, pp. 667–672 (2024)
16. Qiu, Y.H., et al.: Non-linearly weighted pheromone updating for ant colony optimization. In: IEEE International Conference on Systems, Man, and Cybernetics, pp. 653–658 (2024)
17. Cao, H., et al.: Random pairwise competition based ant selection for pheromone updating in ant colony optimization. In: IEEE International Conference on Systems, Man, and Cybernetics, pp. 1455–1460 (2023)
18. Zheng, J., et al.: Ant colony optimization for route planning of multiple tourists. In: Proceedings of the Genetic and Evolutionary Computation Conference Companion, pp. 971–974 (2025)
19. Xu, L.-T., et al.: Ant colony optimization for tourist route planning. In: Proceedings of the Genetic and Evolutionary Computation Conference, pp. 349–357 (2025)
20. Wu, D.M., et al.: Adapted ant colony optimization for large-scale orienteering problem. In: Proceedings of the Genetic and Evolutionary Computation Conference Companion, pp. 223–226, (2024)
21. Wu, D.M., et al.: Adapted ant colony optimization for team orienteering problem. In: International Conference on Machine Intelligence Theory and Applications, pp. 1–8 (2024)
22. Chen, Y., et al.: Multimodal ant colony optimization for finding multiple different routes for autonomous underwater vehicles. In: Proceedings of the Genetic and Evolutionary Computation Conference Companion, pp. 943–946 (2025)
23. Shi, X.L., et al.: A max-min ant system with repetitive influence reduction strategy for interactive dissemination of positive and negative information. IEEE Trans. Comput. Soc. Syst. **11**, 3255–3267 (2024)
24. Liao, X.C., et al.: Crowd management through optimal layout of fences: an ant colony approach based on crowd simulation. IEEE Trans. Intell. Transp. Syst. **24**, 9137–9149 (2023)
25. Jia, Y.H., et al.: An intelligent cloud workflow scheduling system with time estimation and adaptive ant colony optimization. IEEE Trans. Syst. Man Cybern.: Syst. **51**, 634–649 (2021)
26. Huang, Z.M., et al.: Ant colony evacuation planner: an ant colony system with incremental flow assignment for multipath crowd evacuation. IEEE Trans. Cybern. **51**, 5559–5572 (2021)

27. Wu, Q.H., You, X.M., Liu, S.: Multi-ant colony optimization algorithm based on game strategy and hierarchical temporal memory model. Cluster Comput. - J. Netw. Softw. Tools Appl. **27**, 3113–3133 (2024)
28. Skinderowicz, R.: Improving ant colony optimization efficiency for solving large TSP instances. Appl. Soft Comput. **120**, 108653 (2022)
29. Ghimire, B., Mahmood, A., Elleithy, K.: Hybrid parallel ant colony optimization for application to quantum computing to solve large-scale combinatorial optimization problems. Appl. Sci.-Basel **13** (2023)
30. Liao, E., Liu, C.: A hierarchical algorithm based on density peaks clustering and ant colony optimization for traveling salesman problem. IEEE Access **6**, 38921–38933 (2018)
31. Yu, J., You, X., Liu, S.: Dynamic reproductive ant colony algorithm based on piecewise clustering. Appl. Intelll. **51**, 8680–8700 (2021)
32. Dorigo, M., Maniezzo, V., Colorni, A.: Ant system: optimization by a colony of cooperating agents. IEEE Trans. Syst. Man Cybern. Part B Cybern. **26**, 29–41 (1996)
33. Bullnheimer, B., Hartl, R.F., Strauss, C.: A new rank based version of the ant system: a computational study. Cent. Eur. Oper. Res. (1997)
34. Stützle, T., Hoos, H.H.: MAX–MIN ant system. Future Gener. Comput. Syst. **16**, 889–914 (2000)
35. Dorigo, M., Gambardella, L.M.: Ant colony system: a cooperative learning approach to the traveling salesman problem. IEEE Trans. Evol. Comput. **1**, 53–66 (1997)
36. Tan, H., Wu, Y., Zhang, J., Zhang, J.: Study on a hybrid algorithm combining enhanced ant colony optimization and double improved simulated annealing via clustering in the traveling salesman problem (TSP). PeerJ Comput. Sci. **9**, e1609 (2023)
37. Jiang, Z.-H., et al.: Clustering-assisted ant colony optimization for large-scale travelling salesman problem. In: Proceedings of the Genetic and Evolutionary Computation Conference Companion, pp. 227–230 (2025)

A Comparative Analysis of Ant Colony Optimization for Mobile Robot Route Optimization

Wen-Jun Zheng[1], Qiang Yang[1(✉)], Dan-Ting Duan[2], Zhen-Yu Lu[1], and Jun Zhang[2,3,4,5]

[1] Nanjing University of Information Science and Technology, Nanjing 210044, China
qiangyangmmmyq@126.com

[2] Hanyang University, ERICA, Ansan 15588, South Korea

[3] Nankai University, Tianjin 300071, China

[4] Zhejiang Normal University, Jinhua 321004, China

[5] Chaoyang University of Technology, Taichung 41349, Taiwan

Abstract. This paper adapts the five classical ACOs, namely ant system (AS), max-min AS (MMAS), elite AS (EAS), rank-based AS (RAS), and ant colony system (ACS), to solve mobile robot path planning problems. Specifically, this paper leverages a directional position selection strategy to adapt the path construction. Then, instead of depositing pheromone on edges, this paper maintains a pheromone matrix with the same size of the environment and deposits pheromone on grids. By considering the path length first and the number of turns second, this paper evaluates the path constructed by each ant comprehensively. With the above adaption, the five ACOs are expected to address the mobile robot path planning problem effectively. Extensive experiments have been conducted on totally 10 environments with different scales and different degrees of obstacles. The experimental results have proved that as compared with two traditional algorithms, namely A* and Dijkstra, the five adapted ACOs and the two traditional algorithms all find the shortest paths with respect to the path length. However, the shortest paths found by the five ACOs have much fewer turns than those found by the two traditional algorithms. Particularly, among the five adapted ACOs, ACS performs the best concerning the path length and the number of turns.

Keywords: Ant Colony Optimization · Mobile Robot Path Planning · Route Optimization · Discrete Optimization · Evolutionary Algorithms

1 Introduction

Mobile robot path planning problems aim to find a shortest path for a robot from the starting position to the target position [9,25]. To model this problem, in the literature [1,24,37], researchers usually utilize a square of grids to simulate the environment for the robot. Then, the mobile robot path planning problem

I. Awan et al. (Eds.): WISE 2025, LNCS 16368, pp. 135–149, 2026.
https://doi.org/10.1007/978-981-95-7251-9_10

turns to finding an optimal sequence of grids from the starting position to the target position. During the search for the optimal path, one algorithm needs to avoid obstacles located in the grids. As a result, the optimization of the mobile robot path is essentially an NP-hard optimization problem [23,40].

Traditionally, to find the optimal path of robots in small-scale environments, A* [16] and Dijkstra [22] are most widely used thanks to their fast efficiency. However, in face of large-scale environments, the two traditional algorithms usually lose their effectiveness and efficiency. As a result, researchers have turned to swarm intelligence algorithms, which keep a swarm of individuals to cooperatively search the optimal route for robots [17,18,37].

Particularly, among swarm intelligence algorithms, ant colony optimization (ACO) is the most popularly researched one for path optimization [9,10,25,27,30,35]. Inspired by the foraging behavior of ants [19], ACO maintains a swarm of ants to iteratively find the optimal path. Thanks to its strong global search ability, ACO has been employed to successfully solve various optimization problems [8,36,41] and deployed in the real-world applications [20,29,31].

In face of the mobile robot path planning problem, researchers have also developed a lot of ACO variants [6,21,25]. Though these ACO variants have shown very promising performance in solving this problem, there are very few studies paying attention to taking a comparative analysis of ACO in solving the mobile robot path planning problem, especially in large-scale environments.

To fill this gap, this paper systematically compares the performance of the five classical ACOs, namely ant system (AS) [12], max-min AS (MMAS) [32], elite AS (EAS) [26], rank-based AS (RAS) [5], and ant colony system (ACS) [11], in solving the mobile robot path planning problem. For this paper, this paper first adapts the five classical ACOs by introducing a directional position selection strategy for effectively constructing paths for the robot and slightly changing the pheromone update rule.

To investigate the efficacy of the five ACOs in solving the mobile robot path planning problem, we have conducted extensive experiments on totally 10 environments of different scales and different degrees of obstacles to compare the five ACOs with the two traditional algorithms, namely A* [16]and Dijkstra [22]. For comprehensive evaluation, we not only compare the path length, but also compare the number of turns in the found shortest paths by the 7 algorithms.

In the following, this paper is structured as follows: Sect. 2 gives the mathematical model for the mobile robot path planning problem. Section 3 elucidates the adapted five ACOs for mobile robot path planning. Section 4 provides experiments to demonstrate the efficacy of the adapted ACOs for mobile robot path planning. At last, Sect. 5 summarizes this paper.

2 Mathematical Model of Mobile Robot Path Planning

In the literature [4,9,37], as shown in Fig. 1, the environment of the mobile robot path planning problem is usually modeled as a square of grids. Among these grids, some are obstacles, where the robot cannot cross. Given the starting position S and the target position T, the objective of the mobile robot path planning is to find the shortest path with the fewest turns for the robot from the starting position to the target position. Such a path is actually a sequence of feasible grids.

Given the environment is of scale $N \times N$, this paper identifies each grid by a coordinate system and a serial number system. As displayed in Fig. 1, each grid is associated with a unique serial number n. Based on this number, its coordinates are calculated as follows:

$$\begin{cases} x_n = \mathrm{mod}(n-1,\ N) + 1 \\ y_n = \left\lfloor \dfrac{n-1}{N} \right\rfloor + 1 \end{cases} \tag{1}$$

where x_n and y_n represent the horizontal and the vertical coordinates of the nth grid, respectively; $\mathrm{mod}(\cdot,\cdot)$ and $\lfloor \cdot \rfloor$ represent the modulo function and the floor function, respectively.

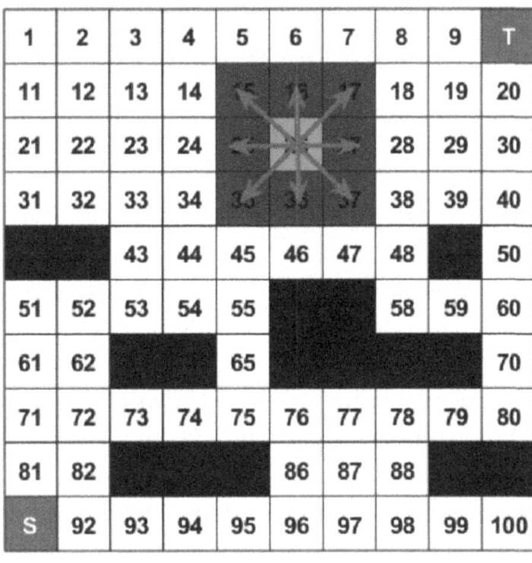

Fig. 1. An example of the eight candidate positions.

With the coordinates, we then compute the distance between two positions (grids m and n) as follows:

$$d(n,m) = \sqrt{(x_m - x_n)^2 + (y_m - y_n)^2} \tag{2}$$

Based on the above distances, given that the grid sequence of one path is $path_i = \{S, 1, ..., n, n+1, ...m, T\}$, we then get its path length as follows:

$$L(\mathrm{path}_i) = \sum_{n=1}^{m-1} \sqrt{(x_{n+1} - x_n)^2 + (y_{n+1} - y_n)^2} + \sqrt{(x_S - x_1)^2 + (y_S - y_1)^2} + \sqrt{(x_T - x_m)^2 + (y_T - y_m)^2} \tag{3}$$

Besides, evaluating the length of a path, we also evaluate the number of turns in this path. Specifically, a turn is identified when the direction from $n-1$ to n and the direction from n to $n+1$ are not identical. Particularly, a turn is identified by the following formula:

$$Turn_{flag} = \begin{cases} 1, & \text{if } (x_n - x_{n-1} \neq x_{n+1} - x_n) \vee (y_n - y_{n-1} \neq y_{n+1} - y_n), \\ 0, & \text{otherwise.} \end{cases} \tag{4}$$

Based on the above turn identification rule, we can get the number of turns in one path from S to T.

In general, the shorter length one path has, the better it is; the fewer turns one path has, the better it is. Between the two criteria, the path length has a higher superiority to the number of turns. Therefore, in this paper, we consider the path length first and the number of turns second to compare the quality of paths. That is, no matter how many turns two paths have, the path with a shorter length is better. However, once two paths have the same length, the path with fewer turns is better.

3 Adapted ACO for Mobile Robot Path Planning

ACO has been successfully employed to address various path optimization problems [2,13–15,38,42]. Therefore, it is also promising to solve the mobile robot path planning problem. For this purpose, this paper adapts the classical ACO with the overall framework shown in Algorithm 1.

Specifically, given that the environment is of $N \times N$ grids, the starting position is S, the target position is T, and the ant colony size in ACO is M, the adapted ACO works as follows: First, it uses the greedy strategy to construct a feasible path and then uses the length of this path to initialize the pheromone matrix. It deserves mentioning that different from the classical ACO for solving traveling salesman problems (TSP) [3,33,39], which deposits pheromone on edges, the adapted ACO deposits pheromone on the grids in the environment. Therefore, the adapted ACO maintains a pheromone matrix of $N \times N$, with each element initialized as follows:

$$\tau_0 = \frac{M}{L_{\text{greedy}}} \tag{5}$$

where L_{greedy} is the length of the path constructed by the greedy algorithm and M is the number of ants.

After the initialization, ACO enters the main iteration to seek for the optimal path. Particularly, in each iteration, the ants in the ant colony construct their paths position by position. Specifically, given that the mth ant ant_m is currently at grid i, from Fig. 1, it is observed that if there is no any obstacle, the maximum number of candidate positions for ant_m to select is 8. However, further observation shows that since the target T is at the right upper corner, to ensure that ant_m moves towards the target T, only at most three positions are meaningful for it to select, namely the upper position, the right position and the upper right position, as shown in Fig. 2.

Algorithm 1 Adapted ACO for mobile robot path planning

Initialize the pheromone matrix using greedy strategy;
while $fes \leq FES_{Max}$ **do**
  for $i = 1 : M$ **do**
    ant_i starts from the beginning position;
    while ant_i does not reach the target position **do**
      ant_i chooses the next position based on the associated selection rule;
      if ant_i reaches a dead position **then**
        ant_i returns to the previous position;
      end if
    end while
    Calculate the number of turns of ant_i and its path length; $fes++$;
  end for
  Find the best ant ant_{best} among the M ants;
  if the path length of ant_{best} is smaller than the best path $path_{gbest}$ **then**
    Update $path_{gbest}$ by ant_{best};
  else if the path length of ant_{best} is the same as $path_{gbest}$ but the number of turns of ant_{best} is smaller than that of $path_{gbest}$ **then**
    Update $path_{gbest}$ by ant_{best};
  end if
  Update the pheromone matrix by the pheromone update rule;
end while
return the discovered best path along with its number of turns and path length.

Based on this, in the path construction of each ant, at each position, actually at most three candidate positions should be considered. With these candidate positions, each ant selects the next position to visit by the roulette wheel selection rule with the probabilities calculated as follows:

$$p_{ij} = \begin{cases} \dfrac{[\tau_j]^\alpha * [\eta_j]^\beta}{\sum_{s \in J_m} [\tau_s]^\alpha * [\eta_s]^\beta}, & \text{if } j \in J_m \\ 0, & \text{otherwise} \end{cases} \tag{6}$$

$$\eta_j = \frac{1}{d_{Sj} + d_{jT}} \tag{7}$$

where J_m represents the candidate positions for ant m to select. Its size is at most 3. α and β are the pheromone and heuristic factors, respectively. p_{ij} is the probability that ant_m moves from position i to position j in J_m. τ_j is the pheromone on position j. η_j is the heuristic information of position j, which is the inverse of its distance d_{Sj} to the starting position S and the distance d_{jT} to the target position T.

Here, it should be mentioned that if there are obstacles around the current position i, the number of the candidate positions in J_m is fewer than 3. If, however, J_m is empty, it means that there is no feasible position to visit for ant_m at the current position i and thus it reaches a dead position. In this case,

1	2	3	4	5	6	7	8	9	T
11	12	13	14	15	16	17	18	19	20
21	22	23	24	25	26	27	28	29	30
31	32	33	34	35	36	37	38	39	40
		43	44	45	46	47	48	49	
51	52	53	54	55			58	59	60
61	62			65					70
71	72	73	74	75	76	77	78	79	80
81	82				86	87	88		
S	92	93	94	95	96	97	98	99	100

Fig. 2. An example of the candidate positions for an ant to select in the adapted ACO.

ant_m returns to the last position before the current position i to select another candidate position to visit instead of position i.

Based on the above selection probabilities, ant_m randomly picks a position to visit and then continues this position selection process until it reaches the target position T. At this point, ant_m finishes its path construction. Then, the path length and the number of turns of this ant are calculated.

Subsequently, the other ants construct their paths in the same way. After all ants complete their path construction, the best ant ant_{best} among the M ants is found. Then, it compares with the global best path $path_{gbest}$. If the path length of ant_{best} is shorter than $path_{gbest}$, we directly replace $path_{gbest}$ with ant_{best}. If ant_{best} has the same path length with $path_{gbest}$, we then compare the number of turns in these two paths. Only when ant_{best} has fewer turns, $path_{gbest}$ is replaced by ant_{best}.

Subsequently, the pheromone matrix is updated by using the M ants. In the literature, five classical ACO, namely AS [12], EAS [26], RAS [5], MMAS [32], and ACS [11] are developed by designing different pheromone update rules. In the following, we elucidate their pheromone rules:

3.1 Ant System (AS)

AS utilizes the whole ant colony to update the pheromone matrix as follows:

$$\tau_j = (1-\rho) * \tau_j + \sum_{m=1}^{M} \Delta\tau_j^m \tag{8}$$

$$\Delta\tau_j^m = \begin{cases} \frac{1}{L_m}, & \text{if } j \in path_m \\ 0, & \text{otherwise} \end{cases} \tag{9}$$

where τ_j is the pheromone on position j, ρ represents the pheromone evaporation factor, which is within [0,1], $\Delta\tau_j^m$ is the pheromone deposited by the m-th ant on position j, and L_m represents the path length of the m-th ant.

3.2 Elite AS (EAS)

The pheromone update rule of EAS is based on AS. Besides using all ants to update the pheromone, EAS additionally deposits pheromone on the global best path. Particularly, EAS updates the pheromone matrix as follows:

$$\tau_j = (1-\rho) * \tau_j + \sum_{m=1}^{M} \Delta\tau_j^m + e * \Delta\tau_j^{gbest} \tag{10}$$

$$\Delta\tau_j^{gbest} = \begin{cases} \frac{1}{L_{\text{gbest}}}, & \text{if } j \in path_{gbest} \\ 0, & \text{otherwise} \end{cases} \tag{11}$$

where e is a weight parameter to enlarge the pheromone $\Delta\tau_j^{gbest}$ deposited on the global best path $path_{gbest}$, and L_{gbest} is the length of the global best path $path_{gbest}$ found so far.

3.3 Rank-Based AS (RAS)

Different from AS and EAS, RAS only utilizes several top best ants to update the pheromone matrix. Particularly, RAS updates the pheromone matrix as follows:

$$\tau_j = (1-\rho)\,\tau_j + \textstyle\sum_{k=1}^{w-1} (w-k)\,\Delta\tau_j^k + w * \Delta\tau_j^{gbest} \tag{12}$$

where $w-1$ is the number of the top best ants used to update the pheromone.

It should be mentioned that we sort the ants based on two criteria, namely the path length and the number of turns. Firstly, all ants are sorted according to their path lengths. The shorter length one ant has, the better this ant is. Secondly, for those ants with the same path length, we further sort them based on the number of turns. The fewer turns one ant has, the better this ant is.

Additionally, Eq. (12) indicates that RAS also additionally deposits pheromone on the global best path $path_{gbest}$ found so far.

3.4 Max-Min AS (MMAS)

Different from the above AS variants, MMAS first limits the pheromone on each position within a range $[\tau_{min}, \tau_{max}]$. Particularly, τ_{max} and τ_{min} are calculated as follows:

$$\tau_{max} = \left(\frac{1}{2*(1-\rho)} * \frac{1}{L_{\text{gbest}}} + \frac{1}{L_{\text{gbest}}}\right) \times 200 \tag{13}$$

$$\tau_{min} = \frac{\tau_{max}}{500} \tag{14}$$

where τ_{max} and τ_{min} are the largest and smallest values of τ_j, respectively. L_{gebst} is the path length of the global best path $path_{gbest}$ found so far.

In addition, in the initial stage, the pheromone is initialized as τ_{max}. Then, during the evolution, MMAS utilizes the current best ant in each generation to update the pheromone matrix as follows:

$$\tau_j = (1 - \rho) * \tau_j + \Delta\tau_j^{best} \tag{15}$$

$$\Delta\tau_j^{best} = \begin{cases} \frac{1}{L_{\text{best}}}, & \text{if } j \in ant_{best} \\ 0, & \text{otherwise} \end{cases} \tag{16}$$

where L_{best} is the path length of the best ant ant_{best} in the current generation.

3.5 Ant Colony System (ACS)

ACS is very different from the above four AS variants not only concerning the pheromone update, but also regarding the path construction.

Specifically, ants in ACS pick the next position to visit via the following rule:

$$J = \begin{cases} \arg\max\left(\tau_j^{\alpha} * \eta_j^{\beta}\right), & j \in J_m, \quad \text{if } rand(0,1) \le q_0 \\ J*, & \text{otherwise} \end{cases} \tag{17}$$

where q_0 is a probability offered by users, J is the selected position to be visited, and $J*$ is the selected position by the roulette wheel selection strategy as in AS.

Equation (17) indicates that the ant in ACS uses the greedy strategy to select the next position to visit with a probability q_0 and utilizes the roulette wheel selection strategy to select the next position with a probability $1 - q_0$.

As for the pheromone update, ACS has two kinds of pheromone update, namely local pheromone update and global pheromone update. Particularly, in the initial stage, the pheromone matrix is initialized as follows:

$$\tau_0 = \frac{1}{N * L_{\text{greedy}}} \tag{18}$$

where N is the scale of the environment and L_{greedy} is the length of the path built by the greedy strategy.

During the path construction, once an ant selects a position to visit, ACS immediately utilizes the following local pheromone update rule to update the pheromone on the selected position:

$$\tau_j = (1 - g) * \tau_j + g * \tau_0 \tag{19}$$

where $g \in (0, 1)$ denotes the local pheromone evaporation rate.

Here, it deserves mentioning that this local pheromone update only occurs on the selected position by one ant during the path construction. The pheromone on the other positions keeps unchanged.

After all ants finish their path construction, the global best path $path_{gbest}$ is updated and then ACS utilizes $path_{gbest}$ to globally update the pheromone matrix as below:

$$\tau_j = (1-\rho) * \tau_j + \rho * \Delta\tau_j^{gbest}, j \in path_{gbest} \tag{20}$$

where ρ is the global pheromone evaporation rate.

Here, it also deserves mentioning that the global pheromone update only occurs on the positions belonging to the global best path $path_{gbest}$. The pheromone on the other positions keeps unchanged as well.

With the above adapted position selection rule and the pheromone update rule, the five ACOs are expected to solve the mobile robot path planning problem effectively, which is to be verified in the following section.

Table 1. Parameter settings of the five adapted ACOs for the 20×20 environments

Algorithm	Parameters
ACS	M=10, $\rho = 0.02$, $\alpha = 1$, $\beta = 5$, $g = 0.01$, $q_0 = 0.5$
EAS	M=20, $\rho = 0.02$, $\alpha = 1$, $\beta = 5$, $e = 1$
RAS	M=20, $\rho = 0.02$, $\alpha = 1$, $\beta = 5$, $w = 6$
MMAS	M=20, $\rho = 0.02$, $\alpha = 1$, $\beta = 5$
AS	M=20, $\rho = 0.02$, $\alpha = 1$, $\beta = 5$

Table 2. Parameter settings of the five adapted ACOs for the 30×30 environments

Algorithm	Parameters
ACS	M=15, $\rho = 0.02$, $\alpha = 1$, $\beta = 5$, $g = 0.01$, $q_0 = 0.5$
EAS	M=30, $\rho = 0.02$, $\alpha = 1$, $\beta = 5$, $e = 1$
RAS	M=30, $\rho = 0.02$, $\alpha = 1$, $\beta = 5$, $w = 6$
MMAS	M=30, $\rho = 0.02$, $\alpha = 1$, $\beta = 5$
AS	M=30, $\rho = 0.02$, $\alpha = 1$, $\beta = 5$

4 Experiments

This section conducts experiments to compare the five adapted ACOs with two traditional algorithms for mobile robot path planning, namely A* and Dijkstra. For this purpose, as shown in Fig. 3 and Fig. 4, we build totally 10 environments with 5 of scale 20×20 and another 5 of scale 30×30. These 10 environments

Fig. 3. The best paths found by the 7 algorithms with the shortest lengths and the smallest numbers of turns on the 5 environments of 20×20.

Fig. 4. The best paths found by the 7 algorithms with the shortest lengths and the smallest numbers of turns on the 5 environments of 30×30.

consist of different numbers of obstacles to simulate different scenarios in real-world applications.

To effectively address the mobile robot path planning problem in the two scales of environments, the parameter settings of the five adapted ACOs are listed in Tables 1 and 2 for the 20 × 20 and 30 × 30 environments, respectively.

Table 3 presents the average path lengths and the average numbers of turns of all the 7 algorithms over 10 independent runs on the 20 × 20 and 30 × 30 environments, while Fig. 3 and Fig. 4 display the best paths of all the 7 algorithms with the shortest path length and the smallest number of turns on the 5 environments of scale 20 × 20 and scale 30 × 30, respectively.

Table 3. The average lengths and the average number of turns of the paths found by the 7 algorithms on the 10 environments

Scale	Scenario	Evaluation	AS	MMAS	RAS	EAS	ACS	Dijkstra	A*
20 × 20	Scenario 1	Path Length	**29.2132**	**29.2132**	**29.2132**	**29.2132**	**29.2132**	**29.2132**	**29.2132**
		Number of Turns	**9**	**9**	**9**	**9**	11	10	12
	Scenario 2	Path Length	**32.1421**	**32.1421**	**32.1421**	**32.1421**	**32.1421**	**32.1421**	**32.1421**
		Number of Turns	**11**	**11**	**11**	**11**	**11**	12	13
	Scenario 3	Path Length	**30.3848**	**30.3848**	**30.3848**	**30.3848**	**30.3848**	**30.3848**	**30.3848**
		Number of Turns	6	8	**4**	6	8	6	10
	Scenario 4	Path Length	**28.6274**	29.2132	29.2132	29.2132	**28.6274**	**28.6274**	**28.6274**
		Number of Turns	**4**	**4**	5	5	**4**	**4**	**4**
	Scenario 5	Path Length	**28.0416**	**28.0416**	**28.0416**	**28.0416**	**28.0416**	**28.0416**	**28.0416**
		Number of Turns	**6**	8	**6**	**6**	**6**	8	**6**
30 × 30	Scenario 1	Path Length	**43.9411**	**43.9411**	44.5269	**43.9411**	**43.9411**	**43.9411**	**43.9411**
		Number of Turns	9	**8**	10	10	10	11	12
	Scenario 2	Path Length	45.6985	**44.5269**	**44.5269**	**44.5269**	**44.5269**	**44.5269**	**44.5269**
		Number of Turns	**9**	**9**	11	**9**	**9**	15	13
	Scenario 3	Path Length	46.8701	46.2843	45.6985	**44.5269**	**44.5269**	**44.5269**	**44.5269**
		Number of Turns	**5**	7	13	9	9	11	10
	Scenario 4	Path Length	**46.2843**	**46.2843**	47.8701	46.8701	**46.2843**	**46.2843**	**46.2843**
		Number of Turns	**14**	17	22	18	16	18	20
	Scenario 5	Path Length	**48.6274**	**48.6274**	**48.6274**	**48.6274**	**48.6274**	**48.6274**	**48.6274**
		Number of Turns	18	**16**	18	18	17	17	24

From Table 3, Fig. 3 and Fig. 4, we get the following observations: 1) Regarding the path length, all the 7 algorithms find the shortest paths of most of the 10 environments. Specifically, Dijkstra, A*, and ACS find the shortest paths of all the 10 environments. AS, MMAS, RAS, and EAS find the shortest paths of 8, 8, 6, and 8 environments, respectively. Therefore, with respect to the path length, ACS performs the best among the 5 adapted ACOs. 2) In terms of the number of turns, we find that on the condition that the shortest path length is the same, the 5 ACOs find the shortest paths with fewer turns than Dijkstra and A*. Specifically, on the 5 20 × 20 environments, AS, ACS, Dijkstra, and A* all find the shortest paths of these environments. However, the number of turns of the paths found by AS and ACS is much smaller than Dijkstra and A*. On the 5 30×30 environments, ACS, Dijkstra, and A* all find the shortest paths of these environments. However, the number of turns of the paths found by ACS is much smaller than Dijkstra and A*. 3) Regarding the best path, Fig. 3 and Fig. 4 show that the shortest paths found by the 5 ACOs are a little different from those found by Dijkstra and A*. Such little difference may contribute to the superiority of the 5 ACOs to Dijkstra and A* concerning the number of turns in the shortest paths.

In summary, the above experimental discoveries have proved that the five adapted ACOs are very promising in solving the mobile robot path planning problem. Particularly, as compared with the two traditional algorithms, namely Dijkstra and A*, the five ACOs find the shortest paths with the same path lengths as them, but with fewer turns. Among the five ACOs, ACS performs the best regarding both the path length and the number of turns.

5 Conclusion

This paper has adapted the five classical ACOs, namely ACS, EAS, RAS, MMAS, and AS, with small modifications on the pheromone update, to tackle the mobile robot path planning problem. Then, extensive experiments have been conducted on 10 built environments with different scales and different numbers of obstacles to compare the five adapted ACOs with two traditional algorithms, namely A* and Dijkstra, to investigate the effectiveness of the five adapted ACOs in solving the mobile robot path planning problem. Experimental discoveries have revealed that the five adapted ACOs are very promising for solving the mobile robot path planning problem. Particularly, compared with the two traditional algorithms, the five ACOs find the best path with the same shortest length as the two traditional algorithms, but the paths found by the five ACOs have fewer turns than those by the two traditional algorithms. In particular, among the five ACOs, we find that ACS performs the best with respect to the path length and the number of turns.

In the future, we aim at adapting more advanced ACO variants [7,28,34] to tackle the mobile robot path planning problem, so as to improve the performance of ACO in addressing the mobile robot path planning problem.

Acknowledgments. This work was supported in part by the National Natural Science Foundation of China under Grant 62576172, in part by the National Research Foundation of Korea under Grant RS-2025-00555463, in part by the Tianjin Top Scientist Studio Project under Grant 24JRRCRC00030, and in part by the Tianjin Belt and Road Joint Laboratory under Grant 24PTLYHZ00250.

Disclosure of Interests. The authors have no competing interests to declare that are relevant to the content of this article.

References

1. Ali, Z.A., Zhangang, H., Zhengru, D.: Path planning of multiple UAVs using MMACO and de algorithm in dynamic environment. Meas. Control **56**(3–4), 459–469 (2023)
2. Bai, H.L., Yang, Q., Yuan, P.Y., Duan, D.T., Li, T., Liu, D., Zhang, J.: Destination-oriented route construction for ant colony optimization to solve minmax multiple travelling salesmen problems. In: Proceedings of the Genetic and Evolutionary Computation Conference Companion, pp. 199–202 (2025)
3. Bao, C., Yang, Q., Gao, X.D., Lu, Z.Y., Zhang, J.: Ant colony optimization with shortest distance biased dispatch for visiting constrained multiple traveling salesmen problem. In: Proceedings of the Genetic and Evolutionary Computation Conference Companion, pp. 77–80 (2022)
4. Brand, M., Masuda, M., Wehner, N., Yu, X.H.: Ant colony optimization algorithm for robot path planning. In: International Conference on Computer Design and Applications, vol. 3, pp. V3–436. IEEE (2010)
5. Bullnheimer, B., Hartl, R., Strauss, C.: A new rank based version of the ant system: a computational study. CEJOR **7**(1), 25–38 (1999)
6. Cai, Z., Liu, J., Xu, L., Wang, J.: Cooperative path planning study of distributed multi-mobile robots based on optimised ACO algorithm. Rob. Auton. Syst. **179**, 104748 (2024)
7. Cao, H., Yang, Q., Gao, X.D., Xu, P.L., Lu, Z.Y., Zhang, J.: Random pairwise competition based ant selection for pheromone updating in ant colony optimization. In: 2023 IEEE International Conference on Systems, Man, and Cybernetics (SMC), pp. 1455–1460. IEEE (2023)
8. Chen, W.N., Tan, D.Z., Yang, Q., Gu, T., Zhang, J.: Ant colony optimization for the control of pollutant spreading on social networks. IEEE Trans. Cybern. **50**(9), 4053–4065 (2019)
9. Chen, X., Kong, Y., Fang, X., Wu, Q.: A fast two-stage ACO algorithm for robotic path planning. Neural Comput. Appl. **22**, 313–319 (2013)
10. Chen, Y., et al.: Multimodal ant colony optimization for finding multiple different routes for autonomous underwater vehicles. In: Proceedings of the Genetic and Evolutionary Computation Conference Companion, pp. 943–946 (2025)
11. Dorigo, M., Gambardella, L.M.: Ant colony system: a cooperative learning approach to the traveling salesman problem. IEEE Trans. Evol. Comput. **1**(1), 53–66 (2002)
12. Dorigo, M., Maniezzo, V., Colorni, A.: Ant system: optimization by a colony of cooperating agents. IEEE Trans. Syst. Man Cybern. Part B (Cybern.) **26**(1), 29–41 (1996)
13. Jia, Y.H., Mei, Y., Zhang, M.: A bilevel ant colony optimization algorithm for capacitated electric vehicle routing problem. IEEE Trans. Cybern. **52**(10), 10855–10868 (2021)
14. Jia, Y.H., Mei, Y., Zhang, M.: Confidence-based ant colony optimization for capacitated electric vehicle routing problem with comparison of different encoding schemes. IEEE Trans. Evol. Comput. **26**(6), 1394–1408 (2022)
15. Jiang, Z.H., et al.: Clustering-assisted ant colony optimization for large-scale travelling salesman problem. In: Proceedings of the Genetic and Evolutionary Computation Conference Companion, pp. 227–230 (2025)
16. Ju, C., Luo, Q., Yan, X.: Path planning using an improved a-star algorithm. In: Proceedings of International Conference on Prognostics and System Health Management, pp. 23–26. IEEE (2020)

17. Kanan, H.R., Faez, K.: An improved feature selection method based on ant colony optimization (ACO) evaluated on face recognition system. Appl. Math. Comput. **205**(2), 716–725 (2008)
18. Li, M., Li, B., Qi, Z., Li, J., Wu, J.: Optimized APF-ACO algorithm for ship collision avoidance and path planning. J. Mar. Sci. Eng. **11**(6), 1177 (2023)
19. Li, W., Xia, L., Huang, Y., Mahmoodi, S.: An ant colony optimization algorithm with adaptive greedy strategy to optimize path problems. J. Ambient Intell. Hum. Comput. 1–15 (2022)
20. Liao, X.C., Chen, W.N., Guo, X.Q., Zhong, J., Hu, X.M.: Crowd management through optimal layout of fences: an ant colony approach based on crowd simulation. IEEE Trans. Intell. Transp. Syst. **24**(9), 9137–9149 (2023)
21. Liu, C., et al.: An improved heuristic mechanism ant colony optimization algorithm for solving path planning. Knowl.-Based Syst. **271**, 110540 (2023)
22. Liu, L.S., et al.: Path planning for smart car based on Dijkstra algorithm and dynamic window approach. Wireless Commun. Mobile Comput. **2021**(1), 8881684 (2021)
23. Liu, L., Li, L., Nian, H., Lu, Y., Zhao, H., Chen, Y.: Enhanced grey wolf optimization algorithm for mobile robot path planning. Electronics **12**(19), 4026 (2023)
24. Miao, C., Chen, G., Yan, C., Wu, Y.: Path planning optimization of indoor mobile robot based on adaptive ant colony algorithm. Comput. Ind. Eng. **156**, 107230 (2021)
25. Mukherjee, D., Acharyya, S.: ACO variants in solving mobile ad hoc network routing. In: Proceedings of International Conference on Emerging Applications of Information Technology, pp. 366–371. IEEE (2012)
26. Negulescu, S.C., Oprean, C., Kifor, C.V., Carabulea, I.: Elitist ant system for route allocation problem. In: Proceedings of the 8th conference on Applied Informatics and Communications, Greece: World Scientific and Engineering Academy and Society (WSEAS), pp. 62–67 (2008)
27. Nie, Z.H., Yang, Q., Zhang, E., Liu, D., Zhang, J.: Ant colony optimization for electric vehicle routing problem with capacity and charging time constraints. In: 2022 IEEE International Conference on Systems, Man, and Cybernetics (SMC), pp. 480–485. IEEE (2022)
28. Qiu, Y.H., et al.: Non-linearly weighted pheromone updating for ant colony optimization. In: 2024 IEEE International Conference on Systems, Man, and Cybernetics (SMC), pp. 653–658. IEEE (2024)
29. Shi, W., Wei, F.F., Bo, X., Bi, Z., Xi, J., Chen, W.N.: Asynchronous storming-norming ant colony system for project scheduling under scenario perturbation of activity attributes. Swarm Evol. Comput. **98**, 102141 (2025)
30. Shi, X.L., Chen, W.N., Wei, F.F., Zhang, J.: A distributed ant colony system with pheromone transfer for multiagent traveling salesmen problem. IEEE Trans. Evol. Comput. (2025)
31. Shi, X.L., Chen, W.N., Zhong, J.H., Zhang, J.: A max-min ant system with repetitive influence reduction strategy for interactive dissemination of positive and negative information. IEEE Trans. Comput. Soc. Syst. **11**(3), 3255–3267 (2023)
32. Stützle, T., Hoos, H.H.: Max-min ant system. Futur. Gener. Comput. Syst. **16**(8), 889–914 (2000)
33. Sun, B., Wang, C., Yang, Q., Liu, W., Yu, W.: Ant colony optimization for balanced multiple traveling salesmen problem. In: 2021 International Conference on Computational Science and Computational Intelligence (CSCI), pp. 476–481. IEEE (2021)

34. Wang, B., et al.: Adaptive ant selection for pheromone update in ant colony optimization. In: 2024 IEEE International Conference on Systems, Man, and Cybernetics (SMC), pp. 667–672. IEEE (2024)
35. Wu, D.M., Duan, D.T., Yang, Q., Liu, X.F., Zhou, C.J., Zhao, J.M.: Adapted ant colony optimization for team orienteering problem. In: 2024 11th International Conference on Machine Intelligence Theory and Applications (MiTA), pp. 1–8. IEEE (2024)
36. Wu, D.M., Yang, Q., Zhou, C.J., Zheng, Z.L., Zhang, J.: Adapted ant colony optimization for large-scale orienteering problem. In: Proceedings of the Genetic and Evolutionary Computation Conference Companion, pp. 223–226 (2024)
37. Wu, L., Huang, X., Cui, J., Liu, C., Xiao, W.: Modified adaptive ant colony optimization algorithm and its application for solving path planning of mobile robot. Expert Syst. Appl. **215**, 119410 (2023)
38. Xu, L.T., et al.: Ant colony optimization for tourist route planning. In: Proceedings of the Genetic and Evolutionary Computation Conference, pp. 349–357 (2025)
39. Xu, N., et al.: Ant colony optimization for multiple travelling salesmen problem with pivot cities. In: 2023 15th International Conference on Advanced Computational Intelligence (ICACI), pp. 1–8. IEEE (2023)
40. Xue, Y., Sun, J.Q.: Solving the path planning problem in mobile robotics with the multi-objective evolutionary algorithm. Appl. Sci. **8**(9), 1425 (2018)
41. Yang, Q., et al.: Adaptive multimodal continuous ant colony optimization. IEEE Trans. Evol. Comput. **21**(2), 191–205 (2016)
42. Zheng, J., et al.: Ant colony optimization for route planning of multiple tourists. In: Proceedings of the Genetic and Evolutionary Computation Conference Companion, pp. 971–974 (2025)

An Effective Multi-hop Ride-Sharing Algorithm on Large-Scale Road Networks

Junwei Liu and Detian Zhang(✉)

Institute of Artificial Intelligence, School of Computer Science and Technology, Soochow University, Suzhou, China
{jwliu055,20235227055}@stu.suda.edu.cn, detian@suda.edu.cn

Abstract. This paper addresses the multi-hop ride-sharing problem in large-scale road networks. Traditional ride-sharing (i.e., single-hop ride-sharing) is constrained by limited flexibility and rider convenience, whereas multi-hop ride-sharing significantly enhances adaptability by allowing riders to transfer between multiple vehicles during their trips. We construct a Feasible Matching Graph (FMG) to systematically represent the potential matching relationships between drivers and riders, capturing feasible areas and possible path constraints for drivers. To efficiently organize and store paths within the FMG and avoid redundant calculations during repeated searches, we introduce a Guide-Tree based on the Trie data structure, which captures the hierarchical relationships among paths and allows shared subpaths to be stored only once, thereby substantially improving search efficiency. Building on the Guide-Tree, we propose the Guide Search (GS) algorithm, which leverages the Guide-Tree to identify optimal multi-hop paths, significantly reducing the search space and improving computational efficiency. Extensive experiments on two real-world datasets show that our algorithms consistently outperform current state-of-the-art methods in both computational efficiency and scalability.

Keywords: Multi-Hop Ride-Sharing · Large-Scale Road Networks · Transportation Transfer

1 Introduction

With the rapid development of the economy and society, global vehicle ownership has increased significantly[1], exacerbating urban traffic congestion issues. Despite the growing number of vehicles, the utilization rate remains relatively low. Data indicates that over 60% of vehicles are occupied by only the driver [19]. This low utilization rate implies that, for the same travel demand, more vehicles are required on the road, which further intensifies urban traffic congestion [14].

Ride-sharing allows multiple riders to share the same vehicle [13,21,26] and is widely regarded as an effective solution for alleviating urban traffic congestion [15]. Its popularity stems from its economic and environmental benefits,

[1] https://www.gov.cn/lianbo/bumen/202401/content_6925362.htm.

I. Awan et al. (Eds.): WISE 2025, LNCS 16368, pp. 150–164, 2026.
https://doi.org/10.1007/978-981-95-7251-9_11

as it reduces travel costs [8] and fuel consumption [25], and mitigates environmental pollution [4]. However, traditional ride-sharing services, i.e., single-hop ride-sharing, only consider direct trips for riders, where a rider is picked up and dropped off by a single driver throughout the ride-sharing process. This model significantly limits rider flexibility and creates accessibility challenges in areas with sparse driver availability, where riders often fail to secure adequate transportation through single-hop services. For example, in Fig. 1, since no driver's route passes near both the source B and destination F of rider r, no driver can provide a single-hop ride-sharing service for r.

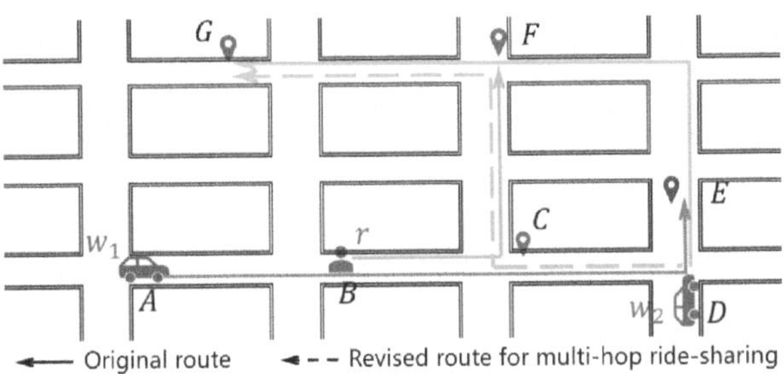

Fig. 1. An example of multi-hop ride-sharing.

Multi-hop ride-sharing allows riders to transfer between different vehicles as needed during a trip [6,12,22]. In this model, riders' travel requests are divided into multiple trip segments, with different vehicles responsible for completing the pick-up and drop-off services for each segment. For example, the trip of rider r in Fig. 1 can be divided into two segments: in the first segment, driver w_1 transports r from source B to location C, while in the second segment, driver w_2 transports r from location C to destination F. Studies [6,16] have demonstrated that, compared to single-hop ride-sharing, multi-hop ride-sharing offers a more flexible travel option for riders. This flexibility improves the matching rate and contributes to alleviating traffic congestion effectively [7,23].

While multi-hop ride-sharing demonstrates considerable potential in transportation optimization, its algorithmic implementation faces critical challenges in driver-rider matching mechanisms. The fundamental challenge resides in designing effective multi-hop matching algorithms that systematically coordinate sequential trip segments. Most existing studies [7,16,22] primarily address this problem by exhaustively searching all possible combinations of riders and drivers, which leads to exponential computational complexity. Furthermore, as influencing factors such as the scale of the road network and the number of drivers increase, the computational difficulty of multi-hop driver-rider matching escalates substantially [23]. This complexity growth pattern fundamentally constrains practical implementations in large-scale road networks.

In this paper, we study the multi-hop ride-sharing problem in large-scale road networks. To achieve efficient driver-rider matching for multi-hop ride-sharing services, we first construct a Feasible Matching Graph (FMG) to represent the potential matching relationships between riders and drivers. Effective paths in the FMG are used to represent the matching between drivers and riders. Subsequently, inspired by the Trie data structure [2], we design a Guide-Tree to efficiently organize and store paths in the FMG, thereby reducing redundant path searches. To compute the optimal multi-hop path with transfer points, we propose a Guide Search (GS) algorithm based on the Guide-Tree. The GS leverages the Guide-Tree to effectively guide the search direction, significantly improving the efficiency of path computation.

In summary, our contributions are as follows:

- We construct the **Feasible Matching Graph (FMG)** to represent potential multi-hop connections between riders and drivers.
- We design the **Guide-Tree** that can organize the paths in the FMG in a low-redundancy form to avoid repeated searches.
- We propose the **Guide Search (GS)** algorithm, which uses the Guide-Tree to efficiently calculate the optimal multi-hop path with transfer points.
- We conduct extensive experiments on two real-world datasets to validate the efficiency of the proposed algorithms.

The rest of this paper is organized as follows. We summarize the related work in Sect. 2. In Sect. 3, we formally define the key concepts of the paper. Section 4 presents our proposed algorithms in detail. Extensive experimental results and our findings are reported in Sect. 5. Section 6 concludes the paper.

2 Related Works

In this section, we review related work on ride-sharing, which can be categorized into single-hop and multi-hop depending on whether riders are allowed to transfer.

2.1 Single-Hop Ride-Sharing

Most current ride-sharing research focuses on single-hop (i.e., 1-hop) ride-sharing scenarios [9,13,20,27]. Ta et al. [20] modeled the ride-sharing problem as a maximum weighted bipartite graph matching problem and proposed the Best-First algorithm to identify driver-rider pairs with the most shared paths. Zou et al. [27] introduced a clustering-based matching algorithm that leverages spatiotemporal information from the road network to reduce computational complexity. Guo et al. [9] proposed a variable neighborhood search method to match drivers and riders across cities. Ke et al. [13] developed a single-driver-multiple-rider matching model and devised an efficient algorithm for rapid computation of the matches.

However, single-hop ride-sharing restricts riders to being served by only one driver during their trip, which significantly limits their flexibility.

2.2 Multi-hop Ride-Sharing

Some works [6,10,11,16] use time-extended graph (TEG) to model multi-hop ride-sharing. Herbawi et al. [10] first applied TEG to the multi-hop ride-sharing problem and designed an evolutionary algorithm to calculate feasible paths. Herbawi et al. [11] further studied the TEG model, considering time and vehicle capacity constraints, and designed a genetic algorithm to calculate feasible paths. Drews et al. [6] designed an A* algorithm on TEG to calculate feasible paths. Masoud et al. [16] reduced the TEG size by restricting the feasible area and designed a dynamic programming algorithm to calculate feasible paths. However, due to TEG's limitations, these algorithms only support vehicles serving at most two riders on a predefined path and are restricted to small-scale road networks with at most 10,000 nodes [23].

Other works [7,22] limit the number of hops to 2 (i.e., 2-hop ride-sharing), which means that riders are allowed to transfer once during the trip. The core of these studies is to determine the possible vehicle transfer options for riders, that is, vehicle matching. Fevre et al. [7] proposed a multi-agent system that uses R-tree for perception indexing and performs vehicle matching based on perception. Wei et al. [22] proposed a vehicle pairing graph (VPG) and used the Blossom algorithm to calculate vehicle matching on the VPG.

Different from the aforementioned works [6,10,11,16], our approach does not rely on a predefined path for the driver and supports scenarios where multiple riders share the same vehicle. Unlike the methods [7,22] that are limited to 2-hop ride-sharing, our approach flexibly accommodates higher hop counts. Furthermore, leveraging the efficiency of the proposed algorithm, our work is applicable to large-scale road scenarios that require real-time performance.

3 Definitions

This section introduces all definitions and symbols used in this paper.

Definition 1 (Road Network). *A road network is defined as an undirected graph $G(V, E)$, where V and E denote the vertex and edge sets, respectively. For $u, v \in V$, the shortest travel time from u to v is denoted by $t(u, v)$.*

Definition 2 (Transfer Point). *A transfer point in a road network $G(V, E)$ is defined as a vertex $p \in V$, where riders can transfer between vehicles. The set of all transfer points is denoted by P.*

Definition 3 (Driver Request). *A driver request is defined as $w = \langle s_w, e_w, tr_w, td_w, c_w \rangle$, where s_w and e_w are the source and destination, tr_w is the release time, td_w is the deadline to reach e_w, and c_w is the vehicle's capacity for accommodating riders. The set of all driver requests is denoted as W.*

Definition 4 (Rider Request). *A rider request is defined as $r = \langle s_r, e_r, tr_r, td_r \rangle$, where s_r and e_r are the source and destination, tr_r is the release time, and td_r is the deadline to reach e_r.*

Definition 5 (Multi-Hop Path). *Given a rider request r, a set of driver requests W, and a set of transfer points P, a multi-hop path for the rider request $r = \langle s_r, e_r, tr_r, td_r \rangle$ is defined as:*

$$\mathcal{L}_r = \{(l_i, l_{i+1}, w_i)\}_{i=1}^{h}, \tag{1}$$

where h is the number of transfers, l_1 is the source s_r, l_{h+1} is the destination e_r, and $l_2, \ldots, l_h \in P$ are the locations where rider r transfers. Each tuple (l_i, l_{i+1}, w_i) denotes that rider r is served by driver $w_i \in W$ on the trip segment from location l_i to location l_{i+1}.

Definition 6 (Multi-Hop Rider-Sharing Problem (MHRSP)). *Given a road network $G(V, E)$, transfer points P, driver requests W, a rider request r, and a hop limit h_{max}, the objective of MHRSP is to find a multi-hop path $\mathcal{L}_r = \{(l_i, l_{i+1}, w_i)\}_{i=1}^{h}$ with the shortest travel time for rider r, i.e.,*

$$\min \sum_{i=1}^{h} t(l_i, l_{i+1}), \tag{2}$$

*where $h \le h_{max}$. Subject to the following **feasibility constraints**:*

1. ***Deadline constraint:*** *The rider request r and all drivers serving r must arrive at their respective destinations before their deadlines.*
2. ***Capacity constraint:*** *The rider capacity of all drivers serving r must not exceed the capacity of their vehicles.*
3. ***Multi-hop constraint:*** *The number of transfers for rider r must not exceed the maximum hop limit h_{max}.*

4 Algorithms

In this section, we introduce the proposed algorithms for solving MHRSP.

4.1 Algorithm Overview

Figure 2 shows the algorithm overview. Users first send requests to the server, which processes rider requests sequentially under the First-Come First-Served (FCFS) principle [7,21], updating driver capacity dynamically with each match. For incoming requests, the server employs the graph generation module to construct an FMG (see Sect. 4.2), which models potential driverâĂŞrider matches by incorporating feasible areas and path constraints.

Next, the server employs the guidance module to build a Guide-Tree (see Sect. 4.3), which provides path search guidance. By representing FMG matching paths as a Trie structure [2], it efficiently organizes path data and avoids duplicate searches.

Then, the server uses the search module to search for the optimal multi-hop path under the guidance of the Guide-Tree. The core of the search module is

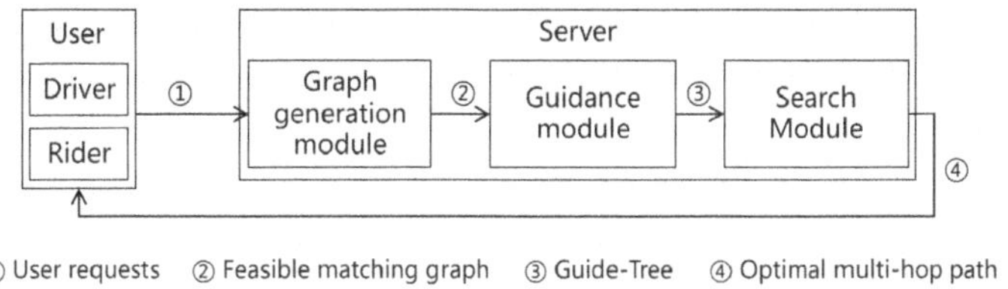

Fig. 2. The Algorithm Overview.

to quickly search for the optimal path solution based on the rider's source and destination, as well as the guidance of the Guide-Tree, using the Guide Search (GS) algorithm (see Sect. 4.4). The GS comprehensively considers the feasible area for drivers and the setting of transfer points, ensuring that riders can choose the shortest path while meeting time constraints.

Finally, the server sends the calculation results of the optimal multi-hop path to the riders and corresponding drivers.

4.2 Feasible Matching Graph

To efficiently represent the potential multi-hop connections between riders and drivers, we propose the Feasible Matching Graph (FMG). The core idea of the FMG is to abstract drivers and riders as nodes in the graph, which is similar to the approach in VPG [22]. VPG is mainly used to calculate driver pairs, focusing on the connection between drivers and ignoring the connection between riders and drivers. In the FMG, in addition to considering the connection between drivers, it is also necessary to consider the connection between riders and drivers.

The FMG is constructed based on the feasible area of the driver. A large number of ride-sharing related studies [1,7,16,22,23] usually use the feasible area to represent the maximum range that a driver can reach within his/her deadline constraint. Pruning the road network through the feasible area can effectively reduce the search space, so as to improve the efficiency of path planning.

Definition 7 (Feasible Area). *A feasible area $\mathcal{A}_w$ of a driver w is defined as the set of all locations that w can visit while ensuring that the deadline constraint for reaching their destination is satisfied.*

The detour ellipse method is one of the mainstream methods to calculate the feasible area of drivers, which is widely used in the field of ride-sharing [1,16,22,23]. In this paper, we use GeoPrune [24], which is currently the most efficient algorithm designed based on the detour ellipse method, to calculate the feasible area of the driver.

After calculating the feasible area, we start to build the FMG. First, all drivers are added to the FMG as virtual nodes.

Next, for any two drivers $w_a = \langle s_a, e_a, tr_a, td_a, c_a \rangle$ and $w_b = \langle s_b, e_b, tr_b, td_b, c_b \rangle$ whose feasible areas intersect, if there is a transfer point in their intersection area, and w_a and w_b can both reach the transfer point under their respective deadline constraints, i.e., satisfy Eq. 3, then connect the virtual nodes representing w_a and w_b.

$$\begin{aligned} &\mathcal{A}_{w_a} \cap \mathcal{A}_{w_b} \neq \emptyset, \\ &t(s_a, p) + t(p, e_a) \leq td_a - tr_a, \\ &t(s_b, p) + t(p, e_b) \leq td_b - tr_b, \end{aligned} \tag{3}$$

where $p \in (\mathcal{A}_{w_a} \cap \mathcal{A}_{w_b}) \cap P$, and P is the set of all transfer points.

Finally, the source s_r and the destination e_r of rider r are added to the FMG as virtual nodes, and connected to the virtual nodes corresponding to the drivers whose feasible areas cover s_r and e_r. In this way, FMG can not only represent the potential matches between drivers, but also reflect the pairing relationship between rider and drivers.

Algorithm 1: Constructing the FMG

Input: Driver set W, Rider request r, Road network $G(V, E)$, Transfer point set P.
Output: FMG $\Gamma(\mathcal{V}_\Gamma, \mathcal{E}_\Gamma)$.

Use GeoPrune to compute each driver $w \in W$'s feasible area $\mathcal{A}_w$.
Initialize $\mathcal{V}_\Gamma, \mathcal{E}_\Gamma \leftarrow \emptyset$.
foreach $w_i \in W$ **do**
  $\mathcal{V}_\Gamma \leftarrow \mathcal{V}_\Gamma \cup \{w_i\}$.
foreach $w_i \in W$ **do**
  foreach $w_j \in W,\ j \neq i$ **do**
    if *Constraint 3 holds* **then**
      $\mathcal{E}_\Gamma \leftarrow \mathcal{E}_\Gamma \cup \{\text{edge}(w_i, w_j)\}$.
$\mathcal{V}_\Gamma \leftarrow \mathcal{V}_\Gamma \cup \{s_r, e_r\}$.
foreach $w_i \in W$ **do**
  if $s_r \in \mathcal{A}_{w_i}$ **then**
    $\mathcal{E}_\Gamma \leftarrow \mathcal{E}_\Gamma \cup \{\text{edge}(s_r, w_i)\}$.
  if $e_r \in \mathcal{A}_{w_i}$ **then**
    $\mathcal{E}_\Gamma \leftarrow \mathcal{E}_\Gamma \cup \{\text{edge}(e_r, w_i)\}$.
return $\Gamma(\mathcal{V}_\Gamma, \mathcal{E}_\Gamma)$.

Time Complexity. Adding drivers to the FMG takes $O(|W|)$ time. Enumerating driver pairs takes $O(|W|^2)$, and checking Constraint 3 for each pair requires $O(|P|)$. Connecting virtual nodes to drivers takes another $O(|W|)$. Therefore, the overall time complexity of Algorithm 1 is $O(|W|^2|P|)$.

4.3 Guide-Tree

To efficiently store the paths in the FMG and avoid recalculating redundant parts during subsequent searches, we have designed a Guide-Tree based on Trie [2]. The

Trie is a classic data structure for storing multiple strings in a low-redundancy manner and supporting efficient retrieval of strings. In this paper, we treat paths as strings and use the Trie to store them, thereby forming a Guide-Tree. We utilize the Trie to implement two key operations in the Guide-Tree:

- $Insert(T, path)$: Inserts $path$ into the Guide-Tree T, with a time complexity of $O(|path|)$.
- $Find(T, node)$: Returns all child nodes of $node$ in the Guide-Tree T, with a time complexity of $O(\delta)$, where δ is the maximum out-degree of the node in the FMG.

To construct the Guide-Tree, we start from the rider's source and gradually expand paths by exploring adjacent nodes along the edges in the FMG. At each step, the algorithm maintains a queue to store the paths to be processed and the current number of hops. Whenever a rider's destination is reached and the transfer count does not exceed the maximum hop limit, the current path is inserted into the Guide-Tree. Finally, the construction of the Guide-Tree is completed.

Algorithm 2: Constructing the Guide-Tree

Input: FMG $\Gamma(\mathcal{V}_\Gamma, \mathcal{E}_\Gamma)$, Rider request r, Maximum hop count $h_{\max}$.
Output: Guide-Tree T.

Initialize the Guide-Tree $T \leftarrow \emptyset$, and the queue $Q \leftarrow \emptyset$.
Q.push($\{s_r, \langle s_r \rangle, 1\}$).
while $Q \neq \emptyset$ **do**
  $\{u, current\_path, len\} \leftarrow Q$.pop().
  if $len > h_{\max} + 2$ **then**
    continue.
  if $u == e_r$ **then**
    T.insert($current\_path$).
    continue.
  foreach $edge\ (u, v) \in \mathcal{E}_\Gamma$ **do**
    if $v \notin current\_path$ **then**
      $new\_path \leftarrow Addvtocurrent\_path$.
      Q.push($\{v, new\_path, len + 1\}$).
return T.

In FMG, when there is an edge between two driver nodes, riders can transfer between these two drivers. Thus, the maximum hop count $h_{\max}$ depends on the length of the FMG path. Previous studies have shown that when the number of transfers exceeds four, the marginal improvement in matching rate becomes negligible, while the computational cost increases significantly [6]. Moreover, high-hop scenarios are rarely observed in real-world urban transportation. Therefore, it is reasonable to assume that $h_{\max}$ is a small constant.

Time Complexity. The maximum path length in the FMG is $O(h_{max})$, and each extension visits at most $O(\delta)$ nodes, leading to $O(\delta^{h_{max}})$ paths. Since inserting each path into the Guide-Tree costs $O(h_{max})$, the overall complexity of Algorithm 2 is $O(h_{max}\delta^{h_{max}})$.

4.4 Guide Search Algorithm

To calculate the optimal multi-hop path for a rider, we propose the Guide Search (GS) algorithm. The GS leverages the branching structure of the Guide-Tree to prune and guide the search space, allowing it to quickly determine whether a rider can transfer from the current driver to another driver offering multi-hop ride-sharing services without enumerating all drivers.

Algorithm 3: GS Algorithm

Input: Driver set W, Rider request r, Road network $G(V, E)$, Transfer point set P, Maximum hop $h_{\max}$.
Output: Multi-hop path $\mathcal{L}$.

$\Gamma(\mathcal{V}_\Gamma, \mathcal{E}_\Gamma) \leftarrow$ Alg. 1$(W, r, G(V, E), P)$, $T \leftarrow$ Alg. 2$(\Gamma, r, h_{\max})$.
Initialize $Q \leftarrow \emptyset, \mathcal{L}_{opt} \leftarrow \emptyset$, $dis_{opt} \leftarrow \infty$.
Q.push$(\{s_r, s_r^T, \emptyset, 0\})$.
while $Q \neq \emptyset$ **do**
  $\{u, w^T, \mathcal{L}, dis\} \leftarrow Q$.pop().
  if $u == e_r$ **then**
    if $dis < dis_{opt}$ **then**
      $\mathcal{L}_{opt} \leftarrow \mathcal{L}$.
      $dis_{opt} \leftarrow dis$.
    continue.
  $childNodes \leftarrow$ Find(T, w^T).
  foreach $w'^T \in childNodes$ **do**
    foreach $p \in \mathcal{A}_w \cap \mathcal{A}_{w'}$ **do**
      $\mathcal{L}' \leftarrow \mathcal{L} \cup \{(u, p, w')\}$.
      $newDis \leftarrow \max(dis + t(u, p), tr_{w'} + t(s_{w'}, p))$.
      Q.push$(\{p, w'^T, \mathcal{L}', newDis\})$.
return $\mathcal{L}_{opt}$.

Specifically, the GS uses a queue to maintain the search states of paths. Each search state contains the current location, the corresponding node in the Guide-Tree (distinguished by a superscript T), the current path, and the accumulated travel time. At each step, the GS uses the branching information of the Guide-Tree to determine whether there is a transfer opportunity, i.e., whether the rider can transfer from the current node to one of its child nodes in the Guide-Tree. If such a transfer is possible, the GS extends the current search state along the Guide-Tree and updates it to reflect the new state after transferring to the target child node, thereby progressively constructing feasible paths.

Time Complexity. Constructing $\Gamma(\mathcal{V}_\Gamma, \mathcal{E}_\Gamma)$ requires $O(|W|^2|P|)$, while constructing T requires $O(h_{max}\delta^{h_{max}})$. For each node in T, computing feasible transfer points costs $O(|P|)$. Since the maximum depth of the tree is $O(h_{max})$, the overall complexity of Algorithm 3 is $O(|P| \cdot (|W|^2 + h_{max}\delta^{h_{max}}))$.

Table 1. Dataset and Experimental Parameter Settings.

	NYC	CD
Road Network	161,608 vertices, 1,023,705 edges	111,148 vertices, 559,417 edges
Capacity	1, 2, **3**, 4, 5	
Num. of drivers	100, 200, **300**, 400, 500	
Num. of transfer points	500, 750, **1000**, 1250, 1500	
Detour rate	1.3, 1.4, **1.5**, 1.6, 1.7	
Maximum hop	1, **2**, 3, 4	
Dataset Date	May 1, 2015	Nov. 27, 2016

5 Experiments

In this section, we empirically evaluate the algorithms described in Sect. 4. We first present the experimental setting and then analyze the experimental results.

5.1 Experimental Settings

Datasets. We evaluated our algorithms using two real-world datasets: the NYC Taxi and Limousine Commission Trip Record Data [17] and the Chengdu trajectory data from the Didi GAIA open dataset [5]. Both datasets contain rider and driver requests. For both rider and driver requests, the source s, destination e, and release time tr are provided. For rider requests, the request deadline td is defined as $tr + \alpha \cdot t(s, e)$, where $t(s, e)$ is the shortest travel time, and α is the detour rate. This setting is widely used in related research [22, 27]. The road networks for New York (NY) and Chengdu (CD) were extracted from Open Street Map [18] using OSMNX [3].

In the experiment, we perform online matching for 1,000 rider requests starting at 10:00 AM. Similar to previous studies [22,27], we transform the coordinates to the Universal Transverse Mercator (UTM) and adopt the Euclidean distance as the shortest distance between nodes. Table 1 summarizes the experimental settings, with default parameters highlighted in bold.

Compared Algorithms. In our experiments, we evaluated the performance of the following algorithms:

- **GS.** The Guide Search (GS) algorithm described in Sect. 4.4. GS supports multi-hop ride-sharing. The time complexity of GS for 2-hop ride-sharing is $O(|P| \cdot (|W|^2 + \delta^2))$.

- **BBVP.** The Blossom-Based Vehicle Pairing (BBVP) [22] algorithm transforms the driver-rider matching problem into a general graph matching problem. The drivers are paired using the Blossom algorithm to form driver pairs, which can provide transfer services. BBVP is specifically designed for 2-hop ride-sharing. The time complexity of BBVP is $O(|W|^3|P|)$.
- **VFRS.** The Verify Feasibility of Ride-Sharing (VFRS) [7] algorithm utilizes an R-tree to identify drivers near the rider's source and destination locations. It then enumerates combinations of these drivers and verifies feasibility. VFRS is specifically designed for 2-hop ride-sharing. The time complexity of VFRS is $O(|W|^2|P|^2)$.

Implementation. All algorithms are implemented in C++17 and run on a computer with an Intel(R) Core(TM) i7-10700 CPU@2.90 GHz and 32 GB RAM.

Metrics. We evaluated the performance of the above algorithms from two aspects:

- **Matches:** The num. of riders successfully matched with drivers.
- **Runtime:** The average CPU time required to complete the matching for a rider.

5.2 Experiment Results

Benefits of Multi-hop Ride-Sharing. Figure 3 reveals the benefits of multi-hop ride-sharing. As the maximum number of hops increases, the number of matches increases. This improvement is most significant during the transition from 1-hop to 2-hop, as the additional flexibility enables many previously unmatched riders to find feasible matches. However, as the number of hops continues to increase, the marginal benefit gradually diminishes.

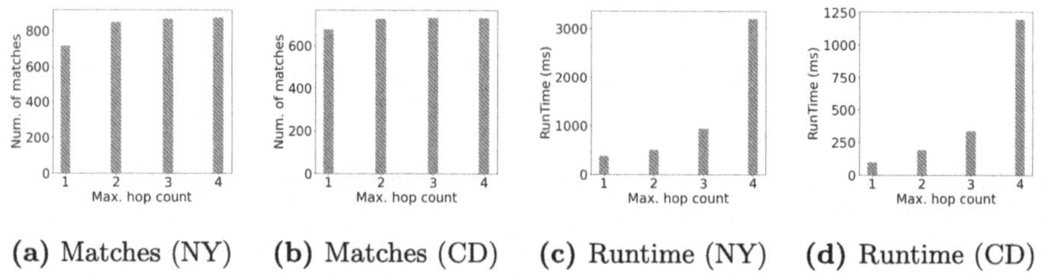

(a) Matches (NY) **(b)** Matches (CD) **(c)** Runtime (NY) **(d)** Runtime (CD)

Fig. 3. Benefit of multi-hop ride-sharing.

On the other hand, the computational cost increases rapidly with the maximum number of hops. 1-hop achieves the shortest runtime due to its limited search space. 2-hop and 3-hop maintain reasonable runtimes, but when the maximum number of hops exceeds four, the runtime becomes impractical.

Impact of the Capacity. Figure 4 reveals the impact of the capacity. The number of matches of each algorithm increases with the increase in capacity. Among them, GS consistently shows the highest number of matches because it uses an accurate feasibility area algorithm. Since VFRS cannot accurately calculate the feasible area of the vehicle, its number of matches is slightly lower than that of GS. However, compared to GS and VFRS, BBVP has a significantly lower number of matches because it is limited to paired driver combinations and cannot fully exploit multi-hop matching opportunities.

Regarding running time, GS is the fastest thanks to efficient Guide-Tree pruning. BBVP ranks second by using a general graph matching algorithm without enumerating all driver combinations. VFRS is the slowest due to exhaustive enumeration and verification of all possible driver sets. These results align with the theoretical time complexity of each method.

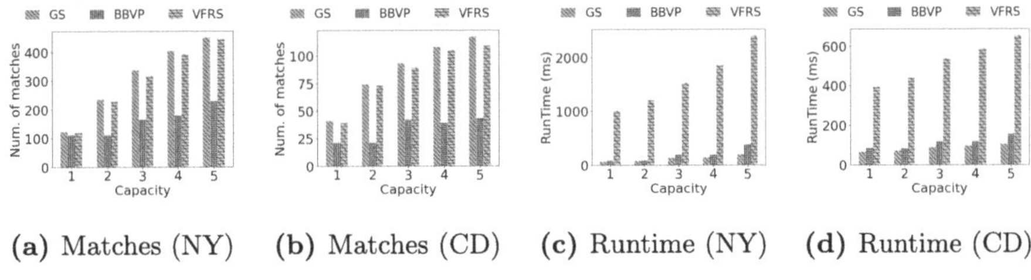

(a) Matches (NY) **(b)** Matches (CD) **(c)** Runtime (NY) **(d)** Runtime (CD)

Fig. 4. Impact of the capacity.

Impact of the Number of Drivers. Figure 5 reveals the impact of the number of drivers. As the number of drivers increases, the number of matches of all algorithms exhibits an upward trend, though the rate of increase gradually tapers off. This is because the number of matches approaches its upper limit as more drivers become available.

On the other hand, as the number of drivers increases, the runtime of VFRS becomes increasingly unacceptable, while BBVP always maintains a low runtime overhead due to its limited search range. In contrast, the GS always has the lowest runtime overhead.

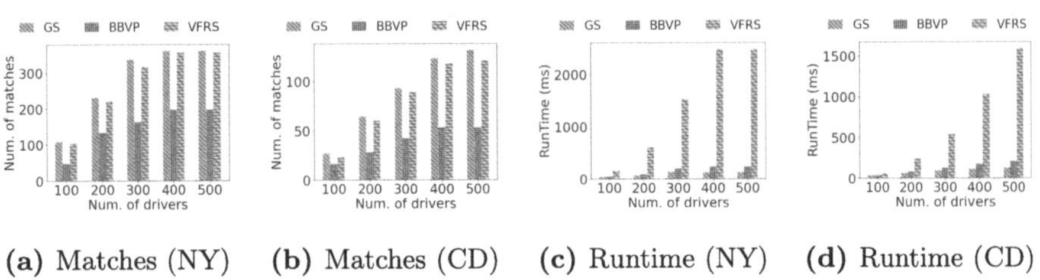

(a) Matches (NY) **(b)** Matches (CD) **(c)** Runtime (NY) **(d)** Runtime (CD)

Fig. 5. Impact of the number of drivers.

Impact of the Number of Transfer Points. Figure 6 reveals the impact of the number of transfer points. As the number of transfer points increases, the number of matches for all algorithms exhibits an upward trend. When the transfer point count is low, there are fewer, or even no, transfer points within the feasible areas of the drivers, leading to matching failures. As the number of transfer points increases, matching opportunities grow, but at the same time, the computational overhead for all algorithms also rises. Among them, VFRS consistently exhibits the highest runtime, followed by BBVP. GS consistently maintains the lowest runtime across all configurations.

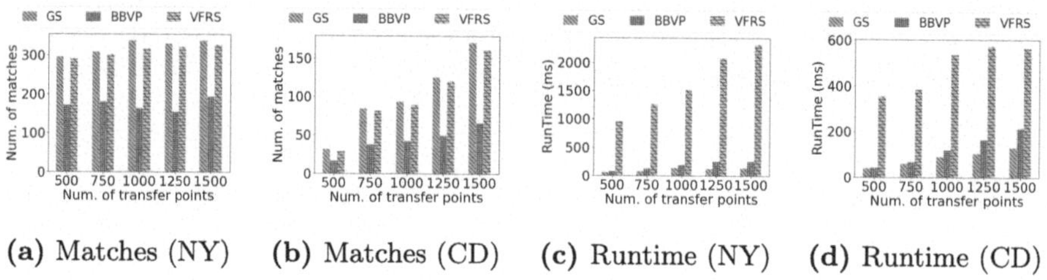

(a) Matches (NY) (b) Matches (CD) (c) Runtime (NY) (d) Runtime (CD)

Fig. 6. Impact of the number of transfer points.

Impact of the Detour Rate. Figure 7 reveals the impact of the detour rate. As the detour ratio increases, the number of matches for all algorithms exhibits an upward trend. This is because a higher detour ratio allows drivers to accept longer detour distances, thereby expanding their feasible areas. The expansion of feasible areas increases the likelihood of matches between drivers and riders, contributing to an overall improvement in the matching rate. However, larger feasible areas also mean that more transfer points need to be computed, which increases computational overhead. Among the algorithms, the runtime of VFRS grows rapidly as the detour ratio increases, while BBVP experiences relatively slower growth. In contrast, the runtime of the GS increases the slowest and consistently maintains the lowest runtime.

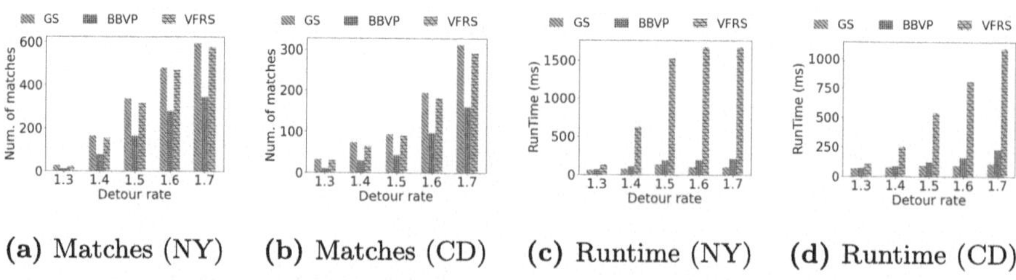

(a) Matches (NY) (b) Matches (CD) (c) Runtime (NY) (d) Runtime (CD)

Fig. 7. Impact of the detour rate.

6 Conclusion

This paper proposes an effective solution to the multi-hop ride-sharing problem on large-scale road networks. We design the Feasible Matching Graph (FMG) to model rider-driver connections and introduce a Guide-Tree based on a Trie to optimize path storage and search. The proposed Guide Search (GS) algorithm uses this structure to efficiently compute optimal multi-hop paths, reducing search space and improving performance. Experiments on real-world datasets show that GS consistently achieves the highest number of matches and shortest runtime, outperforming state-of-the-art methods in efficiency and scalability.

Acknowledgments. This work is supported by the Collaborative Innovation Center of Novel Software Technology and Industrialization and the Priority Academic Program Development of Jiangsu Higher Education Institutions.

Disclosure of Interests. The authors have no competing interests to declare that are relevant to the content of this article.

References

1. Ackermann, C., Rieck, J.: Multiple plan approach for a dynamic dial-a-ride problem. OR Spectrum 1–35 (2025)
2. Aoe, J.I., Morimoto, K., Sato, T.: An efficient implementation of trie structures. Softw.: Pract. Exp. **22**(9), 695–721 (1992)
3. Boeing, G.: OSMnx: new methods for acquiring, constructing, analyzing, and visualizing complex street networks. Comput. Environ. Urban Syst. **65**, 126–139 (2017)
4. Caulfield, B.: Estimating the environmental benefits of ride-sharing: a case study of Dublin. Transp. Res. Part D: Transp. Environ. **14**(7), 527–531 (2009)
5. Didi Chuxing (2023). https://outreach.didichuxing.com/
6. Drews, F., Luxen, D.: Multi-hop ride sharing. In: Proceedings of the International Symposium on Combinatorial Search, vol. 4, pp. 71–79 (2013)
7. Fevre, C., Zgaya-Biau, H., Mathieu, P., Hammadi, S.: Multi-agent systems and R-trees for dynamic and optimised ridesharing. In: 2021 IEEE International Conference on Systems, Man, and Cybernetics (SMC), pp. 1352–1358. IEEE (2021)
8. Furuhata, M., Dessouky, M., Ordóñez, F., Brunet, M.E., Wang, X., Koenig, S.: Ridesharing: the state-of-the-art and future directions. Transp. Res. Part B: Methodol. **57**, 28–46 (2013)
9. Guo, J., Long, J., Xu, X., Yu, M., Yuan, K.: The vehicle routing problem of intercity ride-sharing between two cities. Transp. Res. Part B: Methodol. **158**, 113–139 (2022)
10. Herbawi, W., Weber, M.: Evolutionary multiobjective route planning in dynamic multi-hop ridesharing. In: Evolutionary Computation in Combinatorial Optimization: 11th European Conference, EvoCOP 2011, Torino, Italy, 27–29 April 2011, Proceedings 11, pp. 84–95. Springer (2011)
11. Herbawi, W., Weber, M.: Modeling the multihop ridematching problem with time windows and solving it using genetic algorithms. In: 2012 IEEE 24th International Conference on Tools with Artificial Intelligence, vol. 1, pp. 89–96. IEEE (2012)

12. Hou, Y., Zhong, W., Su, L., Hulme, K., Sadek, A.W., Qiao, C.: TASeT: improving the efficiency of electric taxis with transfer-allowed rideshare. IEEE Trans. Veh. Technol. **65**(12), 9518–9528 (2016)
13. Ke, H., Li, H.: Multi-rider ridesharing stable matching optimization. Soft Comput. 1–16 (2024)
14. Li, T., Ge, Y., Xiong, J., Xu, M., Wu, J., Sun, H.: Ridesharing user equilibrium model without the EN-route transfer: an OD-based link-node formulation. Transp. Res. Part E: Logist. Transp. Rev. **187**, 103599 (2024)
15. Li, Z., Liang, C., Hong, Y., Zhang, Z.: How do on-demand ridesharing services affect traffic congestion? The moderating role of urban compactness. Prod. Oper. Manag. **31**(1), 239–258 (2022)
16. Masoud, N., Jayakrishnan, R.: A real-time algorithm to solve the peer-to-peer ride-matching problem in a flexible ridesharing system. Transp. Res. Part B: Methodol. **106**, 218–236 (2017)
17. NYC (2022). https://www1.nyc.gov/site/tlc/about/tlc-trip-record-data.page
18. OpenStreetMap (2023). http://www.openstreetmap.org
19. Sprung, M.J., Chambers, M., Smith-Pickel, S., et al.: Transportation statistics annual report 2018. Bureau of Transportation Statistics DoT, United States (2018)
20. Ta, N., Li, G., Zhao, T., Feng, J., Ma, H., Gong, Z.: An efficient ride-sharing framework for maximizing shared routes. In: 2018 IEEE 34th International Conference on Data Engineering (ICDE), pp. 1795–1796. IEEE (2018)
21. Tong, Y., Zeng, Y., Zhou, Z., Chen, L., Xu, K.: Unified route planning for shared mobility: an insertion-based framework. ACM Trans. Database Syst. (TODS) **47**(1), 1–48 (2022)
22. Wei, X., Li, P., Huang, W., Liu, Z., Liu, Q.: Two-stage vehicle pair dispatch in multi-hop ridesharing. In: 2023 26th International Conference on Computer Supported Cooperative Work in Design (CSCWD), pp. 255–260. IEEE (2023)
23. Xu, Y., Kulik, L., Borovica-Gajic, R., Aldwyish, A., Qi, J.: Highly efficient and scalable multi-hop ride-sharing. In: Proceedings of the 28th International Conference on Advances in Geographic Information Systems, pp. 215–226 (2020)
24. Xu, Y., Qi, J., Borovica-Gajic, R., Kulik, L.: GeoPrune: efficiently matching trips in ride-sharing through geometric properties. In: Proceedings of the 32nd International Conference on Scientific and Statistical Database Management, pp. 1–12 (2020)
25. Yu, B., et al.: Environmental benefits from ridesharing: a case of Beijing. Appl. Energy **191**, 141–152 (2017)
26. Zhao, Y., Zheng, K., Cui, Y., Su, H., Zhu, F., Zhou, X.: Predictive task assignment in spatial crowdsourcing: a data-driven approach. In: 2020 IEEE 36th International Conference on Data Engineering (ICDE), pp. 13–24. IEEE (2020)
27. Zuo, H., Cao, B., Zhao, Y., Shen, B., Zheng, W., Huang, Y.: High-capacity ride-sharing via shortest path clustering on large road networks. J. Supercomput. **77**(4), 4081–4106 (2021)

Interval Based Constrained Path Optimization in Time-Dependent Road Networks

Kousik Kumar Dutta[1(✉)] and Venkata M. V. Gunturi[2]

[1] Indian Institute of Technology Ropar, Rupnagar 140001, India
kousik.21csz0004@iitrpr.ac.in
[2] Loughborough University, Leicestershire LE11 3TU, UK

Abstract. In the realm of urban mobility, the increasing availability of large-scale transportation data has paved the way for advanced and sophisticated routing queries. Among these, the time-dependent constrained path optimization (TD-CPO) problem optimizes route selection based on user-defined preferences such as safety, navigability, road width, or scenic value, while adhering to specific constraints (travel time). This problem has broad applications in urban navigation, helping commuters and travelers find paths that align with their individual needs. However, solving the TD-CPO problem is challenging, as it can be reduced to the NP-hard arc-orienteering problem. Existing state-of-the-art research has predominantly focused on solving the TD-CPO problem for a single departure time. However, this approach is often too limiting for users who prefer to depart within a time range. Extending these methods to handle a range of departure times typically results in redundant computations and inefficiencies. This paper proposes an extension of the TD-CPO query, called interval TD-CPO, that accounts for a range of departure times. This extension aims to identify the most suitable path and a corresponding departure time that maximizes the user's preference metric within the given constraints. Experimental results on real-world graphs show that our algorithm delivers comparable solution quality in just 5 s, a major improvement over the 120 s needed by state-of-the-art methods adapted for interval TD-CPO.

Keywords: Route Planning · Temporal Graphs · Road Networks · Interval Query

1 Introduction

Background: The Constrained Path Optimization (CPO) problem [3,8] involves finding a path in a road network represented as a directed graph, where each edge is annotated with a cost value (travel time or distance) and a score that reflects a user-defined preference metric (scenic value, navigability, or safety). Input to the CPO problem consists of (a) a road network, (b)

I. Awan et al. (Eds.): WISE 2025, LNCS 16368, pp. 165–176, 2026.
https://doi.org/10.1007/978-981-95-7251-9_12

a source-destination pair, and (c) a budget. The objective is to identify a path from the source to the destination that maximizes the cumulative score while ensuring that the total cost does not exceed the given budget. CPO queries have significant applications in urban transportation. For example, a traveler may prioritize a scenic route within a two-hour limit [1,9,10], or require a highly navigable path or a safer path [7] without exceeding a predefined distance [3,8].

However, solving the CPO problem is inherently complex, as it reduces to the NP-hard Arc-Orienteering Problem (AOP) [11]. Prior research [3,8] on the CPO problem has primarily modeled the underlying road networks as static graphs. However, travel times on road segments fluctuate due to congestion, and the attractiveness of scenic routes also varies based on factors like attraction hours. Similarly, factors like safety and navigability may also change with time. To capture the dynamic nature of the underlying road network, a recent study [4] introduced the time-dependent CPO (TD-CPO) problem.

Point TD-CPO and Interval TD-CPO Problem: Existing research relevant to time-dependent constrained path optimization [1,4,9] has primarily focused on what we refer to as the point TD-CPO queries. Here, the goal is to determine a solution for a fixed departure time. However, this approach is often too restrictive for commuters and travelers who have flexibility in their departure time. In this paper, we introduce the *interval TD-CPO problem.* Unlike point TD-CPO, interval TD-CPO considers a discrete departure-time interval as input and computes the "best solution" over the specified departure-time interval.

Limitations of the Related Works: A naive way to handle interval TD-CPO queries is to run point TD-CPO algorithms [4] for every discrete departure time in the interval. However, this is computationally expensive and redundant. Additionally, temporal pruning techniques from [4] are no longer applicable due to the departure time range.

The 2TD-AOP problem is closely related but permits repeated visits to vertices and edges [9], introducing loops that are generally undesirable in applications like commuting. Moreover, 2TD-AOP is also designed for point queries and would incur similar redundancy when extended to intervals.

CSP problem [12–14] aims to minimize travel time under additional constraints, differing fundamentally from interval TD-CPO, which seeks to maximize a preference score within a time budget. Moreover, CSP algorithms use dominance-based pruning [12–14], which is ineffective for interval TD-CPO.

Our Contributions: This paper makes the following contributions:

(a) To the best of our knowledge, we are the first to study the interval TD-CPO problem and develop an algorithm called $i\mathcal{SCOPE}$.
(b) $i\mathcal{SCOPE}$ constructs *path functions* that capture travel time and score for a range of departure times and optimizes computations by minimizing the function's temporal footprints based on budget constraints. To further enhance efficiency, $i\mathcal{SCOPE}$ merges nearby breakpoints, reducing the number of processed breakpoints by over 50% during interval TD-CPO query execution.

(c) We conducted extensive experiments to evaluate $i\mathcal{SCOPE}$ on three large-scale road networks. We compared $i\mathcal{SCOPE}$ against baseline approaches ([2]) and the state-of-the-art related works [4,9,13].
(d) Our experimental results demonstrate that $i\mathcal{SCOPE}$ achieves the same solution quality in just 5 s, whereas the state-of-the-art (when adapted for interval TD-CPO problem) requires 120 s.

Outline: The rest of this paper is organized as follows: Sect. 2 introduces the fundamental concepts and formally defines the problem. Section 3 presents our proposed solution, $i\mathcal{SCOPE}$. Section 4 provides the experimental evaluation, and Sect. 5 concludes the paper.

2 Problem Definition

Time-dependent Graph: We model the input road network $G(V, E)$ as a time-dependent (TD) graph, where nodes $v \in V$ represent road intersections, and directed edges $e \in E$ correspond to road segments. Each edge $e(x, y)$ is associated with two time-dependent functions: arrival time function ($\Gamma_e(t)$) and score function ($\Phi_e(t)$). In our implementation, we model the arrival time function as a continuous, non-decreasing, piecewise-linear function and score function as a piecewise-constant function. This paper assumes the First-In-First-Out (FIFO) property on the arrival time data for all edges.

Path Arrival Time Function ($\Gamma_{\mathcal{P}}(t)$): Given a simple path $\mathcal{P}$ consisting of edges $\{e_1(x_1, x_2), \ldots, e_n(x_n, x_{n+1})\}$ and a departure time t, $\Gamma_{\mathcal{P}}(t)$ returns the arrival time at the end node (x_{n+1}) of the path $\mathcal{P}$ for a journey that starts at time t from the start node (x_1). $\Gamma_{\mathcal{P}}(t)$ is determined by composing the arrival time functions of its constituent edges, i.e., $\Gamma_{\mathcal{P}}(t) = \Gamma_{e_n}(\ldots \Gamma_{e_2}(\Gamma_{e_1}(t)) \ldots)$.

Path Score Function ($\Phi_{\mathcal{P}}(t)$): Given a simple path $\mathcal{P}$ consisting of edges $\{e_1(x_1, x_2), \ldots, e_n(x_n, x_{n+1})\}$ and a departure time t, $\Phi_{\mathcal{P}}(t)$ returns the total score obtained on a journey (along the path $\mathcal{P}$) that starts at time t from the start node (x_1). $\Phi_{\mathcal{P}}(t)$ is the sum of the score values of the component edges. Here, the score value of an edge e_i is taken at the time when the journey (starting at time t along $\mathcal{P}$) arrives at that particular edge e_i. Mathematically, this can be represented using the following recursive function: $\Phi_{\mathcal{P}}(t) = \Phi_{\mathcal{P}'}(t) + \Phi_{e(x_n, x_{n+1})}(\Gamma_{\mathcal{P}'}(t))$, where $\mathcal{P}' = \{e_1(x_1, x_2), \ldots, e_{n-1}(x_{n-1}, x_n)\}$. The path arrival time and path score functions are the same as defined in [13].

2.1 Interval Based Time-Dependent Constrained Path Optimization

Input. (1) A TD graph, $G = (V, E)$, where each directed edge $e(x, y) \in E$ is associated with an arrival time function (Γ) and a score function (Φ).
(2) A source $s \in V$ and a destination $d \in V$.
(3) A discrete departure time interval $[t_{depS}, t_{depE}]$ at node s.
(4) A positive value *overhead*, which corresponds to the maximum permissible

travel time allowed over the fastest path from s to d. "Budget" ($\mathcal{B}$) denotes the sum of the overhead and the travel time of the fastest path from s to d.

Output. A departure time t^*_{dep} and corresponding path $\mathcal{P}^*$ such that: (a) $t^*_{dep} \in [t_{depS}, t_{depE}]$ and, (b) $\Gamma_{\mathcal{P}^*}(t^*_{dep}) \leq t^*_{dep} + \mathcal{B}$.

Objective.

$$\Phi_{\mathcal{P}^*}(t^*_{dep}) = \max_{\mathcal{P}, t_{dep} \in [t_{depS}, t_{depE}]} \Phi_{\mathcal{P}}(t_{dep}).$$

Here, $\mathcal{P}$ is any $s - d$ path that satisfies the given budget constraint. Note that the fastest path refers to the $s - d$ path that has the minimum travel time over the entire given departure time interval $[t_{depS}, t_{depE}]$ ([2,6]).

3 Proposed Approach

3.1 Overview of $i\mathcal{SCOPE}$

We initialize the source node s with the label $\langle s, NULL, NULL, NULL \rangle$. Each label consists of four components: (1) current node, (2) path arrival time function, (3) path score function, and (4) predecessor list tracking the path history. Note that the path arrival time and score functions represent the functions for the partial path up to the current node. Since the search starts at s, the arrival time and score are initially set to $NULL$. The algorithm recursively explores all possible labels for the destination node d and retrieves the interval TD-CPO path $\mathcal{P}^*$ for a departure time t^*_{dep} that satisfies: 1) $t_{dep}S \leq t^*_{dep} \leq t_{dep}E$, 2) $\Gamma_{\mathcal{P}^*}(t^*_{dep}) \leq t^*_{dep} + \mathcal{B}$, 3) $\Phi_{\mathcal{P}^*}(t^*_{dep})$ is maximized among all paths meeting conditions 1 and 2. Here, $[t_{dep}S, t_{dep}E]$ represents the discrete departure time interval from the source, and $\mathcal{B}$ is the maximum permissible budget.

During the ith recursive call of $i\mathcal{SCOPE}$, given the label $\langle u, \Gamma_{curr}, \Phi_{curr}, u_{pred} \rangle$, the algorithm expands u to each adjacent node v. Before expansion, it checks if v is already in u_{pred} to prevent loops. If not, it computes the path arrival time function Γ_{next} and path score function Φ_{next} as explained in Sect. 2.1. A new predecessor list v_{pred} is created by referencing u_{pred}, except in one instance where it is copied. Node v is added to v_{pred} with u as its predecessor. The algorithm then generates a new label $\langle v, \Gamma_{next}, \Phi_{next}, v_{pred} \rangle$ and recursively calls $i\mathcal{SCOPE}$ with this label.

Recursion terminates when $u = d$, yielding a valid $s \rightsquigarrow d$ path as $\langle d, \Gamma_{curr}, \Phi_{curr}, d_{pred} \rangle$. As recursion unwinds, different destination labels are collected and returned to the previous recursion level. At the end of all the recursions, we would have all the paths from s to d stored in $destLabels$.

Path Retrieval: To obtain the final interval TD-CPO path $\mathcal{P}^*$ and the corresponding departure time t^*_{dep}, we iterate through all the destination labels returned by $i\mathcal{SCOPE}$. Each destination label i contains the following information: 1) destination d, 2) path arrival time function $\Gamma_{\mathcal{P}_i}$, 3) path score function $\Phi_{\mathcal{P}_i}$, and 4) predecessor information $d_{pred}(i)$, where $\mathcal{P}_i$ is the path corresponding to $d_{pred}(i)$. Next, the algorithm iterates through all the breakpoints in

$\Phi_{\mathcal{P}_i}$. It is unnecessary to check every discrete departure time within the range $[t_{dep}S, t_{dep}E]$, as the score remains constant between two consecutive breakpoints (as defined in Sect. 2.1). For each breakpoint, we verify whether the corresponding arrival time falls within the budget limit and whether it results in a better score. If both conditions are met, we update t^*_{dep} and the best score. Finally, if any breakpoint of the current destination label yields a better score, we update $\mathcal{P}^*$ with $\mathcal{P}_i$.

As the algorithm explores all feasible paths between s and d, it incurs a high computational cost, which is impractical for real-time navigation. The next section analyzes path function behavior and introduces two optimizations to significantly improve efficiency.

3.2 Observations on Path Functions and Corresponding Optimization Techniques

Observation 1: Figure 1 illustrates a sample arrival time path function $\Gamma_p(t)$ at a node v (for path $p = s \rightsquigarrow v$) over the departure time interval $[0, 15]$ with breakpoints at $(0, 5, 15)$. Now, given an overall budget value $\mathcal{B}$, we compute an upper bound on allowed arrival time at node v. Any arrival time (at v) that is more than this upper bound cannot result in a feasible path to the destination. This upper bound is computed in the following way:

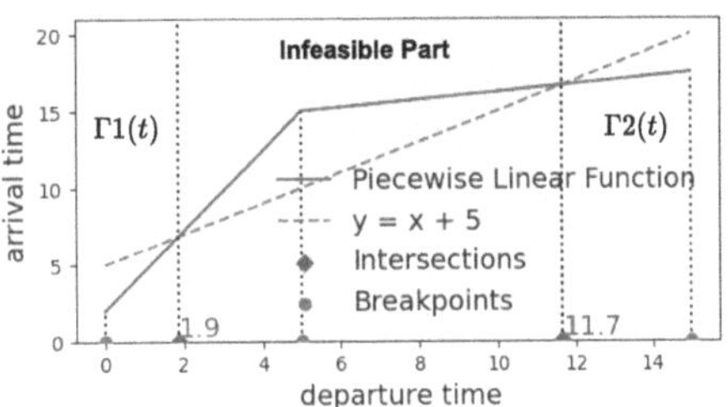

Fig. 1. Split function example.

Let the Euclidean distance between node v and the destination d be $dist(v, d)$, and the maximum allowed speed on the road network be $maxSpeed$. Therefore, the minimum time required (from a theoretical perspective) to reach d from v would be $minTime(v, d) = \frac{dist(v,d)}{maxSpeed}$. Now, if the total permissible budget for the journey is $\mathcal{B}$, then any valid path arriving at v which has a total travel time greater than $\mathcal{B} - minTime(v, d)$ cannot give us a feasible path to the destination. We convert this upper bound on travel time into an *arrival time bound function* by adding the departure time. For the example shown in Fig. 1, the value of $\mathcal{B} - minTime(v, d)$ is 5. This gives us the following arrival time bound function: $y = x + 5$ (y is the upper bound arrival time, x is the departure time). Given this arrival time bound function, any portion of $\Gamma_p(t)$ that lies above this line cannot give a feasible path to the destination. In other words, in Fig. 1, the path p is infeasible for the departure time interval $[1.9, 11.7]$.

***Opt 1.* Split Functions:** To incorporate Observation 1 effectively, we introduce the concept of a *split function* to represent the arrival time and score functions of a path. Unlike a single path function, this approach constructs separate path functions for each feasible segment of the original function, allowing us to discard infeasible portions while preserving valid ones.

Figure 1 visually illustrates this concept. The shaded region represents the infeasible portion of the arrival time function $\Gamma_P(t)$. Instead of considering the entire function as a whole, we decompose $\Gamma_P(t)$ within the interval $t \in [0, 15]$ into two distinct feasible segments: $\Gamma 1(t)$ for $t \in [0, 1.9]$ and $\Gamma 2(t)$ for $t \in [11.7, 15]$.

By using the split function technique, we significantly reduce unnecessary computations while maintaining accuracy in path selection. This method ensures that infeasible segments are discarded early, improving both the efficiency and effectiveness of $i\mathcal{SCOPE}$.

Observation 2: Figure 2 displays a partial arrival time path function for a random interval TD-CPO query in the New York road network. The figure reveals that breakpoints tend to form clusters. This occurs because road network properties fluctuate during rush hours, and these variations are generally consistent across all edges. In a piecewise linear function, breakpoints signify changes in function properties. Consequently, most breakpoints in a road network are concentrated around similar time points (primarily during rush hours). As edge functions are combined to generate path functions, breakpoints occurring at nearly the same times lead to clustering in the final path functions.

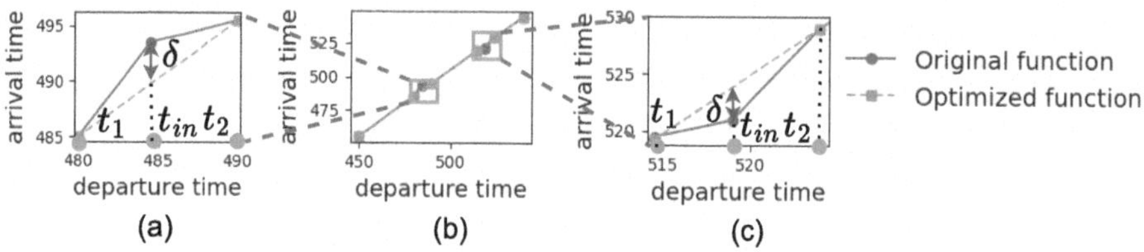

Fig. 2. Merging of breakpoints example.

***Opt 2.* Merge breakpoints:** To efficiently reduce the number of processed breakpoints, we introduce a breakpoint merging technique. This technique clusters nearby breakpoints (e.g., t_1, t_{in}, and t_2 in Fig. 2) and merges them. The merging process retains only the boundary breakpoints (t_1 and t_2), while intermediate breakpoints (t_{in}) are merged with the starting boundary point. The clustering of breakpoints is detailed in the following example.

Suppose a rush hour begins at time unit 480 and ends at 515. As a result, breakpoints will appear on every edge at these two time points. After processing the breakpoints at time 480 across a sequence of consecutive edges in a path, we obtain a set of breakpoints t_1, t_{in}, t_2 as shown in Fig. 2a. Similarly, processing the breakpoints at time 515 for the same edges produces another set of breakpoints t_1, t_{in}, t_2 in Fig. 2b.

As shown in Fig. 2, the optimized function closely approximates the original function, simplifying breakpoint processing while maintaining travel time accuracy within a δ error margin. This arrival time error can manifest in two ways, as depicted in Fig. 2a and 2c. In the first case, the optimized function underestimates the arrival time, potentially exceeding the allotted budget by δ time units. Thus, for an interval TD-CPO query with a maximum budget of $\mathcal{B}$, the resulting interval TD-CPO path may require up to $\mathcal{B} + \delta$. Conversely, in the second case, the optimized function overestimates the arrival time, effectively reducing the available budget by δ time units. As a result, this function can be pruned earlier. In both cases, the value of δ can be computed as

$$\delta = |a_{in} - \frac{(t_{in} - t_1)}{(t_2 - t_1)} \cdot (a_2 - a_1) + a_1|.$$

In the experiments (Sect. 4), we observed that the maximum value of δ reaches up to `5 min`, while the minimum remains around `1 min`.

Once breakpoints are merged, we must determine an appropriate score for the new segment. To do this, we adapt the roulette-wheel selection algorithm [5], a probabilistic technique that assigns breakpoints a likelihood of selection proportional to their scores.

In the example in Fig. 2a, we want to merge t_1 and t_{in} with associated scores s_1 and s_{in}. First, we calculate the percentage-based probability distribution of the scores using the following formulas:

$$P_1 = \frac{s_1}{s_1 + s_{in}} \times 100, \quad P_{in} = \frac{s_{in}}{s_1 + s_{in}} \times 100.$$

Here, s_1 and s_{in} represent the scores associated with breakpoints t_1 and t_{in}, respectively. These probabilities reflect the relative contribution of each score to the total. Next, a random integer v_{rand} is generated uniformly in the range $[0, 100]$. If v_{rand} falls within the interval $0 \leq v_{rand} \leq P_1$, the new score at breakpoint t_1 is updated with the value s_1. Otherwise, it is updated with s_{in}.

This probabilistic score assignment ensures that the merged breakpoints preserve the original distribution of scores, thereby maintaining fairness in representation. Moreover, reducing the number of breakpoints contributes to lower computational complexity without introducing bias into the scoring process.

The impact of these optimizations is further evaluated in our experimental results (Sect. 4). When both optimizations are applied, we observe up to a 1.4× increase in score and approximately 50% reduction in memory usage compared to $i\mathcal{SCOPE}$ without optimizations.

Time and Space Complexity Analysis: The time and space complexities of $i\mathcal{SCOPE}$ are both $O(b^n \cdot n \cdot k)$, where b is the average graph degree, n is the number of nodes in the search space, and k is the number of breakpoints per edge. Despite the exponential bounds, the algorithm performs efficiently on real-world road networks due to the small value of b and the proposed optimizations. Experiments show that $i\mathcal{SCOPE}$ achieves comparable solution quality in 5 s, compared to 120 s required by state-of-the-art methods. A detailed proof is omitted due to page limits.

4 Experimental Evaluation

Dataset: We use the following three large road networks: New York City, Florida, and California-Nevada[1]. Table 1 provides network details. We synthetically generate time-varying travel times and scores in these datasets. We create temporal information for a full day ($T = [0, 1440]$) and assume that this repeats with a periodicity of 24 h.

Table 1. DATASETS

Road Network	#Nodes	#Edges	Morning Rush Hour	Evening Rush Hour
New York City (NY)	264346	733846	7:30a.m.–9:30a.m.	4:00p.m.–6:30p.m.
Florida (FLA)	1,070,376	2,712,798	7:30a.m.–9:30a.m.	5.00p.m.–7:00p.m.
California and Nevada (CAL)	1,890,815	4,657,742	8:00a.m.–9:45a.m.	5.00p.m.–7:00p.m.

We generate $\Gamma_e(t)$ for an edge e by partitioning the rush hour time corresponding to the dataset into 30-min sub-intervals. Travel time remains constant outside rush hours. Starting at its original value $\Gamma_e(t_0)$, within each sub-interval, $\Gamma_e(t)$ follows a linear function, increasing by $(1+f/100)$ before peaking mid-rush hour and then decreasing by $(1 - f/100)$. We ensure the FIFO property. The factor f is randomly selected from $[10, 30]$.

With regard to generating $\Phi_e(t)$, we first randomly select some edges (varied in experiments) and assign a score value randomly between 0 and 15 for each sub-interval (sub-intervals are created in the same fashion as discussed for $\Gamma_e(t)$). All other edges receive a score of 0.

Candidate Algorithms: (a) TD-A* [2] (baseline), (b) SCOPE [4], (c) ICSP [13], (d) REC-INSERT [9].
We adapted SCOPE [4] and REC-INSERT [9] to run for all discrete departure times in the input interval. Note that both SCOPE and REC-INSERT have a notion of an execution time limit. We divide the time limits evenly across the entire input interval in our experiments. For ICSP, we generate a converted graph corresponding to each dataset mentioned in Table 1 by inverting the sign of score values. Each of the candidate algorithms, except TD-A* and REC-INSERT (as these are serial algorithms), is executed using multiple threads. For a multi-threaded execution of $i\mathcal{SCOPE}$, we utilized a "work-stealing" scheduler, which is particularly effective for tasks with multiple levels of recursive calls.

Query Sets: We generate six query sets per dataset based on fastest path costs: 1-10, 11-20, 21-30, 31-40, 41-50, and 51-60 min. Each set contains 100 randomly selected source-destination pairs. The start departure time $t_{dep}S$ is randomly selected within a rush hour period. The end departure time $t_{dep}E$ is then calculated by adding the departure time interval to $t_{dep}S$.

[1] https://www.diag.uniroma1.it/challenge9/download.shtml.

Metrics Measured: We report the average runtime (seconds), output path scores, and static memory consumption (MB) across all queries in all query sets. Note that an execution time limit is also put on *iSCOPE* to handle various user preferences (similar to current works [4,9]).

Experimental Setup: All the algorithms are implemented in Java and executed on an Intel Xeon Gold 6258R server with 28 cores (56 threads), 360GB of RAM, a base frequency of 2.7GHz, and a maximum frequency of 4GHz.

4.1 Experimental Results

Effects of Optimization Techniques: Figure 3 illustrates the impact of the *iSCOPE* optimization techniques discussed in Sect. 3.2. Although Opt 1 reduces the function footprint, it does not significantly decrease the number of breakpoints that need to be processed (Fig. 3b). This is because, when a function is split, additional boundary breakpoints must be created, as seen in Fig. 1 (e.g., adding boundary breakpoints 1.9 for $\Gamma_1(t)$ and 11.7 for $\Gamma_2(t)$). Our experiments reveal that Opt 1 is able to reduce $\sim$ 20% of breakpoints. If we combine Opt 1 and Opt 2, our algorithm reduces more than $\sim$ 50% of breakpoints (Fig. 3b). Consequently, static memory usage is significantly reduced through our optimizations, as shown in Fig. 3c.

With a reduction in the number of breakpoints, we also reduce processing times. Thus, *iSCOPE* gets more time to explore a larger search space within

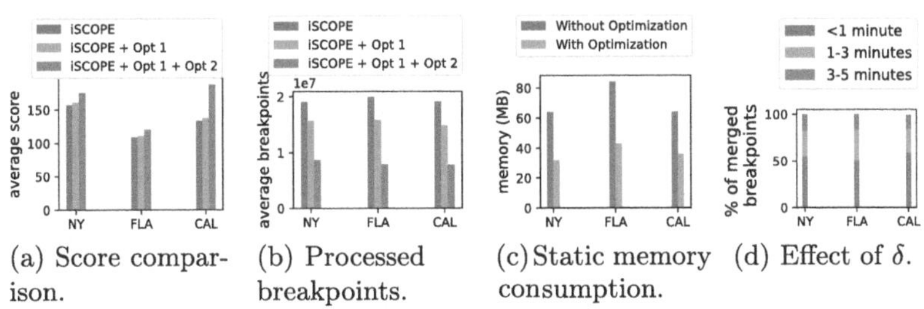

(a) Score comparison. (b) Processed breakpoints. (c) Static memory consumption. (d) Effect of δ.

Fig. 3. Effects of optimization techniques on *iSCOPE*.

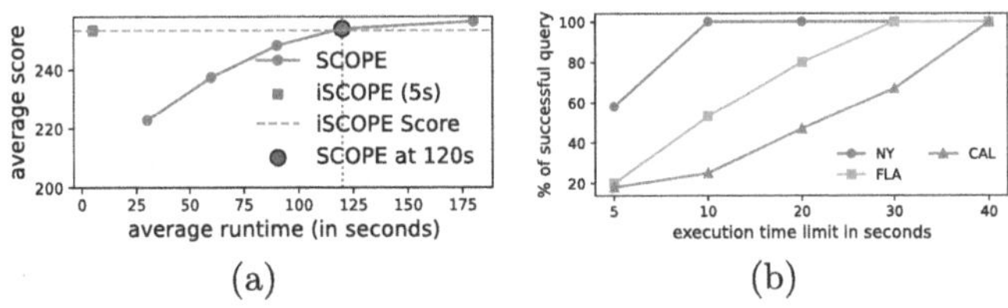

Fig. 4. (a) Average runtime of *SCOPE* to match the average score achieved by *iSCOPE* in 5 s on NY network, (b) Minimum time required by *SCOPE* to produce a feasible solution for all the queries on different road networks.

the same time constraints, thereby leading to improved scores. When both optimizations are applied, $i\mathcal{SCOPE}$ achieves a score improvement of 140%. Whereas using only Opt 1 results in a score improvement of only 110%, as the execution time is capped at 5 s for this experiment (Fig. 3a).

Figure 3d presents the error introduced in the arrival time function due to merging. More than $\sim$ 50% of merged breakpoints cause less than 1 min of error across all three networks, while around $\sim$ 20% result in a maximum error of 3-5 min. Given the effectiveness of the merging technique in real-world road networks, these errors could be acceptable. For the subsequent experiments, we refer to $i\mathcal{SCOPE}$ with both optimizations applied simply as $i\mathcal{SCOPE}$.

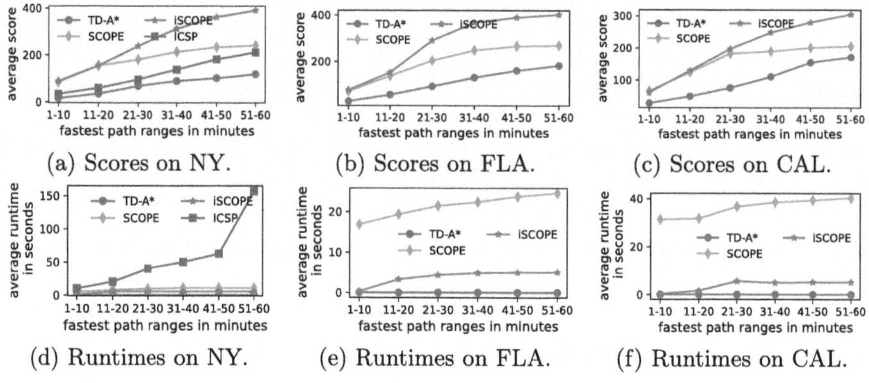

(a) Scores on NY. (b) Scores on FLA. (c) Scores on CAL.

(d) Runtimes on NY. (e) Runtimes on FLA. (f) Runtimes on CAL.

Fig. 5. Comparison between the candidate algorithms for 30% overhead, 20% edges with a non-zero score, running time limit of 5 s, 48 threads and departure time interval of 360 min.

Comparison with the Candidate Algorithms: In Fig. 4a, we fix the score to the value achieved by $i\mathcal{SCOPE}$ in 5 s and run *SCOPE* with execution time limits to determine the time required to reach the same score. The results show that *only after* 120 s, *SCOPE* begins to exceed the score achieved by $i\mathcal{SCOPE}$ in 5 s. Moreover, as shown in Fig. 4b, *SCOPE* requires at least 10, 30, and 40 s to generate a feasible solution for all queries in NY, FLA, and CAL network respectively. Consequently, for further experiments, we limit *SCOPE*'s runtime to the minimum duration required to produce a feasible solution for all queries and compare both score and runtime.

In all the networks (Fig. 5), $i\mathcal{SCOPE}$ consistently achieved the highest score, followed by *SCOPE*. A key observation is that at higher budget levels, $i\mathcal{SCOPE}$ reached the 5-second runtime limit, leading to a limited score. However, at lower budgets, both *SCOPE* and $i\mathcal{SCOPE}$ achieved similar scores, despite *SCOPE* having a significantly higher runtime. This is because for lower budget, both algorithms finish their execution completely within the allotted execution time limit. At higher budgets, $i\mathcal{SCOPE}$ achieved nearly twice the score of *SCOPE* while maintaining a much lower runtime.

ICSP exhibited exponential runtime growth (up to `156 s`, compared to `5 s` by *iSCOPE* for queries with fastest path ranges between `51-60 min`) as the budget increased, due to its reliance on Dijkstra's fastest path algorithm (which was invoked twice for each breakpoint of every edge under its computation strategy). Additionally, the dominance rule led to a lower score value (at best about half of *iSCOPE*). As a result, we ran ICSP only on the `NY` network. Meanwhile, TD-A* had a runtime in **`milliseconds`** across all networks and achieved a maximum of *50%* and a minimum of *16%* of the score obtained by *iSCOPE*. This is understandable as TD-A* focuses on finding the fastest path without considering the score values on edges.

While comparing with REC-INSERT, we report single-core results for *iSCOPE* for a fair evaluation (figure omitted due to space constraint). *iSCOPE* outperforms REC-INSERT, achieving nearly 2× higher average score across all road networks. However, both algorithms exhibit similar average runtimes of approximately `4 s`. REC-INSERT processes all discrete departure times within the given range and incurs a higher runtime. When we eliminate loops (as needed by interval TD-CPO), we end up with solutions with a low score.

5 Conclusion

This paper explores the novel problem of interval queries in time-dependent constrained path optimization (interval TD-CPO), a non-trivial extension of the point query formulation. The key contribution of this work lies in analyzing the properties of continuous path functions, particularly in road networks. Leveraging these insights, we propose a scalable algorithm designed to efficiently handle large time-dependent graphs. Experimental results demonstrate that our proposed algorithm achieves a comparable score in just `5 s`, whereas the state-of-the-art method requires `120 s`.

Acknowledgments. This research is supported by Indian Institute of Technology Ropar, 2022 Qualcomm Faculty Award and Loughborough University.

References

1. Chen, C., et al.: Enjoy the most beautiful scene now: a memetic algorithm to solve two-fold time-dependent arc orienteering problem. Front. Comp. Sci. **14**(2), 364–377 (2019)
2. Ding, B., et al.: Finding time-dependent shortest paths over large graphs, p. 205–216. EDBT '08 (2008)
3. Dutta, K.K., et al.: A multi-threading algorithm for constrained path optimization problem on road networks. In: WISE 2022, pp. 110–118 (2022)
4. Dutta, K.K., Gunturi, V.M.V.: Constrain path optimization on time-dependent road networks. In: WISE 2024 (2024)
5. Goldberg, D.E.: Genetic Algorithms in Search. Optimization and Machine Learning. Addison-Wesley Longman Publishing Co., Inc (1989)

6. Gong, Z., et al.: Querying shortest path on large time-dependent road networks with shortcuts. In: 2024 IEEE 40th ICDE, pp. 4532–4544 (2024)
7. Islam, F.T., et al.: A crowd-enabled approach for privacy-enhanced and personalized safe route planning for fixed or flexible destinations. TKDE **35**(11), 10922–10936 (2023)
8. Kaur, R., et al.: Finding the most navigable path in road networks. GeoInformatica **25**(1), 207–240 (2021)
9. Lu, Y., et al.: Scenic routes now: efficiently solving the time-dependent arc orienteering problem. In: Proc. of the 2017 ACM CIKM, pp. 487–496 (2017)
10. Lu, Y., Shahabi, C.: An arc orienteering algorithm to find the most scenic path on a large-scale road network. In: Proc. of the 23rd SIGSPATIAL (2015)
11. Verbeeck, C., et al.: An extension of the arc orienteering problem and its application to cycle trip planning. Trans. Res. Part E: Logi. Trans. Rev. **68**, 64–78 (2014)
12. Wang, Y., et al.: Constrained route planning over large multi-modal time-dependent networks. In: Proc. of the 37th IEEE ICDE, pp. 313–324 (2021)
13. Yuan, Y., et al.: Constrained shortest path query in a large time-dependent graph. Proc. VLDB Endow. **12**(10), 1058–1070 (2019a)
14. Yuan, Y., et al.: Weight-constrained route planning over time-dependent graphs. In: 2019 IEEE 35th ICDE, pp. 914–925 (2019)

Large Language Models II

HALIFacts: Evaluating Large Language Models for Domain-Specific Fact-Checking and Their Carbon Impact

Théophile Mandon[1,3](✉), Sandra Bringay[1,2], Pascal Poncelet[1], and Maximilien Servajean[1,2]

[1] LIRMM - Université de Montpellier, CNRS, Montpellier, France
{theophile.mandon,sandra.bringay,pascal.poncelet,maximilien.servajean}@lirmm.fr
theophile.mandon@lirmm.fr, sandra.bringay@lirmm.fr, pascal.poncelet@lirmm.fr, maximilien.servajean@lirmm.fr

[2] AMIS - Université Montpellier Paul-Valéry, Montpellier, France

[3] ACELYS, Montpellier, France

Abstract. Fact-checking has emerged as a crucial and in-demand field in recent years. Advances in machine learning and pretrained language models have enabled natural language processing techniques to assist in automating this task. Tailored neural architectures have previously been employed for fact-checking to address the dual objectives of veracity prediction and evidence selection. In this work, we demonstrate that comparable or even superior results can be obtained using large language models (LLMs). This is performed at a fraction of the training cost, particularly in terms of CO_2 emissions. We introduce HALIFacts, a LLM training framework that leverages state-of-the-art LLM training techniques, special tokens and prompt engineering for this dual fact-checking task. We show that our approach either outperforms MultiVerS, the current state-of-the-art, or achieves comparable results across three specialised datasets. Furthermore, we demonstrate that it does so while using significantly less training data, resulting in a CO_2 emission cost that is lower by an order of magnitude. The HALIFacts framework is very versatile, and it can thus be applied to any LLM and can scale easily.

Keywords: fact-checking · LLM · carbon analysis · large language model

1 Introduction

Fact-checking has become increasingly important in recent years, especially due to the increased prevalence of misinformation in contexts such as political elections and medical discourse made from unverified or non-expert sources[1]. The

[1] https://www.nytimes.com/2024/01/09/business/media/election-disinformation-2024.html.

I. Awan et al. (Eds.): WISE 2025, LNCS 16368, pp. 179–193, 2026.
https://doi.org/10.1007/978-981-95-7251-9_13

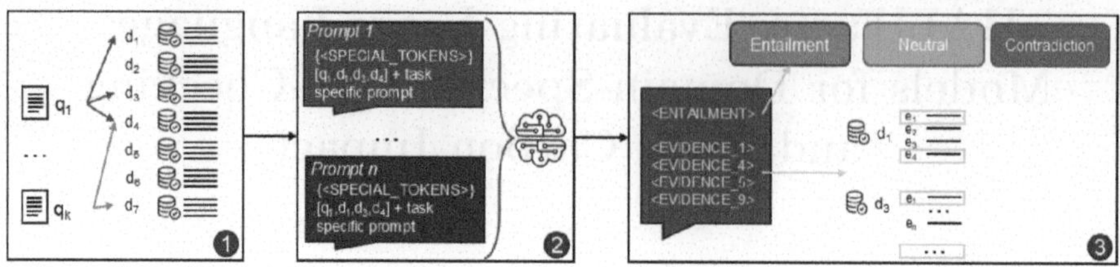

Fig. 1. HALIFacts: fact-checking pipeline (Icons are from the Carbon Design System and reused under the Apache 2 license). (1) For each query q_i, similar documents d_i are retrieved; each d_i is composed of candidate evidence sentences e_i that may or may not address the query. (2) An LLM is finetuned using diverse prompts, with task-specific tokens injected to guide the fact verification process. (3) The model's output—delimited by the injected tokens—is used to infer both the claim's veracity label and the relevant supporting evidence.

emergence of large language models (LLMs) has contributed both to the spread of misinformation and to efforts to counter it, further increasing the need for reliable verification tools. However, manual fact-checking – as carried out by platforms like Snopes[2] – cannot scale to meet the volume of misinformation, due to inherent limitations in human resources. Automation has therefore become essential to support human fact-checkers [15]. One of the most challenging aspects of this process is claim veracity prediction, which continues to drive the development of new model architectures [4].

Fact-checking is a broad and complex task that involves several subtasks. Its complexity depends on the type of data being verified, the underlying technology or the specific step within the verification pipeline. Scientific fact-checking is particularly challenging, as it requires domain-specific knowledge and often relies on evidence spread across multiple sources. Regarding the scientific and medical fields, modern fact-checking models trained on scientific articles have been shown to be insufficient to select evidence relevant to a claim [6].

To address these challenges, we introduce HALIFacts (Heterogeneous Analysis using LLMs with Injected tokens for Fact-checking), a novel approach designed to improve claim verification in closed-domain scientific and biomedical contexts. HALIFacts leverages large language models to perform two critical tasks: (1) identifying the most relevant sentences within a candidate evidence set, and (2) determining whether that evidence supports or contradicts a given claim. The method emphasises both performance and environmental sustainability, aiming to reduce the carbon footprint typically associated with large-scale model training. Figure 1 provides an overview of the fact-checking pipeline and highlights where HALIFacts intervenes in the verification process.

We evaluated HALIFacts on three benchmark datasets from the scientific and biomedical domains. Despite relying on larger models during training, our approach achieved performance comparable to, or exceeding that of recent state-of-

[2] https://www.snopes.com/.

the-art methods. Notably, this was achieved with a significantly reduced carbon footprint, thanks to efficient finetuning strategies and the intrinsic generalisation capabilities of large pretrained LLMs. These results demonstrate that, when properly tuned, large models can deliver high accuracy without incurring excessive environmental cost.

To achieve these results, HALIFacts combines two key techniques: (1) the insertion of special tokens that encode abstract verification concepts, and (2) the use of prompting templates randomly sampled during training. Combining these techniques is our novel contribution to improving fact-checking accuracy. This design encourages the model to learn generalisable verification logic rather than overfit to specific prompt patterns. We add special tokens to elicit task-specific and structured outputs with consistent syntax that are easy to parse, which goes beyond plain prompt engineering.

We conducted extensive ablation studies to quantify the effect of these tokens across multiple LLM backbones, and we compared the CO_2 emissions of our training pipeline with a recent state-of-the-art model. The carbon analysis reports emissions in standard units and documents the underlying assumptions, which enables reproducible comparisons across everyday activities and specialised research workloads. It also provides a clear view of the magnitude of training costs.

Although recent trends emphasise zero-shot or few-shot prompting as more efficient alternatives to finetuning, our results suggest otherwise. In fact, HALIFacts demonstrates that finetuning remains highly relevant for structured tasks such as scientific fact-checking. Moreover, our use of special tokens plays a dual role: encoding verification logic and reducing hallucinations by constraining generation via task-specific signals. Our code is available for reproduction and reuse[3].

2 Related Work

Fact-checking pipelines are typically structured into three main steps: abstract retrieval, sentence selection, and label prediction. Several models have been developed to optimise these steps. VerT5erini [18] trains T5 models to handle all three tasks using generative objectives, each task being handled by a separately finetuned model. ARSJoint [28] introduces a joint learning framework that pools all evidence and uses a dedicated head for each task. Similarly, ParagraphJoint [13] applies a multi-task learning approach at the paragraph level rather than the sentence level. MultiVerS [25] leverages a Longformer model to process multiple pieces of evidence simultaneously, incorporating additional attention mechanisms to enhance interactions between them. Like ARSJoint, it also uses one head per subtask in the pipeline.

These pipelines were designed primarily around smaller models such as BERT [2]. However, larger generative models, such as LLMs, have achieved significant progress in natural language processing. Recent models like LLaMA [3]

[3] https://github.com/theophilem-acelys/HALIFacts.

and Mistral [9] have been shown to achieve state-of-the-art results in various applications. These models rely on distinct attention mechanisms and training corpora, enabling more efficient pretraining and improved generalisation. However, they remain prone to hallucinations [17], where generated content is not grounded in factual knowledge.

To address this, the retrieval-augmented generation (RAG) paradigm [12] was introduced, allowing models to incorporate external sources of information during inference. This approach has proven effective in tasks such as text classification [26] and model pretraining [5].

Building on this, several recent approaches have explored how RAG principles can be applied to fact-checking. For instance, Atlas [8] implements a RAG-like architecture, though it is not explicitly described as such. RAFTS [27] enhances fact verification through contrastive arguments, outperforming prompt-engineered LLMs. Additionally, it improves prompt performance by retrieving similar training examples and incorporating them into the input prompt.

Despite these advances, finetuned transformers still outperform LLMs on many fact-checking tasks, depending on the dataset and language [21]. Even black-box models such as GPT-4 have been evaluated for fact-checking, with studies highlighting differences in error patterns and uncertainty handling compared to traditional transformer-based architectures [16]. This evaluation focused on data beyond GPT-4's training cutoff, particularly in non-English contexts.

Since closed-domain fact-checking already involves a retrieval phase prior to evidence selection and label prediction, RAG-based pipelines are particularly well suited for this task. This insight inspired our approach, which integrates LLMs with retrieval mechanisms to improve sentence selection and veracity prediction, which are two key components of the fact-checking pipeline.

3 Our Approach

3.1 Task Definition

We adopt the scientific fact-checking task defined by SciFact [24]. Given a claim c and a set of abstracts $a \in A$, where each abstract consists of several sentences $a = \{s_1, \ldots, s_n\}$, the system must predict a label $y(c, a) \in \{\text{Entailment}, \text{Contradiction}, \text{Neutral}\}$. It must also identify rationale sentences $R(c, a) = \{s_i, \ldots, s_j\}$ as supporting evidence. These sentences may belong to different abstracts. All information required for prediction is available in advance; the system does not access external web resources.

This closed-domain formulation imposes a different paradigm from traditional web-dependent fact-checking pipelines. While modern systems often rely on zero-shot LLMs that retrieve and process up-to-date web content, our approach instead uses trained transformers with a task-specific architecture tailored to static, trusted corpora. Such a setting is well suited to scientific and medical applications, where curated internal sources are more reliable than general-purpose web searches. It is also particularly valuable when handling confidential or sensitive documents.

3.2 HALIFacts

HALIFacts combines these two fact-checking approaches – the reasoning capabilities of LLMs and model training – to achieve superior performance. HALIFacts combines the reasoning capabilities of LLMs with finetuning techniques to optimise fact-checking performance in closed-domain settings, particularly for scientific and biomedical claims. We therefore train LLMs for our task and explored two strategies to further tailor them to the fact-checking pipeline:

- the introduction of special task-specific tokens learnt during finetuning,
- prompt engineering, using multiple prompt templates during training to encourage generalisation and avoid overfitting to specific phrasings.

We designed our framework to produce generative outputs, thereby enhancing flexibility and meeting fact-checking needs. Our system generates two outputs: a veracity label and a list of supporting evidence sentences. The evidence list may be empty and has no predefined length. Both objectives can be fulfilled through text generation. Sentence selection is particularly well-suited for text generation, as it involves outputs of variable length.

We introduce task-specific tokens – `<ENTAILMENT>`, `<CONTRADICTION>`, `<NEUTRAL>`, `<CLAIM>`, `<EVIDENCE>`, and `<EVID_1>` to `<EVID_i>` – to structure the input and guide the model toward the fact-checking objective. These tokens replace plain-text markers to explicitly encode task semantics while preserving the model's generative and reasoning capabilities. As shown in Fig. 2, they are embedded in the prompt, input, and output to enhance the effectiveness of finetuning.

We trained the LLMs to generate both the veracity label and the corresponding evidence using our set of special tokens. Each task used a distinct subset of tokens: class tokens were used for label prediction, while evidence tokens identified the relevant supporting sentences. This joint generation strategy allows the model to learn both objectives in a unified framework, without requiring separate heads or task-specific architectures. This is particularly advantageous for datasets where neutral labels may or may not be associated with explicit evidence, depending on the annotation scheme.

We designed our prompts based on previously developed tools, such as FactGPT [1], which uses GPT to assist online fact-checkers on Twitter, as well as five approaches proposed at SemEval-2024 [10]. The latter workshop explored the use of LLMs for biomedical natural language inference, i.e. a task closely related to fact-checking. In this context, most submissions developed specific prompts aligned with their workflows, incorporating techniques such as chain-of-thought reasoning, self-consistency, or model ensembling with LLMs and smaller transformers. These prompts were made available in the technical reports or in their code. We also instructed LLMs to generate prompts by specifying the task, input, and output. All of our eight prompts required a LLM assistant to use our special tokens when generating responses. Some prompts presented all instructions first, followed by the data, while others interleaved instructions with the data. Additionally, some prompts incorporated a mix of instructions, data, and examples within the same prompt.

```
Given the following <CLAIM> and <EVIDENCE>:
[INPUT DATA]
Describe the relationship between <CLAIM> and <EVIDENCE>:
answer <ENTAILMENT> if some <EVIDENCE> confirms <CLAIM>,
answer <CONTRADICTION> if some <EVIDENCE> refutes <CLAIM>
else answer <NEUTRAL> if no <EVIDENCE> confirms
or refutes <CLAIM>.
Then add any <EVIDENCE> used for your reasoning.
```

Fig. 2. Example of a prompt used in our system, with our added special tokens in tag format

In addition to prompt engineering and other textual data preprocessing, we integrated different prompts into the training loop. This was achieved by randomly selecting a prompting template from our predefined list of eight prompts and applying it to the examples before tokenization. This step was performed prior to tokenization, rather than on-the-fly during training, in order to reduce the training time by tokenizing all examples only once.

While these modifications were intended for finetuned models, we also evaluated a zero-shot pipeline using the prompt that yielded the best results during finetuning. This pipeline did not incorporate our special tokens, as it was not trained on them. Instead, we replaced the special tokens with their equivalent English-language text, since the data were in English and LLMs are primarily trained on English. This approach therefore appeared to be better suited to a zero-shot setting.

4 Results

4.1 Experimental Setup

Datasets. We compared our approach with several baseline models and the state-of-the-art model across three datasets: SciFact [24], HealthVer [19], and HealthFC [23]. Additionally, we used FEVER [22], i.e. a general-domain dataset based on Wikipedia, for model pretraining in some of our experiments. These datasets were selected because they all include veracity classification and evidence selection, the two key subtasks in fact-checking. Furthermore, the datasets operate in a closed-domain setting, where all relevant knowledge is contained within a fact database. Thus there is no need for an external retrieval, such as search engines. This feature is particularly relevant in domain-specific fact-checking, such as in a biomedical context, where online information may be less reliable than institutional sources, such as patient records.

Baseline Models. We compared our approach with MultiVerS, the state-of-the-art biomedical fact-checking model. Based on the Longformer architecture, this model is specifically designed for fact-checking and has achieved state-of-the-art results on several biomedical datasets.

We assessed HALIFacts using several LLMs. The following LLMs were evaluated within our framework:

- Mistral v0.2: An open-source European model that has demonstrated state-of-the-art performance under various generative benchmarks.
- LLaMA 3.1: The LLaMA family has achieved strong results across multiple model sizes, enabling a wider range of experiments.
- DeepSeek R1 distilled into LLaMA 3.1: DeepSeek models have recently gained traction in the community due to their reasoning capabilities. Since fact-checking relies on reasoning, we included the smaller distilled models in our experiments.

Implementation Details. We finetuned our models in two stages: first on a modified version of FEVER with balanced classes, and then on the target dataset. This balanced FEVER dataset was created by selecting the first 30,000 records from each class. All training was performed using low-rank adaptation (LoRA) [7], and we leveraged quantized models when available. The initial training on balanced FEVER was conducted for one epoch, using a cosine scheduler with a learning rate of 5e−05, a weight decay of 0.05, and LoRA-specific hyperparameters: $R = 25$, $\alpha = 16$, and a dropout rate of 0.1. For finetuning of the target dataset, we used the same hyperparameters, except for an extended training duration of 15 epochs. We used CodeCarbon to monitor CO_2 equivalent emissions[4].

The LoRA hyperparameters were selected from the default configuration. The other hyperparameters were selected after a brief hyperparameter search on LLaMA-1B during which we tested five different learning rate values and five different epoch numbers. We applied the selected hyperparameters consistently across all training runs and models. Since pretraining lasted only one epoch, we maintained the same learning rate for both pretraining and finetuning.

We re-ran the training for MultiVerS using the official codebase of the authors[5]. We used the same settings reported in their paper and we used default values for parameters that were not mentioned in the paper. All finetuning was conducted using their publicly released pretrained model. Although we followed this procedure, we obtained slightly different results (±5%) than those reported in their paper.

4.2 Performance Results

Performance results are presented in Table 1. All experiments were performed only once. The results indicate that the HALIFacts performance was comparable to that of the state-of-the-art MultiVerS model, despite being finetuned only on the target dataset without prior training on a larger dataset. This further highlights that LLMs require less data due to their generalisation capabilities, though they still require more parameters to support this generalisation.

Brief pretraining (one epoch) led to slight improvements, especially for the claim veracity prediction task. The sentence selection task appeared to be less

[4] https://github.com/mlCO2/codecarbon/.

[5] https://github.com/dwadden/multivers/.

Table 1. Performance assessments with different biomedical fact-checking datasets. The best results are shown in **bold**, and the second-best results are underlined. The first three columns show the results on the classification task on all three datasets, while the remaining columns show the results on the sentence selection task for these same three datasets. The experiment names have been shortened: HALI-L1 means HALIFacts using LLaMA-1B, HALI-L8q is HALIFacts using LLaMA-8B-quant, HALI-DL8q represents our framework using DeepSeek-LLaMA-8B-quant, and HALI-M7 is the version using Mistral-7B.

Models	Macro F1			Sentence selection F1		
	SciFact	HealthVer	HealthFC	SciFact	HealthVer	HealthFC
pretraining + finetuning						
MultiVerS	0.68	**0.68**	0.75	0.72	0.69	**0.60**
HALI-L1	0.35	0.50	0.47	0.61	0.77	0.29
HALI-L8q	0.49	0.50	0.27	0.64	0.66	0.29
HALI-DL8q	0.46	0.58	0.41	0.74	0.75	0.32
HALI-M7	**0.69**	0.67	**0.81**	0.81	**0.89**	0.42
only finetuning						
HALI-L1	0.45	0.59	0.41	0.66	0.86	0.32
HALI-L8q	0.48	**0.68**	0.78	0.64	0.85	0.26
HALI-DL8q	0.37	0.54	0.42	0.65	0.83	0.24
HALI-M7	0.61	0.62	0.80	**0.85**	0.88	0.48
zero-shot						
LLaMA-1B	0.20	0.23	0.16	0.48	0.36	0.42
LLaMA-8B-quant	0.20	0.23	0.27	0.46	0.36	0.27
DeepSeek-LLaMA-8B-quant	0.36	0.37	0.15	0.48	0.52	0.43
Mistral-7B	0.44	0.20	0.32	0.49	0.41	0.27

impacted. We believe that two factors could explain this trend. Either this pretraining was too short to really improve these metrics, or the FEVER dataset is more suited for claim veracity prediction than for sentence selection, thereby improving the results on that subdomain while not impacting the other.

Our analysis of LLaMA models showed that increasing the number of parameters improved results while reducing the training effort required. The performance of the 8-billion-parameter model was comparable to the 1-billion-parameter model, despite being finetuned only on the target dataset. In contrast, the smaller model required both pretraining and finetuning. Moreover, the DeepSeek-distilled model obtained lower results than those of its base versions. While it has shown strong performance in other tasks, it may be less suitable for fact-checking.

Overall, our trained LLMs outperformed the MultiVerS model for sentence selection while remaining comparable for label prediction. With two trainings and Mistral-7B used as the base model, HALIFacts outperformed MultiVerS in four of six tasks. Although the label classification performance margins were narrow, our approach substantially outperformed MultiVerS on the sentence selection task on two datasets. However, MultiVerS significantly outperformed HALIFacts on the third dataset.

We hypothesise that HALIFacts was less effective on sentence selection for HealthFC because this dataset often includes more textual evidence per claim than the others. This made it harder for the LLM to keep track of all the evidence and mark it as relevant or not. In contrast, MultiVerS is specifically tailored for that task, so it is better suited for handling longer texts.

Another notable difference between HALIFacts and MultiVerS is that MultiVerS performance seemed consistent throughout the two tasks, with close F1 scores, while HALIFacts performance results were inconsistent. MultiVerS demonstrated similar F1 scores for both sentence selection and veracity prediction, in contrast, HALIFacts showed less consistency between these subtasks. This was probably because MultiVerS is trained using several, equally weighted losses for each objective. Thus, it aims to optimise all tasks in equal measure. In contrast, our method uses a standard generative loss function that does not explicitly distinguish between tasks, which can hence lead to unbalanced metrics.

Finally, our zero-shot results were relatively low, suggesting that this strategy may not be well suited for this context. However, the DeepSeek model distilled into LLaMA achieved relatively strong zero-shot performance, with a smaller performance gap between zero-shot and fine-tuned results compared to other models.

4.3 Ablation Study

We assessed the impact of various techniques used to train LLMs for label prediction in scientific fact-checking. Specifically, we analysed the effects of finetuning and pretraining, special token integration, prompting strategies, and their combined use on veracity label prediction performance. The ablation results are shown in Table 2.

Table 2. Ablation study on SciFact using LLaMA-8B-quant as backbone model.

Models	Macro F1
pretraining + finetuning	
additions applied to both trainings unless specified	
base	<u>0.61</u>
+ random prompt training (RPT)	0.54
+ RPT only for pretraining	**0.63**
+ special tokens	0.49
+ RPT only for pretraining & special tokens	0.42
+ RPT & special tokens	0.38
finetuned	
base	<u>0.47</u>
+ random prompt training (RPT)	0.37
+ special tokens	**0.48**
+ RPT & special tokens	0.42

The addition of random prompt training did not yield the results we expected, i.e. lower results were obtained in all situations except for pretraining without special tokens. Although mixing prompts seemed like a promising way to encourage task generalisation, we hypothesise that the model's original pretraining already provided sufficient generalisation capabilities. Random prompt training merely added a few less efficient prompts into the training loop, thus reducing its impact and effects. Similar effects were observed regardless of the presence of special tokens.

The benefits of adding special tokens were not clear-cut. These special tokens seemed to slightly improve the results with only one finetuning. In both instances where fine-tuning was performed without pretraining, the inclusion of special tokens resulted in improved performance. Otherwise, the addition of tokens seemed to dampen the pretraining and finetuning results. With these two trainings, the special tokens significantly lowered the performance and did not seem to have the expected positive effect.

We hypothesise that the reduced efficiency of special tokens stems from the different nature of the two training datasets. The FEVER dataset is mainly geared towards veracity prediction, the sentence selection objective being easier in this dataset than in the three target datasets and thus less important during the training. Moreover, FEVER contains less evidence irrelevant to veracity prediction. However, SciFact, and all the target datasets, have a more diverse

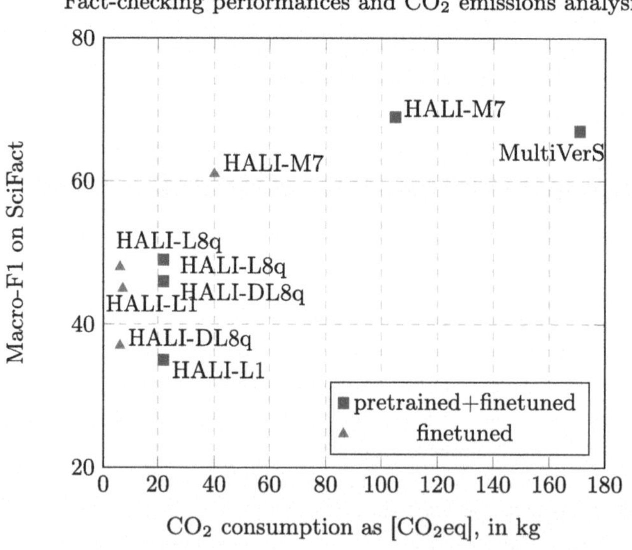

Fig. 3. Comparative CO_2 emissions and SciFact results analysis on different versions of our pipeline HALIFacts and state-of-the-art MultiVerS. Higher macro-F1 values reflect better performance, while lower CO_2 consumption indicates better training time and less pollution.

complexity, as both objectives seem equally difficult. This might have been the root cause of the differences in performance of the special tokens with or without pretraining.

Pretraining on the balanced version of FEVER enhanced the veracity prediction performance of SciFact, as demonstrated here. Pretraining improved performance in most cases. Interestingly, pretraining was more effective without the inclusion of special tokens. Pretraining with special tokens slightly improved the results in one situation while it slightly worsened them in another. However, pretraining without special tokens consistently resulted in significant performance gains across all backbones.

In this ablation study, we have assessed the benefits and drawbacks of our addition of special tokens and random prompt training. The results indicated that the addition of random prompt training did not improve them. However, the addition of special tokens seemed to slightly improve the results only when using one finetuning, as they did not show the same behaviour when the model was first pretrained and then finetuned.

5 Carbon Emissions Analysis

We monitor the carbon footprint of the selected experiments to identify the model that achieved the best performance with a reasonable environmental impact. All training was conducted using two A100 GPUs and 16 AMD Milan EPYC 7543 CPUs. We compared the emissions generated during training for all models tested in our performance analysis, while considering both finetuning and pretraining settings.

We evaluated only the training footprint specific to each method, excluding the carbon cost of general pretraining. For MultiVerS, we monitored emissions from pretraining on three datasets over three epochs, and the finetuning emissions on the target datasets over 20 epochs. We did not account for emissions related to Longformer pretraining on non-fact-checking tasks.

Similarly, for our method, we excluded the carbon footprint associated with general LLM pretraining or any operations performed before our use of the model, such as quantization. However, we measured emissions from the one-epoch pretraining on FEVER, as well as the 15-epoch finetuning on the SciFact dataset across all configurations.

We conducted that experiment on a broad range of backbone models to get a better overview of the impact of the different choices made during our pipeline. First, we examined the effect of the model size, while checking if the models were quantized or not, mainly to highlight the differences between quantized 8-billion-parameter models and non-quantized 1-billion-parameter models. Then Mistral and LLaMA were compared to assess the differences in model architecture. Thirdly, we evaluated the impact of pretraining on both performance and carbon emissions. These results are presented in Fig. 3.

We highlighted the efficiency of quantized models: the emissions of quantized 8-billion-parameter models were similar to those of regular 1-billion-parameter models. Mistral, with 7 billion parameters and no quantization, consumed over sixfold more energy than the quantized 8-billion-parameter models.

Despite its lighter architecture, MultiVerS consumed more energy than any configuration of our pipeline. This was mainly due to its extensive pretraining, which involved three datasets over three epochs. By comparison, our pipeline used only one of those datasets for a single epoch. We hypothesise that similar performance could be achieved with shorter pretraining owing to the inherent capabilities of LLMs.

Moreover, when applied to quantized 8-billion-parameter models, our framework consumed less energy than MultiVerS finetuning alone (excluding prior pretraining). This suggests that comparable performance could be attained at significantly lower computational and environmental cost—even with basic finetuning.

6 Limitations

Despite focusing on automated fact-checking, our approach exhibits limitations in certain areas critical to this task. Although we trained and assessed our model on a small dataset, our experiments were restricted to scientific fact-checking, and we did not assess its applicability to other domains. Fact-checking is a broad field, and other subdomains of fact-checking, while distinct and less knowledge-intensive than scientific fact-checking, remain important and should not be overlooked. Furthermore, we ran each experiment only once, which means that some favourable results may reflect random variation rather than, or in addition to, the strength of the method.

Although we use generative models for this task, they are not prompted to produce explanations, although such outputs could be advantageous to human fact-checkers [11]. Providing justifications might also improve model performance, as demonstrated by the effectiveness of chain-of-thought (CoT) prompting techniques.

7 Conclusion

This paper introduces HALIFacts, a lightweight framework for training LLMs on fact-checking tasks. Leveraging modern training and optimisation techniques, it efficiently trains models to jointly learn two objectives: veracity prediction and sentence selection – while preserving the generative capabilities of the underlying LLM. The use of special tokens and prompt engineering allows for better results.

Using a backbone of Mistral v0.2 7B, HALIFacts achieves better results than MultiVerS, the current state-of-the-art, on four out of six measured tasks using a combination of pretraining and finetuning. Additionally, HALIFacts still achieves superior results on three out of six tasks even without pretraining. Furthermore, results indicate that even in the full setup – pretraining and finetuning – HALIFacts obtains reduced CO_2 emissions compared to MultiVerS.

Future work could explore several extensions of our framework. A key direction is to automate fact-checking while also providing explanations for automated decisions, in order to support human fact-checkers [20]. Although LLMs are well suited for this purpose, our current framework deliberately omits explanation generation to mitigate the risks of hallucinations. Implementing LLMs in a multi-agent setup could be another promising direction for future work, as this method has already shown potential in fact-checking contexts [14]. For instance, LLM agents could generate clarifying questions about claims and evidence to better assess the veracity and identify supporting content.

Acknowledgments. This work was granted access to the HPC/AI resources of IDRIS under the allocation 20XX- AD011014040R2 made by GENCI.

Disclosure of Interests. The authors have no competing interests to declare that are relevant to the content of this article.

References

1. Choi, E.C., Ferrara, E.: Fact-GPT: fact-checking augmentation via claim matching with LLMs. In: Companion Proceedings of the ACM Web Conference 2024. Association for Computing Machinery (2024)
2. Devlin, J., Chang, M.W., Lee, K., Toutanova, K.: BERT: pre-training of deep bidirectional transformers for language understanding. In: Proceedings of the 2019 Conference of the North American Chapter of the Association for Computational Linguistics (2019)
3. Dubey, A., Jauhri, A., Pandey, A., Kadian, A., et al.: The LLaMA 3 herd of models (2024)
4. Eldifrawi, I., Wang, S., Trabelsi, A.: Automated justification production for claim veracity in fact checking: a survey on architectures and approaches. In: Proceedings of the 62nd Annual Meeting of the Association for Computational Linguistics. Association for Computational Linguistics (2024)
5. Guu, K., Lee, K., Tung, Z., Pasupat, P., Chang, M.: Retrieval augmented language model pre-training. In: Proceedings of the 37th International Conference on Machine Learning. PMLR (2020)
6. Hafid, S., Ammar, W., Bringay, S., Todorov, K.: Cite-worthiness detection on social media: a preliminary study. In: International Workshop on Natural Scientific Language Processing and Research Knowledge Graphs. Springer, Cham (2024)
7. Hu, E.J., et al.: LoRA: low-rank adaptation of large language models. In: International Conference on Learning Representations (2022)
8. Izacard, G., et al.: Atlas: Few-shot learning with retrieval augmented language models. J. Mach. Learn. Res. **24**(251) (2023)
9. Jiang, A.Q., et al.: Mistral 7b (2023)
10. Jullien, M., Valentino, M., Freitas, A.: SemEval-2024 task 2: safe biomedical natural language inference for clinical trials. In: Proceedings of the 18th International Workshop on Semantic Evaluation (SemEval-2024). Association for Computational Linguistics (2024)
11. Kim, K., Lee, S., Huang, K.H., Chan, H.P., Li, M., Ji, H.: Can LLMs produce faithful explanations for fact-checking? Towards faithful explainable fact-checking via multi-agent debate (2024)

12. Lewis, P., t al.: Retrieval-augmented generation for knowledge-intensive nlp tasks. In: Proceedings of the 34th International Conference on Neural Information Processing Systems, NIPS 2020 (2020)
13. Li, X., Burns, G., Peng, N.: A paragraph-level multi-task learning model for scientific fact-verification (2021)
14. Li, X., Zhang, Y., Malthouse, E.C.: Large language model agentic approach to fact checking and fake news detection. In: ECAI 2024. IOS Press (2024)
15. Nakov, P., et al.: Automated fact-checking for assisting human fact-checkers. In: Proceedings of the Thirtieth International Joint Conference on Artificial Intelligence, IJCAI-21. International Joint Conferences on Artificial Intelligence Organization (2021)
16. Pelrine, K., et al.: Towards reliable misinformation mitigation: generalization, uncertainty, and GPT-4. In: Proceedings of the 2023 Conference on Empirical Methods in Natural Language Processing. Association for Computational Linguistics (2023)
17. Peng, B., et al.: Check your facts and try again: Improving large language models with external knowledge and automated feedback (2023)
18. Pradeep, R., Ma, X., Nogueira, R., Lin, J.: Scientific claim verification with VerT5erini. In: Proceedings of the 12th International Workshop on Health Text Mining and Information Analysis. Association for Computational Linguistics (2021)
19. Sarrouti, M., Ben Abacha, A., Mrabet, Y., Demner-Fushman, D.: Evidence-based fact-checking of health-related claims. In: Findings of the Association for Computational Linguistics: EMNLP 2021. Association for Computational Linguistics (2021)
20. Schmitt, V., et al.: Evaluating human-centered ai explanations: introduction of an XAI evaluation framework for fact-checking. In: Proceedings of the 3rd ACM International Workshop on Multimedia AI against Disinformation. Association for Computing Machinery (2024)
21. Setty, V.: Surprising efficacy of fine-tuned transformers for fact-checking over larger language models. In: Proceedings of the 47th International ACM SIGIR Conference on Research and Development in Information Retrieval, SIGIR 2024. Association for Computing Machinery (2024)
22. Thorne, J., Vlachos, A., Christodoulopoulos, C., Mittal, A.: FEVER: a large-scale dataset for fact extraction and VERification. In: Proceedings of the 2018 Conference of the North American Chapter of the Association for Computational Linguistics: Human Language Technologies, Volume 1 (Long Papers). Association for Computational Linguistics (2018)
23. Vladika, J., Schneider, P., Matthes, F.: HealthFC: verifying health claims with evidence-based medical fact-checking. In: Proceedings of the 2024 Joint International Conference on Computational Linguistics, Language Resources and Evaluation (LREC-COLING 2024). ELRA and ICCL (2024)
24. Wadden, D., et al.: Fact or fiction: verifying scientific claims. In: Proceedings of the 2020 Conference on Empirical Methods in Natural Language Processing (EMNLP). Association for Computational Linguistics (2020)
25. Wadden, D., Lo, K., Wang, L.L., Cohan, A., Beltagy, I., Hajishirzi, H.: MultiVerS: improving scientific claim verification with weak supervision and full-document context. In: Findings of the Association for Computational Linguistics: NAACL 2022. Association for Computational Linguistics (2022)

26. Xu, R., Yu, Y., Ho, J., Yang, C.: Weakly-supervised scientific document classification via retrieval-augmented multi-stage training. In: Proceedings of the 46th International ACM SIGIR Conference on Research and Development in Information Retrieval, SIGIR 2023. Association for Computing Machinery (2023)
27. Yue, Z., Zeng, H., Shang, L., Liu, Y., Zhang, Y., Wang, D.: Retrieval augmented fact verification by synthesizing contrastive arguments. In: Proceedings of the 62nd Annual Meeting of the Association for Computational Linguistics (Volume 1: Long Papers). Association for Computational Linguistics (2024)
28. Zhang, Z., Li, J., Fukumoto, F., Ye, Y.: Abstract, rationale, stance: a joint model for scientific claim verification. In: Proceedings of the 2021 Conference on Empirical Methods in Natural Language Processing (2021)

A Hybrid AI System for Evaluating Media Representation of Violence and Inequality

Zhan Liu(✉) and Nicole Glassey Balet

Media Innovation Lab, University of Applied Sciences and Arts Western Switzerland HES-SO Valais-Wallis, Sierre, Switzerland
{zhan.liu,nicole.glassey}@hevs.ch

Abstract. Media coverage of gender-based violence plays a critical role in shaping public understanding and policy, yet often perpetuates stereotypes and biases. We present a hybrid AI approach to analyze how French-language media represent gender-based violence. Combining rule-based Natural Language Processing (NLP) with Large Language Models (LLMs), the system applies expert-defined criteria across analytical categories, with each criterion assigned to the most effective method based on empirical performance. This strategy achieves 87.1% overall accuracy, surpassing previous models. GPT-4 led general performance (77.9%), while NLP delivered exceptional results in structural and language-sensitive categories. Our findings demonstrate that combining complementary AI techniques enables near-human accuracy in evaluating media narratives and contributes to advancing web-based text mining for socially relevant media analysis.

Keywords: Hybrid AI · Large language models · Natural language processing · Web text mining · Social bias in media representation · Gender-based violence

1 Introduction

Media representation of gender remains a critical factor in shaping public perceptions and reinforcing—or challenging—societal norms. Despite increased attention to gender equality, media coverage of gender-based violence (GBV) continues to exhibit stereotypes, bias, and misrepresentation, necessitating rigorous scrutiny and systematic evaluation methodologies. As [4] demonstrate, news media consistently produce content reinforcing traditional gender hierarchies despite growing awareness of inequality issues.

According to [19], GBV affects roughly one in three women globally, ranging from psychological abuse to femicide. Media portrayals significantly influence public understanding of violence's causes, severity, and solutions. [11] highlight that sensational coverage of isolated incidents often distorts reality and hinders effective policy responses.

Swiss media outlets differ markedly in their GBV framing, showing variable adherence to ethical guidelines from organizations such as the Council of Europe-

I. Awan et al. (Eds.): WISE 2025, LNCS 16368, pp. 194–209, 2026.
https://doi.org/10.1007/978-981-95-7251-9_14

[7] and [9]. Systematic implementation and monitoring remain limited, creating a clear opportunity for scalable technological solutions, precisely the challenge addressed in this research.

Current methods for evaluating gender representation suffer from three main limitations: (1) lack of comprehensive, standardized evaluation frameworks, (2) limited understanding of how different AI techniques handle culturally-specific gender narratives, and (3) absence of hybrid approaches integrating complementary strengths of traditional NLP and advanced LLM technologies.

To address these gaps, this study introduces a structured taxonomy refining analytical criteria, significantly broadening coverage of gender representation dimensions. It also compares four prominent large language models—GPT-4, Llama 3, Gemma 3, and DeepSeek R1—to elucidate trade-offs in performance and accessibility. Finally, the proposed hybrid analytical strategy optimizes the integration of NLP and LLM methods based on empirical effectiveness, substantially improving accuracy and closely approaching expert human assessments.

Results show no single AI approach excels across all evaluation dimensions. Traditional NLP methods outperform LLMs in structural analysis, while LLMs excel at identifying implicit bias and contextual framing. Among tested models, GPT-4 achieved the highest overall accuracy, though open-source alternatives like Gemma demonstrated competitive performance, suggesting viable pathways for more accessible implementations.

Collectively, these contributions yield a robust, hybrid AI framework, significantly enhancing analytical capabilities in evaluating media narratives on gender-based violence.

2 Related Work

2.1 Gender Stereotypes and Media Representation

A substantial body of research demonstrates that news media coverage of gender-based violence (GBV) often reinforces harmful stereotypes. For example, political discourse in news frequently assigns gendered blame [3]. Many narratives perpetuate victim-blaming tropes [10], and news reports often emphasize individual pathology in GBV cases rather than examining broader societal factors [5]. These patterns perpetuate the misconception that incidents of GBV are isolated occurrences rather than manifestations of systemic inequality. Such biases also extend beyond textual content. AI-generated news imagery, for instance, overrepresents men and frequently portrays women in passive roles [6], indicating that emerging digital media platforms replicate the same gender stereotypes found in traditional journalism.

Structural factors within the media industry may further contribute to biased representation. Women occupy only about one-quarter of top editorial roles in news organizations, despite comprising roughly 40% of the journalism workforce [16]. This imbalance likely influences which voices and perspectives dominate coverage. These representational problems are deeply intertwined with organizational cultures and professional norms [9], implying that remedies must involve changes at both individual and institutional levels. However, despite extensive documentation of media biases, there is still no comprehensive framework to systematically evaluate the nuanced and implicit ways GBV is framed in media coverage.

2.2 AI Applications in Media Analysis

The rise of artificial intelligence (AI) and NLP has opened new opportunities for large-scale media analysis, but these tools are not inherently neutral and often reflect or amplify biases from their training data [15], highlighting the need for socio-technical caution.

News organizations are increasingly deploying AI for various newsroom tasks [12], but this adoption often occurs without sufficient scrutiny of algorithmic biases or ethical implications. Interviews with journalists indicate that many newsrooms implement AI without fully understanding its limitations [17]—an oversight that can inadvertently perpetuate the inequalities these tools are meant to mitigate. As a result, most AI-driven media analysis systems fail to account for the nuanced cultural context of gender narratives, especially in multilingual or sensitive settings.

2.3 Challenges in Automated Content Evaluation

Despite progress, significant challenges persist in the development of automated systems to evaluate media content for gender bias. Bias can infiltrate every stage of the AI pipeline, often in ways that are not transparent [14]. LLMs may further amplify these biases, acting as "stochastic parrots" that reproduce biased patterns without true understanding [2]. For example, ChatGPT has been observed to default to male pronouns for "programmer" and female for "nurse" even when instructed otherwise [18]. Such outcomes illustrate the limitations of LLMs in producing unbiased language and underscore the need for continual bias evaluation and mitigation.

Frameworks like the Council of Europe's guidelines [7] provide benchmarks for fair and sensitive reporting, but translating these principles into concrete, automatable criteria remains difficult. Furthermore, few approaches combine rule-based NLP with LLMs, so subtle framing biases often go undetected. Hence, methods that operationalize ethical standards and integrate NLP and LLM approaches are crucial for advancing automated content evaluation.

2.4 Evolution from Our Previous Work

The current study substantially extends previous research [13], which introduced a preliminary NLP-LLM hybrid approach for evaluating media coverage of gender-based violence. While that work demonstrated the potential of hybrid methods (76% accuracy across 27 evaluation criteria), several critical limitations remain.

First, our earlier framework used a simplistic binary assignment of criteria (NLP vs. GPT), resulting in suboptimal alignments. We now empirically assign each criterion to its most effective method, greatly improving performance alignment. Second, the prior study relied only on GPT-4. We now evaluate multiple LLMs (Llama 3-12B, Gemma 3-12B, DeepSeek-R1-14B), highlighting performance, cost, and accessibility trade-offs between commercial and open-source models. Third, the previous work focused mainly on explicit content. The current framework expands to 32 criteria in 9 categories to capture implicit bias, linguistic framing, and systemic patterns. Finally, our hybrid method reaches 87.1% overall accuracy, an 11-point gain over the prior 76%, demonstrating the effectiveness of this optimized approach.

2.5 Research Gap and Contributions

Based on this literature review, we identify three primary research gaps:

1. Most existing studies focus narrowly on particular aspects of gender bias without offering an integrated framework capable of holistic evaluation.
2. Comparative evaluations of emerging open-source LLMs for media analysis (especially in non-English contexts like Swiss French journalism) remain scarce.
3. Prior work typically uses either traditional NLP or LLMs; few employ a hybrid approach leveraging each method's strengths.

This paper addresses these gaps by introducing a comprehensive, taxonomically structured evaluation framework, benchmarking commercial and open-source LLMs alongside traditional NLP tools, and implementing a hybrid methodology designed to maximize reliability and accuracy in gender representation analysis.

3 Dataset Description

3.1 Data Collection and Sources

To capture the evolving landscape of GBV representation in Swiss French-language media, we expanded our data collection approach both in scope and in methodology. Our previous study relied on a narrower selection of media sources and keyword-based retrieval; the current study adopts a more comprehensive, multi-source strategy integrating both mainstream and emerging platforms.

We sourced articles from the Swissdox database, complemented by API integrations with digital news outlets and monitoring tools from gender equality organizations. This triangulated method enhanced both the breadth and timeliness of our corpus, allowing us to include dynamic content such as comment sections and associated multimedia.

Our dataset spans from 2022 to early 2025, encompassing three full years of news coverage. We collected 5,517 French-language articles from 25 Swiss media outlets. In addition to our previous sources, we added six prominent digital-native platforms: *M Le Média*, *Heidi.news*, *La Côte*, *Blue News*, *aJour*, and *Frapp*. These platforms bring editorial diversity and introduce alternative framing practices that enrich our analysis.

This expansion significantly improves upon our previous dataset (1,752 articles, 19 outlets, 2022), offering greater size, media diversity, and temporal coverage for identifying longitudinal patterns in GBV representation.

3.2 Data Preprocessing and Refinement

We implemented a multi-phase preprocessing pipeline to ensure the dataset's quality and relevance, building on earlier improvements in semantic filtering and normalization.

- Semantic filtering: We augmented keyword matching with word embeddings and semantic networks to capture thematically related content, improving recall for GBV content expressed implicitly or in varied language.
- Relevance scoring and review: Each article received an automated relevance score, with low-scoring ones flagged for manual review to eliminate false positives.
- Metadata extraction: Using source-specific parsers, we standardized article metadata into 14 structured fields (e.g., date, source, section, tags) and noted whether articles contained images or videos for potential future analysis.
- Deduplication: We removed exact and near-duplicate articles (e.g., syndicated content with minor edits) using a similarity detection algorithm.

This preprocessing yielded 3,684 unique and relevant articles with complete metadata. Article lengths ranged from 43 to 1,919 words (mean 457), spanning brief news items to in-depth analyses. This diverse corpus provides a robust basis for evaluating GBV representation across content types.

3.3 Annotation Process

To support model training and evaluation, we developed a comprehensive annotation framework based on our taxonomy of 32 expert-defined criteria across 9 categories. We created detailed annotation guidelines with specific examples and edge cases for each criterion. Each of the 32 expert-defined criteria was operationalized as a numeric weighting criterion using a binary scale. This uniform coding scheme ensures consistency across criteria and allows straightforward computation of evaluation metrics such as accuracy and F1-score. [1] provide methodological foundations for assessing inter-coder agreement in computational linguistics, which we applied to ensure reliability in our annotation process.

A team of three subject-matter experts in journalism, gender studies, and media analysis annotated the dataset. For the gold-standard test set (300 randomly selected articles), each article was independently labeled by at least two annotators. Inter-annotator agreement, measured using Cohen's kappa, averaged

0.81, indicating substantial agreement across criteria. For criteria with lower initial agreement ($\kappa < 0.7$), calibration sessions were held to resolve discrepancies and refine the annotation guide. This iterative process improved consistency without oversimplifying expert judgment.

The remaining articles were distributed for single annotation, with 20% overlap to monitor reliability throughout. This dataset serves two functions: as ground truth for evaluating model performance and as a source of in-context examples for few-shot prompting in the hybrid framework.

4 Methodology and Implementation

4.1 Expanded Evaluation Framework

We expanded our previous evaluation framework from 27 to 32 criteria, organized into nine categories to enable more targeted and interpretable analysis of GBV media coverage:

1. Classification and Context of Violence (**CCV**): Identification and contextualization of different forms of violence.
2. Article Structure and Presentation (**ASP**): Headline framing, article layout, and citation practices.
3. Reporting Balance (**RB**) – Narrative symmetry between victims and perpetrators.
4. Societal Context (**SC**): Broader social framing and systemic patterns.
5. Victim Characterization (**VC**): Description of victims, including implicit victim-blaming.
6. Perpetrator Characterization (**PC**): How perpetrators are described or justified.
7. Power Dynamics (**PD**): References to control, coercion, or power imbalances.
8. Psychological and Health Factors (**PHF**): Inclusion and framing of mental health or addiction.
9. Linguistic Choices (**LC**): Language analysis, including euphemisms, passive constructions, and emotional tone.

Each criterion is accompanied by guidelines and examples to ensure consistent coding. For example, Linguistic Choices goes beyond word-level analysis to examine how grammar and metaphors shape narratives, revealing subtle biases.

Table 1 presents the distribution of our criteria across categories, showing actual criteria from our framework.

In our hybrid approach, each evaluation criterion is handled by the method (rule-based NLP or LLM) that performs best for it. For instance, in Societal Context, statistical references are captured by NLP, whereas nuanced cultural references (e.g., rape culture) are better interpreted by an LLM. This allocation leverages the precision of deterministic NLP for explicit content and the contextual understanding of LLMs for implicit narratives, yielding a more nuanced and robust analysis than a single-method approach.

Table 1. Distribution of evaluation criteria by category

Category	Count	Example criteria
CCV	3	Type and context of violence, mention of femicide
ASP	5	Title framing, sourcing, case linkage, accuracy
RB	3	Expert consultation, victim resources
SC	4	Statistical framing, systemic context, cultural references
VC	4	Victim behavior, identity, consequences
PC	5	Perpetrator identity, language, consequences
PD	3	Control relationships, escalation patterns
PHF	3	Mental health, substance use, trauma
LC	2	Minimization vs. explicit framing

4.2 Technical Implementation

We adopted a hybrid system architecture that strategically assigns each criterion to either traditional NLP methods or LLMs, depending on which approach yields better performance for that specific task.

Processing Architecture. Figure 1 illustrates the full processing architecture of our hybrid evaluation system. The system processing pipeline begins with article ingestion and tokenization. Articles then proceed through two parallel analytical pipelines:

- A rule-based NLP pipeline, built in Python using libraries such as SpaCy, NLTK, and scikit-learn.
- An LLM analysis pipeline, integrating multiple models including GPT-4, Llama 3-12B, Gemma 3-12B, and DeepSeek-R1-14B.

Key components of the architecture include:

- Embedding search and key phrase extraction to identify relevant content segments.
- Dynamic prompt generation, incorporating evaluation feedback for continuous optimization.
- Model-specific processing, using standardized few-shot prompting strategies for LLMs.
- Results integration, applying a weighted ensemble logic—using criterion-specific weights derived from validation accuracy—to consolidate outputs.

This architecture promotes modular scalability and analytical flexibility, allowing future model upgrades or the addition of other language pipelines. As shown in Fig. 1, the system integrates both rule-based and language model-driven processes, from article ingestion and segmentation to final evaluation synthesis, with feedback loops for continual prompt optimization during development and domain adaptation for evaluation. Domain adaptation here means tailoring prompts and instructions to the task, not fine-tuning model weights.

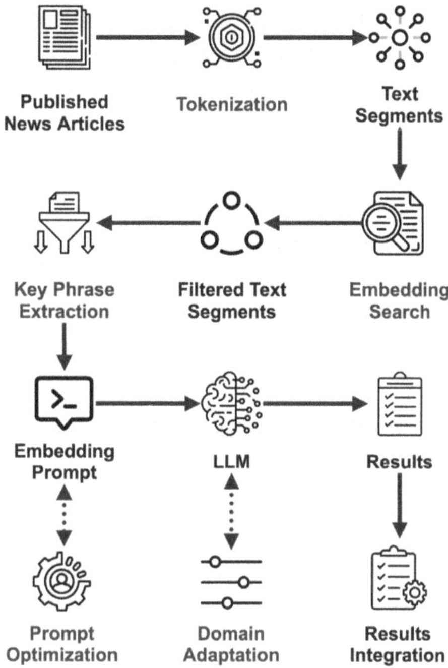

Fig. 1. System architecture integrating NLP and LLM pipelines.

NLP Implementation. For the 14 criteria suited to structured and terminological analysis, we used a deterministic NLP approach. Components included:

- French-language lemmatization and stemming.
- Named Entity Recognition with custom tags relevant to GBV.
- TF-IDF and contextual embeddings for statistical analysis.
- Custom sentiment calibration models for sensitive topics.

These techniques proved especially effective in structurally well-defined categories, where traditional NLP methods achieved high accuracy—up to 96% for article-related structure and 99% for linguistic framing—demonstrating the strength of rule-based approaches when patterns are explicit and consistent.

The high performance in these categories can be attributed to the explicit, pattern-based nature of the criteria involved, which align well with the strengths of deterministic NLP techniques. However, as noted in our results, NLP methods struggled with more interpretive categories such as Reporting Balance, Victim Characterization and Power Dynamics, where implicit language and framing devices required deeper semantic understanding.

LLM Implementation and Comparison. We evaluated each LLM's performance across the 18 remaining criteria, focusing on contextual interpretation, ambiguity resolution, and implicit framing.

- GPT-4 served as the baseline and demonstrated high performance, especially on nuanced categories like Victim and Perpetrator Characterizations.
- Gemma 3-12B showed strong generalization across tasks, particularly in multilingual prompts.
- DeepSeek-R1-14B performed well in inferencing Psychological and Health Factors.
- Llama 3-12B, while more lightweight, delivered competitive results in categories with shorter content structures.

All LLMs were tested using the few-shot prompting strategy proposed by [8], incorporating our own expert-annotated examples and domain-specific context. Prompt engineering was an iterative development process guided by performance logs and expert feedback. The best-performing prompt from this process was then fixed and used for all final evaluations.

Hybrid Approach Integration. Rather than relying on uniform application, we developed a decision framework to assign each criterion to its optimal analytical technique. Criteria were evaluated using performance benchmarks and qualitative error analyses. The results integration layer used:

- Criterion-specific weighting, based on accuracy scores from validation sets.
- Ensemble averaging, where both NLP and LLM outputs contributed proportionally.

We selected accuracy as our primary evaluation metric because our annotation framework was designed to achieve balanced class distributions across evaluation criteria, making accuracy a straightforward and intuitive representation of model correctness. In contrast, metrics like F1-score are typically preferred for imbalanced datasets to balance precision and recall, a scenario less applicable here due to our careful criterion selection and data balancing strategies. Moreover, accuracy provides clearer interpretability, particularly when communicating results to media professionals.

This hybrid configuration outperformed any single-method system. The modular design also facilitates future research extensions, such as integrating multimodal data or adapting criteria for cross-linguistic media studies.

5 Experimental Setup and Results

5.1 Experimental Environment

To ensure a fair and reproducible evaluation, all experiments were conducted in a controlled environment using Python 3.12. NLP components leveraged libraries such as SpaCy 3.5, scikit-learn, and NLTK. Contextual embeddings were generated using the SentenceTransformers library with multilingual models.

LLMs were accessed via standardized APIs or deployed locally using optimized configurations. GPT-4 was accessed through OpenAI's API with temperature set to 0.2 to prioritize deterministic outputs. Open-source models—Llama 3-12B, Gemma 3-12B, and DeepSeek-R1-14B—were run on local inference servers with 16-bit precision and prompt caching for efficiency.

We selected these models to compare performance across both commercial and open-source options. GPT-4 served as a high-performance benchmark. Gemma and Llama were chosen for their strong multilingual capabilities and accessibility, while DeepSeek was included for its reported strength in inferential reasoning.

All models were evaluated on identical inputs, and all code, prompts, and outputs were version-controlled for reproducibility.

5.2 Evaluation Methodology

We employed a multi-metric evaluation strategy centered on a manually annotated gold-standard test set. This set consisted of 300 articles randomly sampled from our corpus, each annotated by at least two domain experts using the 32 evaluation criteria across 9 categories. Model selection was not based on this annotated dataset. Instead, we selected GPT-4, Gemma, Llama, and DeepSeek based on prior benchmarks, reported domain strengths, and accessibility considerations. The 300-article set was used exclusively as a held-out test set for final benchmarking, ensuring no overlap between model choice and evaluation data.

Evaluation metrics included:

- Accuracy: Correct classifications over total evaluations.
- Precision and Recall: Measured per criterion, averaged by category.
- F1-score: Harmonic mean of precision and recall.

For LLM-based tasks, we used few-shot prompting with in-context examples drawn from annotated data. NLP components were benchmarked using predefined rules and validated classifiers. To assess the statistical significance of performance differences between methods, we conducted paired t-tests with a significance level of $\alpha = 0.05$.

5.3 Comparative Model Analysis

We conducted a detailed performance comparison across traditional NLP techniques, GPT-4, and three open-source LLMs (Gemma 3-12B, Llama 3-12B, and DeepSeek-R1-14B). This evaluation spanned all 32 criteria, yielding both category-level and individual criterion performance metrics. Table 2 presents the core performance results of the hybrid system, which achieved an overall accuracy of 87.1% - an 11% point improvement over our previous framework's 76.1% accuracy. The precision, recall, and F1-score are also high, reflecting the system's robust and balanced performance. The hybrid approach maintained consistently strong results across evaluation dimensions, with particularly high accuracy in

Table 2. Performance metrics for the hybrid system

Metric	Score
Accuracy	87.1%
Precision	83.2%
Recall	79.5%
F1-score	77.7%

certain categories (notably Linguistic Choices and Article Structure and Presentation).

Traditional rule-based NLP techniques excelled in structurally well-defined categories. For example, the NLP-only pipeline achieved near-perfect accuracy in Linguistic Choices (99%), Article Structure and Presentation (96%), and Psychological and Health Factors (95%). However, NLP struggled on criteria requiring deeper semantic understanding and context: it performed poorly on Reporting Balance (32% accuracy), Victim Characterization (36%), and Power Dynamics (39%), where implicit language and framing cues are crucial. In contrast, GPT-4 handled these interpretive dimensions much more effectively – for instance, GPT-4 attained 81% accuracy in Victim Characterization, 88% in Perpetrator Characterization, and 83% in Classification and Context of Violence. The open-source LLMs also showed solid (if slightly lower) performance, with overall accuracies of 75.0% for Gemma 3-12B, 72.4% for DeepSeek-R1-14B, and 67.0% for Llama 3-12B. Each model demonstrated unique strengths in certain categories, as summarized in Table 3.

Table 3. Model accuracy and strongest performing categories

Model	Accuracy	Strongest categories
GPT-4	77.9%	CCV, PC
Gemma 3-12B	75.0%	PC, PHF
DeepSeek-R1-14B	72.4%	ASP, VC
Llama 3-12B	67.0%	ASP, LC

No single model or method excelled across all dimensions; each has specific strengths (for example, GPT-4 in nuanced interpretation, Gemma in multilingual context adaptation, and NLP in structure-sensitive patterns). These complementary strengths motivated our hybrid approach. Indeed, the results validate assigning each evaluation criterion to the most suitable method: the rule-based NLP was most effective for explicit, repetitive patterns (e.g. Linguistic Choices and Article Structure), while LLMs outperformed on context-dependent criteria (e.g. Victim Characterization and Reporting Balance) that require implicit bias detection and broader reasoning.

Table 4 provides a detailed accuracy breakdown per category for each method, including the hybrid. As shown, the hybrid model achieves the highest accuracy in every category, effectively combining the advantages of both approaches. Notably, the hybrid reaches 87% accuracy in Reporting Balance and 86% in Victim Characterization, dramatically higher than the NLP-only results for those categories (which were 32% and 36%, respectively). Overall, the hybrid approach consistently matches or exceeds the best individual model in each category.

Table 4. Per-category accuracy comparison across models

Category	NLP only	GPT-4	Llama-3	Gemma-3	DeepSeek-R1	Hybrid
CCV	54%	83%	69%	78%	73%	89%
ASP	96%	81%	75%	72%	80%	95%
RB	32%	82%	54%	65%	72%	87%
SC	74%	65%	68%	75%	66%	79%
VC	36%	81%	62%	77%	77%	86%
PC	63%	88%	66%	82%	70%	88%
PD	39%	78%	67%	76%	68%	77%
PHF	95%	68%	70%	78%	78%	86%
LC	99%	75%	72%	72%	68%	99%
Overall average	**65%**	**78%**	**67%**	**75%**	**72%**	**87%**

Statistical tests (paired t-tests, $\alpha = 0.05$) confirm that the hybrid model's improvement is significant. The hybrid's overall accuracy advantage over every individual method is statistically significant ($p < 0.01$). It also achieved uniformly high accuracy across all categories, with stand-out performance in Linguistic Choices (99%), Article Structure and Presentation (95%), and Psychological and Health Factors (86%). The only category where the rule-based NLP was on par with the hybrid is Linguistic Choices (both 99% accuracy, difference not significant). In addition, GPT-4 and DeepSeek each came close to the hybrid on one category (Article Structure and Societal Context, respectively), but those differences were not statistically significant. These findings underscore the benefit of selectively combining rule-based and neural techniques to leverage their complementary strengths in media analysis.

Compared to a purely LLM-driven approach, our hybrid system shows clear advantages. If an LLM alone were used for all criteria, performance would suffer in areas where structured analysis is crucial. For example, GPT-4 alone achieved about 78% overall accuracy (see Table 4), noticeably below the hybrid's 87%. It also struggled with structurally defined categories – attaining only 81% in Article Structure (versus 95% by the hybrid). These gaps illustrate that even a state-of-the-art LLM cannot fully replicate the hybrid's balanced strengths across diverse criteria.

Furthermore, to our knowledge no existing hybrid system in the literature directly mirrors our integration of rule-based NLP with LLMs for media analysis, underlining the novelty of this framework. One could alternatively employ a transformer model fine-tuned specifically for fairness or media framing tasks. While such a specialized model (e.g., a BERT variant trained on bias detection) can excel at targeted classifications, it would address a narrower set of biases or frames and require extensive labeled data for each nuance. In contrast, our hybrid method leverages a general-purpose LLM's broad knowledge alongside rule-based precision, covering a wide spectrum of 32 criteria without task-specific retraining. This comparative perspective confirms that our combined approach captures nuanced media representations more comprehensively than either a purely generative LLM pipeline or a single fine-tuned model alone.

6 Discussion

6.1 Interpretation of Results

The findings confirm that a hybrid evaluation system, combining NLP and LLMs, can approach human-level performance in assessing GBV representation in media. Traditional NLP techniques remain highly effective in handling structurally explicit criteria, especially when patterns are rule-based or linguistically predictable. However, their limitations become apparent when faced with subtle semantic framing, implicit bias, or nuanced social commentary—areas where LLMs, particularly GPT-4, excel.

The comparative analysis demonstrated the added value of open-source LLMs, with Gemma 3-12B and DeepSeek-R1-14B providing competitive alternatives to GPT-4. Their performance in select categories—such as Psychological and Health Factors and Societal Context—suggests that with appropriate prompting and domain-specific context, open models can offer cost-effective and privacy-friendly options for large-scale media analysis.

Our results also highlight the importance of tailored evaluation strategies. By assigning criteria based on the analytical strengths of each method and refining prompts and embeddings accordingly, we achieved substantial performance gains (+11 points over baseline). This validates the hypothesis that hybrid integration is not only feasible but advantageous in socially sensitive AI applications.

6.2 Practical Implications

This study contributes to the emerging field of algorithmic media evaluation by offering a scalable, adaptable framework for assessing gender representation in journalism. Newsrooms, NGOs, and media regulators could adopt this framework to monitor coverage of GBV more systematically. Because the system is designed with modular inputs, it can be adapted to other languages, countries, or thematic focuses with limited reconfiguration.

From a technological standpoint, our approach underscores the potential for synergistic use of deterministic and generative models. As LLMs continue to evolve and become more accessible, integrating them strategically with rule-based systems will offer flexible solutions in both high- and low-resource environments.

6.3 Limitations and Future Work

Several limitations warrant attention. First, although our dataset is large and diverse, it remains geographically bounded to Swiss French-language media, limiting generalizability. Second, while expert annotations provide a solid ground truth, some evaluation criteria remain interpretative, potentially introducing variability in LLM outputs. Third, the system struggled with certain content types: short articles (under 150 words) often lacked sufficient context for reliable assessment, and dialectal variations (regionalisms in Swiss French) caused vocabulary mismatches that undermined NLP accuracy. Fourth, hybrid narrative formats blending reporting with opinion introduced additional ambiguity, particularly in evaluating criteria like balance and systemic framing; these challenges persisted despite targeted mitigation efforts (e.g., length-sensitive thresholds and regional lexicons) that achieved only moderate success, highlighting the complexity of automating nuanced media evaluations.

Future research could address these limitations by:

- Extending the framework to multilingual and cross-regional media corpora.
- Incorporating human-in-the-loop evaluation to combine expert feedback with automated analysis.
- Enhancing interpretability tools for LLM outputs.
- Exploring multimodal media analysis by integrating image and video content.

7 Conclusion

This paper presented a novel hybrid AI framework for evaluating gender representation in media reporting on gender-based violence. By combining NLP and LLM methods across 32 expert-defined criteria in 9 categories, our system achieves a new state-of-the-art in this domain. The approach is not only more accurate than prior methods but also more flexible and extensible.

Beyond performance metrics, this framework demonstrates how different computational approaches—deterministic and generative—can be strategically integrated to complement each other. Such a methodology is especially valuable in analyzing socially sensitive topics, where linguistic nuance and contextual framing are essential.

Our results suggest not only the feasibility of hybrid automation for media analysis but also its relevance for promoting more equitable journalism practices. As AI continues to evolve, interdisciplinary solutions like ours will be central to ensuring that technological tools contribute meaningfully to democratic discourse, ethical media practices, and public accountability.

Acknowledgments. This research was supported by the University of Applied Sciences and Arts Western Switzerland (HES-SO) under grant number 133851. We are especially grateful to our project partner DécadréE, and in particular to its director, Valérie Vuille, for their dedicated collaboration and invaluable support.

References

1. Artstein, R., Poesio, M.: Inter-coder agreement for computational linguistics. Comput. Linguist. **34**(4), 555–596 (2008)
2. Bender, E.M., Gebru, T., McMillan-Major, A., Shmitchell, S.: On the dangers of stochastic parrots: can language models be too big? In: Proceedings of the 2021 ACM conference on fairness, accountability, and transparency, pp. 610–623 (2021)
3. Berns, N.: Degendering the problem and gendering the blame: political discourse on women and violence. Gender Soc. **15**(2), 262–281 (2001)
4. Byerly, C.M., Ross, K.: Women and media: a critical introduction. John Wiley and Sons (2008)
5. Carll, E.K.: News portrayal of violence and women: implications for public policy. Am. Behav. Sci. **46**(12), 1601–1610 (2003)
6. Chen, Y., Zhai, Y., Sun, S.: The gendered lens of ai: examining news imagery across digital spaces. J. Comput. Mediated Commun. **29**(1), zmad047 (2024)
7. COE: The council of Europe convention on preventing and combating violence against women and domestic violence. (2011). https://www.coe.int/en/web/gender-matters
8. Dang, H., Mecke, L., Lehmann, F., Goller, S., Buschek, D.: How to prompt? opportunities and challenges of zero-and few-shot learning for human-ai interaction in creative applications of generative models. arXiv preprint arXiv:2209.01390 (2022)
9. DécadréE: Report 2023: Media coverage of sexist violence. (2023). https://decadree.com/wp-content/uploads/2023/11/2023_Rapport_ViolenceSexistes_NV-1.pdf
10. Easteal, P., Holland, K., Judd, K.: Enduring themes and silences in media portrayals of violence against women. In: Women's Studies International Forum, vol. 48, pp. 103–113. Elsevier (2015)
11. Flood, M., Pease, B.: Factors influencing attitudes to violence against women. Trauma Violence Abuse **10**(2), 125–142 (2009)
12. Forja-Pena, T., García-Orosa, B., López-García, X.: A shift amid the transition: towards smarter, more resilient digital journalism in the age of AI and disinformation. Soc. Sci. **13**(8), 403 (2024)
13. Liu, Z., Darbellay, A., Balet, N.G., Vuille, V.: Advancing gender equality in media: tackling stereotypes and biases with AI. In: International KES Conference on Intelligent Decision Technologies, pp. 413–424. Springer (2024)
14. Manasi, A., Panchanadeswaran, S., Sours, E.: Addressing gender bias to achieve ethical AI. (2023). https://theglobalobservatory.org/2023/03/gender-bias-ethical-artificial-intelligence/
15. O'Connor, S., Liu, H.: Gender bias perpetuation and mitigation in ai technologies: challenges and opportunities. AI Soc. **39**(4), 2045–2057 (2024)
16. Arguedas, A.R., Mukherjee, M., Nielsen, R.K.: Women and leadership in the news media 2024: Evidence from 12 markets. (2024). https://reutersinstitute.politics.ox.ac.uk/women-and-leadership-news-media-2024-evidence-12-markets

17. Simon, F.: Artificial intelligence in the news: How AI retools, rationalizes, and reshapes journalism and the public arena (2024)
18. Tilawat, M.: AI bias report 2025: LLM discrimination is worse than you think! (2025). https://www.allaboutai.com/resources/ai-statistics/ai-bias/
19. WHO: Violence against women (2024). https://www.who.int/news-room/fact-sheets/detail/violence-against-women

TCM-Eval: A Multi-dimensional Benchmark Framework for Evaluating Large Language Models in Traditional Chinese Medicine

Meihan Zhang[1], Xin Wang[2(✉)], Yuqian Wang[3], Hanshuo Xing[3], Pengwei Zhuang[4], and Xiangyu Ji[5]

[1] International Joint Institute of Tianjin University, Fuzhou, China
zescy_11bun@tju.edu.cn
[2] College of Intelligence and Computing, Tianjin University, Tianjin, China
wangx@tju.edu.cn
[3] School of Chinese Materia Medica, Tianjin University of Traditional Chinese Medicine, Tianjin, China
[4] First Teaching Hospital of Tianjin University of Traditional Chinese Medicine, Tianjin, China
[5] Tianjin International Engineering Institute, Tianjin, China
jixiangy123@tju.edu.cn

Abstract. Recently, domain-specific large language models (LLMs) have been rapidly developed and prosperous in many specialized fields, yet their performance in traditional Chinese medicine (TCM) remains unclear because of the lack of a reliable and user-friendly benchmarking framework. In this paper, we propose TCM-Eval, an automated, scalable, and open-source system for evaluating LLMs on TCM scenarios. In TCM-Eval, we design six core dimensional tasks modules plus 1 integrated module, and standardize a total of 6,813 questions covering 29 specialized data sources. Furthermore, we integrate 16 LLMs, including the popular commercial, open-source, and state-of-the-art proprietary LLMs, into TCM-Eval. To provide a fine-grained and systematic assessment, we also design 4 multi-dimensional metrics across 7 types of questions. Our framework shapes a new standard for TCM LLM evaluation, offering a robust foundation for the relevant studies and clinical applications.

Keywords: Traditional Chinese Medicine · Benchmark · Large Language Models

1 Introduction

Large language models (LLMs), with their remarkable performance in natural language understanding and processing, are facilitating the emergence of extensive expert models across every professional domain. Traditional Chinese

I. Awan et al. (Eds.): WISE 2025, LNCS 16368, pp. 210–225, 2026.
https://doi.org/10.1007/978-981-95-7251-9_15

medicine (TCM) is no exception. To scientifically evaluate their reliability in this field, it is crucial to establish a comprehensive, standardized and fair evaluation framework, not only aligning with the disciplinary characteristics of TCM, but also establishing a differentiated distinction from the evaluation metrics of western medicine.

Despite a considerable effort being put into the construction of TCM datasets, there are still many deficiencies for the existing works, such as insufficiently detailed evaluation granularity, inaccessibility of evaluation data, and low usability of evaluation tools.

To tackle these potential issues, we propose TCM-Eval, a comprehensive benchmarking system that includes the entire diagnostic process in TCM. The evaluation procedure involves six independent modules throughout TCMs diagnosis and treatment, as well as an overall assessment module that takes all six aspects into consideration.

We summarize our contributions as follows:

- **Detailed multi-dimensional coverage:** the framework provides a *systematic assessment* aligned with TCM capability, designating six evaluation dimensions and an integrated assessment to ensure the professionalism and comprehensiveness.
- **Streamlined, modular workflow:** the framework features multi-modal input formats and accommodates pre-defined TCM-specific tasks.
- **Open source:** the entire evaluation framework, including *benchmark curation*, *source code*, and *LLM instructions*, will be publicly released to communities. TCM-Eval is publicly available at https://github.com/Zescy1/TCM-Eval.git.

The rest of this paper is organized as follows. Section 2 reviews related work, offering contextual background to facilitate a complete understanding of the research. Section 3 elaborates on the evaluation framework in detail, encompassing the assessment architecture, task categories, benchmark datasets, and evaluation metrics. Section 4 presents the models evaluated, the experimental results and an in-depth analysis of the findings. Finally, Sect. 5 concludes the study and proposes directions for future work.

2 Related Work

2.1 Limitations of Existing Medical Benchmarks

Currently, English medical benchmarks are well-established, such as MedQA [1], MedMCQA [2], and PubMedQA [3], covering a broad spectrum of scenarios including basic medicine and clinical diagnosis, with rigorous evaluation systems and update mechanisms, but they are not well-suited to address Chinese-English differences. In the Chinese medical field, Medbench [4], though widely used, fails to address theoretical differences between Chinese and Western medicine; TCM-Bench [5], the first Chinese medical benchmark, includes basic TCM questions but has coarse classification; TCM-3CEval [6] enables multimodal tongue diagnosis evaluation but lacks granularity; MTCMB [7], with five evaluation dimensions, overlooks the dynamic reasoning in inquiry and syndrome differentiation. Furthermore, there are major issues affecting the TCM benchmarks, including difficult access to datasets, and insufficient evaluation granularity, which urgently need optimization.

2.2 Question Types Classifications

Based on authoritative assessment frameworks, including the National Licensed TCM Practitioner Qualification Examination [8], TCM Professional Technical Qualification Examination [9], and Assistant TCM Practitioner Qualification Examination [10], we systematically collated and categorized existing standardized question types. These include: A1-type single-choice questions (A1), A2-type clinical case-based single-choice questions (A2), B1-type matching questions (B1), and X-type multiple-select questions (X). Through the integration of the Shennong TCM Knowledge Dataset [11] and the Traditional Chinese-Medicine-Dataset-SFT [12] we finally distilled 3 core question types: question-answer (QA), fill-in-the-blank (F) and true-false (T), which comprehensively cover the full-dimensional assessment scenarios from basic TCM theories and classic texts to clinical syndrome differentiation and treatment.

2.3 NLP Evaluation Metrics

The BLEU [13] score is based on n-gram matching but is sensitive to word order variations and prone to common word interference. While ROUGE-L [14] can better reflect sentence similarity, its reliance on the longest common subsequence inherently favors longer sentences, compromising fairness. To address this limitation, a dynamic ROUGE-L algorithm is introduced to mitigate text length bias. To accommodate the demand for deep semantic understanding in Chinese, BERTScore [15], which captures semantic similarity using Chinese-BERT [16], and CosSim [17], which computes vector space similarity, are integrated as complementary evaluation metrics to form a multi-dimensional assessment framework.

3 Evaluation Framework

To enhance the efficiency and scalability of the evaluation framework, multiple deployment strategies are supported within the evaluation workflow architecture. Once configured via script, the system executes the entire pipeline autonomously, from model loading to metric computation, and delivers results through four standardized output formats. The task taxonomy of benchmark is designed to mirror six core diagnostic dimensions of Traditional Chinese Medicine (TCM), aligning with its classical theoretical perspectives while enabling comprehensive, multi-angle model assessment.

3.1 Evaluation Workflow Architecture

The evaluation framework is structured around five core modules: Models Layer, Datasets Layer, Method Layer, Automated Evaluation Process, and Forms of Results. Among them, the models layer provides technical support for interactive dialogue; the datasets layer enables multi-faceted assessment; the method layer adopts a comprehensive evaluation approach; the automated process ensures the orderly progress of the work; and the evaluation results guarantee accuracy and authority through multiple means. Together, they form a complete evaluation system. Figure 1 shows the architecture of the evaluation workflow.

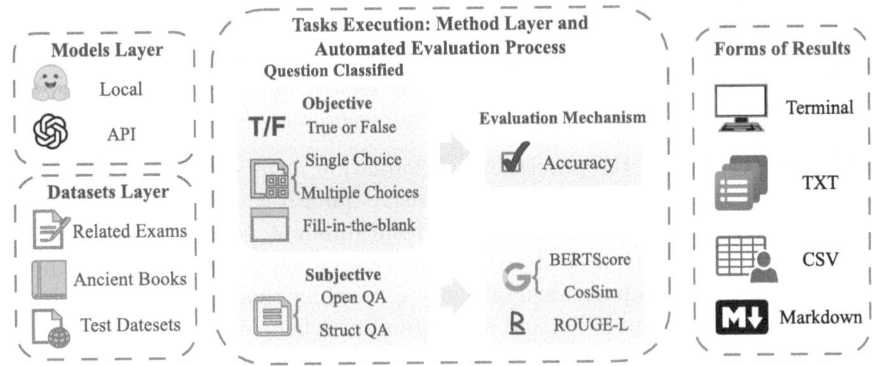

Fig. 1. TCM Large Model Evaluation Workflow Architecture.

Models Layer: it enables interaction with models through diverse implementation approaches. This includes establishing communication via standardized API interfaces, directly loading and executing pre-trained model weights for local or distributed computation. These strategies collectively ensure robustness and high efficiency in model interaction workflows.

Datasets Layer: Datasets Layer: it possesses multi-faceted assessment capabilities enabled by the construction of targeted datasets. On one hand, it can conduct comprehensive and in-depth assessments of the multi-dimensional capabilities involved in the field of traditional Chinese medicine, covering various specific aspects such as traditional Chinese medicine theories, diagnostic and treatment methods, and knowledge of medicinal materials. On the other hand, it can also assess text reasoning ability and language understanding ability. Text reasoning involves logical deduction, information integration, etc., while language understanding includes the accurate grasp of semantics and context, thereby achieving a comprehensive evaluation of relevant capabilities. The specific capability assessments, corresponding tasks, and datasets will be introduced in the following sections.

Method Layer: the evaluation methodology prioritizes subjective assessment, where open responses are scored based on semantic alignment with expert-validated reference answers. This approach emphasizes nuanced understanding and reasoning capabilities by analyzing coherence, clinical relevance, and adherence to TCM principles in the generated outputs.

Automated Evaluation Process: the entire evaluation process forms a complete automated workflow, consisting of four core stages. Firstly, the configuration stage, where the settings of various parameters, data, and environment required for the evaluation are completed. Secondly, the reasoning stage, where the model performs calculations and deductions based on the input information to obtain corresponding results. Then, the evaluation stage, where the reasoning results are analyzed and judged according to the set standards and indicators. Finally, the visualization stage, where the evaluation results are presented in an intuitive and clear form. These four stages are closely linked, forming a complete automated closed-loop, ensuring the orderly progress of the evaluation work.

Forms of Results: in the processing of evaluation results, a variety of evaluation metrics have been used for comprehensive quantitative analysis, and these metrics measure the evaluation situation from different perspectives. However, considering the distinct particularity of the Traditional Chinese Medicine field, there is still a certain gap between ordinary natural language processing technology and professional expression and understanding when dealing with traditional Chinese medicine terminology. To make up for this deficiency, experts in the field of traditional Chinese medicine are specially invited to conduct sampling inspections. Through the professional judgment and review of experts, the evaluation results are further calibrated and verified to effectively ensure the accuracy and authority of the evaluation results.

3.2 Tasks Dimensions

The TCM-Eval benchmark datasets are divided into six parallel dimensions and a comprehensive evaluation, which are architecturally arranged in a ring-shaped configuration around the TCM-Eval Wheel. Developed by postgraduate professional students in traditional Chinese medicine based on standard diagnostic procedures and essential practitioner competencies, each module is specifically designed to evaluate a core competency within TCM. These modules are intentionally interdependent, reflecting the logical structure of TCM diagnostic reasoning. As illustrated in Fig. 2, each assessment task module maps to a specific core dimension of the TCM-Eval Wheel, serving as the concrete realization of competency assessment.

Basic Theory: it focuses on assessing LLMs of classical TCM theoretical systems. Based on foundational texts including *Yellow Emperor's Inner Canon* and *Treatise on Cold Damage*, this dimension quantitatively evaluates memorization accuracy and comprehension depth of core concepts of the model, including *yin-yang* (representing the dualistic balance of opposing yet complementary

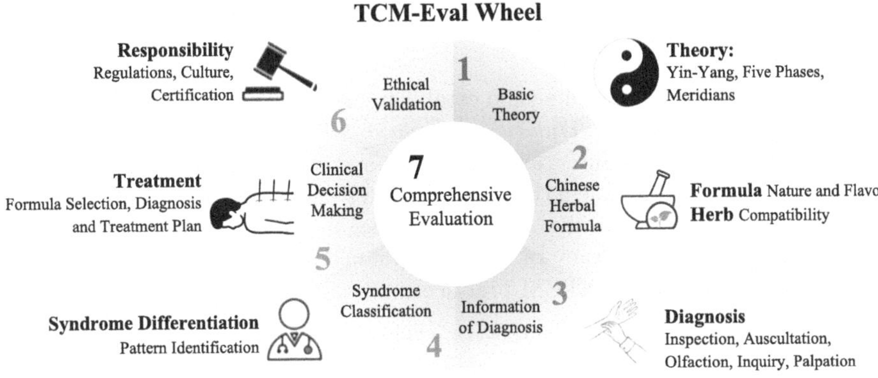

Fig. 2. The TCM-Eval Wheel presents the distribution of tasks modules within the TCM-Eval benchmark across six primary dimensions and a comprehensive evaluation.

forces) theory and *zang-fu* organs (the TCM functional system of the internal organs) systems.

Chinese Herbal Formula: it emphasizes evaluating ability of the model to transform theoretical knowledge into clinical practice. It assesses the accurate identification of herbal properties and meridian tropism, appropriate application of formula composition principles, and accurate dosage adjustment based on meridian tropism, with particular attention to the logical consistency of *herb-syndrome correspondence* (the therapeutic alignment between single herbs and TCM syndrome patterns) and *formula-syndrome matching* (the suitability of a herbal formula for treating a specific syndrome pattern).

Information of Diagnosis: it examines capability of the model to process multi-source clinical data. Through technical approaches such as interrogation text parsing, this dimension evaluates structured processing of TCM diagnostic information of the model and its analytical proficiency in syndrome differentiation methods.

Syndrome Classification: it focuses on assessing clinical thinking ability of the model. Through tasks including symptom combination analysis, syndrome pattern deduction, and disease mechanism interpretation, this dimension systematically evaluates application of the model in differentiation methods such as *eight-principle pattern identification* (a fundamental TCM diagnostic framework based on *yin-yang*, exterior-interior, cold-heat, and deficiency-excess) and *six-channel pattern differentiation* (a pattern-differentiation method that traces disease progression across six stages, rooted in the Six-Channels theory of *Yellow Emperor's Inner Canon*), particularly its competence in analyzing complex syndromes.

Clinical Decision Making: it evaluates the complete ability of the model to formulate treatment plans. Assessment covers multiple aspects including formula selection appropriateness, dosage adjustment accuracy, and treatment principle compatibility.

Ethical Validation: this dimension establishes a structured ethical assessment framework grounded in the *Traditional Chinese Medicine Law* (TCM Law) and regulatory guidelines. By integrating industry-specific norms, historical medical ethics, and cultural principles, the framework systematically assesses the understanding and adherence of the model to the legal standards of TCM through metrics including the accuracy of legal compliance, alignment of ethical principles and fidelity to classical TCM practices.

Comprehensive Evaluation: the comprehensive evaluation dimension integrates evaluation results from all dimensions, referencing the certification standards for TCM practitioners and herbalists.

3.3 Benchmark Metrics and Datasets

To comprehensively evaluate the capabilities of large language models across the entire TCM diagnostic workflow, seven core modules are devised. Six are precisely aligned with the six pivotal clinical stages: basic theory, herbal formula, diagnostic information, syndrome classification, clinical decision making, and ethical validation; the seventh is dedicated to comprehensive evaluation. For each task, a corresponding set of evaluation metrics is paired with a purpose-built dataset to enable rigorous, domain-specific performance evaluation.

Metrics: to enhance the rigor of evaluation, a dynamic coefficient β is defined based on the length ratio between a predicted answer Q and a reference answer R , as formalized in Eq. 1. By dynamically balancing the weights of recall and precision, the ROUGE-L metric is adapted to compute a length-aware variant, termed dynamic ROUGE-L, as specified in Eq. 2. This adjustment accommodates the flexible and often heterogeneous answer lengths characteristic of Traditional Chinese Medicine responses.

$$\beta = 1 + \log\left(\frac{\max(\text{len}(Q), \text{len}(R))}{\min(\text{len}(Q), \text{len}(R))}\right) \tag{1}$$

$$\text{ROUGE-}L_{\text{dynamic}} = \frac{(1+\beta^2)\cdot \text{LCS}(Q,R)}{\beta^2 \cdot \text{len}(R) + \text{len}(Q)} \tag{2}$$

Datasets: based on the theoretical framework outlined in Sect. 3.2, the evaluation datasets are categorized into seven components: six competency-specific dimensions and a comprehensive evaluation module. The specific details of the datasets are depicted in Table 1.

1. **Base Theory:** it evaluates ability of the model aims to memorize and understand TCM key concepts and basic knowledge.

- Base-CH: 118 single-choice questions, cover basic fields such as *yin-yang*, Five Phases (Five Elements in TCM), *zang-fu* organs, and meridians.

Table 1. Summary of tasks, datasets, question types and evaluation metrics in TCM-Eval.

Tasks Modules	#	Dataset	Question Types	Evaluation Metrics
Base Theory	1	Base-CH	A1, A2, B1	Accuracy
	2	Base-TF	T	Accuracy
	3	Book	F	Accuracy
	4	Reason	QA	ROUGE-L, BERTScore, CosSim
Chinese Herbal Formula	5	Herb-CH	A1, A2, B1	Accuracy
	6	Herb-TF	T	Accuracy
	7	Logic-CH	A1, A2, B1	Accuracy
	8	Logic-TF	T	Accuracy
	9	Pro-Herb	QA	ROUGE-L, BERTScore, CosSim
Diagnosis	10	Four	F	Accuracy
Syndrome Classification	11	ShenNong	QA	ROUGE-L, BERTScore, CosSim
	12	Prac-CH	A1, A2, B1	Accuracy
	13	Prac-TF	T	Accuracy
Clinical Decision Making	14	Acup-CH	A1, A2	Accuracy
	15	Derm-CH	A1, A2	Accuracy
	16	Gyne-CH	A1, A2	Accuracy
	17	Inter-CH	A1, A2	Accuracy
	18	Orth-CH	A1, A2	Accuracy
	19	Otorh-CH	A1, A2	Accuracy
	20	Pedi-CH	A1, A2	Accuracy
	21	Rehab-CH	A1, A2	Accuracy
	22	Tuina-CH	A1, A2	Accuracy
Ethical Validation	23	Law-MCH	X	Accuracy
	24	Law-CH	A1, A2	Accuracy
Comprehensive Assessment	25	TCM-CH	A1, A2, B1	Accuracy
	26	Licen-MCH	X	Accuracy
	27	Licen-CH	A1, A2, B1	Accuracy
	28	Open-Com	QA	ROUGE-L, BERTScore, CosSim
	29	Struct-Cli	QA	ROUGE-L, BERTScore, CosSim

- Base-TF: 41 true/false questions, are used for rapid screening of conceptual accuracy.
- Book: 970 fill-in-the-blank questions, are extracted from classic ancient texts such as *Synopsis of the Golden Chamber* and *Treatise on Febrile Diseases*, as well as modern TCM works.
- Reason: 291 open-ended questions, require interpretation of classic passages and explanation of basic disease conditions.

2. **Chinese Herbal Formula:** it evaluates proficiency of the model in applying herbal properties, herb compatibility principles, formula-syndrome alignment, and pharmacological knowledge.

- Herb-CH: 104 single-choice questions, involve the nature, flavor, and meridian tropism of Chinese medicinal herbs.
- Herb-TF: 28 true/false questions, focus on descriptions of medicinal properties and processing essentials.
- Logic-CH: 93 single-choice questions, examine the logic of formula compatibility.
- Logic-TF: 29 true/false questions, verify the rationality of the *sovereign, minister, assistant and guide* compatibility principle.
- Pro-Herb: 620 question-and-answer tasks, include generating complete prescriptions for given syndromes, explaining compatibility ideas, and describing medicinal processing methods.

3. **Information of Diagnosis:** it evaluates the ability of models to judge and extract diagnostic information.

- Four: 160 fill-in-the-blank questions, convert descriptions from inspection, auscultation-olfaction, inquiry, and palpate into standardized answer labels.

4. **Syndrome Classification:** it evaluates chain reasoning ability of the model from symptoms to syndrome types and etiologies.

- ShenNong: 1026 question-and-answer items, test reasoning ability in symptom chain analysis, syndrome type determination, and etiology deduction.
- Prac-TF: 59 true/false questions, verify the correspondence between symptoms and syndrome differentiation.
- Prac-CH: 94 single-choice questions, cover the content of 200 common diseases and syndromes.

5. **Clinical Decision Making:** it evaluates ability of the model to generate reasonable diagnosis and treatment plans in real department scenarios.

- Acup-CH: 132 single choice questions, involve acupuncture point selection and combination decisions in the acupuncture department.
- Derm-CH: 150 single-choice questions, include diagnosis and treatment of dermatological diseases.
- Gyne-CH: 137 single-choice questions, examine the treatment of gynecological diseases.

- Inter-CH: 124 single-choice questions, examine the management of internal medicine syndromes.
- Orth-CH: 150 single-choice questions, examine diagnosis and treatment decisions in orthopedics.
- Otorh-CH: 170 single-choice questions, examine the treatment of otolaryngological diseases.
- Pedi-CH: 100 single-choice questions, examine the treatment of pediatric diseases.
- Rehab-CH: 121 single-choice questions, examine the treatment of rehabilitation conditions such as functional recovery, rehabilitation assessment, and therapeutic techniques.
- Tuina-CH: 100 single-choice questions, involve indication and manipulation selection in the *Tuina* (a form of traditional Chinese manipulative therapy involving massage and acupressure).

6. **Ethical Validation:** it evaluates adherence of the model to TCM regulations, culture, and industry standards.

- Law-MCH: 50 multiple-choice questions, focus on regulatory content such as clinic registration and medicinal material management.
- Law-CH: 50 single-choice questions, examine knowledge related to the *Traditional Chinese Medicine Law* and cultural inheritance.

7. **Comprehensive Evaluation:** it conducts cross-departmental blind testing and capability revalidation.

- TCM-CH: 298 single-choice questions, originate from the question bank of the qualification examination for Chinese materia medica professionals.
- Licen-MCH: 70 multiple-choice questions, originate from the question bank of the TCM practitioner qualification examination.
- Licen-CH: 240 single-choice questions, originate from the question bank of the TCM practitioner qualification examination.
- Open-Com: 1000 question-and-answer scenarios simulate free consultation by patients.
- Struct-Cli: 296 question-and-answer tasks based on standardized medical records, reply syndrome differentiation, prescription generation, and medication dispensing.

4 Experiments and Analysis

The TCM-Eval benchmark evaluates a diverse set of large language models using multi-dimensional datasets to comprehensively assess their capabilities in Traditional Chinese Medicine. Model details are provided for reference. Given the large number of datasets involved in this benchmark, detailed scores are provided for the comprehensive module. Results across the six diagnostic dimensions are also analyzed using radar charts (Table 2).

Table 2. Evaluated Models in TCM-Eval: The Model Categories column categorizes models into five domains, while the Access column and Parameters indicate whether models are locally deployable or limited to API-only access.

Model Categories	Model Names	*Access*	*#Parameters*
Chinese General Model	DeepSeek-R1	Local	*671B*
	Qwen-max	API	undisclosed
	Doubao-seed-1-6	API	undisclosed
	Zhipu-4-plus	API	undisclosed
General Model	Claude-3-7	API	undisclosed
	ChatGPT-4	API	undisclosed
	Llama-3	Local	*32B*
Chinese General Model with medical fine-tuning	Baichuan-3-turbo	API	undisclosed
	Spark-lite	API	undisclosed
Chinese Medical Model	Huatuo	Local	*7B*
	Mingyi	Local	*7B*
	Sunsimiao	Local	*7B*
	WiseDiag	API	undisclosed
Traditional Chinese Medicine Model	Biancang	Local	*13B*
	Qibo	API	*7B*
	Zhongjing	Local	*13B*

4.1 Evaluation Models

The evaluated models fall into five distinct categories. General models serve as baselines because of their robust semantic and text-generation capabilities. Chinese General models, adapted to the linguistic characteristics of Chinese, demonstrate improved suitability for processing Chinese medical texts. Another category comprises general models fine-tuned on medical corpora, integrating broad foundational knowledge with domain-specific expertise to achieve a balance between cross-domain flexibility and clinical proficiency. Specialized medical large models focus on acquiring deep medical knowledge, while their Chinese medical counterparts are further customized. These model categories offer a diverse and representative sample for comparative analysis of how training methodologies influence performance in Chinese medical language tasks. (1) Chinese General Model: DeepSeek-R1 [18], Doubao-seed-1-6 [19], Qwen-max [20], Zhipu-4-plus [21]; (2) General Model: Claude-3-7 [22], ChatGPT-4 [23], Llama-3 [24]; (3) Chinese General Model with medical fine-tuning: Baichuan-3-turbo [25], Spark-lite [26]; (4) Chinese Medical Model: Huatuo [27], Mingyi [28], Sunsimiao [29], WiseDiag [30]; (5) Traditional Chinese Medical Model: Biancang [31], Qibo [32], Zhongjing [33].

Table 3. Comprehensive Performance Comparison (Note: table is split vertically for layout; data rows are continuous and should be analyzed horizontally as a single row. Max/min values are computed across the full row.)

Datasets	Metric	Deep-seek	Dou-Bao	Qwen-max	Zhipu	Claude	GPT-4	Llama3	Bai-chuan3
Open-Com	BERTScore	0.72	0.72	0.77	0.77	0.76	0.77	0.77	0.79
	CosSim	0.76	0.76	0.82	0.83	0.81	0.82	0.82	**0.85**
	ROUGE-L	0.27	0.15	0.33	0.33	**0.72**	0.3	0.44	0.46
Struct-Cli	BERTScore	0.66	0.67	0.68	0.67	0.67	0.69	0.68	0.67
	CosSim	0.75	0.73	0.72	0.71	0.77	0.74	0.71	0.66
	ROUGE-L	0.5	0.53	0.53	0.5	0.54	0.53	0.56	0.52
TCM-CH	Accuracy	89.26	**97.99**	89.26	87.92	57.38	69.13	56.38	91.61
Licen-MCH	Accuracy	8.86	84.75	8.86	**89.83**	64.41	8.86	6.33	21.52
Licen-CH	Accuracy	86.67	**94.17**	86.67	81.67	67.92	68.75	55.42	84.58
Average	**Avg Score**	62.88	67.93	65.25	**69.33**	68.82	61.62	60.66	67.46
Datasets	Metric	Spark	Wise-Diag	Hua-tuo	Ming-yi	Sun-simiao	Bian-cang	Qibo	Zhong-jing
Open-Com	BERTScore	0.78	0.74	0.56	0.75	0.77	**0.8**	0.77	0.67
	CosSim	0.82	0.74	0.32	0.71	0.81	0.83	0.8	0.48
	ROUGE-L	0.4	0.4	0.2	0.08	0.53	0.58	0.54	0.09
Struct-Cli	BERTScore	0.68	0.65	0.68	0.66	0.65	**0.74**	0.67	0.63
	CosSim	0.68	0.57	0.67	0.71	0.62	**0.8**	0.67	0.52
	ROUGE-L	0.54	0.53	0.5	0.31	0.52	**0.57**	0.55	0.03
TCM-CH	Accuracy	91.28	25.5	58.72	21.14	74.5	40.27	49.46	16.78
Licen-MCH	Accuracy	20.51	1.27	12.68	18.27	2.53	1.27	8.33	5.56
Licen-CH	Accuracy	85	37.5	59.17	23.75	76.67	40	60	36.5
Average	**Avg Score**	66.75	50.99	48.46	45.52	63.01	61.61	60.45	34.98

4.2 Results

As presented in Tables 3 and 4, substantial performance variations are evident across model categories. Within the comprehensive evaluation module (Table 3), Chinese purpose models, including DeepSeek-R1 and Qwen-Max, achieve the highest precision on multiple choice tasks (TCM-CH: 89. 26% - 91. 61%). In contrast, TCM models such as Biancang and Sunsimiao, achieve the highest BERTScore on open-ended clinical reasoning tasks (Struct-Cli: 0.74–0.80). Hybrid models (e.g., DouBao, Zhipu-4-plus) exhibit balanced performance across task types, with average scores of 69.33%. TCM models, including Huatuo and Mingyi, perform strongly in knowledge recall (TCM-CH: 91.61%) but significantly underperform in complex reasoning (Licen-MCH: 16.78%).

Consistent with these findings, Table 4 reveals that the top three models across all six diagnostic dimensions are predominantly Chinese general or medical-finetuned Chinese models, indicating superior overall capability in multi-dimensional TCM assessment.

Table 4. Top 3 Models in Six Dimensions

Model	Basic Theory	Chinese Herbal Formula	Information of Diagnosis	Syndrome Classification	Clinical Decision Making	Ethical Validation	**Average Score**
Qwen-max	64.97	74.13	86.67	51.53	91.12	71.33	73.47
Baichuan3	56.75	70.06	89.92	52.92	86.67	69.79	72.71
DouBao	59.75	72.04	85.26	54.32	87.30	70.81	70.37

4.3 Analysis

Experimental results reveal certain limitations of large language models in specific traditional Chinese medicine tasks. As illustrated in Fig. 3, the six-dimensional TCM competency spectral map demonstrates significant variations in capability profiles across model categories. Notably, general models exhibit overall superior performance compared to domain-specific models, primarily because of their robust knowledge reasoning capabilities and extensive knowledge storage capacity. These findings demonstrate that TCM models, despite their strength in open-ended clinical reasoning, remain limited in performance on standardized examinations and health literacy communication.

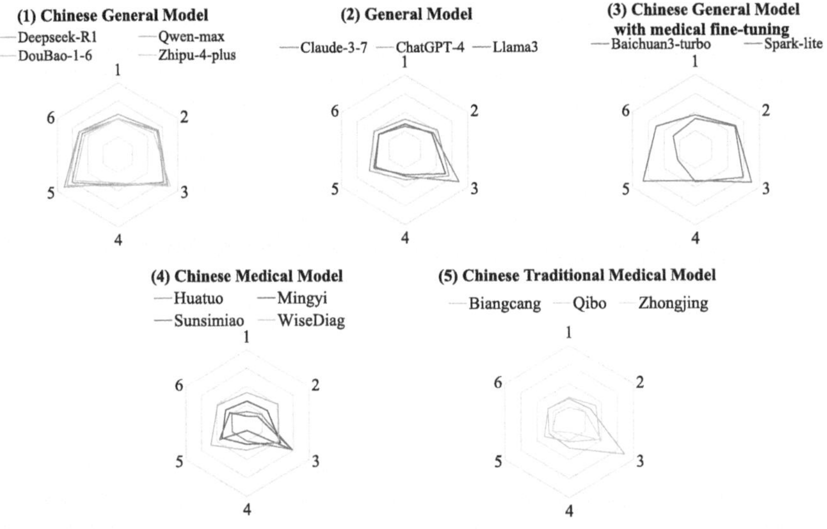

Fig. 3. Six-Dimensional TCM Competency Spectral Map for Large Language Models. The meaning of the label of each axis is as follows, listed in numerical ascend order: Basic Theory, Chinese Herbal Formula, Information of Diagnosis, Syndrome Classification, Clinical Decision Making, and Ethical Validation.

Three major reasons are proposed to explain the performance gap. Firstly, we identify inadequate handling of non-Chinese terminology and symbols as a critical issue. Table 3 (Sect. 4.2) reveals that Chinese medical and TCM models lag significantly behind general-purpose and medical-fine-tuned counterparts in standardized examination tasks, with radar plots (Fig. 3) highlighting particularly weak performance in core clinical and diagnostic competencies. In the experiments, Huatuo mainly demonstrates insufficient parsing capability while encountering inputs containing English terminology or special symbols. This leads to misinterpretation of multiple-choice questions, resulting in incorrect answers and consequently reduced overall evaluation scores. Secondly, instruction following failure in semantic interpretation is also observed. For example, Zhongjing frequently fails to grasp the core intent of a query. This results in semantically misaligned responses, revealing persistent challenges in semantic understanding and instruction-response alignment within current TCM LLMs. Thirdly, progressive decline in answer quality under sequential query scenarios is revealed: both Chinese medical and TCM models show a systematic degradation in answer quality over successive interactions. The phenomenon occurred even if the context windows is long enough, or the knowledge is still preserved, showing the accumulation of internal reasoning state drift and the failure of server-side session state reset mechanisms, which leads to progressive inference instability.

These findings demonstrate the necessity of improved robustness in cross-lingual input processing and enhanced instruction-aware training paradigms for Traditional Chinese Medicine models.

5 Conclusion

TCM-Eval evaluates five categories of models in six capability dimensions and an integrated assessment in Traditional Chinese Medicine. General models and medical-finetuned models excel in foundational theories and common knowledge; Chinese medical models and TCM models focus deeply on core TCM knowledge in text-based question answering, demonstrating the unique value of domain-specialized architectures. However, both medical-oriented models suffer from weak parsing of English terminology, declining answer quality in multi-turn dialogues, and semantic misalignment, limiting their effectiveness in standardized examinations and health information dissemination contexts. Future work must prioritize enhancing semantic robustness, instruction adherence, and conversational consistency. We will focus on refining evaluation granularity and extending to multimodal applications in the TCM domain.

References

1. Yang, H., et al.: LLM-MedQA: Enhancing Medical Question Answering Through Case Studies in Large Language Models. arXiv preprint arXiv:2501.05464 (2024)
2. Pal, A., Umapathi, L. K., Sankarasubbu, M.: MedMCQA: A large-scale multi-subject multi-choice dataset for medical domain question answering. In: Proceedings of the Conference on Health, Inference, and Learning, pp. 248–260. PMLR (2022)

3. Jin, Q., Dhingra, B., Liu, Z., Cohen, W.W., Lu, X.: PubMedQA: A Dataset for Biomedical Research Question Answering. arXiv preprint arXiv:1909.06146 (2019)
4. Cai, Y., et al.: MedBench: a large-scale chinese benchmark for evaluating medical large language models. In: Proceedings of the AAAI Conference on Artificial Intelligence, vol. 38, no. 16, pp. 17709–17717 (2024)
5. Yue, W., et al.: TCMBench: A Comprehensive Benchmark for Evaluating Large Language Models in Traditional Chinese Medicine. arXiv preprint arXiv:2406.01126 (2024)
6. Huang, T., et al.: TCM-3CEval: A Triaxial Benchmark for Assessing Responses from Large Language Models in Traditional Chinese Medicine. arXiv preprint arXiv:2503.07041 (2025)
7. Kong, S., Yang, X., Wei, Y., et al.: MTCMB: A Multi-Task Benchmark Framework for Evaluating LLMs on Knowledge, Reasoning, and Safety in Traditional Chinese Medicine. arXiv preprint arXiv:2506.01252 (2025)
8. National Administration of Traditional Chinese Medicine: National Licensed TCM Practitioner Qualification Examination Syllabus (2023)
9. Ministry of Human Resources and Social Security: TCM Professional Technical Qualification Examination Guidelines (2022)
10. National Health Commission: Assistant TCM Practitioner Qualification Examination Standards (2023)
11. Zhu, W., Yue, W., Wang, X.: ShenNong-TCM: A Traditional Chinese Medicine Large Language Model. GitHub repository (2023). https://github.com/michael-wzhu/ShenNong-TCM-LLM, Accessed 13 July 2025
12. Traditional-Chinese-Medicine-Dataset-SFT (2024). https://huggingface.co/datasets/SylvanL/Traditional-Chinese-Medicine-Dataset-SFT, Accessed 13 July 2025
13. Papineni, K., Roukos, S., Ward, T., Zhu, W.J.: BLEU: a method for automatic evaluation of machine translation. In: Proceedings of the 40th Annual Meeting of the Association for Computational Linguistics, pp. 311–318 (2002)
14. Lin, C.Y.: ROUGE: a package for automatic evaluation of summaries. In: Proceedings of the ACL-04 Workshop: Text Summarization Branches Out, pp. 74–81 (2004)
15. Zhang, T., Kishore, V., Wu, F., Weinberger, K. Q., Artzi, Y.: BERTScore: Evaluating Text Generation with BERT. arXiv preprint arXiv:1904.09675 (2019)
16. Devlin, J., Chang, M. W., Lee, K., Toutanova, K.: BERT: Pre-training of Deep Bidirectional Transformers for Language Understanding. arXiv preprint arXiv:1810.04805 (2019)
17. Jiang, H.: Short-Text semantic similarity model of BERT-Based Siamese network. In: Proceedings of the 10th International Conference on Wireless Communication and Sensor Networks, pp. 145–149 (2023)
18. Guo, D., et al.: DeepSeek-R1: Incentivizing Reasoning Capability in LLMs via Reinforcement Learning. arXiv preprint arXiv:2501.12948 (2025)
19. ByteDance: Doubao Large Language Model (2023). https://www.doubao.com, Accessed 13 July 2025
20. Yang, A., et al.: Qwen3 Technical Report. arXiv preprint arXiv:2505.09388 (2025)
21. Zhipu AI: Zhipu-4-Plus Technical Report. Technical Report (2024). https://www.zhipuai.cn/, Accessed 13 July 2025
22. Anthropic: Claude 3 Model Family: Technical Overview and Capabilities. Technical Report (2024). https://www.anthropic.com/news/claude-3-family, Accessed 13 July 2025

23. OpenAI: GPT-4 Technical Report. Technical Report (2023). https://cdn.openai.com/papers/gpt-4.pdf, Accessed 13 July 2025
24. Touvron, H., et al.: Llama: Open and Efficient Foundation Language Models. arXiv preprint arXiv:2302.13971 (2023)
25. Baichuan Intelligence: Baichuan 3 Technical Report. Technical Report (2024). https://www.baichuan-ai.com/, Accessed 13 July 2025
26. iFLYTEK: SparkDesk: The Large Language Model by iFLYTEK. Technical Report (2023). https://xinghuo.xfyun.cn/, Accessed 13 July 2025
27. Wang, H., et al.: Huatuo: Tuning Llama Model with Chinese Medical Knowledge. arXiv preprint arXiv:2304.06975 (2023)
28. Liao, Y., Jiang, S., Wang, Y., Wang, Y.: MING-MOE: Enhancing Medical Multi-Task Learning in Large Language Models with Sparse Mixture of Low-Rank Adapter Experts. arXiv preprint arXiv:2404.09027 (2024)
29. Yan, X., Xue, D.: Sunsimiao: Chinese Medicine LLM. GitHub repository (2023). https://github.com/thomas-yanxin/Sunsimiao, Accessed 13 July 2025
30. Wisediag: Wisediag: AI-Powered Medical Diagnostics Platform. Technical Report (2024). https://www.wisediag.com/, Accessed 13 July 2025
31. Wei, S., et al.: Biancang: A Traditional Chinese Medicine Large Language Model. arXiv preprint arXiv:2411.11027 (2024)
32. Jia, Y., Ji, X., Wang, X., et al.: Qibo: a large language model for traditional Chinese medicine. Expert Syst. Appl. **284**, 127672 (2025). https://doi.org/10.1016/j.eswa.2025.127672
33. Yang, S., et al.: Zhongjing: enhancing the Chinese medical capabilities of large language models through expert feedback and real-world multi-turn dialogue. In: Proceedings of the AAAI Conference on Artificial Intelligence, vol. 38, no. 17, pp. 19368–19376 (2024)

Boosting Pre-trained Language Models for Temporal Knowledge Graph Reasoning via Joint Structure and Recurring Patterns

Zihao Jiang[1], Miao Peng[2], Wenjie Xu[1], Ben Liu[1], Yao Xiao[1], Kai Liu[1], and Min Peng[1](✉)

[1] School of Computer Science, Wuhan University, Wuhan, China
{jiangzihao,vingerxu,liuben123,y.xiao,zerkvii,pengm}@whu.edu.cn
[2] The Hong Kong University of Science and Technology (Guangzhou), Guangzhou, China
mpeng885@connect.hkust-gz.edu.cn

Abstract. Temporal Knowledge Graph (TKG) reasoning aims to infer missing facts based on historical information. Pre-trained Language Models (PLMs) have excelled in knowledge-intensive tasks, motivating numerous studies to explore their semantic modeling capability for TKG reasoning. However, existing PLM-based methods primarily focus on temporal semantic modeling while neglecting structural dependencies and global historical patterns, which limits their effectiveness. To address these challenges, we propose PSG, a **P**LM-based framework that takes into account **S**tructure and **G**lobal information for TKG reasoning. Specifically, we design specific contextualized *time-aware soft prompts* to combine and balance semantic and structural information, which are then processed by both the frozen PLMs and the graph model. Besides, based on our analysis, we capture timely and relevant global information by utilizing global frequency, which emphasizes interactions involving recent historical facts. We evaluate PSG on three datasets and conduct extensive analysis, validating the effectiveness of PSG in TKG reasoning.

Keywords: temporal knowledge graph reasoning · pre-trained language models · soft prompts

1 Introduction

Temporal knowledge graphs (TKGs) serve as a vital mechanism to store facts with dynamic temporal information, playing a crucial role in applications like financial analysis [20] and question answering [4]. Each fact in TKGs is represented by a quadruple *(subject, relation, object, timestamp)*. However, due to the inherent incompleteness of existing TKGs, temporal knowledge graph reasoning (TKGR) has gained significant attention for its ability to predict missing or new quadruples. TKGR tasks are typically classified into two categories: interpolation and extrapolation [9]. Interpolation focuses on predicting missing facts within

I. Awan et al. (Eds.): WISE 2025, LNCS 16368, pp. 226–240, 2026.
https://doi.org/10.1007/978-981-95-7251-9_16

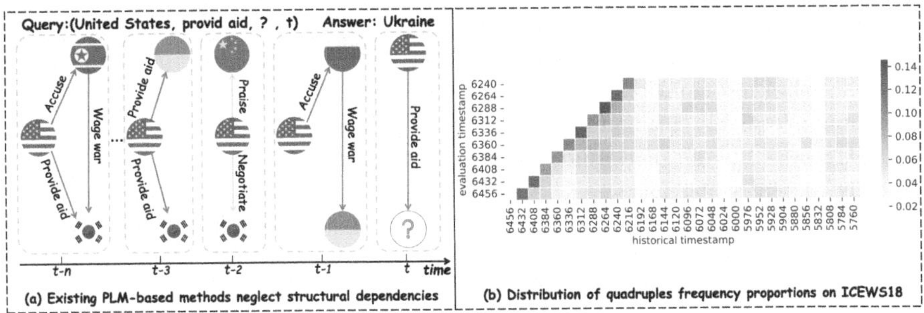

Fig. 1. Two challenges faced by existing PLM-based methods in capturing structural dependencies and global information. In figure (a), the **blue lines** represent the target *provide aid* relationship, but existing models struggle to infer the query based on the structural dependencies indicated by the two-order **red lines**. In figure (b), the y-axis represents the evaluation timestamps, while the x-axis shows the historical timestamps, ordered from nearest to furthest. (Color figure online)

known timestamps, while extrapolation aims to infer future facts at unknown timestamps. This work focuses on the extrapolation task.

To solve the problem of TKGR task, many efforts have been made to model the various characteristics of TKGs for future event prediction. Early works [9,13,25] mainly rely on graph neural networks (GNNs) to capture the temporal and structural dependencies within TKGs. However, these graph-based methods are fall short in temporal semantic modeling. Recently, with the success of pre-trained language models (PLMs) in temporal semantic modeling, they have garnered increasing attention. Works such as [15,22,26] focus on leveraging historical text within the graph to enhance the model's semantic understanding. Despite the advancements achieved, we argue that these PLM-based methods still have two significant drawbacks that need to be addressed.

Firstly, these PLM-based methods struggle to effectively capture **structural dependencies** within TKGs. Taking Fig. 1(a) as an example, existing models rely on first-order historical data related to the *United States* to enhance their inference capabilities when considering the query *(United States, provide aid, ?, t)*. However, these approaches are limited as they fail to capture more complex relationships that are not directly apparent in the history. For instance, the correct answer may depend on a two-order relationship, such as the graph at time $t-n$: *the United States accuses North Korea of waging war against South Korea and provides aid to South Korea*. Without capturing such structural dependencies, the model struggles to infer the correct answer *Ukraine*. In contrast, by learning the structural dependencies and incorporating the historical graph at time $t-1$, the model can make more accurate inferences.

Secondly, previous PLM-based methods do not explicitly incorporate **global information** from recurring historical facts. These methods typically use query text with sampled historical quadruples as input for PLMs but fail to capture the trending patterns of historical interactions. In fact, many recurring historical facts provide valuable global information. As shown in Fig. 1(a), historical interactions involving entities that *have received aid* from the *United States* can serve as global information for the query *(United States, provide aid, ?, t)*. Furthermore, effectively utilizing global information from a temporal perspective is non-trivial. Our detailed analysis of distribution of quadruple frequency proportions in real-word facts, as illustrated in Fig. 1(b), reveals that the recent historical facts are more relevant for prediction. This observation highlights the importance of leveraging recent historical facts to improve the predictions.

To this end, we propose **PSG**, a **P**LM-based framework that takes into account **S**tructure and **G**lobal information derived from recurring historical facts for TKG reasoning. Specifically, PSG first utilizes entity and relation embeddings from the graph space to generate *time-aware soft prompts*, which are then equipped with specific temporal text and fed into the frozen PLMs. Subsequently, these *time-aware soft prompts* from PLM's last layer serve as input for the graph model, obtaining preliminary inference results. Besides, based on our analysis, we design the time factor and time window in PSG to compute additional predictions based on global frequency, placing greater emphasis on recent historical facts. In the inference stage, the answers inferred by two modules are adaptively fused to make the final prediction more comprehensive. To summarize, the contributions of this paper are as follows:

- We propose a PLM-based framework that utilize specific temporal contextualized *time-aware soft prompts* to combine and balance semantic and structural information.
- Based on a detailed analysis of the quadruple frequency distribution, we effectively utilize global information, with a focus on emphasizing recent historical facts.
- We achieve state-of-the art performance on three datasets and conduct extensive analysis, demonstrating the effectiveness of our method in TKGR.

2 Related Work

Graph-Based TKGR Models. Graph-based models aim to capture both structure and temporal dynamics. Some methods [3,10,11] attempt to incorporate temporal information based on static knowledge graph reasoning models but often overlook latent temporal patterns. Furthermore, RE-NET [9] and RE-GCN [13] use GNNs to model structural and temporal evolution. CyGNet [27] and SiMFy [14] incorporate frequency learning for historical event interactions, while CENET [23] applies contrastive learning to identify likely entities. However, these methods struggle to model semantic information.

PLM-Based TKGR Models. Recently, PLM-based models have been utilized to obtain contextualized knowledge embeddings from external textual information. PPT [22] frames the task as masked token prediction, ECOLA [7] further enriches temporal knowledge embeddings by concurrently optimizing for the

TKG reasoning. Additionally, ChapTER [15] enhances reasoning across diverse complex scenarios with time prefix tokens. CoPET [26] addresses the issue by incorporating time-invariant information through a contrastive learning framework. Nonetheless, they overlook both structural dependencies and global recurring patterns.

3 Preliminary

Let $\mathcal{E}$, $\mathcal{R}$, $\mathcal{F}$ represent the set of entities, relations and facts respectively. TKG can be defined as an ordered KG sequence $\mathcal{G} = \{\mathcal{G}_0, \mathcal{G}_1, \dots, \mathcal{G}_n\}$. Each $\mathcal{G}_t = \{\mathcal{E}_t, \mathcal{R}_t, \mathcal{F}_t\}$, where $\mathcal{E}_t \subseteq \mathcal{E}$, $\mathcal{R}_t \subseteq \mathcal{R}$, and $\mathcal{F}_t$ represent facts that occur at time t. Each fact is represented as a quadruple (s, r, o, t), in which $s \in \mathcal{E}_t$ is a subject entity, $o \in \mathcal{E}_t$ is an object entity, and $r \in \mathcal{R}_t$ is the interactive relation. Given a query $q = (s, r, ?, t_q)$, TKGR extrapolation task aims to forecast the missing object entity o based on the historical KG sequence $\mathcal{G}_{t<t_q} = \{\mathcal{G}_0, \mathcal{G}_1, \dots, \mathcal{G}_{t_q-1}\}$. For each quadruple (s, r, o, t), we add its inverse quadruple (o, r^{-1}, s, t) for subject prediction, where r^{-1} represents the inverse predicate of r.

4 Methodology

As illustrated in Fig. 2, PSG is composed of two core modules: the Graph-PLM Synergy (GPS) module and the Global Recurring Patterns (GRP) Learning module. In this section, we first explain how the GPS module combines and balances semantic and structural information. Next, we describe how the GRP Learning module captures timely and relevant global information. Finally, we discuss the training and inference processes of the PSG model.

4.1 Graph-PLM Synergy Module

(1) Input Constructions. Given the query $q = (s, r, ?, t_q)$, our input for PLMs include two components: subject entity (relation) embedding and textual information. Specifically, we introduce subject entity embedding $\boldsymbol{E}_s \in \mathbb{R}^d$ and relation embedding $\boldsymbol{E}_r \in \mathbb{R}^d$ from the graph model (e.g., ConvTransE [17]), where d is embedding size. These graph-dependent embeddings are then concatenated with textual information, enabling interactions between them through PLMs. To provide $\boldsymbol{E}_s$ and $\boldsymbol{E}_r$ with temporal contextualized representations, we incorporate two types of textual information: **factual description** and **historical context**.

Factual Descriptions. In the dataset ICEWS (*Integrated Crisis Early Warning System*) [1], entities are represented by their names, such as "*China*". However, these names are often short and lack detail, whereas the relation in quadruple itself typically conveys more informative semantics [15]. To address this issue, we introduce enriched descriptions for the entities, enhancing their semantic information. For example, for the entity "*China*", the description is "*East Asian, world's most populous, rich history*". We then concatenate the original text with

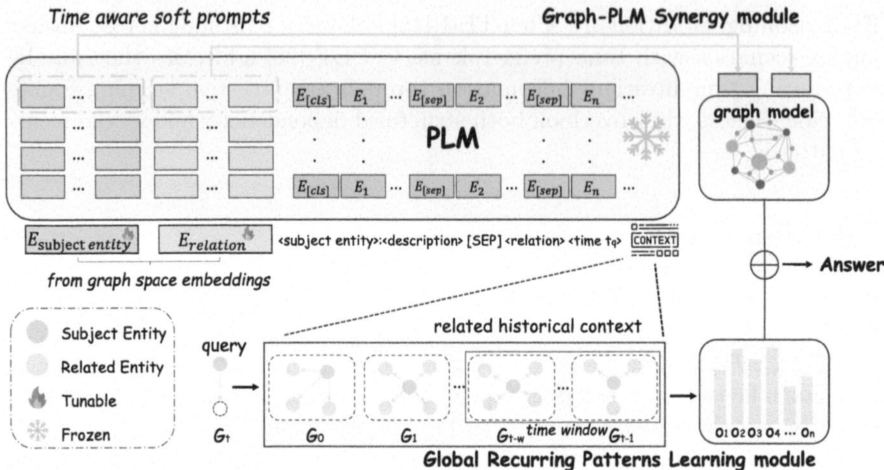

Fig. 2. Overall illustration of the PSG model. Given the query $(s, r, ?, t_q)$, the Graph-PLM Synergy module uses the embeddings for *subject entity* and *relation* from graph space to generate specific contextualized *time-aware soft prompts*, which are then processed by the frozen PLMs and graph model to obtain results. The Global Recurring Patterns Learning module calculates global frequency results, assigning higher scores to interactions within the specified time window. By combining two module results, the model predicts the final answer.

the entity description to form the subject text $\mathcal{Q}_s$. For relation text $\mathcal{Q}_r$, we use their name text directly. For timestamp text $\mathcal{Q}_{t_q}$, we adopt the format "yyyy-mm-dd" to form text.

Historical Context. To incorporate historical context, we sample some relative historical quadruples for the query q and convert them into historical text. Specifically, we define the set of historical quadruples $\mathcal{H}(s, r, t_q)$ as follows:

$$\mathcal{H}(s, r, t_q) = \{(s, r, o, t) | (s, r, o, t) \in \mathcal{F}, t < t_q\}. \tag{1}$$

Subsequently, we reorder all historical contexts in temporal ascending order and construct input textual prompts $\mathcal{P}(q)$ to PLM as follows:

$$\langle cls \rangle\ \mathcal{Q}_s \mid \mathcal{Q}_r \mid \mathcal{Q}_{t_q}\ \langle sep \rangle\ \mathcal{H}(s, r, t_q)\ \langle sep \rangle$$

(2) Align Text Representation with Graph Space. Previous studies [2,12] have demonstrated that the soft prompt tuning method can achieve comparable performance with minimal parameter adjustments in downstream tasks. Building on this, we introduce a novel *time-aware soft prompts tuning* method. Specifically, we input the *time-aware soft prompts* (TS) and constructed textual prompts $\mathcal{P}(q)$ that account for temporal dependencies into the frozen PLMs. To obtain the TS, we apply linear transformations to $\boldsymbol{E}_s$ and $\boldsymbol{E}_r$ as follows:

$$TS = \left[F\left(\boldsymbol{E}_s\right); F\left(\boldsymbol{E}_r\right)\right], \tag{2}$$

$$F(x) = \mathbf{W}_{x_2} \cdot (\mathrm{ReLU}(\mathbf{W}_{x_1} \cdot (x \parallel \psi(\boldsymbol{t}_q))), \tag{3}$$

where $\boldsymbol{W}_{x_1} \in \mathbb{R}^{d_h \times 2d}$, $\boldsymbol{W}_{x_2} \in \mathbb{R}^{(l*H*m)\times d_h}$ are trainable weight matrices, d_h is the middle hidden size for the mapping layers, l is the sequence length, H is the hidden size for the transformer layers, $\parallel$ denotes the concatenation operation and $\psi(\cdot)$ is the generic time encoding function [21].

Denoting $\boldsymbol{h}^{(j)} \in \mathbb{R}^{n\times d}$ as the output embeddings of all tokens in input text prompts $\mathcal{P}(q)$ after j-th transformer layer, we concatenate *time-aware soft prompts* with m-length token embeddings to the text token embeddings in each transformer layer as follows:

$$\widetilde{\boldsymbol{h}}^{(j)} = \boldsymbol{p}^{(j)} \parallel \boldsymbol{h}^{(j)}, 0 \le j \le L, \tag{4}$$

where $\boldsymbol{p}^{(j)}$ indicates the TS token embeddings of jth layer and $\widetilde{\boldsymbol{h}}$ is the concatenated input token embeddings. Formally, the ith input token of the jth layer $\widetilde{\boldsymbol{h}}^{(j)} \in \mathbb{R}^H$ is defined as:

$$\widetilde{\boldsymbol{h}}_i^{(j)} = \begin{cases} \boldsymbol{p}_i^{(j)}, & 0 \le i < m \\ \boldsymbol{e}_i^{(j)}, & (i \ge m) \wedge (j = 0) \\ \mathrm{FFN}(\widetilde{\boldsymbol{h}}^{(j-1)})_i, & \text{Otherwise} \end{cases} \tag{5}$$

Finally, we feed the outputs of TS from the frozen PLMs into the graph model and apply the softmax function to obtain the predicted results from the GPS module, as follows:

$$\mathcal{S}_{syn}^{(s,r)} = \mathrm{softmax}\left(f\left(\boldsymbol{E}_s, \boldsymbol{E}_r\right)\right), \tag{6}$$

where $\mathcal{S}_{syn}^{(s,r)} \in \mathbb{R}^{|\mathcal{E}|}$ denotes the score for candidate entities, and $f(\cdot)$ is the scoring function of the graph model.

4.2 Global Recurring Patterns Learning Module

The Global Recurring Patterns Learning module aims to obtain global frequency results based on KG sequence $\mathcal{G}_{t<t_q}$. Specifically, we compute the frequency score $\mathbf{z}_{t'}^{(s,r)} \in \mathbb{R}^{|\mathcal{E}|}$ for every timestamp $t' < t_q$. This score includes all entities served as the objects in facts with subject entity s and relation r at timestamp t', and is calculated as follows:

$$\mathbf{Z}_{t'}^{(s,r)}(o) = \sum_{x\in\mathcal{G}_{t'}} \mathbb{I}[x = (s, r, o, t')], \tag{7}$$

where $\mathbb{I}[\cdot]$ is an indicator function that returns 1 if the condition inside is true and 0 otherwise. Furthermore, based on our detailed analysis of the distribution

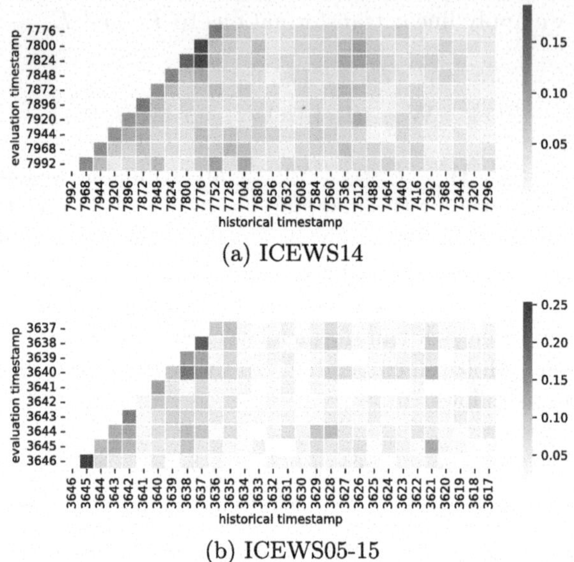

(a) ICEWS14

(b) ICEWS05-15

Fig. 3. Attention weights for the ICEWS14 and ICEWS05-15.

of quadruple frequency proportions in Fig. 1(b) and Fig. 3, we introduce a time window and time factor to aggregate frequency scores from all timestamps $t < t_q$ as follows:

$$\mathbf{Z}_{t_q}^{(s,r)} = \mathbf{Z}_{t'<t_q-w}^{(s,r)} + k \cdot \mathbf{Z}_{t_q-w\leq t'<t_q}^{(s,r)}, \tag{8}$$

where $\mathbf{Z}_{t_q}^{(s,r)} \in \mathbb{R}^{|\mathcal{E}|}$, w represents the time window size, and $k \geq 1$ is a time factor that assigns higher scores for interactions within the time window. For a more comprehensive discussion of the rationale behind this design, please refer to Sect. 6.1. Finally, we use the softmax function to obtain the scores with timely and relevant global information for candidate entities, as formalized below:

$$\mathcal{S}_{freq}^{(s,r)} = \text{softmax}\left(\mathbf{Z}_{t_q}^{(s,r)}\right). \tag{9}$$

4.3 Training and Inference

Given the query $q = (s, r, ?, t_q)$, predicting the object entity can be viewed as a multi-class classification task. We apply standard cross-entropy loss based on the output score from the graph model, as described below:

$$\mathcal{L} = -\sum_{t\in\mathcal{T}} \sum_{(s,r,o,t)\in\mathcal{G}_t} \log f(\boldsymbol{E}_s, \boldsymbol{E}_r). \tag{10}$$

For inference, we use a weighted coefficients $\alpha \in [0, 1]$ to balance the output scores from Graph-PLM Synergy module and Global Recurring Patterns

Learning module, generating the final probability as follows:

$$\mathbf{P}(o|s,r,t_q) = \alpha \cdot \mathcal{S}_{syn}^{(s,r)}(o) + (1-\alpha) \cdot \mathcal{S}_{freq}^{(s,r)}(o), \tag{11}$$

where $\mathbf{P}(o|s,r,t_q) \in \mathbb{R}^{|\mathcal{E}|}$ represents the final predicted distribution probability of candidate entities. The final prediction o_{t_q} will be the entity that receives the highest combined probability, as follows:

$$o_{t_q} = \arg\max_{o\in\mathcal{E}} \mathbf{P}(o|s,r,t_q). \tag{12}$$

5 Experiments

5.1 Experimental Setup

We conduct experiments on three representative TKG datasets: ICEWS14 [5], ICEWS18 [6], and ICEWS05-15 [5], all sourced from the *Integrated Crisis Early Warning System* [1]. The details of these benchmark datasets are summarized in Table 1. To evaluate model performance in TKGR, we use two widely adopted metrics: Mean Reciprocal Rank (MRR) and Hits@N ($N \in 1, 3$). For fair comparison, all model results are calculated using the raw settings [8]. For the hyper-parameters, the dimension d of entity and relation embeddings are set to 200; weighted coefficients α is set to 0.001; soft prompt length m is set to 5; time factor k is set to 14,8,26 and the window size w is set to 3,5,15 on ICEWS14, ICEWS18 and ICEWS05-15, respectively. All experiments are carried out on NVIDIA A800 GPU using PyTorch. We adopt AdamW optimizer, and our model employs *bert-base-cased* as the pre-trained language model, with ConvTransE [17] serving as the graph model. Detailed descriptions of baselines are provided in the Sect. 2, with factual descriptions added for PLM-based baselines to ensure fairness.

Table 1. The statistics of datasets.

Dataset	$\|\mathcal{E}\|$	$\|\mathcal{R}\|$	Train	Valid	Test	Timegap
ICEWS14	7128	230	74,845	8514	7371	24 h
ICEWS18	23,033	256	373,018	49,545	23,033	24 h
ICEWS05-15	10,488	251	368,868	46,302	46,159	1 day

5.2 Main Results

The experimental results of our model and other baselines are presented in Table 2, from which the following observations can be drawn.

Table 2. Main results on the ICEWS14, ICEWS18, and ICEWS05-15. The best results are highlighted in **bold**, and the second best results are underlined. Results marked with * are reimplementations using their open-source codes, while others are taken from the literature [13,22].

Model	ICEWS14			ICEWS18			ICEWS05-15		
	MRR	Hits@1	Hits@3	MRR	Hits@1	Hits@3	MRR	Hits@1	Hits@3
Static Graph-based models									
DistMult [24]	20.32	6.13	27.59	13.86	5.61	15.22	19.91	5.63	27.22
RotatE [18]	25.71	16.41	29.01	14.53	6.47	15.78	19.01	10.42	21.35
ConvTransE [17]	31.50	22.46	34.98	23.22	14.26	26.13	30.28	20.79	33.80
Temporal Graph-based models									
RE-NET [9]	35.77	25.99	40.10	26.17	16.43	29.89	36.86	26.24	41.85
RE-GCN [13]	37.78	27.17	42.50	27.51	17.82	31.17	38.27	27.43	43.06
CyGNet [27]	35.45	26.05	39.91	26.46	16.62	30.57	35.46	25.44	40.20
SiMFy* [14]	39.48	29.26	44.61	28.61	18.74	32.50	41.92	31.18	47.33
CENET* [23]	37.96	28.46	42.23	27.39	17.46	31.45	40.37	30.01	45.61
PLM-based models									
SimKGC* [19]	27.39	19.90	29.72	19.87	12.77	21.85	29.52	21.20	32.15
KGT5* [16]	33.36	24.36	37.48	23.77	15.02	26.86	32.81	23.75	36.85
PPT [22]	38.42	28.94	42.50	26.63	16.94	30.64	38.85	28.57	43.35
CoPET* [26]	31.04	21.53	35.29	22.36	13.83	24.76	31.34	22.05	34.78
ChapTER* [15]	32.81	23.27	36.67	22.82	14.23	25.72	31.77	22.00	35.63
PSG (Ours)	**43.13**	**33.79**	**48.03**	**30.69**	**21.31**	**34.63**	**45.00**	**35.13**	**50.33**

Comparison with Graph-Based Model. PSG surpasses static graph-based models, which fail to leverage temporal information. Although temporal graph-based models utilize message-passing mechanisms to make reasoning, they struggle to capture semantic information. In contrast, PSG integrates both semantic and structural information, enabling it to outperform temporal graph-based models. Specifically, PSG achieves improvements of 3.65%, 2.08%, and 3.08% in the MRR metric over the best temporal Graph-based model SiMFy, respectively.

Comparison with PLM-based Model. PSG significantly outperforms PLM-based models across all evaluation metrics. Notably, most PLM-based baselines struggle to achieve results comparable to temporal graph-based models. This is because PLM-based models, relying solely on textual semantics, struggle to capture the complex structural characteristics of TKGs. This underscores the necessity of incorporating additional structural and global information from historical facts to tackle more complex TKG reasoning tasks. Compared with PPT, which has the best results among PLM-based baselines, PSG improve 4.71% , 4.06%, and 6.15% in the MRR metric, respectively.

5.3 Ablation Study

The ablation study results are presented in Table 3, lines 2–6, where each ablative variant showing varying degrees of performance degradation. We evaluate

Table 3. Ablation study of PSG on ICEWS14, ICEWS18, and ICEWS05-15.

No.	Model	ICEWS14		ICEWS18		ICEWS05-15	
		MRR	Hits@1	MRR	Hits@1	MRR	Hits@1
1	**PSG**	**43.13**	**33.79**	**30.69**	**21.31**	**45.00**	**35.13**
2	*w/o* factual descriptions	41.88	32.23	29.16	20.27	43.96	34.95
3	*w/o* historical context	42.02	33.19	29.50	20.63	44.41	35.05
4	*w/o* graph model	39.91	31.39	27.88	19.54	40.97	30.76
5	*w/o* GRP Learning module	39.65	29.64	27.51	17.91	41.11	30.06
6	*w/o* time factor k	40.75	30.76	28.86	19.16	42.33	31.24

the contributions of key components in the PSG model, including input text prompts (lines 2–3), the graph model (line 4), and the GRP Learning module (lines 5–6). Specifically, PSG *w/o factual descriptions* results in MRR drops of 1.25%, 1.53%, and 1.04%, respectively. Furthermore, the results for PSG *w/o graph model*, which uses the PLM output directly as the graph model output, reveal that excessive reliance on textual semantic information negatively impacts performance. In contrast, incorporating structural information helps achieve a balance between semantics and structure. Line 5 demonstrates that removing the GRP Learning module causes substantial performance drops, highlighting the module's crucial role in capturing up-to-date global information. Finally, line 6 presents results for PSG *w/o time factor* k, which treats all historical facts equally (with $k = 1$). This result supports our analysis from Fig. 1(b) and Fig. 3, confirming that recent historical facts are more relevant for prediction.

6 Discussion

In this section, we analyze the quadruple frequency distributions to validate the rationale behind the design of the Global Recurring Patterns Learning module in Sect. 4.2. Besides, we analyze the impact of the frozen parameter training strategy, the adaptability to different graph models and PLMs, various sampling strategies, and the sensitivity to key hyper-parameters on PSG.

6.1 Analysis of Quadruple Frequency Distributions

In this section, we provide a detailed analysis of the distribution of quadruple frequency proportions to validate the rationale behind this design. The algorithm is summarized in Algorithm 1. Specifically, we compute attention weights for evaluation timestamps, where the attention weight quantifies the *degree of correlation* between a historical timestamp t_x and an evaluation timestamp t_y.The attention weight is calculated as the proportion of overlapping triples (s, r, o) present in both timestamps t_x and t_y. A higher attention weight indicates that a greater fraction of triples from the historical timestamp t_x also appear in the evaluation timestamp t_y, reflecting stronger temporal correlation between these two

Algorithm 1: Frequency Proportions for Evaluation Timestamps

Input: TKG validation set data $\mathcal{D} = \{(s, r, o, t)\}$, Evaluation timestamps $\mathcal{Y} = \{t_y \mid \forall t_y \in \mathcal{D}\}$, Historical timestamps $\mathcal{X} = \{t_x \mid t_x < t_y, \forall t_y \in \mathcal{Y}, \forall t_x \in \mathcal{D}\}$.
Output: Frequency Proportions matrix $\mathbf{A} \in \mathbb{R}^{|\mathcal{Y}| \times |\mathcal{X}|}$.
foreach $t_y \in \mathcal{Y}$ **do**
  foreach $t_x \in \mathcal{X}$ **do**
    Compute OverlapRatio $= \frac{|\{(s,r,o) \in \mathcal{D}_{t_x} \cap \mathcal{D}_{t_y}\}|}{|\mathcal{D}_{t_y}|}$;
    Assign $\mathbf{A}[t_y, t_x] \leftarrow$ OverlapRatio;
  end
end
Replace $\mathbf{A}[i, j] = 0$ with NaN for all i, j;
return A;

timestamps. The results of this analysis on three datasets are shown in Fig. 1(b) and Fig. 3, which reveal that facts associated with evaluation timestamps tend to cluster within more recent time periods. This suggests that, when predicting future events, it is crucial to focus on recent historical quadruples.

6.2 Frozen Parameter Training Strategy Analysis

To validate the impact of the frozen parameter training strategy, we conduct experiments with different levels of parameter frozen. The results are presented in Table 4. As the number of trainable parameters in the PLM increases, the performance of PSG declines. Notably, "PSG w/ fully tuned" experiences a significant drop, with a 6.95% decrease in MRR. These results indicate that freezing the PLM parameters enables PSG to better maintain semantic and structural correlations. Moreover, comparing Table 4 lines 2-3 and lines 4-5 reveals that freezing parameters from the bottom layers yields better than from the top layers. This is likely because the lower layers contain more crucial semantic features [2].

Table 4. Performance of PSG with different frozen parameter training strategies on ICEWS14.

No.	Model	MRR	Hits@1
1	**PSG**	**43.13**	**33.79**
2	*w/* first layer tuned	41.95	33.19
3	*w/* first 6 layer tuned	38.61	31.22
4	*w/* last layer tuned	41.56	32.90
5	*w/* last 6 layer tuned	36.81	30.72
6	*w/* fully tuned	36.18	30.24

Table 5. Performance of PSG with different graph models on ICEWS14.

Methods	MRR	Hits@1
DistMult	20.32	6.13
+ PSG	$41.60_{\uparrow 21.28}$	$32.78_{\uparrow 26.65}$
RotatE	25.71	16.41
+ PSG	$41.76_{\uparrow 16.05}$	$32.91_{\uparrow 16.50}$
ConvTransE	31.50	22.46
+ PSG	$43.13_{\uparrow 11.63}$	$33.79_{\uparrow 11.33}$

6.3 Adaptability to Graph Models

To confirm the robustness and flexibility of PSG, we conduct experiments using different graph models. Specifically, we select three representative graph models: ConvTransE [17], DistMult [24], and RotatE [18]. As shown in Table 5, PSG achieves excellent performance on the ICEWS14 dataset, demonstrating that our approach is not dependent on a specific graph model and generalizes effectively. Notably, compared to the DistMult alone, PSG achieves a significant improvement in MRR and an over fivefold increase in Hits@1 (from 6.13 to 32.78).

6.4 Adaptability to PLMs

To evaluate the robustness of our proposed method, we conduct experiments using different PLMs, including bert-base-uncased, bert-large-cased, and roberta-base. As shown in Fig. 4, we can observe that PSG with these PLM models all achieve close high performance. Specifically, PSG integrated with roberta-base achieved performance of 42.14, 32.68, and 46.87 on MRR, Hits@1, and Hits@3, respectively. These results indicate that our PSG is robust to different PLMs with varying parameters and agnostic to PLM size.

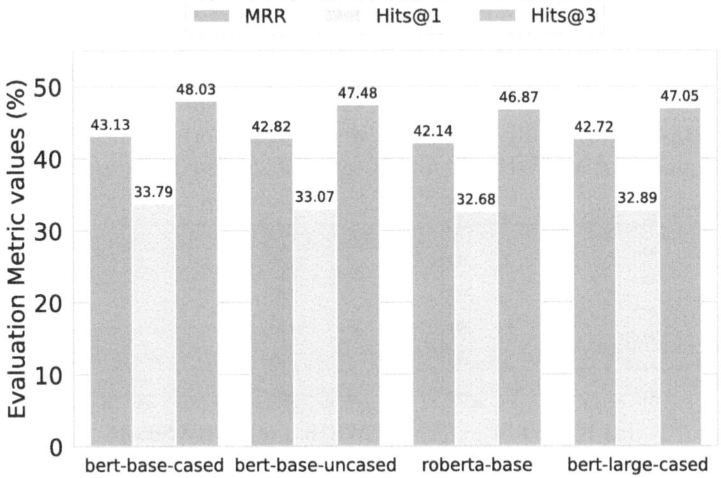

Fig. 4. Performance of PSG with different PLMs on ICEWS14. The x-axis denotes different PLMs, and the y-axis shows Evaluation Metric values.

6.5 Sampling Strategies

Given the query $= (s, r, ?, t_q)$, we explore three sampling strategies for selecting relevant historical quadruples: *entity-related* (historical facts related to **subject entity**), *relation-related* (historical facts related to **relation**), and *pair-related* (historical facts involving both **subject entity** and **relation**). As shown in

Table 6, the pair-related strategy achieves the best performance. Notably, It outperforms the second-best entity-related strategy, with improvements of 0.60%, 0.24%, and 0.71% in MRR, Hits@1, and Hits@3, respectively. The advantage becomes even more significant when compared to the relation-related strategy, where the gains reach 0.90%, 0.68%, and 1.38%. We believe this is because pair-related historical facts provides more contextualized background information.

Table 6. Performance comparison of different sampling strategies on the ICEWS14 dataset.

Sampling Strategy	MRR	Hits@1	Hits@3
pair-related	**43.13**	**33.79**	**48.03**
entity-related	42.53	33.55	47.32
relation-related	42.23	33.11	46.65

6.6 Parameter Sensitivity Analysis

To investigate the impact of the time factor k and time window size w on model performance, we conduct experiments with various values of k and w across all three datasets. The results, presented in Fig. 5, show that increasing the time factor k significantly enhances entity prediction accuracy. Furthermore, considering recent historical facts within an appropriate time window improves model performance, while excessively large w values can negatively impact the main prediction task. Specifically, PSG achieves optimal performance on ICEWS14, ICEWS18, and ICEWS05-15 when w is set to 3, 5, and 15, respectively.

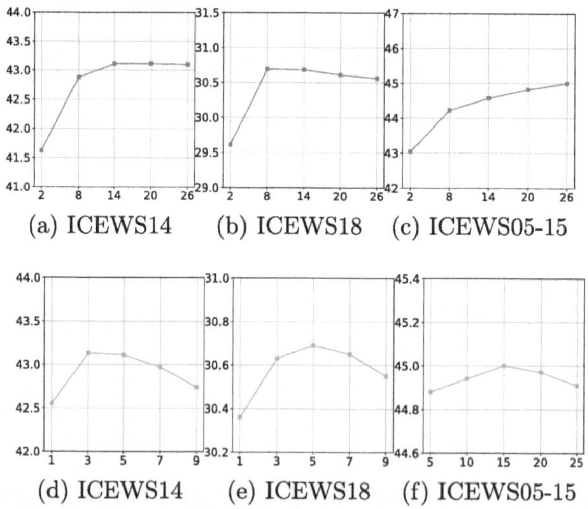

Fig. 5. Sensitivity analysis of time factors k (blue curves) and time window w (yellow curves). The x-axis denotes the respective values of k or w, and the y-axis shows corresponding MRR(%) values. (Color figure online)

7 Conclusion

In this paper, we propose PSG, a PLM-based framework that takes into account structure and global information for TKG reasoning. The model not only effectively integrates semantic and structural information, but also introduces timely and relevant global information in a simple manner. The experimental results demonstrate that our proposed method outperforms existing graph-based methods and PLM-based methods. Moving forward, how to design an adaptive fusion strategy that optimally enhances the performance of PSG without compromising efficiency is worth exploring.

Ackowledgment. We would like to thank all the anonymous reviewers and area chairs for their comments. This research is supported by National Natural Science Foundation of China (U23A20316) and founded by Joint&Laboratory on Credit Technology.

References

1. Boschee, E., et al.: Integrated Crisis Early Warning System (ICEWS) coded event data (2015). https://dataverse.harvard.edu/dataverse/icews
2. Chen, C., Wang, Y., Sun, A., Li, B., Lam, K.: Dipping PLMs sauce: bridging structure and text for effective knowledge graph completion via conditional soft prompting. In: Proceedings of the ACL Findings, pp. 11489–11503 (2023)
3. Dasgupta, S.S., Ray, S.N., Talukdar, P.P.: Hyte: Hyperplane-based temporally aware knowledge graph embedding. In: Proceedings of the EMNLP, pp. 2001–2011 (2018)
4. Gao, Y., et al.: Two-stage generative question answering on temporal knowledge graph using large language models. In: ACL (Findings), pp. 6719–6734 (2024)
5. García-Durán, A., Dumancic, S., Niepert, M.: Learning sequence encoders for temporal knowledge graph completion. In: Proceedings of the EMNLP, pp. 4816–4821 (2018)
6. Han, Z., Chen, P., Ma, Y., Tresp, V.: Explainable subgraph reasoning for forecasting on temporal knowledge graphs. In: Proceedings of the ICLR (2021)
7. Han, Z., et al.: ECOLA: enhancing temporal knowledge embeddings with contextualized language representations. In: Proceedings of the ACL Findings, pp. 5433–5447 (2023)
8. He, Y., et al.: HIP network: Historical information passing network for extrapolation reasoning on temporal knowledge graph. In: Proceedings of the IJCAI, pp. 1915–1921 (2021)
9. Jin, W., Qu, M., Jin, X., Ren, X.: Recurrent event network: autoregressive structure inferenceover temporal knowledge graphs. In: Proceedings of the EMNLP, pp. 6669–6683 (2020)
10. Lacroix, T., Obozinski, G., Usunier, N.: Tensor decompositions for temporal knowledge base completion. In: Proceedings of the ICLR (2020)
11. Leblay, J., Chekol, M.W.: Deriving validity time in knowledge graph. In: Proceedings of the WWW, pp. 1771–1776 (2018)
12. Li, X.L., Liang, P.: Prefix-tuning: optimizing continuous prompts for generation. In: Proceedings of the ACL, pp. 4582–4597 (2021)

13. Li, Z., et al.: Temporal knowledge graph reasoning based on evolutional representation learning. In: Proceedings of the SIGIR, pp. 408–417 (2021)
14. Liu, Z., et al.: Simfy: a simple yet effective approach for temporal knowledge graph reasoning. In: Proceedings of the EMNLP Findings, pp. 3825–3836 (2023)
15. Peng, M., et al: Deja vu: contrastive historical modeling with prefix-tuning for temporal knowledge graph reasoning. In: Proceedings of the ACL Findings, pp. 1178–1191 (2024)
16. Saxena, A., Kochsiek, A., Gemulla, R.: Sequence-to-sequence knowledge graph completion and question answering. In: ACL (1), pp. 2814–2828 (2022)
17. Shang, C., et al.: End-to-end structure-aware convolutional networks for knowledge base completion. In: Proceedings of the AAAI, pp. 3060–3067 (2019)
18. Sun, Z., Deng, Z., Nie, J., Tang, J.: Rotate: Knowledge graph embedding by relational rotation in complex space. In: Proceedings of the ICLR (2019)
19. Wang, L., Zhao, W., Wei, Z., Liu, J.: Simkgc: simple contrastive knowledge graph completion with pre-trained language models. In: Proceedings of the ACL, pp. 4281–4294 (2022)
20. Xiang, S., Cheng, D., Shang, C., Zhang, Y., Liang, Y.: Temporal and heterogeneous graph neural network for financial time series prediction. In: Proceedings of the CIKM, pp. 3584–3593 (2022)
21. Xu, D., Ruan, C., Körpeoglu, E., Kumar, S., Achan, K.: Inductive representation learning on temporal graphs. In: Proceedings of the ICLR (2020)
22. Xu, W., Liu, B., Peng, M., Jia, X., Peng, M.: Pre-trained language model with prompts for temporal knowledge graph completion. In: Proceedings of the ACL Findings, pp. 7790–7803 (2023)
23. Xu, Y., Ou, J., Xu, H., Fu, L.: Temporal knowledge graph reasoning with historical contrastive learning. In: Proceedings of the AAAI, pp. 4765–4773 (2023)
24. Yang, B., Yih, W., He, X., Gao, J., Deng, L.: Embedding entities and relations for learning and inference in knowledge bases. In: Proceedings of the ICLR (2015)
25. Zhang, M., Xia, Y., Liu, Q., Wu, S., Wang, L.: Learning long- and short-term representations for temporal knowledge graph reasoning. In: WWW, pp. 2412–2422 (2023)
26. Zhang, Y., et al.: Bring invariant to variant: a contrastive prompt-based framework for temporal knowledge graph forecasting. In: Proceedings of the COLING, pp. 2526–2536 (2024)
27. Zhu, C., Chen, M., Fan, C., Cheng, G., Zhang, Y.: Learning from history: Modeling temporal knowledge graphs with sequential copy-generation networks. In: Proceedings of the AAAI, pp. 4732–4740 (2021)

Knowledge Graphs II

On Large-Scale Evaluation of Embedding Models for Knowledge Graph Completion

Nasim Shirvani-Mahdavi(✉), Farahnaz Akrami, and Chengkai Li

University of Texas at Arlington, Arlington, TX 76019, USA
{nasim.shirvanimahdavi2,farahnaz.akrami}@mavs.uta.edu, cli@uta.edu

Abstract. Knowledge graph embedding (KGE) models are extensively studied for knowledge graph completion, yet their evaluation remains constrained by unrealistic benchmarks. Standard evaluation metrics rely on the closed-world assumption, which penalizes models for correctly predicting missing triples, contradicting the fundamental goals of link prediction. These metrics often compress accuracy assessment into a single value, obscuring models' specific strengths and weaknesses. The prevailing evaluation protocol, link prediction, operates under the unrealistic assumption that an entity's properties, for which values are to be predicted, are known in advance. While alternative protocols such as property prediction, entity-pair ranking, and triple classification address some of these limitations, they remain underutilized. Moreover, commonly used datasets are either faulty or too small to reflect real-world data. Few studies examine the role of mediator nodes, which are essential for modeling n-ary relationships, or investigate model performance variation across domains. This paper conducts a comprehensive evaluation of four representative KGE models on large-scale datasets FB-CVT-REV and FB+CVT-REV. Our analysis reveals critical insights, including substantial performance variations between small and large datasets, both in relative rankings and absolute metrics, systematic overestimation of model capabilities when n-ary relations are binarized, and fundamental limitations in current evaluation protocols and metrics.

Keywords: Knowledge graph embedding · Knowledge Graph Completion · Large-Scale Evaluation · Evaluation Metrics · Evaluation Protocols

1 Introduction

Knowledge graphs (KGs), such as Freebase [5] and Wikidata [39], represent real-world information in the form of triples, denoted as (head entity (subject), *relation*, tail entity (object)). KGs are indispensable resources for a wide range of artificial intelligence applications [19], such as question answering [46] and recommender systems [12]. Despite their size and utility, KGs are inherently incomplete, which can hinder their effectiveness in practical applications. Researchers have developed numerous automatic knowledge graph completion techniques to address

I. Awan et al. (Eds.): WISE 2025, LNCS 16368, pp. 243–259, 2026.
https://doi.org/10.1007/978-981-95-7251-9_17

this limitation. Among these approaches, knowledge graph *embedding* (KGE) models [7] have been extensively studied. These models aim to infer missing information by leveraging the latent representations of entities and relations.

This paper presents a comprehensive large-scale evaluation of KGE models for KG completion. Although these models have been extensively evaluated to assess their efficacy and applicability in real-world applications, we demonstrate fundamental limitations in current evaluation methodologies that result in inaccurate assessments of model performance. Our investigation focuses particularly on large-scale analysis, examining two main interrelated issues: 1) shortcomings of standard rank-based evaluation metrics and 2) inherent weaknesses in evaluation protocols. Our findings reveal that these methodological limitations substantially affect how KGE models are understood and compared. We also examine how data representation choices affect performance outcomes by using two datasets that employ different data modeling approaches in all our experiments.

Many existing evaluations of KGE models rely on datasets, such as FB15k-237 [6] and WN18RR [9], both of which exhibit several limitations. First, they fail to capture n-ary relationships among entities, which are modeled using mediator nodes (also called CVT nodes) in the Freebase data dump [25] and statement nodes in Wikidata. Our earlier findings [34] indicate that the conversion of n-ary relationships to binary ones, as implemented in FB15k-237, leads to substantial overestimation of KGE models' performance. Second, these datasets are considerably smaller than real-world datasets. Experiment results from previous studies [34,47] reveal significant differences in the performance of models between small-scale and large-scale datasets, with relative performance rankings among models also varying based on dataset size. Our experiments are conducted on two large-scale datasets, FB-CVT-REV and FB+CVT-REV [34]. While FB+CVT-REV represents n-ary relationships using CVT nodes, FB-CVT-REV converts n-ary relationships into binary ones, similar to FB15k-237. This distinction allows us to assess how KGE model performance varies when data is modeled differently. These datasets, derived from Freebase, are large-scale, represent real-world scenarios, and do not include the data redundancy that exists in FB15k. A discussion of these two datasets and other benchmarks is provided in Sect. 3.

(1) *Shortcomings of standard rank-based evaluation metrics*: KG completion methods aim to identify missing but correct triples in a KG. However, current evaluation metrics paradoxically penalize models for correctly predicting triples that are missing from the evaluation dataset. Standard ranking-based metrics such as Mean Rank (MR) and Mean Reciprocal Rank (MRR) [45] operate under the *closed-world assumption*, treating all predictions outside the KG as incorrect. This contradicts the *open-world assumption*, which acknowledges that absent facts are not necessarily false [28]. Furthermore, each of these metrics aggregates performance across all relations and triples into a single value, obscuring models' strengths and weaknesses on different relations. In Sect. 4, we explore the shortcomings of existing evaluation metrics with supporting experimental evi-

dence discussed in Sect. 5. We illustrate how these shortcomings impact models' performance and propose refinements to improve evaluation reliability.

(2) *Inherent weaknesses in evaluation protocols*: The standard evaluation protocol for KGE models, *link prediction* [6], evaluates models by predicting the missing h in triple (?, *r*, t) or missing t in (h, *r*, ?). It assesses whether a model prioritizes correct answers over incorrect ones. However, as Wang et al. [40] pointed out, this approach can be misleading because it does not verify whether correct triples are ranked better than all type of false and nonsensical ones. For example, for a test triple (James Ivory, *director/film*, A Room With A View), evaluation by link prediction does not rank the nonsensical triple (A Room With A View, *director/film*, James Ivory). Wang et al. [40] showed that models often assign high scores to such invalid triples. To assess how models rank all possible triples, even the nonsensical ones, for a given relation, we performed the *entity-pair ranking* evaluation protocol on the two datasets mentioned above. Another limitation of link prediction is its assumption that an entity's properties are already known, focusing only on retrieving the correct object or subject entities. In practice, determining whether a property applies to an entity is itself a challenge. To address this gap, we introduce a new evaluation protocol, *property prediction*. A third alternative evaluation protocol to link prediction, *triple classification* [35,41], assesses whether a given triple is a true or false fact. This requires negative triples in the test and validation sets. Traditionally, these negative triples are generated by randomly replacing a head or tail entity, an approach that does not sufficiently challenge the models [35,41]. Inspired by *hard negatives* suggested by Pezeshkpour et al. [26] and Safavi et al. [31], we propose focusing on generating *type-consistent* negatives using the Freebase type system as models generally excel at identifying entity types, making *type-inconsistent* negatives easier to classify and providing less meaningful evaluation challenges. Further details on the limitations of link prediction can be found in Sect. 4, while experiments involving alternative evaluation protocols are presented in Sect. 5.

In summary, this paper makes the following contributions:

- We present a comprehensive large-scale evaluation of KGE models on FB-CVT-REV and FB+CVT-REV datasets.
- We provide quantitative results indicating that metrics based on the closed-world assumption underestimate models' accuracy.
- We develop comprehensive global metrics revealing hidden performance patterns, including macro-averaging by relation or domain, analysis of left and right entity link predictions, and quantitative evidence showing how n-ary to binary conversion leads to overestimation of model performance.
- We highlight the limitations of link prediction as an evaluation protocol for KGE models, and demonstrate how dataset size affects model performance and relative rankings among different KGE approaches.
- We introduce a new evaluation protocol, property prediction, and evaluate the KGE models on this protocol, entity-pair ranking, and triple classification as alternatives to link prediction.

All the scripts and datasets used in our experiments, and additional details on the experimental setup, are publicly available at https://github.com/idirlab/largeKGEeval.

2 Related Work

Prior research has investigated various aspects of KGE evaluation. Several studies have explored the impact of training strategies on KGE models' performance [3]. Evaluation metrics for KGE models have been extensively studied. For instance, Hoyt et al. [14] proposed desiderata for improved metrics to enhance interpretability and comparability of existing metrics across datasets of different sizes and properties. Similarly, Hubert et al. [17] proposed *Sem@K*, a semantic-oriented metric, to evaluate the semantic-awareness of KGE models. Other studies explored different evaluation protocols [30, 40] and assessed KGE models from an information retrieval perspective [48]. Additionally, KGE models have been evaluated via real-world applications, such as recommendation systems [13]. ReliK [10] introduced a framework to quantify a KGE model's reliability for specific downstream tasks without requiring their direct execution. Furthermore, some studies focused on what the embeddings learn and whether similar entities have similar embeddings [18]. Others examined biases in KGE benchmarks [2,32]. The most closely related work to ours is [34], which investigates the impact of various data modeling idiosyncrasies, such as representing n-ary relations via mediator nodes, on the performance of KGE models at scale. Additionally, they provide several well-processed datasets that facilitate more realistic assessments of KGE models, two of which are used in our experiments. In this paper, we primarily focus on the limitations of evaluation metrics and protocols, rather than solely on data modeling. Nevertheless, all our experiments place emphasis on large-scale evaluation and systematically examine the effect of different data modeling choices on model performance as well.

3 Background

3.1 Common Evaluation Protocols and Evaluation Metrics

KG embedding-based methods consist of two key components: (1) a score function that evaluates the plausibility of triples $(\mathsf{h}, r, \mathsf{t})$ by assigning a real-valued score based on relation and entity embeddings, and (2) a learning process to generate the representations (i.e., embeddings) of entities and relations. These models are evaluated on several KG completion tasks such as link prediction, triple classification, relation extraction [21,43], and relation prediction [33]. However, link prediction remains the most widely used. The goal of link prediction is to infer the missing entity h or t in a triple $(\mathsf{h}, r, \mathsf{t})$. For each test triple $(\mathsf{h}, r, \mathsf{t})$, the head entity h is replaced with every other entity $\mathsf{h}' \in \mathcal{E}$ to form *corrupted* triples, where $\mathcal{E}$ represents the set of all entities in the dataset. The original test triple and its corresponding corrupted triples are ranked by their scores according to the score function and the rank of the original test triple is denoted $rank_{\mathsf{h}}$.

The same procedure is used to calculate $rank_{\mathtt{t}}$ for the tail entity t. The ideal score function and embeddings should rank the test triple at top.

The commonly used metrics for measuring the accuracy of embedding models are: (1) $\mathtt{Hits@k}^{\uparrow}$,[1] the percentage of top k results that are correct; (2) Mean Rank ($\mathtt{MR}^{\downarrow}$), the mean of the test triples' ranks, defined as $\frac{1}{2\,|T|}\sum_{(\mathtt{h},r,\mathtt{t})\in T}(rank_{\mathtt{h}} + rank_{\mathtt{t}})$ in which $|T|$ is the size of the test set; and (3) Mean Reciprocal Rank ($\mathtt{MRR}^{\uparrow}$) [45], the average inverse of harmonic mean of the test triples' ranks, defined as $\frac{1}{2\,|T|}\sum_{(\mathtt{h},r,\mathtt{t})\in T}(\frac{1}{rank_{\mathtt{h}}} + \frac{1}{rank_{\mathtt{t}}})$. In addition to these raw metrics, their corresponding *filtered* versions [6] are commonly used to exclude the corrupted triples that already exist in the training, validation, or test sets. Throughout the paper, all mentions of the metrics refer to their filtered versions.

3.2 Evaluation Datasets and Frameworks

The most commonly used datasets for evaluating KGE models are derived from knowledge bases such as Freebase [5], WordNet [23], YAGO [36], Wikidata [39], NELL [8], and DBpedia [4]. Among them, FB15k, FB15k-237 [6], WN18, WN18RR [9], NELL-995 [8], and YAGO3-10 [22] are the most widely used benchmarks. However, these datasets have two key limitations. First, they do not capture n-ary relationships among entities. Second, they are substantially smaller than real-world datasets. Large-scale datasets have been introduced to address scalability concerns, yet they also have drawbacks. For instance, Freebase86m [47] includes numerous non-subject matter triples from Freebase's implementation domains and suffers from high data redundancy due to reverse triples [34]. WikiKG90Mv2 [15] and ogbl-wikikg2 [16] do not include n-ary relationships, i.e., statement nodes in Wikidata. JF17k [42] and WikiPeople [11], albeit small in scale, are also commonly used in the literature. However, these datasets explicitly capture hyper-relational structures [29] and are primarily used to evaluate hyper-relational models.

Several frameworks have been developed to scale up the training and evaluation of KGE models, including DGL-KE [47], PyTorch-BigGraph [20], and Marius [24]. While each framework offers distinct advantages, we selected DGL-KE for our experiments due to its ease of use, efficient negative sampling strategies, and high performance. In this study, we trained and evaluated four well-known KGE models—TransE [6], DistMult [44], ComplEx [38], and RotatE [37]—using the settings and hyperparameters recommended in [47]. TransE and RotatE are selected as representatives of translational distance models, while DistMult and ComplEx represent semantic matching models [47]. To overcome the limitations of the datasets mentioned above, we employ the FB-CVT-REV and FB+CVT-REV datasets. As mentioned in Sect. 1, these datasets are large-scale and do not include the data redundancy that exists in FB15k. FB+CVT-REV explicitly

---

[1] Throughout the paper, we always place an upward (downward, respectively) arrow beside a measure to indicate that methods with greater (smaller, respectively) values by that measure possess higher accuracy.

represents n-ary relationships using CVT nodes, whereas FB-CVT-REV converts an n-ary relationship centered at a CVT node into $\binom{n}{2}$ binary relationships between every pair of entities by concatenating the edges that connect the entities through the CVT node.

4 Limitations of Current Evaluation Methodologies

4.1 Shortcomings of Standard Evaluation Metrics

Closed-World Assumption. The aforementioned performance metrics are designed to evaluate a model's performance based on the closed-world assumption. Suppose that the total knowledge of a domain is available. Then it is not necessary to explicitly represent negative facts; they are inferred from the absence of their positive counterparts. This concept of closed-world assumption, first introduced by Reiter [27,28], can be stated as "if a positive fact P is not provable from the knowledge base, assume $\neg P$." This assumption is far from realistic due to the incompleteness of real-world knowledge graphs and thus has flaws when a model correctly predicts a triple that does not exist in a dataset. More specifically, if a corrupted triple of a given test triple does not exist in the current dataset, it is considered false. However, the corrupted triple might actually be valid. If a model ranks the correct corrupted triple higher than the test triple itself, its accuracy measures will be penalized, which contradicts the primary goal of link prediction—finding correct triples that do not already exist in the dataset.

Global Metrics. Another limitation of the current metrics is that they aggregate the accuracy of all predicted triples into a single value—the micro-average accuracy—which masks the specific strengths and weaknesses of the models. The Freebase dataset exhibits a highly skewed distribution, with a few high-frequency relations and a large number of low-frequency ones [1]. Thus, the micro-average accuracy is predominantly influenced by the most frequent relations. Moreover, the practice of reporting a single, overall accuracy neglects important sources of variability, such as asymmetries between predicting head versus tail entities and performance variation across semantic domains, which can all affect a model's real-world utility. Furthermore, in the presence of n-ary relationships (i.e., CVT nodes), link prediction becomes more challenging since these nodes are often long-tail entities with limited connectivity [34]. This limited connectivity stems from the fact that each CVT node typically represents the specific attributes or relationships of just a single main entity, inherently restricting its connections within the graph. However, their impact on the effectiveness of current link prediction models remains underexplored.

4.2 Inherent Weaknesses in Evaluation Protocols

Link prediction is a widely used evaluation protocol for assessing KGE models. However, it has certain limitations. *First*, its evaluation setup can be misleading as we cannot verify if a model ranks all types of false or nonsensical triples lower than correct triples. For example, consider a test triple (James Ivory, *director/film*, A Room With A View). Evaluation by link prediction only seeks responses to two sensible questions: "who directed the film A Room With A View?", i.e., (?, *director/film*, A Room With A View), and "which film(s) are directed by James Ivory?", i.e., (James Ivory, *director/film*, ?). It does not verify if a model would rank false or nonsensical triples, such as (A Room With A View, *director/film*, James Ivory) lower than the correct one. In this triple, the subject and object entities are swapped, resulting in an incorrect direction for the relation. Wang et al. [40] discussed this problem and proposed to use an alternative protocol called entity-pair ranking. *Second*, link prediction is based on the assumption that the presence of a particular property on an entity is already known. The evaluation focuses on whether a model can derive the correct property values. In reality, though, it remains a challenge to determine whether a property is valid for a given entity in the first place. Therefore, we propose the property prediction task as another evaluation protocol. Both entity-pair ranking and property prediction, along with a third alternative protocol, triple classification, are discussed in Sect. 5.2.

5 Experiments

In conducting our experiments, we utilized the provided training, validation, and test sets of the FB-CVT-REV and FB+CVT-REV datasets, with the split ratio of 90/5/5. Our experiments were performed on an NVIDIA H100 80GB GPU.

5.1 Empirical Analysis and Improvements of Evaluation Metrics

This section presents a series of experiments demonstrating the limitations that render commonly used evaluation metrics (cf. Section 3.1) inadequate for assessing KGE models. For each limitation, we propose a set of recommendations for improving the evaluation process to obtain more realistic results.

Closed-World Assumption. To verify whether the conventional metrics operate under the closed-world assumption and to assess the correctness of the predicted triples absent from the current dataset, we conducted two sets of experiments, one on FB+CVT-REV and the other on FB-CVT-REV. For each set of experiments, we created a subset dataset by randomly selecting 10% of the full dataset. The models were trained on this subset, and the evaluation was performed twice, using the subset or the full dataset as the ground truth, respectively. A corrupted triple for a test instance in the subset was considered correct if it exists in the ground-truth dataset. We then filtered out these valid corrupted triples from the ranked predictions in order to avoid penalizing the models for correctly predicting them over the actual test triple. The full dataset provides a more comprehensive knowledge base, and thus, using it as the ground truth helps better assess whether a model is incorrectly penalized due to the closed-world assumption. While FB+CVT-REV and FB-CVT-REV are still far from complete, this method was employed for a more realistic evaluation of the models' performance and to demonstrate the limitations associated with the closed-world assumption.

The results of this experiment are presented in Table 1. Using the full datasets to filter out correct predictions from the ranked list led to improved performance. The models' MRR$^{\uparrow}$ increased by varying degrees, ranging from 3.94% to 6.98% across different models and datasets, with the performance improvement being slightly lower on the dataset with n-ary relationships. This increase in accuracy demonstrates that models are penalized for predicting correct triples and that metrics based on the closed-world assumption underestimate models' accuracy. This poses an intrinsic challenge in evaluating KGE models—We would ideally need an absolute ground-truth dataset which is impossible to come by given any large-scale knowledge graph, and such a ground-truth dataset will not require completion anyways.

Table 1. Link prediction results (micro-averaged) on FB-CVT-REV and FB+CVT-REV, using their subsets vs. the full datasets as ground-truth to filter out correct predictions from the ranked list to avoid penalizing the models for valid predictions

	ground-truth: FB-CVT-REV subset				ground-truth: FB-CVT-REV			
Model	MRR$^{\uparrow}$	MR$^{\downarrow}$	Hits@1$^{\uparrow}$	Hits@10$^{\uparrow}$	MRR$^{\uparrow}$	MR$^{\downarrow}$	Hits@1$^{\uparrow}$	Hits@10$^{\uparrow}$
TransE	0.73	74.33	0.67	0.83	0.77 (6.01%)	73.80	0.67	0.84
DistMult	0.68	69.93	0.63	0.78	0.72 (6.98%)	69.03	0.64	0.80
ComplEx	0.69	71.83	0.65	0.78	0.73 (6.90%)	71.10	0.65	0.81
RotatE	0.69	132.13	0.65	0.75	0.73 (6.41%)	131.54	0.65	0.78
	ground-truth: FB+CVT-REV subset				**ground-truth: FB+CVT-REV**			
Model	MRR$^{\uparrow}$	MR$^{\downarrow}$	Hits@1$^{\uparrow}$	Hits@10$^{\uparrow}$	MRR$^{\uparrow}$	MR$^{\downarrow}$	Hits@1$^{\uparrow}$	Hits@10$^{\uparrow}$
TransE	0.50	98.39	0.44	0.62	0.51 (3.94%)	98.04	0.44	0.63
DistMult	0.43	134.29	0.38	0.55	0.45 (4.76%)	133.55	0.39	0.57
ComplEx	0.42	141.86	0.36	0.52	0.44 (4.82%)	140.00	0.37	0.54
RotatE	0.40	209.93	0.35	0.47	0.41 (4.10%)	208.66	0.35	0.50

Macro-averaging by Relation. To establish a metric that provides equal weight to all relations in the evaluation, we propose incorporating the macro-average of per-relation accuracy. The macro-averaged MRR$^{\uparrow}$ is defined as $\frac{1}{|R|}\sum_{r\in R}(\frac{1}{2}\frac{1}{|T_r|}\sum_{(\mathsf{h},r,\mathsf{t})\in T_r}(\frac{1}{rank_{\mathsf{h}}}+\frac{1}{rank_{\mathsf{t}}}))$, where $|R|$ is the total number of distinct relations and $|T_r|$ is the size of the test triples in relation r. Table 2 compares micro- and macro-averaged MRR$^{\uparrow}$. As observed, MRR$^{\uparrow}$ improves across all models with macro-averaging, indicating that treating all relations equally results in higher overall performance. This suggests that models perform relatively well even on low-frequency relations.

Left Vs. Right Entity Link Prediction. We propose evaluating left and right entity link prediction—(?, r, t) and (h, r, ?), respectively—separately for each relation, instead of relying solely on the overall average accuracy of test triples. Table 2 shows that models have considerably higher accuracy on right entity link predictions than left entity link predictions. This distinction reveals important asymmetries in model performance; thus, examining predictions in both directions separately provides a more nuanced understanding of model capabilities.

N-Ary Vs. Binary Relations. To investigate the impact of n-ary relationships on link prediction, we categorized relations into two types—binary relations, which connect two regular entities, and n-ary (or concatenated) relations. In FB+CVT-REV, n-ary relations link regular entities to CVT nodes, while in FB-CVT-REV concatenated relations represent binary conversions of n-ary relations. Table 3 presents the results for both relation types, with the "all" columns aggregating them. The results indicate that evaluation on concatenated relations yields overestimated accuracy metrics for most models compared to their performance on n-ary ones. This may result from decomposing n-ary relations into several binary relations through Cartesian product-like conversions. The decomposition allows models to more easily learn these simplified patterns when evaluated separately, creating an illusion of higher capability of the models. Moreover, across all models and datasets, the accuracy on concatenated/n-ary relations is significantly higher than binary relations because they exhibit more consistent structural patterns with lower variability, making them easier for models to learn despite their origin in complex relationships.

Table 2. Link prediction accuracy measured by micro-average vs. macro-average on FB-CVT-REV and FB+CVT-REV

FB-CVT-REV	Micro-average			Macro-average		
Model	Left MRR↑	Right MRR↑	Overall MRR↑	Left MRR↑	Right MRR↑	Overall MRR↑
TransE	0.46	0.74	0.67	0.48	0.77	0.69
DistMult	0.51	0.85	0.70	0.52	0.89	0.74
ComplEx	0.56	0.87	0.71	0.59	0.90	0.74
RotatE	0.58	0.90	0.80	0.60	0.92	0.82
FB+CVT-REV	**Micro-average**			**Macro-average**		
Model	Left MRR↑	Right MRR↑	Overall MRR↑	Left MRR↑	Right MRR↑	Overall MRR↑
TransE	0.35	0.65	0.57	0.38	0.68	0.60
DistMult	0.41	0.73	0.61	0.43	0.75	0.63
ComplEx	0.45	0.78	0.62	0.47	0.80	0.65
RotatE	0.49	0.83	0.73	0.50	0.85	0.74

Table 3. Micro-averaged MRR$^{\uparrow}$ on FB-CVT-REV and FB+CVT-REV, binary vs. n-ary/concatenated relations

	FB-CVT-REV			FB+CVT-REV		
Model	**binary**	**concatenated**	**all**	**binary**	**n-ary**	**all**
TransE	0.60	0.90	0.67	0.57	**0.96**	0.57
DistMult	0.64	0.89	0.70	0.61	0.77	0.61
ComplEx	0.66	0.90	0.71	0.62	0.80	0.62
RotatE	**0.76**	**0.92**	**0.80**	**0.73**	0.88	**0.73**

Macro-averaging by Domain. Freebase is a cross-domain common fact KG that comprises factual information in a broad range of domains [34], such as music, sports, biology, etc. We analyzed link prediction performance on the 12 most frequent domains in FB-CVT-REV, which together account for nearly 95% of all subject-matter triples—those representing real-world facts, as opposed to metadata that describes the data itself [34]. Table 4 reports the number of distinct relations, triples, and MRR$^{\uparrow}$ for each domain. The results show significant variance in models' accuracy across domains, with overall micro-averaged accuracy heavily influenced by dominant domains, particularly *music*, which accounts for over 60% of the triples. This highlights the importance of incorporating macro-average evaluation alongside micro-average evaluation to give equal weight to each domain, a factor largely overlooked in the existing literature. Here, the macro-average is defined at the domain level rather than the relation level. The domain-level macro-averaged MRR$^{\uparrow}$ is $\frac{1}{|D|}\sum_{d\in D}(\frac{1}{2}\frac{1}{|T_d|}\sum_{(\mathsf{h},r,\mathsf{t})\in T_d}(\frac{1}{rank_{\mathsf{h}}}+\frac{1}{rank_{\mathsf{t}}}))$, where $|D|$ is the total number of distinct domains and $|T_d|$ is the size of the test triples in domain d. Given the large variance of performance across different domains, it is also important to understand the models' performance on a domain is influenced by each domain's characteristics. For instance, the models had almost perfect accuracy on domain *measurement_unit*. Most of the frequent relations in this domain are *1-to-n* relations—relations in which a single head entity can be associated with multiple tail entities. One example is */measurement_unit/dated_integer/source-/location/hud_foreclosure_area/estimated_number_foreclosures*, which is a concatenated property. For instance, when the subject is United States Department of Housing and Urban Development, the objects are Lake Barcroft, Van Vleck, Fort Ahby, and so on. Given the similarity between the objects, it could be easier to predict the subject. On the other hand, the models had particularly low accuracy on domains such as *book*. One of the most prevalent relations in this domain is */book/book_edition/isbn*. An ISBN value mostly appears in one triple only, with highly rare exceptions, and that triple would be an instance of */book/book_edition/isbn*. To predict either the book or the ISBN value, without the ISBN value being connected to anything else, the model would be helpless.

Table 4. Link prediction performance (MRR↑) on the most frequent subject-matter domains in FB-CVT-REV

Domain	#Triples	#Relations	TransE MRR↑	DistMult MRR↑	ComplEx MRR↑	RotatE MRR↑
/music/	76,853,315	119	0.752	0.674	0.694	0.819
/film/	8,099,424	113	0.943	0.788	0.815	0.871
/people/	7,737,375	71	0.853	0.638	0.652	0.659
/tv/	5,276,787	148	0.970	0.922	0.929	0.945
/book/	5,258,889	90	0.590	0.284	0.268	0.290
/measurement_unit/	4,496,699	239	**0.999**	**0.994**	**0.995**	**0.990**
/location/	3,198,389	157	0.900	0.791	0.810	0.835
/award/	3,112,556	60	0.995	0.981	0.984	0.987
/biology/	1,459,238	71	0.814	0.596	0.606	0.560
/organization/	1,223,205	55	0.883	0.710	0.734	0.766
/education/	1,083,133	82	0.866	0.740	0.658	0.696
/sports/	996,040	105	0.973	0.871	0.902	0.910

5.2 Mitigating Weaknesses in Evaluation Protocols

In this section, we reproduce link prediction results and present the results from alternative evaluation protocols, including entity-pair ranking, property prediction, and triple classification. Our results indicate that the models perform poorly on these alternative evaluations, and there is some mismatch between link prediction accuracy and performance on other tasks. For instance, while RotatE achieves the highest link prediction scores, DistMult and ComplEx excel in triple classification. These findings highlight the need for better training and evaluation strategies for KGE models.

Link Prediction. We conducted link prediction experiments using the four aforementioned KGE models in the DGL-KE framework on datasets FB-CVT-REV, FB+CVT-REV, and FB15k-237. Table 5 presents the results, revealing a significant performance gap between large- and small-scale datasets. On the FB15k-237 dataset, the performance differences between models are mostly marginal. However, on the larger datasets, their performances diverge more significantly, and the ranking of models differs from that observed on the smaller FB15k-237. For instance, ComplEx performs the worst on small-scale data but surpasses TransE and DistMult on larger datasets. This highlights that results from small-scale data may not provide a realistic evaluation of the models. Although we originally reported these results in [34], they are reproduced here to emphasize the importance of experimenting with large-scale datasets rather than small-scale ones. Additionally, these results are included to provide a basis for comparing the performance of KGE models on link prediction with other evaluation protocols.

Table 5. Link prediction results (micro-averaged) on FB15k-237, FB-CVT-REV, and FB+CVT-REV

	FB15k-237				FB-CVT-REV				FB+CVT-REV			
Model	MRR↑	MR↓	Hits@1↑	Hits@10↑	MRR↑	MR↓	Hits@1↑	Hits@10↑	MRR↑	MR↓	Hits@1↑	Hits@10↑
TransE	**0.24**	**257.75**	0.14	**0.44**	0.67	**48.49**	0.61	0.78	0.57	**36.12**	0.49	0.75
DistMult	**0.24**	385.12	0.14	0.43	0.70	70.49	0.66	0.77	0.61	81.84	0.56	0.70
ComplEx	0.23	425.38	0.14	0.42	0.71	67.74	0.68	0.78	0.62	83.20	0.57	0.70
RotatE	**0.24**	288.43	**0.16**	0.42	**0.80**	75.72	**0.78**	**0.84**	**0.73**	68.43	**0.69**	**0.80**

Entity-Pair Ranking. Wang et al. [40] discussed the first limitation with link prediction, mentioned in Sect. 4.2 and proposed to use an alternative protocol called entity-pair ranking. Following this evaluation protocol, we would create all possible combinations of entities for a relation and then rank them based on their scores. Specifically, Wang et al. [40] proposed using Weighted Mean Average Precision (WMAP@K↑) and Weighted Precision (WP@K↑). To treat each relation equally, we employ macro-averaging, which corresponds to reporting the unweighted version of these metrics.

Specifically, the unweighted version of $WMAP@K$ is defined as $MAP@K = \sum_{r \in \mathcal{R}} AP_r@K$, where R is the set of all relations in the test set and $AP_r@K$ is defined as $AP_r@K = \frac{1}{NP_r} \sum_{k \in K} P_r@k \times relv_r[k]$ in which NP_r is the lesser of K and $|T_r|$ (the number of test triples for relation r), $P_r@k$ is the precision among top k predictions for relation r, and $relv_r[k]$ is a Boolean indicator of whether the kth prediction is correct (1) or not (0). Furthermore, we define the unweighted version of $WP@K$ as $P@K = \sum_{r \in \mathcal{R}} P_r@K$ where R is the set of all relations in the test set and $P_r@K$ is the precision among top K predictions for relation r.

Tables 6 shows the results. The overall observation is that the models have low performance on entity-pair ranking, especially when CVT nodes exist in the data. DistMult is the worst-performing model, while ComplEx has the best $P@100$ and RotatE has the best $MAP@100$.

Table 6. Entity-pair ranking results

	FB-CVT-REV		FB+CVT-REV	
Model	MAP@100↑	P@100↑	MAP@100↑	P@100↑
TransE	0.12	15.6	0.07	10.4
DistMult	0.11	7.7	0.04	1.1
ComplEx	0.17	**17.0**	0.11	**14.7**
RotatE	**0.20**	15.4	**0.13**	11.2

Table 7. Property prediction results

	FB-CVT-REV		FB+CVT-REV	
Model	MRR↑	MR↓	MRR↑	MR↓
TransE	0.10	120.1	0.07	145.1
DistMult	0.27	93.1	0.26	99.8
ComplEx	0.33	94.5	0.31	98.8
RotatE	**0.40**	**80.9**	**0.37**	**97.0**

Property Prediction. To conduct property prediction, it is imperative to modify the test set. Specifically, we need to restructure the test data to consist only of (h, r) pairs. A pair (h, r) is included in the test set only if no triples of the form (h, r, t') exist in the training set. This ensures that the property r for entity h is not already observed during training, which preserves the integrity of the evaluation. Given a test case (h, r), a KGE model is applied to calculate the scores of all such triples (h, r', t') where t' $\in \mathcal{E}$, $r' \in \mathcal{R}$, $\mathcal{E}$ is the set of all entities, and $\mathcal{R}$ is the set of all relations. The scores are used to evaluate whether the correct relation r is assigned a high rank among all candidate relations. Table 7 shows that the models have deficient performance on this task and struggle to accurately predict the properties of entities. The MRR$^{\uparrow}$ of the best-performing model, RotatE, is 0.40 on FB-CVT-REV and 0.37 on FB+CVT-REV. However, when evaluating the models using the link prediction protocol, the MRR$^{\uparrow}$ of the best-performing model, RotatE, is 0.80 on FB-CVT-REV and 0.73 on FB+CVT-REV. This underscores the need for diverse evaluation protocols as assessing models across different tasks provides a more comprehensive understanding of their strengths and limitations.

Triple Classification. Triple classification is the binary classification of triples regarding whether they are true or false facts. To conduct this task, we need to create negative samples for the test and validation sets and then learn a classification threshold for each relation on validation data. After learning the thresholds, each test triple with a score higher than the specific threshold for its relation is considered positive and negative otherwise. Some of the earlier KGE models were evaluated using triple classification [35,41]. However, their negative triples were generated by randomly corrupting head or tail entities of test and validation triples. Randomly generated negative test cases fail to provide sufficient challenges because they are often semantically implausible triples that models can trivially identify as false, resulting in inflated performance measures. Pezeshkpour et al. [26] and Safavi et al. [31] noted this problem and created some hard negative samples for their benchmark datasets. Inspired by their work, for both the test and validation sets of each dataset, we generated a suite of four sets of negative samples. Two of these sets adhere to type constraints—one involving tail entity corruption and the other involving head entity corruption—while the remaining two sets violate these constraints. This distinction is necessary because models tend to perform well in recognizing entity types, making *type-inconsistent* negatives easier to classify and thus offering a less challenging evaluation(Table 8).

Each entity in Freebase has one or more types and these types are denoted by the special relation *object/type* [34]. We used the type information and the ranked list of predictions generated by an embedding model for tail or head entity link prediction to create the aforementioned two sets. To generate a type consistent negative triple for a test triple (h, r, t), we scan the ranked list generated for tail entity prediction to identify the first entity t' that shares at least one entity type with t. We then verify that the corrupted triple (h, r, t') is negative by checking whether it exists anywhere in the whole dataset. If it does not exist in the dataset, triple (h, r, t') is added to the set of type-consistent negative triples for tail entities. We repeat the same procedure and create another set of

Table 8. Triple classification results on FB-CVT-REV

	consistenth				inconsistent h			
Model	Precision	Recall	Accuracy	F1	Precision	Recall	Accuracy	F1
TransE	0.56	0.60	0.57	0.60	0.87	0.75	0.80	0.79
DistMult	0.57	0.54	0.58	0.57	0.95	0.90	0.93	0.92
ComplEx	0.60	0.54	0.59	0.57	0.96	0.93	0.94	0.94
RotatE	0.60	0.58	0.58	0.58	0.94	0.89	0.92	0.92
	consistentt				inconsistent t			
Model	Precision	Recall	Accuracy	F1	Precision	Recall	Accuracy	F1
TransE	0.63	0.56	0.60	0.60	0.95	0.86	0.91	0.90
DistMult	0.65	0.59	0.61	0.62	0.96	0.93	0.94	0.94
ComplEx	0.65	0.61	0.62	0.64	0.96	0.94	0.95	0.95
RotatE	0.68	0.55	0.62	0.59	0.93	0.84	0.90	0.88

type-consistent negative triples by corrupting the head entities of test triples. The same procedure is used to create negative samples for validation data. To generate type-violating negative triples, we just make sure that the types of the entity that is used to corrupt a positive triple do not overlap with the original entity's types.

The results of triple classification on all these new test sets, for both FB-CVT-REV and FB+CVT-REV, are presented in Table 9. It can be observed that the models have low performance on type-consistent negative test samples, while their performance on type-violating ones is satisfactory. The scores of positive and negative triples differ clearly when negative test samples are type-violating.

Table 9. Triple classification results on FB+CVT-REV

	consistenth				inconsistent h			
Model	Precision	Recall	Accuracy	F1	Precision	Recall	Accuracy	F1
TransE	0.54	0.59	0.54	0.57	0.83	0.71	0.77	0.76
DistMult	0.56	0.54	0.54	0.54	0.95	0.88	0.92	0.91
ComplEx	0.58	0.52	0.55	0.53	0.96	0.90	0.94	0.93
RotatE	0.56	0.57	0.54	0.54	0.91	0.86	0.89	0.90
	consistentt				**inconsistent t**			
Model	Precision	Recall	Accuracy	F1	Precision	Recall	Accuracy	F1
TransE	0.61	0.57	0.59	0.58	0.91	0.83	0.88	0.87
DistMult	0.61	0.58	0.60	0.59	0.95	0.91	0.93	0.92
ComplEx	0.64	0.60	0.62	0.62	0.96	0.91	0.95	0.94
RotatE	0.65	0.52	0.61	0.57	0.89	0.80	0.86	0.84

These results suggest that the models primarily learn basic entity type compatibility, rather than capturing deeper semantic distinctions between entities of the same type.

6 Conclusion

This study exposes critical flaws in current KGE evaluation practices. Our large-scale experiments reveal major performance gaps between small and large datasets, systematic overestimation from binarizing n-ary relations, and shortcomings in standard metrics. Existing metrics assume a closed world—penalizing correct predictions of missing triples—and rely on micro-averaging, which overweights frequent relations while obscuring variation across relations, types, and domains. Alternative evaluations (entity-pair ranking, property prediction, and triple classification) showed consistently poor results, underscoring the disconnect between link prediction scores and real KG completion. These findings highlight the need for more realistic evaluation protocols and KGE methods suited to real-world challenges.

Acknowledgments. This work was supported by NSF Grant TIP-2333834 and used computing resources provided by the Texas Advanced Computing Center.

References

1. Akrami, F.: On the efficacy of knowledge graph completion methods, accuracy measures and evaluation protocols. Ph.D. Dissertations, The University of Texas at Arlington (2021)
2. Akrami, F., Saeef, M.S., Zhang, Q., Hu, W., Li, C.: Realistic re-evaluation of knowledge graph completion methods: an experimental study. In: SIGMOD, pp. 1995–2010 (2020)
3. Ali, M., et al.: Bringing light into the dark: a large-scale evaluation of knowledge graph embedding models under a unified framework. IEEE Trans. Pattern Anal. Mach. Intell. **44**(12), 8825–8845 (2021)
4. Auer, S., Bizer, C., Kobilarov, G., Lehmann, J., Cyganiak, R., Ives, Z.: DBpedia: a nucleus for a web of open data. In: ISWC + ASWC, pp. 722–735 (2007)
5. Bollacker, K., Evans, C., Paritosh, P., Sturge, T., Taylor, J.: Freebase: a collaboratively created graph database for structuring human knowledge. In: SIGMOD, pp. 1247–1250 (2008)
6. Bordes, A., Usunier, N., Garcia-Durán, A., Weston, J., Yakhnenko, O.: Translating embeddings for modeling multi-relational data. In: NeurIPS, pp. 2787–2795 (2013)
7. Cai, H., Zheng, V.W., Chang, K.C.C.: A comprehensive survey of graph embedding: Problems, techniques, and applications. TKDE **30**(9), 1616–1637 (2018)
8. Carlson, A., Betteridge, J., Kisiel, B., Settles, B., Hruschka Jr, E.R., Mitchell, T.M.: Toward an architecture for never-ending language learning. In: AAAI, pp. 1306–1313 (2010)
9. Dettmers, T., Pasquale, M., Pontus, S., Riedel, S.: Convolutional 2D knowledge graph embeddings. In: AAAI, pp. 1811–1818 (2018)

10. Egger, M.K., et al.: ReliK: a reliability measure for knowledge graph embeddings. In: WWW, pp. 2009–2019 (2024)
11. Guan, S., Jin, X., Wang, Y., Cheng, X.: Link prediction on n-ary relational data. In: The Web Conference, pp. 583–593 (2019)
12. Guo, Q., et al.: A survey on knowledge graph-based recommender systems. TKDE, pp. 3549–3568 (2020)
13. Heist, N., Hertling, S., Paulheim, H.: KGrEaT: a framework to evaluate knowledge graphs via downstream tasks. In: CIKM, pp. 3938–3942 (2023)
14. Hoyt, C.T., Berrendorf, M., Galkin, M., Tresp, V., Gyori, B.M.: A unified framework for rank-based evaluation metrics for link prediction in knowledge graphs. arXiv:2203.07544 (2022)
15. Hu, W., Fey, M., Ren, H., Nakata, M., Dong, Y., Leskovec, J.: OGB-LSC: a large-scale challenge for machine learning on graphs. arXiv:2103.09430 (2021)
16. Hu, W., et al.: Open graph benchmark: datasets for machine learning on graphs. NeurIPS **33**, 22118–22133 (2020)
17. Hubert, N., Monnin, P., Brun, A., Monticolo, D.: Sem@ K: is my knowledge graph embedding model semantic-aware? Semantic Web **14**(6), 1273–1309 (2023)
18. Hubert, N., Paulheim, H., Brun, A., Monticolo, D.: Do similar entities have similar embeddings? In: ESWC, pp. 3–21. Springer (2024)
19. Ji, S., Pan, S., Cambria, E., Marttinen, P., Philip, S.Y.: A survey on knowledge graphs: representation, acquisition, and applications. IEEE Trans. Neural Netw. Learn. Syst. **33**(2), 494–514 (2021)
20. Lerer, A., et al.: PyTorch-BigGraph: A large-scale graph embedding system. In: SysML, pp. 120–131 (2019)
21. Lin, Y., Liu, Z., Sun, M., Liu, Y., Zhu, X.: Learning entity and relation embeddings for knowledge graph completion. In: AAAI, pp. 2181–2187 (2015)
22. Mahdisoltani, F., Biega, J., Suchanek, F.M.: YAGO3: a knowledge base from multilingual Wikipedias. In: CIDR (2015)
23. Miller, G.A.: WordNet: a lexical database for english. CACM **38**(11), 39–41 (1995)
24. Mohoney, J., Waleffe, R., Xu, H., Rekatsinas, T., Venkataraman, S.: Marius: learning massive graph embeddings on a single machine. In: OSDI, pp. 533–549 (2021)
25. Pellissier Tanon, T., Vrandečić, D., Schaffert, S., Steiner, T., Pintscher, L.: From Freebase to Wikidata: the great migration. In: WWW, pp. 1419–1428 (2016)
26. Pezeshkpour, P., Tian, Y., Singh, S.: Revisiting evaluation of knowledge base completion models. In: AKBC (2020)
27. Reiter, R.: Deductive question-answering on relational data bases. In: Logic and data bases, pp. 149–177. Springer (1978)
28. Reiter, R.: On closed world data bases. In: Gallaire H., Minker J. (eds) Logic and Data Bases, pp. 55–76. Elsevier (1978)
29. Rosso, P., Yang, D., Cudré-Mauroux, P.: Beyond triplets: hyper-relational knowledge graph embedding for link prediction. In: WWW, pp. 1885–1896 (2020)
30. Ruffinelli, D., Gemulla, R.: Beyond link prediction: on pre-training knowledge graph embeddings. In: RepL4NLP, pp. 136–162 (2024)
31. Safavi, T., Koutra, D.: CoDEx: A comprehensive knowledge graph completion benchmark. In: EMNLP, pp. 8328–8350 (2020)
32. Sawischa, S.F.: Bias assessments of benchmarks for link predictions over knowledge graphs. B.S. thesis, Hannover: Gottfried Wilhelm Leibniz Universität (2023)
33. Shi, B., Weninger, T.: ProjE: embedding projection for knowledge graph completio. In: AAAI, pp. 1236–1242 (2017)

34. Shirvani-Mahdavi, N., Akrami, F., Saeef, M.S., Shi, X., Li, C.: Comprehensive analysis of freebase and dataset creation for robust evaluation of knowledge graph link prediction models. In: ISWC, pp. 113–133. Springer (2023)
35. Socher, R., Chen, D., Manning, C.D., Ng, A.: Reasoning with neural tensor networks for knowledge base completion. In: NeurIPS, pp. 926–934 (2013)
36. Suchanek, F.M., Kasneci, G., Weikum, G.: YAGO: a large ontology from Wikipedia and WordNet. Web Semantics **6**(3), 203–217 (2008)
37. Sun, Z., Deng, Z.H., Nie, J.Y., Tang, J.: RotatE: knowledge graph embedding by relational rotation in complex space. In: ICLR, pp. 926–934 (2019)
38. Trouillon, T., Welbl, J., Riedel, S., Gaussier, É., Bouchard, G.: Complex embeddings for simple link prediction. In: ICML, pp. 2071–2080 (2016)
39. Vrandečić, D., Krötzsch, M.: Wikidata: a free collaborative knowledgebase. CACM **57**(10), 78–85 (2014)
40. Wang, Y., Ruffinelli, D., Gemulla, R., Broscheit, S., Meilicke, C.: On evaluating embedding models for knowledge base completion. In: RepL4NLP, pp. 104–112 (2019)
41. Wang, Z., Zhang, J., Feng, J., Chen, Z.: Knowledge graph embedding by translating on hyperplanes. In: AAAI, pp. 1112–1119 (2014)
42. Wen, J., Li, J., Mao, Y., Chen, S., Zhang, R.: On the representation and embedding of knowledge bases beyond binary relations. arXiv:1604.08642 (2016)
43. Weston, J., Bordes, A., Yakhnenko, O., Usunier, N.: Connecting language and knowledge bases with embedding models for relation extraction. In: EMNLP, pp. 1366–1371 (2013)
44. Yang, B., Yih, W.t., He, X., Gao, J., Deng, L.: Embedding entities and relations for learning and inference in knowledge bases. In: ICLR (2015)
45. Yang, H., Lin, Z., Zhang, M.: Rethinking knowledge graph evaluation under the open-world assumption. NeurIPS **35**, 8374–8385 (2022)
46. Information extraction over structured data: Yao, X., Van Durme, B. Question answering with freebase. In: ACL. **1**, 956–966 (2014)
47. Zheng, D., et al.: DGL-KE: Training Knowledge Graph Embeddings at Scale. In: SIGIR, pp. 739–748 (2020)
48. Zhou, Y., Chen, X., He, B., Ye, Z., Sun, L.: Re-thinking knowledge graph completion evaluation from an information retrieval perspective. In: SIGIR, pp. 916–926 (2022)

Analysis of Neuro-Symbolic Embedding Approaches: Assessing Knowledge Representation and Latent Space Reasoning Capabilities

Ludwig de Sousa[1,2](✉), Salima Benbernou[1], and Mourad Ouziri[1]

[1] Université Paris Cité, LIPADE, 75006 Paris, France
{ludwig.de-sousa,salima.benbernou,mourad.ouziri}@u-paris.fr
[2] Ministère de l'Europe et des affaires étrangères, 75007 Paris, France
ludwig.de-sousa@diplomatie.gouv.fr

Abstract. The main objective of the analysis is to assess the effectiveness of current neuro-symbolic approaches, with a focus on their capabilities in knowledge representation and reasoning in latent space for web applications. Today, neuro-symbolic approaches are increasingly influential in bridging neural representation learning and symbolic reasoning, particularly for knowledge graph completion and semantic interoperability in web engineering. A central challenge in this field is the lack of methods that simultaneously link word embeddings capturing semantic information from unstructured text and concept embeddings encoding formal knowledge from ontologies such as OWL and RDF(S), while enabling unified approximate deductive inference across both modalities. This disconnection limits the potential to perform integrated reasoning over textual data and structured knowledge bases. In this paper, we analyze whether state-of-the-art neuro-symbolic inference methods can represent symbolic entities in a shared vectorial space while preserving the formal semantics dictated by ontologies. Our analysis examines how well these models align the geometry of learned embeddings with ontological constraints, and whether this alignment supports effective inference over knowledge graphs. Finally, we conclude with a discussion of open research directions, including the need for joint embedding models that combine neural and symbolic reasoning for heterogeneous web data, as well as diversification strategies to enhance inference robustness and retrieval effectiveness.

Keywords: Neuro-symbolic AI · Semantic embeddings · Ontology embeddings · Latent space reasoning

1 Introduction

Recent years have witnessed a dramatic leap forward in natural language processing (NLP) driven by large, pre-trained transformer models. The advent of such

I. Awan et al. (Eds.): WISE 2025, LNCS 16368, pp. 260–274, 2026.
https://doi.org/10.1007/978-981-95-7251-9_18

architectures and their attendant scaling laws [10] have precipitated a paradigm shift in NLP: very large language models exhibit emergent capabilities ranging from reading comprehension [24] to open-domain question answering [13,16] and dense retrieval [15]. Yet these models operate primarily by inductive pattern-matching (i.e., "System 1" cognition [14]) and remain prone to hallucinatory output, brittle when presented with out-of-distribution inputs, and effectively opaque—lacking guarantees of logical consistency or traceable explanations for their predictions.

By contrast, ontologies are mainly rooted in Description Logics with formally and explicitly defined semantics embodying domain-specific, rule-based knowledge that supports sound and complete deductive inference (i.e., "System 2" cognition [14]) via tableau algorithms or rule-based engines. Ontologies are inherently explainable, modular, and amenable to rigorous consistency checking. Such reasoning-based methods are indispensable in high-stakes applications (e.g. healthcare, law, and scientific discovery), where incorrect or unverified inferences are critical. However, purely symbolic systems are often too rigid to handle noisy and ambiguous data, demand extensive expert curation, and fail to exploit the rich contextual information embedded in textual data.

Bridging these paradigms, a variety of neuro-symbolic methods have emerged to endow neural models with structured domain knowledge. Ontology embedding approaches enable new solutions for ontology engineering, such as inductive inference through operations in continuous latent spaces. Differentiable logical reasoning methods and neural theorem proving systems (e.g. [9,18,33]) implement differentiable proof-search by operating on embedding spaces to perform symbolic unification. Neural text-based reasoning frameworks integrate multi-hop reasoning techniques, few-shot learning capabilities, and text retrieval mechanisms with language model decoding processes. These frameworks mitigate hallucination by grounding generated outputs in verifiable factual information. Yet none of the existing approaches satisfy the full desiderata: (i) an accurate approximation of the deductive closure within decidable OWL fragments; (ii) a unified latent representation that integrates both logical and semantic aspects to enable joint reasoning over symbolic and textual data; and (iii) support for natural language querying over ontologies and corpus data.

Numerous application domains, including biomedicine, law, and regulatory compliance, require high-assurance information retrieval from large domain-specific corpora. Users must locate not only explicitly stated facts, but also those implicitly entailed by a formal theory. Purely symbolic information retrieval methods lack scalability when applied to unstructured documents, while purely inductive approaches cannot ensure logical coherence. An ideal system would integrate grounded retrieval, extend it through approximate deduction, and ensure that every returned inference is well-grounded.

Contributions of this work are summarized as follows:

- We identify paradigms exploited by state-of-the-art for knowledge representation and reasoning in latent space

- We provide a brief survey of the SOTA. We describe their design principles and pinpoint their strengths and limitations.
- We analyze the experimental evaluation of eight SOTA methods using synthetic and real-world datasets from different domains. We provide a discussion of the results.
- Based on the results of the comprehensive experimental study, we pinpoint some promising research directions to advance neuro-symbolic in latent space.

The paper is organized as follows: in Sect. 2 we provide the background related to the terminology used through the paper. In Sect. 3, we review the main SOTA and selected some of them to be analyzed in the next section. Section 4 provides, the analysis on main existing methods based on their capabilities on latent space through their experiments, and a discussion of open research directions. Finally, Sect. 5 concludes the paper.

2 Background

2.1 Symbolic Knowledge Representation Formalisms: Knowledge Graph and Ontology

Symbolic knowledge representation is central to neuro-symbolic AI, providing the structural and semantic grounding for inference and reasoning. Ontologies and knowledge graphs are among the most widely used symbolic representation formalisms. Description logics, a type of formal logic, provide the foundational frameworks that define the underlying representation languages and semantics used to encode and reason about this symbolic knowledge.

Ontologies represent domain knowledge in terms of classes (concepts), properties (roles), and individuals (instances). They are typically encoded in languages such as OWL (Web Ontology Language) [19]. Ontologies are used to support reasoning tasks such as subsumption, consistency checking, and instance classification. The formal foundations of OWL are rooted in description logics [2], a family of decidable fragments of first-order logics. Ontology axioms are divided into: TBox (Terminological Box): Contains concept definitions and general axioms, and ABox (Assertional Box): Contains instance assertions

Example 1. The ontology presented below represents a basic family domain:

$$\begin{aligned}\mathcal{T} = \{&Father \sqsubseteq Parent \sqcap Male, Mother \sqsubseteq Parent \sqcap Female,\\ &Child \sqsubseteq \exists hasParent.Father,\ Child \sqsubseteq \exists hasParent.Mother,\\ &hasParent \sqsubseteq relatedTo\ \}\\ \mathcal{A} = \{&Father(William), Child(Georges), hasParent(Georges, William)\ \}\end{aligned}$$

The TBox defines a father as a male parent, a mother as a female parent, and states that every child has at least one father and one mother. It also specifies that having a parent implies a relational connection. The ABox asserts that William is a father, Georges is a child, and William is a parent of Georges.

Knowledge graph (KG) is a graph-based representation of entities and their relationships [11]. Formally defined as a directed, labeled graph $G = (E, R, T)$, where E denotes a set of entities, R a set of relation types, and $T \subseteq E \times R \times E$ a set of factual triples representing binary relations among entities. Unlike ontologies, which focus on conceptual structuring and logical entailment, KGs aim to represent factual knowledge to be processed with data-driven systems. Initially popularized in industrial applications, KGs have become a cornerstone for neuro-symbolic reasoning, combining logical inference with embedding-based learning [22] [31].

2.2 Symbolic Reasoning: Logical Inference

Logical inference plays a central role in symbolic AI and is particularly crucial in neuro-symbolic systems. It provides deductive reasoning, enabling tasks such as consistency checking, fact entailment, classification, and query answering. Many ontological reasoning systems are based on description logics (DLs), a family of logic-based knowledge representation languages that are decidable fragments of first-order logic. DLs offer a balance between expressive power and computational decidability, making them particularly suitable for automated reasoning.

Description logics come in various fragments, each defined by a set of constructors such as conjunction ($\sqcap$), disjunction ($\sqcup$), negation ($\neg$), existential ($\exists$), universal ($\forall$) quantifiers, and number restrictions, with varying levels of expressivity and reasoning complexity [25]. Some of the most common DLs include EL, ALC, SHIQ and SROIQ [2]. Tableau algorithm is among the most widely used reasoning techniques in Description Logics. It enables checking the satisfiability of concepts, facts, or entire knowledge bases. It is designed to determine the satisfiability of a concept C with respect to a TBox $\mathcal{T}$ and, optionally, an ABox $\mathcal{A}$. All core reasoning tasks in Description Logics—such as subsumption ($T \models C \sqsubseteq D$), instance checking ($\mathcal{T}, \mathcal{A} \models C(a)$, a is not an instance of $\neg C$ in any model), and consistency—are reducible to concept satisfiability. This reduction makes satisfiability the central problem in DL reasoning.

2.3 Embedding Definitions

Embedding techniques map symbolic data (e.g., words, entities, or concepts) into continuous vector spaces. These vector representations capture semantic similarities and structural relationships, enabling machine learning models to process discrete symbolic information in a differentiable and scalable manner. Formally, Embedding techniques are as functions that map discrete symbolic objects such as words, entities, or ontological concepts into points in a continuous, high-dimensional vector space R^d.

Embeddings are fundamental in bridging symbolic reasoning with sub-symbolic approaches like neural networks [30]. A notable subclass of these methods is Knowledge graph embeddings (KGE), where entities and relations from a KG are represented as vectors while preserving the graph's structural and semantic properties. Formally, an entity $e \in E$ and $r \in R$ in a knowledge graph

$G = (E, R, T)$ are embedded into R^d. Each triple $(h, r, t) \in T$ is assigned a plausibility score by a differentiable scoring function ϕ. Thus, embeddings enable efficient reasoning and inference. During inference, embeddings enable efficient computation of similarity or relatedness between entities or concepts through vector operations such as dot product $(v1, v2)$ or cosine similarity $cos - sim(v1, v2)$. This continuous representation space supports downstream tasks—such as link prediction [32], recommendation, and question answering, providing a bridge between symbolic knowledge and neural methods.

3 Related Work and Gap Analysis

We now present an overview of the main SOTA approaches for knowledge representation and reasoning in latent space.

3.1 Embedding Symbolic Knowledge Into Vector Spaces

Building on the success of distributional word embeddings, such as Word2Vec [20] and GloVe [23], which learn dense vectors by exploiting co-occurrence statistics in text, ontology embedding methods (including concept embedding) extend this idea to structured, symbolic knowledge. This paradigm was first applied to structured data in knowledge graph embedding frameworks such as TransE, DistMult, and ComplEx [5,27,32], where entities and relations are embedded into $\mathbb{R}^d$ so that simple algebraic operations approximate graph traversal and relational inference. Ontology embeddings extend this approach by incorporating both TBox axioms and ABox assertions. Concepts, roles, and individuals are all assigned continuous representations, and logical constructors (e.g., subsumption, conjunction, existential restriction) are enforced via differentiable geometric constraints.

In practice, these methods can fall into three broad families [8]:

Sequence modeling. Sequence modeling approaches in ontology embeddings aim to transform structured ontology knowledge, typically represented in OWL axioms into linear sequences or token streams. This linearization enables the use of NLP models (e.g., Word2Vec and Transformers) to learn meaningful embeddings. By treating axioms as sentences, these models capture both symbolic structure and rich textual annotations in ontologies. However, Word2Vec generates non-contextual embeddings, assigning each token a fixed vector representation regardless of its surrounding context. OPA2Vec [26] further enriches ontology axioms with annotation properties. It processes these axioms using Word2Vec to produce embeddings that reflect both logical and linguistic information. OWL2Vec [7] extends this by transforming the ontology into a graph and performing random walks to generate sequences that preserve the structural semantics before training embedding models. In contrast, BERTSubs [6] applies pre-trained Transformer encoders (e.g., BERT) directly to serialized OWL axioms, using attention mechanisms to model complex dependencies and relationships. These sequence-based models have shown promising results in tasks such as similarity estimation, entity classification, and reasoning, by embedding ontological knowledge into continuous vector spaces that capture both formal semantics and contextual nuances.

Geometric models. Embedding entities and ontologies embeddings and queries using geometric shapes has recently emerged as a promising approach, as these shapes naturally capture answer sets and the logical relationships between them. Unlike sequence modeling, geometric models interpret each concept as a convex region (e.g., an n-dimensional ball, box, cone, or hyperbolic disk) and each role as an affine transformation or translation, so that logical entailment correspond to region-containment or distance-based inequalities. These models aim to project concepts, individuals, and roles into a continuous vector space (e.g., $\mathbb{R}^n$), where they are represented as points or geometric regions. This enables the capture of certain semantic aspects of the underlying ontology through the geometric structure of the embedding space. In other words, axioms can usually be inferred by calculating the geometric relationship of vectors, exemplified by methods like Box2EL, Order Embeddings, and Hyperbolic Entailment Cones [1,12,33].

The work in [33] proposes a geometry-based query embedding model, namely Cone Embeddings (ConE), to answer multi-hop first-order logical (FOL) queries over knowledge graphs. spaces. Given a query, QE models generate query embeddings following the corresponding computation graph. Then, they determine whether an entity is a correct answer based on similarities between the query embeddings and entity embeddings. The entity sets are represented as Cartesian products of cones and the corresponding logical operations are designed including conjunction, disjunction, and negation.

Recent work [12] addresses ontology completion reasoning, focusing on limitations in previous geometric ontology embeddings. These earlier methods fail to faithfully model one-to-many, many-to-one, and many-to-many relations, as well as role inclusion axioms. The proposed approach called Box^2EL aims to learn ontology embeddings in a latent vector space. Here, both concepts and roles are represented as boxes (i.e., axis-aligned hyperrectangles), and models inter-concept relationships using a bumping mechanism. In Fig. 1 is presented an example of the embeddings learned by Box^2EL [8].

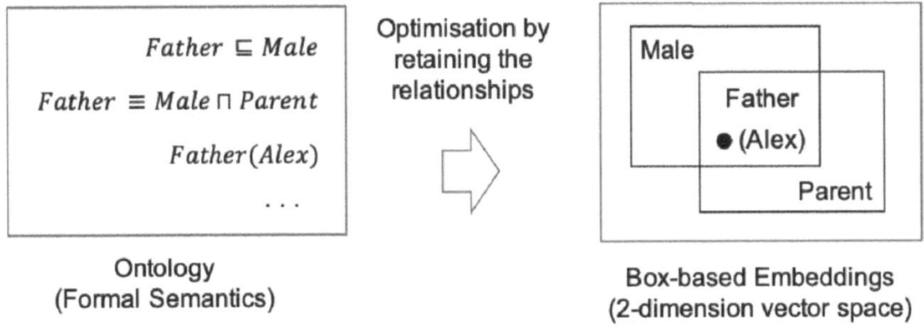

Fig. 1. Visualization of the embeddings learned by Box2EL.

The box embedding simulates the hierarchical ordering with hyperrectangles, where a child entity's box is contained within its parent entity's box, and box embeddings require two vectors representing the minimal and maximal coordinates in the hyperrectangle

Graph propagation models. Graph propagation methods represent ontologies as (multi-relation) graphs and employ graph neural networks or propagation algorithms to learn embeddings through neighborhood aggregation and message passing. The work in [17] encodes ontologies as a graph where predicates are nodes with initial concept embeddings, and edges capture co-occurrence in rules. A GCN refines node vectors to predict new ontology rules, enabling ontology completion. The work in [28] is specifically designed for multi-relational graphs, this model learns embeddings for both nodes and relations by integrating GNN-style propagation with translational operations used in KG embeddings such as TransE. The work in [29] is a post-processing method that further propagates relation-based context into KG embeddings to enhance them. Although applied to KGs, the underlying machinery mirrors ontology propagation techniques. The work in [4] extends propagation to hyperbolic space and captures hierarchical multi-relational structure, offering strong inductive bias for ontological embeddings.

3.2 Differentiable Logical Reasoning and Theorem Proving

Differentiable logical reasoning aims to integrate symbolic logic with gradient-based learning by relaxing discrete logical operations into continuous, differentiable functions, enabling neural networks to learn and reason over structured knowledge, including TensorLog, Logic Tensor Networks, or Neural Theorem Provers [3,9,21].

TensorLog is a probabilistic deductive database system that supports differentiable reasoning. It transforms logical rules into sparse matrix operations, allowing them to be embedded into deep learning models. Each predicate becomes a matrix, and logical inference is performed using matrix multiplication, enabling gradient-based optimization. Moreover, it is an implementation of a probabilistic first-order logic in which classes of logical queries are compiled into differentiable functions in a neural-network infrastructure such as Tensorflow or Theano. This leads to a close integration of probabilistic logical reasoning with deep-learning infrastructure: in particular, it enables high-performance deep learning frameworks to be used for tuning the parameters of a probabilistic logic. This implementation is used in case of entity linking and knowledge base completion.

Logic Tensor Networks (LTNs) fuse first-order logic with real-valued semantics. Predicates and functions are modeled as differentiable tensor functions, and logical formulas are interpreted using fuzzy logic to allow reasoning under uncertainty. The main idea is to assign truth values in [0,1] to logical formulas, enabling soft logic reasoning. LTN allows constraints and background knowledge to guide learning. It has been used for semantic image interpretation and ontology reasoning.

Neural Theorem Prover (NTP) [21] showcases a practical step toward integrating symbolic logic and neural representations at scale, enabling differentiable theorem proving in real-world, large-scale knowledge bases. The original NTP uses embedding similarity in lieu of exact symbolic unification in backward chaining. It explores every possible unification which is infeasible for large KBs. There is a new version NTP 2.0, a scalable version of NTP that leverages Approximate Nearest Neighbor Search (ANNS). The latter achieves order-of-magnitude speedups and reduced memory usage, enabling training on large ontologies like WordNet.

4 Analysis of Experimentation

In this section, we analyze how selected approaches among those previously discussed perform on the ontology-completion task. Their reasoning power is assessed through experiments on both synthetic and real-world datasets, using a diverse set of metrics.

4.1 Datasets and Evaluation Metrics

We outline the commonly used datasets for KG completion tasks and KG embeddings evaluation with the appropriate metrics.

Datasets. The Table 1 provides an overview of the benchmark ontologies used in the literature to evaluate the methods surveyed in this work. Spanning a broad spectrum of domains from the toy benchmarks of Kinship and Nations to the large-scale world-knowledge subset FB122, the biomedical hierarchies of UMLS and the Gene Ontology, the nutrition taxonomy in FoodOn, and the extensive proteinâĂŞprotein interaction networks in yeast and human—these datasets vary dramatically in schema complexity, number of relations and individuals, and total ground facts. For each resource, we list the count of relation types (Pred.), individual constants (Const.), and known facts, together with a brief description of its domain focus. This heterogeneity highlights both the expressive requirements and the scalability challenges that methods must address across diverse ontology-completion tasks.

Metrics. The comparison of methods is based on three widely adopted, filtered metrics: Mean Reciprocal Rank (MRR), Hits-at-K (H@1, H@3, H@10, H@100) and area under the ROC curve (AUC). MRR averages the inverse rank of correct prediction (values range from 0 to 1, with higher scores indicating more accurate top-ranking), while Hits-at-K reports the fraction of held-out axioms appearing among the top K predictions (for instance, an H@10 of 0.2 signifies that 20% of true facts are recovered within the ten highest-scoring candidates). AUC evaluates a model's ability to discriminate positive from negative predictions across all decision thresholds, yielding a threshold-agnostic performance score between 0 and 1, where higher values denote better overall discrimination.

Table 1. Dataset characteristics and descriptions across different domains.

Dataset	Domain	Pred.	Const.	Facts	Additional Info
Kinship	family relationships	26	104	10,686	models kin types, descent and marriage relations
Nations	geopolitics	167	14	2,565	defines countries, capitals, currencies, political affiliations
UMLS	Biomedical terminology	49	135	6,529	integrates vocabularies into Metathesaurus plus Semantic Network
FB122	world-knowledge	122	9,738	91,638	subset of Freebase (people, places, events, culture)
GO	Biology (molecular functions, processes, components)	1	2,140	1,855	organizes molecular functions, processes and components hierarchically
FoodOn	Nutrition (foods, ingredients, products)	-	-	-	covers food sources, ingredients, categories and processing
Yeast (PPI)	Biology	1	51,679	360,217	protein interactions among five yeast species
Human (PPI)	Biology (Homo sapiens)	1	59,311	1,325,746	experimentally determined protein interactions in humans

4.2 Analysis

In the following sections, we conduct a structured survey of knowledge graph and ontology-based reasoning models for link prediction and subsumption tasks. In addition, we review each paradigm (symbolic embedding and differentiable reasoning) along three fundamental dimensions: expressiveness, symbolic reasoning, and flexibility.

Link Prediction. Link prediction on ontologies is the task of predicting missing or unknown relationships between entities based on existing structured knowledge. This task is crucial for completing incomplete ontologies and enabling more comprehensive reasoning. The results presented in table 2 reveal several key trends in this field: first, there is a clear trade-off between interpretability and performance, where traditional neural link predictors like TransE, DistMult, and ComplEx achieve strong accuracy but operate as black boxes without providing explanations for their predictions. Second, the integration of logical reasoning capabilities directly into neural architectures is becoming increasingly

Table 2. Relational Link Prediction Results on Ontology: $r(a, b)$

Dataset	Model	H@1	H@3	H@5	H@10	MRR
Kinship	NTP	0.240	0.370	-	0.570	0.350
	GNTP+Attention	0.642	0.850	-	0.959	0.759
Nations	NTP	0.450	0.730	-	0.870	0.610
	GNTP+Attention	0.490	0.736	-	0.975	0.645
UMLS	NTP	0.700	0.880	-	0.950	0.800
	GNTP+Attention	0.761	0.947	-	0.983	0.857
FB122	TransE	-	0.360	0.410	0.481	0.269
	DistMult	-	0.360	0.403	0.453	0.313
	ComplEx	-	0.370	0.413	0.462	0.329
	GNTPs	0.260	0.337	0.369	0.412	0.313
FB122 with entailed triples	TransE	-	0.589	0.642	0.702	0.480
	DistMult	-	0.674	0.702	0.729	0.628
	ComplEx	-	0.673	0.695	0.719	0.641
	GNTPs	0.658	0.692	0.711	0.732	0.678

Table 3. Link Prediction as Subsumption on ontology: $p_i \sqsubseteq \exists\, interacts\_with.\, p_j$

Dataset	Model	H@3	H@10	H@100	MRR	AUC
Yeast	OPA2Vec	0.051	0.128	0.543	0.061	0.935
	OWL2Vec*-Sim	0.154	0.301	0.730	0.149	0.967
	Box2EL	0.190	0.435	0.805	0.167	0.969
Human	OPA2Vec	0.071	0.177	0.594	0.080	0.961
	OWL2Vec*-Sim	0.140	0.283	0.639	0.131	0.967
	Box2EL	0.175	0.336	0.683	0.163	0.967

important, as evidenced by GNTPs' ability to automatically discover and utilize logical patterns from data while maintaining competitive performance with other methods.

The experimental results demonstrate distinct performance patterns across different model categories and evaluation scenarios. Neural theorem proving methods show variable performance depending on dataset characteristics and architectural enhancements. On the Kinship dataset, GNTP with attention achieves substantial gains over basic NTP, improving from 24% to 64.2% on Hits@1 and from 35% to 75.9% in MRR. Similar improvements are observed across other datasets, with UMLS showing increases from 70% to 76.1% on Hits@1 and from 80% to 85.7% in MRR, suggesting that attention mechanisms significantly enhance the reasoning capabilities of neural theorem provers.

The most revealing insights emerge when comparing performance on standard FB122 versus FB122 with entailed triples. The latter represents a more

Table 4. Concept Subsumption Prediction on Ontology: $C \sqsubseteq D$

Dataset	Model	H@3	H@10	H@100	MRR	AUC
GO	OPA2Vec	0.112	0.207	0.571	0.112	0.990
	OWL2Vec*-Sim	0.245	0.428	0.881	0.220	0.997
	Box2EL	0.027	0.088	0.305	0.031	0.911
FoodOn	OPA2Vec	0.082	0.136	0.349	0.081	0.926
	OWL2Vec*-Sim	0.267	0.442	0.731	0.233	0.985
	Box2EL	0.051	0.118	0.221	0.039	0.835

challenging evaluation setting where test triples include both standard facts and those that can be inferred via logical rules, essentially testing the models' ability to perform multi-step reasoning. Traditional embedding approaches show dramatic performance improvements on this enhanced dataset: TransE jumps from 26.9% to 48.0% MRR, DistMult from 31.3% to 62.8%, and ComplEx from 32.9% to 64.1%. However, GNTPs demonstrates the most substantial gain, rising from 31.3% to 67.8% MRR, ultimately outperforming all traditional methods. This performance reversal highlights a crucial insight: while embedding-based approaches can handle simple factual recall effectively, explicit reasoning capabilities become essential when predictions require logical inference chains, giving GNTPs a decisive advantage in scenarios demanding multi-step deduction.

Subsumption Prediction. Concept subsumption prediction in ontologies involves determining hierarchical relationships between concepts, formally expressed as $C \sqsubseteq D$ (concept C is subsumed by concept D), which is fundamental for ontology reasoning and knowledge organization. An interesting variant of this task reformulates traditional link prediction as subsumption prediction, where relationship prediction $r(p_i, p_j)$ is cast as $p_i \sqsubseteq \exists\, interacts\_with.\, p_j$ in Table 3, allowing for better ontology alignment by capturing different types of role and cardinality constraints (1-to-1, n-to-1, etc.) that are difficult to model in standard approaches. The results reveal distinct performance patterns across different embedding approaches and reasoning paradigms.

The experimental results demonstrate significant performance variations across model architectures and problem formulations. In the subsumption-based link prediction task (Table 3), Box2EL consistently outperforms other approaches across both datasets, achieving 0.190 H@3 and 0.167 MRR on Yeast compared to OWL2Vec*-Sim's 0.154 H@3 and 0.149 MRR, and OPA2Vec's substantially lower 0.051 H@3 and 0.061 MRR. This pattern suggests that geometric embedding approaches (Box2EL) are particularly well-suited for capturing the logical constraints inherent in subsumption relationships when applied to protein interaction prediction.

However, the performance landscape shifts dramatically in direct concept subsumption prediction tasks (Table 4). OWL2Vec*-Sim emerges as the clear leader, achieving 0.245 H@3 and 0.220 MRR on GO, and 0.267 H@3 and 0.233 MRR on FoodOn, substantially outperforming Box2EL, which drops to 0.027 H@3 and 0.031 MRR on GO. This reversal highlights a crucial insight: while geometric approaches excel at structured relationship prediction, sequence-based similarity methods prove more effective for capturing the semantic hierarchies inherent in direct concept subsumption, particularly in complex domain ontologies like Gene Ontology and food classification systems.

4.3 Research Opportunities

The reported performance gap in our analysis between different model families narrows significantly when logical inference becomes essential, indicating that explicit reasoning capabilities provide substantial advantages when predictions require multi-step logical deduction. This highlights the growing emphasis on handling real-world complexity, including the incorporation of textual mentions alongside structured facts and the ability to scale to larger knowledge bases, suggesting that future advances will focus on neuro-symbolic approaches that combine the representational power of neural methods with interpretable reasoning mechanisms while addressing textual information. The latter being too little addressed in the literature. A promising research direction involves developing neuro-symbolic models capable of performing approximate deductive inference over large-scale textual corpora by leveraging embedding-based representations. Traditional approaches studied previously rely on static embeddings that are trained on fixed ontological structures, making them inflexible to the dynamic nature of real-world data. This limits their ability to accommodate new individuals (entities) or roles (relations) without costly retraining. To address this, future work should explore dynamic embedding frameworks that allow on-the-fly integration of new symbolic knowledge such as new entities or assertions into the latent vector space, while preserving semantic consistency. Moreover, these models should support bidirectional reasoning: using latent patterns in unstructured text to suggest ontology completion (e.g., adding new axioms or role assertions), and conversely, leveraging ontological rules to guide retrieval and disambiguation in noisy or incomplete corpora. Key to this is designing architectures that combine differentiable logical reasoning with context-aware vector updates, enabling approximate symbolic inference that generalizes beyond explicitly seen data. Embedding-based reasoning should be capable of exploiting implicit regularities in the corpus such as co-occurrence statistics or discourse structure to infer missing semantic relations, ultimately enabling scalable, adaptive knowledge representation without reinitializing or retraining the entire model.

5 Conclusion

We presented a comparative analysis of neuro-symbolic paradigms that integrate neural representation learning with symbolic reasoning, focusing on knowledge graph completion and semantic interoperability in web engineering. Our analysis uncovered substantial performance gaps, particularly on tasks requiring logical deduction, and revealed significant variation in each model's ability to preserve ontological semantics during inference. These findings highlight the limitations of current approaches and point to an urgent need for new hybrid frameworks capable of bridging reasoning across both structured and unstructured data. Advances in this direction will be critical for developing more accurate, interoperable, and semantically rich web applications.

Acknowledgments. This work was supported by the Ministère de l'Europe et des affaires étrangères.

Disclosure of Interest. The authors have no competing interests to declare that are relevant to the content of this article.

References

1. Athiwaratkun, B., Wilson, A.G.: Hierarchical density order embeddings. In: 6th International Conference on Learning Representations, ICLR 2018, Vancouver, BC, Canada, April 30 - May 3, 2018, Conference Track Proceedings. OpenReview.net (2018)
2. Baader, F., Calvanese, D., McGuinness, D.L., Nardi, D., Patel-Schneider, P.F. (eds.): The description logic handbook: theory, implementation, and applications. Cambridge University Press, Cambridge (2003)
3. Badreddine, S., d'Avila Garcez, A.S., Serafini, L., Spranger, M.: Logic tensor networks. Artif. Intell. **303**, 103649 (2022)
4. Balazevic, I., Allen, C., Hospedales, T.M.: Multi-relational poincaré graph embeddings. In: Wallach, H.M., Larochelle, H., Beygelzimer, A., d'Alché-Buc, F., Fox, E.B., Garnett, R. (eds.) Advances in Neural Information Processing Systems 32: Annual Conference on Neural Information Processing Systems 2019, NeurIPS 2019, December 8-14, 2019, Vancouver, BC, Canada. pp. 4465–4475 (2019)
5. Bordes, A., Usunier, N., García-Durán, A., Weston, J., Yakhnenko, O.: Translating embeddings for modeling multi-relational data. In: Burges, C.J.C., Bottou, L., Ghahramani, Z., Weinberger, K.Q. (eds.) Advances in Neural Information Processing Systems 26: 27th Annual Conference on Neural Information Processing Systems 2013. Proceedings of a meeting held December 5-8, 2013, Lake Tahoe, Nevada, United States, pp. 2787–2795 (2013)
6. Chen, J., He, Y., Geng, Y., Jiménez-Ruiz, E., Dong, H., Horrocks, I.: Contextual semantic embeddings for ontology subsumption prediction. World Wide Web (WWW) **26**(5), 2569–2591 (2023)
7. Chen, J., Hu, P., Jiménez-Ruiz, E., Holter, O.M., Antonyrajah, D., Horrocks, I.: Owl2vec*: embedding of OWL ontologies. Mach. Learn. **110**(7), 1813–1845 (2021)
8. Chen, J., Mashkova, O., Zhapa-Camacho, F., Hoehndorf, R., He, Y., Horrocks, I.: Ontology embedding: a survey of methods, applications and resources. IEEE Trans. Knowl. Data Eng. **37**(7), 4193–4212 (2025)
9. Cohen, W.W., Yang, F., Mazaitis, K.: Tensorlog: a probabilistic database implemented using deep-learning infrastructure. J. Artif. Intell. Res. **67**, 285–325 (2020)
10. Hoffmann, J., et al.: Training compute-optimal large language models (2022). https://doi.org/10.48550/arXiv.2203.15556, http://arxiv.org/abs/2203.15556, arXiv:2203.15556

11. Hogan, A., et al.: Knowledge graphs. ACM Comput. Surv. **54**(4), 1–37 (2021). https://doi.org/10.1145/3447772
12. Jackermeier, M., Chen, J., Horrocks, I.: Dual box embeddings for the description logic el^{++}. In: Chua, T., Ngo, C., Kumar, R., Lauw, H.W., Lee, R.K. (eds.) Proceedings of the ACM on Web Conference 2024, WWW 2024, Singapore, May 13-17, 2024, pp. 2250–2258. ACM (2024)
13. Joshi, M., Choi, E., Weld, D.S., Zettlemoyer, L.: Triviaqa: a large scale distantly supervised challenge dataset for reading comprehension. In: Barzilay, R., Kan, M. (eds.) Proceedings of the 55th Annual Meeting of the Association for Computational Linguistics, ACL 2017, Vancouver, Canada, July 30 - August 4, Volume 1: Long Papers, pp. 1601–1611. Association for Computational Linguistics (2017)
14. Kahneman, D.: Thinking, fast and slow. Thinking, fast and slow, Farrar, Straus and Giroux, New York, NY, US (2011), p. 499
15. Karpukhin, V., Oguz, B., Min, S., Lewis, P., Wu, L., Edunov, S., Chen, D., Yih, W.: Dense passage retrieval for open-domain question answering. In: Webber, B., Cohn, T., He, Y., Liu, Y. (eds.) Proceedings of the 2020 Conference on Empirical Methods in Natural Language Processing, EMNLP 2020, Online, November 16-20, 2020, pp. 6769–6781. Association for Computational Linguistics (2020)
16. Kwiatkowski, T., et al.: Natural questions: a benchmark for question answering research. Trans. Ass. Comput. Linguis. **7**, 452–466 (2019). https://doi.org/10.1162/tacl_a_00276, https://aclanthology.org/Q19-1026/, place: Cambridge, MA Publisher: MIT Press
17. Li, N., Bouraoui, Z., Schockaert, S.: Ontology completion using graph convolutional networks. In: Ghidini, C., et al, (eds.) The Semantic Web - ISWC 2019 - 18th International Semantic Web Conference, Auckland, New Zealand, October 26-30, 2019, Proceedings, Part I. Lecture Notes in Computer Science, vol. 11778, pp. 435–452. Springer (2019)
18. Manhaeve, R., Dumancic, S., Kimmig, A., Demeester, T., Raedt, L.D.: Deepproblog: neural probabilistic logic programming. CoRR **abs/1805.10872** (2018)
19. McGuinness, D.L., van Harmelen, F.: Owl web ontology language overview. W3C Recommendation (2004). https://www.w3.org/TR/owl-features/, w3C Recommendation, 10 February 2004
20. Mikolov, T., Chen, K., Corrado, G., Dean, J.: Efficient estimation of word representations in vector space. In: Bengio, Y., LeCun, Y. (eds.) 1st International Conference on Learning Representations, ICLR 2013, Scottsdale, Arizona, USA, May 2-4, 2013, Workshop Track Proceedings (2013)
21. Minervini, P., Bosnjak, M., Rocktäschel, T., Riedel, S.: Towards neural theorem proving at scale. CoRR **abs/1807.08204** (2018)
22. Nickel, M., Murphy, K., Tresp, V., Gabrilovich, E.: A review of relational machine learning for knowledge graphs. Proc. IEEE **104**(1), 11–33 (2016). https://doi.org/10.1109/JPROC.2015.2483592
23. Pennington, J., Socher, R., Manning, C.D.: Glove: global vectors for word representation. In: Moschitti, A., Pang, B., Daelemans, W. (eds.) Proceedings of the 2014 Conference on Empirical Methods in Natural Language Processing, EMNLP 2014, October 25-29, 2014, Doha, Qatar, A meeting of SIGDAT, a Special Interest Group of the ACL, pp. 1532–1543. ACL (2014)
24. Rajpurkar, P., Zhang, J., Lopyrev, K., Liang, P.: Squad: 100, 000+ questions for machine comprehension of text. In: Su, J., Carreras, X., Duh, K. (eds.) Proceedings of the 2016 Conference on Empirical Methods in Natural Language Processing, EMNLP 2016, Austin, Texas, USA, November 1-4, 2016, pp. 2383–2392. The Association for Computational Linguistics (2016)

25. Sattler, U., Horrocks, I., Baader, F.: Complexity of reasoning in expressive description logics. In: International Joint Conference on Automated Reasoning (IJCAR), pp. 146–151. Springer (2006)
26. Smaili, F.Z., Gao, X., Hoehndorf, R.: Opa2vec: combining formal and informal content of biomedical ontologies to improve similarity-based prediction. Bioinform. **35**(12), 2133–2140 (2019)
27. Trouillon, T., Welbl, J., Riedel, S., Gaussier, É., Bouchard, G.: Complex embeddings for simple link prediction. In: Balcan, M., Weinberger, K.Q. (eds.) Proceedings of the 33nd International Conference on Machine Learning, ICML 2016, New York City, NY, USA, June 19-24, 2016. JMLR Workshop and Conference Proceedings, vol. 48, pp. 2071–2080. JMLR.org (2016)
28. Vashishth, S., Sanyal, S., Nitin, V., Talukdar, P.P.: Composition-based multi-relational graph convolutional networks. In: 8th International Conference on Learning Representations, ICLR 2020, Addis Ababa, Ethiopia, April 26-30, 2020. OpenReview.net (2020)
29. Wang, H., et al.: Simple and effective relation-based embedding propagation for knowledge representation learning. In: Raedt, L.D. (ed.) Proceedings of the Thirty-First International Joint Conference on Artificial Intelligence, IJCAI 2022, Vienna, Austria, 23-29 July 2022, pp. 2755–2761. ijcai.org (2022)
30. Wang, Q., Mao, Z., Wang, B., Guo, L.: Knowledge graph embedding: a survey of approaches and applications. IEEE Trans. Knowl. Data Eng. **29**(12), 2724–2743 (2017). https://doi.org/10.1109/TKDE.2017.2754499
31. Wang, X., Ren, Z., Wang, J., Cai, Y., Su, Y., Wang, W.: Logical rule-based knowledge graph reasoning: a comprehensive survey. Mathematics **11**(21), 4486 (2023). https://doi.org/10.3390/math11214486, https://www.mdpi.com/2227-7390/11/21/4486
32. Yang, B., Yih, W., He, X., Gao, J., Deng, L.: Embedding entities and relations for learning and inference in knowledge bases. In: Bengio, Y., LeCun, Y. (eds.) 3rd International Conference on Learning Representations, ICLR 2015, San Diego, CA, USA, May 7-9, 2015, Conference Track Proceedings (2015)
33. Zhang, Z., Wang, J., Chen, J., Ji, S., Wu, F.: Cone: cone embeddings for multi-hop reasoning over knowledge graphs. In: Ranzato, M., Beygelzimer, A., Dauphin, Y.N., Liang, P., Vaughan, J.W. (eds.) Advances in Neural Information Processing Systems 34: Annual Conference on Neural Information Processing Systems 2021, NeurIPS 2021, December 6-14, 2021, virtual, pp. 19172–19183 (2021)

RAG-KT: Retrieval Augmented Generation Based Difficulty Estimation for Knowledge Tracing

Hui Ma[1], Tiancheng Zhang[1(✉)], Wangyue Lu[1], Fan Li[1], Minghe Yu[2], Yifang Yin[3], and Ge Yu[1]

[1] School of Computer Science and Engineering, Northeastern University, Shenyang, China
{mah6,luwy,lif21}@mails.neu.edu.cn, {tczhang,yuge}@mail.neu.edu.cn
[2] Software College, Northeastern University, Shenyang, China
yuminghe@mail.neu.edu.cn
[3] Institute for Infocomm Research (I2R), A*STAR, Singapore, Singapore
yin_yifang@i2r.a-star.edu.sg

Abstract. Knowledge Tracing (KT) is a key task in online education that aims to model the dynamic knowledge states of students. To achieve high-quality KT, question difficulty estimation plays an important role during the information extraction phase. However, most existing methods based on statistical models face two major challenges: (1) unstable estimates across different datasets, and (2) the cold-start problem when estimating the difficulty of new questions. To address these issues, we propose a Retrieval-Augmented Generation-based Knowledge Tracing framework (RAG-KT). This framework introduces a novel RAG-based difficulty estimation method that generates stable and accurate difficulty scores, and can estimate the difficulty of unseen questions by referencing semantically similar ones. The LLM-generated scores, along with other relevant information from students' learning histories, are then fed into a KT model for the prediction task. Specifically, to improve the quality of difficulty estimation, we apply contrastive learning to fine-tune a domain-specific embedding model for RAG in educational contexts. We also carefully design task-specific prompts to guide LLMs for better difficulty estimation performance. Extensive experimental results demonstrate that RAG-KT achieves stable difficulty estimation and effectively addresses the cold-start problem. With more reliable difficulty estimates, the performance of KT models can be significantly improved.

Keywords: Knowledge Tracing · Retrieval-Augmented Generation · Difficulty Estimation

1 Introduction

In recent years, the rapid growth of large-scale online education has enabled platforms to provide richer resources, immediate formative feedback, and more

I. Awan et al. (Eds.): WISE 2025, LNCS 16368, pp. 275–290, 2026.
https://doi.org/10.1007/978-981-95-7251-9_19

personalized learning services [2,26]. In this context, Knowledge Tracing (KT) has emerged as a key research area at the intersection of education and data mining, aiming to model students' evolving knowledge states and predict their future performance based on learning histories [10].

Early knowledge tracing began with Bayesian Knowledge Tracing (BKT) [3]. With deep learning advances, Deep Knowledge Tracing (DKT) [15] employed Recurrent Neural Networks (RNNs) [17] to model students' sequential learning behaviors. Subsequently, researchers emphasized the importance of difficulty estimation in assessing student progress, especially in dynamic knowledge tracing models [13]. Accurate difficulty estimation enables a more comprehensive understanding of student mastery and significantly enhances learning outcomes. In recent years, an increasing number of models have incorporated difficulty factors into their designs to improve prediction accuracy. For example, EKT [11] and RKT [14] implicitly estimate difficulty from question text, while AKT [5] incorporates IRT-based item embeddings to enhance difficulty representation. Difficulty is estimated by models such as DIMKT [19], PEBG [24] and DL4KT [9] based on correctness rate. These methods have made significant progress in question representation and prediction accuracy.

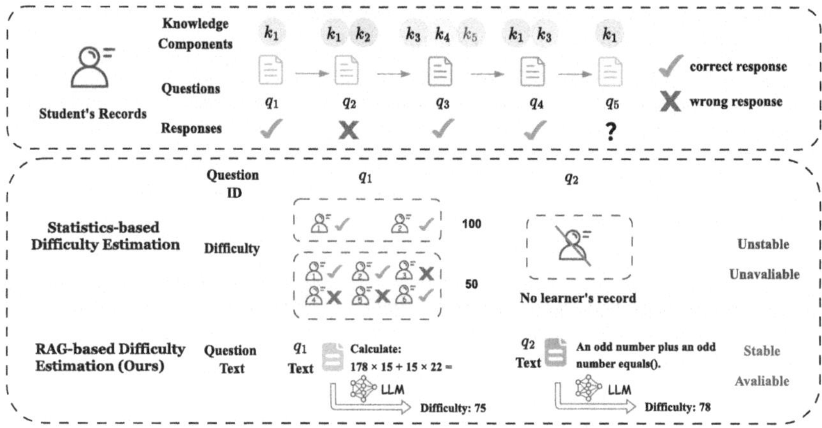

Fig. 1. An example of knowledge tracing (Top). Comparison between statistical-based and RAG-based difficulty estimation methods (Bottom). Question q_2 is a new question that has not appeared in any learning history.

However, these methods rely heavily on student response data such as correctness or response time, which introduces inherent limitations. As shown in Fig. 1, the **instability of difficulty estimation** arises from its high sensitivity to individual student performance, resulting in inconsistent predictions across varying sample sizes. Moreover, for newly introduced questions with limited data available, traditional methods often fail to provide accurate estimates, leading to the **cold-start problem** (refer to Sect. 3).

Intuitively, integrating Retrieval-Augmented Generation (RAG) with Large Language Models (LLMs) provides an effective solution to the instability of difficulty estimation and the cold-start problem. RAG retrieves k semantically similar questions from the training set as context, and LLMs combine these with known difficulty values to produce new, more stable estimates. This approach enables reliable difficulty prediction for new questions even without historical data, effectively addressing the cold-start problem. However, directly applying existing RAG and LLMs frameworks presents two key limitations: **(1) Semantic Similarity Challenge**: General embedding models often lack awareness of the education field, which limits their ability to capture subtle differences in teaching content. **(2) Limitations of Predefined Templates**: Standard RAG templates are not made for educational tasks and often miss key features like question type and difficulty, reducing the accuracy of difficulty estimates.

In this paper, we are the first to analyze the limitations of traditional difficulty estimation methods from a data perspective, revealing their instability with limited samples and cold-start problem for new questions lacking historical responses. To overcome these challenges, we propose RAG-KT, a Retrieval-Augmented Generation framework for difficulty estimation in knowledge tracing. We fine-tune an embedding model via contrastive learning on public and KT datasets to better capture semantic similarities in educational texts. Given a target question, the model retrieves the top-k semantically similar questions from a database. These retrieved texts, their difficulty labels, and the target question are input to a LLM, mitigating instability and cold-start problem. For difficulty generation, the LLM receives the target question, retrieved texts with difficulty values, and a task description via a specialized prompt template, enabling more flexible and adaptive inference. Finally, the generated difficulty scores are integrated into students' learning sequences and fed into a knowledge tracing model (KTM), enhancing knowledge state modeling and improving future performance prediction accuracy. The main contributions are summarized as follows:

- Through data analysis, we reveal new challenges in difficulty estimation for knowledge tracing. Existing methods are highly sensitive to sample size variations, often leading to unstable and inaccurate estimates.
- Based on these findings, we propose a novel difficulty estimation framework that combines RAG. This framework aims to improve the stability of difficulty estimation and alleviate cold-start problem.
- To address these challenges, we propose the following solutions: (1) Enhancing estimation stability by retrieving and jointly processing semantically similar texts with the target question to strengthen inference robustness. (2) Mitigating the cold-start problem by incorporating contextual information from retrieved texts, enabling effective reasoning without historical data. (3) Improving semantic representation by fine-tuning embeddings on public datasets, thereby boosting retrieval accuracy and semantic matching. (4) Increasing model adaptability by designing task-specific input templates, overcoming the limitations of predefined prompt templates.

- Extensive experiments on two public datasets demonstrate the effectiveness of RAG-KT. In addition, we validate its generalizability across different datasets, LLMs, and KT models.

2 Related Works

2.1 Knowledge Tracing

Knowledge Tracing (KT), as a core task in online education, has been extensively studied for several decades [20]. One of the early classic approaches is Bayesian Knowledge Tracing (BKT) [3], which models students' knowledge states using Hidden Markov Models (HMMs) to capture and update their learning progress.

With the advent of deep learning, Deep Knowledge Tracing (DKT) [15] pioneered the use of RNNs [17] or LSTMs [7] to model student knowledge states. Subsequent works like DKVMN [22] employed memory networks to capture latent knowledge concepts, while EKT [11] and RKT [14] implicitly estimated question difficulty from textual content. AKT [5] incorporated question difficulty via IRT-based embeddings to enrich representations. Many KT models further integrate difficulty as auxiliary information: DIMKT [19] fuses question and concept difficulty from response data, and DL4KT [9] employs BERT to estimate difficulty attributes, MAKT [6] models difficulty via attempt and hint-based behaviors with multi-task attention. These studies demonstrate the growing attention to incorporating question difficulty.

With the rapid development of LLMs, the direction of difficulty modeling and knowledge tracing research has shifted. The powerful representational capabilities of large models offer promising prospects for applications in KT. For example, SINKT [4] generates a concept-question heterogeneous graph using LLMs, extracting semantic and structural information between questions and concepts. KPLLM-STE [29] applies knowledge-enhanced large language models to better capture semantic and contextual information.

2.2 Retrieval-Augmented Generation

RAG is particularly well-suited for tasks that require retrieving external information to enhance performance. By incorporating relevant data, RAG can improve the effectiveness of large language models in specific contexts, leading to more accurate outputs [23]. In decision support, the PlanRAG [8] combines LLMs with RAG via an iterative plan-retrieve-replan cycle, enhancing accuracy and efficiency in complex tasks. In education, the RAMO [16] retrieves relevant course data from a vector database and uses LLMs with prompt templates to provide personalized, dynamic learning recommendations. Furthermore, RAG has broad applications in other fields, such as RA-DT [18] and CaseGPT [28]. Therefore, we have reason to believe that RAG also holds great potential in knowledge tracing, as it can more accurately estimate question difficulty by retrieving relevant question sets. To the best of our knowledge, we are the first to apply RAG in knowledge tracing.

3 Data Analysis

In this section, we evaluate the limitations of traditional question difficulty estimation methods through experiments, focusing on estimate instability and the cold-start problem under insufficient student samples.

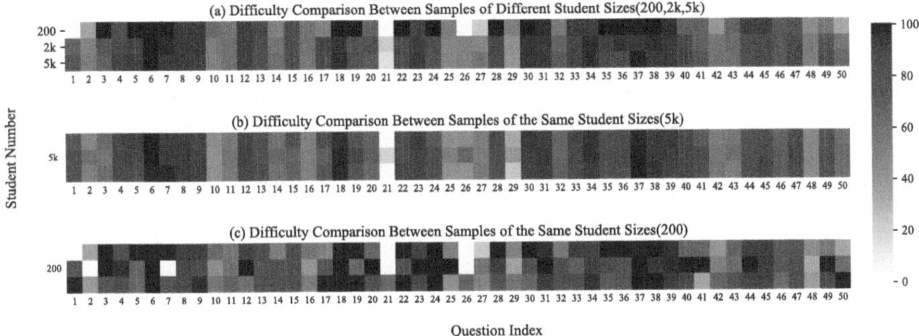

Fig. 2. Variation in question difficulty across student sample sizes.

3.1 Experimental Purpose

We argue that relying solely on statistical features is insufficient, as it cannot effectively address the cold start problem for new questions without historical data. This experiment aims to obtain data-driven insights to guide model design, specifically targeting difficulty estimation instability and the cold start problem.

3.2 Experimental Method

We analyze the impact of student sample size on difficulty estimation using the XES3G5M dataset by randomly selecting three student groups of different sizes (200, 2000, and 5000) and computing question difficulty based on performance (e.g., accuracy). For each group, 50 questions answered by all students are chosen, and their difficulties are estimated and visualized with heatmaps to demonstrate how sample size affects estimation stability.

3.3 Experimental Results and Analysis

Sample Size-Induced Instability in Difficulty Estimation. Fig. 2(a) compares difficulty estimation under different student sample sizes (200, 2000, 5000). As the sample size increases, estimates become more stable and less variable. In Fig. 2(b), with 5000 students, the results are highly consistent, indicating reduced estimation variance. Conversely, Fig. 2(c) shows that with only 200 students, estimates fluctuate significantly, leading to potential errors.

Cold Start Problem. In the absence of historical data, traditional methods struggle to estimate the difficulty of new questions. When a question has not yet been attempted by any students, its difficulty value remains undefined, indicating that traditional approaches lack the capacity to effectively estimate the difficulty of unseen items.

Therefore, traditional methods suffer from instability in difficulty estimation with limited samples and cannot reliably support new questions in cold-start scenarios. These limitations restrict their applicability in dynamic data environments. To address this, the next chapter investigates RAG-based difficulty estimation methods to better handle data insufficiency and cold-start challenges.

4 Method

In this section, we define the knowledge tracing (KT) task and introduce question representation methods used in existing KT models. We then present the proposed method and illustrate its framework in Fig. 3, divided into offline and online phases. In the offline phase, the embedding model is fine-tuned via contrastive learning on open educational resources and KT datasets, and training texts are stored in a vector database for efficient retrieval. In the online phase, question texts similar to the target question are retrieved from the vector database, and two inference strategies using a LLM estimate difficulty for historical and new questions. These estimates are then integrated into the knowledge tracing model (KTM) to enhance predictions of students' future performance.

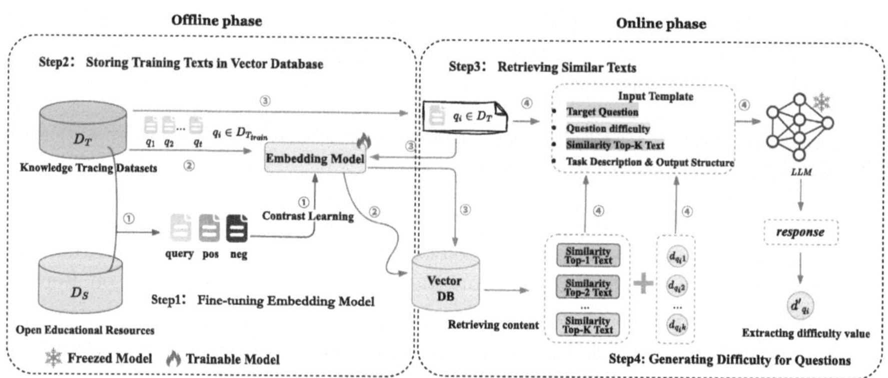

Fig. 3. The RAG-KT framework and its detailed process. The process is divided into two phases: offline phase and online phase.

4.1 Preliminary

Problem Definition. In an online learning system, let $S = \{s_1, s_2, \ldots, s_I\}$ represent the set of students, $Q = \{q_1, q_2, \ldots, q_J\}$ denote the set of questions and

$K = \{k_1, k_2, \ldots, k_M\}$ be the set of knowledge components (KCs). Each question is associated with one or more specific KCs, and students practice different questions to achieve knowledge mastery. The learning history of a student $s \in S$ is represented as: $R_s = \{(q_1, r_1), (q_2, r_2), \ldots, (q_T, r_T)\}$where $q_t \in Q$ refers to the question answered by the student at time step t, and $r_t \in \{0, 1\}$ indicates whether the student s answered q_t correctly (1 for correct, 0 for incorrect).

Task Definition. Given the student's learning history R_s and a new question q_{T+1}, the goal of the KT task is to predict the probability that the student will correctly answer the new question, expressed as $p(r_{T+1} = 1|R_s, q_{T+1})$.

Difficulty Definition. Question difficulty is a widely studied attribute. Typically, the difficulty of a problem is not provided in the dataset. Inspired by Classical Test Theory(CTT) and some previous studies, the initial difficulty value is calculated using an objective statistical method as follows:

$$d_i = \sum_{j=1}^{|A_i|} \frac{\{a_{ij} = 1\}}{|A_i|} \cdot g \tag{1}$$

where d_i is the difficulty estimate for question q_i, A_i represents the set of answers related to question q_i, $a_{ij} = 1$ indicates the correct answer within that set, and the constant g is a predefined difficulty level (e.g., if g is set to 100, there are 100 different difficulty levels).

4.2 Fine-Tuning Embedding Model

we present a fine-tuning approach for the embedding model using contrastive learning to enhance its semantic representation capabilities in a specific domain. This study employs a joint fine-tuning strategy that integrates both the source dataset and the target dataset, where the training data is derived from the open educational resources (D_S) and the knowledge tracing dataset (D_T).

$$\min_{(q,p)} \sum -\log \frac{e^{\langle e_q, e_p \rangle/\tau}}{e^{\langle e_q, e_p \rangle/\tau} + \sum e^{\langle e_q, e_n \rangle/\tau}} \tag{2}$$

where (q, p) denotes a positive sample pair, τ is the temperature parameter, $\langle e_q, e_p \rangle$ represents the similarity between the embedding vectors of the query text and the positive sample, and $\langle e_q, e_n \rangle$ represents the similarity between the embedding vectors of the query text and a negative sample. A key aspect of contrastive learning is selecting negative samples. Instead of mining hard negatives, we use in-batch negative sampling, where other batch samples serve as negatives. We follow the sample construction strategy outlined in [27], which helps the fine-tuned embedding model better capture semantic relationships and provides a strong basis for efficient retrieval in the online phase.

4.3 Storing Training Texts in Vector Database

In the offline phase, we convert training texts into high-dimensional vectors using the fine-tuned embedding model and store them in a vector database. Specifically, each text q_i from the knowledge tracing dataset D_T is encoded as e_{q_i} and stored in the Chromadb vector database. The database builds a dense vector index, enabling fast similarity computations and efficient retrieval of similar texts during the online phase.

4.4 Retrieving Similar Texts

In the online phase, the system performs efficient retrieval of similar texts using the fine-tuned embedding model and the vector database constructed in the offline phase. Specifically, when a target question $q_i \in D_T$ is input, the embedding model first maps the question to a high-dimensional vector representation. The system then uses this vector as a query to perform retrieval in the vector database. With the help of the text index space, the vector database quickly calculates the similarity between the target question and the stored text vectors, returning the top-k most similar texts. These retrieved similar texts provide semantic support for subsequent difficulty estimation and question analysis, ensuring the accuracy and effectiveness of the retrieval results.

4.5 Generating Difficulty for Questions

In the online phase, the system generates the difficulty evaluation of the target question by combining the retrieved similar texts with the LLM. Specifically, the target question q_i, the top-k similar texts and their difficulty values $d_{q_i,1}, d_{q_i,2}, \ldots, d_{q_i,K}$, along with a predefined input template, serve as input to the LLM. This template includes the target question, similar texts, task description, and output format, providing context to guide the LLM in producing accurate evaluations. The LLM then generates the difficulty analysis, from which the final difficulty value d'_{q_i} is extracted. This approach ensures accurate and interpretable difficulty estimation by effectively integrating information from similar texts with the LLM's generative capability.

4.6 Integrating Difficulty and Prediction

In this study, we propose the RAG-KT framework, which integrates difficulty estimation into knowledge tracing to better predict student performance. As shown in Fig. 4, RAG-KT retrieves historical questions semantically similar to the target question, along with their difficulty values, and uses them in a prompt for a LLM to generate an enhanced difficulty representation d'. The framework applies two inference strategies based on whether the target question is in the training set:

1)Historical Questions. For history questions that have appeared in the training data, the model first estimates an initial difficulty based on students'

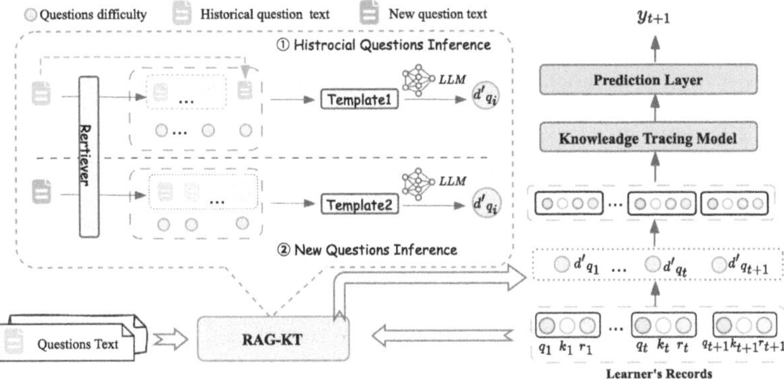

Fig. 4. Overall workflow of RAG-KT. The process is divided into two main phases: historical questions inference and new questions inference.

past responses. It then retrieves similar historical questions and their difficulty values, constructs a prompt including this information, and uses the LLM to refine the estimate, generating a more accurate and stable result. **2)New Questions.** For new questions not present in the training data, the system retrieves semantically similar questions based on the input text and uses their known difficulty values to construct a prompt. The LLM then infers the difficulty of the new question by leveraging semantic similarity and prior difficulty patterns.

The enhanced difficulty representation d' and the student's learning sequence X_s are fed into the knowledge tracing model (KTM) to predict student knowledge states and future performance. In this study, KTM is instantiated with DL4KT [9] and DIMKT [19], while remaining compatible with other KT models. This process can be formalized as:

$$\hat{y} = \mathrm{KTM}(X_s, d') \tag{3}$$

where KTM denotes the base knowledge tracing model, which is compatible with various difficulty-aware KT methods and exhibits strong generalization ability. The model takes X_s and d' as input, and outputs $\hat{y}_{t+1}$, the predicted probability that the student will correctly answer the next question at time step $t + 1$.

5 Experiment

5.1 Dataset

We select two publicly available real-world datasets from different subjects to evaluate our method: (1) XES3G5M [12] and (2) DBE-KT22 [1]. These datasets provide important textual features related to questions and knowledge concepts (KCs) in the field of Knowledge Tracing (KT). To the best of our knowledge, these are the only two publicly available knowledge tracing datasets that contain question texts. In addition, we use two open educational resources, Math23K [25] and Database System Concepts [21], to fine-tune the embedding models.

XES3G5M[1] is created by the TAL Education Group. It covers the academic performance of third-grade students in mathematics and records over 5 million interactions. The original text data is in Chinese.

DBEKT22[2] consists of exercise data from undergraduate students enrolled in the Database course at the Australian National University from 2018 to 2021.

Math23K[3] contains Chinese arithmetic word questions for elementary school students, sourced from multiple online education websites. It includes 23,161 Chinese arithmetic word questions.

Database System Concepts.[4] is a widely recognized textbook on relational databases. We select 262 exercises from this book to create an open educational resource for fine-tuning embedding models(Table1).

Table 1. Dataset statistics.

Statistic	XES3G5M	DBE-KT22
Students	18,066	212
Questions	7,652	1,361
Knowledge Concepts	845	98
Interactions	5,549,635	167,222
Avg. Questions per KCs	9.06	13.89
Avg. Records per Question	725.25	122.87

5.2 Baselines

Deep Learning Models. To demonstrate the effectiveness of our model and its improvements over existing deep KT models, we conduct a comparative evaluation of KT models that utilize difficulty information.

DIMKT [19]: DIMKT leverages difficulty and concept information to model the problem-solving process. By integrating difficulty features into question modeling and utilizing student interaction data, it improves prediction accuracy.

DL4KT [9]: DL4KT introduces a difficulty-centered contrastive learning method that uses BERT to model question representations and employs LLMs to optimize and predict difficulty from unseen data.

1 https://github.com/ai4ed/XES3G5M.
2 https://dataverse.ada.edu.au/dataset.xhtml?persistentId=doi:10.26193/6DZWOH.
3 https://opendatalab.org.cn/Math23K.
4 https://www.db-book.com/Practice-Exercises/index-solu.html.

Embedding Models. We employ two embedding models, bge-base-zh-v1.5 and bge-base-en-v1.5 [27], for representing Chinese and English texts, respectively. Both models are specifically optimized for their respective languages and demonstrate strong performance in semantic representation and similarity computation tasks.

Large Language Models. To ensure a comprehensive evaluation of large language models in the context of knowledge tracing, we select four diverse and representative models: GPT-4o mini, GPT-4o, GLM-4, and DeepSeek-V3.

5.3 Experimental Setup

In this study, student practice records are sorted by answer time, and input sequences are fixed to a length of 100. Longer sequences are split, and shorter ones are zero-padded. Problems with fewer than three responses are removed. The dataset is divided into training, validation, and test sets in an 8:1:1 ratio. The model is trained on the training set, the best model is selected based on validation results, and evaluation is conducted on the test set. Early stopping is applied after 10 validation steps without improvement. The Adam optimizer is used with a learning rate of 1×10^{-4}, with other settings following the original knowledge tracing model.

5.4 Overall Performance

Table 2 reports the average AUC (Area Under the Curve) and RMSE (Root Mean Square Error) of all evaluated models on the XES3G5M and DBE-KT22 datasets. The results highlight several key observations. First, our proposed RAG-KT model achieves the highest AUC and the lowest RMSE across both datasets, demonstrating its superior performance in knowledge tracing tasks. These results indicate that the integration of RAG and LLMs enables more accurate difficulty estimation, which in turn enhances the modeling of students' knowledge states. Furthermore, RAG-KT outperforms DL4KT and DIMKT in predictive capability, achieving higher accuracy. These findings further validate the effectiveness of large language model-driven approaches in improving the accuracy of knowledge tracing.

5.5 The Impact of Different Large Language Models

As shown in the Table 2, we observe that our proposed method achieves stable performance when combined with different large language models, consistently outperforming the corresponding baseline models. The performance differences across various LLMs are relatively minor, indicating that the performance gains primarily stem from our framework itself rather than reliance on any specific language model. This consistency across different LLMs demonstrates the strong adaptability and generalization capability of our approach, enabling it to function robustly with diverse language understanding modules.

Table 2. Performance comparison between RAG-KT and traditional baselines on student performance prediction. Best results are in bold. * denotes statistically significant improvement ($p < 0.05$, t-test).

Model		XES3G5M		DBE-KT22	
KT	RAG-KT	AUC	RMSE	AUC	RMSE
DL4KT		0.7974	0.3538	0.7607	0.4298
	GPT-4o mini	0.8274	0.3442	0.7714	**0.4246***
	GPT-4o	0.8274	0.3445	0.7704	0.4265
	DeepSeek-v3	**0.8297***	**0.3434***	0.7706	0.4262
	GLM4	0.8282	0.3441	**0.7721***	0.4253
DIMKT		0.7388	0.3962	0.6454	0.4765
	GPT-4o mini	0.7726	0.3944	0.6497	0.4763
	GPT-4o	0.7658	0.3948	0.6576	0.4768
	DeepSeek-v3	0.7710	0.3946	0.6569	0.4765
	GLM4	**0.7736***	**0.3943***	**0.6623***	**0.4757***

5.6 Ablation Study

In this section, we conduct an ablation study to assess the contribution of each model component. As shown in Table 3, the experimental results demonstrate that incorporating the retrieval (retr.) module improves performance in terms of AUC and RMSE, indicating a stronger ability to capture question difficulty and, consequently, better predictive accuracy. Building on this, fine-tuning the embedding model further enhances performance by improving adaptability to domain-specific data. Finally, integrating the LLM (GLM-4) in the DL4KT-Retr-FT variant yields the best results on both datasets, further confirming the effectiveness of LLMs in enhancing difficulty estimation. Overall, each module contributes positively to performance, with embedding fine-tuning and the LLM integration providing the most substantial improvements.

Table 3. Ablation Study of all datasets. ✓ indicates the inclusion of the corresponding component.

Model	Components				XES3G5M		DBE-KT22	
	KT	Retr.	FT	LLM	AUC	RMSE	AUC	RMSE
DL4KT	✓				0.7974	0.3538	0.7607	0.4298
DL4KT-Retr	✓	✓			0.8136	0.3496	0.7674	0.4262
DL4KT-Retr-FT	✓	✓	✓		0.8243	0.3461	0.7689	0.4240
DL4KT-Retr-FT-LLM(RAG-DL4KT)	✓	✓	✓	✓	0.8282	0.3441	0.7721	0.4253

5.7 The Impact of Fine-Tuning the Embedding Model

To examine the impact of embedding model fine-tuning on retrieval performance in knowledge tracing, this section compares performance before and after fine-tuning in a question-text retrieval task. A two-stage fine-tuning strategy is employed: first, semantic-level adaptation on open educational resources, followed by task-specific tuning on knowledge tracing datasets. For the Chinese embedding model, bge-base-zh-v1.5 is fine-tuned on Math23K and subsequently on XES3G5M. For the English embedding model, bge-base-en-v1.5 is adapted on Database System Concepts, followed by tuning on DBE-KT22.This process enhances both general semantic comprehension and task-specific representation. DL4KT is used as the baseline, with experimental settings, metrics, and results discussed below.

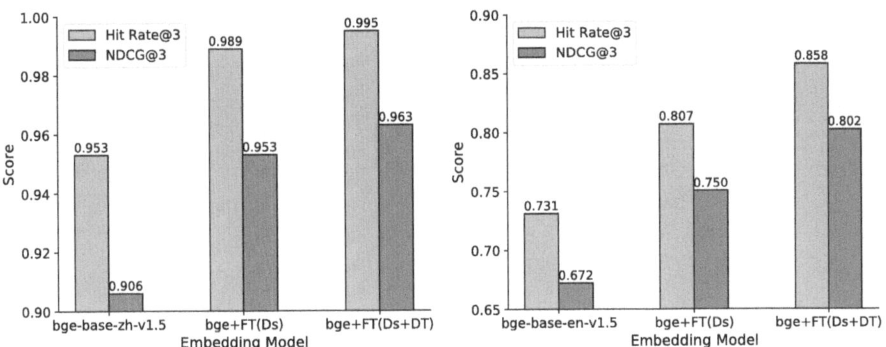

Fig. 5. Evaluation Results of Embedding Models.

HR@k (Hit Rate): Evaluates whether the correct item appears in the top-k results. Higher values indicate better retrieval accuracy.

NDCG@k (Normalized Discounted Cumulative Gain): Measures ranking quality by comparing cumulative gain with an ideal ranking. Values closer to 1 indicate more accurate and stable retrieval performance.

As shown in Fig. 5, we compare the performance of different embedding models in both Chinese and English settings, evaluated by Hit Rate@3 and NDCG@3. Results indicate that sequential fine-tuning, first on open educational resources (D_S), followed by knowledge tracing datasets (D_T), significantly improves retrieval accuracy and enhances the stability of difficulty estimation across languages. In the Chinese setting (left), the base model bge-base-zh-v1.5 achieves strong initial performance, which further improves after tuning on Math23K and reaches the best scores following additional tuning on XES3G5M. In the English setting (right), bge-base-en-v1.similarly benefits from fine-tuning on Database System Concepts, yielding notable gains in both metrics.

5.8 Cold-Start Experiment

To investigate the cold-start problem in knowledge tracing, we conduct an experimental analysis. Specifically, we construct training sets of varying sizes on the XES3G5M dataset, containing student histories of 200, 2000, 5000, and 18,066 (full dataset). We train DL4KT and DIMKT, along with their enhanced variants RAG-DL4KT and RAG-DIMKT (both incorporating GLM4 as the language model), on these subsets and evaluate all models on the full test set.

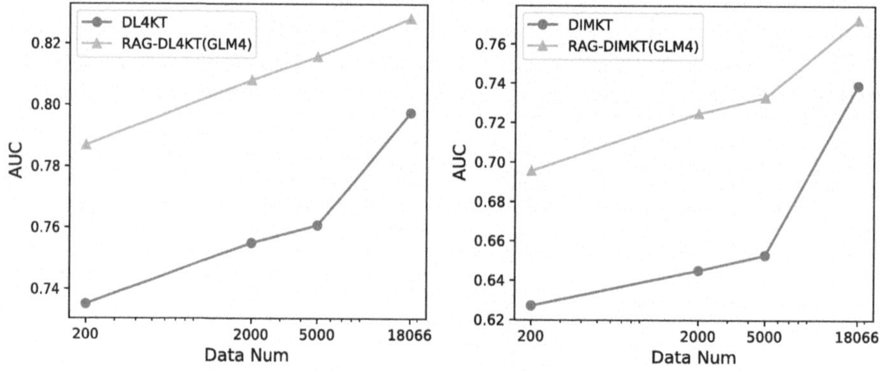

Fig. 6. Cold start analysis of RAG-KT.

As shown in Fig. 6, the performance of baseline models DL4KT and DIMKT declines significantly as the amount of training data decreases. In contrast, our RAG-enhanced models maintain relatively stable performance across different data scales and consistently outperform their baselines. The performance gap is especially pronounced in low-resource scenarios (e.g., 200 or 2000 students), further validating the effectiveness of our method under limited data. These results suggest that even with constrained training data, our proposed RAG-KT framework generates stable and reliable difficulty representations, improving predictive performance in knowledge tracing tasks.

6 Conclusion

In this paper, we introduce the RAG-KT framework, which combines Retrieval-Augmented Generation (RAG) and Large Language Models (LLMs) for more stable difficulty estimation in knowledge tracing tasks. The framework effectively addresses two major challenges in existing models: the instability of difficulty estimation caused by small sample sizes and the cold-start problem for new questions. We propose a dual-stage fine-tuning strategy to enhance the embedding model's semantic representation capabilities. By integrating specialized difficulty estimation templates with LLMs, the model generates reliable difficulty estimates for both historical and new questions. Extensive experiments validate the effectiveness of the proposed method. Moreover, the framework's generalizability is demonstrated across multiple datasets, large language models, and knowledge tracing architectures. In the future, we will explore optimizing retrieval strategies and leveraging multimodal learning to further improve model efficiency and applicability across diverse educational contexts.

References

1. Abdelrahman, G., Abdelfattah, S., Wang, Q., Lin, Y.: DBE-KT22: a knowledge tracing dataset based on online student evaluation. CoRR **abs/2208.12651** (2022)
2. Anderson, A., Huttenlocher, D.P., Kleinberg, J.M., Leskovec, J.: Engaging with massive online courses. In: WWW, pp. 687–698. ACM (2014)
3. Corbett, A.T., Anderson, J.R.: Knowledge tracing: modeling the acquisition of procedural knowledge. User Model. User-Adap. Inter. **4**, 253–278 (1994)
4. Fu, L., et al.: SINKT: A structure-aware inductive knowledge tracing model with large language model. In: CIKM, pp. 632–642. ACM (2024)
5. Ghosh, A., Heffernan, N.T., Lan, A.S.: Context-aware attentive knowledge tracing. In: KDD, pp. 2330–2339. ACM (2020)
6. He, L., Li, X., Wang, P., Tang, J., Wang, T.: Integrating fine-grained attention into multi-task learning for knowledge tracing. World Wide Web **26**(5), 3347–3372 (2023)
7. Hochreiter, S., Schmidhuber, J.: Long short-term memory. Neural Comput. **9**(8), 1735–1780 (1997)
8. Lee, M., An, S., Kim, M.: Planrag: a plan-then-retrieval augmented generation for generative large language models as decision makers. In: NAACL-HLT, pp. 6537–6555. Association for Computational Linguistics (2024)
9. Lee, U., et al.: Difficulty-focused contrastive learning for knowledge tracing with a large language model-based difficulty prediction. In: LREC/COLING, pp. 4891–4900. ELRA and ICCL (2024)
10. Liu, H., et al.: Advancing knowledge tracing by exploring follow-up performance trends. arXiv preprint arXiv:2508.08019 (2025)
11. Liu, Q.: EKT: exercise-aware knowledge tracing for student performance prediction. IEEE Trans. Knowl. Data Eng. **33**(1), 100–115 (2021)
12. Liu, Z., et al.: XES3G5M: a knowledge tracing benchmark dataset with auxiliary information. In: NeurIPS (2023)
13. Minn, S., Zhu, F., Desmarais, M.C.: Improving knowledge tracing model by integrating problem difficulty. In: ICDM Workshops, pp. 1505–1506. IEEE (2018)
14. Pandey, S., Srivastava, J.: RKT: relation-aware self-attention for knowledge tracing. In: CIKM, pp. 1205–1214. ACM (2020)
15. Piech, C., et al.: Deep knowledge tracing. In: NIPS, pp. 505–513 (2015)
16. Rao, J., Lin, J.: RAMO: retrieval-augmented generation for enhancing moocs recommendations. In: HEXED/L3MNGET@EDM. CEUR Workshop Proceedings, vol. 3840. CEUR-WS.org (2024)
17. Rumelhart, D.E., Hinton, G.E., Williams, R.J.: Learning representations by back-propagating errors. nature **323**(6088), 533–536 (1986)
18. Schmied, T., Paischer, F., Patil, V., Hofmarcher, M., Pascanu, R., Hochreiter, S.: Retrieval-augmented decision transformer: external memory for in-context RL. CoRR **abs/2410.07071** (2024)

19. Shen, S., Huang, Z., Liu, Q., Su, Y., Wang, S., Chen, E.: Assessing student's dynamic knowledge state by exploring the question difficulty effect. In: SIGIR, pp. 427–437. ACM (2022)
20. Shen, S., et al.: A survey of knowledge tracing: models, variants, and applications. IEEE Trans. Learn. Technol. **17**, 1898–1919 (2024)
21. Silberschatz, A., Korth, H.F., Sudarshan, S.: Database system concepts (2011)
22. Sun, X., Zhao, X., Li, B., Ma, Y., Sutcliffe, R.F.E., Feng, J.: Dynamic key-value memory networks with rich features for knowledge tracing. IEEE Trans. Cybern. **52**(8), 8239–8245 (2022)
23. Wang, C., Ong, J., Wang, C., Ong, H., Cheng, R., Ong, D.: Potential for GPT technology to optimize future clinical decision-making using retrieval-augmented generation. Ann. Biomed. Eng. **52**(5), 1115–1118 (2024)
24. Wang, W., Ma, H., Zhao, Y., Yang, F., Chang, L.: PERM: pre-training question embeddings via relation map for improving knowledge tracing. In: DASFAA (3). Lecture Notes in Computer Science, vol. 13247, pp. 281–288. Springer (2022)
25. Wang, Y., Liu, X., Shi, S.: Deep neural solver for math word problems. In: EMNLP, pp. 845–854. Association for Computational Linguistics (2017)
26. Wu, Z., Jiang, H., Cheng, X., Huang, H., Yang, Q., Zhang, J.: Metacognition-driven user-to-project recommendation for online education services. World Wide Web **26**(5), 2311–2327 (2023)
27. Xiao, S., Liu, Z., Zhang, P., Muennighoff, N., Lian, D., Nie, J.: C-pack: Packed resources for general chinese embeddings. In: SIGIR, pp. 641–649. ACM (2024)
28. Yang, R.: Casegpt: a case reasoning framework based on language models and retrieval-augmented generation. CoRR **abs/2407.07913** (2024)
29. Zhong, H., Zhang, Q., Li, W., Lin, R., Tang, Y.: Kpllm-ste: knowledge-enhanced and prompt-aware large language models for short-text expansion. World Wide Web **28**(1), 1–25 (2025)

BiRKGC: Bidirectional Relation and Graph-Aware Model for Knowledge Graph Completion

Yicheng Zhang, Jiwei Qin(✉), Shengguo Kang, Duxiang Chen, Haichao Li, Li Zhang, and Qiangsheng Feng

School of Computer Science and Technology, Xinjiang University, Urumqi, Xinjiang 830046, China

jwqin@xju.edu.cn

Abstract. In recent years, many studies have focused on improving knowledge graph completion (KGC) using pre-trained language models (PLMs). Most PLM-based methods focus on encoding textual triples but fail to account for relation directionality and structural context, which are crucial for capturing complex relational semantics. To address this limitation, we propose BiRKGC, a Bidirectional Relation and Graph-Aware model for KGC. The framework consists of three collaborative components: a Bidirectional Relation Encoder (BiR) for explicit direction modeling, a Graph-Aware Sequence Encoder (GaS) for integrating subgraph-level structure, and a Masked Token Modeling (MTM) task for semantic pre-training. Together, these components enhance the model's ability to fuse textual semantics with structural information for more effective reasoning. In addition, BiRKGC introduces a dynamic subgraph sampling mechanism to improve structural adaptability. Experiments on WN18RR and FB15k-237 show that BiRKGC consistently improves MRR, Hits@1, and other metrics over strong baselines, while also narrowing the performance gap between forward and backward reasoning. Ablation studies validate the effectiveness of each module, demonstrating BiRKGC's potential and competitiveness in KGC tasks.

Keywords: Knowledge Graph Completion · Pre-trained Language Model · Bidirectional Relation Modeling · Graph-Aware Modeling

1 Introduction

Knowledge Graphs (KGs) are multi-relational structures composed of (head entity, relation, tail entity) triples, capturing real-world entities and their semantic connections. KGs have shown strong performance in recommender systems [1], search engines [2], question answering [3], and knowledge discovery. However, both manual construction and automated extraction [4] lead to missing triples, affecting completeness and downstream task performance. To address

I. Awan et al. (Eds.): WISE 2025, LNCS 16368, pp. 291–305, 2026.
https://doi.org/10.1007/978-981-95-7251-9_20

this, Knowledge Graph Completion (KGC) aims to predict missing head or tail entities, enriching KGs' structure and semantics.

Early methods for knowledge graph completion (KGC) primarily rely on knowledge graph embedding (KGE) techniques, including classic models such as TransE [5], RotatE [6], and Tucker [7]. These approaches map entities and relations into continuous vector spaces and define scoring functions to evaluate the plausibility of triples. While effective in modeling simple graph structures and relation patterns, they struggle with complex relation types—such as symmetric, inverse, and compositional relations—and often fail to capture rich semantic information. To enhance structural representation, subsequent work has introduced graph neural network (GNN) techniques, such as R-GCN [8] and CompGCN [9], which aggregate neighborhood information to improve the structural awareness of entity and relation embeddings. These GNN-enhanced methods partially overcome the limitations of traditional KGE models and achieve better prediction performance. However, embedding-based methods still generally overlook the abundant textual information associated with entities and relations in knowledge graphs, limiting their capability for semantic understanding and complex reasoning.

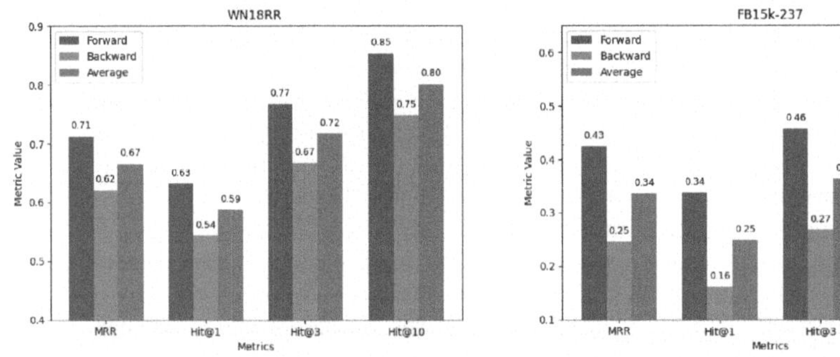

Fig. 1. Evaluation of SimKGC's Forward, Backward, and Average Metrics on WN18RR and FB15k-237.

In recent years, with the advent of pre-trained language models (PLMs) such as BERT [10] and T5 [11], PLM-based methods for knowledge graph completion have received increasing attention. Representative approaches like KG-BERT [12], SimKGC [13], and CSProm-KG [14] convert triples into textual sequences and leverage PLMs' powerful language understanding abilities to capture contextual semantics. These methods have significantly advanced the semantic modeling of knowledge graphs. Nevertheless, most PLM-based approaches still fail to effectively integrate graph structural information and often lack the ability to capture complex relational patterns or the interaction between structure and semantics. In particular, many of them do not explicitly model inverse relations, resulting in significant performance gaps between forward and backward predictions for the same triple. For example, experimental results from SimKGC [13] on WN18RR and FB15k-237 show noticeable discrepancies in metrics such as MRR and Hits@1 between forward and backward settings (Fig. 1), which leads to degraded average performance. This phenomenon underscores the limitations of current PLM-based approaches in modeling relation directionality and highlights the need for new architectures that can explicitly capture directional features of relations.

To address these issues, this paper proposes BiRKGC. First, we design the Masked Token Modeling (MTM) pre-training task, which maps special tokens for entities and relations to their textual descriptions, enhancing the model's understanding of entity and relation semantics. Second, we propose the Bidirectional Relation Encoder (BiR), which uses bidirectional special tokens to explicitly model semantic differences in relation directionality and improve the model's ability to distinguish the same relation in different directions. Finally, we introduce the Graph-Aware Sequence Encoder (GaS) and the Dynamic Subgraph Sampling Pool, which generate diverse subgraph sequences through random walks and dynamically select the optimal subgraph, improving the model's perception of complex graph structures and contextual semantics.

The major contributions of this work are three-fold:

- We introduce a new framework for knowledge graph completion called BiRKGC, which leverages pre-trained language models to build bidirectional relation modeling and graph structure awareness mechanisms. This design enables effective joint modeling of semantic and structural information.
- We develop two main modules: the Bidirectional Relation Encoder (BiR) and the Graph-Aware Sequence Encoder (GaS). We also design a Dynamic Subgraph Sampling Pool to further enhance the model's ability to capture structural patterns in knowledge graphs.
- We present a pre-training task, Masked Token Modeling (MTM), to improve the model's ability to encode special tokens and their textual descriptions. Experiments on the benchmark datasets WN18RR and FB15k-237 show that our method significantly outperforms baselines across multiple evaluation metrics.

2 Methodology

2.1 Notations

A knowledge graph (KG) is a data structure that describes real-world facts in a structured way, usually represented as a directed graph $G = (E, R, T)$. Here, E denotes the set of entities, where each entity $e \in E$ corresponds to an object in the real world. R denotes the set of relations, where each relation $r \in R$ describes a semantic connection between two entities. $T \subseteq E \times R \times E$ represents the set of factual triples in the graph, where each triple $(h, r, t) \in T$ represents a directed edge from head entity h to tail entity t with relation r. To handle both head and tail entity missing inference tasks, this paper adopts the inverse relation modeling approach proposed by SimKGC [13]. Specifically, for each triple (h, r, t), we introduce an inverse triple (t, r^{-1}, h), where $r^{-1} \in R$ represents the inverse of relation r. In knowledge graph completion, the core task is link prediction, where the goal is to predict the most probable missing entity in a query triple. In mainstream evaluation, tail entity prediction is typically done by scoring all candidate entities and ranking them, aiming to rank the true entity as high as possible in the candidate list.

2.2 The Overall Architecture

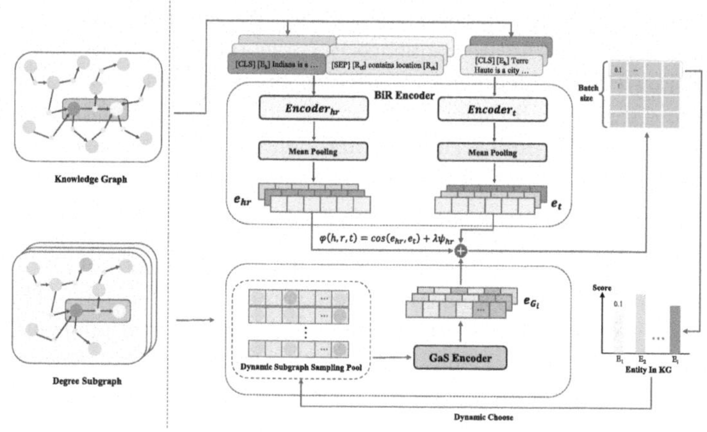

Fig. 2. Overall architecture of BiRKGC. The model integrates a Bidirectional Relation Encoder (BiR) and a Graph-Aware Sequence Encoder (GaS). BiR encodes head-relation and tail entity pairs with bidirectional tokens, while GaS dynamically selects and encodes subgraph sequences from the knowledge graph using a dynamic subgraph sampling pool.

As shown in Fig. 2, the proposed BiRKGC contains a Bidirectional Relation Encoder (BiR encoder) and an additional Graph-Aware Sequence Encoder (GaS encoder). In the BiR encoder part, we use two separate pre-trained language models to encode the head entity-relation pair and the candidate tail entity in the query. The initial weights during formal training are determined by the pre-training task MTM. For the GaS encoder, we also build it based on a pre-trained language model. By defining special tokens for entities and relations, we map subgraph sequences into token sequences as model input to capture structural contextual information. The specific hyperparameter settings and training details of the above encoders will be described in the experimental section.

2.3 Masked Token Modeling

To enable the model to understand the connection between special tokens and their corresponding textual semantics before performing the link prediction task, we design a pre-training task called Masked Token Modeling (MTM). As shown in Fig. 3, we define special tokens ($[h]$, $[t]$, $[r]$, $[r^{-1}]$) and their textual descriptions for each entity and relation. Compared to the original relation token, we additionally introduce inverse relation tokens. For the same relation r, we introduce r^{-1} to distinguish the direction of the relation when constructing triple samples later. During the pre-training phase, we concatenate the constructed [MASK]âĂŞtext description pairs into a complete input sequence and feed it into the pre-trained language model encoder. Unlike full-parameter fine-tuning, we freeze the attention layers (Frozen Attention Layer) and only train the embedding layer. In the subsequent construction of path information, we use the sequences composed of special tokens as the input to the GaS encoder, rather than the complete textual descriptions.

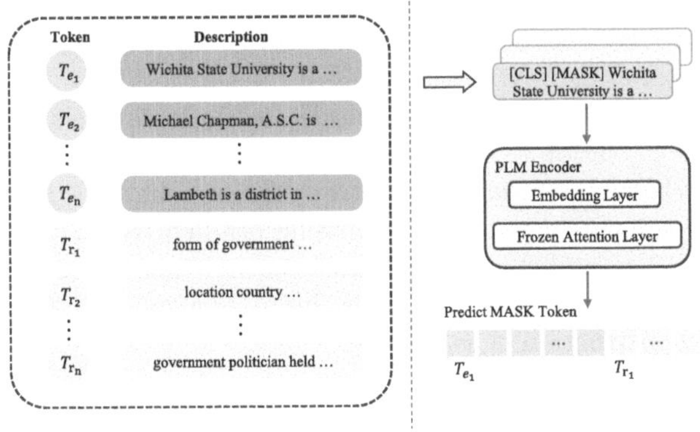

Fig. 3. Illustration of the Masked Token Modeling (MTM) pre-training task in BiRKGC. Special tokens for entities and relations are masked and predicted using the PLM encoder.

2.4 BiR Encoder

For each original triple sample (h, r, t), we construct two samples during training: tail entity prediction $(h, r, ?)$ and head entity prediction $(?, r, t)$. As shown in Fig. 4, traditional methods usually simulate different prediction directions by adjusting the order of entities in the input, while keeping the relation representation mostly unchanged. For example, in SimKGC, the reverse relation is represented by simply prepending the word *Inverse* to the original forward relation description. For the same triple (h, r, t), the input sequences hr and tr are encoded by $Encoder_{hr}$. Since the difference in their relation descriptions is only the additional word *Inverse*, the resulting embeddings of hr and tr are primarily influenced by the textual descriptions of the entities, while the directionality of the relation is not well captured. This approach, therefore, partially ignores the semantic differences caused by relation directionality.

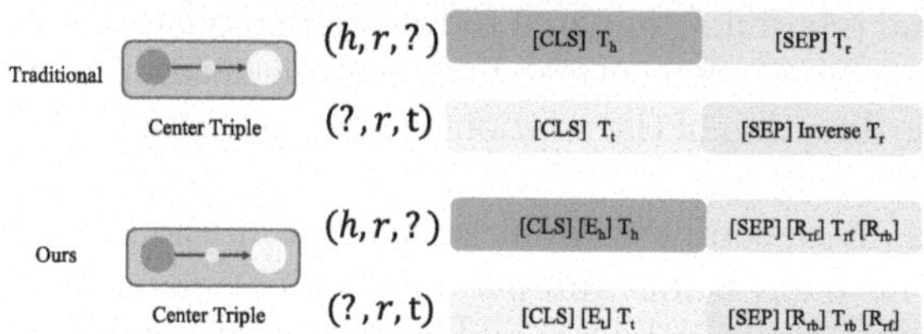

Fig. 4. Comparison of $Encoder_{hr}$ input sequences between traditional and BiRKGC.

To better model the directionality of relations, we introduce special tokens for bidirectional relations in the input sequences. Specifically, E_h and E_t denote the special tokens for the head entity h and the tail entity t, respectively. T_h and T_t denote the corresponding text descriptions of the entities. $[R_{rf}]$ and $[R_{rb}]$ denote the forward relation token (relation forward) and backward relation token (relation backward) for relation r, and T_{rf} and T_{rb} denote the text descriptions of the forward and backward relations, respectively. In our method, for the inference tasks of missing tail entity $(h, r, ?)$ and missing head entity $(?, r, t)$, we construct input sequences X_{hr} and X_{tr}, which are both fed into $Encoder_{hr}$. Additionally, for the tail entity t, we construct the input sequence X_t, which is fed into $Encoder_t$. The construction is as follows:

$$X_{hr} = [\text{CLS}][E_h]T_h[\text{SEP}][R_{rf}]T_{rf}[R_{rb}] \tag{1}$$

$$X_{tr} = [\text{CLS}][E_t]T_t[\text{SEP}][R_{rb}]T_{rb}[R_{rf}] \tag{2}$$

$$X_t = [\text{CLS}][E_t]T_t \tag{3}$$

In the link prediction task, the initial weights of $Encoder_{hr}$ and $Encoder_t$ come from the training results of the MTM task. Taking tail entity prediction as an example, the input sequences X_{hr} and X_t are fed into $Encoder_{hr}$ and $Encoder_t$, respectively. The final embeddings e_{hr} and e_t are obtained through mean pooling:

$$e_{hr} = \text{Pool}(Encoder_{hr}(X_{hr})) \tag{4}$$

$$e_t = \text{Pool}(Encoder_t(X_t)) \tag{5}$$

Our method explicitly introduces forward and backward relation tokens in the input, allowing the model to effectively distinguish between the different semantics of the same relation in forward and backward directions. Compared with traditional approaches that rely only on changes in entity positions, this design provides independent semantic information for different relation directions. Formally, given a triple (h, r, t), treating r and r^{-1} as two independent relation tokens effectively doubles the relational space from $|R|$ to $2|R|$, enabling the model to construct distinct embeddings for forward and backward semantics with only a constant-factor increase in complexity. It forms clearer boundaries in the embedding space and enhances the recognition of relation directionality. Tail entity prediction and head entity prediction are encoded through different input sequences, and the resulting embeddings e_{hr} and e_t effectively reflect the directional properties of the relation.

2.5 GaS Encoder with Dynamic Subgraph Sampling Pool

Traditional static subgraph sampling methods often introduce redundant or noisy neighbors, limiting the adaptability of the model to diverse graph structures. To address this issue, we propose a dynamic subgraph sampling pool that adaptively selects informative subgraphs during training. In our model, each target triple (h, r, t) undergoes random walks guided by the degree information of neighboring nodes to generate multiple candidate subgraph sequences. Specifically, we start from the head entity h, randomly selecting connected nodes and relations based on the degree distribution of its neighbors. This step-by-step process constructs node-relation-node paths, forming subgraph sequences. By repeating the random walks multiple times, we obtain a diverse set of candidate subgraphs. To select the optimal subgraph from these candidates, we design a dynamic subgraph sampling pool. During each training iteration, the model randomly selects a subset of candidate subgraphs for learning and dynamically updates the pool based on their performance in training. After several iterations, the model automatically selects the most representative subgraph sequences from the candidates to capture the most valuable structural information in the triple. Through this dynamic selection and optimization, the model fully utilizes the diverse subgraph structures, enhancing its ability to perceive graph structural information and improving its performance in link prediction tasks.

Each subgraph sequence consists of node-relation-node triples, formally expressed as:

$$G_i = \{(v_{i1}, r_{i1}, v_{i2}), (v_{i2}, r_{i2}, v_{i3}), \dots\} \tag{6}$$

Here, v_{ij} represents an entity node in the subgraph, and r_{ij} denotes the relation connecting nodes v_{ij} and $v_{i(j+1)}$. For each target triple (h, r, t), we generate multiple subgraph sequences, each representing structural information derived from different neighboring nodes. These subgraph sequences are stored in a dynamic subgraph sampling pool Q_{sub}, defined as:

$$Q_{sub} = \{G_1, G_2, \dots, G_N\} \tag{7}$$

Here, G_i denotes the i-th subgraph sequence, composed of multiple node-relation-node triples. During training, the subgraph sampling pool dynamically updates based on the model's current learning state, selecting the most relevant or representative subgraphs for further training. To integrate graph structural information into the model, we map each entity and relation in a subgraph sequence into corresponding special tokens. Specifically, each entity v is mapped to a special token $[E_v]$, and each relation r is mapped to a corresponding relation token $[R_r]$. The tokenized input format of each subgraph sequence is:

$$X_{G_i} = [E_{v_{i1}}][R_{r_{i1}}][E_{v_{i2}}][R_{r_{i2}}][E_{v_{i3}}]\cdots \tag{8}$$

In this process, the mapping of nodes and relations to special tokens combines the structural and semantic features of the subgraph, which the encoder processes. Finally, the tokenized subgraph sequence is fed into the GaS Encoder, which extracts structural information and maps it into a high-dimensional embedding space. The final embedding representation of each subgraph sequence after encoding is:

$$e_{G_i} = GaS\ Encoder(X_{G_i}) \tag{9}$$

To further enable dynamic selection of subgraphs, we introduce a queue-based update mechanism during training. For each target triple (h, r, t), suppose M candidate subgraph sequences are initially generated, and a subgraph sampling rate α is specified. The capacity of the dynamic queue is therefore $L = \lfloor \alpha M \rfloor$. At each training iteration, the model randomly selects one candidate subgraph that has not yet been added to the queue, obtains its encoded representation e_{G_i}, and performs a similarity evaluation with the tail entity representation e_t to assess the structural relevance of the subgraph. If the evaluation score is higher than the current minimum score in the queue, G_i replaces that subgraph and the threshold is updated; otherwise, the sample is discarded. Through this "retain-the-best" dynamic update strategy, the queue consistently preserves the top-L most representative subgraph sequences, gradually converging to a set of candidates that best capture structural information. At the end of training, the subgraphs retained in the queue for each (h, r) serve as structural auxiliary evidence for the final prediction.

2.6 Training and Inference

During the training phase, the model learns optimal parameters by minimizing a comprehensive loss function to achieve accurate entity prediction. We first construct positive and negative samples, where positive samples come from known triples in the knowledge graph and negative samples are generated by replacing entities in the triples. To prevent information leakage and ensure the model's generalization ability, we filter out target entities during neighborhood sampling and perform subgraph sampling only within the training set, ensuring that head and tail entities do not appear in the sampled neighborhoods of training samples.

To integrate text similarity and subgraph structural features, we define the final scoring function as:

$$\varphi(h, r, t) = \cos(e_{hr}, e_t) + \lambda \psi_{hr} \tag{10}$$

Here, $\cos(e_{hr}, e_t)$ denotes the cosine similarity between the head-relation pair embedding and the tail entity embedding from the text encoder, and ψ_{hr} denotes the structural contribution factor calculated by the subgraph encoder, measuring the structural similarity with the tail entity. λ is a learnable weight parameter used to balance the contributions of text similarity and structural information. The structural contribution factor ψ_{hr} is obtained by averaging the similarity between sampled subgraph sequence embeddings e_{G_i} and the tail entity embedding e_t:

$$\psi_{hr} = \frac{1}{k}\sum_{i=1}^{k} \cos(e_{G_i}, e_t) \tag{11}$$

The model's training objective is to minimize the cross-entropy loss based on the final scoring function $\varphi(h, r, t)$, defined as:

$$\mathcal{L} = -\log\left(\frac{e^{(\varphi(h,r,t)-\gamma)/\tau}}{e^{(\varphi(h,r,t)-\gamma)/\tau} + \sum_{i=1}^{N} e^{\varphi(h,r,t_i)/\tau}}\right) \tag{12}$$

where γ is an additive margin that penalizes the positive triple to encourage greater separation from negatives, τ is a temperature parameter that controls the sharpness of the distribution, and N is the number of negative samples.

During inference, the model scores and ranks all candidate entities using the final scoring function $\varphi(h, r, t_i)$ to predict missing entities. The prediction result is obtained by selecting the entity t_i that achieves the highest score among all candidates in the set $\mathcal{E}$:

$$\arg\max_{t_i \in \mathcal{E}} \varphi(h, r, t_i) \tag{13}$$

3 Experiments

3.1 Experimental Setup

Table 1. Statistics of datasets used in the experiments.

Dataset	# Entity	# Relation	# Train	# Valid	# Test
WN18RR	40,943	11	86,835	3,034	3,134
FB15k-237	14,541	237	272,115	17,535	20,466

Datasets. In this study, we use two widely adopted benchmark datasets to evaluate the performance of the proposed model: WN18RR and FB15k-237. Table 1 shows the detailed statistics of these datasets. The WN18RR dataset [15] is constructed based on the WordNet knowledge base [16] for link prediction tasks. It contains entities represented by English phrases and their semantic relations. The FB15k-237 dataset [17] is a subset derived from the Freebase knowledge base [18], which mainly includes real-world entities and their relations. For textual descriptions, we use the descriptions provided by WordNet and KG-BERT [12] for WN18RR and FB15k-237, respectively.

Evaluation Metrics. We adopt standard metrics for knowledge graph completion, including Hits@1, Hits@3, Hits@10, and MRR. Hits@K evaluates whether the target triple is ranked among the top-K candidates, while MRR (Mean Reciprocal Rank) reflects overall prediction quality by averaging the reciprocal ranks of the correct triples. To ensure fair and accurate evaluation, we follow the filtered ranking protocol proposed in [5], which excludes training triples from the candidate set. Additionally, we adopt the randomized evaluation protocol from [19] to enhance robustness and reliability.

3.2 Main Results

Table 2. Experimental results of link prediction on WN18RR and FB15k-237 datasets. Results marked with * are from [20], while other results are from the original papers. The best results are highlighted in **bold** and the second-best results are underlined.

Models	WN18RR				FB15k-237			
	Hits@1	Hits@3	Hits@10	MRR	Hits@1	Hits@3	Hits@10	MRR
Embedding-based method								
TransE [5]*	0.043	0.441	0.532	0.243	0.198	0.376	0.441	0.279
DistMult [21]*	0.412	0.470	0.504	0.444	0.199	0.301	0.446	0.281
RotatE [6]*	0.428	0.492	0.571	0.476	0.241	0.375	0.533	0.338
TuckER [7]*	0.443	0.482	0.526	0.470	0.266	0.394	0.544	0.358
CompGCN [9]	0.443	0.494	0.546	0.479	0.264	0.390	0.535	0.355
HittER [22]	0.462	0.516	0.584	0.503	<u>0.279</u>	0.409	0.558	<u>0.373</u>
CompoundE [23]	0.452	0.510	0.570	0.492	0.262	0.390	0.547	0.350
KRACL [24]	0.482	0.547	0.613	0.527	0.266	0.395	0.548	0.360
DaBR [25]	0.450	0.538	0.622	0.510	0.274	<u>0.410</u>	<u>0.572</u>	<u>0.373</u>
PLM-based method								
KG-BERT [12]*	0.041	0.302	0.524	0.216	-	-	0.420	-
StAR [20]*	0.243	0.491	0.709	0.401	0.205	0.322	0.482	0.296
KG-S2S [26]	0.531	0.595	0.661	0.574	0.257	0.373	0.498	0.336
SimKGC [13]	<u>0.585</u>	<u>0.731</u>	<u>0.817</u>	<u>0.671</u>	0.246	0.362	0.510	0.333
LP-BERT [27]	0.343	0.563	0.752	0.482	0.223	0.336	0.490	0.310
CSProm-KG [14]	0.522	0.596	0.678	0.575	0.269	0.393	0.538	0.358
PEMLM-F [28]	0.509	0.573	0.648	0.556	0.264	0.389	0.538	0.355
BiRKGC(Ours)	**0.591**	**0.736**	**0.823**	**0.682**	**0.289**	**0.418**	**0.576**	**0.381**

We compared BiRKGC with a range of competitive baseline models, including representative embedding-based methods such as HittER [22], KRACL [24], and

Table 3. Comparison of SimKGC and BiRKGC on FB15k-237 and WN18RR datasets with Forward-Backward Gap.

	Model	SimKGC				BiRKGC			
Dataset	Metric	F	B	A	Gap	F	B	A	Gap
WN18RR	MRR	0.712	0.619	0.666	0.093	0.726	0.639	0.682	**0.087**
	Hits@1	0.631	0.542	0.587	0.089	0.633	0.549	0.591	**0.084**
	Hits@3	0.766	0.667	0.717	0.099	0.784	0.688	0.736	**0.096**
	Hits@10	0.853	0.748	0.800	0.105	0.873	0.772	0.823	**0.101**
FB15k-237	MRR	0.425	0.246	0.336	0.179	0.457	0.304	0.381	**0.153**
	Hits@1	0.337	0.161	0.249	0.176	0.363	0.216	0.289	**0.147**
	Hits@3	0.457	0.267	0.362	0.190	0.506	0.330	0.418	**0.176**
	Hits@10	0.604	0.418	0.511	0.186	0.658	0.494	0.576	**0.164**

DaBR [25], as well as PLM-based approaches such as SimKGC [13], CSPromKG [14], and PEMLM-F [28]. As summarized in Table 2, BiRKGC consistently achieves the best performance across all evaluation metrics.

On WN18RR, we observe that BiRKGC reaches a Hits@1 of 0.591 and an MRR of 0.682, outperforming the strongest PLM baseline SimKGC by 1.0 and 1.6% points, respectively, and clearly surpassing all embedding-based models. On the more challenging FB15k-237 dataset—characterized by higher relation diversity and denser structure—BiRKGC maintains strong generalization, achieving 0.289 in Hits@1 and 0.381 in MRR, with gains of 3.5 and 2.1% points over the second-best model, respectively.

To further assess performance across reasoning directions, we compared BiRKGC with the representative PLM-based method SimKGC under forward and backward prediction settings. As shown in Table 3, SimKGC suffers from a significant forward-backward gap on both datasets. For example, on FB15k-237, its MRR drops from 0.425 (forward) to 0.246 (backward), yielding a gap of 0.179. In contrast, BiRKGC reduces the gap substantially, achieving 0.087 on WN18RR and 0.153 on FB15k-237. In addition, BiRKGC shows lower variance across Hits@1, Hits@3, and Hits@10, indicating greater directional stability and more consistent reasoning behavior.

3.3 Ablation Studies

We conducted ablation studies on WN18RR and FB15k-237 to assess the contributions of the three core components in BiRKGC: the MTM pre-training task, the BiR module for relation directionality, and the GaS module for structure-aware encoding. As shown in Table 4, removing any module results in a clear drop in performance, confirming its importance.

Specifically, removing MTM reduces the MRR to 0.656 and 0.363 on WN18RR and FB15k-237, respectively, indicating its role in enhancing semantic representation via pre-training. Excluding BiR leads to MRRs of 0.662 and

Table 4. Ablation studies on link prediction, evaluating the contributions of MTM, BiR, and GaS modules.

Dataset	Method	Hits@1	Hits@3	Hits@10	MRR
WN18RR	w/o MTM	0.564	0.703	0.782	0.656
	w/o BiR	0.577	0.710	0.793	0.662
	w/o GaS	0.539	0.680	0.769	0.631
	Ours	**0.591**	**0.736**	**0.823**	**0.682**
FB15k-237	w/o MTM	0.271	0.394	0.547	0.363
	w/o BiR	0.282	0.411	0.569	0.375
	w/o GaS	0.258	0.382	0.533	0.357
	Ours	**0.289**	**0.418**	**0.576**	**0.381**

0.375, highlighting its effectiveness in modeling relation directionality. Combined with the forward-backward gap analysis, this shows that BiR also improves reasoning consistency across directions. The largest performance drop occurs when removing GaS (MRR drops to 0.631 and 0.357), confirming its critical role in injecting structural context for complex graph reasoning. In summary, MTM, BiR, and GaS contribute complementary strengths—semantic, directional, and structural—that together underpin BiRKGC's strong performance on multi-relational and structurally rich knowledge graphs.

3.4 Effect of Sampling Ratio and Subgraph Size

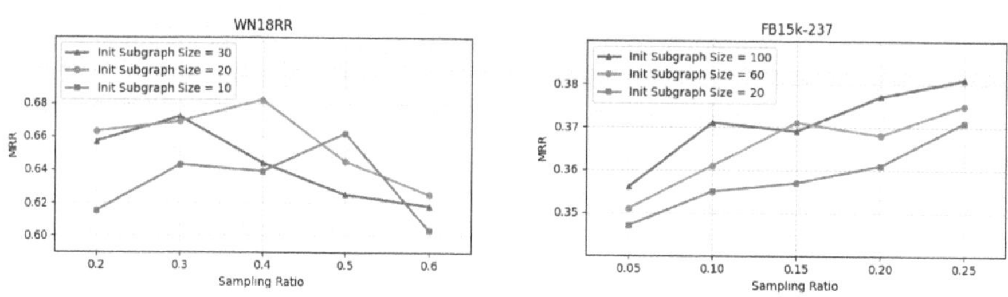

Fig. 5. MRR performance of BiRKGC on WN18RR (left) and FB15k-237 (right) under different sampling ratios and initial subgraph sizes.

To investigate how subgraph construction strategies affect model performance, we evaluate BiRKGC under different initial subgraph sizes and sampling ratios. The results are shown in Fig. 5.

On the WN18RR dataset, the results indicate that both overly large and overly small initial subgraphs are suboptimal. The best performance (MRR = 0.682) is achieved when the initial subgraph size is 20 and the sampling ratio is 0.4. Further increasing the sampling ratio leads to performance degradation, suggesting that WN18RR, as a structurally sparse knowledge graph, may suffer from noise or redundancy when excessive structural information is included. In contrast, compact and informative subgraphs are more beneficial for generalization in such sparse scenarios.

On the FB15k-237 dataset, model performance consistently improves with larger initial subgraph sizes and higher sampling ratios. The best MRR (0.381) is obtained when the initial subgraph size is 100 and the sampling ratio is 0.25. This demonstrates that FB15k-237, as a denser and more complex graph, can better leverage rich structural context. However, larger subgraphs and higher sampling ratios also introduce additional computational cost, which suggests a need to balance performance with efficiency in real-world deployment.

In summary, subgraph sampling strategies should be adapted to the structural characteristics of the dataset: sparse graphs benefit from compact and focused subgraphs, while dense graphs require broader structural coverage to exploit their rich contextual information.

4 Conclusions and Future Work

In this paper, we presented BiRKGC, a novel framework for knowledge graph completion that jointly models semantic and structural information through three key components: a Masked Token Modeling (MTM) pre-training task, a Bidirectional Relation Encoder (BiR), and a Graph-Aware Sequence Encoder (GaS). BiRKGC effectively captures relation directionality and structural context, addressing limitations in existing PLM-based methods. Comprehensive experiments on WN18RR and FB15k-237 demonstrate that BiRKGC achieves state-of-the-art performance across all standard metrics and substantially reduces the forward-backward prediction gap, validating the effectiveness of its bidirectional relation modeling and structure-aware design. In future work, we plan to apply the proposed framework to downstream tasks based on knowledge graphs, such as multi-hop question answering and recommendation systems.

Acknowledgments. This work was supported by the General Program of the Natural Science Foundation of Xinjiang Uygur Autonomous Region (No. 2022D01C433) and by the National Science Foundation of China (Grant No. 62467008) and the Xinjiang Uygur Autonomous Region Outstanding Graduate Students Innovation Project NO. XJDX2025YJS081

References

1. Guo, Q., et al.: A survey on knowledge graph-based recommender systems. IEEE Trans. Knowl. Data Eng. **34**(8), 3549–3568 (2020)
2. Vu, T., et al.: Freshllms: Refreshing large language models with search engine augmentation. arXiv preprint arXiv:2310.03214, 2023

3. Wang, Y., Lipka, N., Rossi, R.A., Siu, A., Zhang, R., Derr, T.: Knowledge graph prompting for multi-document question answering. In: Proceedings of the AAAI Conference on Artificial Intelligence, vol. 38, pp. 19206–19214 (2024)
4. Yuan, L., Cai, Y., Wang, J., Li, Q.: Joint multimodal entity-relation extraction based on edge-enhanced graph alignment network and word-pair relation tagging. In: Proceedings of the AAAI Conference on Artificial Intelligence, vol. 37, pp. 11051–11059 (2023)
5. Bordes, A., Usunier, N., Garcia-Duran, A., Weston, J., Yakhnenko, O.: Translating embeddings for modeling multi-relational data. Adv. Neural Inf. Process. Syst. **26** (2013)
6. Sun, Z., Deng, Z.-H., Nie, J.-Y., Tang, J.: Rotate: knowledge graph embedding by relational rotation in complex space. arXiv preprint arXiv:1902.10197 (2019)
7. Balažević, I., Allen, C., Hospedales, T.M.: Tucker: Tensor factorization for knowledge graph completion. arXiv preprint arXiv:1901.09590 (2019)
8. Schlichtkrull, M., et al.: Modeling relational data with graph convolutional networks. In: Gangemi, A., et al. (eds.) The Semantic Web: 15th International Conference, ESWC 2018, Heraklion, Crete, Greece, June 3–7, 2018, proceedings 15, pp. 593–607. Springer, Cham (2018). https://doi.org/10.1007/978-3-319-93417-4_38
9. Vashishth, S., Sanyal, S., Nitin, V., Talukdar, P.: Composition-based multi-relational graph convolutional networks. arXiv preprint arXiv:1911.03082 (2019)
10. Devlin, J., Chang, M.-W., Lee, K., Toutanova, K.: Bert: pre-training of deep bidirectional transformers for language understanding. In: Proceedings of the 2019 Conference of the North American Chapter of the Association for Computational Linguistics: Human Language Technologies, vol. 1 (long and short papers), pp. 4171–4186 (2019)
11. Raffel, C., et al.: Exploring the limits of transfer learning with a unified text-to-text transformer. J. Mach. Learn. Res. **21**(140), 1–67 (2020)
12. Yao, L., Mao, C., Luo, Y.: Kg-bert: bert for knowledge graph completion. arXiv preprint arXiv:1909.03193 (2019)
13. Wang, L., Zhao, W., Wei, W., Liu, J.: Simkgc: Simple contrastive knowledge graph completion with pre-trained language models. arXiv preprint arXiv:2203.02167 (2022)
14. Chen, C., Wang, Y., Sun, A., Li, B., Lam, K.-Y.: Dipping plms sauce: bridging structure and text for effective knowledge graph completion via conditional soft prompting. arXiv preprint arXiv:2307.01709 (2023)
15. Dettmers, T., Minervini, P., Stenetorp, P., Riedel, S.: Convolutional 2d knowledge graph embeddings. In: Proceedings of the AAAI Conference on Artificial Intelligence, vol. 32 (2018)
16. Fellbaum, C., Miller, G.: Wordnet: An electronic lexical database (language, speech, and communication) (1998)
17. Toutanova, K., Chen, D., Pantel, P., Poon, H., Choudhury, P., Gamon, M.: Representing text for joint embedding of text and knowledge bases. In: Proceedings of the 2015 Conference on Empirical Methods in Natural Language Processing, pp. 1499–1509 (2015)
18. Bollacker, K., Evans, C., Paritosh, P., Sturge, T., Taylor, J.: Freebase: a collaboratively created graph database for structuring human knowledge. In: Proceedings of the 2008 ACM SIGMOD International Conference on Management of Data, pp. 1247–1250 (2008)
19. Sun, Z., Vashishth, S., Sanyal, S.,Talukdar, P., Yang,Y.: A re-evaluation of knowledge graph completion methods. arXiv preprint arXiv:1911.03903 (2019)

20. Wang, B., Shen, T., Long, G., Zhou, T., Wang, Y., Chang, Y.: Structure-augmented text representation learning for efficient knowledge graph completion. In: Proceedings of the Web Conference, vol. 2021, pp. 1737–1748 (2021)
21. Yang, B., Yih, W., He, X., Gao, J., Deng, L.: Embedding entities and relations for learning and inference in knowledge bases. arXiv preprint arXiv:1412.6575 (2014)
22. Chen, S., Liu, X., Gao, J., Jiao, J., Zhang, R., Ji, Y.: Hitter: hierarchical transformers for knowledge graph embeddings. arXiv preprint arXiv:2008.12813 (2020)
23. Ge, X., Cheng Wang, Y., Wang, B., Jay Kuo, C.-C.: Compounding geometric operations for knowledge graph completion. In: Proceedings of the 61st Annual Meeting of the Association for Computational Linguistics (Vol. 1: Long Papers), pp. 6947–6965 (2023)
24. Tan, Z., Chen, Z., Feng, S., Zhang, Q., Zheng, Q., Li, J., Luo, M.: Kracl: contrastive learning with graph context modeling for sparse knowledge graph completion. In: Proceedings of the ACM Web Conference, vol. 2023, 2548–2559 (2023)
25. Wang, W., Liang, Q., Bao, F., Gao, G.: Distance-adaptive quaternion knowledge graph embedding with bidirectional rotation. arXiv preprint arXiv:2412.04076 (2024)
26. Chen, C., Wang, Y., Li, B., Lam,K.-Y.: Knowledge is flat: a seq2seq generative framework for various knowledge graph completion. arXiv preprint arXiv:2209.07299 (2022)
27. Li, D., Zhu, B., Yang, S., Kele, X., Yi, M., He, Y., Wang, H.: Multi-task pre-training language model for semantic network completion. ACM Trans. Asian Low-Res. Lang. Inf. Process. **22**(11), 1–20 (2023)
28. Qiu, C., et al.: Joint pre-encoding representation and structure embedding for efficient and low-resource knowledge graph completion. In: Proceedings of the 2024 Conference on Empirical Methods in Natural Language Processing, pp. 15257–15269 (2024)

Information Retrieval and Keywords

MAGIC-Enhanced Keyword Prompting for Zero-Shot Audio Captioning with CLIP Models

Vijay Govindarajan[1], Pratik Patel[2], Sahil Tripathi[3], Md Azizul Hoque[4], and Gautam Siddharth Kashyap[4(✉)]

[1] Expedia Group, Seattle, USA
vigovindaraja@expediagroup.com
[2] California Universities of Management and Sciences, Fairfax, USA
Pratik.bigdata@gmail.com
[3] Jamia Hamdard, New Delhi, India
sahilkrtr@gmail.com
[4] Macquarie University, Sydney, Australia
mdazizul.hoque@students.mq.edu.au, officialgautamgsk.gsk@gmail.com

Abstract. Automated Audio Captioning (AAC) generates captions for audio clips but faces challenges due to limited datasets compared to image captioning. To overcome this, we propose the zero-shot AAC system that leverages pre-trained models, eliminating the need for extensive training. Our approach uses a pre-trained audio CLIP model to extract auditory features and generate a structured prompt, which guides a Large Language Model (LLM) in caption generation. Unlike traditional greedy decoding, our method refines token selection through the audio CLIP model, ensuring alignment with the audio content. Experimental results demonstrate a 35% improvement in NLG mean score (from 4.7 to 7.3) using MAGIC search with the WavCaps model. The performance is heavily influenced by the audio-text matching model and keyword selection, with optimal results achieved using a single keyword prompt, and a 50% performance drop when no keyword list is used.

Keywords: Automated Audio Captioning · Large Language Model · CLIP · WavCaps

1 Introduction

Automated Audio Captioning (AAC) aims to generate natural language descriptions of audio content, distinguishing it from related tasks in machine listening [28] and audio pattern recognition [10]. Unlike Automatic Speech Recognition (ASR) [19], which transcribes speech, AAC describes entire auditory scenes while excluding speech. It also differs from Audio Tagging (AT) [29], which classifies predefined audio events, Sound Event Detection (SED) [1], which localizes these events, and Acoustic Scene Classification (ASC) [5], which categorizes audio into

I. Awan et al. (Eds.): WISE 2025, LNCS 16368, pp. 309–323, 2026.
https://doi.org/10.1007/978-981-95-7251-9_21

predefined scene types. AAC can be viewed as an inter-modal translation task, where captions provide structured descriptions of sequences of audio events. The Detection and Classification of Acoustic Scenes and Events (DCASE) [30] challenges have driven advancements in AAC, leading to improved models and larger datasets. Standard AAC systems utilize an encoder to extract meaningful audio representations and a decoder to generate natural language descriptions, with neural networks playing a central role. AAC has diverse applications, including video subtitling and accessibility support for individuals with hearing impairments [23].

Recently, Large Language Models (LLMs) have gained prominence in various applications, including machine translation [13] and summarization [38], and conversational agents such as ChatGPT[1]. Traditional AAC approaches integrate LLMs as trainable components, requiring significant computational resources and raising concerns about generalization. Furthermore, recent advancements in Computer Vision (CV) address similar challenges by leveraging pre-trained models without gradient updates. Socratic Models (SMs) [37] prompt LLMs with modality-specific information, while frameworks like MAGIC (Image-Guided Text Generation with CLIP) [31] use visual data to guide text generation.

Inspired by these developments, we propose the zero-shot AAC framework, utilizing pre-trained AudioCLIP [14] model to guide language generation. Our approach follows a Socratic-style—keyword-guided prompting strategy combined with an audio-guided MAGIC search [31] for caption generation. By exclusively employing publicly available pre-trained models, our system ensures flexibility and ease of adaptation as new models emerge. We evaluate our framework on the AudioCaps [15] and Clotho [7] datasets, achieving significant improvements over an unguided baseline. To enhance the Socratic keyword-guiding mechanism, we extend an AudioSet-based keyword list using GPT-3.5 Turbo, expanding it from 512 to 1987 keywords. We further analyze the impact of varying keyword usage and the strength of audio guidance in the MAGIC search [31]. Therefore, following are the contributions of the paper:

1. We introduce the zero-shot AAC framework, inspired by State-of-the-Art (SOTA) zero-shot image captioning techniques, and demonstrate its empirical effectiveness by significantly outperforming a baseline on the AudioCaps and Clotho datasets using standard Natural Language Generation (NLG) metrics.
2. We present an expanded AudioSet-based keyword list, generated with GPT-3.5 Turbo, and make it publicly available for future research, while also providing a comprehensive qualitative analysis of the generated captions, highlighting both the strengths and limitations of our model and suggesting directions for future work.

2 Related Works

This section reviews key research in AAC, drawing inspiration from Xu et al. [36] and Mei et al. [21]. We also discuss the latest advancements in zero-shot classifi-

[1] https://openai.com/index/chatgpt/.

cation and AAC with LLMs. Since our approach is on the zero-shot method for AAC, we explore relevant work in zero-shot image captioning, which has greatly influenced the design of our model. Zero-shot methods in image captioning have shown significant promise by leveraging pre-trained models, offering a powerful framework for applying similar techniques to the AAC task.

2.1 Existing Studies on Automated Audio Captioning

Early approaches to AAC utilized Recurrent Neural Network (RNN) encoders and decoders, first introduced by Drossos et al. [6]. RNNs were favored for their sequential modeling capabilities, and despite their declining usage, they demonstrated competitive performance in early DCASE challenges [35]. Given the structural similarities between spectrograms and visual data, research shifted towards Convolutional Neural Networks (CNNs) for feature extraction [24]. Kong et al. [18] introduced Pre-Trained Audio Neural Networks (PANNs), which have since become widely adopted in AAC [4,9,22]. CNN encoders have also been combined with contrastive loss methods to enhance representation learning [2]. Transformer-based models have gained prominence due to their superior performance in language generation [20,26,27]. Initially used as decoders [33], they are now employed as encoders, with architectures such as the Hierarchical Token-Semantic Audio Transformer (HTSAT) achieving SOTA results [3,22]. Beyond direct encoding, recent studies have explored methods to enhance AAC performance. One approach involves extracting keywords that capture key audio characteristics [9,12,16], while another, proposed by Koizumi et al. [17], incorporates ground truth captions from acoustically similar audio clips to improve decoding.

2.2 Existing Studies via CLIP

Contrastive representation learning has emerged as a key approach in zero-shot classification for CV. Radford et al. [25] introduced Contrastive Language-Image Pre-Training (CLIP), which jointly trains an image encoder and a text encoder. The model learns a multimodal embedding space by optimizing cosine similarity between correct image-text pairs while minimizing similarity for incorrect pairs. During inference, classification is performed by encoding candidate class names within a prompt and selecting the label with the highest cosine similarity to the image embedding. Given CLIP's [25] success in vision-language tasks, similar methods have been adapted for zero-shot audio classification. Guzhov et al. [14] extended CLIP [25] by integrating a ResNeXt-based audio encoder (EsResNeXt), creating a multimodal system for joint audio, image, and text representation learning. Their method enabled zero-shot audio classification, though more recent CLIP-based models [25] have achieved superior performance. Wu et al. [34] built on Contrastive Language-Audio Pre-Training (CLAP) [8], improving encoding and preprocessing for longer audio clips. Their approach combines global and local features, where a learnable parameter balances the two. The global feature is obtained by down-sampling the audio, while the local feature is extracted by segmenting the clip, enabling a unified representation. Beyond model design, dataset scale and quality play a crucial role. LAION's models, trained on extensive datasets such as LAION-Audio-630K [34], have demonstrated significant improvements. Mei et al. [22] introduced WavCaps, compiling audio data from FreeSound[2], BBC Sound Effects[3], and SoundBible[4]. They refined textual descriptions using ChatGPT, improving data quality.

2.3 Existing Studies via Large Language Models

While CLIP-based [25] systems excel in zero-shot tagging and classification, they are limited in generating detailed captions, often producing short snippets rather than complete sentences. To address this, researchers have explored methods where CLIP [25] guides LLMs in zero-shot image captioning without directly fine-tuning LLMs. Instead, visually guided decoding techniques leverage pre-trained LLMs' generalization capabilities while preserving model flexibility. ZeroCap [32] introduces a method where each step of auto-regressive language generation is influenced by visual input. The token distribution at each decoding step is adjusted using image features derived from a context cache in the attention mechanism. A CLIP-based [25] cosine similarity loss ensures alignment between image embeddings and generated tokens, while another term maintains fluency with the LLM's natural output distribution. However, this approach requires significant computational resources due to gradient-based optimization during inference. To improve efficiency, MAGIC [31] eliminates gradient-based optimization while maintaining competitive performance. The MAGIC search [31] process integrates three key components: model confidence, degeneration penalty, and MAGIC score. Model confidence reflects the LLM's probability distribution, the degeneration penalty discourages repetitive tokens, and the MAGIC score measures cosine similarity between image and token embeddings. A weighted combination of these components determines the next token, significantly reducing computational overhead compared to ZeroCap [32]. Socratic Models (SMs), introduced by Zeng et al. [37], employ a multi-model approach for zero-shot image captioning. CLIP [25] first performs zero-shot classification, selecting top-l tags for image type, objects, and locations based on cosine similarity. These tags form a structured prompt fed into an LLM, which generates multiple candidate captions. CLIP [25] then evaluates and selects the caption with the highest alignment to the image embedding. This structured interaction between CLIP [25] and LLMs enhances captioning performance without fine-tuning.

3 Methodology

In this section, we introduce our zero-shot AAC method–our approach is built upon the MAGIC [31] framework, with key modifications to enhance its perfor-

[2] https://freesound.org/.

[3] https://sound-effects.bbcrewind.co.uk/.

[4] https://soundbible.com/.

Algorithm 1: Proposed Zero-Shot AAC Method

Input: A: Audio clip, K: Keyword list, α, β, γ: Hyperparameters
Output: C: Generated caption
Step 1: Keyword Selection
$E_A \leftarrow \text{AudioEncoder}(A)$
$E_K \leftarrow \text{KeywordEmbeddings}(K)$
$S_{k,a} \leftarrow \text{cos\_sim}(E_K, E_A)$ for all $k \in K$
$K_{top} \leftarrow \text{Top}_k(S_{k,a})$
Step 2: Prompt Enhancement
$P \leftarrow \text{SPE}(K_{top})$
Step 3: Candidate Token Generation
$T \leftarrow \text{LLM}(P)$
For each $t_i \in T$, compute:
$S_{c,p} \leftarrow \text{cos\_sim}(t_i, p)$ for all previously generated tokens p
$T_{final} \leftarrow \text{SelectTokens}(S_{c,p})$
Step 4: MAGIC Search and Sequence Evaluation
For each candidate token c in T_{final}, compute:
$\text{final\_score}(c) =$
$\alpha \times \text{model\_confidence}(c) + \beta \times \text{degeneration\_penalty}(c) + \gamma \times \text{MAGIC}(c)$
$c_{selected} \leftarrow \arg\max(\text{final\_score}(c))$
Step 5: Sequence Construction
$S \leftarrow \text{ConstructSequence}(c_{selected})$
Repeat until EndOfSentence or maximum length reached.
Step 6: Truncation and Output Generation
$C \leftarrow \text{Truncate}(S)$
$C \leftarrow \text{PenalizePrematureEnding}(C)$

mance. Specifically, we replace MAGIC's [31] image-text matching component, CLIP [25] with a zero-shot audio classification model (AudioCLIP [14]). Additionally, to improve the quality of prompts fed into the LLMs—we incorporate keyword-based enhancements. These keywords are selected from a predefined list using the same zero-shot audio classification model that powers MAGIC search [31]. Finally, we apply a modified version of MAGIC search [31], incorporating a penalty mechanism to refine the generated output sequence. Algorithm 1 provides an overview of our proposed model.

3.1 Modeling

We leverage the pre-trained CLIP [25] model's audio encoder and text encoder to identify the most relevant keywords from a designated keyword list, referred to as Zero-Shot Keyword Selection (ZSKS). These keywords enhance the prompt through Socratic Prompt Enhancement (SPE) before being processed by LLMs. Based on the likelihood scores, the top k candidate tokens are selected, and an aural-guided search, MAGIC search [31], is employed to select the subsequent token. Tokens that signify the end of a sentence are penalized to avoid premature termination. ZSKS serves as the initial phase in generating captions, starting with the encoding of the raw audio waveform using the audio encoder of the pre-trained CLIP [25] model. To align audio and text, we use the pre-trained CLIP [25] text encoder to derive a representation for matching with the audio encoding, based on cosine similarity. The compatibility of each keyword with the AudioCLIP [14] is evaluated using the cosine similarity between the keyword embeddings and the audio embedding as shown in Eq. (1).

$$\text{cos\_sim}(k, a) = \frac{k \cdot a}{\|k\| \|a\|} \tag{1}$$

where k is the keyword embedding and a is the audio embedding. The top matches are extracted and incorporated into the prompt for the LLM, where the hyperparameter top is optimized to influence caption quality, as validated by our ablation studies in Sect. 5.2. To refine the output, MAGIC search [31] is applied after prompting the LLMs. The top k output tokens are selected based on their probability distribution. The generation follows an auto-regressive process, conditioned on previously generated tokens. For each candidate token, we compute the cosine similarity with previously generated tokens to evaluate the alignment of each candidate with the evolving context as shown in Eq. (2).

$$\text{cos\_sim}(c, p) = \frac{c \cdot p}{\|c\| \|p\|} \tag{2}$$

where c is a candidate token and p is the previously generated token. This allows the model to assess contextual relevance. In the original MAGIC [31] framework, the rationale behind the parameter selection was unclear. Therefore, we introduce the tunable hyperparameter τ, which directly influences the computation of the MAGIC score [31] as shown in Eq. (3).

$$\text{MAGIC}(c, p, \tau) = \text{cos\_sim}(c, p) \times \tau \tag{3}$$

A key innovation in our method is replacing the image component used in MAGIC [31] with the audio embedding, which is also used to identify relevant keywords. Each candidate sequence is formed by concatenating the previously generated tokens with the top k predictions from the LLM. We evaluate the relevance of each candidate sequence to the audio by computing the cosine similarity between the sequence embedding and the audio embedding as shown in Eq. (4).

$$\text{cos\_sim}(s, a) = \frac{s \cdot a}{\|s\| \|a\|} \tag{4}$$

where s is a candidate sequence and a is the audio embedding. A final score for each candidate token is computed by combining the model confidence, degeneration penalty, and the MAGIC score [31] as shown in Eq. (5).

$$\begin{aligned} \text{final\_score}(c) &= \alpha \times \text{model\_confidence}(c) \\ &+ \beta \times \text{degeneration\_penalty}(c) \\ &+ \gamma \times \text{MAGIC}(c) \end{aligned} \tag{5}$$

where α, β, γ are trainable weights. The token with the highest score is selected using the argmax function. To address the issue of excessively long sequences, we introduce a truncation step that uses natural sentence-ending punctuation to limit the output to a single coherent sentence. Additionally, to prevent overly short outputs, we implement a penalty vector that discourages premature sentence-ending tokens as shown in Eq. (6).

$$\text{penalty}(c) = \frac{1}{1 + \text{num\_tokens\_generated}} \tag{6}$$

where num_tokens_generated is the count of previously generated tokens. This balance ensures that the generated captions are both structurally and semantically complete, aligning with the intuitive principle that sentence length should be constrained while maintaining content richness.

4 Experimental Setup

4.1 Dataset Analysis

We evaluate our AAC system on two widely used datasets, AudioCaps [15] and Clotho [7], both of which provide five ground truth captions per audio clip. AudioCaps [15] consists of uniform 10-second clips, while Clotho [7] features variable-length samples (1530 s, avg. 22.4 s) with greater complexity due to overlapping sound events. This disparity impacts system performance, with AudioCaps [15] favoring shorter, well-segmented inputs, whereas Clotho [7] presents a more challenging benchmark for generating concise captions. Our model, utilizing HTSAT [3,22] pre-trained on WavCaps [22], applies random cropping to clips exceeding 10 s. While this approach aligns with AudioCaps [15], it may discard critical sound events in Clotho [7], potentially affecting performance.

Keyword Sets. To enhance audio captioning through augmented prompts, we constructed a comprehensive keyword set encompassing diverse audio objects. Given that AudioCaps [15] is a subset of AudioSet [11], and our audio-text matching models were trained on AudioSet or its subsets [14,22,34], we leveraged the publicly available AudioSet [11] keyword list, which originally contained 527 audio classes across various categories. By refining this list and separating compound classes, we get 512 unique categories. Recognizing the need for broader coverage, we further enriched the keyword pool using GPT-3.5 Turbo[5] with a structured prompting approach as shown in Table 1. The model, set to a deterministic temperature of 0, systematically generated additional audio-related keywords in batches, iterating over the original AudioSet [11] classes. Despite occasional omissions and duplicates, we integrated the generated keywords with the original list, yielding an augmented set—AudioSet+GPT3.5 KW—comprising 1987 unique audio classes as shown in Table 2. This expanded set enhances prompt diversity, improving system performance in capturing complex sound events.

[5] https://platform.openai.com/docs/models/gpt-3.5-turbo.

Table 1. Structured prompting used to expand AudioSet classes using GPT-3.5 Turbo. The model was queried with a deterministic temperature of 0 to ensure reproducibility.

Prompt Template:

```
For the audio category ``{AudioSet Class}", list 5 related sound
event keywords that can co-occur in real-world soundscapes. Ensure
these keywords are distinct from the original category and describe
relevant sounds or acoustic contexts.
```

Example (Input Class = "Rain"):

```
1. Thunder, 2. Raindrops on window, 3. Wind gusts, 4. Distant
traffic, 5. Water splashing
```

Table 2. Comparison of keyword set sizes. The expanded AudioSet+GPT3.5 set introduces significantly more keyword diversity to improve prompt coverage and representation.

Keyword Set	Number of Unique Classes
Original AudioSet (refined) [11]	512
AudioSet + GPT-3.5 Expansion (Ours)	**1987**

4.2 Hyperparameters

We conducted hyperparameter sweeps using the AudioSet [11] validation set to optimize model performance while maintaining consistency with the original MAGIC [31] framework. Key hyperparameters tuned included α, β, k, l, τ, and γ, with k fixed at 45, the keyword prompt set to "Objects", and the basic prompt as `` `This is a sound of" `` following CLIP's approach. While all parameters are theoretically tunable, we limited experiments on predefined components, leaving them for future exploration. Notably, the optimal degeneration penalty weight α was found to be 0, suggesting that omitting it improved performance by preventing undue suppression of LLM probability scores. This result aligns with the imbalance where MAGIC scores [31], subjected to softmax normalization, dominate over unnormalized LLM probabilities. Lower temperature τ and penalty strength γ consistently led to higher scores, with minimal impact from β variations when τ and γ were well-tuned. The best performance was achieved with $\beta = 0.5$, as $\beta = 0.6$, despite comparable NLG Mean Scores. Adjusting τ to 10 further improved results compared to the MAGIC [31] default of 18.6612, underscoring the importance of modality-specific tuning. ***Note:*** The code will be made available post-review for reproducibility.

4.3 Evaluation Metrics

AAC systems are evaluated by comparing generated captions to ground truth captions using NLG metrics. These metrics, originally designed for machine translation, assess both syntactic structure and semantic relevance. N-gram-based metrics such as BLEU computes n-gram precision up to $n = 4$, emphasizing exact matches. Whereas, CIDEr assigns higher weights to distinctive n-grams, prioritizing informativeness. METEOR improves upon BLEU by incorporating stemming, synonyms, unigram alignment, and word order penalties. It computes precision, recall, and an F1-score, with a penalty term ensuring fluency and coherence.

Table 3. Performance comparison on the AudioCaps [15] dataset. The mean score is calculated as the average of all listed metrics for our model.

Model	BLEU-2	BLEU-3	METEOR	CIDEr	Mean Score
Baseline Model	0.267	0.179	0.215	0.434	0.274
ACB [7]	0.251	0.162	0.198	0.386	0.249
TAC [15]	0.276	0.188	0.222	0.428	0.279
CLAP-based [34]	0.290	0.205	0.231	0.449	0.294
WavCaps [22]	–	–	0.242	0.471	–
Our Model	**0.314**	**0.238**	**0.247**	**0.502**	**0.325**

Table 4. Performance comparison on the Clotho [7] dataset. As with Table 3, the mean score for our model is the average of all available metrics.

Model	BLEU-2	BLEU-3	METEOR	CIDEr	Mean Score
Baseline Model	0.192	0.111	0.198	0.295	0.199
ACB [7]	0.178	0.102	0.187	0.264	0.183
TAC [15]	0.201	0.121	0.198	0.287	0.202
CLAP-based [34]	0.219	0.138	0.212	0.309	0.220
WavCaps [22]	–	–	0.218	0.331	–
Our Model	**0.251**	**0.163**	**0.229**	**0.348**	**0.248**

5 Result Analysis

5.1 Baseline Experiments

The highest scores were achieved using the WavCaps [22] model, combined with a penalized MAGIC search [31] and the original AudioSet [11] keyword list. Performance comparisons between our optimized model, the current supervised SOTA system [7,15,22,34], and a baseline are presented in Tables 3 and 4. The NLG mean score for our model was computed as the average of all available metrics, including BLEU-2 and BLEU-3. However, since the creators of the existing SOTA system [22] did not report these BLEU values, a direct computation of their mean score was not possible. To analyze the strengths and limitations of our best-performing model, Table 5 presents qualitative examples. The first five columns contain ground truth captions, while the last column displays the model's predictions. Predictions fall into the following categories: 1.) Irrelevant Predictions (GT Caption 1): Some outputs show no similarity to the ground truth, indicating potential limitations in the audio encoding process. 2.) Shorter Captions (GT Caption 2): Some predictions are shorter than the ground truth captions despite length penalty tuning. 3.) Repetitive Captions (GT Caption 3): The model sometimes correctly identifies subjects but fails to provide additional relevant details, often producing redundant tokens. 4.) Unusual Tokens (GT Caption 4): The model occasionally generates the token likely due to tokenization artifacts. 5.) Missed Events in Multi-Event Clips (GT Caption 5): The model struggles to recognize multiple concurrent audio events, such as detecting a car but missing a barking dog.

Table 5. Qualitative examples from the best-performing model. GT = Ground Truth.

GT Captions	Model Prediction
1. A car engine starts 2. A vehicle is starting 3. The sound of a car ignition 4. Car engine noise 5. Automobile starts up	The engine is making noise repeatedly
1. Children are playing 2. Kids laughing loudly 3. Children making joyful noises 4. Laughing and yelling of kids 5. Happy children playing	Happy `asdfasdf` children children
1. Dog barking with traffic 2. Barking sound overlaps car 3. Vehicle and dog sounds 4. Car honks and dog bark 5. Traffic with barking	A car drives fast
1. Footsteps on wood 2. Walking on a wooden floor 3. Shoes tapping rhythmically 4. Steps echo indoors 5. Someone walks on hardwood	Footsteps
1. Water splashing 2. Splashing in a pool 3. People playing with water 4. Splash sound event 5. Water droplets fall	Water water splashing splash

5.2 Ablation Studies

Table 6 presents the performance metrics obtained by varying key components, including MAGIC [31] guiding, the audio-text matching module, and the keyword list. We conducted experiments using three audio CLIP models: WavCaps [22], LAION [34], and AudioCLIP [14]. The evaluation primarily relies on the NLG mean score. Replacing WavCaps [22] with LAION [34] and AudioCLIP [14] resulted in performance drops of approximately 1.7 and 11.6, respectively, on the AudioCaps [15] test set, highlighting the importance of the audio-text matching component in zero-shot audio classification. Notably, WavCaps [22] and LAION [34], trained on similarly-sized datasets, outperformed AudioCLIP [14], suggesting that a robust CLIP-like component is crucial for accurate captions. However, a weaker audio-text matcher can generate misleading keywords, potentially affecting caption quality. The keyword list plays a critical role, as an advanced list underperformed compared to the original AudioSet [11] tags. Despite containing more sophisticated alternatives, it led to suboptimal keyword selection, likely due to limitations in prompt design or the audio-text matcher's encoding quality. AudioCLIP's [14] training data, which lacks variations such as "car alarm" alongside "vehicle" may contribute to this issue. The most significant performance drop occurred when no keyword list was used, reducing the NLG mean score for AudioCLIP [14] from 9.6 to 4.7, a 50% decrease, reinforcing the necessity of a keyword-enhanced prompt. MAGIC search [31] did not consistently improve performance across all models. For weaker models, its impact was negligible, suggesting that its effectiveness depends on the quality of the CLIP model [25]. However, when applied to stronger models like LAION [34] and WavCaps [22], MAGIC search [31] led to clear improvements. For instance, with WavCaps [22], MAGIC search [31] increased the NLG mean score from 4.7 to 7.3, a 35% gain. ***Note:*** We limited our ablation study to the AudioCaps [15] dataset due to its well-aligned and diverse audio-caption pairs, which make it particularly suitable for analyzing the effect of individual components in a controlled setting. Unlike Clotho [7], which often includes longer and more descriptive captions with higher variability in linguistic structure, AudioCaps [15] provides more consistent and constrained descriptions. This allows us to isolate the impact of changes such as keyword selection and audio-text matching quality more effectively, leading to more interpretable results in the ablation context.

5.3 Additional Experiments

Tables 7 and 8 present the ablation study results for the hyperparameters β and the number of keywords l on the AudioCaps [15] test set. Qualitative analysis indicates that most captions remained unchanged across different β values, suggesting stable token ranking. Since $\alpha = 0$, the only active components were the MAGIC score [31], model confidence, and their respective weights. Consequently, varying β had minimal impact on rankings. However, quantitative evaluation using the NLG Mean Score revealed that $\beta = 1.1$ yielded the best results, differing from the optimal $\beta = 0.5$ on the AudioSet [11] validation data. This

Table 6. Ablation study results showing the effect of key components: audio-text matching model, keyword list, and MAGIC search [31]. The metric used is NLG Mean Score on the AudioCaps [15] test set.

Model	Keyword List	MAGIC Search	NLG Mean Score
WavCaps (Ours)	AudioSet Tags	✓	**9.0**
WavCaps [22]	AudioSet Tags	✗	7.3
WavCaps [22]	Advanced Keywords	✓	8.2
WavCaps [22]	None	✗	4.7
LAION (Ours)	AudioSet Tags	✓	**7.3**
LAION [34]	AudioSet Tags	✗	6.2
LAION [34]	Advanced Keywords	✓	6.9
LAION [34]	None	✗	3.8
AudioCLIP (Ours)	AudioSet Tags	✓	**6.3**
AudioCLIP [14]	AudioSet Tags	✗	5.1
AudioCLIP [14]	Advanced Keywords	✓	5.7
AudioCLIP [14]	None	✗	4.7

discrepancy highlights that while MAGIC search [31] enhances performance, it is not the primary performance driver but rather an auxiliary refinement mechanism. The number of keywords l significantly impacts performance. As shown in Table 9, the most substantial improvement occurred when the prompt contained a single keyword. Adding a second keyword provided a smaller but still positive gain, leading to optimal system performance. These findings validate the effectiveness of Socratic-style prompt refinement. However, including more than two keywords degraded performance, likely due to increased noise or irrelevant information. With three or more keywords, contradictions or ambiguities in the prompt became more frequent, potentially misleading the LLM. This suggests that excessive keywords may dilute relevance, reducing caption quality.

Table 7. Qualitative caption stability across varying β values. Captions were largely invariant to changes in β, suggesting stable token ranking under MAGIC [31].

β Value	Generated Caption (example)
0.3	A dog is barking in the distance.
0.5	A dog is barking in the distance.
1.1	A dog is barking in the distance.
1.5	A dog is barking in the distance.

Table 8. Effect of varying β on NLG Mean Score using AudioCaps [15] test set. $\alpha = 0$ is fixed.

β Value	NLG Mean Score
0.3	8.3
0.5	8.7
1.1	**9.0**
1.5	8.5

Table 9. Effect of number of keywords l on NLG Mean Score on AudioCaps [15]. Excessive keywords reduce performance due to prompt noise.

Number of Keywords (l)	NLG Mean Score
0	4.7
1	8.3
2	**9.0**
3	7.6
4	6.9

6 Conclusion and Future Work

The proposed AAC system integrates pre-trained language models and CV techniques to enable zero-shot audio-visual captioning without additional training. By employing an AudioCLIP model for zero-shot classification, the system extracts keywords to construct enhanced prompts, which are processed by a pre-trained LLM to generate token probabilities. MAGIC search refines token selection by ranking candidates based on cosine similarity to the audio representation, ensuring better alignment. Additionally, a tunable penalty mechanism regulates caption length, improving relevance. Evaluated on AudioCaps and Clotho, the system surpasses an audio-agnostic baseline but remains behind task-specific AAC models. Ablation studies underscore the critical role of keyword selection and audio model quality, while MAGIC search offers only marginal improvements. Hyperparameter tuning, particularly in keyword selection, significantly influences performance, highlighting the importance of effective prompt engineering. Future work will focus on refining model components and optimizing hyperparameters to bridge the performance gap, enhancing system accuracy and applicability in real-world scenarios.

References

1. Bhosale, S., Nag, S., Kanojia, D., Deng, J., Zhu, X.: Diffsed: sound event detection with denoising diffusion. In: Proceedings of the AAAI Conference on Artificial Intelligence, vol. 38, pp. 792–800 (2024)
2. Chen, C., Hou, N., Hu, Y., Zou, H., Qi, X., Chng, E.S.: Interactive audio-text representation for automated audio captioning with contrastive learning. arXiv preprint arXiv:2203.15526 (2022)
3. Chen, K., Du, X., Zhu, B., Ma, Z., Berg-Kirkpatrick, T., Dubnov, S.: Hts-at: A hierarchical token-semantic audio transformer for sound classification and detection. In: ICASSP 2022-2022 IEEE International Conference on Acoustics, Speech and Signal Processing (ICASSP), pp. 646–650. IEEE (2022)
4. Chen, K., et al.: Audio captioning based on transformer and pre-trained CNN. In: DCASE, pp. 21–25 (2020)
5. Chen, Z., Shao, Y.F., Ma, Y., Wei, M., Zhang, L., Zhang, W.Q.: Improving acoustic scene classification in low-resource conditions. In: ICASSP 2025-2025 IEEE International Conference on Acoustics, Speech and Signal Processing (ICASSP), pp. 1–5. IEEE (2025)

6. Drossos, K., Adavanne, S., Virtanen, T.: Automated audio captioning with recurrent neural networks. In: 2017 IEEE Workshop on Applications of Signal Processing to Audio and Acoustics (WASPAA), pp. 374–378. IEEE (2017)
7. Drossos, K., Lipping, S., Virtanen, T.: Clotho: an audio captioning dataset. In: ICASSP 2020-2020 IEEE International Conference on Acoustics, Speech and Signal Processing (ICASSP), pp. 736–740. IEEE (2020)
8. Elizalde, B., Deshmukh, S., Al Ismail, M., Wang, H.: Clap learning audio concepts from natural language supervision. In: ICASSP 2023-2023 IEEE International Conference on Acoustics, Speech and Signal Processing (ICASSP), pp. 1–5. IEEE (2023)
9. Eren, A.Ö., Sert, M.: Automated audio captioning with topic modeling. IEEE Access **11**, 4983–4991 (2023)
10. Fischer, J., Orescanin, M., Eckstrand, E.: Vi-pann: harnessing transfer learning and uncertainty-aware variational inference for improved generalization in audio pattern recognition. IEEE Access (2024)
11. Gemmeke, J.F., et al.: Audio set: an ontology and human-labeled dataset for audio events. In: 2017 IEEE international Conference on Acoustics, Speech and Signal Processing (ICASSP), pp. 776–780. IEEE (2017)
12. Gontier, F., Serizel, R., Cerisara, C.: Automated audio captioning by fine-tuning bart with audioset tags. In: DCASE 2021-6th Workshop on Detection and Classification of Acoustic Scenes and Events (2021)
13. Guerreiro, N.M., Rei, R., Stigt, D., Coheur, L., Colombo, P., Martins, A.F.: xcomet: transparent machine translation evaluation through fine-grained error detection. Trans. Assoc. Comput. Linguist. **12**, 979–995 (2024)
14. Guzhov, A., Raue, F., Hees, J., Dengel, A.: Audioclip: extending clip to image, text and audio. In: ICASSP 2022-2022 IEEE International Conference on Acoustics, Speech and Signal Processing (ICASSP), pp. 976–980. IEEE (2022)
15. Kim, C.D., Kim, B., Lee, H., Kim, G.: Audiocaps: Generating captions for audios in the wild. In: Proceedings of the 2019 Conference of the North American Chapter of the Association for Computational Linguistics: Human Language Technologies, Vol. 1 (Long and Short Papers), pp. 119–132 (2019)
16. Koizumi, Y., Masumura, R., Nishida, K., Yasuda, M., Saito, S.: A transformer-based audio captioning model with keyword estimation. arXiv preprint arXiv:2007.00222 (2020)
17. Koizumi, Y., Ohishi, Y., Niizumi, D., Takeuchi, D., Yasuda, M.: Audio captioning using pre-trained large-scale language model guided by audio-based similar caption retrieval. arXiv preprint arXiv:2012.07331 (2020)
18. Kong, Q., Cao, Y., Iqbal, T., Wang, Y., Wang, W., Plumbley, M.D.: Panns: Large-scale pretrained audio neural networks for audio pattern recognition. IEEE/ACM Trans. Audio Speech Lang. Process. **28**, 2880–2894 (2020)
19. Kuhn, K., Kersken, V., Reuter, B., Egger, N., Zimmermann, G.: Measuring the accuracy of automatic speech recognition solutions. ACM Trans. Access. Comput. **16**(4), 1–23 (2024)
20. Lewis, M., et al.: Bart: Denoising sequence-to-sequence pre-training for natural language generation, translation, and comprehension. arXiv preprint arXiv:1910.13461 (2019)
21. Mei, X., Liu, X., Plumbley, M.D., Wang, W.: Automated audio captioning: an overview of recent progress and new challenges. EURASIP J. Audio Speech Music Process. **2022**(1), 26 (2022)

22. Mei, X., et al.: Wavcaps: A Chatgpt-Assisted Weakly-Labelled Audio captioning dataset for audio-language multimodal research. IEEE/ACM Trans. Audio Speech Lang. Process. (2024)
23. Patel, P., Pampaniya, S., Ghosh, A., Raj, R., Karuppaih, D., Kandasamy, S.: Enhancing accessibility through machine learning: a review on visual and hearing impairment technologies. IEEE Access (2025)
24. Perez-Castanos, S., Naranjo-Alcazar, J., Zuccarello, P., Cobos, M.: Listen carefully and tell: an audio captioning system based on residual learning and gammatone audio representation. arXiv preprint arXiv:2006.15406 (2020)
25. Radford, A., et al.: Learning transferable visual models from natural language supervision. In: International Conference on Machine Learning, pp. 8748–8763. PmLR (2021)
26. Radford, A., Narasimhan, K., Salimans, T., Sutskever, I., et al.: Improving language understanding by generative pre-training (2018)
27. Radford, A., Wu, J., Child, R., Luan, D., Amodei, D., Sutskever, I., et al.: Language models are unsupervised multitask learners. OpenAI blog **1**(8), 9 (2019)
28. Ren, Z., Chang, Y., Bartl-Pokorny, K.D., Pokorny, F.B., Schuller, B.W.: The acoustic dissection of cough: diving into machine listening-based covid-19 analysis and detection. J. Voice **38**(6), 1264–1277 (2024)
29. Singh, S., Steinmetz, C.J., Benetos, E., Phan, H., Stowell, D.: Atgnn: Audio tagging graph neural network. IEEE Signal Process. Lett. **31**, 825–829 (2024)
30. Stowell, D., Giannoulis, D., Benetos, E., Lagrange, M., Plumbley, M.D.: Detection and classification of acoustic scenes and events. IEEE Trans. Multimedia **17**(10), 1733–1746 (2015)
31. Su, Y., et al.: Language models can see: Plugging visual controls in text generation. arXiv preprint arXiv:2205.02655 (2022)
32. Tewel, Y., Shalev, Y., Schwartz, I., Wolf, L.: Zerocap: Zero-shot image-to-text generation for visual-semantic arithmetic. In: Proceedings of the IEEE/CVF Conference on Computer Vision and Pattern Recognition, pp. 17,918–17,928 (2022)
33. Vaswani, A., et al.: Attention is all you need. Adv. Neural Inf. Process. systems **30** (2017)
34. Wu, Y., Chen, K., Zhang, T., Hui, Y., Berg-Kirkpatrick, T., Dubnov, S.: Large-scale contrastive language-audio pretraining with feature fusion and keyword-to-caption augmentation. In: ICASSP 2023-2023 IEEE International Conference on Acoustics, Speech and Signal Processing (ICASSP), pp. 1–5. IEEE (2023)
35. Xu, X., Xie, Z., Wu, M., Yu, K.: The sjtu system for dcase2022 challenge task 6: Audio captioning with audio-text retrieval pre-training. Technical Report, DCASE2022 Challenge (2022)
36. Xu, X., Xie, Z., Wu, M., Yu, K.: Beyond the status quo: a contemporary survey of advances and challenges in audio captioning. IEEE/ACM Trans. Audio Speech Lang. Process. **32**, 95–112 (2023)
37. Zeng, A., et al.: Socratic models: Composing zero-shot multimodal reasoning with language. arXiv preprint arXiv:2204.00598 (2022)
38. Zhang, H., Yu, P.S., Zhang, J.: A systematic survey of text summarization: From statistical methods to large language models. arXiv preprint arXiv:2406.11289 (2024)

ESGTabQA: Open-Domain Question Answering on High-Cardinality ESG Tables

Adam Binks[1], Basem Suleiman[2(✉)], and Jinglin Sun[2]

[1] School of Computer Science, The University of Sydney, Sydney, Australia
abin2135@uni.sydney.edu.au

[2] School of Computer Science and Engineering, The University of New South Wales, Sydney, Australia
{b.suleiman,jinglin.sun}@unsw.edu.au

Abstract. The analysis of Environmental, Social, and Governance (ESG) data presents significant challenges for traditional question answering (QA) systems. These systems, typically designed for small and well-structured tables, struggle to handle the high-cardinality, ambiguity, and constant updates that characterize real-world ESG datasets. To address this, we present ESGTabQA, a table-based question-answer system capable of handling online, open-domain, natural language queries over high-cardinality ESG tables. The system integrates three key components: an MPNet-based retriever to identify relevant data segments, the TAPAS model to extract answers from tables, and GPT-4 to generate clear responses in natural language. A central innovation of our system is an entity-specific query decomposition that breaks down complex multi-entity queries into parallel, independent sub-queries that align with the data's structure. This is particularly effective for comparative questions, allowing the system to locate and reason over data spread across multiple sections of a large dataset. We evaluate ESGTabQA on 32 real-world ESG queries, covering simple, ambiguous, and comparative scenarios. The proposed system achieves strong results, including a semantic similarity score of 0.876, 79.5% keyword inclusion, and an F1-score of 0.597. These results demonstrate ESGTabQA's ability to scale QA to real-world datasets, supporting more efficient information retrieval and analysis in evolving data environments.

Keywords: Tabular Question Answering · Query Decomposition · High-Cardinality Data · ESG Analytics · Retrieval-Augmented Generation

1 Introduction

Environmental, Social and Governance (ESG) analysis has become essential for financial stakeholders evaluating investment sustainability and ethical impact. However, current ESG datasets present significant analytical challenges. The

I. Awan et al. (Eds.): WISE 2025, LNCS 16368, pp. 324–339, 2026.
https://doi.org/10.1007/978-981-95-7251-9_22

EUROFIDAI ESG Raw Data on Corporations dataset exemplifies these issues, containing over 1 million records across 57000 companies with 105 metrics, where data exhibits high cardinality, ambiguous structure, and inconsistent reporting formats [14]. These characteristics make traditional information retrieval inadequate for ESG analysis. Manual data extraction is time-consuming and error-prone, while existing automated approaches fail to handle the scale and ambiguity of real-world ESG datasets. Financial analysts need tools that can perform comparative analysis across multiple companies and metrics while generating comprehensive insights from complex data points. Furthermore, making such tools accessible on web-based platforms is critical for enhancing corporate transparency and enabling wider societal and regulatory oversight (Fig. 1).

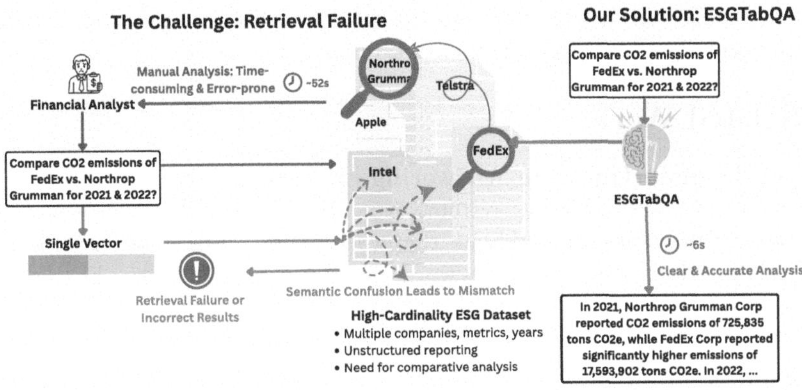

Fig. 1. Challenges in Question Answering over High-Cardinality Tabular ESG Data.

Existing tabular question answering systems primarily target small, well-structured tables with clear semantics. The dominant Retriever-Reader architecture [30] works effectively for datasets like Wikipedia tables but faces critical limitations with high-cardinality data. Current table reading models like TAPAS [10] have token constraints that prevent processing large tables, while retrieval models struggle with semantic ambiguity when thousands of similar rows exist. Most importantly, no existing solutions support comparative queries across multiple entities within a single, large-scale, homogeneous table, limiting their applicability to real-world financial analysis.

To bridge this gap, this paper introduces ESGTabQA, a novel architecture designed to address semantic ambiguity in high-cardinality tables. The system resolves complex comparative queries by decomposing them into focused, single-entity sub-queries, preventing semantic dilution of the query vector and enabling accurate information retrieval across millions of rows. Our system makes three key contributions:

1. We propose entity-specific query decomposition, an architectural approach that processes queries by breaking them into independent sub-queries aligned

with data structure. This eliminates semantic interference in high-cardinality tables, enabling precise parallel retrieval across different table regions.
2. We integrate state-of-the-art models—MPNet-table for retrieval [23] and TAPAS for reading [10]—with large language models to generate analysis while maintaining accuracy in numerical extraction from ambiguous data.
3. We evaluate our system on a large-scale financial dataset rather than synthetic benchmarks, demonstrating practical applicability and addressing unique challenges of high-cardinality data often overlooked in existing work.

Our evaluation shows that entity-specific query decomposition achieves a 29.53% average performance improvement across all metrics compared to baseline methods. The system delivers a semantic similarity score of 0.876 and keyword inclusion accuracy of 79.53%, while reducing analysis time by approximately 9x versus manual approaches. These results demonstrate that specialized decomposition architectures are essential for effective question answering on real-world complex, high-cardinality tabular data.

2 Related Work

- **Open-Domain Question Answering on Tabular Data:** Modern open-domain question answering systems typically employ retriever-reader architectures with dense embeddings that capture semantic relationships more effectively than traditional keyword-matching methods like TF-IDF and BM25 [20,21]. Dense Passage Retrieval (DPR) enhanced retrieval accuracy through dual encoder architectures for query-document similarity comparison [13]. For tabular data, specialized models are essential to understand structural relationships between cells, rows, and columns [12]. MPNet-table generates semantic embeddings that capture table content meaning, enabling flexible querying where users can ask about "emissions" and retrieve relevant data regardless of terminology, significantly outperforming keyword-based methods when handling varied ESG terminology [23,27]. TAPAS adapts BERT architecture for table processing through cell selection and numerical aggregation capabilities, directly processing semi-structured data unlike alternatives such as TAPEX or TaBERT [10,16,26]. However, existing tabular QA systems target small, independent tables rather than large-scale datasets [9,19,25]. When information is scattered across millions of similar rows, these systems struggle with comparative queries requiring data integration from distant locations within vast datasets, highlighting the need for enhanced approaches to handle high-cardinality tabular question answering.
- **Query Decomposition for High-Cardinality Data:** High-cardinality datasets pose a fundamental challenge: queries spanning multiple entities produce semantically diluted query vectors, making it difficult to retrieve scattered relevant information [3]. This becomes critical in ESG corporate data, where comparative queries must retrieve information about different companies and metrics separated by millions of rows. While multi-hop question answering addresses similar challenges in textual domains by decomposing complex queries into sequential sub-questions [18,24], it relies on

sequential reasoning through logical chains. This differs fundamentally from high-cardinality tabular data challenges: comparative queries require parallel retrieval of similar information for different entities within the same dataset, rather than sequential reasoning through connected documents [4,6]. Traditional multi-hop approaches fail because they optimize for context-dependent reasoning, not entity-specific information gathering. Recent RAG frameworks have also explored alternative decomposition strategies, such as K^2 RAG's divide-and-conquer approach of generating sub-questions for topics identified by a knowledge graph [17]. As encoding effectiveness decreases with increasing row counts and decreasing record distinctiveness [3], current tabular QA systems lack mechanisms to handle multi-entity queries within large, homogeneous datasets. This gap necessitates query decomposition methods specifically designed for high-cardinality tabular structures.

- **Retrieval-Augmented Generation for Analysis:** Retrieval-Augmented Generation (RAG) enables language models to access external knowledge without expensive retraining, making it ideal for complex analytical tasks requiring diverse data integration [8,15]. However, standard RAG assumes a single query can retrieve all necessary context through one vector encoding. This assumption fails for multi-entity comparative queries in high-cardinality datasets, where mixed intents cause semantic dilution and retrieval failures. Our architecture addresses this limitation by integrating query decomposition as a preprocessing module. This transforms complex queries into focused atomic sub-queries, enabling precise retrieval for each component and unified analytical synthesis [2,11].

3 Methodology

3.1 System Overview

To enable complex, comparative analysis directly on tabular ESG data with high cardinality, we propose ESGTabQA, an end-to-end question answering (QA) system. The primary innovation of our system lies in the integration of a novel, entity-specific query decomposition stage with a Retriever-Reader architecture [9]. This approach enables the system to systematically deconstruct a single complex query into multiple, manageable sub-queries, thereby facilitating targeted data retrieval and analysis across vast and disparate sections of a large-scale dataset. The complete architecture is illustrated in Fig. 2.

The ESGTabQA workflow is organized into two distinct phases: an Offline Preparation phase and an Online Query Processing phase. In the offline phase, the raw, monolithic ESG dataset is pre-processed and indexed for efficient retrieval. The dataset is first partitioned into semantically coherent table chunks, an approach that aligns with the principle of semantic chunking in text-based RAG frameworks [28], with each chunk typically representing a single metric for a single company. These chunks are then encoded into high-dimensional dense vectors using the MPNet-table sentence transformer [23], and subsequently stored in a vector database to serve as the system's external knowledge base.

The Online Query Processing phase is initiated when a user submits a natural language query. As shown in the "Online Query Processing" section of Fig. 2, the query first enters a Query Decomposer module. This component, powered by a Large Language Model (LLM) through few-shot prompting-based inference [22], analyzes the query for multiple entities or data points and splits it into a series of atomic sub-queries. Following decomposition, the system iteratively processes each sub-query through a Retriever-Reader pipeline. The retriever, also using MPNet-table [23], identifies the most relevant table chunks from the vector database via dense vector search [13]. These retrieved chunks are then passed as context to the TAPAS model [10], a transformer-based reader specifically designed for tabular data, which extracts the precise answer cells. Finally, once all sub-queries have been answered, the extracted data points are aggregated and passed to a final Answer Synthesizer module. This LLM-based component is responsible for collating the individual pieces of information and generating a single, cohesive, and analytical response in natural language. This architecture not only overcomes the inherent context-size limitations of table reader models when faced with massive datasets but also provides a scalable framework for complex, multi-entity question answering on real-world tabular data.

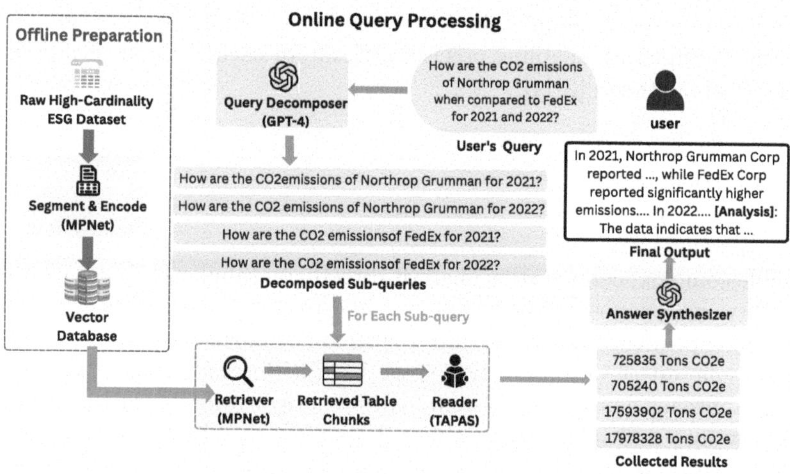

Fig. 2. ESGTabQA System Architecture.

3.2 Data Preprocessing and Filtering

Our system targets financial analysts who need efficient tools for ESG data analysis without manually searching through complex datasets. We evaluate ESGTabQA using the EUROFIDAI ESG Raw Data on Corporations dataset, curated by ClarityAI [5]. This dataset contains 105 ESG metrics across Environmental, Social, and Governance pillars, covering data from Q1 2016 onwards with both quantitative measures (e.g., CO2 emissions) and qualitative policies (e.g., board diversity policies). The original dataset presents significant preprocessing challenges due to its scale and structure. With over 4.5 million rows covering over 57000 companies across 137 countries, the data exhibits high cardinality with many similar rows differing only in company names and metric values. Additionally, the raw format includes redundant columns and inconsistent value representations that complicate semantic retrieval. To ensure a robust evaluation focused on companies with the most substantial ESG data, we filtered the dataset to retain only those with over 200 data points from the top 10 countries by company count. This resulted in a final dataset of 4200 companies and over 1 million data points.

We implemented several transformations to optimize the data for semantic search. First, we simplified the column structure by removing redundant identifiers and combining related fields. Metric values were merged with their units using natural language formatting (e.g., "Yes/No" for boolean values, "per" instead of "/" for ratios). We grouped data by company and metric type to create meaningful table segments, with each segment representing one company's data for one specific metric. The processed data was segmented into 353635 table chunks, each small enough for the TAPAS reader model while maintaining semantic coherence. We attached metadata (company name, ESG pillar, country) to each vector to enable filtered searches, improving retrieval precision by reducing the search space for specific queries. This preprocessing approach addresses the fundamental challenge of applying question answering systems to high-cardinality financial data, where traditional methods fail due to ambiguous structure and scale.

3.3 Online Query Processing and Answer Synthesis

Once the vector database is prepared, the system is ready for the online query processing phase, which transforms a user's online natural language query into a data-driven analytical answer. This process involves a multi-stage pipeline designed to deconstruct, retrieve, verify, and synthesize information, as detailed below.

- **LLM-Driven Query Decomposition:** Our system addresses comparative questions through an entity-specific query decomposition approach in the Query Decomposer module. This design choice stems directly from our dataset's structure: each database entry contains a single atomic fact (CompanyName, Metric, Value, Year). When users pose complex comparative queries, the resulting query vector semantically combines multiple entities and metrics, creating a diluted representation that poorly matches individual database entries. Our decomposition strategy solves this by breaking complex queries into atomic sub-queries, each designed to align with specific data points in our vector database. This structural alignment optimizes

retrieval performance by ensuring each sub-query can precisely target relevant database entries through cosine similarity search, eliminating the semantic ambiguity inherent in blended query representations.
The LLM is guided using few-shot prompting [22], where the prompt template provides a clear task description alongside several illustrative examples. For instance, the prompt includes examples to demonstrate the desired output format, such as decomposing the query "What are the emissions for COMPANY A versus COMPANY B?" into two distinct sub-queries: "What are the 'emissions' for 'COMPANY A'?" and "What are the 'emissions' for 'COMPANY B'?". This technique ensures the model consistently identifies and separates the distinct entities within the user's request. The decomposer also extracts the entity names (e.g., company names) from the query, which are used for verification in a later stage. While our final evaluation employed GPT-4 for accessibility reasons, validation tests with the smaller 1.1B parameter TinyLlama model confirmed that our entity-specific decomposition mechanism functions effectively across different model scales, demonstrating the architecture's robustness and adaptability.

- **Iterative Retrieval with MPNet-table:** For each sub-query generated by the decomposer, the system initiates a retrieval process. We employ MPNet-table [23] as our retriever, a model fine-tuned for tabular data that consistently outperforms earlier transformer architectures. The retriever encodes each sub-query into a 768-dimension dense vector and executes a cosine similarity search against the vector database to find the top-k most relevant table chunks. This dense retrieval approach [13] is critical for understanding the semantic nuance of a query beyond simple keyword matching. Furthermore, during preprocessing we attached metadata (e.g., company or country) to each vector, which allows users to optionally pre-filter the search space. Importantly, these manual filters were not used in our reported results; the performance we present reflects the system itself. Exploratory trials only suggested that such filters could improve efficiency and reduce semantic dilution by narrowing the candidate set.
- **Program-Aided Reading and Verification:** The retrieved table chunks for each sub-query are then passed to the reader module. We selected TAPAS (TAble PArSing) [10] as our reader due to its strong performance in weakly supervised tabular QA and its native aggregation capabilities, which are vital for numerical ESG data. Before passing the data to TAPAS, we implement a crucial programmatic guardrail: the company name extracted from the query is compared against the company name in the retrieved table chunk using Levenshtein distance. Chunks that fail this verification are discarded, preventing the reader from processing irrelevant information and reducing the likelihood of hallucination. After verification, TAPAS parses the correct table and returns the coordinates of the answer cell(s). This entire stage exemplifies a program-aided language model approach [7], where programmatic logic complements the neural model to ensure higher fidelity.
- **Answer Synthesis and Composition:** In the final stage, an Answer Synthesizer module, powered by GPT-4, transforms the extracted data into a

coherent analytical response. This module receives structured context strings, each containing the key data for a sub-query—such as the company name, metric, value, and year. Guided by a carefully designed prompt, GPT-4 synthesizes these discrete facts into a two-part answer: a direct factual summary, followed by a brief, objective analysis based strictly on the provided data. For instance, after processing the context for Northrop Grumman and FedEx, the synthesizer generates a factual comparison of their emissions followed by a brief analysis of potential operational reasons for the disparity.

4 Results

4.1 Experimental Setup

To evaluate the performance of ESGTabQA, we developed a comprehensive experimental setup designed to test its capabilities on a large-scale, high-cardinality dataset that differs significantly from standard academic benchmarks. Unlike publicly available datasets such as WTQ (Wiki Table Questions) or SQA (Sequential Question Answering), which consist of many small, well-structured tables, the EUROFIDAI ESG dataset is a single, large table with over a million rows, where data points for different entities are separated by vast regions. This structure presents unique challenges for comparative analysis and necessitates a custom evaluation framework.

Our evaluation is centered around a custom suite of 32 queries, designed to simulate realistic online use cases. These are categorized into three distinct sets to systematically assess the system's performance across different use cases: **Question Set 1 (Simple Queries):** Assesses baseline performance on direct, single-entity information retrieval. **Question Set 2 (Ambiguous Queries):** Tests the system's robustness in handling vague or conversationally phrased questions, highlighting the effectiveness of semantic search over traditional keyword matching. **Question Set 3 (Complex Comparative Queries):** Evaluates the core contribution of this work—the system's ability to answer questions requiring comparison across multiple entities or metrics.

To isolate and measure the impact of our primary contribution, we conduct a comparative analysis of our full ESGTabQA system against a baseline version, ESGTabQA-Naive. The Naive baseline deliberately omits the query decomposition stage; it encodes the entire complex query into a single vector and attempts to retrieve all relevant information in one step by fetching the top-k (k=5) most similar table segments. This contrasts with the full ESGTabQA approach, which first decomposes a complex query into multiple, simpler sub-queries, retrieves the top results for each sub-query individually, and then synthesizes a final answer. This direct comparison is designed to demonstrate that without decomposition, the query's semantic meaning becomes "clouded," leading to poor retrieval performance on complex tasks.

For evaluation, ground truths were systematically generated by extracting only objective keywords (e.g., company names, metric values, years) from the source data to ensure objectivity. This methodology is critical for creating reliable evaluations in specialized domains that lack pre-existing annotated datasets. Performance is measured using Precision, Recall, F1-Score, and a Keyword Inclusion percentage to assess factual accuracy. Additionally, Semantic and Cosine Similarity are used to evaluate the contextual integrity of the generated natural language answers.

4.2 Baseline Performance

Before assessing the system's performance on complex comparative queries, we first establish its baseline effectiveness on foundational retrieval tasks. This was accomplished by evaluating the system against two distinct query sets: simple, direct queries (QS1) and ambiguous, conversational queries (QS2). The results confirm that the core architecture of ESGTabQA is robust and accurate for standard use cases.

The first set, Simple Queries (QS1), was designed to emulate straightforward lookup scenarios. This set included direct questions requiring the retrieval of a specific data point for a single entity, such as "What was the total amount of waste produced by Intel Corp in 2021?" and "What is the percentage of females on the board of Asian Paints Ltd in 2021?". In these tests, ESGTabQA demonstrated high accuracy, achieving a semantic similarity of 0.897 and a Keyword Inclusion rate of 84.95%.

The second set, Ambiguous Queries (QS2), presented a more challenging scenario by testing the system's ability to interpret vague or colloquially phrased questions. This is a critical capability, as users often lack precise knowledge of underlying data schemas. For example, the system was challenged with conversational queries like "How much does Apple recycle?", which it had to correctly map to the formal metric "Total waste that is generated by the company and is recycled, reused or composted". Similarly, it had to interpret "Are there many female managers?" to retrieve data from the "Percentage of women managers" metric, a task where simple keyword matching would fail. Despite the increased ambiguity, performance remained high, achieving an F1-Score of 0.614 and a Keyword Inclusion of 84.43%. The consistently high performance across both simple and ambiguous queries, summarized in Table 1, validates that the core components of ESGTabQA are well-suited for this high-cardinality dataset.

Table 1. Average Performance on Baseline Query Sets

Question Set	Type	Semantic Similarity	Cosine Similarity	Precision	Recall	F1-Score	Keyword Inclusion (%)
QS1	Simple	0.897	0.669	0.534	0.709	0.599	84.95%
QS2	Ambiguous	0.864	0.629	0.562	0.698	0.614	84.43%

4.3 Performance on Complex Comparative Queries

Table 2. Performance Comparison on Complex Comparative Queries (QS3)

Query	ESGTabQA						ESGTabQA-Naive					
	Semantic	Cosine	Precision	Recall	F1-Score	Keyword Inc.	Semantic	Cosine	Precision	Recall	F1-Score	Keyword Inc.
21	0.939	0.681	0.655	0.704	0.679	73.91%	0.811	0.548	0.577	0.556	0.566	60.87%
22	0.921	0.689	0.647	0.667	0.657	84.00%	0.459	0.231	0.389	0.212	0.275	32.00%
23	0.773	0.514	0.762	0.457	0.571	51.61%	0.483	0.224	0.524	0.314	0.393	32.26%
24	0.868	0.652	0.625	0.833	0.714	86.67%	0.645	0.625	0.760	0.528	0.623	60.00%
25	0.840	0.511	0.311	0.583	0.406	61.90%	0.608	0.214	0.311	0.583	0.406	57.14%
26	0.966	0.545	0.821	0.793	0.807	84.00%	0.734	0.491	0.632	0.828	0.716	80.00%
27	0.812	0.429	0.333	0.351	0.342	36.36%	0.701	0.191	0.364	0.324	0.343	33.33%
28	0.932	0.741	0.556	0.714	0.625	87.50%	0.860	0.700	0.526	0.714	0.606	83.33%
29	0.831	0.506	0.484	0.417	0.448	46.88%	0.815	0.416	0.311	0.389	0.346	40.63%
30	0.809	0.613	0.471	0.466	0.444	62.00%	0.846	0.314	0.478	0.344	0.400	44.00%
31	0.857	0.617	0.528	0.792	0.633	100.00%	0.784	0.447	0.421	0.667	0.516	73.91%
32	0.910	0.580	0.710	0.537	0.611	55.88%	0.557	0.202	0.500	0.366	0.423	38.24%
Average	**0.871**	**0.590**	**0.575**	**0.610**	**0.578**	**69.23%**	**0.692**	**0.384**	**0.483**	**0.485**	**0.468**	**52.98%**

Having established the system's baseline competence, we now evaluate its core innovation: the ability to process complex comparative queries (QS3). This task represents a significant challenge for standard tabular QA systems operating on large, high-cardinality datasets. When a single query contains multiple entities (e.g., comparing emissions for "FedEx" versus "Telstra"), the resulting query vector becomes a semantic blend, failing to align closely with any single, specific table segment in the vector database. This "semantic clouding" leads to poor retrieval performance, a limitation that our entity-specific query decomposition is designed to overcome. To measure the efficacy of our approach, we conducted a head-to-head comparison between the full ESGTabQA system and the ESGTabQA-Naive baseline on the QS3 test suite. The performance disparity was stark. For instance, when asked to compare the CO2 emissions for Northrop Grumman and FedEx across two different years, ESGTabQA correctly decomposed the query, retrieved all four required data points, and synthesized an accurate comparative answer. In contrast, the naive model, overwhelmed by the query's complexity, failed to retrieve any correct information.

The quantitative results, detailed in Table 2, confirm this substantial performance gap across the entire test set. The introduction of query decomposition led to dramatic improvements across all evaluation metrics. As highlighted in Fig. 3, ESGTabQA outperformed the naive baseline by an average of 29.53% overall. The most pronounced gain was a 53.79% increase in Cosine Similarity, indicating a vastly more accurate retrieval of semantically relevant table segments. Furthermore, Keyword Inclusion rose by 30.68%, while Semantic Similarity, Recall, and F1-Score all saw substantial increases of over 23%. This improvement is primarily driven by the enhanced performance of the retriever stage. By breaking down a complex query into focused, unambiguous sub-queries, the retriever's accuracy

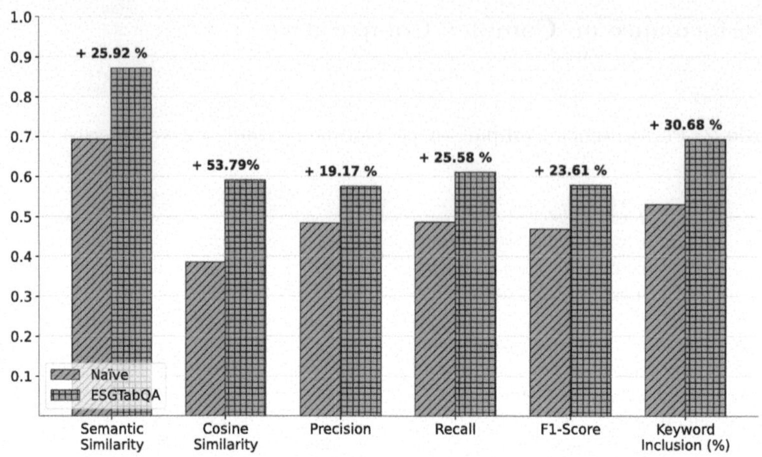

Fig. 3. Performance Gain from Entity-Specific Query Decomposition.

in identifying the correct table segments soared from 0.31 for the naive model to 0.94 for ESGTabQA. The naive model's frequent retrieval failures left its reader stage with irrelevant data, leading to incorrect or incomplete answers. In summary, these findings provide clear evidence that for complex analytical tasks on large-scale tabular data, entity-specific query decomposition is a necessary and highly effective architectural enhancement.

4.4 Overall Performance Summary

Across all 32 test queries, encompassing simple, ambiguous, and complex comparative scenarios, ESGTabQA demonstrated consistently high performance (shown in Table 3). The system achieved an overall F1-Score of 0.597, a semantic similarity of 0.876, and a factual Keyword Inclusion rate of 79.53%. These comprehensive results underscore the system's effectiveness and robustness as a generative QA solution for navigating complex, high-cardinality tabular data in specialized domains like ESG analytics.

Table 3. Overall metric performance

Metric	QS1	QS2	QS3	Overall
Semantic Similarity	0.897	0.864	0.868	**0.876**
Cosine Similarity	0.669	0.629	0.590	**0.629**
Precision	0.534	0.562	0.575	**0.557**
Recall	0.709	0.698	0.610	**0.672**
F1-Score	0.599	0.614	0.578	**0.597**
Keyword Inclusion (%)	84.95%	84.43%	69.23%	**79.53%**

5 Discussion

5.1 Analysis and Implications

Our research addresses the critical limitation of existing question-answering systems, which rely on small, well-structured datasets [12] and consequently fail to handle the massive, complex data volumes required for real-world ESG analysis. The central technical finding demonstrates that entity-specific query decomposition is essential for high-cardinality data, as evidenced by the 29.53% average performance increase on comparative queries, which avoids the semantic diffusion that plagues single-vector approaches. By successfully decomposing, retrieving, and synthesizing answers within an RAG framework, our system provides a robust architecture for complex questions within large-scale, homogeneous tables.

This architectural approach diverges from conventional systems like T-RAG and Dense Passage Retrieval (DPR) [13], which employ unified training pipelines that prevent the insertion of crucial intermediary steps needed for complex table analysis. ESGTabQA's modular architecture enables this core innovation through specialized components designed for purely tabular, ambiguous data, leveraging a powerful semantic encoder (MPNet-table) to interpret vague natural language queries—a significant advancement over earlier systems like TableQA [25]. This specialization differentiates our work from hybrid models like TAT-QA [29], which are architected for small, well-defined tables embedded within text rather than monolithic datasets exceeding a million rows. These deliberate architectural choices enable our system to achieve a robust F1-score of 0.597 on tasks beyond the design scope of existing models.

The practical implications extend beyond academic contributions, as deploying our system as a web service makes powerful data analysis directly accessible within analysts' daily platforms, enhancing corporate transparency and regulatory oversight. This automation dramatically increases efficiency, with queries answered in 5.7 s by our system compared to an average of 52.3 s for manual completion by human analysts.

5.2 Case Study

The value of our entity-specific query decomposition is best illustrated with a complex comparative online query that standard models cannot handle, such as: "How are the CO2 emissions of Northrop Grumman when compared to FedEx for 2021 and 2022?" A standard approach that encodes this entire query into a single vector fails completely. The resulting query vector contains a mixture of semantic intents—two companies, two years, one metric—making it too diluted to precisely match any single-entity data segment in the database.

In contrast, ESGTabQA first decomposes this query into four focused sub-queries (e.g., "What are the CO2 emissions of Northrop Grumman for 2021?"), as detailed in Fig. 2. This ensures each query vector sent to the retriever has a clear, unambiguous target. As a result, the system successfully retrieves all four required data points from disparate locations in the dataset and synthesizes them into a correct, coherent answer. This case concretely demonstrates that resolving semantic ambiguity before retrieval is critical for enabling complex, multi-entity analysis on high-cardinality data.

Conversely, analyzing the system's failure modes reveals **two primary error categories**: The first category involves **retriever errors**, which typically occur with short, semantically ambiguous queries. For instance, the query "Does Kopper Holdings have any policy to reduce emissions?" prompted the retriever to select a metric for "total CO2 emissions" instead of the correct "policy" metric. This error arises from "semantic confusion," where the vague query vector is similarly close to multiple thematically related but distinct table chunks in the high-cardinality dataset. This underscores the difficulty of precise retrieval when queries lack specific detail. The second category stems from **reader errors**, where the TAPAS model fails to adhere to precise constraints even with the correct table context. When asked for board diversity data for "Dril Quip in 2016", the system retrieved the correct table but returned the data from 2017. The reader model prioritized matching the numerical value ("0%"), which was the same for both years, over the explicit year constraint mentioned in the query.

5.3 Limitations and Future Work

While ESGTabQA demonstrates strong performance, several **limitations** point to clear research directions. The primary bottleneck lies in retriever accuracy, particularly for semantically ambiguous queries, a challenge inherent to high-cardinality datasets. Our initial evaluation focused on a limited set of queries to ensure ground truth quality for this novel task. We evaluated against a naive baseline rather than existing benchmarks like TAPEX or TAT-QA due to fundamental architectural differences. These systems target many small, structured tables, while ESGTabQA operates on single, monolithic, semi-structured tables with millions of rows. Direct comparison would require substantial re-engineering, fundamentally altering their original designs. Although we did not empirically test performance at varying scales, the system architecture supports large-scale operation. The reader component maintains constant workload by processing only small retrieved chunks, regardless of dataset size. Scalability depends on the retriever, which uses inherently scalable vector database technologies, providing a robust architectural foundation for scaling to even larger datasets. **Future research** will proceed along three axes. First, we will integrate Query Disambiguation as a pre-retrieval step to address retriever limitations. Additionally, future work could explore dedicated re-ranking modules to optimize retrieval results, an approach proven effective in adjacent domains like long-context modelling [1]. Second, comprehensive scalability experiments will empirically validate architectural performance under increasing data loads. Finally, we will explore adapting external benchmarks to our data paradigm, establishing common ground for extensive and rigorous comparative analysis.

6 Conclusion

The paper addressed the critical challenge of applying question answering systems to high-cardinality ESG datasets—a context where standard architectures fail due to data scale and ambiguity. We demonstrated that enhancing the Retriever-Reader pipeline with an entity-specific query decomposition stage is a highly effective strategy for overcoming these limitations.

Our work validates that for complex, comparative analysis over large, homogeneous datasets, entity-specific query decomposition is an essential architectural component, not merely an incremental improvement. By resolving semantic confusion before retrieval, the system's accuracy on such tasks improved by an average of 29.53%, confirming the critical role of specialized pre-retrieval processing. The strong overall performance, including an F1-Score of 0.597 and an approximate 9x efficiency gain over manual analysis in our simulated evaluation, further validates the practical viability of this approach. Ultimately, ESGTabQA serves as a validated blueprint for extending QA systems beyond clean academic benchmarks to the noisy, complex data common in web-based enterprise applications. This research highlights a key principle for the field: to build powerful and practical information systems for data-intensive domains like finance, the focus must shift towards sophisticated pre-retrieval processing that accommodates the structural realities of real-world data.

References

1. Alselwi, G., et al.: Long context modeling with ranked memory-augmented retrieval (2025). https://arxiv.org/abs/2503.14800
2. Borgeaud, S., et al.: Improving language models by retrieving from trillions of tokens (2022). https://arxiv.org/abs/2112.04426
3. Cerda, P., Varoquaux, G.: Encoding high-cardinality string categorical variables. IEEE Trans. Knowl. Data Eng. **34**(3), 1164–1176 (2022). https://doi.org/10.1109/tkde.2020.2992529
4. Deng, Z., Zhu, Y., Chen, Y., Witbrock, M., Riddle, P.: Interpretable amr-based question decomposition for multi-hop question answering (2022). https://arxiv.org/abs/2206.08486
5. EUROFIDAI: Esg raw data on corporations. EUROFIDAI (September)
6. Fu, R., Wang, H., Zhang, X., Zhou, J., Yan, Y.: Decomposing complex questions makes multi-hop qa easier and more interpretable (2021). https://arxiv.org/abs/2110.13472
7. Gao, L., et al.: Pal: Program-aided language models (2023). https://arxiv.org/abs/2211.10435
8. Gao, Y., et al.: Retrieval-augmented generation for large language models: a survey (2024). https://arxiv.org/abs/2312.10997
9. Herzig, J., Müller, T., Krichene, S., Eisenschlos, J.: Open domain question answering over tables via dense retrieval. In: Proceedings of the 2021 Conference of the North American Chapter of the Association for Computational Linguistics: Human Language Technologies, pp. 512–519 (2021). https://doi.org/10.18653/v1/2021.naacl-main.43

10. Herzig, J., Nowak, P.K., Müller, T., Piccinno, F., Eisenschlos, J.: Tapas: weakly supervised table parsing via pre-training. In: Proceedings of the 58th Annual Meeting of the Association for Computational Linguistics (2020). https://doi.org/10.18653/v1/2020.acl-main.398
11. Izacard, G., Grave, E.: Leveraging passage retrieval with generative models for open domain question answering (2021). https://arxiv.org/abs/2007.01282
12. Jin, N., Siebert, J., Li, D., Chen, Q.: A survey on table question answering: Recent advances (2022). https://arxiv.org/abs/2207.05270
13. Karpukhin, V., et al.: Dense passage retrieval for open-domain question answering. In: Proceedings of the 2020 Conference on Empirical Methods in Natural Language Processing (EMNLP), pp. 6769–6781 (2020). https://doi.org/10.18653/v1/2020.emnlp-main.550
14. Kotsantonis, S., Serafeim, G.: Four things no one will tell you about esg data. J. Appl. Corp. Financ. **31**(2), 50–58 (2019)
15. Lewis, P., et al.: Retrieval-augmented generation for knowledge-intensive nlp tasks. In: Proceedings of the 34th International Conference on Neural Information Processing Systems. NIPS '20 (2020)
16. Liu, Q., et al.: Tapex: Table pre-training via learning a neural sql executor (2022). https://arxiv.org/abs/2107.07653
17. Markondapatnaikuni, H., Suleiman, B., Erradi, A., Chen, S.: Keyknowledgerag (k^2 rag): An enhanced rag method for improved llm question-answering capabilities (2025). https://arxiv.org/abs/2507.07695
18. Mavi, V., Jangra, A., Jatowt, A.: Multi-hop question answering (2024). https://arxiv.org/abs/2204.09140
19. Pan, F., Canim, M., Glass, M.R., Gliozzo, A., Hendler, J.A.: End-to-end table question answering via retrieval-augmented generation. ArXiv abs/2203.16714 (2022). https://api.semanticscholar.org/CorpusID:247839624
20. Robertson, S., Zaragoza, H.: The probabilistic relevance framework: Bm25 and beyond. Found. Trends Inf. Retr. **3**(4), 333–389 (2009). https://doi.org/10.1561/1500000019
21. Salton, G., Buckley, C.: Term-weighting approaches in automatic text retrieval. Inf. Process. Manage. **24**(5), 513–523 (1988). https://doi.org/10.1016/0306-4573(88)90021-0
22. Schick, T., Schütze, H.: True few-shot learning with prompts – a real-world perspective (2021). https://arxiv.org/abs/2111.13440
23. Song, K., Tan, X., Qin, T., Lu, J., Liu, T.Y.: Mpnet: Masked and permuted pre-training for language understanding (2020). https://arxiv.org/abs/2004.09297
24. Trivedi, H., Balasubramanian, N., Khot, T., Sabharwal, A.: Interleaving retrieval with chain-of-thought reasoning for knowledge-intensive multi-step questions (2023). https://arxiv.org/abs/2212.10509
25. Vakulenko, S., Savenkov, V.: Tableqa: Question answering on tabular data (2017). https://arxiv.org/abs/1705.06504
26. Yin, P., Neubig, G., tau Yih, W., Riedel, S.: Tabert: Pretraining for joint understanding of textual and tabular data (2020). https://arxiv.org/abs/2005.08314
27. Zhang, L., Zhang, S., Balog, K.: Table2vec: Neural word and entity embeddings for table population and retrieval. In: Proceedings of the 42nd International ACM SIGIR Conference on Research and Development in Information Retrieval, pp. 1029–1032. SIGIR'19 (2019). https://doi.org/10.1145/3331184.3331333
28. Zhong, K., Suleiman, B., Erradi, A., Chen, S.: Semrag: Semantic knowledge-augmented rag for improved question-answering (2025). https://arxiv.org/abs/2507.21110

29. Zhu, F., et al.: TAT-QA: A question answering benchmark on a hybrid of tabular and textual content in finance. In: Proceedings of the 59th Annual Meeting of the Association for Computational Linguistics and the 11th International Joint Conference on Natural Language Processing (Volume 1: Long Papers), pp. 3277–3287 (2021). https://doi.org/10.18653/v1/2021.acl-long.254
30. Zhu, F., Lei, W., Wang, C., Zheng, J., Poria, S., Chua, T.S.: Retrieving and reading: a comprehensive survey on open-domain question answering (2021). https://arxiv.org/abs/2101.00774

Finding Top-K Keywords-Aware Optimal Routes: A Splice-Based Expansion Approach

Yang Song[1], Jiajia Li[1(✉)], Lei Li[2], Linlin Ding[3], and Chengcheng Chen[1]

[1] Shenyang Aerospace University, Shenyang, China
songyang2@stu.sau.edu.cn, lijiajia@sau.edu.cn
[2] HKUST(GZ), Guangzhou, China
thorli@ust.hk
[3] Liaoning University, Shenyang, China
dinglinlin@lnu.edu.cn

Abstract. Given a start point s, a destination t, and the set of keyword types that must be satisfied, the goal of *Top-k Keywords-Aware Optimal Route* (*k-KAOR*) query is to return top-k shortest routes that covers all query keyword types. Existing solutions can be divided into two classes: candidate based algorithms and path expansion based algorithms. However, they all face a trade-off between query efficiency and route quality. To solve this problem, in this paper, we further study the *k-KAOR* problem and introduce a Splice-Based Expansion (*SBE*) algorithm. The *SBE* algorithm efficiently integrates the ideas of candidate set and path expansion. First, to avoid a vast search space, we introduce a Point of Interest (POI) filtering refinement strategy based on the spatial index *IG-Tree*. Then, to cover more combinations of POIs while avoiding brute-force enumeration, we pre-construct a keyword distance matrix and splice POIs using the graph partitioning of the *IG-Tree*. Finally, we perform path expansion by concatenating different POI combinations until the top-k paths are discovered. Extensive experiments on real-world road networks show that our method can reduces response time by an order of magnitude and improves result quality by 25%.

Keywords: Keywords Aware Route · Spatial Index · Road Networks

1 Introduction

With the rapid development of location-based services [6,15] in urban areas and the widespread proliferation of mobile devices, the demand for route planning in road networks increases sharply. Among them, the *Keywords-Aware Optimal Routing* (*KAOR*) query [5,7–9,13,14] have been widely studied for their ability to plan routes that meet user requirements. Specifically, given a road network G, where one Point of Interest (POI) may contain one or several keywords, a starting point s, a destination t, and a user-specified keywords type list, *KAOR* query returns the shortest route that cover all the query keyword types.

Such queries are common in real-life Web applications, as shown in Fig. 1. A user drives from start point s to destination t, buys some fruits and vegetables,

I. Awan et al. (Eds.): WISE 2025, LNCS 16368, pp. 340–355, 2026.
https://doi.org/10.1007/978-981-95-7251-9_23

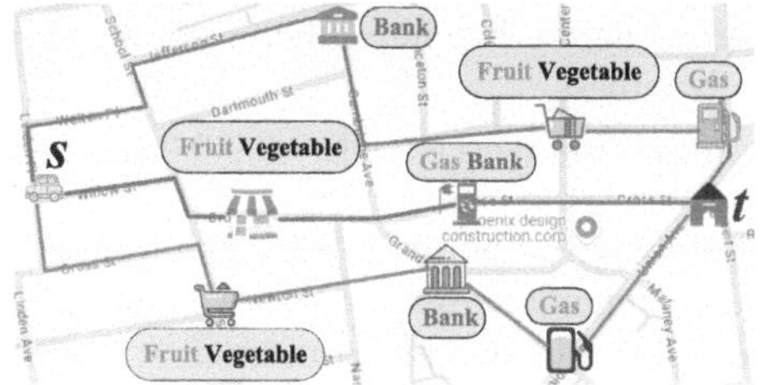

Keywords Requirement: {Fruit ,Vegetable , Gas , Bank}	
Route	**Distance**
R1	6.4km
R2	5.5km
R3	6.1km

Fig. 1. Example of user route selection

deposits money in the bank, and fuels his car. It is worth noting that the user does not fixed the order in which these services are accessed, allowing them to be visited in any order. Therefore, the three routes R_1, R_2, R_3 are all valid routes because each route can satisfy the {*Fruit, Vegetable, Gas, Bank*} needs. However, different users have diverse preferences. Therefore, a more practical solution is to return multiple routes to the user and allow users to choose from them. Motivated by this, in this paper, we study the *Top-k Keyword-Aware Optimal Routes* (*k-KAOR*) query, which returns top-k shortest routes that satisfy the user's keyword type requirements.

Existing methods to solving *k-KAOR* query can be divided into two classes: candidate based methods [5,7,8,14] and path expansion based methods [9,13]. Candidate based methods first build a POI candidate set based on the query location and then construct a route from the starting point using a greedy nearest-neighbor strategy. Although these methods have fast response times, they often suffer from poor route quality because the greedy strategy overlooks a large number of possible POI combinations. In addition, to find the top-k routes, each nearest neighbor strategy needs to find at least k POIs, which further increases the computational cost. Therefore, it is non-trivial to use candidate based methods to efficiently answer *k-KAOR* queries. On the other hand, path expansion-based methods gradually extend from the starting point to different POIs to construct a large set of candidate paths, and then use heuristic functions to search for the top-k routes. However, these methods require computing the global POI distance when calculating the heuristic cost of each candidate path, which further increases the execution time of the algorithm. Therefore, while path expansion-based methods can return shorter routes, this often comes at the cost of longer response times.

Therefore, existing solutions face a trade-off between query efficiency and route quality, which makes it hardly for them to efficiently plan shorter routes for users. To address this problem, in this paper, we propose a Splice-Based Expansion (*SBE*) algorithm. The core idea of the *SBE* algorithm is to splice POIs that are closer in distance to construct a large number of POI combinations, and to further splice different combinations again during the path extension phase. By splicing different combinations, during the path expansion phase, each path can able to satisfy a set of keywords rather than just a single keyword, effectively improving query efficiency while ensuring result quality. However, the large number of POIs in the road network results in a massive number of POI combinations, which directly impacts query efficiency. Therefore, we propose the following strategies to reduce this hardness.

First, we utilize an efficient spatial index *IG-Tree* [5] construct a candidate set of POIs that satisfy the query keyword types. This effectively filters out a large number of distant POIs, thereby reducing the number of POI combinations. Secondly, we integrate the state-of-the-art shortest distance algorithm, *H2H* [17], to perform nearest-neighbor (*NN*) queries and quickly construct a feasible route. Since the *NN* strategy only considers the single nearest combination, this feasible route can serve as an effective upper bound for the optimal solution. Thirdly, by calling *H2H*, we filter out POIs with detour distances greater than the upper bound, further narrowing the search range. Next, we first splice two POIs that satisfy different query keyword types to construct POI routes. In order to avoid brute-force enumeration between POIs, we efficiently utilize the subgraph partitions in *IG-Tree*, expanding the subgraph layer by layer to search for POIs that can be spliced, pruning the subgraph that are farther apart. This naturally raises a question: which pairs of POIs can be spliced? Therefore, in order to determine the conditions for splicing POIs, we introduce a splice distance threshold. During the *IG-Tree* index construction phase, we construct a keyword distance matrix that stores the average distance of POI combinations covering different keyword types. Finally, in the path extension phase, different POI routes are further splice until top-k routes satisfies all the query keyword types. Besides, we introduce a new heuristic function that simultaneously considers the distance of the POI routes and the number of covered keywords, enhancing the efficiency of path extension. The specific contributions of this paper are as follows:

- We further study the *k-KAOR* problem and proposed a splice-based extension algorithm *SBE* to answer *k-KAOR* query in road network.
- We proposed several optimization strategies, such as POI filtering, *H2H* refinement and the *IG-Tree* partition pruning to reduce the search range.
- We introduce a novel heuristic function that simultaneously considers the distance of the POI routes and the number of covered keyword types to accelerate path expansion.
- Our experiment on real road networks show that our method can reduces response time by an order of magnitude and improves result quality by 25%.

2 Related Work

2.1 Candidate Based Methods for *k-KAOR*

Candidate-based methods first filter out a large number of POIs using spatial indexing or precomputation. Then, starting from the start point, construct the optimal route using a nearest neighbor strategy. *MRRP* [14] filters POIs by distance from start point and destination for each POI. The *GOD* algorithm [8] uses grid index [19] to filter POIs and further considers the distribution of POIs for different keywords. The *OptDist* algorithm [5] uses the graph partitioning algorithm METIS [18] to divide the road network into multiple subgraphs, and then retrieves the POI set based on the query's spatial relationships. However, they all construct only one optimal route by executing greedy strategies. Therefore, they cannot directly answer *k-KAOR* queries.

2.2 Path Expansion Based Methods for *k-KAOR*

Path expansion based methods start from the start point and gradually extend to different POIs, constructing a large number of candidate paths. Then, by calculating the heuristic cost, guiding the search for the top-k optimal routes. *OSScaling* algorithm [4,10] uses the Breadth-First Search method to constructs candidate paths. The *ROSE* algorithm [11,20] uses the idea of dynamic programming to gradually construct candidate paths. Therefore, they cannot be applied to large-scale road networks, as their method would result in significant search costs and memory overhead. *KOSR-MA* [13] constructs candidate paths by iteratively obtaining neighboring POIs from the starting point. However, it only supports fixed-order keyword access and cannot be directly applied to scenarios where keywords access in arbitrary order. The *DA-Prune* [9] algorithm draws on the idea of the *KSP* algorithm [12,16] by deviating each point on the shortest path to the nearest POI, thus constructing a large number of candidate paths. However, it preprocesses the global road network by contracting it into a POI subnet before expansion. Therefore, it cannot quickly respond to scenarios when POI data in the road network are changed.

3 Problem Definition

In this section, we define the problem and the corresponding concepts formally. A road network is an undirected graph $G(V, E)$, where V is a set of vertices and $E \subseteq V \times V$ is a set of edges with each edge $(u, v) \in E$ having a positive weight $\omega(u, v)$. Each POI in road network contains one or multiple keyword types. A path p is a sequence of vertices $\langle v_0, \ldots, v_n \rangle$, where $(v_i, v_{i+1}) \in E, \forall i \in [0, n-1]$. The distance of p is denoted as $D(p) = \sum_{i=0}^{n-1} \omega(v_i, v_{i+1})$. Let $K(\cdot)$ be the set of keyword types for a POI or a path. Moreover, we maintain an inverted list $O(kw_i)$ for each type of keyword kw_i to store the all POIs that contain keywords type kw_i. For a set of POIs that satisfy the query keyword sets Q_{kw}, we use C_{POI} to represent its POI candidate set. We summarize the notations in Table 1.

Table 1. Important Notations.

Notation	Definition
$p = \langle v_0, ..., v_n \rangle$, $D(p)$	A path from v_0 to v_n and the path distance
$sp(v_i, v_j)$, $\delta(v_i, v_j)$	Shortest path from v_i to v_j and its distance
$K(\cdot)$	Keyword type set of for a POI or a path
$O(kw_i)$	POI set containing the keyword type kw_i
Q_{kw}	User-specified keywords type set of query Q
C_{POI}	a POI candidate set that satisfy Q_{kw}

Definition 1. (Detour Distance (*DD*)) *Given a starting vertex s and a destination t, the Detour Distance from s to t via a POI p, denoted as $\delta^D(s, p, t)$, and calculated by*

$$\delta^D(s, p, t) = \delta(s, p) + \delta(p, t) \tag{1}$$

Definition 2. (POI Route (*PR*)) *Given a route $P = \langle v_0, \ldots, v_n \rangle$, if each vertex in P contains one or more keyword types, i.e., $\forall v_i \in P$, $|K(v_i)| > 0$. We define the route P as a POI Route, denoted as PR.*

Definition 3. (Top-k Keywords-Aware Optimal Routes (k-*KAOR*)) *Given a road network $G(V, E)$, a source vertex s, a destination t, an integer k, and a set of keyword types $Q_{kw} \subseteq K(V)$, let P be all possible valid paths w.r.t Q_{kw} from s to t. The k-KAOR query of $Q(s, t, Q_{kw}, k)$ is to return a size-k subset $P_k \subseteq P$ such that: i) $\forall p \in P_k$, $\omega(p) \leq \omega(p')$, for all $p' \in P \setminus P_k$, and ii) $\forall p_i, p_j \in P_k$, $(i \neq j)$, we have $R_{p_i} \neq R_{p_j}$.*

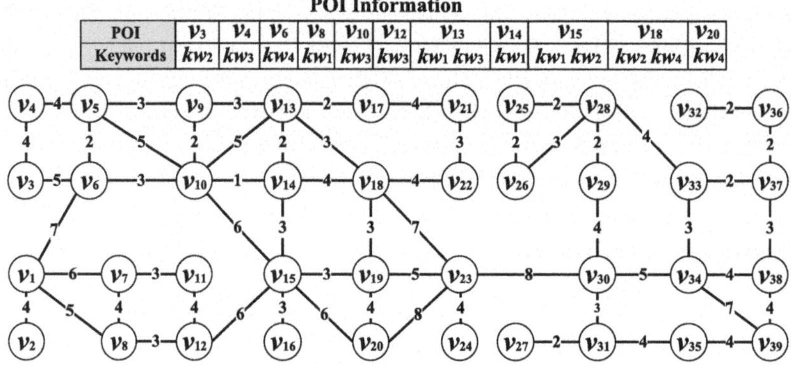

POI Information

POI	v_3	v_4	v_6	v_8	v_{10}	v_{12}	v_{13}	v_{14}	v_{15}	v_{18}	v_{20}
Keywords	kw_2	kw_3	kw_4	kw_1	kw_3	kw_3	kw_1 kw_3	kw_1	kw_1 kw_2	kw_2 kw_4	kw_4

Fig. 2. An Example of Road Network with POIs and Keyword types

Figure 2 shows an example of road network with POIs and corresponding keyword types. Given a 2-*KAOR* query $Q(v_1, v_{23}, \{kw_1, kw_2, kw_3, kw_4\}, 2)$. Many paths can cover the query keyword types, such as $p_1 = \{v_1, v_6, v_5, v_9, v_{13}, v_{18}, v_{23}\}$, $D(p_1) = 25$; $p_2 = \{v_1, v_8, v_{12}, v_{15}, v_{20}, v_{23}\}$, $D(p_2) = 28$, $p_3 = \{v_1, v_6, v_{10}, v_{14}, v_{18}, v_{23}\}$, $D(p_3) = 22$; $p_4 = \{v_1, v_6, v_{10}, v_{15}, v_{19}, v_{23}\}$, $D(p_4) = 24$. Therefore, we can obtain the query result set $P_k = \{p_3, p_4\}$.

4 *SBE* Algorithm for *k-KAOR* Query

In this section, we will introduce our algorithm *SBE* for solving *k-KAOR* query. *SBE* is mainly divided into three stages, i) **Candidate Set Filtering and Refinement**: In Sect. 4.1, based on the user's specified query Q, we propose a POI filtering refinement strategy based on the *IG-Tree* index. ii) **Splicing of two POIs**: In Sect. 4.2, we first splice two POIs with different keyword types to construct a large number of POI routes. iii) **POI Route Expansion**: In Sect. 4.3, we gradually expand the POI routes and then using a novel heuristic function to construct the query result set. The details of each stage are as follows.

4.1 Candidate Set Filtering and Refinement

In the road network, there are numerous POIs that can satisfy the user's query keyword types. However, some POIs are far from the query starting point and destination, and the routes passing through these POIs may be very long, making them unlikely to become top-k routes. Therefore, quickly filtering these POIs based on their spatial relationships can not only improve the search efficiency but also enhance the quality of the results. In this paper, we use an efficient spatial index structure, *IG-Tree*, to filter POIs. The details will be shown below.

Candidate Set Filtering: Specifically, *IG-Tree* recursively divides the global road network into multiple subgraphs through a multi-layer partitioning algorithm [18] and establishing a tree structure according to the relationship between subgraphs. The lowest-level leaf nodes of the tree represent each physical vertices in the road network. From bottom to top, there are partition nodes composed of multiple leaf nodes. In addition, binary code also used in each partition node to efficiently manage keywords information. Figure 3 shows an example of *IG-Tree* corresponding to the road network in Fig. 1. G_0 represents the entire road network, and subsequent layers of partitions are recursively constructed. In addition, the subgraph stores the current included keyword information. For example, G_9 covers the keyword types kw_2 and kw_3, so the binary code is 0110. Given a query $Q(s, t, Q_{kw}, k)$, *IG-Tree* first finds the least common ancestor (LCA) node of the s and t, and checks whether the binary code of the LCA contains all the query keywords. If the POIs in LCA partition do not encompass all query keywords, the search continues upward to the parent nodes of the LCA until Q_{kw} is fully satisfied. Subsequently, all POIs under this partition node that satisfy Q_{kw} are added to C_{POI}.

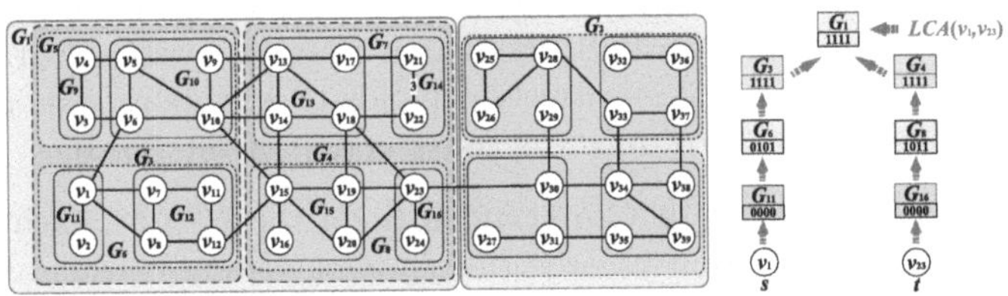

Fig. 3. An example of *IG-Tree* Index

For example in Fig. 3, given a query $Q(v_1, v_{23}, \{kw_1, kw_2, kw_3, kw_4\}, 2)$, we first find the $LCA(v_1, v_{23}) = G_1$, and G_1 can satisfy all the query keywords. Therefore, all POIs under G_1 that contain the query keywords form the candidate set C_{POI}, $C_{POI} = \{v_3, v_4, v_6, v_8, v_{10}, v_{12}, v_{13}, v_{14}, v_{15}, v_{18}, v_{20}\}$. This process avoids accessing the subgraph G_2, thus reducing the search space effectively.

Candidate Set Refinement: Next, we propose a POI candidate set refinement strategy to further filter POIs in C_{POI}. First, by integrating the *H2H* index and performing nearest neighbor queries, we construct two greedy paths bidirectionally to quickly obtain feasible paths that satisfy all query keywords. The greedy strategy starts from the origin node and iteratively selects the nearest POI that satisfies the remain query keywords. Then, we select the shorter path as the upper bound *UB* for the optimal route length. This is because the greedy path represents only one possible combination of the current POIs. Therefore, the length of the optimal path will not exceed the upper bound. Next, for each POI in the C_{POI}, we calculate its detour distance and filter out those POIs with a detour distance greater than the *UB*. This is because if $\delta^D(s,p,t) > UB$, then the distance of the path passing through this POI p that satisfies the remaining keywords will certainly be greater than *UB*. Therefore, this POI can be safely filtered out. Finally, we construct the refined candidate set CR_{POI}.

For example, given a query $Q(v_1, v_{23}, \{kw_1, kw_2, kw_3, kw_4\}, 2)$. After obtaining the C_{POI}, we construct two greedy paths, $P_s(s,t)$ and $P_t(s,t)$. P_s starts from the source v_1 , while P_t starts from the destination v_{23}. Because the path distances $D(P_s)$ is 28 and $D(P_t)$ is 25. Therefore, the upper bound *UB* is determined to be 25. At this time, we calculate the detour distance *DD* for each POI in C_{POI}. Based on the *DD*, the distance of v_3, v_4 and v_{20} are 31, 32 and 27 respectively, which exceed the *UB*, 25. Therefore, they are further filtered out. Finally, we construct the refined candidate set $CR_{POI} = \{v_6, v_8, v_{10}, v_{12}, v_{13}, v_{14}, v_{15}, v_{18}\}$.

4.2 Splicing of Two POIs

After obtaining the CR_{POI}, we begin splicing two POIs in CR_{POI} that contain different keyword types to construct the POI routes. To determine the splice distance threshold, we build keywords distance matrix (KDM) during the *IG-Tree* index construction. This matrix effectively evaluates the distances resulting from different partition POI combinations, thereby determining the distance threshold for POI splicing. Then, for each POI, the search starts from the subgraph where the current POI is located and iteratively expands to neighboring subgraphs via boundary points. We first introduce the construction of the *KDM*.

Keywords Distance Matrix Construction: In the *IG-tree*, each subgraph stores a "distance matrix" that records the shortest distances from all vertexes within the subgraph to its boundary vertexes. A vertex that have edges connecting it to other subgraphs is defined as boundary vertex. Therefore, we can progressively access adjacent subgraphs via boundary vertex to construct *KDM*.

Specifically, the construction of the *KDM* starts from the smallest subgraph partition and then progressively builds upon the upper-level subgraph partitions. In each smallet partition S_{par}, we utilize the inverted index of POIs constructed for the current partition to retrieve all POI pairs corresponding to different keyword type combinations. Suppose there are n POI pairs in S_{par} that can cover $\{kw_a, kw_b\}$, then the corresponding matrix value in the *KMD* of S_{par} is update to $\sum_{i=0}^{n-1} \delta(v_a, v_b)/n$, where $\delta(v_a, v_b)$ is the shortest distance between each POI pair. After constructing the *KDM* for all the samllest partitions, we begin iteratively constructing the *KDM* for the upper-level partitions. For each upper-level partition S_p, we retrieve the *KDM* of the two sub-partitions, S_{lp} and S_{rp}. Then, the value in the *KDM* of S_p is first updated to $(S_{lp} + S_{rp})/2$. This is because the upper-level partition S_p, also contains the keyword combinations of its corresponding two sub-partitions S_{lp} and S_{rp}. Next, we construct new POI pairs formed by the POIs from different sub-partitions. Their distances can further update the *KDM* of S_p. Specifically, we use the boundary vertexes to efficiently calculate the shortest distance between POI pairs across partitions. Assume that POI v_a is in S_{lp} and POI v_b is in S_{rp}, then the shortest distance of POI pair $< v_a, v_b >$ can be calculated by:

$$\delta(v_a, v_b) = \min_{b_1 \in B(S_{lp}), b_2 \in B(S_{rp})} (\delta(v_a, b_1) + \delta(b_1, b_2) + \delta(b_2, v_b)) \tag{2}$$

where $B(S_p)$ is the boundary vertex set for each partition S_p in *IG-Tree*. Because $\delta(v_a, b_1)$ and $\delta(b_2, v_b)$ have already been pre-stored in the distance matrix, this process avoids redundant distance calculations. Finally, by calculating the distances of all new POI pairs, we progressively update the *KDM* of S_p.

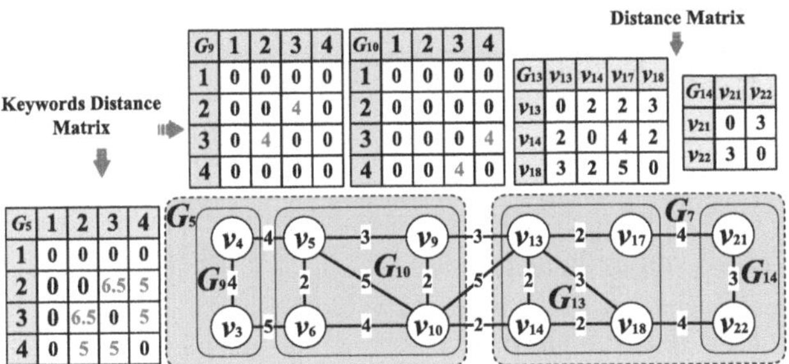

Fig. 4. Keywords Distance Matrix in *IG-Tree*

Figure 4 shows an example of distance matrix and keywords distance matrix. In the distance matrix, rows represent the vertexes within the partition, columns represent the boundary vertexes, and each value denotes the shortest distance between them. For keywords distance matrix, the rows and columns of the matrix represent the keyword type IDs, while the values indicate the average distance of different keyword type combinations within the current partition. For example in G_5, we first compute the keyword distance matrices for its sub-partitions G_9 and G_{10}. In G_9, only one POI pair $< v_3, v_4 >$ can cover $\{kw_2, kw_3\}$, so the corresponding matrix value in G_9 is $\delta(v_3, v_4) = 4$. In G_{10}, the value of matrix for keywords combination $\{kw_3, kw_4\}$ is $\delta(v_6, v_{10}) = 4$. Then, for the newly formed POI combinations such as $\{v_3, v_{10}\}$, by utilizing the distance matrices, the total distance can be calculated as $\delta(v_3, v_3)+\delta(v_3, v_6)+\delta(v_6, v_{10}) = 9$. For the keyword type combinations $\{kw_2, kw_3\}$, the new distance is update to $(9 + 4)/2 = 6.5$.

The Process of Splicing two POIs: Now, we begin splicing two POIs to build POI routes. A brute-force method is to combine all two POIs and then evaluate them against a distance threshold. However, the number of combinations increases exponentially with the size of the CR_{POI}, which will result in substantial computational costs. Therefore, we propose a *IG-Tree* partition pruning strategy. By pruning distant POIs through boundary vertex, we avoid blind enumeration and improve the splicing efficiency.

Algorithm 1 shows the process of splicing two POIs. First, use P_{dist} to store all POI routes (line 1). Then, for each POI p_i in CR_{POI}, start the splice process from the current partition T_{node} (lines 2–7). For each pair of POIs, if their shortest distance is not greater than the corresponding average distance in the *KMD*, they are spliced together (lines 8–11). Then, the splice process extends to the adjacent partitions of the T_{node} (lines 12–13). For each partition P_{adj}, we evaluate the shortest distance d_{min} between p_i and its boundary vertexes (line 14). If d_{min} exceeds the average distance d_{ave} of the corresponding keywords combination in the LCA partition matrix, we can prune this partition safely. This is because the shortest distance to the boundary vertexes can serve as a lower bound for the exact distance. Finally, when the d_{min} of all extended partitions exceeds the corresponding distance threshold, the splicing process for the current POI ends.

Algorithm 1: The Splicing of two POIs

Input: POI Candidate Set CR_{POI}
Output: All POI routes that distance smaller than the distance threshold

1 $P_{list} \leftarrow \emptyset$;
2 **for** *each POI* p_i *in* CR_{POI} **do**
3     $U_{kw} \leftarrow Q_{kw} \setminus (Q_{kw} \cap K(p_i))$;
4     $T_{node} \leftarrow$ *IG-Tree* partition where p_i is located;
5   **if** $T_{node}.bit \cap U_{kw} \neq \emptyset$ **then**
6         $N_{list} \leftarrow$ Obtain all POIs that $K(v) \cap U_{kw} \neq \emptyset$;
7   **for** *each POI* p_j *in* N_{list} **do**
8             $d_{kw} \leftarrow$ Distance threshold in the *KMD* of T_{node};
9   **if** $\delta(p_i, p_j) <= d_{kw}$ **then**
10                 $P_{pair} \leftarrow$ Splicing p_i and p_j;
11   Add P_{pair} into the P_{list};
12     $IG_{adj} \leftarrow$ Get all partitions adjacent to T_{node};
13   **for** *each partition* P_{adj} *in* IG_{adj} **do**
14         $d_{min} \leftarrow$ The shortest distance from p_i to boundary vertexes of P_{adj};
15         $d_{ave} \leftarrow$ The distance of the *KMD* for the partition $LCA(P_{adj}, T_{node})$;
16   **if** $P_{adj}.bit \cap U_{kw} \neq \emptyset$ *and* $d_{min} <= d_{ave}$ **then**
17   same as lines 6-11;
18   Add all partitions adjacent to the P_{adj} to IG_{adj};
19 **return** P_{list};

For example in Fig. 4, the splicing process begins from the partition G_{10}, which contains the POI v_6. Then, we splice v_6 and v_{10} because both are located with in partition G_{10} and satisfy the distance threshold. Next, we gradually

Table 2. The cost of POI Route ($\beta = 0.7$) in Fig. 2.

PR	$D(PR)$	$Min(PR)$	$Num(PR)$	$Cost(PR)$
$< v_6, v_{10} >$	3	23	2	$0.7 * 23 + 0.3 * (1/2) = 16.25$
$< v_{10}, v_{14} >$	1	22	2	$0.7 * 22 + 0.3 * (1/2) = 15.55$
$< v_{14}, v_{18} >$	4	22	3	$0.7 * 22 + 0.3 * (1/3) = 15.50$
$< v_{13}, v_{14} >$	2	26	2	$0.7 * 26 + 0.3 * (1/2) = 18.30$
$< v_{10}, v_{15} >$	6	24	3	$0.7 * 24 + 0.3 * (1/3) = 16.90$

extend the G_{10} to its adjacent partitions G_9, G_{11} and G_{13}. Because POIs from CR_{POI} are not within G_9 and G_{10}, so we do not access them. For G_{13} and G_{15}, since both $LCA(G_{10}, G_{13})$ and $LCA(G_{10}, G_{15})$ are G_1, we determine the splice distance threshold using the *KMD* of G_1. Finally, we obtain all POI pairs that satisfy the distance threshold.

4.3 POI Route Expansion

Through the splicing POIs from CR_{POI}, we construct a large number of POI routes that can cover different keyword types. In order to satisfy all query keywords as early as possible, we integrate the route distance and keywords types number that has satisfied into a heuristic function and apply the best-first paradigm to guild POI route expansion. We first introduce the heuristic function and then introduce the best-first route expansion. Finally, we present the overall process of *SBE* algorithm.

Heuristic Function: From the perspective of route distance, for a POI route $PR(v_a, ..., v_b)$, if it is located far from s and t, even if its own distance is relatively short, it may result in a longer overall route distance. Therefore, we further consider the positional relationship of the POI route with respect to the query's location. We first calculate the shortest distance to visit it, denoted as $Min(PR)$, $Min(PR)$ is calculated by:

$$Min(PR) = min((\delta(s, v_a) + D(PR) + \delta(v_b, t)), (\delta(s, v_b) + D(PR) + \delta(v_a, t))) \quad (3)$$

It is worth noting that since we have already computed the detour distance for each POI during the refinement phase. Therefore, we only need to compute $D(PR)$, which further improves the efficiency of the heuristic function.

Next, we further consider the number of keyword types that the current POI route $PR(v_a, v_b)$ has already satisfied, denoted as $Num(PR) = |K(PR) \cap Q_{kw}|$. Finally, for each POI route PR, we integrate them into a heuristic function through weighted calculation, denoted as $Cost(PR)$ that is calculated by:

$$Cost(PR) = \beta * Min(PR) + (1 - \beta) * (1/Num(PR)) \quad (4)$$

For example, consider a *k-KAOR* query $Q(v_1, v_{23}, \{kw_1, kw_2, kw_3, kw_4\}, 2)$, Table 2 shows the costs of some POI routes constructed through Algorithm 1

Algorithm 2: SBE Algorithm

Input: $G(V, E)$, $Q(s, t, Q_{kw}, k)$
Output: The Top-k Optimal Routes Ψ

1 $C_{POI} \leftarrow$ Construct the POI candidate set based on the *IG-Tree* index;
2 $CR_{POI} \leftarrow$ Calculate the detour distance refinement of the C_{POI};
3 $PR_{set} \leftarrow$ Splicing the POIs based Algorithm 1;
4 $\Psi \leftarrow \emptyset$, Initialize the priority queue PQ;
5 **for** *each POI route PR in* PR_{set} **do**
6 $\quad PQ.insert(PR, Cost(PR))$;
7 **while** *PQ is not empty and* $|\Psi| < k$ **do**
8 $\quad PR_m \leftarrow PQ.extractMin()$;
9 $\quad$ **if** $K(PR_m) \cap Q_{kw} = Q_{kw}$ **then**
10 $\quad\quad R_{ABE} \leftarrow$ Obtain the route with a shorter distance between $s \oplus PR_m \oplus t$ and $s \oplus PR_m.reverse() \oplus t$;
11 $\quad\quad \Psi \leftarrow \Psi \cup R_{ABE}$;
12 $\quad$ **else**
13 $\quad\quad v_a, v_b \leftarrow$ Obtain the starting and ending POIs of PR_m;
14 $\quad\quad$ **for** *each POI route* PR_s *that end POI is* v_a **do**
15 $\quad\quad\quad$ **if** $|K(PR_s) \cup K(PR_m)| > K(PR_m)$ **then**
16 $\quad\quad\quad\quad PR_{new} \leftarrow PR_s \oplus PR_m$;
17 $\quad\quad\quad\quad PQ.insert(PR_{new}, Cost(PR_{new}))$;
18 $\quad\quad$ **for** *each POI route* PR_t *that start POI is* v_b **do**
19 $\quad\quad\quad$ same as lines 14-16;
20 $\quad\quad$ **for** *each POI* p_i *in* $O(kw_i)$ *that* $kw_i \in Q_{kw} \setminus K(PR_m)$ **do**
21 $\quad\quad\quad P_{dis} \leftarrow$ Calculate the distance threshold for $K(v_a) \cup K(v_b) \cup K(p_i)$;
22 $\quad\quad\quad$ **if** $\delta(PR_m \oplus p_i)$ *or* $\delta(p_i \oplus PR_m) <= P_{dis}$ **then**
23 $\quad\quad\quad\quad P_{new} \leftarrow$ Obtain the route with a shorter distance between $PR_m \oplus p_i$ and $p_i \oplus PR_m$;
24 $\quad\quad\quad\quad PQ.insert(PR_{new}, Cost(PR_{new}))$;
25 return Ψ

when $\beta = 0.7$. First, through POI filtering and refinement, we obtain the POI candidate set $CR_{POI} = \{v_6, v_8, v_{10}, v_{12}, v_{13}, v_{14}, v_{15}, v_{18}\}$. Then, for each POI route, we compute $D(PR)$, $Min(PR)$, and $Num(PR)$, respectively. Finally, by computing $Cost(PR)$, the POI route $< v_{14}, v_{18} >$ has the minimum cost and is therefore prioritized for expansion.

Best-First Route Expansion: Now we are able to describe our algorithm *SBE*, the details are provided in Algorithm 2.

SBE first filters and refines the POIs, and then splices two POIs to construct the initial POI route set PR_{set} (lines 1–3). PQ is used to manage the candidate POI routes expanded so far and Ψ is the top-k optimal routes set (line 4). Then, *SBE* insert each POI route in PR_{set} into the PQ to await subsequent expansion (lines 5–6). Subsequently, the PQ ranks the PR with $Cost(PR)$ and pops the minimum one PR_m at each step (lines 7–8). If PR_m satisfies all the query keyword types Q_{kw}, we determine the its visit order, and then add it to the result set Ψ (lines 9–11). Otherwise, we extend PR_m to satisfy more query keyword types. Specifically, the expansion of each PR_m consists of two steps: (i) we splice the current POI route PR_m with other POI route to form a new POI route that covers more query keyword type (lines 12–19). This process can further satisfy a set of query keyword types; (ii) Using the inverted index, we insert the new POI p_i at the beginning or the end of the current POI route to construct a new POI route PR_{new} (lines 20–24).

5 Experiment Evaluation

Table 3. Real Road Networks

Maps	|V|	|E|	#POI
CAL	21K	43K	12K
NY	**264K**	**733K**	**20K**
COL	435K	1057K	32K

Table 4. Parameters

Parameters	Values
$\|Q_{kw}\|$	2, 4, **6**, 8, 10
k	1, 3, **5**, 7, 9
Density	2%, 4%, **8%**, 16%, 32%
β	0.5, 0.6, **0.7**, 0.8, 0.9

Datasets: We selected three real road networks from [1], and then obtained the real POI data as a foundation from OpenStreetMap [2] as shown in Table 3. To gain insight into the performance of the algorithm in different settings, we vary some parameters, such as the number of query keywords, k and POI density, etc. We choose *NY* as the default road network to test the effect of the other parameters, which are listed in Table 4, with the default settings marked in bold.

Evaluation Criteria: To align with real-life query scenarios, we randomly extracted 1K trajectories with lengths ranging from 20 to 50 km from a real trajectory dataset [3], then use their starting and ending points as our query locations. Then, based on the dwell time of the trajectory, determine the query keywords types. Next, we record the response time for each query and the average distance of the top-k routes. All results are average from 1K queries.

Methods and Implementation Details: We implemented the following algorithms in C++ under Ubuntu 18.04 LTS, 64-bit as baselines for comparison: 1)*k-OptDist* [5]: The state-of-the-art candidate based algorithm, we modify it by searching k required POIs that can collectively cover all the needed keyword types; 2) *KOSR-MA* [13]: The state-of-the-art path expansion based algorithm in terms of query efficiency; 3) *DA-Prune* [9]: The state-of-the-art path expansion based algorithm in terms of result quality. 4) *SBE*: Algorithm 2 in our paper.

5.1 Experimental Results

Effect of $|Q_{kw}|$: Fig. 5 shows the results when varying $|Q_{kw}|$. In terms of response time (Fig. 5 (a)-(c)), in the most case, the *SBE* consistently outperforms the *KOSR-MA* and *DA-Prune*. This is because the *SBE* algorithm reduces the search space and accelerates path expansion through POI filtering and subgraph pruning strategies. In the *CAL* and *NY*, the response time of the *k-OptDist* is slightly faster than the *SBE*, because *k-OptDist* incrementally replaces POIs in a direct greedy manner, thereby overlook a large number of POI combinations. In the *COL*, the response time of the *SBE* is comparable to the *k-OptDist*, indicating that *SBE* performs efficiently in larger road networks. However, in terms of route distance (Fig. 5 (d)-(f)), the *SBE* is consistently outperforms that of all baselines. Specifically, the candidate set-based algorithm *k-OptDist* is the worst, followed by the path expansion-based algorithm *KOSR-MA*, *DA-Prune*, and our *SBE* is the best. This is because all baselines rely on greedy expansion strategies, while *SBE* uses a splice-based expansion strategy that ensures POI combination coverage and effectively improves result quality. Overall, the result quality of the *SBE* is better than that of *k-OptDist*, *KOSR-MA*, and *DA-Prune* by 33%, 28%, and 15%, respectively.

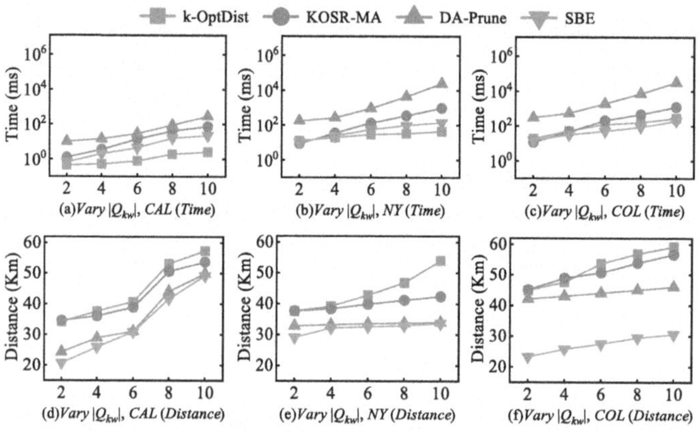

Fig. 5. Comparison of the number of various query keywords

Effect of k**:** Fig. 6 shows the results when varying the number of return routes k. In terms of response time (Fig. 6 (a)-(c)), as k increases, the response time of *KOSR-MA*, *DA-Prune*, and *SBE* slowly increases. This is because these algorithms are all based on route expansion using priority queues, and once the first feasible route is found, more valid routes can be searched with relatively low extra time cost. For *k-OptDist*, especially when $k > 5$, its response time increases significantly. While *k-OptDist* is based on the POI candidate set, and larger k results in more POI combinations, thereby increasing the time cost of top-k POI search. Specifically, the *SBE* is on average 63% faster than the *KOSR-MA* and 1–2 orders of magnitude faster than the *DA-Prune*. *k-OptDist* is initially slightly faster than *SBE*, but *SBE* eventually achieves the best performance. In terms of route distance (Fig. 6 (d)-(f)), *SBE* performs the best under all settings. This is because the *SBE* cover a wider range of POI combinations, rather than only considering the neighbor POI for each candidate path. This indicates that the *SBE* achieves better result quality.

Effect of POI Density: Fig. 7-(b) shows the results when varying the POI density. Overall, as the POI density increases, the response time of all baselines increases. This is because more POIs means more POI combinations, which require higher time costs for the search process. However, for the *SBE* algorithm, the response time initially decreases slowly and then increases gradually. This is because the number of POIs affects both the time cost of candidate set construction and the cost of path expansion. At lower densities, due to fewer POI combinations, more time is required to search for splicing the POI routes. As the POI density increases, more POI routes can satisfy the query keyword types, allowing more POI routes to be spliced, which also increases the cost of path expansion. However, in most cases, the *SBE* is still on average 80% faster than all baselines. This validates the efficiency of our algorithm, especially under higher POI density conditions.

Effect of parameter β: Fig. 7-(b) shows the effect of varying β. For response time, the variation is negligible. For result quality, experimental results demonstrate that the result quality is optimal when $\beta = 0.7$. Therefore, we set the heuristic function parameter β to 0.7.

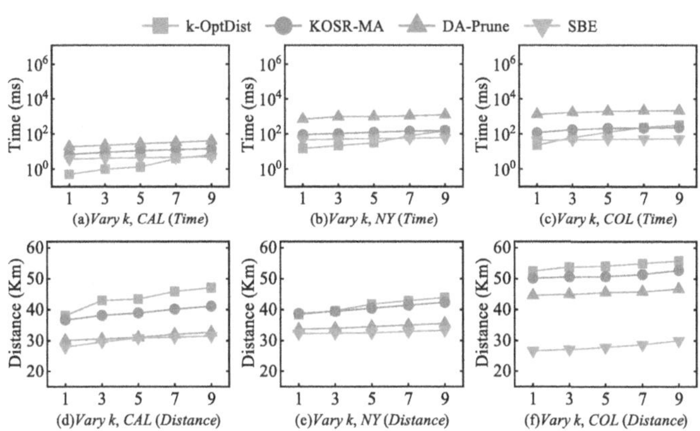

Fig. 6. Comparison of the number of k

Strategy Ablation Results: Finally, Fig. 7-(b) shows the ablation results of the optimization strategy. By removing the POI filtering strategy (*SBE-NoFilter*), the response time of the *SBE* is most significantly affected, increasing by approximately 1–2 orders of magnitude. For the case that the POI refinement strategy (*SBE-NoRefinement*) is removed, the response time also increases by an average of 62%. This is because they both lead to more POIs need to search,

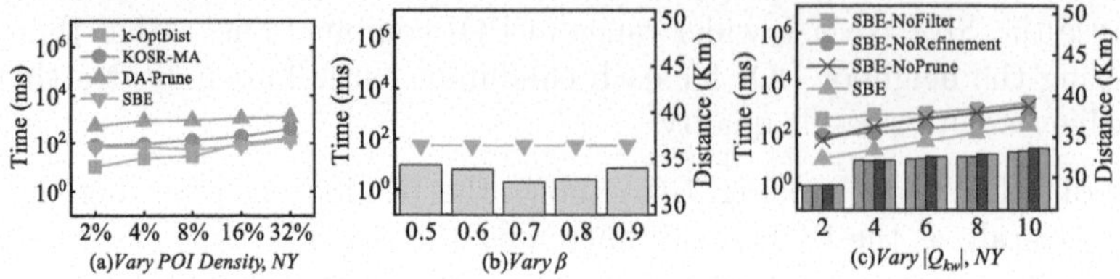

Fig. 7. Comparison of the POI Density, β and Strategy Ablation

which increase the cost of path expansion. By removing the partition pruning strategy (*SBE-NoPrune*), the response time increased by an average of 84%. Especially when $Q_{kw} = 10$, the response time increased by one order of magnitude. This is because the number of POI combinations increases exponentially with the number of query keyword types. Therefore, the more query keyword types there are, the more effective our pruning strategy becomes. Besides, the results quality of removing each optimization strategy, showing that although a large number of POIs were filtered out, the quality of the results is still ensured.

6 Conclusion

In this paper, we propose an efficient algorithm *SBE* to answer the *k-KAOR* problem. The *SBE* algorithm first filters and refines a large number of POIs by quickly constructing the feasible route. Then, we construct a keyword distance matrix to guide the splicing between different POIs. Finally, by iteratively calculating route costs and expanding the routes, until the top-k optimal routes are found. Extensive experimental validate that our algorithm outperforms other methods, both in terms of efficiency and quality.

Acknowledgments. This research was supported in part by the Key Research and Development Program of Liaoning Province under Grant No. 2023JH26/10300022, in part by the National Natural Science Foundation of China No. 52574191, 62072220 and the youth talent support program of Xing Liao Talent Program No. XLYC2203003.

References

1. 9th dimacs implementation challenge - shortest paths. http://users.diag.uniroma1.it/challenge9/download.shtml
2. Openstreetmap. https://www.openstreetmap.org/
3. Real historical trajectory data. https://transitfeeds.com/
4. Cao, X., Chen, L., Cong, G., Xiao, X.: Keyword-aware optimal route search. Proc. VLDB Endowment **5**(11) (2012)
5. Haryanto, A.A., Islam, M.S., Taniar, D., Cheema, M.A.: Ig-tree: an efficient spatial keyword index for planning best path queries on road networks. World Wide Web **22**, 1359–1399 (2019)

6. Hu, D., Chen, L., Fang, H., Fang, Z., Li, T., Gao, Y.: Spatio-temporal trajectory similarity measures: A comprehensive survey and quantitative study. TKDE (2023)
7. Li, J., An, Q., Zhao, Y., Zhu, R., Guo, N.: Keywords and stops aware optimal routes on road networks. In: APWeb-WAIM (1), pp. 299–314. Springer, Cham (2023)
8. Li, J., Hu, J., Li, L., Xiong, X., Xia, X.: Efficient multi-request route planning on road network. In: ISPA, pp. 617–624. IEEE (2020)
9. Li, J., Xiong, X., Li, L., He, D., Zong, C., Zhou, X.: Finding top-k optimal routes with collective spatial keywords on road networks. In: ICDE, IEEE (2023)
10. Li, J., Yang, Y.D., Mamoulis, N.: Optimal route queries with arbitrary order constraints. TKDE **25**(5), 1097–1110 (2012)
11. Li, W., Zhu, H., Liu, W., Yin, J., Xu, J.: Optimal sequenced route query with poi preferences. In: Jensen, C.S., et al. (eds.) DASFAA, vol. 12681, pp. 457–473. Springer, Cham (2021). https://doi.org/10.1007/978-3-030-73194-6_31
12. Liu, H., Jin, C., Yang, B., Zhou, A.: Finding top-k shortest paths with diversity. TKDE **30**(3), 488–502 (2017)
13. Liu, H., Jin, C., Yang, B., Zhou, A.: Finding top-k optimal sequenced routes. In: ICDE, pp. 569–580. IEEE (2018)
14. Lu, E.H.C., Chen, H.S., Tseng, V.S.: An efficient framework for multirequest route planning in urban environments. TITS **18**(4), 869–879 (2016)
15. Luo, C., Jin, L., Liu, Q., Gao, Y., Chen, L.: Tasks: a real-time query system for instant error-tolerant spatial keyword queries on road networks. In: ICDE. pp. 5409–5412. IEEE (2024)
16. Luo, Z., Li, L., Zhang, M., Hua, W., Xu, Y., Zhou, X.: Diversified top-k route planning in road network. VLDB, pp. 3199–3212 (2022)
17. Ouyang, D., Qin, L., Chang, L., Lin, X., Zhang, Y., Zhu, Q.: When hierarchy meets 2-hop-labeling: Efficient shortest distance queries on road networks. In: SIGMOD, pp. 709–724 (2018)
18. Selvakkumaran, N., Karypis, G.: Analysis of multilevel graph partitioning. In: Supercomputing, IEEE/ACM Sc95 Conference (1995)
19. Zheng, B., Xu, J., Lee, W.C., Lee, D.L.: Grid-partition index: a hybrid method for nearest-neighbor queries in wireless location-based services. VLDB J. **15**, 21–39 (2006)
20. Zhu, H., Li, W., Liu, W., Yin, J., Xu, J.: Top k optimal sequenced route query with poi preferences. Data Sci. Eng. **7**(1), 3–15 (2022)

Backbone-Based Neighbor Transferring Proximity Graph for Fast Inner Product Retrieval

Aoran Chen(✉), Yuchen Ji, Shengzhe Jiao, Yihong Zhang, and Takahiro Hara

The University of Osaka, 1-1 Yamadaoka, Suita, Osaka 565-0871, Japan
{aoran.chen,ji.yuchen,jiao.shengzhe,zhang.yihong,hara}@ist.osaka-u.ac.jp

Abstract. Modern recommender systems usually rely on inner product search to find relevant items. The inner product inherently considers both the norm and direction of vectors, which naturally aligns well with purchasing behavior. Unlike the metric space, the inner product space does not follow the triangle inequality and the identity of indiscernibles. This makes search in the inner product space more challenging as the neighbor transferring is not as stable as metric space, which directly affects the connectivity and efficiency of graph-based methods. Existing representative methods, including ip-nsw and its successors, are insert-based graph construction algorithms. These insert-based algorithms build the edges between non-candidate points which makes them unsuitable for maximum inner product search (MIPS). In this paper, we analyze neighbor transferring in the inner product space and find that normalized points can improve the efficiency of neighbor transferring. Based on this idea, we propose a new inner product search method that has the following advantages: (i) It constructs a highly accurate proximity graph that can help the inner product search and reduce the index size to a minimum of 1%. (ii) Good efficiency: Our algorithm is about 20% faster than other competitors with the same recall. (iii) Stable accuracy: Our algorithm can achieve good accuracy on different datasets and settings. Experiment results on different datasets demonstrate that our algorithm constantly and significantly outperforms other state-of-the-art algorithms. These advantages can significantly improve current recommender systems.

Keywords: Recommendation · maximum inner product search · approximate near neighbor search

1 Introduction

Recommender systems play a central role in modern web platforms by enabling large-scale personalization across services such as search, social feeds, and e-commerce. To support these functionalities, user and item data are projected into high-dimensional embedding spaces, where retrieving similar vectors is a core operation [31]. Users' historical actions are projected into a vector space, and

I. Awan et al. (Eds.): WISE 2025, LNCS 16368, pp. 356–371, 2026.
https://doi.org/10.1007/978-981-95-7251-9_24

matching functions retrieve their corresponding latent item vectors. Traditional matrix factorization methods laid the groundwork by mapping users and items into a shared latent space for similarity-based retrieval [8].

More recent models, such as deep learning-based approaches, further refine this by using non-linear transformations, self-attention, and contrastive learning to capture complex user-item interactions [29,30]. These advances improve embedding quality and retrieval accuracy by better aligning user preferences with relevant items. Despite evolving model architectures, the core principle remains unchanged: both users and items are projected into a shared space, and online retrieval still relies on the same vector search mechanism. In the online stage, given a user's projected vector, the system retrieves item vectors and returns those with the highest matching scores.

In current research, where demonstrating a model's peak capabilities is essential, linear search is often used as a benchmark for accuracy [8]. However, this brute-force method is too slow for large-scale recommender systems due to the vast embedding spaces. For example, datasets like MicroLens [18] and Tenrec [33] include over 5 million users and 1 million items, making exhaustive search take seconds to minutes—unacceptable for real-time services [34]. Thus, approximate search is preferred to balance accuracy and speed.

Many methods have been proposed for approximate vector search, including graph-based methods [4,5,16,19], LSH methods [21,26,27], and quantization-based methods [6,7,22]. Quantization and LSH approaches often suffer from larger index sizes and instability during training. In contrast, graph-based methods offer more efficient search and stable performance, making them well-suited for large-scale recommenders.

For metrics like cosine similarity or Euclidean distance, graph-based algorithms include NSW-based methods [16] and NN-descent methods [3]. NSW algorithms incrementally insert each vertex with a process similar to search, leveraging the *navigable small world* property. NN-descent, on the other hand, relies on the principle that *a neighbor of a neighbor is also likely to be a neighbor*, transferring neighbor information through the graph to improve recall.

The inner product is a widely used similarity metric for retrieving similar vectors in recommender systems, as it captures both the direction of the user vector and the norm of the item vector. However, it does not satisfy the triangle inequality or identity of indiscernibles, making neighbor transfers asymmetric and the approximate Maximum Inner Product Search (MIPS) problem particularly challenging. Lacking these properties, traditional approximate nearest neighbor (ANN) methods often suffer significant efficiency degradation when directly applied to MIPS. Our contributions can be summarized as follows:

- We conduct a thorough reanalysis of the differences between the maximum inner product graph and general metric similarity graphs in both the construction and search phases.
- We introduce a new framework for proximity graph building in inner product space with a neighbor transferring strategy. This framework makes the construction process of the proximity graph have a similar efficiency compared

with the metric similarity NN-descent algorithm and significantly reduces the index size.
- Extensive experiment results on 5 real datasets with different sizes and dimensionality demonstrate that our algorithm is effective and efficient for the approximate MIPS problem.

2 Preliminary

In this section, we aim to formally define the MIPS problem and provide an overview of recent advancements in related works.

2.1 Problem Setting

In the space $X \subset \mathbb{R}^d$, the dimension of queries is d. The set of the queries would be marked as $Q_u = \{q_1, q_2, ..., q_m\}$ and the set of the datasets would be marked as $D_i = \{d_1, d_2, ..., d_n\}$. The main continuous symmetric similarity function would be defined as $f : X \cdot X \longrightarrow \mathbb{R}$. With those definitions, the retrieval of the most optimal similar vectors is defined as

$$p = arg \max_{d_i \in D_i} f(d_i, q) \quad \text{for}\, q \in Q_u \tag{1}$$

As in our paper, we mainly focus on the inner product, $f(d_i, q) = d_i^\top q$. Substituting the inner product into Eq. 1 defines the Maximum Inner Product Search. Since in our algorithm, we also need to use Euclidean similarity. Here, we define Euclidean similarity: $f(d_i, q) = \sum_{j=0}^{d} -(d_{ij} - q_j)^2$.

2.2 Related Work

As the retrieval space expands, the processing time of linear search becomes prohibitively slow for real-time services. Nevertheless, researchers have continued to pursue advancements in exact search methodologies. In this domain, the focus is typically on pruning data and acceleration on matrix computation [1]. LEMP [25] mitigates the need for additional data accesses by leveraging a tree structure and using vectors' norms to transfer the problem into several cosine similarity searches. FEXIPRO [12] employs Singular Value Decomposition (SVD) with an early termination strategy and reduces the dimension that is taken into computing to enhance the performance of LEMP. Additionally, hardware-level optimizations can improve the overall computational efficiency of the algorithm, like MAXIMUS [1] accelerating with an indexing strategy of conditional pruning and OPTIMUS [1] accelerating with blocked matrix multiply skill. Although these exact MIPS methods are significantly more efficient than brute-force scanning, they remain suitable only for datasets of moderate size and dimensionality.

Previous studies on approximate MIPS did not fully align with traditional approximate nearest neighbor (ANN) methods in metric spaces, though their categories remain analogous. Both ANN and MIPS approaches include LSH-based [21,26,32], graph-based [3,19,24], tree-based [9,14], and quantization-based methods [6,7,11]. Recent research [13]has shown that in many recommendation datasets, norms follow a pronounced long-tail distribution, causing most MIPS candidates to cluster around points with larger norms. Based on this insight, several approaches partition data by norm.

Hash-based algorithms have advanced with the growing importance of query-based hashing [26]. Significant progress in random projections and multi-probing has led to methods like Range-LSH [32] and FARGO [36]. In parallel, quantization-based methods have also evolved, with recent trends focusing on learning-based or adaptive quantization techniques to improve accuracy [22]. current hashing and quantization approaches often target ultra-high-dimensional [28] or sparse representations [35], which, despite their theoretical appeal, remain inefficient in recommender systems.

Graph-based algorithms have shown excellent performance in metric similarity. The use of proximity graphs in inner product spaces emerged later. Early methods like ip-nsw [17] applied the NSW strategy by replacing the metric distance with the inner product. Many improvements have built on this, such as ip-nsw+ [13], which uses a cosine proximity graph to generate candidates for NSW search. IPDG [24] and NAPG [23] further refine edge pruning and connection rules: IPDG removes low-norm points, while NAPG introduces a hyperparameter to decide edge inclusion. Generally, graph-based methods share two main steps: (i) offline proximity graph construction, and (ii) online greedy search on the graph (Algorithm 1). The key difference lies in how the proximity graph is built.

In general, for all graph-based algorithms, there are two main steps for handling the ANN problems: (i) the offline step, building a proximity graph, and (ii) the online step, using the greedy search algorithm searching on the graph (Algorithm 1). Thus, the key distinction is in how the proximity graph is constructed.

2.3 Limitations of NSW-Based Algorithms in Inner Product Space

The NSW-based algorithm greedily builds the graph. After inserting the first vertex into the graph, every other vertex uses the greedy search to find the vertices that have the most suitable candidates from the existing graph and insert the vertices into the graph (Algorithm 2).

However, the limitations of insert-based graph construction prevent the NSW-based algorithm from inherently determining whether the insertion point itself is a true MIPS candidate. As shown in Fig. 1a, we can observe that, in the case of ℓ_2 similarity, changing the insertion order results in only limited changes to the set of affected neighbors. On the contrary, in Fig. 1b, we can see that if we insert an MIPS candidate, the insertion of an MIPS candidate will result in a significantly broader range of affected neighbors These factors severely undermine the quality of graph construction. Inserting MIPS candidates during the

Algorithm 1. Greedy Search Algorithm

Input: The query q_i, the proximity graph G, the searching parameter for cache size k

Initialize Candidate set $C \leftarrow \emptyset$
Randomly choose k vertices $d \in D_i$ as unchecked.
while Exist c in C marked as unchecked **do**
  Pick the c with the highest inner product with q_i
  Set c into checked.
  Compute c's neighbors' inner product with q_i
  $C \leftarrow$ suitable amount of new candidates
end while

Output: Candidate set C

Algorithm 2. NSW-based algorithm

Input: The dataset D_i, the maximum vertex degree M, the searching parameter during building's searching k

Initialize graph $G \leftarrow \emptyset$
for each d in D_i **do**
  Canditate set $C \leftarrow \emptyset$
  $C \leftarrow$ Greedy search on index Graph G by Greedy algorithm
  for each c in C **do**
    if between c and d could update a better edge **then**
      add d in to graph G and connect with c
    end if
  end for
end for

Output: the proximity graph G

final phase of graph construction may significantly degrade the overall quality of the resulting graph.

2.4 Why NN-Descent Fails in Inner Product Space

The NN-descent algorithm iteratively updates the neighbor information of each point by exploring the neighbors of its current neighbors. Each point undergoes a conditional greedy random walk [20]. Due to random walk properties, this process efficiently reaches unvisited points that meet specified conditions, with more similar points encountered sooner. In [3], the authors use an R-ball tree to describe the neighbor information exchange process in the NN-descent algorithm. While the principles discussed thus far apply to metric spaces, the shift to inner product spaces introduces additional complexities. The $B_r(v)$ set with the R-ball tree based on the similarity functions' radius in metric space. Therefore, the inner product space could not be established. With the main conceptions not satisfied in inner product spaces, the NN-descent without changes does not work well in this situation.

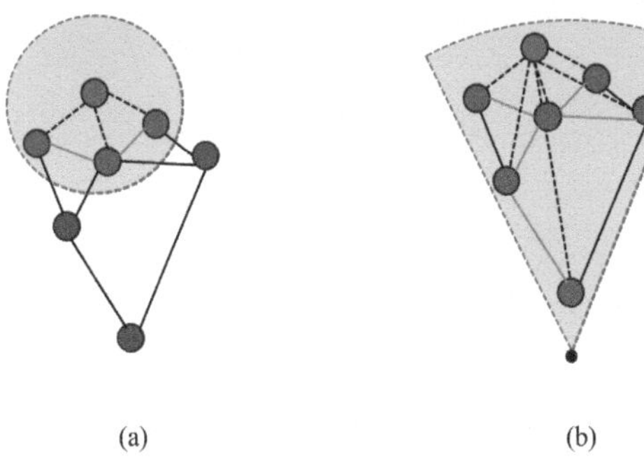

Fig. 1. NSW-based methods work poorly in inner product space. (a) An insertion in Euclidean space. (b) An insertion in the inner product space. The red points are the insertions. The green points are the points that need to change their neighbors. The blue ones are the points that do not need to change and the purple lines are the edges that need to be changed. (Color figure online)

Algorithm 3. Simple NN-descent Algorithm

Input: The dataset D_i, the maximum vertex degree M

Initialize graph $G \leftarrow \emptyset$
Randomly choose k vertices $d \in D_i$ for each d as neighbors
while Conditions for early stop or iteration for required times **do**
    Reserve edges from neighbors for add vertices d_i in D_i
    for all All vertices d_i in D_i **do**
        Updating d_i with their neighbors' neighbor in G
    end for
end while

Output: the proximity graph G

---

3 Backbone Based NN-Descent

Motivated by the insights from our previous analysis of the limitations inherent in NSW-based approaches and the strengths of NN-descent-based methods, we introduce a novel NN-descent-based algorithm that optimally leverages these advantages.

3.1 A New Perspective on NN-Descent

In previous analysis, we noted that the R-ball model does not fit well in the inner product setting. Instead, the descent model more accurately explains the mechanism of NN-descent under inner product similarity. By focusing on the neighbors randomly assigned to each point and the trajectories of their transfers, we can view each assigned neighbor as a starting point: local minima correspond to points that stop updating or are replaced, while the global minimum is the accurate neighbor graph. Each neighbor transfer resembles a descent process, moving toward closer points. Figure 2 illustrates the local minima situations

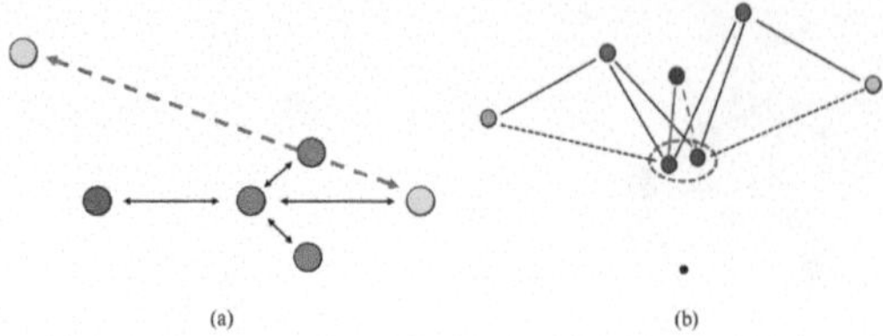

Fig. 2. The samples for ℓ_2 distance's basin of attraction and Inner product distance's basin of attraction. (a) is the situation in ℓ_2 distance when the left yellow point has no path to reach the left red point to update the correct neighbor. (b) is the situation in Inner product distance, when the left blue point could not pass the purple point to the right one as they do not build edges between each other. (Color figure online)

under ℓ_2 and inner product distances. In the inner product case, most points tend to select neighbors with higher norms, causing connections to easily get trapped in local minima. To address this, incorporating additional structures to reduce norm influence could be an effective approach.

3.2 Formalization and Proof

From the previous analysis, we find that the inner product metric have more local minima compared with other metric which makes the importance of reduce the basin of attraction which contains local minimum. First, before diving into the topic of reduction, proving the idealized scenario where local minima do not exist could provide a more stable starting point.

Theorem 1. *Suppose that there exists a K monotony neighbors graph k-G, for each point having at most edges K with other points in the dataset. If we construct a new graph in which each point is randomly assigned neighbors and uses the K-G to transfer the neighbors' information, the new graph will still converge to a KNN graph and have a similar quality to an NN-descent graph.*

Proof. The proof is similar to the one provided by the NN-descent paper and partially provided in Sect. 2.4. We just need to substitute the vertex neighbors with the monotony neighbors graph k-G. Randomly choosing the point to start is similar to using a half-radius of the whole dataset's diameter to scan.

From Theorem 1, we have an efficient way of transferring information which in other words reduces the number of basin of attraction, even though we have different measures, the conclusion provided by NN-descent to construct a high-quality graph still works. Consequently, we need to prove that normalized vectors' neighbors would be a better graph for transferring neighbors than directly using MIPS neighbors. In other words, we aim to establish the possibility that normalized vectors are more likely to share MIPS neighbors than their MIPS neighbors.

Theorem 2. *Suppose we have two measures in the same space* $\mathbb{R}^d$ *for* d *dimensions. We have a dataset (item embedding)* D_i*, and a new dataset is noted as* $D_i^{'}$ *that contains all data points in* D_i *after normalization. Using Euclidean similarity measure, we could build a neighbor graph with* $D_i^{'}$ *as a graph* G_e^k *with* k *neighbors and use the inner product measure with* D_i *as a graph* $G_i^{k'}$ *with* k *neighbors. Then we have* B_i *for the neighbors of every point in* G_e^k *and we have the* $B_i^{k'}$ *for the neighbors of every point in* $G_i^{k'}$*. Define a function* $f(g_i) =$ *the inner product neighbors of the point. We have the conclusion for the neighbor similarity that* $P(\left|\sum_{j=1}^{k} f(g_e^k) \bigcap B_i(g_e^k)_j\right| - \left|\sum_{j=1}^{k} f(g_e^{k'}) \bigcap B_i(g_e^{k'})_j\right|) > 0$ *which means that normalized Euclidean neighbors would share more inner product neighbors compared with original inner product neighbors.*

Proof. Here, we need to provide a lemma to start our proof.

Lemma 1. *If two data points in* D_i a *and* b *are normalized to* $a^{'}$ *and* $b^{'}$ *in* $D_i^{'}$*, then the similarity of their inner product neighbors is independent of the norm.*

It is simple to prove, as we just need to consider two situations to determine if one of the two points would be the MIPS candidate. Whether the point is a candidate or not doesn't affect the conclusion. If two points have the same output after normalization, their MIPS neighbors will be exactly the same as well. After this lemma, we could expand it. Here we first set data point $a^{'}$ as the unit vector and provide a projection for $b^{'}$ to $a^{'}$. With the projection, we could split $b^{'}$ into two parts, $b_1^{'}$ and $b_2^{'}$ where $b_1^{'}$ is the projection part to the $a^{'}$ and $b_2^{'}$ is the part that is linearly different from $a^{'}$. Then, we could write the further proof with another lemma.

Lemma 2. *If we have two data points in* D_i a *and* b *and their normalizations* $a^{'}$ *and* $b^{'}$ *in* $D_i^{'}$*, their MIPS neighbors difference could be judged by a projection transfer for* $b^{'}$ *on* $a^{'}$*, where* $b_1^{'}$ *is the projection part and the* $b_2^{'}$ *is the linearly different part. The part that makes* a *and* b*'s MIPS neighbors different is based on the* $b_2^{'}$ *with Lemma 1.*

By applying Lemma 2 and combining it with Theorem 1 in [13], we can conclude that the larger the linearly independent component, the greater the variation in the probabilities of MIPS neighbors differing.

Based on those two theorems, Using the Euclidean neighbor after normalization is more reasonable as it could reduce the amount of basin of attractions, as normalized Euclidean neighbors could cover more of the same neighbors. This property provides a Euclidean neighbor graph for neighbor transferring, which could help the original NN-descent algorithm to build a high-quality proximity graph for MIPS searching.

3.3 Implementations

We show our framework in Algorithm 4. To build a high-quality and accurate graph, we start building the graph for neighbor transferring with the original NN-descent algorithm (line 1–3 in Algorithm 4). Instead of letting all vertices share their MIPS neighbors which wastes a computation as we previously analyzed in Theorem 2, the normalized Euclidean neighbor has more overlapping neighbors which make the step of sharing neighbor (line 7–12 in Algorithm 4) more efficient. Unlike the original NN descent, providing a reverse edge to the linked point in the updating process which helps every point improve the diversity of the neighbors, our algorithm optimizes the strategy to make it more suitable for MIPS A further step needs to be provided, as the words *the higher your norm is, the more attention you could receive.* We reverse the edge if a point has a larger norm than its connected neighbor. This prevents high-norm points from becoming MIPS neighbors for many others and wasting resources on reverse edge computations. Since many connections to high-norm points are likely meaningless, we filter reverses based on this condition. By controlling the number of reverse edges, we improved efficiency compared to algorithms without this filtering.

Algorithm 4. Backbone based NN-descent

Input: The dataset D_i, the maximum vertex degree M
1: Initialize graph $G_e \leftarrow \emptyset$
2: Normalize all data points $d \in D_i$ to make a new dataset D_{ni}
3: Create an Euclidean neighbor graph with Algorithm 3 and D_{ni} called G_e
4: Initialize graph $G \leftarrow \emptyset$
5: Randomly choose k vertices $d \in D_i$ for each d as neighbors
6: **while** Reached proposed accuracy or reached maximum iterations **do**
7:   **for all** All vertices d_i in D_i **do**
8:     Updating d_i with their neighbors' neighbor in G
9:     **if** norm $d_i >$ d_i's neighbor's norm **then**
10:       Adding the reverse edge to the neighbor
11:     **end if**
12:   **end for**
13: **end while**
Output: the proximity inner product graph G

The index construction complexity of our algorithm is similar to the original NN-descent algorithm in metric spaces. The index size is less than twice that of a standard K-nearest neighbor graph, as we require a normalized graph for neighbor transferring. However, the graph does not need to maintain the same number of neighbors, since smaller degrees do not significantly impact efficiency or accuracy for inner product graphs, similar to using a lower-accuracy graph as discussed earlier. These additional complexities have minimal effect on construction time, as NN-descent in Euclidean space can build highly accurate graphs within about 10 iterations. We demonstrate this empirically in Sect. 4.5. With a highly accurate graph, most inner product graphs can also be constructed in no more iterations. Unlike most existing proximity-graph-based algorithms, which rely on insert-based NSW, our approach uses neighbor transferring, offering a new paradigm that may inspire future research.

4 Experiments

We evaluate our algorithm on five datasets of varying sizes and dimensions to comprehensively assess its performance.

4.1 Datasets

We have 5 datasets, the first 3 are the common datasets with different characterizations, two of which are high-dimensional, demonstrating the potential of our algorithm in other deep learning areas. In recommender systems, embedding dimensions over 100 capture high information entropy, enabling robust representation of complex relationships. Using the 100 dimensions angular datasets[1], the experiment result could prove that our algorithm can achieve strong performance even in modern, high-dimensional recommendation settings.

To ensure that our algorithm is suitable for a recommender system, we use Matrix factorization (MF) with Amazon Moive[2]. We utilize the implementation to generate the vectors for users and items, using the items as the dataset and using the users as the query. To make the experiment more convincing, we use two embedding sizes for those two Amazon datasets with 32 dimensions and 64 dimensions to show the efficiency of our algorithm in most recommender systems' retrieve tasks (Table 1).

Table 1. Dataset Statistics.

	amazonMF32	amazonMF64	angular-25	angular-100	MNIST
Items	120328	119241	1,183,514	1,183,514	60,000
Dimensions	32	64	25	100	784

4.2 Baseline

As baselines, we choose some representative state-of-the-art MIPS algorithms in different categories to evaluate the proposed method.

- Ip-nsw+ is one of state-of-the-art graph-based algorithms [13]. In the ip-NSW paper [17], they mentioned that HNSW, which performs well on general distance metrics, does not achieve effective performance in inner product search. The authors use another layer of cosine similarity to improve the search efficiency.

[1] https://nlp.stanford.edu/projects/glove/.

[2] https://cseweb.ucsd.edu/~jmcauley/datasets.html.

- Range-LSH, is a hash-based method and outperforms previous hash-based methods for MIPS [32]. In the previous plan, we hope to compare with the latest hash-based method FRAGO [36]. However, without using AVX512, a powerful Single Instruction Multiple Data(SIMD) instruction set, the performance of FRAGO is not as good as Range-LSH. Therefore, we pick Range-LSH as the hash-based state-of-the-art algorithm.
- NEQ [2] and scaNN [22] are SOTA quantization-based methods. Quantization-based algorithms use codebooks to reduce the dimensions. NEQ focused on inner product area optimization and scaNN focus on optmizing training result. Therefore, we pick NEQ and as the quantization-based baselines.

4.3 Experimental Settings

The experiments were conducted on a machine with Intel Core i7-12700KF latest update which does not provide AVX-512 and 128 GB memory. In all the experiments, we allow the offline stage like graph building or norm-based rearranging to run on multi-core mode and the online stage, searching, on single-core mode. All comparing methods have parameters that could provide the trade-off between the search speed and accuracy. We adjust all parameters across a detailed grid for each method to ensure a fair comparison.

We use the Top-10 MIPS as the target performance metric, as the recommender systems would normally use recall 10 as its experimental result. For the top-K, the comparison would be the algorithm result with the top-k ground truth, as $recall = |R_{query} \cap R_{groundtruth}| / k$. We present the algorithm's performance in terms of queries per second (QPS) and the corresponding recall.

4.4 Performance Evaluation

From the experiments, we could see that our algorithms work best in most of the cases in Fig. 3. The figure shows that high recall levels [15], such as 88% to 95%, are meaningful to the recommender system's real applications. Besides, our algorithm works robustly on different kinds of vectors in different dimensions. In Amazon datasets and glove datasets, our algorithm provides a distinct advantage in searching performance compared with both graph-based algorithms and quantization-based algorithms. We found that the previous state-of-the-art graph algorithm and quantization-based algorithms achieved varying results, with each outperforming the other in certain cases. The only case where our algorithm does not perform outstandingly is on the MNIST dataset, primarily due to its extremely high dimensionality. Quantization-based algorithms, which reduce dimensionality, can significantly lower the cost of distance computation, offering an advantage in this context. However, in standard recommender systems, embeddings with over 700 dimensions are rarely used. We use the MNIST dataset for the experiment and it shows that our algorithm still works robustly and has competitive performance.

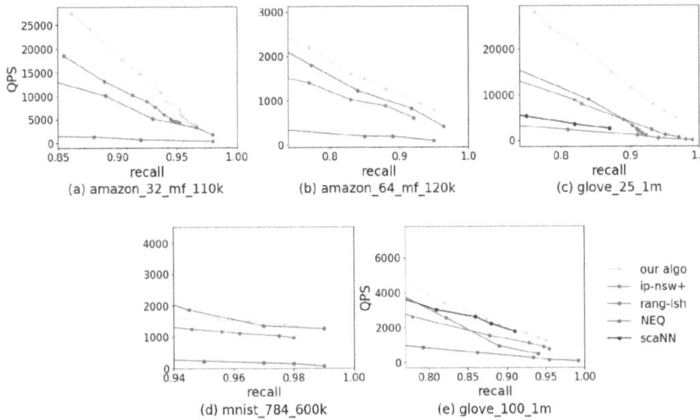

Fig. 3. The comparisons via Recall vs. QPS for all methods, based on top-10.

On the contrary, no baseline works consistently well on different sizes of the dataset. Due to common limitations inherent in graph-based methods, performance tends to degrade as the dataset scales. The hash-based algorithm provides great performance when constructing the index. However, their search performance falls short. The strengths of quantization-based algorithms are complementary to those of hash-based methods. The long training duration naturally limits its applicability in recommender systems. Due to its high training overhead and limited robustness on small datasets, ScaNN is evaluated only on the largest benchmarks. While a fully tuned ScaNN may achieve performance close to ours in certain cases, our method still maintains a consistent advantage. For moderate embedding sizes, quantization approaches both extends training time unnecessarily and achieves lower search efficiency compared to graph-based methods. It might be better to combine quantization-based algorithms with graph-based when the data size and dimensions are relatively large [10].

4.5 Graph Accuracy Evaluation

In this section, we would like to analyze the quality of the graph. In Sect. 3.3, we make the statement that using an inexact normalized graph would not hurt the graph's accuracy. We limited the iteration amount in building the normalized graph to compare the graph accuracy in Fig. 4 (b). We could find that the quality of the normalized graph does affect the upper bound of the graph accuracy. The influence is lower than expected because the number of MIPS candidates is relatively small, allowing many neighbors to provide similar information. As a result, the case that even half of the neighbors are not the closest does not significantly impact the overall performance, as other neighbors could provide the MIPS neighbor information as well. Without a correct way to transfer neighbor information, the original NN-descent is significantly degraded, which results in a markedly low accuracy. Furthermore, we analyze the search recall's relationship

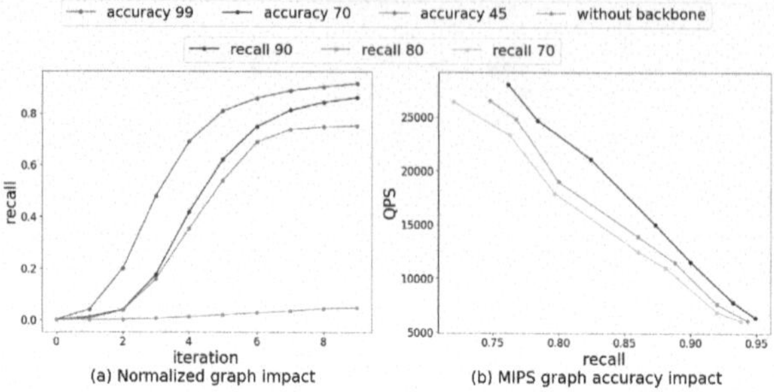

Fig. 4. (a) Study of graph accuracy with different backbone graph accuracies. (b) Study of the influence of MIPS graph accuracy on search efficiency.

with the graph accuracy. We can observe that the accuracy of the graph is closely tied to the search efficiency, especially in the advantage range of our algorithm, between 85% and 90%. We can find that compared with 70% accurate, 90% accurate would have a 25% advantage in search efficiency in 85% recall. As in a more accurate result, the searching cache would have more impact compared with the graph accuracy.

4.6 Index Compression Evaluation

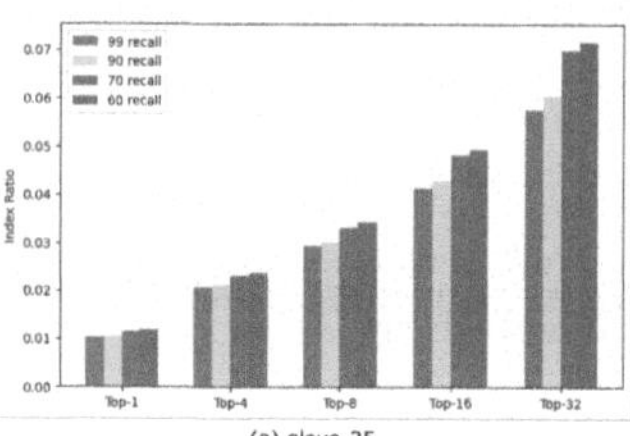

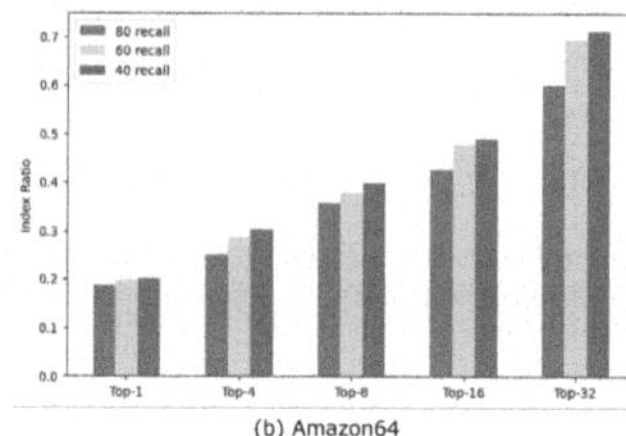

Fig. 5. Impact of Accuracy on Required Points Ratio in angular-25 and amazonMF64.

As in the previous analysis, we have the hypothesis that many points would never be selected as results in many search conditions. From Fig. 5, we could find that our hypothesis is correct. Regardless of the dimensionality of the data, a high-precision graph will always help us filter out the points that won't be search results. From Fig. 5 (a), our algorithms provide extremely high filtering efficiency in low dimensions and large data volumes. It can be observed that even as the search scope expands from Top-1 to Top-32, in a 25-dimensional space with a dataset of one million points, only 1–5% of the data points contribute to the final search results. Figure 5 (b), shows that our algorithm remains effective in mainstream recommender system settings, such as those with a dimensionality of 64. Based on this observation, we hypothesize that applying our algorithm to large-scale recommender systems would enable substantial data filtering, preventing a significant portion of the dataset from entering the search process. This, in turn, would reduce memory requirements for search operations.

5 Conclusion

Fast inner product search is an important topic for modern recommender systems. In this paper, we provide clear proof that normalized vectors provide a better inner product neighbor transfer. This could help us build a high-quality inner product graph without many useless edges provided by insert-based graph algorithms. We use this property to build a new algorithm that could avoid traveling on those non-MIPS candidate points. Experimental results show that our algorithm outperformed the state-of-the-art graph algorithm. With our algorithm, the recommender system will spend less time on the retrieval tasks, significantly improving the system's overall efficiency and responsiveness.

References

1. Abuzaid, F., Sethi, G., Bailis, P., Zaharia, M.: To index or not to index: Optimizing exact maximum inner product search. In: 2019 IEEE 35th International Conference on Data Engineering (ICDE), pp. 1250–1261. IEEE (2019)
2. Dai, X., Yan, X., Ng, K.K., Liu, J., Cheng, J.: Norm-explicit quantization: Improving vector quantization for maximum inner product search. In: Proceedings of the AAAI Conference on Artificial Intelligence (2020)
3. Dong, W., Moses, C., Li, K.: Efficient k-nearest neighbor graph construction for generic similarity measures. In: Proceedings of the 20th international Conference on World Wide Web (2011)
4. Fu, C., Wang, C., Cai, D.: High dimensional similarity search with satellite system graph: Efficiency, scalability, and unindexed query compatibility. IEEE Trans. Pattern Anal. Mach. Intell. (2021)
5. Fu, C., Xiang, C., Wang, C., Cai, D.: Fast approximate nearest neighbor search with the navigating spreading-out graph. arXiv:1707.00143
6. Guo, R., et al.: Accelerating large-scale inference with anisotropic vector quantization. In: International Conference on Machine Learning, pp. 3887–3896. PMLR (2020)
7. Hae-Chan, N., Taeho, K.: Product quantizer aware inverted index for scalable nearest neighbor search. In: CVF International Conference on Computer Vision, ICCV (2021)
8. He, X., Liao, L., Zhang, H., Nie, L., Hu, X., Chua, T.S.: Neural collaborative filtering. WWW '17, International World Wide Web Conferences Steering Committee
9. Hirata, K., Amagata, D., Hara, T.: Cardinality estimation in inner product space. IEEE Open J. Comput. Soc. **3**, 208–216 (2022)
10. Jayaram Subramanya, S., Devvrit, F., Simhadri, H.V., Krishnawamy, R., Kadekodi, R.: Diskann: Fast accurate billion-point nearest neighbor search on a single node. Adv. Neural Inf. Process. Syst. **32** (2019)

11. Johnson, J., Douze, M., Jégou, H.: Billion-scale similarity search with gpus. IEEE Trans. Big Data **7**(3), 535–547 (2019)
12. Li, H., Chan, T.N., Yiu, M.L., Mamoulis, N.: Fexipro: fast and exact inner product retrieval in recommender systems. In: Proceedings of the 2017 ACM International Conference on Management of Data, pp. 835–850 (2017)
13. Liu, J., Yan, X., Dai, X., Li, Z., Cheng, J., Yang, M.C.: Understanding and improving proximity graph based maximum inner product search. In: Proceedings of the AAAI Conference on Artificial Intelligence (2020)
14. Ma, H., Li, J., Zhang, Y.: Reconsidering tree based methods for k-maximum inner-product search: The lrus-covertree. In: 2024 IEEE 40th International Conference on Data Engineering (ICDE). IEEE (2024)
15. Malkov, Y.A., Yashunin, D.A.: Efficient and robust approximate nearest neighbor search using hierarchical navigable small world graphs. IEEE Trans. Pattern Anal. Mach. Intell. (2018)
16. Malkov, Y., Ponomarenko, A., Krylov, V.: Approximate nearest neighbor algorithm based on navigable small world graphs. Inf. Syst. (2014)
17. Morozov, S., Babenko, A.: Non-metric similarity graphs for maximum inner product search. Adv. Neural Inf. Process. Syst. **31** (2018)
18. Ni, Y., et al.: A content-driven micro-video recommendation dataset at scale. arXiv preprint arXiv:2309.15379 (2023)
19. Ootomo, H., Naruse, A., Nolet, C., Wang, R., Feher, T., Wang, Y.: Cagra: highly parallel graph construction and approximate nearest neighbor search for gpus. In: 2024 IEEE 40th International Conference on Data Engineering (ICDE)
20. Orenshtein, T., Shinkar, I.: Greedy random walk. Comb. Probab. Comput. (2014)
21. Paulevé, L., Jégou, H., Amsaleg, L.: Locality sensitive hashing: A comparison of hash function types and querying mechanisms. Pattern Recogn. Lett. (2010)
22. Sun, P., Simcha, D., Dopson, D., Guo, R., Kumar, S.: Soar: Improved indexing for approximate nearest neighbor search. In: Neural Information Processing Systems (2023)
23. Tan, S., Xu, Z., Zhao, W., Fei, H., Zhou, Z., Li, P.: Norm adjusted proximity graph for fast inner product retrieval. In: Proceedings of the 27th ACM SIGKDD Conference on Knowledge Discovery & Data Mining, pp. 1552–1560 (2021)
24. Tan, S., Zhou, Z., Xu, Z., Li, P.: On efficient retrieval of top similarity vectors. In: Proceedings of the 2019 Conference on Empirical Methods in Natural Language Processing and the 9th International Joint Conference on Natural Language Processing (EMNLP-IJCNLP) (2019)
25. Teflioudi, C., Gemulla, R., Mykytiuk, O.: Lemp: Fast retrieval of large entries in a matrix product. In: Proceedings of the 2015 ACM SIGMOD International Conference on Management of Data (2015)
26. Tian, Y., Zhao, X., Zhou, X.: DB-LSH: locality-sensitive hashing with query-based dynamic bucketing. In: ICDE, pp. 2250–2262 (2022)
27. Tian, Y., Zhao, X., Zhou, X.: Db-lsh2.0: locality-sensitive hashing with query-based dynamic bucketing. IEEE Trans. Knowl. Data Eng. (2023)
28. Tiwari, M., et al.: In: Proceedings of the 41st International Conference on Machine Learning. ICML'24
29. Veličković, P., Cucurull, G., Casanova, A., Romero, A., Liò, P.: Graph attention networks. In: International Conference on Learning Representations (2018)
30. Wang, X., He, X., Cao, Y., Liu, M., Chua, T.S.: Kgat: knowledge graph attention network for recommendation. In: Proceedings of the 25th ACM SIGKDD International Conference on Knowledge Discovery & Data Mining. KDD '19, Association for Computing Machinery (2019)

31. Xu, J., He, X., Li, H.: Deep learning for matching in search and recommendation. In: The 41st International ACM SIGIR Conference on Research & Development in Information Retrieval, pp. 1365–1368 (2018)
32. Yan, X., Li, J., Dai, X., Chen, H., Cheng, J.: Norm-ranging lsh for maximum inner product search. Adv. Neural Inf. Process. Syst. **31** (2018)
33. Yuan, G., et al.: Tenrec: A large-scale multipurpose benchmark dataset for recommender systems. In: Thirty-sixth Conference on Neural Information Processing Systems Datasets and Benchmarks Track (2022)
34. Zhang, H., et al.: Cafe: Towards compact, adaptive, and fast embedding for large-scale recommendation models. Proc. ACM Manage. Data (2024)
35. Zhao, X., Chen, Z., Huang, K., Zhang, R., Zheng, B., Zhou, X.: Efficient approximate maximum inner product search over sparse vectors. In: 2024 IEEE 40th International Conference on Data Engineering (ICDE) (2024)
36. Zhao, X., et al.: FARGO: fast maximum inner product search via global multi-probing. PVLDB (2023)

Graph Models and Methods

Counting the Number of Hop-Constrained Simple S-T Paths in Large Graphs

Bocheng Han, Zebin Chen, Yi Ding, Weizhang Jiang, Yizhe Zhang, John Shepherd, Dong Wen, and Zhengyi Yang(✉)

University of New South Wales, Sydney, Australia
{bocheng.han,zebin.chen1,yi.k.ding,weizhang.jiang,yizhe.zhang1, john.shepherd,dong.wen,zhengyi.yang}@unsw.edu.au

Abstract. Graphs are widely used to model complex relationships among entities in domains such as recommendation systems and social networks. A fundamental problem in these applications is quantifying the connectivity between two entities, often formulated as estimating the number of source-to-target (s–t) paths under specific constraints. In this paper, we study the problem of hop-constrained s–t path counting, which aims to estimate the number of paths from a source vertex s to a target vertex t within a given hop bound k. We propose *kPathAssess*, an efficient path counting algorithm inspired by the recent *PathAssess* algorithm. *kPathAssess* balances estimation accuracy and computational complexity by leveraging locally computable lower bounds on path counts. Extensive experiments on real-world graphs demonstrate that *kPathAssess* achieves high estimation efficiency with significantly reduced computation time, particularly as the hop constraint increases.

Keywords: Graph Analysis · Path Counting · Hop-Constrained Path Counting

1 Introduction

Graph-structured data are ubiquitous in modern applications, and analyzing connectivity via paths is a fundamental task [14]. Understanding how pairs of vertices are connected through paths is fundamental in various fields, such as communication networks, social networks, and biological networks [2,3,6]. Counting simple paths between a source s and a target t is a classic $\#P$-hard problem [16,20], but it reveals important connectivity information. Recent work has focused on estimating the number of paths without requiring full enumeration. Notably, Punzi et al. [15] propose a polynomial-time algorithm that estimates the total number of s–t paths by utilizing graph decomposition techniques. This approach transforms the challenging task of listing all paths into a more manageable computation. It primarily focuses on unconstrained paths and does not account for hop constraints, which are crucial in various applications such as recommendation systems and influence modeling. In these contexts, interactions typically occur within a limited number of steps. When hop constraints are introduced, the problem of counting paths becomes computationally expensive. Naive

I. Awan et al. (Eds.): WISE 2025, LNCS 16368, pp. 375–387, 2026.
https://doi.org/10.1007/978-981-95-7251-9_25

methods, such as calculations of recursive adjacency matrix [9,22] or exhaustive enumeration [8,10,18,19], become impractical even for moderate graphs. Furthermore, while some algorithms [1,12,13,18] can enumerate hop-constrained paths with polynomial delays, they often suffer from excessive memory usage and slow runtime, especially when the number of paths is large. As a result, estimating the number of hop-constrained paths continues to be a challenging and unresolved issue.

In this paper, we study the problem of estimating hop-constrained s–t path counting. More specifically, given a graph G, a source vertex s, and a target vertex t, our goal is to efficiently estimate the number of paths between s and t.

Motivation. Despite significant advances in path enumeration and counting, current methods still face challenges when applied to large-scale graphs and hop-constrained scenarios. Two key challenges arise: (1) the number of simple s–t paths grows exponentially with graph size, rendering exact counting infeasible even on moderate graphs; (2) classical approaches, including recursive traversal [10,19] and matrix-based techniques [9,22], require explicit enumeration, while dedicated hop-constrained algorithms [1,18] often incur prohibitive time costs. These challenges highlight the need for scalable algorithms to estimate the number of hop-bounded paths without resorting to exhaustive enumeration.

Applications. Hop-constrained path counting is valuable in domains where local connectivity dominates. By restricting path length, it emphasizes nearby interactions while ignoring tenuous long-range links.

Social networks. Short-hop paths capture close contacts that typically drive strong social influence, while longer indirect ties are less relevant.

E-commerce. In recommendation graphs, short-hop paths between users and items indicate stronger purchasing intent or product similarity. Limiting path length filters noisy indirect associations, improving relevance and accuracy.

Our Approach and Contributions. We propose *kPathAssess*, an estimation framework for hop-constrained path counting inspired by *PathAssess*. The method operates in three stages: (1) a bidirectional BFS extracts a k-bounded subgraph to reduce the search space; (2) preprocessing verifies connectivity and reindexes nodes; (3) a modified *PathAssess* is applied with a restriction on the number of biconnected components considered, ensuring compliance with the hop limit. This design enables efficient lower-bound estimation without full enumeration and scales to large graphs. Our contributions are as follows:

- We formally define the problem of estimating hop-constrained path counts, complementing existing enumeration methods such as PathEnum [18].
- We develop *kPathAssess*, a framework that extends path counting to provide efficient lower-bound estimation under hop constraints.
- We present extensive experiments on real-world graphs, showing that *kPathAssess* outperforms PathEnum, particularly for larger k, with significant gains in runtime and scalability.

Paper Outline. In Sect. 2 we formally define the hop-constrained s–t path counting problem. Section 3 reviews the *PathAssess* algorithm for the unconstrained s–t path counting problem and introduces the key data structures. In

Sect. 4 we review other related work on path counting and enumeration. In Sect. 5 we present our approach *kPathAssess*. Section 6 reports the experimental evaluation. Finally, Sect. 7 concludes the paper.

2 Preliminary

We define a graph as $G = (V, E)$, where V is a set of vertices (or nodes), and $E \subseteq V \times V$ is a set of edges connecting pairs of vertices. In this paper, we consider graphs are undirected and unweighted unless explicitly mentioned otherwise. To formally describe our problem setting, we begin by introducing the basic concepts of paths and hop constraints used throughout this paper.

Definition 1 (Path). *A path p in G is a sequence of vertices $(v_0, v_1, \ldots, v_k)$ such that each pair $(v_i, v_{i+1}) \in E$. The length of a path is defined as the number of edges. A path p is a* ***simple path*** *if all vertices on the path are distinct.*

Definition 2 (s–t Simple Path). *Given two distinct vertices $s, t \in V$, an s–t* ***simple path*** *is defined as a sequence of distinct vertices beginning at vertex s and ending at vertex t, such that consecutive vertices are connected by edges. Formally, an s–t path p can be expressed as: $p = (s, v_1, v_2, \ldots, t)$, where$(v_i, v_{i+1}) \in E$. The length of a path is the number of edges in p.*

Definition 3 (Hop-Constrained s–t Path). *A hop-constrained s–t path is a simple s–t path whose length is at most k, for a given hop bound k. The set of such paths is denoted as $P_{s,t}^{\leq k}(G)$.*

<u>Problem Definition</u>. (Hop-Constrained s–t Path Counting). Given a graph $G = (V, E)$, two vertices $s, t \in V$, and an integer hop constraint k, the hop-constrained path counting problem aims to compute the number of simple s–t paths of length at most k. Formally, the goal is to compute: $|P_{s,t}^{\leq k}(G)|$

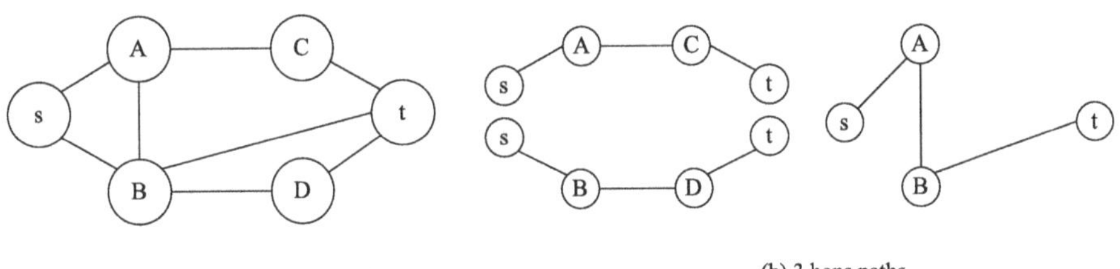

Fig. 1. An undirected graph with hop limit $k = 3$ for s–t path counting.

Example 1. Consider the undirected graph shown in Fig. 1(a). Suppose the hop limit is $k = 3$. Then, we count all simple paths from s to t whose length is at most 3. For paths $p_1 = (s, A, C, t)$, $p_2 = (s, B, D, t)$, $p_3 = (s, A, B, t)$, shown in Fig. 1(b), all of them contain 3 edges and are thus included in $P_{s,t}^{\leq 3}(G)$. Any path from s to t involving more than 3 edges would be ignored.

Formally, for each path $p \in P_{s,t}(G)$, we only include it in our count if $length(p) \leq k$. The goal of the hop-constrained path counting algorithm is to efficiently estimate the number of such paths without explicit enumeration. We now introduce the structural concepts that support our approach.

Definition 4 (Articulation Points and BCCs). *An articulation point is a vertex whose removal increases the number of connected components. A biconnected component (BCC) is a maximal subgraph that cannot be disconnected by removing a single vertex. A BCC is called non-trivial if it is made up of at least three nodes. Every undirected graph can be uniquely decomposed into its BCCs and articulation points.*

Definition 5 (Block-Cut Tree). *The Block-Cut Tree(BC-Tree) B_G is a tree where: Each node is either a BCC (called a graph-vertex) or an articulation point (called a node-vertex); An edge exists between an articulation point a and a BCC B iff $a \in B$. This tree captures connectivity in terms of biconnected component relationships.*

Definition 6 (Bead String). *For a pair of nodes $s, t \in V$, all simple s–t paths are confined to a subgraph formed by a contiguous sequence of BCCs in the BC-tree. This path in the BC-tree is referred to as the bead string $B_{s,t}$. Let the bead string path be denoted as:*

$$B_{s,t} = B_s \xrightarrow{a_0} B_1 \xrightarrow{a_1} \dots \xrightarrow{a_k} B_t$$

where $a_0, a_1, \dots, a_k$ are the articulation points that connect consecutive BCCs. Then the set of all s–t paths can be decomposed as:

$$P_{s,t}(G) = P_{s,a_0}(B_s) \times \left(\prod_{i=1}^{k} P_{a_{i-1},a_i}(B_i) \right) \times P_{a_k,t}(B_t)$$

This formula (referred to in the original paper as Corollary (2.1) [15]) enables recursive and modular computation.

Definition 7 (Lower Bounding Function). *To avoid explicit path enumeration, PathAssess uses a lower bound function $L_{s,t}(G)$ that satisfies:*

$$1 \leq L_{s,t}(G) \leq P_{s,t}(G)$$

In implementation, this function is instantiated as:

$$L_{s,t}(G) = |E| - |V| + 2$$

which is the cyclomatic number, providing a guaranteed lower bound on the number of simple paths in a biconnected graph.

Definition 8 (MSTDS). *The Multi-Source Tree Data Structure (MSTDS) is a dynamic tree structure that organizes the estimation of s–t path counts by decomposing the graph into biconnected components (BCCs) and maintaining a hierarchical path structure from multiple sources to a common target t. The root of the tree is t, and each leaf corresponds to a source node. Each internal node represents a BCC and stores its local path bound, articulation point, and an ancestor-product term to support efficient updates. During execution, MSTDS supports recursive expansion by replacing source leaves with BC-trees of reduced subgraphs, enabling fast updates to the global lower bound $lb_P = \sum_{s' \in S} L_{s',t}$.*

3 PathAssess

Hop-constrained path counting seeks to estimate the number of simple paths from a source node s to a target node t that contain at most k hops. This problem is particularly challenging, as the number of such paths can grow exponentially with k, and the exact enumeration becomes infeasible on large graphs. To address related challenges, recent work has introduced *PathAssess* [15], an efficient path estimation algorithm designed to assess whether the total number of unconstrained simple paths between s and t exceeds a given threshold z. Rather than listing all paths, *PathAssess* leverages the recursive decomposition of the graph into biconnected components (BCCs), combined with a multi-source tree structure, to estimate path counts in a modular and scalable manner. However, *PathAssess* is not designed to incorporate hop constraints and therefore cannot be directly applied to the hop-constrained setting. Inspired by its decomposition-based framework, we propose *kPathAssess* that introducing a hop-aware mechanism into the estimation process. Our approach retains the efficiency of *PathAssess* while enabling a estimation of k-hop path counts without full enumeration.

In the remainder of this section, we describe the algorithm in detail. We first explain the overall idea of the estimation process and then elaborate on two key components: the construction of the BC tree and the recursive expansion of source nodes.

Algorithm 1 Algorithm for Assessing the Number of st-Paths

```
1: procedure PATHASSESS(G = (V, E), s, t, z)
2:     S = {s}
3:     T_G = COMPUTEBCTREE(G, t)
4:     Initialize T as the bead string B_{s,t} in T_G
5:     Add t as the root of T, s as only leaf
6:     if T is trivial then
7:         lb_P ← 1
8:     else
9:         lb_P ← L_{s,t}
10:    end if
11:    while lb_P < z do
12:        if T is trivial then
13:            Output NO
14:        end if
15:        Choose a source s̃ ∈ S
16:        T = EXPLODE(T, s̃)                    ▷ Also updates S, lb_P
17:    end while
18:    Output YES
19: end procedure
```

Overview. The framework of the algorithm, as outlined in Algorithm 1, begins by initializing the source set S with only the starting node s, and constructing the Block-Cut Tree T_G rooted at the target node t using the function `ComputeBCtree()`. It then initializes a bead string configuration in T, setting up a minimal tree with s as a leaf and t as the root (lines 2–5). Next, the algorithm checks whether this tree is trivial, meaning whether there is a direct connection between s and t. If the structure is trivial, it simply sets the lower bound lb_P to 1; otherwise, it computes a more informative lower bound $L_{s,t}$, which helps eliminate unnecessary path enumeration early on by identifying cases where the number of paths is clearly insufficient (lines 6–10). The algorithm then enters a loop in which it repeatedly expands the tree using the `Explode` operation, which selects a source node $\tilde{s} \in S$, removes it, and updates both the BC-tree structure and the path estimates. In each iteration, the source set S and lower bound lb_P are updated accordingly. This process continues until either $lb_P \geq z$, in which case the algorithm returns TRUE, or until the structure remains trivial with $lb_P < z$, in which case it returns FALSE (lines 11–18). Here, TRUE (YES) indicates that the number of simple s–t paths is at least z, while FALSE (NO) means that the total number of such paths is strictly less than z.

BC-Tree Constructing(ComputeBCtree(G, t)). The first step of the algorithm is to decompose the input graph $G = (V, E)$ into its biconnected components (BCCs) and construct the corresponding block-cut tree (BC-tree), rooted at the target node t. This step uses the classical linear-time algorithm by Hopcroft and Tarjan [7] to compute articulation points and BCCs. The BC-tree B_G is a bipartite tree where: Each graph-vertex represents a BCC; Each node-vertex represents an articulation point; Edges exist between a node-vertex a and graph-vertex B iff $a \in B$. The unique path in B_G from the BCC containing s to the BCC containing t is extracted and initialized as the main path in the Multi-Source Tree Data Structure (MSTDS).

Source Node Explosion(Explode(T,s)). The core of *PathAssess* is its ability to recursively refine the current lower-bound estimate of $P_{s,t}(G)$ via a structural expansion over the MSTDS tree. The procedure begins by identifying the biconnected component (BCC) $\widetilde{B}$ that contains $\tilde{s}$. It then computes the BC-tree of the subgraph $\widetilde{B} \setminus \tilde{s}$, rooting it at the articulation point that connects $\widetilde{B}$ in the direction of the target node t. For each neighbor u of $\tilde{s}$ in $\widetilde{B}$, the algorithm determines the corresponding BCC B_u to which u belongs and adds u to the MSTDS as a new source. After introducing all such new sources, the algorithm updates the global lower bound lb_P by subtracting the previous contribution from $\tilde{s}$ and adding the contributions of its neighbors, formally:

$$lb_P := lb_P - L_{\tilde{s},t} + \sum_{u \in N_{\widetilde{B}}(\tilde{s})} L_{u,t}$$

Finally, the node $\tilde{s}$ is replaced in the MSTDS with the subtree structure induced by the newly computed BC-tree, effectively refining the search space and improving the accuracy of the lower-bound estimate.

While *PathAssess* offers an efficient solution for unconstrained path estimation, it does not address hop constraints, which are critical in many real-world applications. We review work that are closely related to hop-constrained path enumeration in the following section.

4 Other Related Work

Path counting. Counting paths is a classical problem in graph theory with broad applications. While shortest paths can be computed efficiently [2,4], counting all simple paths is #P-hard, making exact solutions infeasible for large graphs. Recursive enumeration methods [10,19] suffer from combinatorial explosion, and matrix-based techniques face similar scalability issues. Approximation approaches such as Monte Carlo estimation [17] provide scalable lower bounds, highlighting the trade-off between accuracy and efficiency [5].

Path Enumeration. Hop-constrained path enumeration (HCPE) restricts paths by length and arises in tasks such as fraud detection and knowledge graph completion. Although still NP-hard, practical algorithms have been developed. PathEnum [18] achieves real-time performance through lightweight indexing and cost-aware traversal. EVE [1] improves efficiency by edge-based verification with tight subgraphs, and distributed methods such as DistriEnum [21] extend scalability via graph reduction.

Despite these advances, current methods remain inadequate for efficient hop-constrained path counting, motivating the design of *kPathAssess*, which integrates hop-aware pruning with structural decomposition for real-time estimation.

5 kPathAssess

This section describes our proposed approach *kPathAssess* for estimating the number of k hops s–t simple paths. Our approach is inspired by the *PathAssess* algorithm, with key modifications to support the hop constraint. Figure 2 illustrates the procedure of *kPathAssess*.

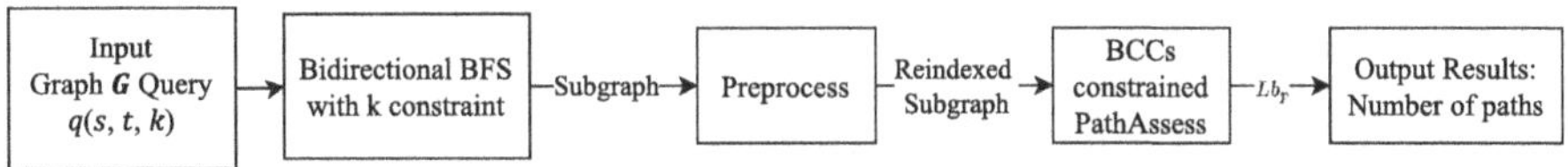

Fig. 2. The procedure of the *kPathAssess*

Main Idea. The central idea of our method is to estimate the number of k-hop s–t paths by restricting the original graph to a k-bounded subgraph using bidirectional BFS and then applying a modified version of *PathAssess* for efficient estimation. Specifically, we use *PathAssess* to decompose the subgraph into biconnected components (BCCs) and estimate the number of paths based on lower bounds across these components. This approach avoids full path enumeration while approximating k-hop path counts with high efficiency. To incorporate the k-hop constraint, we begin by extracting a subgraph using bidirectional BFS from the source node s and target node t, which filters out nodes that cannot appear in any valid k-hop path. This step filters the graph by removing nodes that cannot be on any valid k-hop path, significantly reducing the size of the graph. During the execution of *PathAssess*, we further restrict the number of BCCs considered in the Multi-Source Tree Data Structure (MSTDS). By bounding the number of BCCs, we constrain the potential path lengths, ensuring that only paths conforming to the k-hop requirement are included.

Our approach consists of three major stages: Bidirectional BFS with k Constraint; Preprocess; *PathAssess* with BCC Constraint.

Bidirectional BFS with k Constraint. The goal of the bidirectional BFS algorithm is to efficiently construct a k-bounded subgraph that includes all possible paths of length at most k between a source node s and a target node t. This is achieved by exploring the graph from both ends.

Algorithm 2 Bidirectional k constraint BFS

```
1: procedure BIDIRECTIONALBFS(G, s, t, k)
2:     Q_s, Q_t ← empty queues
3:     E_sub ← ∅                                        ▷ Subgraph edges
4:     Q_s.enqueue({s, 0}); Q_t.enqueue({t, 0})
5:     while Q_s ≠ ∅ OR Q_t ≠ ∅ do
6:         if Q_s ≠ ∅ then
7:             (u, d_s) ← Q_s.dequeue()
8:             if d_s < k/2 then
9:                 for all v ∈ Adj[u] do
10:                    Q_s.enqueue({v, d_s + 1})
11:                    E_sub ← E_sub ∪ {(u, v)}
12:                end for
13:            end if
14:        end if
15:        Similar process for Q_t
16:    end whilereturn E_sub
17: end procedure
```

The algorithm shown in Algorithm 2 begins with the initialization of two queues for bidirectional search from s and t, respectively, where each queue element contains a node and its current depth in the search (Lines 1–3). Then, a bidirectional BFS is performed, with each direction limited to a depth of $k/2$. This significantly reduces the search space compared to unidirectional BFS. During this process, all traversed edges are collected to form a subgraph edge set, and the depth constraint ensures that only paths satisfying the k-hop limit are considered (Lines 4–15). Finally, based on the collected edges, a subgraph is constructed, which can be then passed to *PathAssess* for further processing.

Algorithm 3 Preprocess

```
1: procedure PREPROCESS(G(V, E), s, t)
2:     Store original s, t as s_orig, t_orig
3:     Initialize visited array, node mapping array mapping_id
4:     DFS(t)                                          ▷ Check s-t reachability
5:     if s not reachable from t then
6:         throw error
7:     end if
8:     Find_Caterpillar(s, t)                          ▷ Identify critical components
9:     index ← 0                                       ▷ Remap nodes
10:    for each v ∈ V do
11:        if v is visited and not marked for removal then
12:            mapping_id[v] ← index
13:            index ← index + 1
14:        end if
15:    end for
16:    s_new ← mapping_id[s_orig]                      ▷ Track s-t mapping
17:    t_new ← mapping_id[t_orig]
18:    Output: Reduced graph with new s-t indices
19:    Store: (s_orig, s_new), (t_orig, t_new) mapping
20: end procedure
```

Preprocessing. The preprocess step, as shown in Algorithm 3, begins with the storage of the original source and target nodes as s_{orig} and t_{orig} (Lines 1–3). Then, a depth-first search (DFS) is executed from t to determine whether s is reachable; if it is not, an error is thrown to indicate that no s–t path exists in the current graph (Lines 4–7). Following this check, the `FindCaterpillar`(s, t) procedure is invoked to identify and remove components that are irrelevant to s–t connectivity (Lines 8). Next, each node is re-indexed if it remains valid and unmarked for removal, which helps build a compact representation of the reduced graph (Lines 9–15). Finally, the mapping between the original and new node indices for s and t is updated in order to maintain consistency during subsequent processing (Lines 16–20).

PathAssess with BCC Constraint. In this stage, we extend the *PathAssess* framework (Algorithm 1) to the subgraph obtained in previous steps by fundamentally replacing its original stopping rule with a cutoff based on the number of BCCs. Specifically, we increase the internal threshold z to a value much larger than any feasible path count, effectively neutralizing the original condition $lb_P \geq z$. Instead, we terminate the algorithm when the number of BCCs in the MSTDS exceeds k. At that point, the algorithm halts and returns the current lower bound lb_p as our estimate of the number of simple k-hop paths between nodes s and t. Under hop constraints, the lower bound derived from the cyclomatic number remains applicable and never overestimates the number of hop-constrained paths, although it may become looser because cycles longer than the hop limit are excluded. Restricting the number of BCCs during traversal allows us to maintain an upper bound on path length while preserving valid k-hop paths. This approach allows us to estimate the number of hop-constrained simple paths within the logical framework of *PathAssess*.

Our approach is summarized as follows: We first use **Algorithm 2** to perform bidirectional BFS with k constraint to extract a subgraph. The subgraph is

Table 1. Properties of real-world graphs.

Dataset	$\|V\|$	$\|E\|$	d_{avg}	Type
Soc-Epinion1	75K	508K	13.4	Social
Soc-Slashdot0922	82K	948K	21.2	Social

Table 2. Query performance on *Soc-Epinion1* and *Soc-Slashdot0922*.

	Soc-Epinion1		*Soc-Slashdot0922*	
	Time	Count	Time	Count
PathEnum	0.2886 s	16543423	0.8335 s	18585235
kPathAssess	0.0261 s	11886355	0.1261 s	14942450

then preprocessed using **Algorithm 3**, which verifies reachability and re-indexes valid nodes; Finally, *PathAssess* is executed with BCC count constraints in the MSTDS to compute the number of k-hop s–t paths. By bounding the number of BCCs and restricting the depth from the source and target, the algorithm effectively estimates the number of paths that satisfy the k-hop condition.

6 Evaluation

In this section, We evaluated *kPathAssess* on several graph datasets to assess its performance compared with the PathEnum [18] algorithm.

Experimental Setup. All experiments were conducted on a Linux machine equipped with an AMD Ryzen 7 5800H CPU running at 3.20GHz and 16GB of RAM. The system runs Ubuntu Server with g++ version 11.2.0 used for compiling all C++ implementations. We terminate the algorithm early if the runtime exceeds 120 s.

Datasets. We evaluated algorithms on various real-world graphs from the SNAP dataset repository [11]. Table 1 summarizes the datasets we used.

We conduct extensive experiments to evaluate the efficiency and effectiveness of our algorithm *kPathAssess*. We compare it with PathEnum [18], which is the state-of-the-art solution for hop–constrained shortest path enumeration. The evaluation includes multiple real-world datasets and analyzes performance from three perspectives: (1) comparison on moderate-hop scenarios, (2) scalability under large hop constraints, and (3) time-efficiency in early-stage estimation.

Performance on Social Graphs. We first evaluate both algorithms on two social graphs, Soc-Epinion1 and Soc-Slashdot0922, with a hop constraint of $k = 6$. This setting follows the experimental setup used in PathEnum [18], where $k = 6$ is chosen to reflect typical path lengths observed in real-world social networks. As shown in Table 2, *kPathAssess* achieves a dramatic runtime reduction, saving 91% on Soc-Epinion1 (0.2886 s to 0.0262 s) and 85% on Soc-Slashdot0922 (0.8335 s to 0.1261 s). While *kPathAssess* produces 20–30% fewer paths than PathEnum [18], this is expected since it provides a lower-bound estimate rather than exact enumeration. In many time sensitive graph analysis tasks, obtaining the essential connectivity quickly is more valuable than computing the exact path count. Thus, *kPathAssess* makes a practical trade-off: sacrificing exactness in exchange for substantial efficiency and scalability.

Table 3. Performance when varying hop number

	k=7		*k=10*		*k=15*	
	Time	Count	Time	Count	Time	Count
PathEnum	1.5	484,622,184	F/E		F/E	
kPathAssess	0.227	132,787,851	0.350	347,210,362	0.426	501,838,148

Scalability with Increasing Hop Constraints. To test scalability, we vary the hop constraint k and evaluate performance on dataset Soc-Slashdot0922. Table 3 presents results for $k = 7, 10, 15$. PathEnum fails to execute at $k = 10$ and $k = 15$. In contrast, *kPathAssess* completes all runs within one second. As k increases, the number of paths grows from 132 million at $k = 7$ to 501 million at $k = 15$, while *kPathAssess* maintains stable runtime. These results confirm the scalability of our estimation method under realistic hop settings.

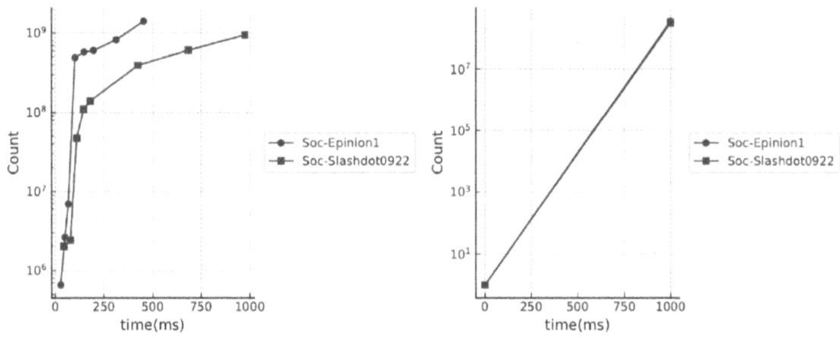

Fig. 3. Path count growth over time for *kPathAssess* and PathEnum.

Time-Sensitive Path Estimation. As shown in Fig. 3, *kPathAssess* rapidly produces lower-bound estimates of s–t paths within milliseconds. It reaches over 10^8 paths in both datasets in under 200 ms, while PathEnum remains much slower. This demonstrates the suitability of *kPathAssess* for applications requiring timely connectivity assessment without full enumeration.

7 Conclusion

We presented *kPathAssess*, a novel algorithm for estimating the number of hop-constrained s–t paths in large graphs. By integrating a bidirectional BFS pruning step with a biconnected component-based counting mechanism, our approach efficiently computes a lower bound on the number of paths up to a given length k. While it provides conservative estimates rather than exact counts, these estimates still offer valuable insights into the graph's connectivity.

References

1. Cai, Y., Liu, S., Zheng, W., Lin, X., Zhang, C., Zhang, X.: Generating k-hop-constrained s-t path graphs. IEEE Trans. Knowl. Data Eng. **PP**, 1–14 (2025). https://doi.org/10.1109/TKDE.2025.3532318
2. Chen, Z., Chen, K., Wen, D., Yang, Z., Li, W., Zhang, Y.: Accelerating shortest path counting on road networks. In: 2025 IEEE 41st International Conference on Data Engineering (ICDE), pp. 3508–3521. IEEE (2025)
3. Chen, Z., Liang, K., Yuan, L., Zhang, W., Yang, Z.: Recent advances in efficient dynamic graph processing. Appl. Sci. **15**(11), 6003 (2025)
4. Dijkstra, E.W.: A note on two problems in connexion with graphs. Numer. Math. **1**(1), 269–271 (1959)
5. Handler, G.Y., Zang, I.: A dual algorithm for the constrained shortest path problem. Networks **10**(4), 293–310 (1980). https://doi.org/10.1002/net.3230100403
6. He, H., Yet al.: A survey on efficient graph reachability queries. In: Pacific-Asia Conference on Knowledge Discovery and Data Mining, pp. 58–77. Springer, Cham (2025)
7. Hopcroft, J.E., Tarjan, R.E.: Algorithm 447: efficient algorithms for graph manipulation. Commun. ACM **16**(6), 372–378 (1973)
8. Johnson, D.B.: Finding all the elementary circuits of a directed graph. SIAM J. Comput. **4**(1), 77–84 (1975)
9. Khomenko, N.P., Golovko, L.D.: Identifying certain types of parts of a graph and computing their number. Ukr. Math. J. **24**(3), 313–321 (1972)
10. Kumar, R., Calders, T.: An efficient algorithm to enumerate all simple temporal cycles. In: Proceedings of the VLDB Endowment, vol. 11, pp. 1233–1244 (2018)
11. Leskovec, J., Krevl, A.: Stanford large network dataset collection (2014). http://snap.stanford.edu/data/
12. Li, X., Hao, K., Yang, Z., Cao, X., Zhang, W.: Hop-constrained s-t simple path enumeration in large uncertain graphs. In: Hua, W., Wang, H., Li, L. (eds.) Australasian Database Conference, pp. 115–127. Springer, Cham (2022). https://doi.org/10.1007/978-3-031-15512-3_9
13. Li, X., et al.: Hop-constrained s-t simple path enumeration in billion-scale labelled graphs. In: Chbeir, R., Huang, H., Silvestri, F., Manolopoulos, Y., Zhang, Y. (eds.) International Conference on Web Information Systems Engineering. pp. 49–64. Springer, Cham (2022). https://doi.org/10.1007/978-3-031-20891-1_5
14. Peng, Y., Zhang, Y., Lin, X., Zhang, W., Qin, L.: Hop-constrained s-t simple path enumeration: Towards bridging theory and practice. In: Proceedings of the VLDB Endowment, vol. 13, pp. 463–476 (2019)
15. Punzi, G., Conte, A., Grossi, R., Marino, A.: An efficient algorithm for assessing the number of st-paths in large graphs. In: Proceedings of the SIAM International Conference on Data Mining (SDM), pp. 289–297 (2023)
16. Read, R.C., Tarjan, R.E.: Bounds on backtrack algorithms for listing cycles, paths, and spanning trees. Networks **5**(3), 237–252 (1975)
17. Roberts, B., Kroese, D.: Estimating the number of s-t paths in a graph. J. Graph Algorithms Appl. **11**(1), 195–214 (2007)
18. Sun, S., Chen, Y., He, B., Hooi, B.: Pathenum: Towards real-time hop-constrained s-t path enumeration. In: Proceedings of the ACM SIGMOD International Conference on Management of Data, pp. 1571–1583 (2021)
19. Tarjan, R.E.: Finding all minimum-cost paths in a graph. Inf. Process. Lett. **16**(1), 17–19 (1983). https://doi.org/10.1016/0020-0190(83)90038-8

20. Valiant, L.G.: The complexity of enumeration and reliability problems. SIAM J. Comput. **8**(3), 410–421 (1979)
21. Zeng, Y., Fang, Y., Ma, C., Zhou, X., Li, K.: Efficient distributed hop-constrained path enumeration on large-scale graphs. Proc. ACM Manage. Data **2**, 1–25 (2024). https://doi.org/10.1145/3639277
22. Zhang, F., Wang, W., Li, G.: Net approach to enumerate all simple paths in a graph. In: Proceedings of the International Conference on Management of Data (SIGMOD), pp. 857–872 (2018)

MambaTSC: Towards Robust Time Series Completion via Multi-scale Temporal Enhancement and Score-Gated Graph Modeling

Linlin Ding[1], Yuhang Hu[1], Mo Li[1(✉)], Zhaosong Zhao[1], and Jiajia Li[2]

[1] School of Information, Liaoning University, Shenyang, China
limo@lnu.edu.cn

[2] School of Computer Science, Shenyang Aerospace University, Shenyang, China

Abstract. Multivariate time series imputation is vital for domains such as meteorology, finance, and transportation. However, most existing approaches employ a separated imputation-then-forecasting pipeline, which struggles to model complex spatio-temporal dependencies effectively and tends to incur significant error accumulation, especially in scenarios with high missing rates. To address these challenges, we propose Mamba-based Time Series Completer (MambaTSC), an end-to-end framework that integrates time series imputation and forecasting within a unified state space modeling architecture. Specifically, we first devise a Multi-Scale Temporal Enhancement Mamba (MS-Mamba) module, which augments state space modeling with multi-scale temporal feature extraction, enabling the capture of both short-term fluctuations and long-term trends. Additionally, we develop a Score-Gated Graph Convolutional Network (SGCN) that dynamically adjusts information propagation based on observation reliability, thereby improving spatio-temporal representation learning. Extensive experimental results on three real-world datasets show that our proposed MambaTSC achieves state-of-the-art performance, demonstrating superior effectiveness and robustness for time series with substantial missing data.

Keywords: Time Series Imputation · Time Series Forecasting · Mamba · Spatiotemporal Dependency

1 Introduction

Time series data are pervasive across critical domains such as meteorology [1], energy systems [20], and transportation networks [27]. Accurate forecasting and anomaly detection rely heavily on data completeness, yet real-world datasets often suffer from missing values due to sensor malfunctions, transmission interruptions, or equipment failures [23,29,30]. These missing values frequently occur in block-wise patterns, leading to biased estimates and degraded model performance.

I. Awan et al. (Eds.): WISE 2025, LNCS 16368, pp. 388–403, 2026.
https://doi.org/10.1007/978-981-95-7251-9_26

Existing methods for handling missing data fall into two main categories: **traditional statistical techniques** and **deep learning-based methods**. Traditional approaches typically adopt a two-stage pipeline, imputing missing values before performing downstream forecasting [3,7], but this separation fails to capture temporal dependencies and often introduces cumulative errors, thereby compromising predictive accuracy. Deep learning-based methods(e.g., GRU-D [4], BRITS [3], Transformer-based models [21], and ODE-driven frameworks such as Neural ODE [5], GraFITi [26], and CRUs [22]) learn expressive representations from incomplete data. However, they often suffer from high computational costs, long convergence times, and limited robustness under high missing rates. Moreover, most existing approaches decouple imputation and forecasting, failing to exploit temporal coherence and leading to significant error propagation.

Recently, State Space Models (SSMs) have emerged as a promising paradigm for sequence modeling [10–13]. These models overcome key limitations of earlier methods, such as the restricted capacity of linear models (e.g., DLinear [28] and TiDE [8]) and the quadratic computational complexity inherent in Transformer-based architectures like iTransformer [17] and PatchTST [19]. By leveraging the structure of linear time-invariant dynamical systems, SSMs enable efficient and scalable inference over long sequences while achieving competitive or superior performance. However, their effectiveness in unified imputation and forecasting tasks remains underexplored, highlighting the need for frameworks that can handle complex temporal dynamics and high missing rates in real-world scenarios.

To address these challenges, we propose an end-to-end time series imputation and forecasting framework, termed ***MambaTSC***, which adopts state space modeling as its foundational architecture. Specifically, MambaTSC incorporates two key components: a ***Multi-Scale Temporal Enhancement Mamba (MS-Mamba)*** module to capture both short-term fluctuations and long-term trends, and a ***Score-Gated Graph Convolutional Network (SGCN)*** to dynamically propagate reliable spatial information. By jointly learning from both observed and incomplete segments, MambaTSC effectively bridges the gap between imputation and forecasting. Extensive experiments conducted on three real-world benchmark datasets demonstrate that MambaTSC consistently outperforms existing state-of-the-art methods across multiple evaluation metrics.

Furthermore, by jointly optimizing imputation and forecasting, MambaTSC effectively reduces error propagation and delivers substantial gains in downstream prediction accuracy, as validated in our experimental results.

The main contributions can be summarized as follows:

- We propose *MambaTSC*, a unified end-to-end framework that seamlessly integrates time series imputation and forecasting, enabling joint modeling of missing value reconstruction and temporal prediction within a single architecture.
- We design the MS-Mamba module, which combines state space modeling with multi-scale temporal enhancement to effectively capture both short-term variations and long-term dependencies. In addition, we develop the SGCN module to dynamically regulate spatiotemporal message propagation based on the reliability of observed data.

- Extensive experiments on multiple real-world benchmark datasets demonstrate that MambaTSC achieves state-of-the-art performance.

The remainder of this paper is organized as follows. Section 2 reviews the related work. Section 3 presents the details of the proposed MambaTSC framework. Section 4 reports the experimental results and performance analysis. Finally, Sect. 5 concludes the paper and discusses future research directions.

2 Related Work

Most time series forecasting models assume that the dataset is complete and focus solely on improving prediction accuracy. However, in real-world scenarios, many multivariate time series (MTS) datasets are incomplete. Therefore, effectively handling MTS data with missing values is a critical issue, as it significantly impacts both data quality and the accuracy of predictive models.

One of the most common approaches to handling MTS data with missing values is imputation, which estimates missing values before performing downstream tasks such as prediction. Early studies in this area proposed simple imputation techniques based on statistics from observed data, such as mean, median, and mode imputation [24]. In addition, several statistical time series models were introduced, including AutoRegressive (AR) models, Moving Average (MA) models, as well as machine learning-based imputation methods such as k-Nearest Neighbors (KNN) and random forests [2,14,16]. More recently, some researchers have explored deep learning approaches to impute missing values in MTS data. For example, Recurrent Neural Network (RNN)-based methods often incorporate time decay since the last observation and utilize hidden states from bidirectional RNNs to estimate missing values. Other approaches have proposed imputation methods based on self-attention mechanisms [9], or leverage spatiotemporal graphs and sparse observations to reconstruct missing data [18]. However, these imputation methods treat the estimation of missing values as a preprocessing step that is decoupled from the forecasting task, resulting in inefficiencies during training and inference. Moreover, an accurate imputation model does not always guarantee improved forecasting performance.

To address the challenges posed by standalone imputation, some studies have proposed state space model-based forecasting methods, such as S4M [15], an end-to-end time series forecasting framework that seamlessly integrates missing data handling into the Structured State Space Sequence (S4) model architecture. Unlike traditional approaches that treat imputation as a separate preprocessing step, S4M leverages the latent space of the S4 model to directly identify and represent missing data patterns, thereby capturing the underlying temporal and multivariate dependencies more effectively.

With the continuous increase in the scale and complexity of time series data, the State Space Model (SSM) has demonstrated enormous potential in the field of time series prediction, leveraging its linear time complexity and efficient long-range dependency modeling capabilities. Inspired by this, we propose an end-to-end time series completion architecture, MambaTSC, to address the challenge of capturing complex spatiotemporal dependencies in time series completion tasks. MambaTSC takes state space modeling as its core and deeply optimizes the basic Mamba model structure. Innovatively, frequency filters are embedded before and after the State Space Model (SSM) module. The adaptive spectral modulation unit is used to filter and enhance the frequency-domain features of the input sequence. This filter can effectively suppress the interference of high-frequency noise on long-term dependency modeling while strengthening key frequency components, enabling the model to better capture the periodic and trend characteristics of time series. Additionally, a residual attention mechanism is introduced during the state update process to focus on key time steps, enhance feature expression capabilities, and improve the model's adaptability to complex time series patterns. The core components of this framework include the multi-scale temporal enhancement Mamba module, which uses parallel temporal convolutions to extract multi-granularity features of time series. Combined with a causal masking strategy, it ensures that the completion process adheres to temporal logic and avoids information leakage. The score-gated graph convolution module dynamically constructs a topological graph structure based on the historical correlation between time series, using an attention scoring mechanism to weight and aggregate features of neighboring nodes, achieving deep fusion of spatial dimension information. The two modules collaboratively optimize through a bidirectional feature interaction mechanism, efficiently modeling the complex spatiotemporal dependencies in missing time series.

3 Methodology

The architecture of MambaTSC is designed to address block-wise missing patterns in multivariate time series (MTS) data. By introducing a progressive imputation process, the model effectively captures long-range spatiotemporal dependencies while suppressing interference from redundant information. As illustrated in Fig. 1, the architecture first takes incomplete multivariate time series as input, applies a progressive imputation mechanism, and finally outputs both reconstructed values and forecasting results, forming a unified pipeline, which primarily consists of two key components: the Multi-Scale Temporal Enhancement Mamba (MS-Mamba) module and the Score-Gated Graph Convolutional Network (SGCN) module. Within this progressive framework, the former component enhances the ability to jointly model local fluctuations and global trends along the temporal dimension by integrating state space modeling with a multi-scale feature extraction mechanism. The latter component introduces a spatiotemporal scoring function to dynamically adjust the propagation weights between nodes, thereby optimizing information flow in the spatial dimension and improving the quality of effective message passing within the graph structure. These two core modules work collaboratively, driving the model toward more accurate and robust recovery of missing values. Moreover, Fig. 1 highlights the bidirectional feature interaction between temporal and spatial modules, ensuring that information flow is not only sequential but also mutually reinforced across dimensions.

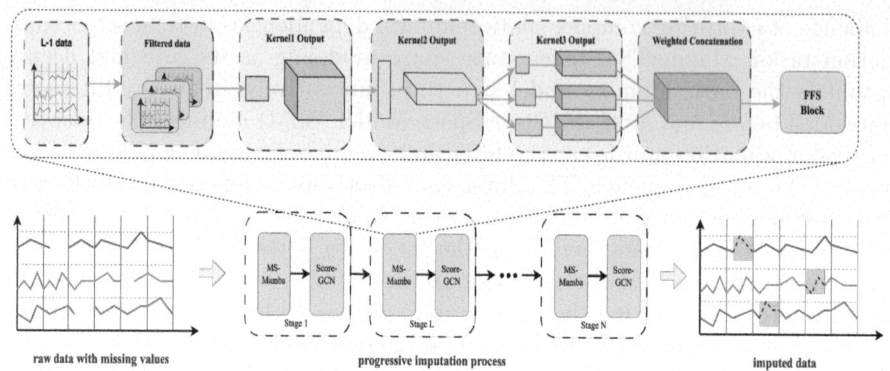

Fig. 1. Architecture of MambaTSC Model

3.1 Multi-scale Temporal Enhancement Mamba Module

We introduce a Multi-Scale Temporal Enhancement Mamba module (MS-Mamba) into our proposed model architecture to effectively capture the complex temporal dynamics and long-term dependency structures in multivariate time series. As a front-end structure of the overall model, this module aims to provide richer and more robust temporal representations for subsequent state space modeling through a parallel convolutional processing mechanism across different temporal scales.

Specifically, the original input data is first transformed into a four-dimensional tensor

$$\boldsymbol{X} \in \mathbb{R}^{B\times C\times N\times T},$$

where B denotes the batch size, C the number of channels, N the number of spatial nodes, and T the time series length. The input is then fed along the channel dimension into multiple dilated convolution branches $i \in \{1, \ldots, S\}$, where each branch corresponds to a different convolutional kernel size k_i and dilation rate d_i, defined as:

$$H_i = \text{Conv1D}(X; k_i, d_i), \quad i = 1, \ldots, S$$

where $\text{Conv1D}(X, k_i, d_i)$ denotes a one-dimensional temporal convolution operation with kernel size k_i and dilation rate d_i. This design allows for multiple receptive fields, thereby capturing temporal dependencies at different scales. The outputs from all scales are concatenated as:

$$H_{\text{multi}} = \text{Concat}(H_1, H_2, \ldots, H_S) \in \mathbb{R}^{B\times C'\times N\times T}$$

To reduce redundant computations, we introduce depthwise separable convolution for dimensionality compression:

$$H_{\text{compressed}} = \text{DWConv}(H_{\text{multi}})$$

Next, we apply the Squeeze-and-Excitation (SE) mechanism to compute attention weights along the temporal dimension:

$$\alpha = \sigma\left(W_2 \cdot \delta\left(W_1 \cdot \mathrm{AvgPool}(H_{\mathrm{compressed}})\right)\right)$$

where δ is the ReLU activation, σ is the sigmoid function, and W_1, W_2 are learnable weight matrices. The final output is:

$$H_{\mathrm{enhanced}} = H_{\mathrm{compressed}} \odot \alpha$$

where $\odot$ denotes channel-wise multiplication. The enhanced feature H_{enhanced} is then fed into the **Frequency Filter Space Block (FFS)** for further modeling.

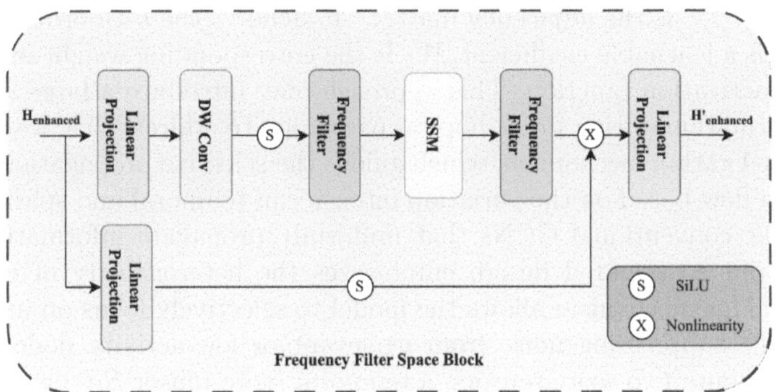

Fig. 2. Architecture of FFS Block

As shown in Fig. 2, the FFS module is designed to enhance the model's ability to capture frequency-domain structural features such as periodic trends, seasonal components, and low-frequency long-term dependencies, thereby compensating for the limitations of state space models in responding to specific frequencies. Frequency filters are inserted before and after the state space model (SSM) in the Mamba module. The filter placed before the SSM is responsible for extracting frequency-domain features as inputs to the state space, by converting the sequence input into the frequency domain and constructing a learnable frequency mask to retain key band information, followed by an inverse Fourier transform to recover the time-domain signal. This enables enhanced modeling of the original input in the frequency domain. This module effectively filters out noise and improves the model's robustness and accuracy under dynamic patterns. The filter placed after the SSM stabilizes the output distribution and smooths abrupt components. In summary, the FFS module introduces learnable frequency-domain operations to provide the state space model with powerful capabilities for frequency feature extraction and regulation, serving as a key innovation for improving the model's overall performance in handling complex time series patterns.

3.2 Score-Gated Graph Convolution Module

To enhance the model's ability to represent key spatiotemporal nodes, we design a Score-Gated Graph Convolution Module (SG-GCN), which introduces a score-based gating mechanism to dynamically adjust the importance of nodes and their adjacency relations in the graph structure, thereby improving the model's capacity to aggregate effective information under high missing rates. Let the input feature be $H \in \mathbb{R}^{B\times C\times N\times T}$. In traditional graph convolution, node feature propagation is typically formulated as:

$$H' = \sigma\left(\sum_{k=0}^{K} \alpha_k A^k H W_k\right)$$

where $A \in \mathbb{R}^{N\times N}$ is the adjacency matrix, A^k denotes the k-th order adjacency matrix, α_k is a learnable coefficient, W_k is the corresponding weight matrix, and $\sigma(\cdot)$ is the activation function. This approach may introduce a large amount of invalid information during multi-hop propagation. To address this, we introduce a score-based gating mechanism, which guides the selective propagation of graph information flow based on the variation intensity in temporal and spatial dimensions. Unlike conventional GCNs that uniformly propagate information across neighbors, our score-gated design emphasizes the heterogeneity of nodes and time steps. This mechanism allows the model to selectively focus on informative regions while suppressing noise from irrelevant or low-activity nodes. Specifically, we compute two score tensors, a temporal score tensor $S_t(t)$ and a spatial score tensor $S_s(n)$, based on the local variation rate V_t and the cross-temporal variance V_s of nodes:

$$S_t(t) = \frac{1}{N\cdot C}\sum_{n=1}^{N}\sum_{c=1}^{C} |H_{b,c,n,t} - H_{b,c,n,t-1}|$$

$$S_s(n) = \frac{1}{T\cdot C}\sum_{t=1}^{T}\sum_{c=1}^{C} \mathrm{Var}(H_{b,c,n,t})$$

The temporal score tensor captures the local variation rate of all nodes at each time step, identifying potential abrupt changes or trend reversals. The spatial score tensor characterizes the magnitude of a node's variation over the entire time series, reflecting the node's activity level. A higher score indicates greater variation and richer information, while long-term stationary nodes with small fluctuations are assigned lower scores and are more likely to be masked.

We further normalize and fuse the scores to obtain the final gating weight graph $G \in \mathbb{R}^{N\times N}$, which is used to modulate the adjacency matrix in graph convolution:

$$\widetilde{A} = A \odot G$$

where $\odot$ denotes element-wise multiplication. The gated graph structure is then used for multi-hop graph convolution to propagate node features:

$$H' = \sigma\left(\sum_{k=0}^{K} \alpha_k \widetilde{A}^k H W_k\right)$$

Under this mechanism, nodes and time steps with lower scores exert weaker influence on propagation, thereby reducing interference from invalid or redundant information. To further enhance the expressive power of the model, we perform residual fusion and layer normalization based on multi-hop propagation:

$$H'' = \text{LayerNorm}(H' + H)$$

The Score-Gated Graph Convolution Module not only models the importance of key nodes but also dynamically adapts to structural noise under different missing patterns, effectively improving the robustness and expressive capacity of graph convolution in the imputation task. By coupling with the MS-Mamba module, the SGCN ensures that temporal dynamics and spatial correlations are reinforced in a coordinated manner, enabling the overall framework to better capture complex spatiotemporal dependencies under high missing rates.

4 Experiments

4.1 Experimental Setup

Datasets. To comprehensively evaluate the performance of the proposed MambaTSC model on multivariate time series imputation tasks, we conducted experiments on three representative real-world datasets, as presented in Table 1. These datasets cover typical scenarios such as energy, meteorology, and industrial control:

(1) **Electricity**: This dataset records electricity load from the California electricity company in the United States, consisting of 321 nodes sampled hourly. It exhibits both long-term periodicity and short-term fluctuations.
(2) **Weather**: Sourced from the U.S. National Weather Service, this dataset includes meteorological variables such as wind speed, humidity, and temperature for 21 cities. It is sampled every 10 min and demonstrates complex dependencies among multiple variables.
(3) **ETTh1**: Collected from the high-frequency industrial time series dataset Electricity Transformer Temperature at the hourly level, this dataset includes multiple physical variables such as temperature, voltage, and current. It features strong sequential regularity and significant inter-dimensional correlations.

All datasets are standardized using Z-score normalization, and block-wise missing values with varying degrees of intensity are introduced into the original data to test the robustness of the model under different missing conditions.

Table 1. Dataset description.

	Electricity	Weather	ETTh1
#Samples (T)	26304	52696	17420
#Instances (N)	321	21	7
Frequency	1 h	10 min	1 h
Mean	2538.79	10.82	4.58
Variance	2.26×10^8	55.78	42.68

Baseline Models. We compare the proposed MambaTSC with several state-of-the-art forecasting methods and classical approaches.

- BRITS [3]: an LSTM-based method, utilizing a bidirectional recurrent model for spatio-temporal imputation.
- GRU-D [4], an RNN-based method, integrating gating mechanisms and temporal decay to account for missingness.
- CRUs [22], a representative prediction model designed for time series with missing values.
- Autoformer [25], a Transformer-based model leveraging self-attention to capture global temporal relationships.
- BiTGraph [6], an end-to-end method specifically designed for missing data forecasting.

To simulate real-world issues such as sensor failures or communication interruptions, we adopt random block missing patterns to construct masks and evaluate model performance under three different missing rates: 0.05, 0.10, and 0.15. For architectures like Autoformer and Transformer that require complete input, we use zero-imputation to initialize missing values before input. To ensure a fair comparison, the historical window length for all baseline models is selected from the set {24, 48, 96, 192}, with the best performance on the validation set reported. For the proposed MambaTSC, a fixed historical window length of 96 is used to fully exploit its advantages in modeling medium- and long-term dependencies.

Evaluation Metrics and Experimental Details. To quantitatively evaluate the performance of the proposed method, we adopt two commonly used metrics: Mean Square Error (MSE) and Mean Absolute Error (MAE). During training, the Adam optimizer is used with a batch size of 32 and a total of 200 training epochs. In each set of experiments, the same masking scheme is applied to ensure fairness, and each experiment is independently run three times on each dataset to report the average results.

Table 2. Comparison of imputation performance (MAE and MSE) under different mask rates r on three datasets.

Models	Metrics	Electricity			Weather			ETTh1		
		r=0.05	r=0.10	r=0.15	r=0.05	r=0.10	r=0.15	r=0.05	r=0.10	r=0.15
BRITS	MAE	0.632	0.793	0.821	0.415	0.428	0.455	0.701	0.744	0.768
	MSE	0.621	0.788	0.818	0.371	0.409	0.419	0.932	0.981	1.104
GRU-D	MAE	0.429	0.443	0.453	**0.361**	0.371	0.394	0.651	0.677	0.712
	MSE	0.361	0.437	0.446	**0.292**	0.336	0.388	0.614	0.642	0.668
CRUS	MAE	0.478	0.497	0.512	0.377	0.401	0.418	0.681	0.694	0.721
	MSE	0.451	0.468	0.498	0.362	0.372	0.385	0.634	0.665	0.682
Transformer	MAE	0.408	0.412	0.421	0.745	0.784	0.829	0.671	0.682	0.683
	MSE	0.401	0.409	0.411	0.715	0.759	0.817	0.633	0.689	0.679
Autoformer	MAE	0.372	0.385	0.417	0.724	0.791	0.849	0.668	0.670	0.674
	MSE	0.368	0.379	0.412	0.719	0.771	0.812	0.624	0.661	0.671
BiTGraph	MAE	0.392	0.397	0.411	0.420	0.455	0.469	0.609	0.612	0.638
	MSE	**0.305**	0.387	0.405	0.411	0.428	0.442	0.601	0.604	0.621
MambaTSC	MAE	**0.369**	**0.377**	**0.409**	0.377	**0.369**	**0.381**	**0.599**	**0.607**	**0.624**
	MSE	0.309	**0.371**	**0.399**	0.311	**0.355**	**0.376**	**0.512**	**0.601**	**0.617**

4.2 Performance Comparison

As shown in Table 2, we conducted a performance comparison between MambaTSC and six baseline models (BRITS, GRU-D, CRU, Transformer, Autoformer, and BITGraph) on three datasets (Electricity, Weather, and ETTh1), using Mean Absolute Error (MAE) and Mean Squared Error (MSE) under mask rates $r = 0.05, 0.10, 0.15$.

Across all datasets, MambaTSC consistently outperforms baseline models in both MAE and MSE under different missing rates. It achieves more accurate imputation with lower errors and greater stability, demonstrating strong adaptability to various temporal patterns. Unlike baselines whose performance degrades notably as the missing rate increases, MambaTSC maintains robust accuracy and reliability, validating its effectiveness and generalizability for time-series imputation tasks.

While Table 2 demonstrates the superiority of MambaTSC in terms of imputation accuracy, it remains unclear whether high-quality completion can further enhance downstream forecasting tasks. To investigate this, we evaluate the forecasting performance after applying different imputation strategies on three benchmark datasets. Specifically, for methods without built-in forecasting capability (e.g., BRITS, GRU-D), we first apply the respective imputation model to recover missing values and then use a unified Autoformer predictor to forecast future time steps. For end-to-end frameworks like BiTGraph and the proposed MambaTSC, we directly adopt their integrated forecasting outputs.

The results are summarized in Table 3. We observe that high-quality imputation consistently leads to improved forecasting performance across all datasets. Notably, MambaTSC achieves the lowest MAE and MSE at different horizons, demonstrating that the proposed model not only recovers missing values more

Table 3. Forecasting performance after applying different imputation methods under missing rate r=0.10 on three benchmark datasets.

Models	Electricity		Weather		ETTh1	
	MAE	MSE	MAE	MSE	MAE	MSE
No Imputation	0.512	0.685	0.488	0.695	0.689	0.945
BRITS	0.438	0.601	0.442	0.648	0.622	0.874
GRU-D	0.410	0.578	0.425	0.621	0.595	0.853
CRUS	0.421	0.589	0.420	0.610	0.605	0.861
Transformer	0.405	0.572	0.417	0.608	0.591	0.849
Autoformer	0.398	0.561	0.411	0.598	0.582	0.832
BiTGraph	0.384	0.547	0.399	0.582	0.567	0.814
MambaTSC	**0.366**	**0.533**	**0.384**	**0.557**	**0.559**	**0.798**

accurately but also provides more reliable inputs for downstream forecasting. This highlights the practical value of jointly optimizing imputation and prediction within a unified framework.

In summary, Tables 2 and 3 jointly demonstrate that accurate imputation substantially benefits downstream forecasting. MambaTSC not only achieves state-of-the-art performance in imputing missing values across all datasets but also delivers the most reliable forecasting results. By integrating imputation and prediction within a unified framework, MambaTSC effectively reduces error propagation and enhances robustness under high missing rates, highlighting its practical value for real-world time-series applications.

4.3 Ablation Study

To verify the effectiveness of the core components proposed in MambaTSC, we conduct systematic ablation studies on the Electricity, Weather, and ETTh1 datasets to evaluate the contribution of each module to the overall performance. The variants focus on two key designs: the Multi-Scale Temporal Enhanced Mamba module (MS-Mamba) and the Score-Gated Graph Convolution module (SGCN).

The following four model variants are evaluated:

- **MambaTSC (Full)**: The complete model including both MS-Mamba and SGCN modules;
- **w/o MS-Mamba**: The multi-scale enhancement module is removed, and only the base Mamba architecture is used for feature modeling;
- **w/o SGCN**: The score-gated graph convolution is removed, reverting to a standard GCN without score-based modulation;
- **w/o Both**: Both MS-Mamba and SGCN modules are removed, retaining only the standard Mamba backbone for modeling.

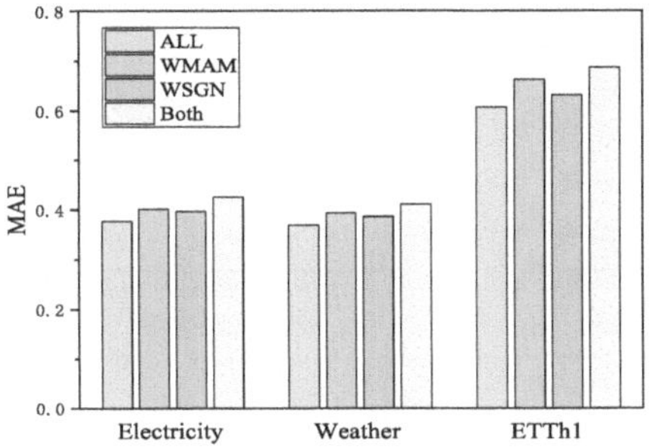

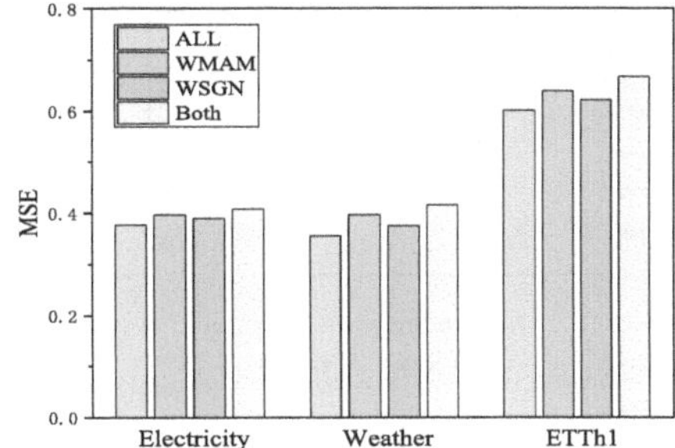

Fig. 3. Ablation Study Results

All models are trained under the same settings, with the historical window length set to 96 and a masking rate of 0.1.

We fix the mask rate at r = 0.10 and report both Mean Absolute Error (MAE) and Mean Squared Error (MSE) across three benchmark datasets: Electricity, Weather, and ETTh1. The results are visualized in Fig. 3, which compares the performance of each variant.

As shown in the figure, the full model consistently achieves the best performance across all datasets, indicating the complementary benefits of the two proposed modules. Removing either MS-Mamba or SGCN leads to a noticeable performance drop in both MAE and MSE, while removing both results in the most significant degradation. These results confirm that the multi-scale temporal modeling and score-based graph information propagation jointly contribute to the overall accuracy and robustness of MambaTSC under incomplete input scenarios. In particular, the ablation results indicate that the SGCN module is more sensitive under high missing rates, while MS-Mamba contributes more significantly to capturing long-term dependencies. This complementary behavior demonstrates that both components are indispensable for robust performance across diverse datasets.

4.4 Hyperparameter Sensitivity Analysis

To further evaluate the robustness and generalizability of MambaTSC under different temporal configurations, we conduct a comprehensive hyperparameter sensitivity analysis focusing on the impact of the historical window length (i.e., input sequence length) on model performance.

Specifically, we select two representative datasets—Electricity and Weather, which exhibit distinct temporal patterns and complexity. We evaluate the Mean Absolute Error (MAE) performance of four MambaTSC variants (Full, w/o MS-Mamba, w/o SGCN, w/o Both) under four different historical window lengths: 24, 48, 96, 192. This experiment is carried out with three different missing ratios: r = 0.05, 0.10, and 0.15, to simulate varying levels of data sparsity and to assess the resilience of the model to different degrees of incompleteness.

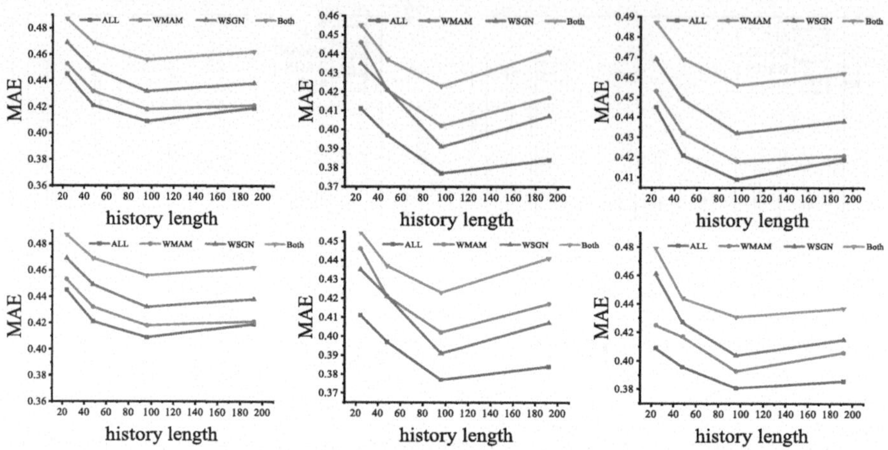

Fig. 4. Hyperparameter Sensitivity Analysis

The results are summarized in Fig. 4, which illustrates the MAE performance of each model variant with different input lengths and missing conditions. We observe the following key findings:

For both datasets, increasing the historical window length generally leads to performance improvements, especially when moving from short windows (24, 48) to medium-length windows (96). This confirms that longer input sequences enable the model to capture more temporal context and latent dependencies.

However, the performance gain tends to saturate or even slightly degrade when the input length is extended to 192, particularly at high missing rates ($r = 0.15$), likely due to the accumulation of irrelevant or noisy information over excessively long temporal intervals.

The full model consistently outperforms its ablated variants across all history lengths, reaffirming the complementary roles of the MS-Mamba and SGCN modules.

Notably, the performance gap between variants becomes more pronounced under longer input lengths, indicating that both multi-scale temporal modeling and score-gated message passing are especially beneficial for leveraging extended temporal context.

These observations highlight the importance of choosing an appropriate window length for different datasets and underline the robustness of MambaTSC in adapting to a wide range of sequence lengths and missing patterns. Furthermore, the relatively stable performance across different window lengths suggests that MambaTSC does not require extensive hyperparameter tuning, which is a desirable property for practical deployment in real-world systems where computational resources and parameter search budgets are limited.

5 Conclusion

In this paper, we propose a novel multivariate time series completion framework, *MambaTSC*, based on state space models. By integrating a multi-scale temporal enhancement module and a score-gated graph convolution mechanism, the framework effectively models long sequences and robustly completes block-missing data. Experiments on multiple real-world datasets demonstrate that the proposed method outperforms existing mainstream baselines in terms of both accuracy and stability. Future work will explore its generalization potential in broader tasks such as forecasting and generation.

Acknowledgement. This study was funded by the National Natural Science Foundation of China (Nos. 52574191, 62072220); the youth talent support program of 'Xing Liao Talent Program' (No. XLYC2203003), the Basic Scientific Research Project of the Department of Education of Liaoning Province (No. LJ232510140001); the Natural Science Foundation of Liaoning Province (No.2022-KF-13-06, 2022-BS-111); Liaoning Provincial Department of Education Youth Project (No. JYTQN2023189); China University Industry-Academia-Research Innovation Fund-Next-Generation Information Technology Innovation Project (No. 2023IT047); Natural Science Foundation of Liaoning University (No. LDZDJC2402).

References

1. Angryk, R.A., Martens, P.C., Aydin, B., Kempton, D., Georgoulis, M.K.: Multivariate time series dataset for space weather data analytics. Scientific Data **7**(1), 227 (2020)
2. van Buuren, S., Groothuis-Oudshoorn, K.: mice: Multivariate imputation by chained equations in r. J. Stat. Softw. **45**(3), 1–67 (2011)
3. Cao, W., Wang, D., Li, J., Zhou, H., Li, L., Li, Y.: Brits: Bidirectional recurrent imputation for time series. In: Advances in Neural Information Processing Systems, vol. 31 (2018)
4. Che, Z., Purushotham, S., Cho, K., Sontag, D., Liu, Y.: Recurrent neural networks for multivariate time series with missing values. Sci. Rep. **8**(1), 6085 (2018)
5. Chen, T.Q., Rubanova, Y., Bettencourt, J., Duvenaud, D.: Neural ordinary differential equations. In: NeurIPS, pp. 6572–6583 (2018)
6. Chen, X., Li, X., Liu, B., Li, Z.: Biased temporal convolution graph network for time series forecasting with missing values. In: The Twelfth International Conference on Learning Representations, ICLR. OpenReview.net (2024)
7. Cini, A., Marisca, I., Alippi, C.: Filling the g_ap_s: Multivariate time series imputation by graph neural networks. In: ICLR (2022)
8. Das, A., Kong, W., Leach, A., Mathur, S.K., Sen, R., Yu, R.: Long-term forecasting with tiDE: Time-series dense encoder. Transactions on Machine Learning Research (2023)
9. Du, W., Côté, D., Liu, Y.: SAITS: self-attention-based imputation for time series. Expert Syst. Appl. **219**, 119619 (2023)
10. Fu, D.Y., Dao, T., Saab, K.K., Thomas, A.W., Rudra, A., Ré, C.: Hungry hungry hippos: towards language modeling with state space models. In: ICLR (2023)

11. Gu, A., Dao, T.: Mamba: Linear-time sequence modeling with selective state spaces. CoRR abs/2312.00752 (2023)
12. Gu, A., Goel, K., Ré, C.: Efficiently modeling long sequences with structured state spaces. In: ICLR (2022)
13. Gu, A., Johnson, I., Goel, K., Saab, K., Dao, T., Rudra, A., Ré, C.: Combining recurrent, convolutional, and continuous-time models with linear state space layers. In: NeurIPS, pp. 572–585 (2021)
14. He, Y., Yucel, R., Raghunathan, T.: A functional multiple imputation approach to incomplete longitudinal data. Statistics in medicine **30**, 1137–56 (05 2011)
15. Jing, P., Yang, M., Zhang, Q., Li, X.: S4M: S4 for multivariate time series forecasting with missing values. In: The Thirteenth International Conference on Learning Representations, ICLR (2025)
16. Karr, A.F.: Statistical matching: A frequentist theory, practical applications and alternative bayesian approaches, susanne rassler. Publ. Am. Stat. Assoc. **102**(477), 386–386 (2007)
17. Liu, Y., Hu, T., Zhang, H., Wu, H., Wang, S., Ma, L., Long, M.: itransformer: inverted transformers are effective for time series forecasting. In: The Twelfth International Conference on Learning Representations, ICLR (2024)
18. Marisca, I., Cini, A., Alippi, C.: Learning to reconstruct missing data from spatiotemporal graphs with sparse observations. In: NeurIPS (2022)
19. Nie, Y., Nguyen, N.H., Sinthong, P., Kalagnanam, J.: A time series is worth 64 words: long-term forecasting with transformers. In: The Eleventh International Conference on Learning Representations, ICLR (2023)
20. Park, D., El-Sharkawi, M., Marks, R., Atlas, L., Damborg, M.: Electric load forecasting using an artificial neural network. IEEE Trans. Power Syst. **6**(2), 442–449 (1991)
21. Qian, Y., Tian, L., Zhai, Shufan Wu, R.: Informer-wgan: high missing rate time series imputation based on adversarial training and a self-attention mechanism. Algorithms **15**(7) (2022)
22. Schirmer, M., Eltayeb, M., Lessmann, S., Rudolph, M.: Modeling irregular time series with continuous recurrent units. In: ICML, vol. 162, pp. 19388–19405 (2022)
23. Sun, Z., Dai, J., Zhao, Y., Zhang, C., Ji, A.: A traffic flow forecasting model using graph convolutional recurrent neural networks with incomplete data. In: IEEE 26th International Conference on Intelligent Transportation Systems (ITSC), pp. 4669–4675 (2023)
24. Tarsitano, A., Falcone, M.: Missing-values adjustment for mixed-type data. J. Probab. Stat. **2011**, 1–20 (2011)
25. Wu, H., Xu, J., Wang, J., Long, M.: Autoformer: Decomposition transformers with auto-correlation for long-term series forecasting. In: Annual Conference on Neural Information Processing Systems, NeurIPS, pp. 22419–22430 (2021)
26. Yalavarthi, V.K., et al.: Grafiti: Graphs for forecasting irregularly sampled time series. In: Thirty-Eighth AAAI Conference on Artificial Intelligence, AAAI 2024, Canada, pp. 16255–16263 (2024)
27. Yang, S.B., Guo, C., Yang, B.: Context-aware path ranking in road networks. IEEE Trans. Knowl. Data Eng. **34**(7), 3153–3168 (2022)
28. Zeng, A., Chen, M., Zhang, L., Xu, Q.: Are transformers effective for time series forecasting? In: Thirty-Seventh AAAI Conference on Artificial Intelligence, AAAI, pp. 11121–11128 (2023)

29. Zhang, X., He, J., Li, Y., Chi, Y., Zhou, Y.: Recovery of corrupted data in wireless sensor networks using tensor robust principal component analysis. IEEE Commun. Lett. **25**(10), 3389–3393 (2021)
30. Zhang, Y., Thorburn, P.J.: Handling missing data in near real-time environmental monitoring: a system and a review of selected methods. Futur. Gener. Comput. Syst. **128**, 63–72 (2022)

Fake News Detection with Hypergraph Neural Networks via Leveraging User-Topic Interactions

Jin Ho Go(✉), Jiaojiao Jiang, and Sanjay Jha

The University of New South Wales, Kensington, NSW 2033, Australia
{jinho.go,jiaojiao.jiang,sanjay.jha}@unsw.edu.au

Abstract. The majority of current approaches to fake news detection seek to improve accuracy by leveraging social context based on pair-wise graph structures. However, these methods encounter two limitations. Firstly, simple graph structures are inherently limited in their ability to capture the complex relational dynamics that exist beyond dyadic associations within social networks. Secondly, social context-based fake news detection research, predominantly focused on user engagement, overlooks the crucial relationship between news content and its author. The author-topic connection is relevant to fake news detection, as author credibility is topic-dependent. To address these, we utilize our model to construct a hypergraph and introduce a hypergraph neural network that reflects both the engagement of spreaders with news, the relationships between news, spreaders, authors, and topics, and, indirectly, the author-topic connections via hyperedge interactions. Experiments on two real-world fake news datasets show that our model outperforms other GNN-based models.

Keywords: Fake news detection · Hypergraph · Graph Neural Network

1 Introduction

The impossibility of manually verifying the authenticity of the vast quantities of news disseminated daily underscores the critical need for automated detection strategies. While there are numerous automatic detection methods, they can broadly be categorized into two main approaches: social context-based and content analysis-based [15]. In essence, social context-based fake news detection offers a crucial advantage over purely content-based methods by leveraging the dynamics of how information spreads online. While content analysis focuses on the article itself, social context examines the reaction to it âĂŞ who is sharing it and with what commentary. Social context is also more resilient to sophisticated deception; even well-written fake news can be revealed by unusual propagation patterns [2,15]. Furthermore, it captures the interaction between entities in social networks and incorporates user engagement [5,11].

I. Awan et al. (Eds.): WISE 2025, LNCS 16368, pp. 404–415, 2026.
https://doi.org/10.1007/978-981-95-7251-9_27

Nevertheless, social context-based approaches for fake news detection are subject to the following two key limitations. Firstly, many social context-based fake news detection methods employ GNNs built on pair-wise structures. Such an approach, however, inadequately captures the complex group dynamics often inherent in fake news dissemination. Consequently, modeling higher-order, group-wise interactions is crucial for comprehensively understanding fake news propagation. Secondly, research in social context-based fake news detection predominantly emphasizes user engagement signals (e.g., likes, shares). This focus often neglects other critical social context dimensions, notably the relationship between news content and its authorial source. Linking authors to topics is crucial because credibility is topic-dependent [3]; an author might be reliable in one domain but biased in another, especially regarding political or social issues [1].

To address these issues, we propose an efficient hypergraph neural network that learns enriched representations from heterogeneous hyperedge connections by deriving Author-Topic connections, utilizing not only user interactions but also inter-hyperedge connections. We construct a hypergraph to group news nodes using different types of hyperedges: spreader-based hyperedges representing spreader activity, author-based hyperedges representing author information, and topic-based hyperedges representing topics contained in the news content. We apply Author-Topic Modeling(ATM) [12] to the datasets to extract word clusters that represent the interaction between author-based and topic-based hyperedges. The resulting hypergraph is then trained through a three-stage process in the hypergraph convolution layer. Crucially, the second stage focuses on learning the interaction between author-based and topic-based hyperedges, thereby capturing and reflecting the author-topic connections in the learned representation. Experimental results on real-world datasets incorporating author information demonstrate the proposed model's outstanding performance over several established baselines.

2 Related Work

Graph Neural Networks (GNNs) have proven highly effective at modeling structural relations in data [8]. However, their focus on simple pairwise connections limits their ability to capture more complex, high-order relationships. To address this limitation, hypergraph learning is emerging as a powerful and flexible technique for modeling such complex relations. The first work that applies GNNs to hypergraphs is HGNN [6]. To leverage complex and high-order relations for better representation learning, it designs a hyperedge convolution operation. HyperGCL [13] is a hypergraph generative model that applies contrastive learning for robust and fair hypergraph representation learning.

Due to its capacity to capture complicated high-order relations, hypergraph neural networks have found applications in various domains. We can conclude that a hypergraph neural network is suitable for numerous real-world scenarios, particularly in the context of complex social networks. However, its application in the domain of detecting fake news in online social networks is relatively limited. SAHyperGAT [4] primarily focuses on news content, lacking the integration of high-order relations of both authors and news. HGFND [9] requires numerous types of hyperedges, increasing the difficulty of dataset construction and impacting real-world practicality. Moreover, it still relies on vanilla GNNs to learn hypergraph representations and is limited in capturing latent high-order relations. Thus, this work is proposed to address such issues.

3 Preliminaries

3.1 Hypergraph

A hypergraph $G = (V, E)$ is a generalization of a standard graph in which each edge, called a hyperedge, can connect any number of vertices—not just two. V denotes the node set, and E denotes the edge set. Instead of connecting only two vertices like a pairwise edge, a hyperedge $e_j \in E$ can connect any subset of nodes in V, i.e., $e_j \subseteq V$. This allows hypergraphs to model complex relationships involving multiple entities simultaneously, extending the pairwise connections found in traditional graphs.

A convenient way to represent the structure of a hypergraph is through an incidence matrix $\mathbf{H} \in \mathbb{R}^{|V| \times |E|}$, with the entries defined as:

$$\mathbf{H}_{i,j} = \begin{cases} 1, & \text{if } v_i \in e_j, \\ 0, & \text{if } v_i \notin e_j. \end{cases}$$

In this paper, we represent each news as a node $v_i \in V$, and we will define three types of hyperedges that group multiple nodes with some common attributes in Sect. 4.1.

3.2 News Propagation Tree

For each article v_i, its propagation tree P_i is defined as a tuple $P_i = (V_i, \mathbf{A}_i)$, where $V_i = \{v_i\} \cup S_i$ denotes the set of users involved in the dissemination of v_i, including the source article and its spreaders. The adjacency matrix $\mathbf{A}_i$ encodes the inferred diffusion network based on the temporal order of user engagements: specifically, $\mathbf{A}_i(j, k) = 1$ if user s_j is inferred to have propagated the news to user s_k, and $\mathbf{A}_i(j, k) = 0$ otherwise. Thus, the propagation tree P_i captures both the engagement of spreaders S_i with the source news v_i and the structure of their interactions as determined by the time-inferred diffusion pattern.

4 Proposed Method

4.1 Hyperedge Construction

To construct a hypergraph that captures higher-order relationships among various types of interactions among news, news authors, and news spreaders, we establish three type of hyperedges (e^S, e^A and e^T) for hypergraph $G = (V, E)$:

- A **spreader**-based hyperedge e^S links multiple news articles through their common spreader, representing the spreader's engagement across different pieces of news. Hence, each hyperedge e^S corresponds to a user.
- An **author**-based hyperedge e^A connects multiple news articles that share the same author, capturing the author's involvement across different pieces of content. Hence, each hyperedge e^A corresponds to an author.
- A **topic**-based hyperedge e^T connects multiple news articles that are associated with the same topic, capturing thematic relationships and enabling the modeling of topic-specific dissemination patterns. Hence, each hyperedge e^T corresponds to a topic (Fig. 1).

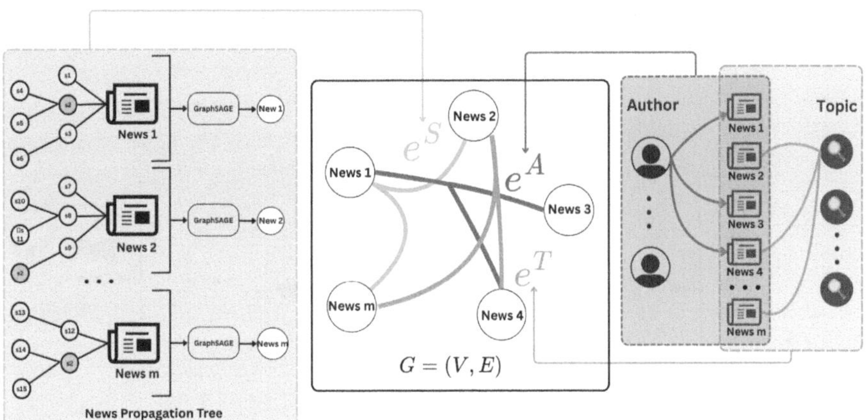

Fig. 1. Hypergraph with three types of hyperedges: (1) spreader-based hyperedges (yellow), (2) author-based hyperedges (blue); (3) topic-based hyperedges (green). (Color figure online)

4.2 Initialize Node Representation via Embedding Propagation Tree

Each node (i.e., news article) v_i is associated with a propagation tree $P_i = (V_i, \mathbf{A}_i)$. To process the propagation structure for each news article v_i, we employ GraphSAGE [7]. From the GraphSAGE output, we extract a compact representation of the propagation pattern, denoted as $\mathbf{x}_i$. This extraction is performed using a function, referred to as ROOT, which summarizes the node embeddings from the final layer of GraphSAGE.

To construct a comprehensive news representation that incorporates both content and propagation information, we concatenate $\mathbf{x}_i$ with the original feature vector of the news article, denoted as $\mathbf{n}_i$.

The resulting vector is then passed through a non-linear activation function, such as ReLU, to introduce non-linearity, followed by a fully connected layer

f, producing the initial node representation $\mathbf{x}_i^0 \in \mathbb{R}$ for the hypergraph. The process is formally defined as:

$$\mathbf{x}_i = \text{ROOT}(\text{GraphSAGE}(P_i)), \tag{1}$$

$$\mathbf{x}_i^0 = f\left(\text{ReLU}(\mathbf{x}_i \oplus \mathbf{n}_i)\right), \tag{2}$$

where $\oplus$ denotes the vector concatenation operation.

4.3 Update Node Representation via Multi-stage Aggregation

The representation of each node is updated via three iterative stages: node-to-hyperedge (**NTH**), hyperedge-to-hyperedge (**HTH**) and hyperedge-to-node (**HTN**), which we will introduce in detail in the following subsections (Fig. 2).

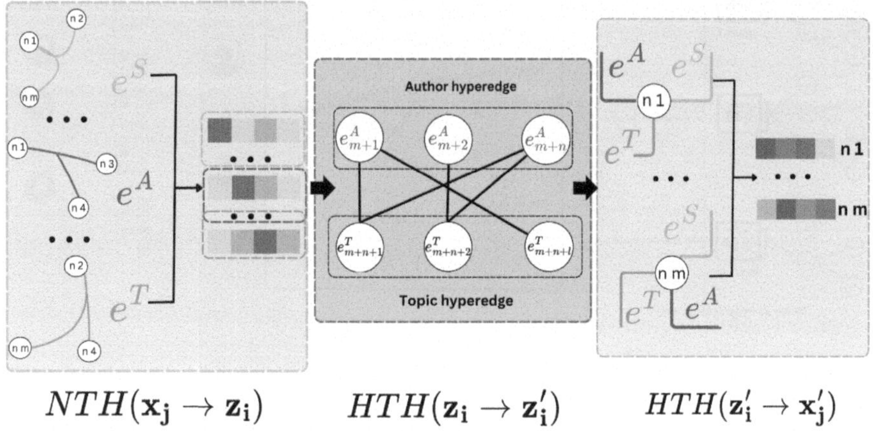

Fig. 2. Multi-Stage Aggregation for Learning representations of nodes and hyperedges: (1)Node-to-Hyperedge (NTH); (2) Hyperedge-to-Hyperedge (HTH); (3) Hyperedge-to-Node (HTN)

(1) Node-to-Hyperedge (NTH). To update a hyperedge embedding, information is aggregated from all incident nodes. Rather than treating all nodes equally, we account for their varying influence, i.e., nodes more aligned with the hyperedge should contribute more. For a given hyperedge e_i^S (e_i^A, or e_i^T), we aggregate node features using a weighted function f_{NTH}, incorporating both node influence and the prior hyperedge feature (denoted $\mathbf{z}_{i-1}^S$, $\mathbf{z}_{i-1}^A$, or $\mathbf{z}_{i-1}^T$ corresponding to Spreader, Author, and Topic, respectively):

$$\mathbf{z}_i^k = f_{\text{NTH}}(\{\mathbf{x}_j^0\}_{v_j \in e_i^k}, \mathbf{z}_{i-1}^k), \quad k \in \{S, A, T\}, \tag{3}$$

where the node-to-hyperedge aggregation function f_{NTH} computes a weighted aggregation of the initial node features within a hyperedge, and S, A, and T correspond to Spreader, Author, and Topic respectively. Given the set of nodes $\{v_j\}$ incident to hyperedge e_i, the contribution of each node is modulated by its relevance to the hyperedge. Specifically, attention weights are learned based on the similarity between each node feature $\mathbf{x}_j^0$ and the current hyperedge representation. Formally:

$$f_{\text{NTH}}(\{\mathbf{x}_j^0\}_{v_j \in e_i^k}, z_{i-1}^k) = \sum_{v_j \in e_i^k} \alpha_{ij}^k \mathbf{x}_j^0 + \mathbf{z}_{i-1}^k, \quad k \in \{S, A, T\}, \tag{4}$$

where α_{ij}^k $(k \in \{S, A, T\})$ is the normalized attention coefficient, computed as:

$$\alpha_{ij}^k = \frac{\exp\left(\phi(\mathbf{x}_j^0, \mathbf{z}_{i-1}^k)\right)}{\sum_{v_l \in e_i^k} \exp\left(\phi(\mathbf{x}_l^0, \mathbf{z}_{i-1}^k)\right)}, \quad k \in \{S, A, T\}, \tag{5}$$

and $\phi(\cdot, \cdot)$ is cosine similarity scoring function.

(2) Hyperedge-to-Hyperedge (HTH). To capture interactions between hyperedges, we introduce an inter-hyperedge learning module. **First**, we construct a bipartite graph $G^{AT} = (V^A \cup V^T, E^{AT})$, where each author-based hyperedge e^A and topic-based hyperedge e^T is treated as a node in sets V^A and V^T, respectively. An edge $e^{AT} \in E^{AT}$ is established between e^A and e^T based on semantic relevance derived from the Author-Topic model (ATM) [12]. Notably, spreader-based hyperedges are excluded from this graph, as the initial node representation $\mathbf{x}_i^0$ already encodes spreader engagement. **Then**, we apply a GNN [7] on G^{AT} to propagate information across author-topic hyperedges and refine their embeddings:

$$(\mathbf{z}_i^A)', (\mathbf{z}_i^T)' = f_{\text{GNN}}(G^{AT}, \mathbf{z}_i^A, \mathbf{z}_i^T), \tag{6}$$

where f_{GNN} denotes the GNN update function over the bipartite structure.

(3) Hyperedge-to-Node (HTN). Finally, we update the representation of each **news article** node v_i in the hypergraph G by aggregating information from all incident hyperedges. This allows each news node to integrate signals from its associated spreaders, authors, and topics:

$$\mathbf{x}_i' = f_{\text{HTN}}(\{\mathbf{z}_j'\}_{e_j \ni v_i}, \mathbf{x}_i^0), \tag{7}$$

where f_{HTN} denotes the hyperedge-to-node aggregation function, which combines the updated hyperedge embeddings $\{\mathbf{z}_j'\}$ with the initial node feature $\mathbf{x}_i^0$. More specifically, f_{HTN} computes an attention-weighted sum over all hyperedges incident to node v_i. Each hyperedge contributes to the updated node embedding proportionally to its relevance, determined by an attention mechanism conditioned on the initial node feature $\mathbf{x}_i^0$ and each hyperedge feature $\mathbf{z}_j'$:

$$f_{\text{HTN}}(\{\mathbf{z}_j'\}_{e_j \ni v_i}, \mathbf{x}_i^0) = \sum_{e_j \ni v_i} \beta_{ij}\mathbf{z}_j' + \mathbf{x}_i, \quad \beta_{ij} = \frac{\exp(\phi(\mathbf{x}_i, \mathbf{z}_j'))}{\sum_{e_k \ni v_i} \exp(\phi(\mathbf{x}_i, \mathbf{z}_k'))}, \tag{8}$$

where β_{ij} is the attention coefficient indicating the importance of hyperedge e_j to node v_i.

4.4 Hypergraph Neural Network Layer

This layer processes the hypergraph incidence matrix $\mathbf{H}$ and the node feature matrix $\mathbf{X}$ as input. The l-th layer of the Hypergraph Neural Network, a core component of this model's architecture, is formally defined through a spectral expression derived from the proposed multi-Stage aggregation methodology. In our experiment, the model receives initial node features as input, denoted by $\mathbf{X}^{(0)} \in \mathbb{R}^{|V| \times d}$, where d refers to the dimension of news attribute vectors. It is necessary to derive initial hyperedge features. This is accomplished by computing the mean of the features of all nodes belonging to each respective hyperedge.

The initial aggregation of node features within a hyperedge is represented by the $\mathbf{H}^\top \mathbf{X}^{(l)}$. However, a more robust approach incorporates normalization, resulting in the expression $\mathbf{D}_e^{-\frac{1}{2}} \mathbf{H}^\top \mathbf{D}_v^{-\frac{1}{2}} \mathbf{X}^{(l)}$. This normalization step enhances stability and performance. Following this aggregation, the resulting node information is combined with the current hyperedge embeddings to produce updated embeddings. Subsequently, the node information is added to the existing information within the hyperedge to update the hyperedge embeddings. A hyperparameter α is introduced to control the influence of the node information. This process can be expressed as follows:

$$\mathbf{Z}^{(l)} = \alpha \mathbf{D}_e^{-\frac{1}{2}} \mathbf{H}^T \mathbf{D}_v^{-\frac{1}{2}} \mathbf{X}^{(l)} + \mathbf{Z}^{(l)} \tag{9}$$

The incorporation of a self-attention mechanism facilitates the automatic learning of weights specific to each node in the aggregation process:

$$e_{ij} = (\mathbf{W}_Q^T \mathbf{x}_i)^T (\mathbf{W}_K^T \mathbf{z}_j), \quad \alpha_{ij} = \frac{\exp(e_{ij})}{\sum_{v_k \in N_{e_i}} \exp(e_{kj})} \tag{10}$$

Let $\mathbf{W}_Q$ and $\mathbf{W}_K$ denote learnable parameter matrices used in the self-attention mechanism. The attention coefficients, calculated between each node v_i and hyperedge e_j, are used to modulate the corresponding entries in the original hypergraph incidence matrix $\mathbf{H}$. Specifically, each non-zero element h_{ij} in $\mathbf{H}$ is replaced by its corresponding attention coefficient, resulting in an attention-weighted incidence matrix $\mathbf{H}_{att}$. Consequently, the output of the l-th stage is given by:

$$\mathbf{Z}_{att}^{(l)} = \sigma\left(\left(\alpha_1 \mathbf{D_e}^{-\frac{1}{2}} \mathbf{H}_{att}^T \mathbf{D_v}^{-\frac{1}{2}} \mathbf{X}^{(\mathbf{l})} + \mathbf{Z}^{(l)}\right) \theta_1^{(\mathbf{l})}\right) \tag{11}$$

where $\mathbf{Z}^{(l)}$ represents the l-th layer hyperedge embeddings, $\mathbf{X}^{(l)}$ is the l-th layer node embeddings, σ denotes a non-linear activation function.

The resulting hyperedge feature matrix $\mathbf{Z}_{att}^{(l)}$ from NTH aggregation is then used as input to the HTH interaction stage. Since the hyperedge interaction graph G_{ed} is a simple graph with edge weights representing the strength of connections between hyperedges, we utilize a Graph Convolutional Network (GCN) with self-loops to model its structure and refine the hyperedge embeddings. This yields the updated hyperedge embeddings $\mathbf{Z}^{(l+1)}$. The output of the HTH stage can be expressed as:

$$\mathbf{Z}^{(l+1)} = \sigma\left(\mathbf{D}_e^{-\frac{1}{2}}(\mathbf{A_{ed}} + \mathbf{I})\mathbf{D}_e^{-\frac{1}{2}}\mathbf{Z}_{att}^{(l)}\boldsymbol{\theta}_2^{(l)}\right) \tag{12}$$

where $\mathbf{Z}_{att}^{(l)}$ has aggregated node information, σ denotes a non-linear activation function, $\mathbf{I}$ represents the identity matrix, and $\boldsymbol{\theta}_2^{(l)}$ is the trainable parameter matrix.

Following a similar methodology to the NTH stage, we aggregate information from hyperedges back to nodes. This is accomplished using a mean aggregation approach, represented by the matrix operation $\mathbf{D}_v^{-1/2}\mathbf{H}\mathbf{D}_e^{-1/2}\mathbf{Z}^{(l+1)}$. The resulting aggregated hyperedge information is then combined with the original node features. A hyperparameter β is introduced to govern the relative contribution of the aggregated hyperedge information and the original node features. The output of this HTN stage is thus given by:

$$\mathbf{X}^{(l+1)} = \beta\mathbf{D}_v^{-\frac{1}{2}}\mathbf{H}\mathbf{D}_e^{-\frac{1}{2}}\mathbf{Z}^{(l+1)} + \mathbf{X}^{(l)} \tag{13}$$

To enhance the representation of hyperedge-to-node relationships, we introduce an attention mechanism. This mechanism refines the incidence matrix $\mathbf{H}$ by learning attention weights, effectively optimizing the hypergraph structure. The resulting information propagation from hyperedges to nodes is then formulated as:

$$\mathbf{X^{(l+1)}} = \sigma\left(\left(\beta\mathbf{D_v}^{-\frac{1}{2}}(\mathbf{H}_{att})\mathbf{D_e}^{-\frac{1}{2}}\mathbf{Z^{(l+1)}} + \mathbf{X^{(l)}}\right)\theta_{\mathbf{3}}^{(\mathbf{l})}\right) \tag{14}$$

where β is a hyperparameter controlling the influence of the aggregated hyperedge information, $\mathbf{W}'_Q$, $\mathbf{W}'_K$, and $\boldsymbol{\theta}_3^{(l)}$ are learnable parameter matrices, and $\mathbf{H}_{att}$ is the attention-weighted incidence matrix computed in this stage.

4.5 Classification

After deriving the updated representation $\mathbf{x}'_i$ for each news article node v_i through the multi-stage aggregation process, we proceed with the classification task using a fully connected (dense) output layer. This layer maps the learned embedding $\mathbf{x}'_i$ to a probability distribution over the target classes. Specifically, we apply a linear transformation parameterized by a trainable weight matrix θ and a bias vector $\mathbf{b}$, followed by a non-linear activation function and a Softmax function to produce the final class probabilities. The computation is formally defined as:

$$\hat{y}_i = \text{Softmax}\left(\text{ReLU}\left(\theta \mathbf{x}_i' + \mathbf{b}\right)\right). \tag{15}$$

The output $\hat{y}_i$ represents the model's predicted probabilities for the binary classification task (i.e., true vs. fake news).

5 Experiments

5.1 Experimental Setup

We perform a comprehensive comparative study against six established baselines. The comparison includes two traditional graph convolutional approaches (**GCN** [10] and **GAT** [16]) as well as four models designed for fake news detection: **UPFD** [5] and **Bi-GCN** [2] which rely on pairwise graph structures, and **HGNN** [6] and **HGFND** [9], which leverage hypergraph representations.

Each model is trained over ten independent runs with different random seeds to ensure robustness. For each run, the model parameters that yield the highest validation accuracy are selected for testing. Performance is measured using standard classification metrics: *accuracy*, *precision*, *recall*, and *F1 score*. The experiments were conducted on a high-performance computing (HPC) cluster. This facility provided access to computational nodes equipped with up to six Nvidia L40S GPUs (each with 48GB of VRAM) and eight CPU cores, running RPM-based Linux distributions.

5.2 Datasets

We utilize two real-world datasets (**PolitiFact** and **GossipCop**) sourced from the FakeNewsNet repository [14], a comprehensive benchmark for studying misinformation in news media. GossipCop contains fact-checked entertainment news from Gossip Cop, focusing on celebrity-related misinformation. PolitiFact consists of political news content verified by the PolitiFact fact-checking website. Due to limited access to X data within FakeNewsNet, we adopt the enriched feature sets provided by UPFD [5], which offer a more accessible and complete alternative (Table 1).

Table 1. Statistics of the datasets in experiments

Dataset	#Graphs (#Fake)	#Total Nodes	#Total Edges	#Avg. Nodes per Graph
Politifact	314 (157)	41,054	40,740	131
Gossipcop	5464 (2732)	314,262	308,798	58

5.3 Experiment Result

Experiment on Original Datasets. As shown in Table 2, our proposed model demonstrates superior performance on both the **PolitiFact** and **GossipCop** datasets when compared with a diverse set of baseline models, including traditional GCNs (GCN and GAT), user preference-based methods (UPFD and Bi-GCN), and hypergraph-based methods (HGNN and HGFND). Specifically, on the **PolitiFact** dataset, our model achieves the highest F1 score of **0.915**, outperforming HGFND, the previous best model, which scored 0.887. Notably, our model exhibits substantial improvements in both precision (0.918) and recall (0.912), indicating its balanced effectiveness in identifying both fake and real news content.

On the **GossipCop** dataset, the results further confirm the robustness of our model. It attains an F1 score of **0.972**, second only slightly to HGFND (0.977). However, our model achieves a better trade-off between recall (0.974) and precision (0.971), suggesting it is more consistent and reliable under varied real-world conditions. While hypergraph-based methods generally outperform traditional GCNs and user-centric baselines, our model takes this a step further by effectively capturing high-order interactions and leveraging enhanced representations. Overall, these results highlight the efficacy of our approach in both standard and complex settings, reinforcing its suitability for the task of fake news detection.

Table 2. The results on the adopted datasets

Method	Politifact				Gossipcop			
	Acc.	Prec.	Recall	F1	Acc.	Prec.	Recall	F1
GCN [10]	0.699	0.711	0.689	0.696	0.931	0.946	0.934	0.940
GAT [16]	0.709	0.721	0.710	0.715	0.935	0.941	0.937	0.938
UPFD [5]	0.813	0.828	0.824	0.825	0.951	0.954	0.954	0.956
Bi-GCN [2]	0.811	0.815	0.814	0.818	0.953	0.958	0.951	0.955
HGNN [6]	0.827	0.838	0.854	0.845	0.959	0.952	0.964	0.956
HGFND [9]	0.884	0.884	0.891	0.887	**0.976**	**0.973**	**0.982**	0.977
Our model	**0.903**	**0.918**	**0.912**	**0.915**	0.969	0.971	0.974	**0.972**

Experiment on Modified Datasets. We conducted additional experiments on a modified dataset, from which news data without associated author information was excluded. Table 3 presents the performance of various models on the modified versions of the **PolitiFact** and **GossipCop** datasets. Across all metrics, our proposed model consistently outperforms the baseline methods. On the **PolitiFact** dataset, our model achieves the highest F1 score of **0.916**, surpassing the previous best model, HGFND, which recorded an F1 score of 0.897.

The improvement is particularly evident in recall (0.910 vs. 0.893), highlighting our model's enhanced capability in identifying fake news. While other models such as UPFD, Bi-GCN, and HGNN also benefit from the modified data, their performance remains noticeably inferior to our approach.

A similar pattern is observed on the **GossipCop** dataset, where our model attains an F1 score of **0.982**, again outperforming HGFND (0.979) and substantially ahead of traditional models like GCN, GAT, and UPFD. The high precision (0.986) and recall (0.977) scores further indicate our model's robustness in minimizing both false positives and false negatives. These results collectively demonstrate not only the effectiveness of our model but also its strong generalization capability when applied to modified or enhanced datasets. The consistent performance gains across two datasets and multiple evaluation metrics underscore the advantages of our model's architecture and its adaptability to diverse fake news detection scenarios.

Table 3. Experimental results on modified datasets

Method	Politifact				Gossipcop			
	Acc.	Prec.	Recall	F1	Acc.	Prec.	Recall	F1
GCN	0.812	0.823	0.802	0.806	0.937	0.943	0.936	0.941
GAT	0.822	0.822	0.815	0.820	0.938	0.939	0.935	0.938
UPFD	0.825	0.831	0.840	0.835	0.961	0.957	0.952	0.956
Bi-GCN	0.820	0.828	0.832	0.830	0.944	0.956	0.959	0.957
HGNN	0.848	0.842	0.851	0.845	0.960	0.954	0.948	0.951
HGFND	0.896	0.912	0.893	0.897	0.978	0.977	0.985	0.979
Our model	**0.912**	**0.924**	**0.910**	**0.916**	**0.984**	**0.986**	**0.977**	**0.982**

6 Conclusion

In this work, we introduce a novel HGNN framework for fake news detection. Its key innovation is the integration of author-topic relationships directly into the hypergraph structure. We construct expressive hyperedges that connect news, users, and their latent topical interests, enabling the model to learn robust, context-aware embeddings. On two real-world datasets, PolitiFact and GossipCop, our method shows significant advantages over existing approaches, especially when author data is present. This work underscores the value of using hypergraphs and indirect signals like author-topic associations, for effective fake news detection.

References

1. Beauvais, C.: Fake news: Why do we believe it? Joint Bone Spine **89**(4), 105371 (2022)
2. Bian, T., et al: Rumor detection on social media with bi-directional graph convolutional networks. In: Proceedings of the AAAI Conference on Artificial Intelligence, vol. 34, pp. 549–556 (2020)
3. Broda, E., Strömbäck, J.: Misinformation, disinformation, and fake news: lessons from an interdisciplinary, systematic literature review. Ann. Int. Commun. Assoc. **48**(2), 139–166 (2024)
4. Dong, D., Lin, F., Li, G., Liu, B.: Sentiment-aware fake news detection on social media with hypergraph attention networks. In: 2022 IEEE International Conference on Systems, Man, and Cybernetics (SMC), pp. 2174–2180. IEEE (2022)
5. Dou, Y., Shu, K., Xia, C., Yu, P.S., Sun, L.: User preference-aware fake news detection. In: Proceedings of the 44th international ACM SIGIR Conference on Research and Development in Information Retrieval, pp. 2051–2055 (2021)
6. Feng, Y., You, H., Zhang, Z., Ji, R., Gao, Y.: Hypergraph neural networks. In: Proceedings of the AAAI Conference on Artificial Intelligence, vol. 33, pp. 3558–3565 (2019)
7. Hamilton, W., Ying, Z., Leskovec, J.: Inductive representation learning on large graphs. In: Advances in Neural Information Processing Systems, vol. 30 (2017)
8. Hu, L., Wei, S., Zhao, Z., Wu, B.: Deep learning for fake news detection: a comprehensive survey. AI Open (2022)
9. Jeong, U., Ding, K., Cheng, L., Guo, R., Shu, K., Liu, H.: Nothing stands alone: relational fake news detection with hypergraph neural networks. In: 2022 IEEE International Conference on Big Data (Big Data), pp. 596–605. IEEE (2022)
10. Kipf, T.N., Welling, M.: Semi-supervised classification with graph convolutional networks. In: International Conference on Learning Representations (ICLR) (2017)
11. Mridha, M.F., Keya, A.J., Hamid, M.A., Monowar, M.M., Rahman, M.S.: A comprehensive review on fake news detection with deep learning. IEEE Access **9**, 156151–156170 (2021)
12. Rosen-Zvi, M., Griffiths, T., Steyvers, M., Smyth, P.: The author-topic model for authors and documents. arXiv preprint arXiv:1207.4169 (2012)
13. Saifuddin, K.M., Ji, J.S., Akbas, E.: HyperGCL: multi-modal graph contrastive learning via learnable hypergraph views. arXiv preprint arXiv:2502.13277 (2025)
14. Shu, K., Mahudeswaran, D., Wang, S., Lee, D., Liu, H.: FakeNewsNet: a data repository with news content, social context, and spatiotemporal information for studying fake news on social media. Big Data **8**(3), 171–188 (2020)
15. Shu, K., Sliva, A., Wang, S., Tang, J., Liu, H.: Fake news detection on social media: a data mining perspective. ACM SIGKDD Explor. Newsl. **19**(1), 22–36 (2017)
16. Veličković, P., Cucurull, G., Casanova, A., Romero, A., Liò, P., Bengio, Y.: Graph attention networks. In: International Conference on Learning Representations (2018)

Aspect-Oriented GraphQL

Curtis Dyreson(✉)

Department of Computer Science, Utah State University, Logan, UT, USA
curtis.dyreson@usu.edu
http://cs.usu.edu/people/CurtisDyreson/

Abstract. In this paper we apply the aspect-oriented programming paradigm to GraphQL, a query language for web services. Aspect-oriented programming is a technique to quickly and easily add support for *cross-cutting concerns* to programs. Data also has cross-cutting concerns such as provenance, versioning, and testing. These cross-cutting data concerns can be represented as *advice* that annotates data. This paper shows how to add support for aspect-oriented advice to GraphQL schemas and queries to create Aspect-oriented GraphQL. We describe a software architecture that leverages GraphQL itself to implement Aspect-oriented GraphQL.

1 Introduction

Web applications rely on *web services* for data management. A web service is an *application programming interface* (API) endpoint that allows a client to interact with a back-end database over the web. Web services are ubiquitous; when online users shop, make dinner reservations, buy airline tickets, vote, or post social media updates each interaction typically invokes several web services.

GraphQL is a technology for improving the development and use of web services [18]. Originally developed by Facebook and widely used in industry, GraphQL is a query language for a web services API. To use GraphQL, a developer specifies a *schema* that describes the *types* of objects provided by the API. GraphQL supports *queries* that read data as well as *mutations* that update data on the types provided by the schema.

GraphQL, however, lacks support for *cross-cutting* data concerns. A cross-cutting data concern is a data need that is *universal* (potentially applicable to an entire data collection) and *widespread* (can be used to enhance many different data collections). Many data collections have cross-cutting data concerns, and as a collection evolves, new concerns may arise. Data *security* and *privacy* policies govern every interaction with a datum [4,10,15]. Security and privacy are of special concern in cloud computing since data is stored and processed in the cloud on potentially untrustworthy computers [6,28,34]. Data quality is another potential cross-cutting concern [1]. Data warehouses aggregate data from a variety of data sources of varying quality and queries that mix low and high quality data should provide a measure of quality along with a result. Data

I. Awan et al. (Eds.): WISE 2025, LNCS 16368, pp. 416–430, 2026.
https://doi.org/10.1007/978-981-95-7251-9_28

provenance [8,9] and *lineage* [2,7] track the data and/or processes that produce a query result, which aids in debugging and understanding complex queries. *Time* is another potential cross-cutting concern, both the time of the transaction that creates a datum and the time that it is valid in the real-world need to be tracked for many applications [27]. Each of these potential cross-cutting concerns has an individual, distinct semantics.

To support cross-cutting data concerns we look to aspect-oriented programming (AOP) to provide a framework that can be adapted to our needs. AOP was developed to extend existing systems with new functionality without having to reprogram the system and has been previously researched in databases [11,13,29,30].

In this paper we model cross-cutting concerns as *data aspects* that are woven into the GraphQL schemas and queries. This paper makes the following contributions.

- We show how to weave data aspects into GraphQL schemas and queries. To the best of our knowledge, this is the first work on weaving data aspects into GraphQL.
- To support Aspect-oriented GraphQL we give a denotational semantics for mapping aspect-oriented schemas and queries into *representational* schemas and queries, which are in standard GraphQL, hence, GraphQL itself can be leveraged to implement Aspect-oriented GraphQL.
- We extend Aspect-oriented GraphQL queries with *slice* and *stepDown* operators that enable users to query the data from different advice perspectives.

This paper is organized as follows. The next section reviews GraphQL. Section 3 introduces Aspect-oriented GraphQL. We then describe a software architecture for Aspect-oriented GraphQL. The final two sections cover related work and conclusions.

2 Review of GraphQL

In this section we review GraphQL. The starting point for GraphQL is a *schema*, which describes the types provided by an API as described in Sect. 2.1. GraphQL supports queries and mutations (updates) on the API. For our purposes mutations are a variation on queries, so this paper focuses exclusively on queries, which are presented in Sect. 2.2.

2.1 GraphQL Schemas

A GraphQL schema describes the types provided by an API. As an example, consider the GraphQL schema specification shown in Fig. 1. The schema is taken from GraphQL's tutorial for learning GraphQL [19] and has three object *types*: `Character`, `Planet`, and `Species`. The miniworld for the types is a science fiction world where a character originates on some planet, is of some species, and

```
type Character {
  name: String!
  friends: [Character]
  homeworld: Planet
  species: Species
}

type Planet {
  name: String
  climate: String
}

type Species {
  name: String
  lifespan: Int
  origin: Planet
}
```

Fig. 1. A GraphQL schema for a science fiction database

```
type Query {
  hero: Character
  characters: [Character]
  planets: [Planet]
}
```

Fig. 2. The `Query` type in GraphQL defines query "entry points"

```
Character = [
  { "id": "id_r2_d2",
    "name": "R2-D2",
    "friends": [
      "characterId": "id_luke_skywalker",
      "characterId": "id_han_solo"
    ],
    "homeworldId": "id_naboo",
    "species": "id_droid" },
   { "id": "id_luke_skywalker",
     "name": "Luke Skywalker",
     ... },
   ...
]
Planet = [
  { "id": "id_naboo",
    "name": "Naboo",
    "climate": "Temperate" },
  ...
]
Species = [
  { "id": "id_droid",
     "name": "Droid",
    ... }
  ...
]
```

Fig. 3. JSON that conforms to the GraphQL schema in Fig. 1 for a science fiction database

has friends who are characters. Each type has one or more properties. A property represents a key-value pair in JSON. The name of the property is the key and the schema records type constraints on the value. The `Character` type has `name`, `friends`, `homeworld`, and `species` properties. The `name` is a `String` type and must be non-null (indicated by the "`!`"). The `friends` property is a list (indicated by the enclosing brackets "`[]`") of references to `Characters`. The relationships among the types are graphically depicted in Fig. 4. The graph shows each type as a node and there is an edge for each type that has a property of another type.

The data is checked during query evaluation to ensure that it conforms to the schema, if not, an error is generated. As an example Fig. 3 shows a fragment of a data instance that conforms to the schema given in Fig. 1. Each JSON object implicitly contains an `id` property that uniquely identifies the object within the database, not just the type (database-wide unique identifiers are used to implement caching of objects). Sub-objects are represented as references, *e.g.*, the `homeworld` property in the `Character` type is a reference to a `Planet` object.

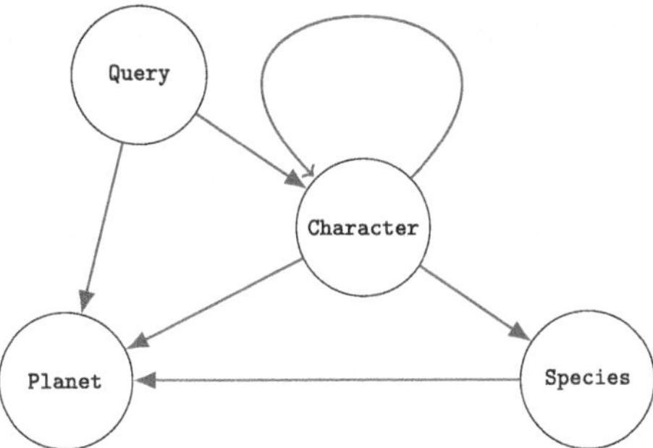

Fig. 4. Graphing the relationships among the schema types

```
query {
  hero {
    name
    friends {
      name
      homeworld {
        name
        climate
      }
    }
  }
}
```

Fig. 5. A query using the `hero` entry point

```
{ "data": {
    "hero": {
      "name": "R2-D2",
      "friends": [
        {  "name": "Luke Skywalker",
           "homeworld": {
             "name": "Tatooine",
             "climate": "Desert"
           }
        },
        ....
      ]
    }
}
```

Fig. 6. A fragment of the result of the GraphQL query in Fig. 5

2.2 Queries

Queries are at the core of GraphQL. Every GraphQL schema must also support an entry point for queries, this type is known as the `Query` type. The `Query` type specifies the root entry point(s) for the database. An example is given in Fig. 2. The `Query` type has three entry points:

1. `hero` reads a `Character`,
2. `characters` yields a list `Characters`, and
3. `planets`, which returns a list of `Planets`.

The entry point is the starting point for the query, more fields can be added to flesh out objects and sub-objects in a query result. An example is given in Fig. 5. In the example, the `hero` entry point is expanded to include the `name` and `friends` properties. The `friends` property is a list of `Characters`, and for each sub-object in the list the `name` and `homeworld` (which is a `Planet` type object) properties are selected. An example of the result of evaluating the query is given in Fig. 6.

Queries can also include *filters*, which are predicates to test the data for membership in the result. For example, suppose that we want to select the character named Luke Skywalker. Then we could filter the hero entry point in a query as follows:

```
hero(filter: { name: { eq: "Luke Skywalker" } }) {
    name
    ...
}
```

Entry points can also be specified to take arguments. For instance, we could modify the hero entry point to match a specific name as follows.

```
type Query {
    hero(name: String) : Character
    ...
}
```

The query to fetch Luke Skywalker would then be as follows.

```
hero(name: "Luke Skywalker") {
    name
    ...
}
```

3 Aspect-Oriented GraphQL

Science fiction data has cross-cutting concerns such as transaction time, quality, and testing. The data changes over time as edits to the data are made and new data is inserted. The changing lifetime can be captured with a transaction time data aspect. Transaction time is the time that the data was present in a data collection. The lifetime of a datum starts when the data is inserted and ends when it is deleted. The data is gathered from various sources and varies in quality. A quality data aspect can record the data's quality as a enum value, from LOW to HIGH. Finally, some data is present only for testing purposes, so should be excluded from consideration in normal queries. A data aspect can be used to distinguish testing data from other kinds of data, and only include testing data in testing scenarios.

This section describes how to capture the cross-cutting concerns. From a developer perspective the concerns add to the GraphQL schema. From a user perspective the concerns must be accounted for in GraphQL queries. We consider each impact in this section.

A key design goal of Aspect-oriented GraphQL is to minimize developer and user time and effort. Ideally a developer will be able to quickly annotate a schema to support data aspects, and for users little effort will need to be expended to write queries on aspect-oriented data. In Sect. 4 we describe the implementation architecture, which leverages GraphQL to support Aspect-oriented GraphQL.

```
# @aod directive declaration
directive @aod() on OBJECT | SCHEMA

# Character type has advice
type Character @aod {
  name: String
  friends: [Character]
  homeworld: Planet
  species: Species
}
...
```

Fig. 7. An Aspect-oriented GraphQL schema for the `Character` type of Fig. 1, additions are represented in a red font (Color figure online)

```
# Aspect-oriented Character
type Character {
  name: String
  friends: [Character]
  homeworld: Planet
  species: Species
  advice: [Advice]
}

# The Advice type has properties for each data aspect
type Advice {
  start: Int
  stop: Int
  quality: QualityEnum
  testing: Boolean
}

type QualityEnum {
  LOW
  MEDIUM
  HIGH
}
...
```

Fig. 8. The representational schema for the Character type adds an `advice` property of type `Advice`, which has properties for each kind of cross-cutting concern, the additions are in a red font (Color figure online)

3.1 Aspect-Oriented Schema

Data aspects augment types and the relationships between types. For example, suppose a `Character` object is edited to correct a misspelled name. Then both versions of the object would be present in the data collection, but each should be marked with a different transaction time period as the transaction time records when the data was live in the collection.

In Aspect-oriented GraphQL the `Character` type can be made aspect-oriented by using an `@aod` directive as shown in Fig. 7. A GraphQL directive is prefixed with the "`@`" character. Directives are essentially decorators in many popular programming languages. The `@aod` directive indicates that the type can have advice. The directive informs a mapping layer to add a data aspect to a type with an additional `advice` property as described further in Sect. 4.2 (and represented in Fig. 8 which will be explained in detail later).

Relationships between types can also have advice. The advice is added as an additional type. Suppose that the `friends` for a `Character` vary in the quality of the relationship, with known friends being of `HIGH` quality information, and unsure friend relationships being of `LOW` quality. The `@aod` directive adds advice to each relationship from a type as described further in Sect. 4.2.

3.2 Aspect-Oriented Queries

Aspect-oriented GraphQL supports queries that explicitly reference the data aspects. There are two kinds of queries, which we call *slice* and *stepDown*. Each kind of query is specified by a GraphQL operator.

- `slice(advice: AdviceFields!)` - A slice query takes all of the properties in an `Advice` object and returns the data, including the data aspects, that have the given advice. The `Advice` type is defined in Sect. 4.2.
- `stepDown(advice: AdviceFields!)` - A stepDown query takes all of the properties in an `Advice` object and returns the data without the data aspects, that have the given advice.

Queries that do not have an explicit aspect-oriented operator default to a slice using the *current* or default advice. For example, suppose the query is part of a set of queries executed in a session in which the client sets the transaction time the current time (the time `now`), an expected quality of `HIGH`, and testing turned `OFF` (these would be the default settings for each kind of advice), then any query would be wrapped in the following `slice` directive.

```
query {
  @slice({start: "now", stop: "now", quality: HIGH, testing: false})
    ...
}
```

4 Implementing Aspect-Oriented GraphQL

In this section we describe how to leverage GraphQL to support Aspect-oriented GraphQL. The key is to the support is a layer of software that maps an Aspect-oriented GraphQL schema (query) to a *representational* schema (query). The representational schema (query) is a GraphQL schema (query). The next section presents the software architecture for Aspect-oriented GraphQL. Following that are sections on the representational schema and representational queries.

4.1 A Software Architecture

Aspect-oriented GraphQL can be implemented as a software layer that wraps a GraphQL implementation. The implementation architecture is depicted in Fig. 9. The architecture has three main components.

1. The *schema mapping* component translates an Aspect-oriented GraphQL schema to a normal GraphQL schema by weaving `Advice` types into the schema as described in Sect. 4.2.
2. The *query mapping* component translates an Aspect-oriented GraphQL query to a GraphQL query as described in Sect. 4.3.
3. The *remove advice* component strips advice from a `stepDown` query since the query should yield a non-aspect-oriented result.

Each component also takes as input the *semantics* of the cross-cutting concerns that are supported. The semantics consist of the properties in the metadata, which in aggregate form the properties of the `Advice` type as well as *filters* on the properties as described further in Sect. 4.3.

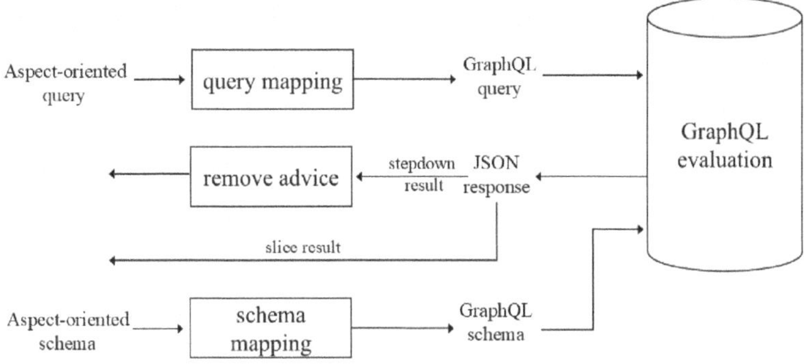

Fig. 9. Software architecture for Aspect-oriented GraphQL

4.2 Representational Schema

An aspect-oriented GraphQL schema is transformed to a representational schema by the schema mapping component. In this section we first describe the transformation informally and then give a denotational semantics for the transformation.

The transformation consists of two parts: transforming each type and transforming each relationship. An example of a type transformation is shown in Fig. 8. The figure shows the result of transforming the `Character` type of Fig. 7. The type is transformed by adding an `advice` property. The property's value is a list of (references to) `Advice` objects (the `Advice` type is given in Fig. 8). Each `Advice` object has properties for each kind of advice. For instance there are `start` and `stop` properties for transaction time advice, representing the start and stop times of the transaction time period. The schema shown in Fig. 8 is the *representational schema*, that is, it is a schema that represents aspect-oriented data. Importantly the representational schema is a GraphQL schema, so aspect-oriented GraphQL can be implemented using GraphQL.

The second part of the transformation is for relationships. Relationships between types can also have advice. The advice is added as an additional type. Suppose that the `friends` for a `Character` vary over time. To record the changing `friends` property changes from `Character` to `CC_AOD`. The `CC_AOD` type pairs `Advice` (an `Advice` type) with `data` (a `[Character]` type). Figure 10 shows the additional types that are added to the representational schema. Figure 12 graphs the representational schema's types and their relationships.

4.3 Aspect-Oriented Queries

Queries, as well as the schema, must be transformed in aspect-oriented GraphQL. We assume that there exist GraphQL resolvers for each type and property to supply the data in an aspect-oriented GraphQL instance from an API, database, or web service. Data is fetched in query evaluation by expanding the pattern of resolvers specified in the query from the root of the query to the leaf.

```
type Character {
  name: String
  friends: [CC_AOD]
  homeworld: [CP_AOD]
  species: [CS_AOD]
  advice: [Advice]
}

type CC_AOD {
  advice: Advice
  data: [Character]
}

type CP_AOD {
  advice: Advice
  data: Planet
}

type CS_AOD {
  advice: Advice
  data: Species
}
```

Fig. 10. A representational schema for an aspect-oriented `Character`, the blue font indicates the property added for advice on the type and the red font is for changes and additions made to represent the relationships with advice.

```
query aod(advice: advice) {
  hero {
    ...AdviceFields
    data {
      ...AdviceFields
      name
      friends {
        ...AdviceFields
        data {
          ...AdviceFields
          name
          homeworld {
            ...AdviceFields
            data {
              ...AdviceFields
              name
              climate
            }
          }
        }
      }
    }
  }
}

fragment adviceFields on Advice {
    advice(filter: {
              start: { ge: $start }
              stop: { le: $stop }
              quality: { ge: $quality }
              testing: { eq: $testing }
          })
        start
        stop
        quality
        testing
}
```

Fig. 11. A representational query for the aspect-oriented query of Fig. 5, changes are marked in red font, `AdviceFields` is a GraphQL query fragment

The query mapper transforms an Aspect-oriented GraphQL query to a representational GraphQL query. As an example of the transformation, consider the query given in Fig. 5 that uses the `hero` entry point. For aspect-oriented GraphQL the query is transformed to that given in Fig. 11.

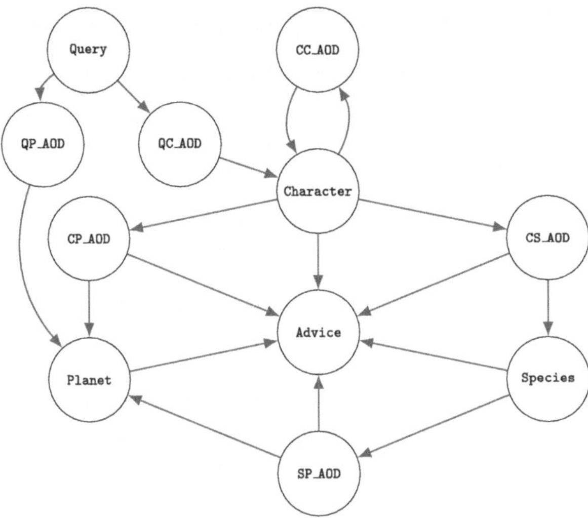

Fig. 12. Relationships among the aspect-oriented schema types

4.4 Remove Advice Component

The remove advice component strips advice-related fields from the result of a query, *i.e.*, it removes `advice` and `data` properties leaving nested properties in place. This is necessary for `stepDown` queries that return non-aspected data, in contrast to a `slice` query that returns the data together with the data aspects. GraphQL lacks functionality to perform this directly, though it is feature that has been proposed for future GraphQL specifications.

4.5 Denotational Semantics

The mappings from aspect-oriented to representational are syntactic transformations and can be formally described by a denotational semantics. The semantics given in Fig. 13 is the denotational semantics for mapping the schema. We assume that the names of the types that are introduced for attaching advice to relationships are generated, but have an `AOD` suffix. Note also that the properties of the `Advice` type depend upon what kind of cross-cutting concerns are supported.

Figure 14 is for mapping a query. Note that `AdviceFields` is a query fragment and its properties depends on the kinds of cross-cutting concerns involved, but it is easy to slot in different kinds of concerns as needed. If the query has an explicit `slice` or `stepDown` then the advice in the operators replaces the advice in the query header.

5 Evaluation

As a preliminary evaluation of the architecture we compared the time of a query run on the aspect-oriented type system versus the same query run on the nor-

```
⟦ type T @aod {
  t_1 : T_1
  t_2 : T_2
  ...
  t_n : T_n }
⟧ ≡ type T {
        t_1 : ⟦T_1⟧
        t_2 : ⟦T_2⟧
        ...
        t_n : ⟦T_n⟧
        advice: Advice
    }

// If T_i is scalar type
⟦T_i⟧ ≡ T_i

// If T_i is non-scalar (object) type
// L is a generated name
⟦T_i⟧ ≡ L_T_i

// For each T_i that is a non-scalar (object) type
⟦T_i⟧ ≡
  type L_T_i {
    advice: Advice
    data: T_i
  }
```

Fig. 13. Denotational rules for translating an AOD schema to a representational schema

```
⟦ query {
   p_1
   ...
   p_n
⟧ ≡ query aod(advice: advice) {
     ⟦p_1⟧
     ...
     ⟦p_n⟧
}

// If p_i is a name
⟦p_i⟧ ≡ p_i

// If p_i = m_i {q_1, ..., q_k} is an object
⟦m_i {q_1, ..., q_k}⟧ ≡
     m_i {
        ..AdviceFields
        data {
          ⟦q_1⟧
          ...
          ⟦q_k⟧
        }
```

Fig. 14. Denotational rules for translating an AOD query to a representational query

mal type system. The difference is that in the aspect-oriented case the representational schema adds advice to each type and splits each relationship into two relationships and an additional type, as well as filtering on the relationship advice. So in the aspect-oriented case there is a larger query pattern with more nesting of types. In database terms, each level of nesting involves an additional join in query evaluation, so the aspect-oriented cost should be higher but offers support for cross-cutting concerns. The idea of the preliminary evaluation is to get a sense of how much higher the cost will be.

The experimental setup uses PostGraphile version 4.14.0 (https://www.graphile.org/postgraphile). PostGraphile is a GraphQL server implementation for a Postgres database (https://www.postgresql.org). PostGraphile automatically constructs a GraphQL schema from a database schema. We used Postgres version 16 and created the Pagila database (https://github.com/neondatabase-labs/postgres-sample-dbs). For the aspect-oriented dataset we populated the database with additional relations to represent the advice and additional aspect-oriented types. Queries are evaluated by translating the GraphQL query to an SQL query. We used default indexes and server configuration for Postgres (*e.g.*, we made no changes to the database buffer size). The experiments were run on a Windows 11 machine with 16GB RAM and an i7-family CPU at 2.8GHz. We

Level of Nesting	GraphQL	Temporal GraphQL	Slowdown Factor
1	153	250	1.63
2	302	732	2.42
3	460	1002	2.17

Fig. 15. Time (in milliseconds) of GraphQL vs. Temporal GraphQL on deepening levels of nesting in a query

used the timings reported by the PostGraphile server. We averaged the times over 5 runs.

We tested with a GraphQL query that specified a hierarchy with deepening levels of nesting from the `rental` relation (16044 rows) to the `customer` (599 rows) and to the `address` relation (603 rows). We included in the result a single property for each field (including fewer properties sharpens the cost comparison since the time is not dominated by projecting all of the data). For the aspect-oriented GraphQL queries we introduced relations for advice on the relationships and added columns to the relations to reference advice. We used transaction time as the only cross-cutting concern. We also added filters to filter the advice (all rows had the same advice values so no results were actually filtered, but the cost of evaluating the filters is included).

The results are shown in Fig. 15. The table charts that Aspect-oriented GraphQL roughly doubles the cost of GraphQL queries, but even large results sizes are still overall "fast" (less than a second).

6 Related Work

To the best of our knowledge there have been no previous papers on Aspect-oriented GraphQL. The database research community has researched models and support for specific kinds of metadata. One of the most important and most widely researched kinds is temporal. Temporal extensions of every data model exist, for instance, relational [32] and XML [16]. Time metadata has also been added to SQL [23] and graph databases [20,33]. Software that supports various kinds of metadata, such as provenance in Postgres, have been developed [31]. We previously proposed Temporal GraphQL [14], which supports only time metadata, unlike Aspect-Oriented GraphQL. Temporal GraphQL also takes a time-centric view of implementing a temporal schema and supporting temporal queries. Queries with value filters would be costly to evaluate, whereas Aspect-oriented GraphQL queries can include efficient value filters. This paper generalizes the work in temporal databases by proposing an infrastructure that supports many kinds of metadata, not just temporal. Other relational model extensions to support security, privacy, probabilities, uncertainty, and reliability have been researched, but there is little previous research on support for manifold kinds of metadata in database management systems, though descriptive metadata has been studied in detail [5,9,17]. Most closely related to this paper are papers on querying different kinds of metadata in a semi-structured data model [12], in XQuery [21,22], the relational algebra [11], and Pig Latin [13]. There are several systems that have support for combining different kinds of metadata in the context of relational DBMSs. Mihaila et al. suggest annotating data with quality and reliability metadata and discuss how to query the data and metadata in combination [25]. The SPARCE system wraps or super-imposes a data model with a layer of metadata [26]. The metadata is active during queries to direct and constrain the search for desired information. Systems that provide mappings between metadata (schema) models are also becoming popular [3,24]. Our approach differs from these systems by focusing on GraphQL support.

7 Conclusions

GraphQL is a widely used technology for making it easier to develop and maintain web applications. GraphQL queries and mutations are used to read and write data to a back-end database through a web services API. But GraphQL lacks support for cross-cutting concerns. In this paper we presented Aspect-oriented GraphQL, a technology that borrows from the aspect-oriented programming paradigm to support cross-cutting data concerns. This paper shows how to weave data aspects into GraphQL schemas and queries. To the best of our knowledge, this is the first work on weaving data aspects into GraphQL. To support Aspect-oriented GraphQL we gave a denotational semantics for mapping aspect-oriented schemas and queries into representational schemas and queries, which are in standard GraphQL, hence, GraphQL itself can be leveraged to implement Aspect-oriented GraphQL. And we extended Aspect-oriented GraphQL queries with `slice` and `stepDown` operators that enable users to query the data from different advice perspectives.

In future we plan to investigate how meta-metadata can be supported, for example, to implement versioned quality where the quality metadata is itself versioned (so a rollback to a previous state of the data rolls back to the quality metadata at the time of the rollback). Meta-metadata involves adding another layer of advice to the advice that annotates data and relationships among the data, which should be a relatively straightforward extension. We also plan to research how data aspects impact GraphQL's pagination model. For instance, how to order the results using advice, *e.g.*, from high quality data first to low quality last. We also plan to work on aspect-oriented GraphQL database resolvers. Resolvers are server-side functions that fetch data from the database by evaluating a query and caching the result. If the database supports cross-cutting concerns then it should be possible to weave data aspects into resolvers. There are also opportunities for exploiting filtering on cached aspect-oriented data.

References

1. Batini, C., Scannapieco, M.: Data Quality: Concepts, Methodologies and Techniques. Data-Centric Systems and Applications. Springer (2006)
2. Benjelloun, O., Das Sarma, A., Halevy, A.Y., Theobald, M., Widom, J.: Databases with uncertainty and lineage. VLDB J. **17**(2), 243–264 (2008)
3. Bernstein, P.A.: Applying model management to classical meta data problems. In: CIDR (2003)
4. Bertino, E., Ghinita, G., Kamra, A.: Access control for databases: concepts and systems. Found. Trends Databases **3**(1–2), 1–148 (2011)
5. Bhagwat, D., Chiticariu, L., Tan, W.C., Vijayvargiya, G.: An Annotation Management System for Relational Databases. In: VLDB, pp. 900–911 (2004)
6. Birman, K., Chockler, G., van Renesse, R.: Toward a cloud computing research agenda. SIGACT News **40**(2), 68–80 (2009)
7. Bose, R., Frew, J.: Lineage retrieval for scientific data processing: a survey. ACM Comput. Surv. **37**(1), 1–28 (2005)
8. Buneman, P., Tan, W.C.: Provenance in databases. In: SIGMOD Conference, pp. 1171–1173 (2007)
9. Chiticariu, L., Tan, W.C., Vijayvargiya, G.: DBNotes: a post-it system for relational databases based on provenance. In: SIGMOD Conference, pp. 942–944 (2005)
10. Denning, D.E., Denning, P.J.: Data security. ACM Comput. Surv. **11**(3), 227–249 (1979)
11. Dyreson, C.E.: Aspect-oriented relational algebra. In: EDBT 2011, 14th International Conference on Extending Database Technology, pp. 377–388. ACM (2011)
12. Dyreson, C.E., Böhlen, M.H., Jensen, C.S.: Capturing and querying multiple aspects of semistructured data. In: VLDB, pp. 290–301 (1999)
13. Dyreson, C.E., Florez, O.U., Thakre, A., Sharma, V.: Supporting data aspects in pig Latin. In: Aspect-Oriented Software Development, AOSD, pp. 13–24. ACM (2013)
14. Dyreson, C.E., Sarkar, B.: Temporal graphQL: a tree grammar approach. In: 32th International Symposium on Temporal Representation and Reasoning, TIME 2025. LIPIcs, vol. 355, pp. 9:1–9:15. Schloss Dagstuhl - Leibniz-Zentrum für Informatik (2025)
15. Fung, B., Wang, K., Chen, R., Yu, P.S.: Privacy-preserving data publishing: a survey of recent developments. ACM Comput. Surv. **42**(4), 14:1–14:53 (2010)
16. Gao, D., Snodgrass, R.T.: Temporal slicing in the evaluation of XML queries. In: VLDB, pp. 632–643 (2003)
17. Geerts, F., Kementsietsidis, A., Milano, D.: MONDRIAN: annotating and querying databases through colors and blocks. In: ICDE, p. 82 (2006)
18. GraphQL: A Query Language for Your API. https://graphql.org. Accessed 10 May 2025
19. Introduction to GraphQL. https://graphql.org/learn. Accessed 10 May 2025
20. Hou, J., et al.: AeonG: an efficient built-in temporal support in graph databases. Proc. VLDB Endow. **17**(6), 1515–1527 (2024)
21. Jin, H., Dyreson, C.E.: Sanitizing using Metadata in MetaXQuery. In: SAC, pp. 1732–1736 (2005)
22. Jin, H., Dyreson, C.E.: Supporting proscriptive metadata in an XML DBMS. In: DEXA, pp. 479–492 (2008)

23. Kulkarni, K.G., Michels, J.-E.: Temporal features in SQL: 2011. SIGMOD Rec. **41**(3), 34–43 (2012)
24. Melnik, S., Rahm, E., Bernstein, P.A.: Rondo: a programming platform for generic model management. In: SIGMOD Conference, pp. 193–204 (2003)
25. Mihaila, G.A., Raschid, L., Vidal, M.-E.: Using quality of data metadata for source selection and ranking. In: WebDB (Informal Proceedings), pp. 93–98 (2000)
26. Murthy, S., Maier, D., Delcambre, L.M.L., Bowers, S.: Superimposed applications using SPARCE. In *ICDE*, p. 861 (2004)
27. Özsoyoglu, G., Snodgrass, R.T.: Temporal and real-time databases: a survey. IEEE Trans. Knowl. Data Eng. **7**(4), 513–532 (1995)
28. Pearson, S., Benameur, A.: Privacy, security and trust issues arising from cloud computing. In: IEEE Cloud Computing (CloudCom), pp. 693–702 (2010)
29. Rashid, A.: Aspect-Oriented Database Systems. Springer (2003)
30. Rashid, A., Loughran, N.: Relational database support for aspect-oriented programming. In: NetObjectDays, pp. 233–247 (2002)
31. Senellart, P., Jachiet, L., Maniu, S., Ramusat, Y.: ProvSQL: provenance and probability management in postgreSQL. Proc. VLDB Endow. **11**(12), 2034–2037 (2018)
32. Snodgrass, R.T. (ed.): The TSQL2 Temporal Query Language. Kluwer (1995)
33. Theodorakis, G., Clarkson, J., Webber, J.: Aion: efficient temporal graph data management. In: EDBT, pp. 501–514 (2024)
34. Zhou, M., Zhang, R., Xie, W., Qian, W., Zhou, A.: Security and privacy in cloud computing: a survey. In: International Conference on Semantics Knowledge and Grid (SKG), pp. 105–112 (2010)

Human-Centred Applications and Services

DIVE - A Neuro-Symbolic and User-Centered Approach for Data Insight Visualization

Jan-David Stütz[1,2(✉)], Selamawit Gegziabher[1], Victor Blaga[1], Oliver Karras[3], Allard Oelen[3], and Sören Auer[2,3]

[1] Robert Bosch GmbH, Gerlingen, Germany
{jan-david.stuetz,selamawit.gegziabher,victor.blaga}@de.bosch.com
[2] Leibniz University Hannover, Hannover, Germany
[3] Leibniz Information Centre for Science and Technology (TIB), Hannover, Germany
{oliver.karras,allard.oelen,soeren.auer}@tib.eu

Abstract. Web-based dashboards are fundamental to digitalization, serving as central components in various organizational processes. However, their development is typically restricted to software engineering teams who must translate domain-specific requirements from stakeholders into functional interfaces. Despite this process often being repetitive and structured in nature, it remains complex and largely inaccessible to non-experts. While template-based tools such as Power BI increase accessibility, they frequently lack the flexibility needed for highly customized and adaptive solutions. To overcome these limitations, we present DIVE (Data Insights and Visualization Engine), a novel stakeholder-driven, hybrid neuro-symbolic framework for generating highly adaptable dashboards. By leveraging natural language interaction and flexible Knowledge Graph (KG) structures, DIVE empowers users to define, query, and visualize data without programming knowledge. At its core, DIVE integrates an interaction of symbolic and neural techniques together with a Retrieval-Augmented Generation (RAG) architecture that integrates coding-relevant context to generate precise queries and synthesize dynamic User Interface (UI) components in real time. To assess DIVE's effectiveness, we conducted a mixed-method evaluation using the NASA Task Load Index (NASA-TLX) and the System Usability Scale (SUS), supplemented by participant and expert interviews for qualitative insights. The results demonstrate that DIVE supports completing complex analytical tasks with high usability and low cognitive load. Study participants and experts emphasized the system's innovative approach, practical applicability, and potential for substantial time and cost savings, thus confirming its capacity to produce customizable, future-proof dashboards.

Keywords: HCI · HAII · Neuro-Symbolic · Dashboard Creation

I. Awan et al. (Eds.): WISE 2025, LNCS 16368, pp. 433–443, 2026.
https://doi.org/10.1007/978-981-95-7251-9_29

1 Introduction

Effective data visualization is essential for deriving insights and making informed decisions [7,9,14]. Its utility, however, strongly depends on the user's data expertise [4,7,14]. Novices often struggle with dashboards designed for experienced analysts [7,14], and even with design thinking, such dashboards are not inherently intuitive [19]. Thus, usability must be shaped by users themselves to accommodate varying levels of expertise.

Despite increasing emphasis on accessibility and personalization, challenges such as customization and data access persist [1,2]. Exploration remains cognitively demanding, particularly for non-experts [2,4,9]. Conventional accessibility methods, such as alternative text or tables, fail to capture the full potential of visualizations. At the same time, existing tools remain limited to static charts and basic filtering, lacking support for dynamic UI elements.

Research shows that effective dashboards improve efficiency, profitability, and cost savings [5,16], yet many current solutions lack flexibility or inclusivity [1,5]. For instance, Hasan et al. created an AI-assisted supply chain dashboard, but it was neither evaluated for usability nor supported dynamic interaction [12]. Similarly, Kazemitabaar et al. showed that iterative workflows enhance AI-assisted analysis [15].

Motivated by these gaps, we propose DIVE (Data Insights and Visualization Engine), a system that enables flexible, dynamic, and user-defined dashboards through natural language interaction. By lowering cognitive and technical barriers, DIVE empowers users to design interfaces suited to their needs, supporting diverse UI elements such as charts, tables, and forms for more personalized workflows.

We evaluated DIVE through usability testing (NASA Task Load Index and System Usability Scale), semi-structured interviews, and expert feedback. Results show that DIVE reduces cognitive load, improves usability across experience levels, and enables dashboards tailored to individual preferences. Overall, our work contributes a user-centered framework that enhances inclusivity, fosters iterative exploration, and increases workflow efficiency in data-driven environments.

The remainder of this paper is structured as follows: Sect. 2 reviews related work, Sect. 3 describes our approach, Sect. 4 outlines the methodology, Sect. 5 presents results, Sect. 6 discusses implications and limitations, and Sect. 7 concludes with future directions.

2 Related Work

A well-designed User Experience (UX) is a critical factor in the success of Generative Artificial Intelligence (GenAI) systems [18]. Kim et al. examined the current state of UI/UX in GenAI applications and emphasized the pivotal role of UX in shaping user interactions with AI-generated content [18]. Their findings suggest that suboptimal UI/UX design can negatively impact the overall effectiveness of AI applications, potentially hindering user engagement and adoption [18].

Dashboard Applications. Elias and Bezerianos show that experts and novices have distinct needs, with novices typically starting with simple views and iteratively refining them [8].

Business intelligence tools such as Tableau, Power BI, Pentaho, Qliksense, Jaspersoft, and Jedox remain widely used [10,17]. While these tools continue to evolve, they still lack advanced customizability, full control over interactions, and clear frameworks for determining appropriate use cases [10,17].

Several studies have also explored AI-based dashboard creation. Swartz et al. presented an NLP tool embedding analysis results, though without personalization [28]. Sequeda et al. emphasize that dashboards are central for data interaction and highlight the importance of organizational availability, proposing KGs as a foundation for warehouses with LLM-based access via natural language [22]. Shen et al. reviewed natural language interfaces and proposed evaluation benchmarks [23], and Srinivasan and Setlur later developed a tool interpreting natural language for dashboard objectives [26].

Code Generation. Code generation today is largely driven by deep learning models such as LLMs [25]. Shin and Nam provided a survey of automatic code generation from natural language, categorizing prior work and outlining future directions [25]. To improve such models, Shen et al. introduced a task augmentation method incorporating domain knowledge [24].

CoLadder enhances user context by allowing programmers to decompose tasks into subtasks through a visual hierarchy [29]. Similarly, Jiang et al. propose a self-planning approach with planning and implementation phases, outperforming direct and chain-of-thought generation [13,29]. Dong et al. extend this idea with a self-collaboration framework, assigning roles such as analyst, coder, and tester, which significantly improves benchmark performance [6].

Beyond scientific research, several industry-oriented applications have emerged, including Vercel's v0, StackBlitz, and Motiff, which provide web-based code generation interfaces.

3 Approach

KGs provide semantic connectivity and have been established as a foundation for downstream applications. Evaluating existing tools and organizational requirements, particularly in procurement, highlighted the potential of a collaborative, user-centered neuro-symbolic approach. This is especially beneficial for novices unfamiliar with data structures. Accordingly, DIVE employs KGs to enable both experts and non-technical users to create personalized, task-specific dashboards that support everyday workflows[1].

Figure 1 illustrates DIVE's workflow. Users specify a panel title and SPARQL endpoint, which is queried to display all KG properties. These can be interactively selected and constrained using natural language (e.g., filtering years from

[1] We published DIVE to provide all technical details here: https://github.com/J-x-D/DIVE.

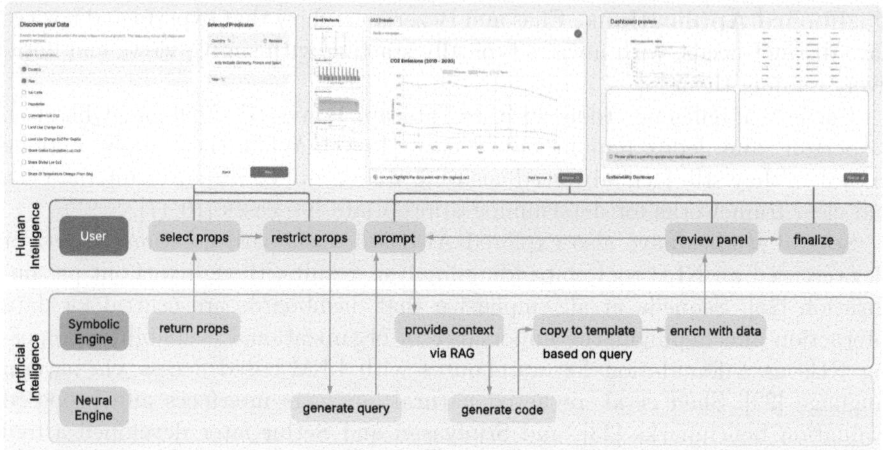

Fig. 1. DIVE's User Flow of Creating Panels involving specific symbolic and neural engine functions.

2010 to 2020). Based on the selection, users either apply a predefined draft or provide a custom prompt to generate an initial panel. The resulting table, chart, or form can then be iteratively refined through natural language until it meets requirements. Finalized panels are added to a dashboard, either newly created or existing, via a shared panel catalog. A demonstration video is available in [27].

Basic Architecture. DIVE connects to a KG and consists of three main components: (1) a *Next.js* frontend for user interaction, (2) a *Bun.js* backend mediating between frontend and development engine, and (3) a *Next.js*-based development engine that executes SPARQL queries and renders panels as React components via iframes. When a new panel is created, the backend initializes a development engine instance, integrates the generated SPARQL query and React code, and renders them dynamically in the frontend.

Setting Up the Generations. For consistency, only *shadcn*-UI and *chart.js* are used. Since GPT-4o occasionally deviates from these libraries, DIVE integrates a Retrieval-Augmented Generation (RAG) mechanism. A *PostgreSQL* database stores vectors of keywords, code snippets, and documentation. The symbolic engine retrieves relevant context (e.g., import statements, usage patterns) via semantic search and appends it to the user prompt before passing it to the neural engine. This ensures adherence to the expected syntax and parameters.

Accessing the Knowledge Graph. As noted by Sequeda et al. and Pan et al. [20,22], KGs are seen as a flexible data storage mechanism. DIVE enhances this by allowing natural language-based selection and restriction of KG elements. All properties are listed for user selection, which can be constrained (e.g., "year 2010âĂŞ2020" or "only Germany and USA"). These inputs and prompts are submitted to GPT-4, which generates a SPARQL query. Queries are validated automatically and if they fail, the system regenerates them and posts them to the SPARQL endpoint (*GraphDB*) for immediate execution.

Creating the User Interface Panels. Validated queries are transferred to the development engine, where panels, such as tables, charts, or forms, are generated. Users may rely on prompt templates or provide custom prompts. The backend then utilizes the RAG mechanism to incorporate relevant code snippets before synthesis. The generated code is integrated into the development engine as a new *Next.js* page and rendered dynamically on the frontend for live interaction. Users can iteratively refine panels via natural language, with each version stored while preserving prior iterations. Only the finalized code is saved in the backend database and added to the panel catalog.

Incorporating Panels Into a Dashboard. Panels are selected from the catalog and arranged in a two-column grid layout. This community-driven catalog prevents redundant creation and promotes reuse. Once the layout is complete, users provide a name and description. A *Next.js* Git repository is then automatically generated and deployed, enabling immediate access to the live dashboard.

4 Methodology

To the best of our knowledge, no other approach allows non-technical users to create fully customized, community-driven dashboards by composing reusable panels through natural language interaction. Therefore, it is not possible to compare DIVE to another approach in terms of all the features and characteristics DIVE provides. Nevertheless, we wanted to investigate DIVE's usability, mental workload, and economic impacts qualitatively and quantitatively. Consequently, we conducted a user study and evaluated DIVE using the SUS, NASA-TLX, and additional expert interviews.

Study Design. To investigate DIVE's usability and technology acceptance, we created a task description that involved creating three panels and adding them to a single dashboard. Therefore, we provided two different KG endpoints. One is about sustainability data taken from the OWID (Our World in Data) dataset [21]. The other dataset was obtained from the work of Stütz et al., who introduced and published a real-world ontology and tabular data related to purchasing. We transformed both tabular datasets into KGs. Based on those KGs, users had to select and restrict specific properties. In the following, users were required to create a suitable visualization with optional interaction features. A summarized and simplified task is: "Visualize the CO2 emissions of Germany and France from 2014 until 2023 in a tabular view with the possibility to filter by emissions". Participants then had to answer questions to verify whether the created visualization provides the desired information. This way, we could validate the successful extraction of relevant data and thus the visualization itself. After using DIVE, participants completed a questionnaire on their general experience, familiarity with similar tools, and filled out the SUS and NASA-TLX. In contrast, experts watched a demonstration video and then provided feedback on their experience, impressions, and DIVE's potential impact. The full task description, KGs, video, and questionnaires are available at [27].

Sample. Our user study involved 20 participants and six domain experts, all voluntarily from the same Fortune 500 company. The participants, comprising 10 males and 10 females, came from purchasing (13) and sustainability (7). The experts, also from the same organization, included researchers and departmental leads specializing in digital transformation, automation, AI, and ERP systems.

Data Analysis. We employed a mixed-methods analytical approach comprising both quantitative and qualitative techniques. Qualitative feedback was analyzed through sentiment scoring via TextBlob and further processed using Frequency-Inverse Document Frequency (TF-IDF) vectorization and Latent Dirichlet Allocation (LDA) topic modeling. Descriptive statistics (means, ranges, and standard scores) were calculated for key variables, including task duration and user-reported intuitiveness and enablement. We analyzed the NASA-TLX [11] questionnaire and the SUS [3] according to the authors. Depending on the data, either Pearson's or Spearman's correlation analysis was used to examine linear associations among usability, workload, task efficiency, and user experience variables, with p-values determined via the t-distribution. To investigate different user groups, we first normalized the SUS, NASA-TLX, duration time, and sentiment and applied Principal Component Analysis (PCA) for dimensionality reduction.

5 Results

Quantitative Results. During the user study, participants were asked a set of verification questions after completing each panel to assess whether their created panels met the intended requirements. All participants were able to answer these questions successfully based on their creations. Across all tasks, participants completed them in an average of 28.78 min, with completion times ranging from 13.5 to 47 min. The system's overall usability, as assessed via the SUS, produced a score of 83.625, which is considered excellent. This high rating was consistent across all experience groups, as shown in Table 2.

Cognitive workload, as measured by the NASA-TLX, produced a mean score of 34.04, indicating a low to moderate perceived workload. We also found several significant correlations, which are listed in Table 1.

Table 1. Significant Correlations Among Key Metrics (N = 20)

Correlation Pair	Correlation (r)	p-value
SUS vs Dashboard Creation Intuitiveness	0.45	<0.05
SUS vs Panel Creation Intuitiveness	0.72	<0.001
SUS vs Enablement	0.41	<0.05
SUS vs NASA-TLX Score	−0.45	<0.05
NASA-TLX vs Dashboard Creation Intuitiveness	−0.45	<0.05
Dashboard Creation vs Panel Creation Intuitiveness	0.39	<0.05
Experience Level vs Dashboard Creation Likelihood	0.60	<0.01
Experience Level vs Independent Question Answering	0.50	<0.05
Dashboard Creation Likelihood vs Independent Question Answering	0.63	<0.01
Dashboard Creation Likelihood vs Experience Level	0.60	<0.01
Dashboard Creation Likelihood vs NASA-TLX Score	−0.45	<0.05

The expert interviews further revealed strong correlations: usability with usefulness ($r \sim 0.94$), empowerment with usefulness ($r \sim 0.90$), and contextual relevance with perceived usefulness ($r \sim 0.85$).

Clustering yielded seven mathematical clusters, salient groups included Efficient Power Users, Positive Explorers, Deliberate Investigators, Critical Navigators, and Overloaded Analysts, with several near-duplicates consolidated as Moderate Generalists, as can be seen here: [27].

Qualitative Insights. Qualitative feedback underscored several strengths of the system. Participants consistently highlighted substantial time and cost savings, emphasizing the interface's intuitive nature, customizability, and speed with which actionable insights could be derived. The system was also praised for its low technical barrier, facilitating access to a wide range of user profiles.

The qualitative feedback from expert interviews echoed these sentiments, with an average sentiment score of 0.095 for advantages, indicating mildly positive feedback emphasizing ease and accessibility. Feedback on disadvantages was also constructive, with a slightly positive average sentiment of 0.049. Additional expert feedback was strongly positive, with an average sentiment score of 0.36, reflecting users' appreciation of the approach and perceived value.

The expert interviews identified several advantages, including eliminating the need for technical expertise, simplifying setup, enabling non-programmers, and providing fast dashboarding capabilities.

Nonetheless, several areas for improvement were identified. Users expressed the need for enhanced user interface support, particularly in the prompting mechanisms and panel configuration. Multiple participants perceived the final dashboard as unpolished or unfinished. Advanced users, in particular, noted the absence of fine-tuning capabilities and expressed a desire to be more involved in the configuration process. Furthermore, participants called for improvements in the prompt design and panel creation workflow, including more precise guidance, additional suggestions, and more extensive customization options.

The expert interviews also highlighted some disadvantages, such as the requirement for knowledge of data structures, limited customization options, unclear prompting, and missing database functions.

Table 2. Cross-Evaluation of Metrics by Experience Level

Experience Level	Avg Time (min)	SUS	TLX	Answer w/o DIVE	Recreate Dashboard	Sentiment
1 (Beginner)	30.00	86.67	37.28	2.33	1.67	+0.12
2 (Basic)	31.12	86.25	**29.96**	3.75	3.75	+0.03
3 (Intermediate)	**26.46**	81.11	34.54	3.67	4.00	-0.03
4 (Advanced)	28.33	**86.67**	35.28	4.67	4.67	0.00
5 (Expert)	38.00	77.50	32.50	**5.00**	**5.00**	+0.12

6 Discussion

DIVE's evaluation demonstrates its efficacy in supporting dashboard creation across a broad spectrum of users, from novices to experts. All user groups were able to construct dashboards suited to their needs, with only minor differences in usability and workload scores. These findings substantiate DIVE's flexibility and adaptability, showing that it effectively bridges the skill gap often seen in traditional dashboarding environments.

A key enabler of adoption is the natural language interface, consistently highlighted by participants and experts as critical for accessing, restricting, and visualizing data. This aligns with prior work on neuro-symbolic interfaces, confirming that reducing technical complexity fosters engagement and empowerment.

DIVE's high usability, reflected in excellent SUS scores, was strongly linked to low cognitive workload (NASA-TLX), underscoring how intuitive design reduces effort and streamlines the user experience. Lower TLX scores also correlated with shorter task durations, suggesting that cognitive simplicity translates into operational efficiency. Participants and experts explicitly confirmed these perceived economic benefits.

Additional correlations reinforced these insights. Usability was positively associated with confidence and goal achievement, while the likelihood of creating similar dashboards was linked to both user expertise and low workload. Intuitiveness of panel and dashboard creation was also correlated, reflecting design consistency. Interestingly, expert users often required longer completion times, likely due to the need for deeper customization and exploration, coupled with higher expectations for manual control.

Qualitative feedback further positions DIVE as a distinctive tool, with no directly comparable systems offering its combination of customization, reusability, and low technical barriers. While alternatives such as Power BI or Excel were noted, DIVE uniquely enables fully custom visualizations beyond predefined templates. Its scalable architecture suggests that cost and time benefits could grow in organizational and public-sector settings.

The most significant implication of these findings is DIVE's contribution to data democratization. By enabling non-technical users to create context-aware visual interfaces without programming, DIVE advances inclusivity beyond existing LLM-based systems, which currently lack query generation, community-driven reuse, and compositional dashboard building capabilities. Importantly, this is achieved without requiring code-level adjustments.

The clusters revealed meaningful variability: Efficient Power Users combined high satisfaction, fast completion, and low workload; Positive Explorers and Deliberate Investigators engaged enthusiastically or deliberately with favorable impressions; Critical Navigators and Overloaded Analysts faced elevated effort or skepticism, indicating a need for clearer guidance and control. Because several clusters were practically indistinguishable in terms of usability, workload, and sentiment, they were grouped as Moderate Generalists, underscoring that statistical separation may not necessarily imply practical differences. These patterns motivate targeted onboarding, suggestion mechanisms, and customization affordances tailored to both confident users and those requiring additional support.

In summary, our neuro-symbolic, user-centric approach enables rapid construction of insightful dashboards that address complex questions across expertise levels. This is accomplished with a low workload, making DIVE a uniquely effective tool for data-driven decision-making.

Limitations. Besides the mentioned advantages, several limitations must be acknowledged. First, DIVE lacks a fine-tuned language model for UI generation, which could further enhance output quality when combined with the RAG mechanism. Second, the absence of a directly comparable baseline system constrained us to internal evaluation only. Third, tasks were restricted to dashboard creation, limiting exploration of other use cases such as form generation. Fourth, the relatively small sample size may reduce statistical power and the generalizability of the results. Finally, DIVE currently relies on user-provided KGs, which may hinder adoption compared to conventional databases. However, explicit knowledge of the KG structure is not always required, since natural language inherently provides selection and restriction mechanisms. Furthermore, we consider our approach readily applicable to SQL query generation as well, rather than being limited to SPARQL queries, since relational databases can be queried using similar natural language-based selection and restriction mechanisms, and the underlying generation process is largely independent of the specific query language employed. Nevertheless, we would like to emphasize that the volume of queried data could affect DIVE's performance, since larger datasets can increase processing time and computational overhead.

7 Conclusion and Future Work

In conclusion, DIVE advances human-centered computing by enabling inclusive, customizable dashboards through intuitive natural language interaction, lowering technical barriers, and fostering the democratization of data visualization. Its hybrid neuro-symbolic architecture, component reusability, and real-time generation capabilities demonstrate strong potential for efficiency gains across enterprise, public, and academic domains. Future work should refine expert-level customization, enhance visualization complexity, expand beyond panel-based compositions, and integrate data persistence and relational database connectivity. These directions will allow DIVE to mature into a comprehensive platform for intelligent user interface construction.

References

1. Amyrotos, C., Andreou, P., Germanakos, P., Polycarpou, I.: Personalization and individual differences in business data analytics, pp. 137–163. Springer, Cham (2024)
2. Bach, B., et al.: Challenges and opportunities in data visualization education: a call to action. IEEE Trans. Visual Comput. Graphics **30**(1), 649–660 (2024)
3. Brooke, J., et al.: Sus-a quick and dirty usability scale. Usabil. Eval. Ind. **189**(194), 4–7 (1996)
4. Burns, A., Lee, C., Chawla, R., Peck, E., Mahyar, N.: Who do we mean when we talk about visualization novices? In: Proceedings of the 2023 CHI Conference on Human Factors in Computing Systems, CHI 2023. Association for Computing Machinery, New York (2023)
5. Bussa, S.: Enhancing bi tools for improved data visualization and insights. Int. J. Comput. Sci. Mob. Comput. **12**(2), 70–92 (2023)
6. Dong, Y., Jiang, X., Jin, Z., Li, G.: Self-collaboration code generation via chatGPT. **33**(7) (2024)
7. Eberhard, K.: The effects of visualization on judgment and decision-making: a systematic literature review. Manage. Rev. Q. **73**(1), 167–214 (2023)
8. Elias, M., Bezerianos, A.: Exploration views: understanding dashboard creation and customization for visualization novices. In: Human-Computer Interaction – INTERACT 2011, pp. 274–291. Springer, Heidelberg (2011)
9. Gorniak, J., Kim, Y., Wei, D., Kim, N.W.: Vizability: enhancing chart accessibility with LLM-based conversational interaction. In: Proceedings of the 37th Annual ACM Symposium on User Interface Software and Technology, pp. 1–19 (2024)
10. Gowthami, K., Kumar, M.P.: Study on business intelligence tools for enterprise dashboard development. Int. Res. J. Eng. Technol. **4**(4), 2987–2992 (2017)
11. Hart, S.G., Staveland, L.E.: Development of NASA-TLX (task load index): results of empirical and theoretical research. In: Hancock, P.A., Meshkati, N. (eds.) Human Mental Workload, pp. 139–183. Advances in Psychology, North-Holland (1988)
12. Hasan, M., Islam, M.Z., Sumon, M.F.I., Osiujjaman, M., Debnath, P., Pant, L.: Integrating artificial intelligence and predictive analytics in supply chain management to minimize carbon footprint and enhance business growth in the usa. J. Bus. Manage. Stud. **6**(4), 195–212 (2024)

13. Jiang, X., et al.: Self-planning code generation with large language models. ACM Trans. Softw. Eng. Methodol. **33**(7) (2024)
14. Jooste, C., Van Biljon, J., Botha, A.: A conceptual framework representing the user experience for business intelligence front-ends. In: 2018 International Conference on Advances in Big Data, Computing and Data Communication Systems (icABCD), pp. 1–8 (2018)
15. Kazemitabaar, M., et al.: Improving steering and verification in AI-assisted data analysis with interactive task decomposition. In: Proceedings of the 37th Annual ACM Symposium on User Interface Software and Technology, pp. 1–19 (2024)
16. Khatri, A., Gupta, N.: Impact of data visualization on management decisions. Lond. J. Res. Manag. Bus. **22**, 53–62 (2022)
17. Khatuwal, V.S., Puri, D.: Business intelligence tools for dashboard development. In: 2022 3rd International Conference on Intelligent Engineering and Management (ICIEM), pp. 128–131 (2022)
18. Kim, T.S., John Ignacio, M., Yu, S., Jin, H., Kim, Y.G.: UI/UX for generative AI: taxonomy, trend, and challenge. IEEE Access **12**, 179891–179911 (2024)
19. Landütama, J., Chowanda, A.: Applied design thinking for kimball lifecycle to improve business intelligence dashboard usability. Int. J. Innov. Comput. Inf. Control **19**(4), 1139–1152 (2023)
20. Pan, S., Luo, L., Wang, Y., Chen, C., Wang, J., Wu, X.: Unifying large language models and knowledge graphs: a roadmap. IEEE Trans. Knowl. Data Eng. **36**(7), 3580–3599 (2024)
21. Ritchie, H., Rosado, P., Roser, M.: Co_2 and greenhouse gas emissions. Our World in Data (2023). https://ourworldindata.org/co2-and-greenhouse-gas-emissions
22. Sequeda, J., Allemang, D., Jacob, B.: Knowledge graphs as a source of trust for LLM-powered enterprise question answering. J. Web Semant. **85** (2025)
23. Shen, L., et al.: Towards natural language interfaces for data visualization: a survey. IEEE Trans. Visual Comput. Graphics **29**(6), 3121–3144 (2022)
24. Shen, S., Zhu, X., Dong, Y., Guo, Q., Zhen, Y., Li, G.: Incorporating domain knowledge through task augmentation for front-end Javascript code generation. In: Proceedings of the 30th ACM Joint European Software Engineering Conference and Symposium on the Foundations of Software Engineering, ESEC/FSE 2022, pp. 1533–1543. Association for Computing Machinery, New York (2022)
25. Shin, J., Nam, J.: A survey of automatic code generation from natural language. J. Inf. Process. Syst. **17**(3), 537–555 (2021)
26. Srinivasan, A., Setlur, V.: Bolt: A natural language interface for dashboard authoring. In: EuroVis (Short Papers), pp. 7–11 (2023)
27. Stütz, J.D., Gegziabher, S., Blaga, V., Karras, O., Oelen, A., Auer, S.: Appendix for dive - a neuro-symbolic user-centric generation approach for data insight visualization (2025). https://doi.org/10.5281/zenodo.17066444
28. Swartz, J., Koziatek, C., Theobald, J., Smith, S., Iturrate, E.: Creation of a simple natural language processing tool to support an imaging utilization quality dashboard. Int. J. Med. Inform. **101**, 93–99 (2017)
29. Yen, R., Zhu, J.S., Suh, S., Xia, H., Zhao, J.: CoLadder: manipulating code generation via multi-level blocks. In: Proceedings of the 37th Annual ACM Symposium on User Interface Software and Technology, pp. 1–20 (2024)

Pose-Guided Feature Restoration Transformer for Occluded Person Re-identification

Jiaqi Li[1], Shaoqian Chen[1], Kangfei Yao[1], Xiaohui Huang[1], Yuewei Wang[1], Jianxin Li[2], and Yunliang Chen[1(✉)]

[1] School of Computer Science, China University of Geosciences, Wuhan, China
chenyunliang@cug.edu.cn

[2] School of Information Technology, Deakin University, Melbourne, Australia

Abstract. The occluded person re-identification (ReID) remains a challenge due to feature loss in occluded regions, which not only introduces noise interference but also poses significant difficulties in feature alignment. To systematically address this issue, we propose an innovative Pose-guided Feature Restoration Transformer (PRT) framework, designed to adaptively restore features within occluded areas. Our approach commences with an occlusion sample augmentation strategy. By integrating real-world images with noisy images, we simulate a wide spectrum of complex occlusion scenarios, enhancing the model's generalization ability across diverse occlusion conditions. Subsequently, based on visibility scores, we develop a method that fuses common and unique features to recover the characteristics of occluded keypoints. To further optimize feature transfer, an adaptive directional graph convolution method is introduced to construct higher-order feature representations, effectively alleviating feature degradation caused by occlusion. Finally, leveraging the attention mechanism of the Transformer, we integrate both global and local contextual information to enhance the overall feature representation comprehensively. Comprehensive experiments conducted on both occluded and holistic datasets demonstrate the superior effectiveness of our PRT framework.

Keywords: Occlusion · Feature Restoration · Person Re-Identification

1 Introduction

Person re-identification (ReID) [1] focuses on identifying individuals across multiple non-overlapping cameras and is extensively applied in behavior analysis, smart cities, and video surveillance [2]. Driven by breakthroughs in deep learning and the proliferation of comprehensive ReID datasets, the accuracy of holistic ReID has made significant progress. However, most existing methods rely on complete pedestrian images and struggle to handle occlusion under real-life conditions [3]. In complex environments such as schools, railway stations and

I. Awan et al. (Eds.): WISE 2025, LNCS 16368, pp. 444–459, 2026.
https://doi.org/10.1007/978-981-95-7251-9_30

commercial centers, occlusion not only reduces the visible regions of pedestrians but may also introduce noise, leading to a decline in recognition accuracy. Therefore, extracting effective features and achieving accurate matching under occlusion has become a key challenge in current ReID research [4].

Compared to complete image matching, occluded person ReID is more challenging in the following aspects. First, due to the scarcity of occlusion samples, the model struggles to capture reliable representations under occlusion conditions [5]. Second, Fig. 1(a) demonstrates that occlusion causes the disappearance of distinguishable visual information, making it difficult to match the extracted features with the real ones. Occlusion also introduces a large amount of noise information, and misleading appearance information from occluded objects may lead to incorrect similarity computation [6]. Recently, some studies have introduced corresponding solutions. In order to overcome the scarcity of occlusion samples, occlusion augmentation strategies have been introduced [7], but these studies fail to address the problem of improving occlusion diversity. For the loss of appearance information, some studies [8–10] try to extract local features through pose estimation or human parsing models, but the reliability of these methods is limited when key points are occluded. For the noise problem, some studies try to recover the appearance of occluded regions through image complementation networks [11], but due to the domain gap, the complementation is often ineffective.

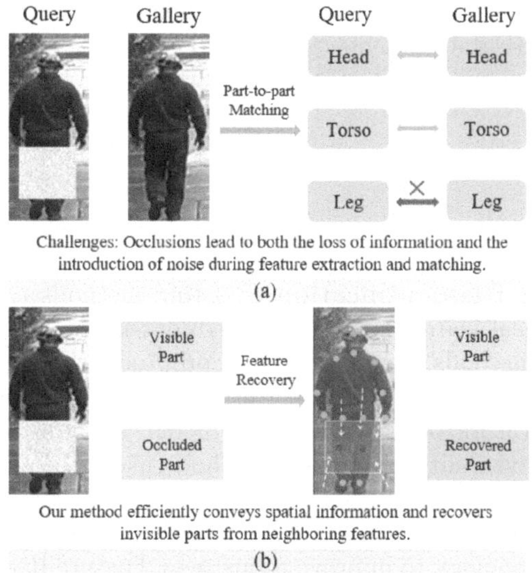

Fig. 1. Illustration of Two Challenges (a) and Our Proposed Method (b).

To resolve the issues above, we propose Pose-guided Feature Restoration Transformer (PRT). As illustrated in Fig. 1(b), our method can adaptively complement the features of the occluded region. Specifically, we determine keypoint visibility based on the confidence scores output by the pose estimation model, and quantify the occlusion degree by calculating the proportion of visible keypoints. It is composed of four stages: occlusion sample augmentation, semantic feature extraction, adaptive feature restoration and global-local feature fusion. First, we generate occlusion samples by combining real and noisy images to simulate a complex occlusion scene. Then, we extract semantic features using CNN backbone and compute visibility scores using Human pose estimation model. In the adaptive restoration phase, we combine the common and unique features of keypoints based on the visibility score. Next, we use Adaptive Graph Convolution Network (AGCN) to establish the relationship of higher-order features and recover the occluded keypoint features. Finally, Transformer is used to fuse the recovered local and global features.

The major contributions of this study are as follows:

- We introduce the Pose-guided Feature Restoration Transformer (PRT), which enhances human keypoint feature transfer and global-local feature fusion to learn robust and aligned features.
- We introduce a novel occlusion sample generation method combining real and noisy images to simulate complex occlusion scenarios.
- We propose an adaptive feature restoration module that combines common and unique human keypoint features, effectively recovering occluded features via AGCN.
- Experimental results consistently show the effectiveness of PRT on holistic and occluded ReID datasets. Specifically, PRT outperforms 4.5% in mAP and 3.5% in Rank-1 compared to state-of-the-art approaches on Occluded-Duke dataset.

2 Related Work

Occluded Person Re-identification. Existing methods can be categorized into three types: local feature matching-based, external cue-based, and feature restoration-based methods. Sun *et al.* [12] proposed the PCB model, which addresses occlusion by dividing the feature map and learning local features. Later, Sun *et al.* [13] introduced the VPM model, using self-supervised learning to perceive the visibility of regions. Methods like PGFA [8] and PVPM [9] leverage pose keypoints to enhance feature representation by focusing on visible regions. Wang *et al.* [10] proposed HOReID, combining higher-order relationships with human body topology to improve robustness. Feature Restoration methods focus on completing occluded regions, with approaches using GANs [11,14] to predict missing parts.

Transformer. Transformer [15] has achieved breakthrough success in natural language processing. Recently, due to its strong feature modeling and disentangling capabilities, it has also received growing attention in person ReID. He *et* *al.* [16] proposed TransReID, a Transformer-based model that integrates auxiliary information, achieving excellent performance in person and vehicle ReID. Li *et al.* [17] introduced the Part-Aware Transformer (PAT), the first to use a Transformer encoder-decoder structure for occluded person ReID, enabling diverse part discovery. Xu *et al.* [18] proposed FRT, which constructs a graph structure to focus on visible regions and recovers features using k-NN samples. Wang *et al.* [7] introduced FCFormer, which uses Occlusion Instance Augmentation and a two-stream architecture to recover occluded region features.

3 Proposed Method

We provides a comprehensive description of our PRT framework in this section. An overall architecture of our PRT is illustrated in Fig. 2.

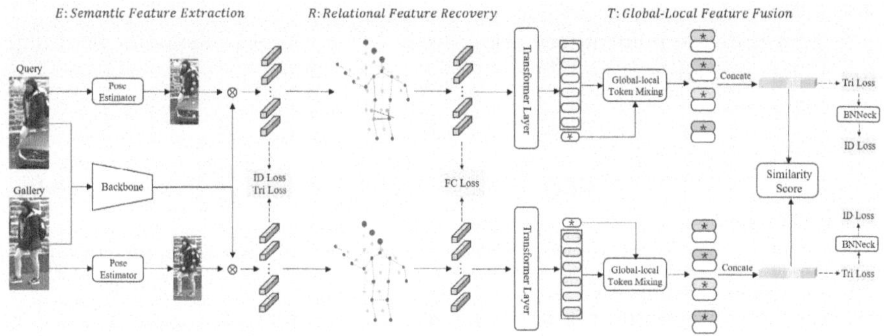

Fig. 2. An overall architecture of our PRT model, including Occlusion Sample Augmentation(OSA), Semantic Feature Extraction (E), Adaptive Feature Restoration (R), and Global-Local Feature Fusion (T).

3.1 Occlusion Sample Augmentation

Occlusion sample augmentation plays a crucial role in occluded ReID. Although current approaches can simulate occlusion to a certain extent, they still suffer from issues such as semantic inconsistency and insufficient diversity of occlusion samples [7].

To address these issues, we propose an intra-batch occlusion augmentation strategy. Specifically, images of different pedestrians in the same training batch are utilized as noise superimposed on the target image. In addition, we introduce a free shape mask to replace the traditional random rectangle mask, which can more realistically model diverse occlusions.

Specifically, given an original image O, we select an image of a different pedestrians from the same batch as noise images N, and generate a random occlusion mask M. The occluded image I is computed according to the formula:

$$I = O \odot (1 - M) + N \odot M \tag{1}$$

where I reprsents the synthesized occluded image, and $\odot$ represents the Hadamard product.

3.2 Semantic Feature Extraction

Person ReID is a fine-grained task [12], which requires precise local feature extraction and accurate feature alignment. We utilize human pose estimation model to identify the critical parts of pedestrians, thus extracting more discriminative features across different body regions.

Given an image, the feature map G is first extracted by a CNN backbone. We use the pre-trained HR-Net for pose estimation to obtain K keypoint heatmaps $\{M_1, M_2, \ldots, M_K\}$, where each M_k represents the confidence distribution of a body part.

To aggregate keypoint information, we combine these K keypoint heatmaps into one foreground heatmap M_f:

$$M_f(i,j) = \max\left(M_1, M_2, \ldots, M_K\right) \tag{2}$$

where K denotes the total count of human body keypoints, such as the shoulders, elbows, and wrists.

After obtaining the foreground heatmap and the K keypoint heatmaps, we perform Global Weighted Average Pooling (GWAP) to fuse the feature map G, extracting the foreground features f_f and local features $\{f_1, \ldots, f_K\}$ based on specific parts of the body:

$$f_i = \mathrm{GWAP}(M_i \odot G), \quad i \in \{f, 1, \ldots, K\} \tag{3}$$

We also extract global features to capture overall information about the pedestrian. Global features are computed by Global Average Pooling (GAP). In addition, we compute the visibility score v_i for each keypoint, which is determined by the median confidence value in the corresponding keypoint heatmap $M_k(h, w)$:

$$v_i = \mathrm{median}_{h,w}\, M_i(h, w), \quad i \in \{1, \ldots, K\} \tag{4}$$

3.3 Adaptive Feature Restoration

Although we have extracted semantic information from different keypoint regions, occlusion not only leads to missing features, but also may introduce invalid noise information [7]. To enhance the quality of features in occluded regions, we design an adaptive feature restoration method as shown in Fig. 3. The method utilizes the common features among keypoints to achieve knowledge sharing, and combine the unique features to compensate the information of the occluded region.

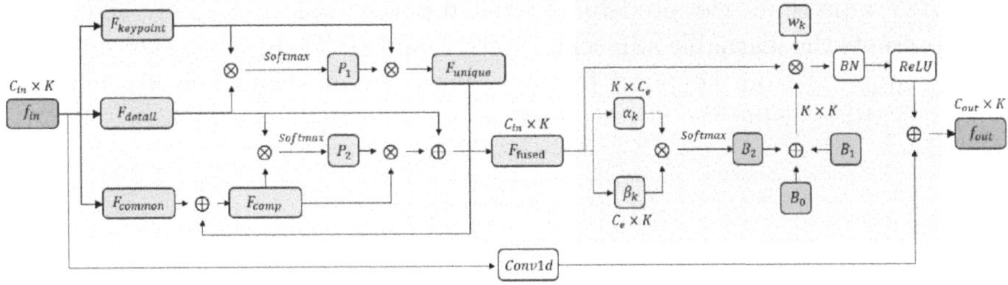

Fig. 3. The framework of the adaptive feature restoration module consists of two main stages: (a) Knowledge-sharing-based Feature Compensation, (b) Adaptive Directional Graph Convolution.

To reduce the interference of occluded keypoints, we weight the local feature of each keypoint f_k using its visibility score v_k:

$$f_{\text{detail},k} = v_k f_k \tag{5}$$

where $f_{\text{detail},k}$ is the weighted detailed feature of the keypoints. This lowers the weight of occluded keypoints to reduce their interference.

Given the high similarity among keypoints of the same person, their shared information compensates for missing features due to occlusion. We represent the global shared features as $f_{\text{common}} = f_g$. Each keypoint also has unique features, extracted as $f_{\text{keypoint},k} = \{f_{\text{detail},k,b}\}_{b=1}^{B}$. We then use similarity-based weighting to select the most relevant unique features:

$$P_1 = \text{Softmax}\left(f_{\text{detail},k} \otimes f_{\text{keypoint},k}^T\right) \tag{6}$$

$$f_{\text{unique},k} = P_1 \otimes f_{\text{keypoint},k} \tag{7}$$

After extracting the f_{common} and f_{unique}, these two are combined to generate the f_{comp}:

$$f_{\text{comp}} = \text{Repeat}\left(f_{\text{common}}\right) + f_{\text{unique}} \tag{8}$$

At last, the f_{comp} are combined with the f_{detail} to obtain the f_{fused}:

$$P_2 = \text{Softmax}\left(f_{\text{detail}} \otimes f_{\text{comp}}^T\right) \tag{9}$$

$$f_{\text{fused}} = P_2 \otimes f_{\text{comp}} + f_{\text{detail}} \tag{10}$$

Through this method, we effectively eliminate obstacle features and combine the global commonality with local specificity of keypoints to enhance feature expression. However, considering the complex spatial relationships between keypoints, we introduce AGCN to model the high-order relationships via graph structures, facilitating semantic feature message passing.

Specifically, we define the graph structure between keypoints as $G = (V, E)$. Unlike traditional fixed adjacency matrices, we decompose the adjacency matrix B into three parts:

$$B = B^{(0)} + B^{(1)} + B^{(2)} \tag{11}$$

where $B^{(0)}$ represents the predefined fixed topology based on body structure, $B^{(1)}$ represents the learnable adjacency matrix, and $B^{(2)}$ represents the similarity matrix computed from keypoint features. We calculate the similarity between keypoint features using the dot product:

$$B_{ij}^{(2)} = \frac{\exp(f_i^T f_j)}{\sum_j \exp(f_i^T f_j)} \tag{12}$$

We use graph convolution to update the compensated keypoint features. The graph convolution computation is:

$$f' = \sigma\left(\tilde{B} f_{\text{fused}} W\right) \tag{13}$$

where f' is the keypoint feature after graph convolution, $\sigma(\cdot)$ denotes ReLU activation function.

To fully capture the higher-order relationships between keypoints, we use multilayer graph convolution and introduce residual connections. The update process of the keypoint features is:

$$f^{(l+1)} = \sigma\left(\tilde{B} f^{(l)} W^{(l)}\right) + f^{(l)} \tag{14}$$

where $f^{(l)}$ is keypoint features of layer l. The adjacency matrix $\tilde{B}$, denoting the symmetrically normalized similarity matrix, is shared among all layers.

3.4 Global-Local Feature Fusion

In occluded ReID, global-local context modeling is crucial for model performance [16]. However, CNN-based methods are difficult to effectively capture the correlations among distant nodes due to the limited sensory field. To mitigate this challenge, we employ a global-local feature fusion method utilizing the Transformer architecture, which can capture long-distance relationships and attention to diverse body parts. Figure 4 is the architecture of our method.

First, $f_{\text{comp}} = f_g$ are input into the Transformer for self-attention to model dependencies between keypoints. The keypoint feature matrix is:

$$F = \{f_1, f_2, \dots, f_K\}, \quad F \in \mathbb{R}^{K \times d} \tag{15}$$

where f_i denotes the i-th keypoint feature vector after compensation, d represents the feature dimension.

To model relationships between keypoints, we design a Relation-Aware Self-Attention (RSA) mechanism that incorporates the topological and similarity information of keypoints into the self-attention computation. The formula is:

$$\text{Attention}(F) = \text{Softmax}(A) \cdot V \tag{16}$$

$$A = \frac{Q \cdot K^T}{\sqrt{d_k}} + B \tag{17}$$

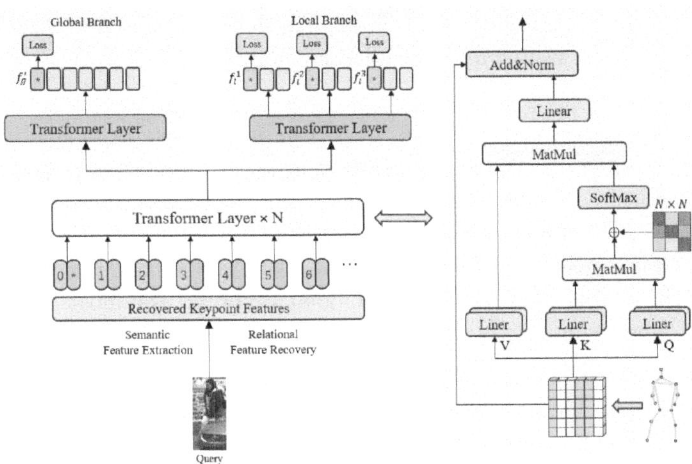

Fig. 4. A detailed illustration of the Transformer-based global-local feature fusion module.

After processing through multiple Transformer layers, the final output feature representation is:

$$\mathcal{Z}^{(L)} = \{z_0, z_1, \ldots, z_N\}, \quad \mathcal{Z}^{(L)} \in \mathbb{R}^{(N+1)\times d} \tag{18}$$

where z_i refers to the output feature of keypoints, and z_0 is global token.

In global branch, f_g extracted by CNN is fused with the keypoint features and processed through a Transformer to model their interactions, resulting in the final global feature representation:

$$\mathcal{Z}' = \{f_g, z_1, \ldots, z_N\}, \quad \mathcal{Z}' \in \mathbb{R}^{(N+1)\times d} \tag{19}$$

$$f_g' = \text{Transformer}(\mathcal{Z}') \tag{20}$$

where f_g' denotes the global branch output after fusion, while the local branch divides the keypoints into three regions based on the human body structure: head $\mathcal{Z}_1$, torso $\mathcal{Z}_2$, and legs $\mathcal{Z}_3$.

Each keypoint region is fused with the global feature z_0 and input to the Transformer to model its local contextual relationships to obtain a region-aware local feature representation:

$$f_l^i = \text{Transformer}\left([\mathcal{Z}_i; z_0]\right), \quad i \in \{1, 2, 3\} \tag{21}$$

In the inference phase, the final feature $f = [f_g', f_l^1, f_l^2, f_l^3]$ is obtained by concatenating the outputs of the global and local branches.

3.5 Overall Training Loss

We introduce the Feature Consistency Loss (FC) to make the direction of the fused features consistent with the visible features. For each keypoint k, its feature vector is f_k and its visibility score is v_k. We define a visibility threshold θ to distinguish between visible and occluded keypoints:

$$\mathcal{V} = \{f_k \mid v_k \geq \theta\}, \quad \mathcal{O} = \{f_k \mid v_k < \theta\} \tag{22}$$

where $\mathcal{V}$ refers to the collection of visible features, and $\mathcal{O}$ refers to the collection of occluded features. For each occluded keypoint, its compensated feature f_{fused} is generated by the adaptive feature restoration module.

The FC Loss ensures the directional consistency between the recovered features and the visible ones. For each occluded keypoint, the most similar visible feature is found using cosine similarity:

$$f_{visible} = \arg\max_{f_v \in \mathcal{V}} \frac{f_{fused} \cdot f_v}{|f_{fused}||f_v|} \tag{23}$$

where $f_{visible}$ is the most similar visible feature, f_v represents the visible features from the set $\mathcal{V}$. The feature consistency loss is computed as:

$$\mathcal{L}_{fc} = -\frac{1}{|\mathcal{O}|} \sum_{k \in \mathcal{O}} \frac{f_{fused} \cdot f_{visible}}{|f_{fused}||f_{visible}|} \tag{24}$$

Finally, the overall loss is formulated as the combination of the following components:

$$\mathcal{L} = \mathcal{L}_{FC} + \mathcal{L}_{ID} + \mathcal{L}_{Tri} \tag{25}$$

where $\mathcal{L}_{fc}$, $\mathcal{L}_{id}$, and $\mathcal{L}_{tri}$ denote the FC, ID, and Triplet Loss [19], respectively.

4 Experiments

4.1 Datasets and Metrics for Evaluation

We carried out the evaluation on four ReID datasets, covering both occluded and holistic pedestrian scenarios. Performance was assessed using the Mean Average Precision (mAP) and Cumulative Matching Characteristic (CMC) curve as the main indicators..

4.2 Implementation Details

Experiments are implemented based on PyTorch. Every image is resized to a dimension of 256 × 128, each ID contains 4 images and the batch size is configured to be 64. To improve generalization, data augmentation methods are used, including cropping and flipping. Feature extraction is based on ResNet-50, excluding the GAP and fully connected layers. The Adam optimizer is utilized in the training process. Human keypoints are detected using HR-Net, which is pretrained on COCO. The learning rate scheduling uses a multi-step decay strategy, which is decayed to 0.1 times of the original in the 40th and 70th rounds, respectively.

Table 1. Evaluation of current models on Occluded-Duke and Occluded-ReID datasets.

Method	Reference	Occluded-Duke		Occluded-ReID	
		Rank-1	mAP	Rank-1	mAP
PCB [12]	ECCV 18	42.6	33.7	-	-
PGFA [8]	ICCV 19	51.4	37.3	-	-
PVPM [9]	CVPR 20	-	-	66.8	59.5
HOReID [10]	CVPR 20	55.1	43.8	80.3	70.2
Pirt [20]	ACM MM 21	60.0	50.9	-	-
BPBreID [21]	WACV 23	75.1	62.5	82.9	75.2
ProFD [22]	ACM MM 24	70.6	63.1	**92.3**	**90.3**
KPR [23]	ECCV 24	79.8	67.1	85.4	79.1
PAT [17]	CVPR 21	64.5	53.6	81.6	72.1
TransReID [16]	ICCV 21	64.2	55.7	-	-
PFD [24]	AAAI 22	69.5	61.8	83.0	81.5
FED [25]	CVPR 22	68.1	56.4	86.3	79.3
FRT [18]	TIP 22	70.7	61.3	80.4	71.0
FCFormer [7]	TMM 24	73.0	63.1	83.6	85.7
PRT *(Ours)*	-	**83.3**	**71.6**	89.1	85.2

4.3 Comparison with State-of-the-Art Methods

Results on Occluded Datasets. Table 1 provides an overview of the experimental results. PRT demonstrates exceptional performance on Occluded-Duke [8] dataset, achieving 83.3% in Rank-1 and 71.6% in mAP, remarkably outperforming handcrafted-based methods. Compared to external model-based methods, while these approaches add extra information to boost performance, Our method continues to outperform them. Compared with FCFormer [7], Our approach combines adaptive feature compensation and local-global context fusion to effectively capture contextual and critical features, resulting a 13.3% increase in Rank-1 and 8.5% increase in mAP. Our method also demonstrates remarkable performance on Occluded-ReID dataset [4]. However, due to the small dataset size and the availability of only a test set, the performance improvement is relatively modest.

Results on Holistic Datasets. Table 2 provides an overview of the experimental results. On Market1501 [2] and DukeMTMC [26] datasets, our method reaches state-of-the-art performance. Even though it is not specifically aimed at holistic person ReID, it still demonstrated outstanding performance to prove its robustness.

Table 2. Evaluation of current models on the Market1501 and DukeMTMC datasets.

Method	Reference	Market1501		DukeMTMC	
		Rank-1	mAP	Rank-1	mAP
PCB [12]	ECCV 18	92.3	77.4	81.8	66.1
PGFA [8]	ICCV 19	91.2	76.8	82.6	65.5
HOReID [10]	CVPR 20	92.4	84.9	86.9	75.6
Pirt [20]	ACM MM 21	94.1	86.3	88.9	77.6
BPBreID [21]	WACV 23	95.7	89.4	82.9	75.2
ProFD [22]	ACM MM 24	96.6	90.8	92.1	84.0
KPR [23]	ECCV 24	95.9	89.6	-	-
PAT [17]	CVPR 21	95.4	88.0	88.8	78.2
TransReID [16]	ICCV 21	95.0	88.2	89.6	80.6
PFD [24]	AAAI 22	95.5	89.6	90.6	82.2
FED [25]	CVPR 22	95.0	86.3	89.4	78.0
FRT [18]	TIP 22	95.5	88.1	90.5	81.7
FCFormer [7]	TMM 24	95.0	86.8	89.7	78.8
PRT *(Ours)*	-	**97.6**	**94.2**	**93.0**	**87.4**

4.4 Ablation Studies

Effectiveness of proposed Modules. Table 3 provides a detailed overview of the experimental results. We built the PRT with HOReID [10] as the baseline. In the occlusion scenario, the baseline model achieved 55.1% Rank-1 and 43.8% mAP. After adding the E module, Rank-1 increased to 59.5% and mAP to 48.6%, indicating that the E module effectively enhanced feature representation. Adding the R module further improved Rank-1 to 67.5% and mAP to 59.8%, effectively compensating for feature loss caused by occlusion. With the addition of the T module, Rank-1 improved to 78.3% and mAP reached 67.7%, demonstrating significant enhancement through global-local feature fusion. The complete model

Table 3. The effectiveness of the three proposed modules: Semantic Feature Extraction (E), Adaptive Feature Recovery (R) and Transformer-based Global-Local Feature Fusion (T).

Index	Baseline	E	R	T	Rank-1	mAP
1	✓				55.1	43.8
2	✓	✓			59.5	48.6
3	✓	✓	✓		67.5	59.8
4	✓	✓		✓	78.3	67.7
5	✓	✓	✓	✓	**83.3**	**71.6**

with E, R, and T modules achieved 83.3% Rank-1 and 71.6% mAP, showing the complementary effect of each module.

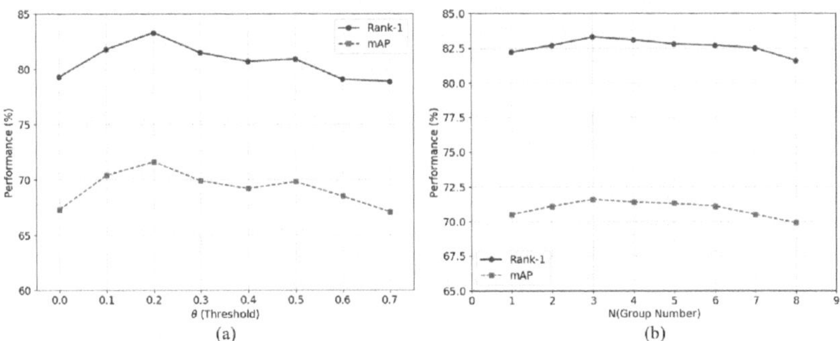

Fig. 5. Parameter sensitivity analysis for θ and N. The optimal performance is observed at $\theta = 0.2$ and $N = 3$.

Analysis of Parameters. We analyze the impact of the visibility threshold and the number of keypoint groups on model performance. As shown in Fig. 5(a), the model performs is best at $\theta = 0.2$, which indicates that a threshold too small may misclassify occluded regions as visible, while too large may discard useful information. Figure 5(b) shows that the model's performance improves as N grows, peaks at $N = 3$ or $N = 4$, and then decreases. This suggests that a moderate number of groups helps capture local details and enhances global-local feature interaction.

4.5 Qualitative Analysis

Visualization of Retrieval Results. Figure 6 visualizes the Rank-5 results for baseline and our PRT. The results indicate that the baseline method struggles with occlusions, often retrieving incorrect targets with similar obstacles, and is easily interfered with by non-target persons in multi-person occlusion scenarios. In contrast, our method effectively utilizes visible information for feature restoration, enabling accurate target identification even in highly occluded scenes.

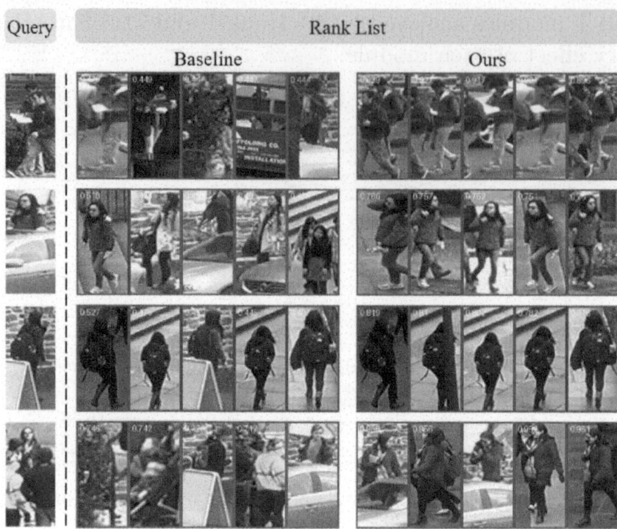

Fig. 6. Retrieval performance between the baseline and proposed PRT on the Occluded-Duke dataset.

Visualization of Feature Distributions. We adopt t-SNE to visualize the effect of each modules on feature distribution. Figure 7(a) shows the distribution after E module, the distribution is more scattered due to the influence of occlusion. Figure 7(b) illustrates the distribution after adding the R module, where samples of the same identity tend to cluster. Figure 7(c) shows the distribution after further adding the T module, where intra-class instances are more tightly clustered and inter-class instances are more separated.

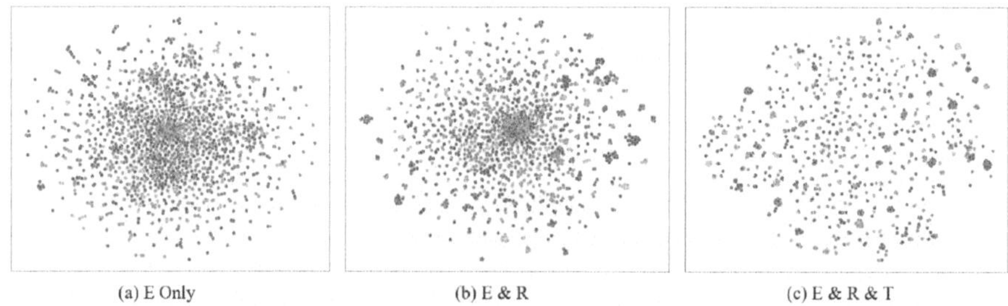

Fig. 7. Feature distributions for different module configurations. Each point represents an image feature extracted from Occluded-Duke dataset, and different colors indicate different identities.

5 Conclusion and Future Work

We introduce a new Pose-guided Feature Restoration Transformer (PRT) framework to tackle feature loss in occluded person ReID. First, we design an occlusion sample augmentation strategy combining real and noise images to simulate complex occlusion scenarios. Next, we extract human keypoints and compute visibility scores for semantic features, which are adaptively recovered by fusing common and unique features. Then, we construct a graph structure based on keypoints and use AGCN to propagate valid features, reducing information loss from occlusion. Finally, we utilize the Transformer to integrate global-local features via multi-head attention, enhancing feature representation. Comprehensive experiments indicate that the PRT framework outperforms existing methods, confirming its effectiveness and advancement.

Despite its promising performance, PRT still has certain limitations. Currently, its training relies on an external pose estimation model, which is particularly constrained under complex backgrounds or severe occlusions. In future work, we plan to explore an end-to-end training scheme. By leveraging a Transformer encoder-decoder architecture, the network can adaptively capture discriminative features of different human body parts in a weakly supervised manner.

Acknowledgements. This paper is partially supported by National Natural Science Foundation of China (No. 62076224).

References

1. Zheng, W.S., Li, X., Xiang, T., Liao, S., Lai, J., Gong, S.: Partial person re-identification. In: Proceedings of the IEEE International Conference on Computer Vision, pp. 4678–4686 (2015)
2. Zheng, L., Shen, L., Tian, L., Wang, S., Wang, J., Tian, Q.: Scalable person re-identification: A benchmark. In: Proceedings of the IEEE International Conference on Computer Vision, pp. 1116–1124 (2015)
3. Gao, G., Shao, H., Wu, F., Yang, M., Yu, Y.: Leaning compact and representative features for cross-modality person re-identification. World Wide Web **25**(4), 1649–1666 (2022)
4. Zhuo, J., Chen, Z., Lai, J., Wang, G.: Occluded person re-identification. In: 2018 IEEE International Conference on Multimedia and Expo (ICME), pp. 1–6. IEEE (2018)
5. Zhu, L., Yu, W., Zhu, X., Zhang, C., Li, Y., Zhang, S.: Mvhaan: multi-view hierarchical attention adversarial network for person re-identification. World Wide Web **27**(5), 59 (2024)
6. Li, J., Cong, Y., Zhou, L., Tian, Z., Qiu, J.: Super-resolution-based part collaboration network for vehicle re-identification. World Wide Web **26**(2), 519–538 (2023)
7. Wang, T., et al.: Feature completion transformer for occluded person re-identification. IEEE Trans. Multimedia (2024)

8. Miao, J., Wu, Y., Liu, P., Ding, Y., Yang, Y.: Pose-guided feature alignment for occluded person re-identification. In: Proceedings of the IEEE/CVF International Conference on Computer Vision, pp. 542–551 (2019)
9. Gao, S., Wang, J., Lu, H., Liu, Z.: Pose-guided visible part matching for occluded person reid. In: Proceedings of the IEEE/CVF Conference on Computer Vision and Pattern Recognition, pp. 11744–11752 (2020)
10. Wang, G., et al.: High-order information matters: Learning relation and topology for occluded person re-identification. In: Proceedings of the IEEE/CVF Conference on Computer Vision and Pattern Recognition, pp. 6449–6458 (2020)
11. Iodice, S., Mikolajczyk, K.: Partial person re-identification with alignment and hallucination. In: Asian Conference on Computer Vision, pp. 101–116. Springer (2018)
12. Sun, Y., Zheng, L., Yang, Y., Tian, Q., Wang, S.: Beyond part models: person retrieval with refined part pooling (and a strong convolutional baseline). In: Proceedings of the European Conference on Computer Vision (ECCV), pp. 480–496 (2018)
13. Sun, Y., et al.: Perceive where to focus: learning visibility-aware part-level features for partial person re-identification. In: Proceedings of the IEEE/CVF Conference on Computer Vision and Pattern Recognition, pp. 393–402 (2019)
14. Ge, Y., Li, Z., Zhao, H., Yin, G., Yi, S., Wang, X., et al.: FD-GAN: pose-guided feature distilling gan for robust person re-identification. Adv. Neural Inf. Process. Syst. **31** (2018)
15. Vaswani, A., et al.: Attention is all you need. Adv. Neural Inf. Process. Syst. **30** (2017)
16. He, S., Luo, H., Wang, P., Wang, F., Li, H., Jiang, W.: Transreid: transformer-based object re-identification. In: Proceedings of the IEEE/CVF International Conference on Computer Vision, pp. 15013–15022 (2021)
17. Li, Y., He, J., Zhang, T., Liu, X., Zhang, Y., Wu, F.: Diverse part discovery: occluded person re-identification with part-aware transformer. In: Proceedings of the IEEE/CVF Conference on Computer Vision and Pattern Recognition, pp. 2898–2907 (2021)
18. Xu, B., He, L., Liang, J., Sun, Z.: Learning feature recovery transformer for occluded person re-identification. IEEE Trans. Image Process. **31**, 4651–4662 (2022)
19. Schroff, F., Kalenichenko, D., Philbin, J.: Facenet: A unified embedding for face recognition and clustering. In: Proceedings of the IEEE Conference on Computer Vision and Pattern Recognition, pp. 815–823 (2015)
20. Ma, Z., Zhao, Y., Li, J.: Pose-guided inter-and intra-part relational transformer for occluded person re-identification. In: Proceedings of the 29th ACM International Conference on Multimedia, pp. 1487–1496 (2021)
21. Somers, V., De Vleeschouwer, C., Alahi, A.: Body part-based representation learning for occluded person re-identification. In: Proceedings of the IEEE/CVF Winter Conference on Applications of Computer Vision, pp. 1613–1623 (2023)
22. Cui, C., Huang, S., Song, W., Ding, P., Zhang, M., Wang, D.: Profd: prompt-guided feature disentangling for occluded person re-identification. In: Proceedings of the 32nd ACM International Conference on Multimedia, pp. 1583–1592 (2024)
23. Somers, V., Alahi, A., Vleeschouwer, C.D.: Keypoint promptable re-identification. In: European Conference on Computer Vision, pp. 216–233. Springer (2024)
24. Wang, T., Liu, H., Song, P., Guo, T., Shi, W.: Pose-guided feature disentangling for occluded person re-identification based on transformer. In: Proceedings of the AAAI Conference on Artificial Intelligence. vol. 36, pp. 2540–2549 (2022)

25. Wang, Z., Zhu, F., Tang, S., Zhao, R., He, L., Song, J.: Feature erasing and diffusion network for occluded person re-identification. In: Proceedings of the IEEE/CVF Conference on Computer Vision and Pattern Recognition, pp. 4754–4763 (2022)
26. Ristani, E., Solera, F., Zou, R., Cucchiara, R., Tomasi, C.: Performance measures and a data set for multi-target, multi-camera tracking. In: European conference on computer vision, pp. 17–35. Springer (2016)

A Fine-Grained Predictive Stress Quantification Framework for Drivers with Autism Spectrum Disorder in Inclusive Smart Mobility

Amadou Djoulde Barry[1(✉)], Nawal Guermouche[1], Viviane Kostrubiec[2], Thouria Ben Haddi[1], Guilhem Baccati[2], Pierre Vincent Paubel[3], and Youcef Belkhiri[4]

[1] LAAS-CNRS, University of Toulouse, INSA, Toulouse, France
{adbarry,nguermou,tbenhaddi}@laas.fr

[2] CERPPS, University of Toulouse, Toulouse, France
{viviane.kostrubiec,guilhem.achard-baccati}@univ-tlse2.fr

[3] CLLE, University of Toulouse, Toulouse, France
paubel@univ-tlse2.fr

[4] Laboratoire LITAN, École supérieure en Sciences et Technologies de l'Informatique et du Numérique, RN 75, 06300 Amizour, Bejaia, Algeria
y_belkhiri@estin.dz

Abstract. Autism Spectrum Disorder (ASD) is a neurodevelopmental condition that significantly heightens the challenges and risks associated with driving. Individuals with ASD often experience increased sensory sensitivities, difficulty adapting to dynamic environments, and heightened vulnerability to unexpected events, which can lead to elevated stress levels, sensory overload, and impaired decision-making on the road. Existing research in stress detection primarily proposes reactive approaches, triggering responses only after stress has escalated. Such strategies limit the possibility for timely and effective intervention. Moreover, most existing studies fail to quantify stress intensity, providing only binary assessments. This lack of granularity hinders the development of proactive and personalized support mechanisms. In this paper, we propose a novel real-time approach for continuous stress prediction and quantification tailored to drivers with ASD. Our method leverages physiological signals and contextual data to anticipate stress escalation and enable proactive stress quantification and provide a proactive, fine-grained assessment of stress levels, paving the way for personalized and context-aware in-vehicle support systems that enhance driving safety and comfort for individuals with ASD.

Keywords: Proactive stress detection · stress quantification · smart mobility · Inclusive mobility · ASD · IoT · deep learning · machine learning

I. Awan et al. (Eds.): WISE 2025, LNCS 16368, pp. 460–475, 2026.
https://doi.org/10.1007/978-981-95-7251-9_31

1 Introduction

Driving is a complex cognitive and emotional activity that requires continuous attention, adaptability, and rapid decision-making in dynamic environments. For individuals with Autism Spectrum Disorder (ASD), these demands are further intensified due to characteristic challenges such as heightened sensory sensitivities, difficulty managing change or unpredictability, and a reduced ability to filter irrelevant stimuli. These factors contribute to elevated stress levels while driving, leading to sensory overload, anxiety, and impaired reaction times, which ultimately compromise safety and autonomy.

Stress is a natural and adaptive physiological response that prepares the body to confront perceived threats through fight, flight, or freeze mechanisms [15]. In individuals with ASD, this system often exhibits heightened reactivity, which can result in diminished situational awareness, impaired executive functioning, and disrupted motor coordination during stress episodes [5,8,14]. These effects are particularly harmful in dynamic and unpredictable driving environments where calm, rapid, and precise responses are critical for ensuring safety.

Despite significant advances in automotive and smart mobility technologies, modern vehicles and road infrastructures are typically designed for individuals with typical neurodevelopment, often overlooking the unique needs of people with ASD. As active members of society, individuals with ASD deserve equitable access to safe and comfortable transportation. This underscores the growing need for inclusive mobility solutions that recognize neurodiversity by integrating adaptive technologies and personalized support systems. Such solutions can help mitigate sensory overload, improve stress regulation, and improve overall driving safety and comfort.

Recent research has explored driver stress detection using physiological signals such as heart rate variability (HRV), skin conductance, and facial expressions [1,16,20]. While these approaches have demonstrated effectiveness in recognizing stress episodes, they are predominantly reactive, responding only after stress has already manifested. This limits their capacity for early intervention and proactive stress management. Moreover, most existing works fail to consider contextual factors, such as traffic density, environmental noise, time pressure, and other situational dynamics that significantly influence stress responses, particularly in individuals with ASD. Without integrating contextual awareness, these systems lack the ability to assess key stress precursors and fall short of providing personalized, anticipatory interventions tailored to the user's specific sensitivities.

To address these limitations, this paper presents a novel fine-grained, proactive stress detection and quantification framework specifically designed for drivers with ASD. The proposed system leverages continuous, real-time data collection through IoT-enabled monitoring and contextual sensing to anticipate stress responses before they escalate. It combines deep learning for temporal modeling with unsupervised learning for stress level segmentation. More specifically, the framework leverages long-short-term memory (LSTM) networks, a specialized type of Deep Neural Network (DNN), which is effective in modeling and capturing temporal dependencies in sequential data [11]. The LSTM model is used to predict heart rate variability (HRV)-driven metrics in response to upcoming road events. These metrics then undergo Exploratory Factor Analysis (EFA) to extract latent stress-related dimensions. The resulting stress factors are then segmented into three meaningful categories, *low*, *moderate*, and *high*, using K-means clustering. These labels serve as ground truth for training and evaluating machine learning classifiers, enabling real-time, anticipatory stress detection and classification.

The main contributions of this study can be summarized as follows: 1) We propose an an inclusive IoT-based smart-mobility framework tailored to meet the specific needs of each individual with ASD. 2) We introduce a hybrid approach that combines deep learning for temporal prediction with unsupervised learning for stress level segmentation, enabling proactive stress detection and quantification based on contextual road events. 3) We implement and evaluate the proposed framework using simulated real-world driving scenarios, demonstrating its effectiveness in anticipating stress responses.

The remainder of the paper is structured as follows. Section 2 introduces a real-life scenario. Section 3 provides a review of related work. Section 4 presents a comprehensive overview of the proposed framework. Section 5 details the proposed approach for proactive stress detection and quantification. Section 6 discusses the experimental results, and Sect. 7 concludes the paper.

2 Motivating Example: ASD Driving Challenge

Let us consider a real-life case shared by a collaborating psychologist. It concerns a woman with ASD, referred to here as Anna. Anna had a scheduled appointment with her psychologist and, as part of her usual routine, meticulously planned her journey in advance to minimize any potential disruptions. To ensure a timely arrival, she left early and carefully followed a familiar, well-rehearsed route, anticipating a smooth and predictable experience. However, as Anna approached a roundabout, she unexpectedly encountered significant traffic congestion. The abrupt change in traffic conditions disrupted her sense of control and routine. The combination of auditory stimuli, such as honking from impatient drivers and sudden lane changes, contributed to a rapid escalation in Anna's stress levels. Unable to manage this situation, she abruptly stopped her vehicle in the middle of the roundabout, experiencing a state of emotional overload. As panic took over, she exited the vehicle and walked away, leaving the car stationary and obstructing the traffic flow. This situation poses a significant safety risk, not only for Anna but for other road users as it increases the likelihood of traffic accidents and contributes to broader roadway disruptions.

This scenario highlights the critical need for a proactive stress prediction system within intelligent transportation frameworks. If Anna's vehicle had been equipped with an IoT-enabled, context-aware stress anticipation mechanism, it could have detected the risk of increased stress before she encountered the congested roundabout. By analyzing real-time road conditions and estimating their potential impact on the driver's stress levels, such a system could have provided timely alerts. This would have enabled Anna to navigate the situation with increased confidence, reduced stress, and improved safety.

3 Related Works

Several initiatives have been defined to contribute to ongoing development of inclusive mobility solutions that address the diverse needs of ASD users, promoting safer and more accessible environments. A substantial body of research has focused on designing solutions tailored to the unique cognitive, sensory, and behavioral characteristics of individuals with ASD across various domains. Padmanaban et al. [13], through a design-thinking approach with caregiver input, developed a personalized system that includes customizable interiors, emotional regulation tools, and an intuitive companion mobile app. This solution has demonstrated a significant enhancement in trust and autonomy for neurodiverse passengers, offering a tailored experience that supports their unique needs and promotes greater independence during mobility.

Other works have studied the stress experienced by individuals with ASD during driving. Cox et al. [5] demonstrated that newly licensed drivers with ASD exhibit greater physiological stress responses and poorer performance in driving simulations compared to their neurotypical peers. Fok et al. [8] conducted a study showing that emerging drivers with ASD report elevated emotional stress and greater difficulty managing challenging driving situations. Other smart mobility systems dedicated to individuals with ASD have also been proposed. In this context, wearable technologies have been increasingly employed to monitor and support individuals with ASD. Benssassi et al. [3] reviewed assistive devices such as smart glasses and proximity sensors, highlighting their potential to enhance real-time social interaction and sensory regulation while pointing out limitations related to usability, feedback design, and ethical implementation. D. Bian et al. [4] introduced a novel adaptive virtual reality (VR) driving simulator for individuals with ASD, which infers user engagement from physiological signals and dynamically adjusts task difficulty in real-time to foster emotionally safe and personalized learning experiences. All these efforts aim to create an ecosystem of mobility solutions that empower individuals with ASD, enhancing their autonomy and inclusivity. However, they fall short in proposing proactive solutions for detecting and anticipating stress states.

Stress detection through physiological signals has been extensively studied. In particular, deep learning techniques have significantly advanced the performance of stress detection models [1,10,17,18,21]. Rastgoo et al. [16] developed a method to process electrocardiogram (ECG) signals for real-time driver stress classification. Similarly, Amin et al. [1] used ECG signals alongside deep transfer learning with fuzzy logic to classify driver stress. Ke Wang et al. [20] presented an ensemble classification model using autoencoders and the AdaBoost framework to classify driving stress levels based on various physiological signals. In a previous work [6], we introduced a framework designed to anticipate whether a driver with ASD is likely to experience stress in the near future. While this approach employed a binary classification scheme (stress vs. no stress), it does not capture the nuanced and continuous nature of stress responses. Its intensity can vary significantly depending on internal states and external conditions. Accurately recognizing these variations is essential for delivering appropriately scaled and personalized interventions. Relying solely on binary classification risks overlooking subtle but meaningful shifts in stress levels, thereby reducing the system's sensitivity and limiting its capacity to deliver effective and timely support in real-world driving scenarios.

While these works have made significant contributions to detecting stress reactively by analyzing observed physiological data, they primarily rely on real-time signals such as ECG to classify stress levels after the stress response has already been triggered. This reactive approach, though effective in many scenarios, presents limitations, particularly within the context of mobility, where it is crucial to anticipate and prevent stress induced by road events and environmental factors before they arise.

4 Global Overview of the IoT-Based Smart Mobility System

Figure 1 illustrates the IoT-based smart mobility framework designed to enable proactive stress detection for drivers with ASD. The system leverages Multi-Access Edge Computing (MEC) servers, which facilitate the acquisition of real-time road event data from geographical areas that the driver is likely to traverse, supporting timely and context-aware decision-making.

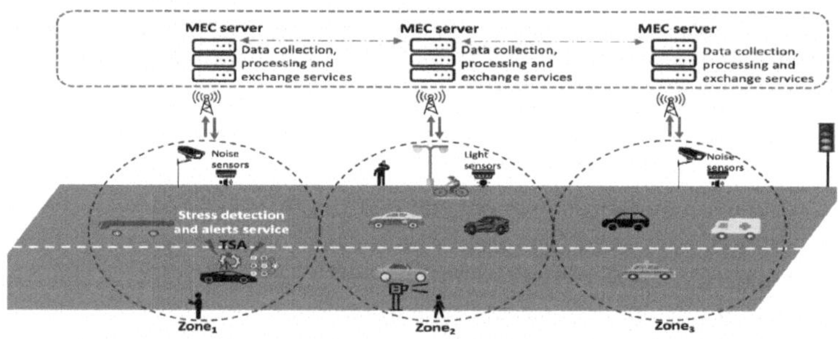

Fig. 1. IoT-based framework for proactive stress detection service.

In this framework, two main categories of data are utilized:

- *Road event data*: Through IoT-enabled services, external environmental and traffic-related conditions, such as noise levels, lighting conditions, weather changes (e.g., fog, rain), and traffic density, are continuously monitored and transmitted to the ASD vehicle analysis system. Moreover, contextual data are also monitored. They refer to information related to the driver's situation and journey progression, such as acceleration patterns, distance traveled, and time elapsed since the start of the trip.

- *Physiological responses*: Stress levels are commonly assessed through various physiological signals, with electrocardiogram (ECG) data being the most widely used due to its reliability in capturing autonomic nervous system responses [22]. In this paper, we focus specifically on heart rate variability (HRV), a critical metric derived from ECG signals, to evaluate physiological stress responses as well as heart rate (HR), which offers a fundamental measure of cardiac activity and is expressed in beats per minute (bpm). To achieve a comprehensive understanding of autonomic nervous system regulation, and informed by non-parametric statistical analyses, specifically the Friedman test [9] applied across all driving experiments, we employ a set of well-established HRV-derived indicators. Each of these metrics offers complementary insights into the complex dynamics of stress [12]:

- *Root Mean Square of Successive Differences (RMSSD)*: It quantifies short-term fluctuations in heart rate, primarily driven by parasympathetic activity, making it a highly sensitive marker for detecting acute stress responses. $\text{RMSSD} = \sqrt{\frac{1}{N-1}\sum_{i=2}^{N}(RR_i - RR_{i-1})^2}$, where RR_i represents the ith RR interval and N is the total number of RR intervals.
- *Standard Deviation of NN Intervals (SDNN)*: measures overall HRV and is considered a robust indicator of long-term stress adaptation. $\text{SDNN} = \sqrt{\frac{1}{N}\sum_{i=1}^{N}(RR_i - \overline{RR})^2}$, where $\overline{RR}$ is the mean of the RR intervals in seconds (i.e., the time between successive R-wave peaks in the ECG signal).
- *Percentage of successive NN intervals differing by more than 50 ms (pNN50)*: reflects parasympathetic activity and short-term variations in heart rate. $\text{pNN50} = \frac{\text{Number of successive RR intervals differing by more than 50 ms}}{N-1} \times 100\%$.
- *Poincaré Plot Standard Deviation 1 (SD1)*: represents short-term variability in heart rate, primarily influenced by parasympathetic activity. It represents the standard deviation of the distances of RR intervals from the line of identity in the Poincaré plot and is sensitive to rapid changes in autonomic regulation. $\text{SD1} = \sqrt{\frac{1}{2}} \cdot \text{RMSSD}$.
- *Cardiac Sympathetic Index (CSI)*: quantifies the balance between sympathetic and parasympathetic activity by capturing the geometrical distribution of RR intervals. It is derived from the Poincaré plot as the ratio between the longitudinal (stress-related) and transverse (parasympathetic-related) axes, offering a non-linear perspective on autonomic modulation. $\text{CSI} = \frac{\text{SD2}}{\text{SD1}}$ where SD2 represents the standard deviation along the line of identity (long-term variability).
- *Detrended Fluctuation Analysis alpha 1 (DFA_alpha1)*: is a non-linear HRV-derived parameter that characterizes the short-term fractal correlation properties of the RR interval time series. It provides a measure of the complexity

and self-correlation of heartbeat fluctuations. A DFA_alpha1 value close to 1.0 reflects well-regulated fractal dynamics, typically associated with stable, low-stress physiological states. In contrast, values approaching 0.5 indicate reduced complexity and a shift toward more random, uncorrelated patterns, features often linked to heightened physiological or psychological stress.

Under stress conditions, SDNN, RMSSD, and pNN50 typically decrease, reflecting a diminished parasympathetic (vagal) activity. Conversely, MeanHR and CSI usually increases, indicating heightened sympathetic nervous system dominance. Similarly, SD1 tends to decrease under stress. Additionally, DFA_alpha1 often decreases during acute psychosocial stress. Together, these changes in HRV metrics provide a multifaceted characterization of autonomic nervous system responses to physiological stress.

Each ASD vehicle is equipped with an onboard AI-driven predictive stress detection model designed to assess the potential impact of context-aware road events on drivers with ASD. The primary objective is to proactively anticipate and quantify stress responses triggered by these events, thereby enabling timely interventions and promoting safer, more adaptive driving experiences.

5 Predictive Stress Detection and Quantification Driven by Roads Events

Figure 2 presents the architecture of the proposed model for proactively assessing stress responses in ASD drivers in the presence of upcoming road events. The framework includes two core components: (1) an LSTM-based prediction module to predict physiological biomarkers (MeanHR, RMSSD, SDNN, pNN50, DFA_alpha1, CSI, and SD1) in response to road and contextual conditions, and (2) a machine learning classification module to infer the driver's stress state from these predicted biomarkers. Each component is described in the subsequent sections.

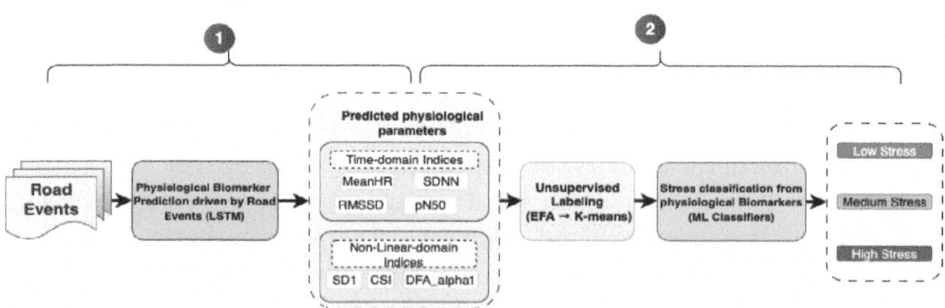

Fig. 2. Global architecture of the proposed stress prediction model.

5.1 Road Events-Driven LSTM Model for Predicting Physiological Biomarkers

The proposed LSTM-based model is illustrated in Fig. 3. It captures temporal dependencies and contextual patterns within the input stream of road events and contextual data. A notable advantage of using LSTM in this setting lies in its capacity to model both immediate and delayed physiological responses. For instance, acute stimuli such as sudden loud noises may trigger instantaneous stress reactions, whereas prolonged exposure to traffic congestion may lead to gradual physiological changes. The model comprises two main components: the *LSTM network* and *a dense layer*, presented below.

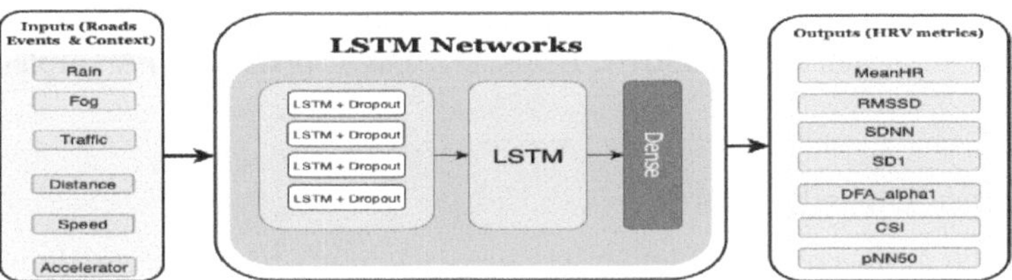

Fig. 3. Architecture of the LSTM-based model.

LSTM Network-Based Context and Road Events Encoding: The model takes as input a sequential stream of road events, each characterized by contextual and environmental factors such as traffic dynamics (e.g., congestion levels), environmental conditions (e.g., noise levels, lighting variations, and weather changes), and emergency events (e.g., roadblocks, sirens, and accidents). These features are encoded as normalized numerical vectors and processed sequentially to reflect their temporal relationships.

Example: Let us consider an ASD driver on a 15-minute urban journey. At a specific moment in time, denoted as t, the vehicle collects and transmits a set of contextual features: Fog (500 m visibility) normalized to 0.92 (assuming a range of 20 m to 6000 m), Rain intensity: 0 (no rain), Noise level (70 dB) normalized to 0.70, Lighting level (40 lux) normalized to 0.45, Traffic: "heavy" as 1.0, Acceleration: -0.4 m/s^2 normalized to 0.35, Driving distance: 2.5 km normalized to 0.42 (assuming a maximum of 6 km trip), and Time elapsed: 6 min normalized to 0.40 (assuming a maximum of 15 min). Considering these subset of features, the feature vector x_i at time t_i is then represented as $x_i =$[0.92, 0, 0.70, 0.45, 1.0, 0.35, 0.42, 0.40].

The normalized input vectors $x_{t_i} \in \mathbb{R}^d$, where d denotes the number of input features, are fed into an LSTM-based model to capture temporal dependencies for forecasting physiological responses. The LSTM architecture comprises stacked layers that progressively learn temporal patterns. A Dropout layer is incorporated to mitigate overfitting by randomly deactivating a subset of neurons during training. The output of the final LSTM layer consists of hidden states $\{h_1, \ldots, h_n\}$, where each $h_i \in \mathbb{R}^d$ encodes the learned temporal and contextual representation of the input at time step t_i.

Final Mapping of Physiological Biomarkers Output Through a Dense Layer: The model incorporates a fully connected *dense* layer that maps the last hidden state output vector$h \in \mathbf{R}^{d_h}$, where d_h is the dimensionality of the final LSTM hidden state, to the final output space corresponding to the predicted physiological biomarkers: MeanHR, RMSSD, SDNN, pNN50, DFA_alpha1, CSI, and SD1. This transformation is defined as: $\hat{y} = W \cdot h + b$, where W is the weight matrix connecting the last hidden state vector h to the output layer, and b is the bias vector. The output vector $\hat{y}$ represents the predicted values of the physiological biomarkers MeanHR, RMSSD, SDNN, pNN50, DFA_alpha1, CSI, and SD1.

5.2 Stress Classification

The predicted physiological biomarkers serve as inputs to a structured analytical pipeline combining Exploratory Factor Analysis (EFA) and K-means clustering to identify distinct stress states. This approach categorizes driver stress levels into three discrete classes, leveraging physiological parameters predicted by an LSTM model. The comprehensive workflow of this stress classification method is detailed in the following.

Exploratory Factor Analysis (EFA): EFA is a powerful multivariate statistical method applied to reduce dimensionality by uncovering latent factors underlying observed variables [19]. EFA simplifies data interpretation by identifying factor loadings that capture core constructs.

Prior to applying EFA, dataset suitability was evaluated via the Kaiser-Meyer-Olkin (KMO) measure and Bartlett's test of sphericity, both of which confirmed sufficient inter-variable correlations to justify reliable and meaningful factor extraction [19]. The results, summarized for each user in Table 1, demonstrate strong inter-parameter correlations, thereby confirming the adequacy of the data for factor analysis

To determine the optimal number of latent factors, the Kaiser criterion, based on retaining factors with eigenvalues greater than 1, was applied [19]. This approach ensures that only factors contributing significantly to the overall variance are retained, thereby improving interpretability while effectively reducing dimensionality. Based on the eigenvalue distribution and the pattern of factor loadings, two distinct latent factors emerged, each capturing a key aspect of the autonomic stress response : *factor 1:* Characterized by strong *parasympathetic activation*, *factor 2:* Reflecting *sympathetic nervous systems activity*.

The composite score used to quantify stress was derived from the three latent factors identified previously. Specifically, the score for each sample i is computed as:

Table 1. Result of Kaiser-Meyer-Olkin (KMO) test and Bartlett's test

User	Kaiser-Meyer-Olkin (KMO)	Bartlett's test
User_01	0.876	$\chi^2 = 34077.1, \quad p < 0.001$
User_02	0.786	$\chi^2 = 28955.3, \quad p < 0.001$
User_03	0.852	$\chi^2 = 36528.4, \quad p < 0.001$
User_04	0.858	$\chi^2 = 56751.6, \quad p < 0.001$
User_05	0.807	$\chi^2 = 64043.0, \quad p < 0.001$
User_06	0.852	$\chi^2 = 23551.9, \quad p < 0.001$
User_07	0.850	$\chi^2 = 31722.6, \quad p < 0.001$
User_08	0.830	$\chi^2 = 55132.7, \quad p < 0.001$
User_09	0.848	$\chi^2 = 35439.4, \quad p < 0.001$
User_10	0.876	$\chi^2 = 31800.4, \quad p < 0.001$
User_11	0.861	$\chi^2 = 33580.5, \quad p < 0.001$
User_12	0.852	$\chi^2 = 31260.3, \quad p < 0.001$
User_13	0.862	$\chi^2 = 33559.8, \quad p < 0.001$
User_14	0.834	$\chi^2 = 28912.5, \quad p < 0.001$
User_15	0.673	$\chi^2 = 32831.8, \quad p < 0.001$

$$SI_i = F_{2i} - F_{1i} \tag{1}$$

where F_{1i}, F_{2i} represent the standardized loadings of sample i on on Factor 1 and Factor 2, respectively. This formula ensures that higher composite scores correspond to heightened stress levels. In fact, it reflects the expected physiological behavior under stress: decreased parasympathetic activity (hence the negative wright on F_1), increased sympathetic dominance (positive weight on F_2).

Stress Labeling: To categorize stress levels based on the normalized Stress Index (SI), K-means clustering was applied to segment the continuous SI values into discrete classes. The optimal number of clusters was determined using the elbow method. Via this analysis, three clusters were identified, corresponding to *Low*, *Medium*, and *High* stress levels.

Based on the clustering results, each data sample was assigned a stress label corresponding to one of the three identified classes: low, moderate, or high stress. These labels were derived from the cluster membership obtained through K-means, using the normalized SI Index as input. Samples grouped within the cluster exhibiting the lowest SI values were labeled as low stress, reflecting relaxed physiological states. Conversely, samples in the cluster with the highest SI values were labeled as high stress, indicative of heightened sympathetic activation and reduced autonomic flexibility. The intermediate cluster was labeled as moderate stress, capturing transitional or mildly elevated physiological responses. This labeling approach provides a data-driven, unsupervised method for quantifying stress levels from physiological signals, facilitating further analysis and model training.

Stress Classification: Following the data labeling process, classification was performed using several well-established machine learning algorithms, including Random Forest, Logistic Regression, Support Vector Machine with an RBF kernel, k-Nearest Neighbors (k-NN), Gradient Boosting, and eXtreme Gradient Boosting. These classifiers were selected based on their effectiveness and consistent robustness across a broad spectrum of classification tasks in various domains. Each algorithm was systematically evaluated to determine the most accurate and reliable model for distinguishing between the defined stress levels.

Once stress is proactively detected and quantified, tailored interventions can be initiated according to the identified stress level. In low stress states, minimal or no intervention is necessary, allowing the driver to maintain optimal focus and comfort. During moderate stress episodes, subtle adaptive feedback, such as calming auditory cues, can be applied to prevent escalation. For high stress levels, more immediate and comprehensive interventions are triggered, including real-time alerts, recommendations to take a break, or suggesting an alternative route. This graduated, context-aware strategy ensures that responses are appropriately scaled to the driver's physiological state, fostering safer, more supportive, and adaptive driving experiences, particularly for vulnerable populations such as drivers with ASD.

6 Experiments and Evaluation

The proposed approach has been implemented and thoroughly evaluated. In the following sections, we present dataset acquisition, experimental setup, and the results obtained across different evaluation metrics.

6.1 Dataset Acquisition and Implementation Setup

Driving Simulator: Data were collected using the *SimulAuto*[1] driving simulator, depicted in Fig. 4, featuring a Renault Zoe car and a 360° visual setup. Several scenarios and simulations were built and executed using SCANeR ™studio 9.8[2], capturing data at 500 Hz.

Participants: In this pilot study, a small convenience sample of fifteen participants (aged between 20âĂŞ28), all licensed drivers with no heart issues, took

[1] https://miroir.univ-tlse2.fr/2019/05/27/com-simulauto-le-simulateur-de-conduite-de-la-plateforme-ccu/.

[2] https://www.avsimulation.com/en/simulators/full-cab/simreal/.

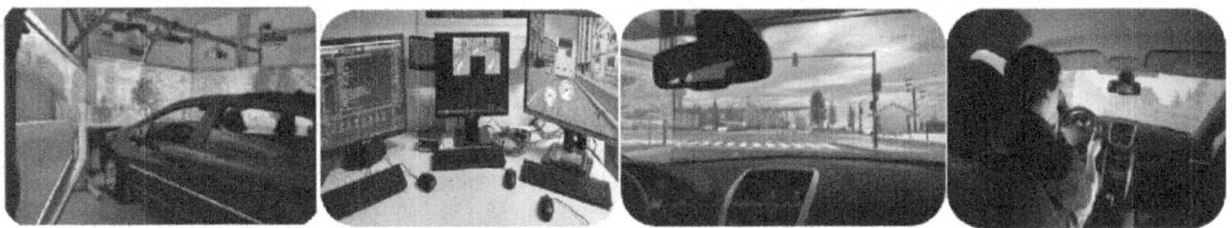

Fig. 4. The car simulator *SimulAuto*.

part. They were recruited via a social media campaign, and in university centers dedicated to supporting individuals with autism. All participants passed the RAADS-14 [7], a screening test designed to identify adults presenting behavioral traits associated with autism. Participants 1, 2, 3, and 10 scored above the cutoff of 14, indicating strong autistic traits; participant 10 was diagnosed with ASD. We note that the study was approved by the University of Toulouse Ethics Committee (CER-2023_709), with consent obtained in line with the Declaration of Helsinki [2].

ECG Acquisition System: The ECG signal was recorded using two pre-gelled Ag/AgCl electrodes (EL 503, BIOPAC), amplified and digitized at 500 Hz with the ActiChamp system (Brain Products), and stored by BrainVision software on a dedicated computer.

Implementation Setup: The approach was implemented in Python 3.11 using PyTorch and tested on a MacBook Pro (M3 Max, 36GB RAM). Data were split into 75% for training and 25% for testing. The Adam optimizer was used for training.

Evaluation Metrics: For evaluating the performance of the LSTM model, we employed two regression metrics: Mean Absolute Error (MAE) and the coefficient of determination (R^2), defined as follows: MAE $= \frac{1}{n}\sum_{i=1}^{n}|y_i - \hat{y}_i|$; $R^2 = 1 - \frac{\sum_{i=1}^{n}(y_i-\hat{y}_i)^2}{\sum_{i=1}^{n}(y_i-\bar{y})^2}$.

For classification models based on machine learning, we utilized various performance metrics, including accuracy, precision, recall, F1-score, and log loss. These metrics were computed using confusion matrix elements: true positives (TP), false positives (FP), true negatives (TN), and false negatives (FN). Their respective formulas are given by: Accuracy $= \frac{TP+TN}{TP+TN+FP+FN}$; Precision $= \frac{TP}{TP+FP}$; F1-score $= \frac{2\times\text{Precision}\times\text{Recall}}{\text{Precision}+\text{Recall}}$.

These metrics collectively provide comprehensive insights into the model's predictive performance, especially under conditions of class imbalance.

6.2 Experimental Evaluations

LSTM model: Figures 5 and 6 show the evolution of the training loss and the coefficient of determination R^2, respectively.

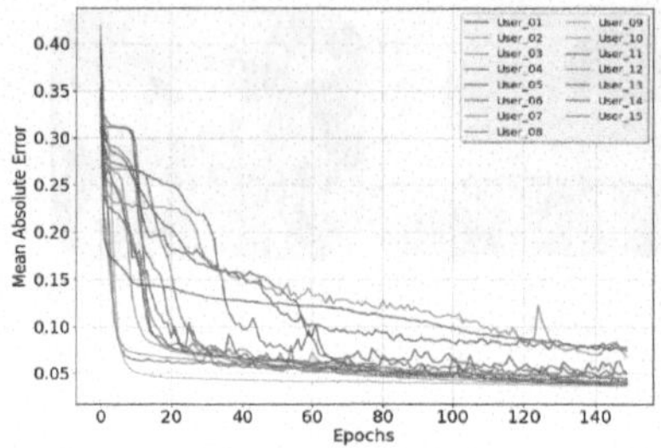

Fig. 5. Training MAE loss of the LSTM model.

Fig. 6. Evaluation of the LSTM model performance using R^2 during training.

These results demonstrate the convergence and learning stability of the model and its effectiveness in capturing the underlying patterns in the physiological data.

Machine Learning Classification Models: Tables 2 and 3 summarize the performance of the different machine learning algorithms evaluated in this study. Specifically, they report the classification accuracy and F1-score, respectively, for each of the fifteen users.

Table 2. Classification Accuracy per User

User	Random Forest	Logistic Regression	SVM	KNN	Gradient Boosting	XGBoost
User_01	0.976	1.000	0.996	0.984	0.968	0.984
User_02	0.972	0.992	0.980	0.964	0.952	0.964
User_03	0.982	0.978	0.978	0.985	0.952	0.952
User_04	0.988	0.993	0.993	0.985	0.968	0.983
User_05	0.987	0.998	1.000	0.998	0.980	0.984
User_06	0.929	0.990	0.975	0.934	0.914	0.939
User_07	0.982	0.989	0.982	0.982	0.975	0.968
User_08	0.987	0.992	0.979	0.987	0.971	0.984
User_09	0.960	0.965	0.960	0.973	0.960	0.969
User_10	0.979	0.986	0.993	0.989	0.964	0.975
User_11	0.939	0.955	0.958	0.962	0.929	0.942
User_12	0.957	0.981	0.977	0.973	0.930	0.961
User_13	0.982	0.985	0.982	0.989	0.974	0.963
User_14	0.981	0.991	0.985	0.991	0.985	0.966
User_15	0.957	0.981	0.977	0.973	0.930	0.961
Average	**0.971**	**0.985**	**0.980**	**0.976**	**0.954**	**0.965**

Table 3. Classification F1 Score per user

User	Random Forest	Logistic Regression	SVM	KNN	Gradient Boosting	XGBoost
User_01	0.979	1.000	0.996	0.986	0.971	0.985
User_02	0.972	0.992	0.980	0.963	0.954	0.965
User_03	0.982	0.978	0.978	0.986	0.952	0.953
User_04	0.988	0.992	0.992	0.986	0.969	0.983
User_05	0.987	0.998	1.000	0.998	0.980	0.985
User_06	0.929	0.990	0.975	0.934	0.913	0.939
User_07	0.982	0.989	0.983	0.983	0.976	0.968
User_08	0.987	0.992	0.978	0.987	0.970	0.984
User_09	0.960	0.964	0.960	0.973	0.960	0.969
User_10	0.979	0.986	0.993	0.990	0.965	0.976
User_11	0.938	0.954	0.958	0.961	0.929	0.942
User_12	0.954	0.978	0.976	0.972	0.924	0.959
User_13	0.982	0.986	0.982	0.989	0.974	0.964
User_14	0.982	0.990	0.984	0.991	0.986	0.967
User_15	0.954	0.978	0.976	0.972	0.924	0.959
Average	**0.971**	**0.985**	**0.981**	**0.977**	**0.954**	**0.966**

The results show that all models achieved relatively high performance across users, with average accuracy and F1-score values consistently exceeding 95%. Among the evaluated algorithms, *logistic regression* demonstrated the highest overall performance (mean accuracy and macro-F1: 98.5%). This likely reflects that our labels are derived from a linear combination (Eq. 1), making the classes near-linearly separable, suggesting that the Logistic Regression is particularly effective in capturing user-specific stress patterns when the data is well-clustered. Similarly, SVM and KNN yielded strong performance, both with average accuracy and F1-scores close to 98%. Overall, the combined analysis of accuracy and F1-score confirms that the proposed framework delivers high precision and reliability in classifying multi-level stress states across a diverse set of users.

7 Conclusion

In this paper, we proposed a fine-grained predictive stress detection and quantification framework for drivers with ASD. Our approach integrates physiological signal modeling, context-aware stressor recognition, and unsupervised labeling to proactively anticipate and quantify individual stress responses in real time. By leveraging HRV features derived from ECG signals and applying LSTM-based prediction combined with EFA and K-means clustering, we derived personalized stress indices and classified stress into interpretable levels.

As part of future work, we plan to extend the framework by integrating additional multimodal physiological signals, such as skin conductance, respiration rate, and pupillometry, coupled with behavioral driving metrics, such as jerk (rate of change of acceleration), pedal pressure, steering variability, and headway distance in drivers with a formal ASD diagnosis. Additionally, we aim to develop a real-time, adaptive intervention system that proactively delivers personalized support and preventive actions based on each driver's ASD profile and current stress state. This will enable a closed-loop system that seamlessly links prediction with individualized, context-sensitive adaptation, thereby fostering safer driving experiences.

Acknowledgment. This work has been supported by the Occitanie region, the European Regional Development Fund (ERDF), and the French government, through the France 2030 project managed by the National Research Agency (ANR) with the reference number "ANR-22-EXES-0015."

References

1. Amin, M., et al.: ECG-based driver's stress detection using deep transfer learning and fuzzy logic approaches. IEEE Access **10**, 29788–29809 (2022)
2. Association, W.M.: World medical association declaration of Helsinki: ethical principles for medical research involving human participants. JAMA **332**(15), 1575–1583 (2024)
3. Benssassi, S., Aitken, J.M., Waraich, A.: Wearable assistive technologies for autism: opportunities and challenges. IEEE Pulse **9**(6), 39–42 (2018)
4. Bian, D., Wade, J.W., Swanson, A., Weitlauf, A.S., Warren, Z., Sarkar, N.: Design of a physiology-based adaptive virtual reality driving platform for individuals with ASD. ACM Trans. Accessible Comput. (TACCESS) **12**, 1–24 (2019)
5. Cox, D., et al.: A pilot study comparing newly licensed drivers with and without autism and experienced drivers in simulated and on-road driving. J. Autism Dev. Disord. **50**, 1258–1268 (2020)
6. Barry, D.A., Guermouche, N., V.K.P.V.P.: Towards IoT-based smart mobility framework for proactive road stress detection for individuals with ASD. In: 36th International Conference on Database and Expert Systems Applications (2025)
7. Eriksson, J.M., Andersen, L.M., Bejerot, S.: RAADS-14 Screen: validity of a screening tool for autism spectrum disorder in an adult psychiatric population. Molecular Autism **4**, 49 (2013)
8. Fok, M., Owens, J., Ollendick, T., Scarpa, A.: Perceived driving difficulty, negative affect, and emotion dysregulation in self-identified autistic emerging drivers. Front. Psychol. **13** (2022)
9. Friedman, M.: The use of ranks to avoid the assumption of normality implicit in the analysis of variance. J. Am. Stat. Assoc. **32**(200), 675–701 (1937)
10. Healey, J., Picard, R.W.: Detecting stress during real-world driving tasks using physiological sensors. IEEE Trans. Intell. Transp. Syst. **6**, 156–166 (2005)
11. Hochreiter, S., Schmidhuber, J.: Long short-term memory. Neural Comput. **9**(8), 1735–1780 (1997)
12. Immanuel, S., Teferra, M.N., Baumert, M., Bidargaddi, N.: Heart rate variability for evaluating psychological stress changes in healthy adults: a scoping review. Neuropsychobiology **82**, 187–202 (2023)

13. Padmanaban, V., Sudhakaran, A., Sabnis, S., Geetha, S.: An autonomous driving system—dedicated vehicle for people with asd and their caregivers. arXiv preprint arXiv:2108.04367 (2021)
14. Patrick, K., Hurewitz, F., McCurdy, M., Agate, F.T., Daly, B., Tarazi, R., Chute, D., Schultheis, M.: Driving comparisons between young adults with autism spectrum disorder and typical development. J. Developmental Behavioral Pediatrics **39**, 451–460 (2018)
15. Porges, S.W.: Polyvagal theory: a science of safety. Front. Integr. Neurosci. **16**, 871227 (2022)
16. Rastgoo, M., Nakisa, B., Maire, F., Rakotonirainy, A., Chandran, V.: Automatic driver stress level classification using multimodal deep learning. Expert Syst. Appl. **138** (2019)
17. Seo, W., Kim, N., Kim, S., Lee, C., min Park, S.: Deep ecg-respiration network (deeper net) for recognizing mental stress. Sensors (Basel, Switzerland) **19** (2019)
18. Seo, W., Kim, N., Park, C., Park, S.M.: Deep learning approach for detecting work-related stress using multimodal signals. IEEE Sens. J. **22**, 11892–11902 (2022)
19. Taherdoost, H., Sahibuddin, S., Jalaliyoon, N.: Exploratory factor analysis; concepts and theory. In: Balicki, J. (ed.) Advances in Applied and Pure Mathematics. Math. Comput. Sci. Eng. Series, vol. 27, pp. 375–382. WSEAS (2014)
20. Wang, K., Guo, P.: An ensemble classification model with unsupervised representation learning for driving stress recognition using physiological signals. IEEE Trans. Intell. Transp. Syst. **22**, 3303–3315 (2020)
21. Wang, K., Murphey, Y., Zhou, Y., Hu, X., Zhang, X.: Detection of driver stress in real-world driving environment using physiological signals. 2019 IEEE 17th International Conference on Industrial Informatics (INDIN) **1**, 1807–1814 (2019)
22. Zepf, S., Hernandez, J., Schmitt, A., Minker, W., Picard, R.W.: Driver emotion recognition for intelligent vehicles: a survey. ACM Comput. Surv. **53**(3), 1–30 (2021)

PersoDPO: Scalable Preference Optimization for Instruction-Adherent, Persona-Grounded Dialogue via Multi-LLM Evaluation

Saleh Afzoon(✉), MohammadHossein Ahmadi, Usman Naseem, and Amin Beheshti

School of Computing, Macquarie University, Sydney, Australia
{saleh.afzoon,mohammadhossein.ahmadi}@hdr.mq.edu.au,
{usman.naseem,amin.beheshti}@mq.edu.au

Abstract. Personalization and contextual coherence are two essential components in building effective persona-grounded dialogue systems. These aspects play a crucial role in enhancing user engagement and ensuring responses are more relevant and consistent with user identity. However, recent studies indicate that open-source large language models (LLMs) continue to struggle to generate responses that are both contextually grounded and aligned with persona cues, despite exhibiting strong general conversational abilities like fluency and naturalness. We present PersoDPO, a scalable preference optimisation framework that uses supervision signals from automatic evaluations of responses generated by both closed-source and open-source LLMs to fine-tune dialogue models. The framework integrates evaluation metrics targeting coherence and personalization, along with a length-format compliance feature to promote instruction adherence. These signals are combined to automatically construct high-quality preference pairs without manual annotation, enabling a scalable and reproducible training pipeline. Experiments on the FoCus dataset show that an open-source language model fine-tuned with the PersoDPO framework consistently outperforms strong open-source baselines and a standard Direct Preference Optimization (DPO) variant across multiple evaluation dimensions.

Keywords: Dialogue Generation · Preference Optimization · Persona-Grounded Dialogue · Contextualized Response Generation · Instruction-Adherent Fine-Tuning

1 Introduction

Dialogue systems have become increasingly integral to a wide range of applications, including virtual assistants, customer service chatbots, and task-oriented agents. As these systems are deployed in more complex and user-centric scenarios, their effectiveness depends not only on producing fluent responses but also

I. Awan et al. (Eds.): WISE 2025, LNCS 16368, pp. 476–486, 2026.
https://doi.org/10.1007/978-981-95-7251-9_32

on delivering meaningful, context-aware, and personalized responses [5]. From a system-level perspective, high-quality dialogue systems must exhibit several critical properties—contextual understanding, persona alignment, and instruction adherence to ensure consistent response structure. Among these, contextualization (the ability to maintain coherence across dialogue turns) and personalization (the ability to tailor responses to individual user personas) are especially important for sustaining user satisfaction and trust. In addition, instruction adherence is crucial in automated pipelines, where consistent response formatting enables seamless downstream processing and system integration.

While recent advances in large language models (LLMs) have significantly improved dialogue fluency and naturalness, their ability to generate responses that are both contextually coherent and persona-aligned remains limited. As shown in the PersoBench benchmark [2], current mid-sized (around 7BâĂŞ8B parameters) instruction-tuned LLMs perform well on surface-level linguistic features but fall short in deeper personalization and multi-turn coherence. To address these limitations, recent works have explored preference-based modeling for improving dialogue quality. A knowledge-grounded dialogue model [19] enhances knowledge selection through supervised contrastive learning, while DPOC [6] focuses on persona alignment by ranking responses from model variants using heuristic quality assessments. Although these studies target specific dimensions such as knowledge integration or persona consistency, they remain limited in scope.

In contrast, our work addresses a broader combination of personalization, contextual coherence, and instruction adherence. By leveraging outputs from both open- and closed-source LLMs and relying on automatic evaluation metrics, our framework enables scalable multi-aspect fine-tuning. We present PersoDPO, a scalable preference optimization framework that inherits complementary strengths from diverse LLMs to jointly enhance coherence, persona alignment, and instruction adherence in dialogue generation. By applying multi-aspect evaluation metrics to responses from diverse LLMs, PersoDPO fine-tunes a robust instruction-tuned model without relying on human-labeled supervision. More specifically, the following are our research contributions:

1. We propose PersoDPO, a preference optimization framework designed to jointly improve coherence, persona alignment, and instruction adherence in dialogue generation.
2. We introduce a scalable method for generating preference pairs from open- and closed-source LLMs, enabling annotation-free supervision while capturing their complementary behaviors.
3. We demonstrate that PersoDPO outperforms strong open-source baselines and a DPO-trained variant on the FoCus dataset across multiple evaluation dimensions.

The implementation of our work—including evaluation results and generated response logs—is publicly available at: github.com/salehafzoon/PersoDPO

2 Related Work

2.1 Persona-Grounded Dialogue Generation

Persona-grounded dialogue generation aims to produce responses that reflect a user's traits or preferences, improving coherence and personalization [1]. Early work relied on pre-defined persona profiles. The PersonaChat dataset facilitated training on persona-description-response triplets [23], and models like Transfer-Transfo [21] fine-tuned transformers for more consistent and engaging responses. Profile Memory Networks [23] used persona facts as memory, though static profiles limited scalability. To overcome these constraints, persona extraction methods emerged. PAED reformulates zero-shot persona extraction as structured triplet extraction, enabling more nuanced personalization [24]. Building on this, DPOC [6] segments dialogue into persona-relevant utterances and generates coherent summaries, which are fused with context using gated attention for dynamic identity modeling.

A parallel line of research focuses on integrating external knowledge and persona cues to enhance empathy and coherence in support-oriented dialogues. A dynamic knowledge filtering mechanism [9], combined with persona extraction, improves emotional understanding in conversational agents. Techniques adapted from recommender systems, such as collaborative filtering, infer user norms implicitly, reducing the need for explicit persona definitions [16]. In mental health contexts, domain-specific personalization has advanced through cross-attentive fusion of persona traits and commonsense knowledge [9]. Context-aware summarization approaches also personalize medical dialogues by tracking psychological states across sessions [12]. These shifts reflect a move from rule-based persona modeling to adaptive, emotionally intelligent systems.

2.2 Evaluation Frameworks and Behavioral Constraints in LLMs

Core Benchmarks and Evaluation Metrics: Evaluating LLMs demands diverse and practical benchmarks that reflect real-world usage. Initial methods relied heavily on automatic metrics such as BLEU, ROUGE, and METEOR, which primarily measure surface-level textual similarity. However, these proved insufficient for assessing complex behaviors like coherence, helpfulness, or factual consistency. To address this, newer evaluations include human preference modeling frameworks such as Helpful and Harmless Assistant (HHA) and Chatbot Arena, which collect pairwise human judgments to assess alignment quality [7].

Importantly, PersoBench [2] introduced a dedicated benchmarking framework for evaluating persona-consistent dialogue generation. It was the first evaluation framework to systematically apply established multi-aspect metrics within a persona-aware benchmark. This framework also highlighted the trade-offs between helpfulness and identity coherence in LLM outputs [22]. Tool-augmented LLM evaluations like Coherence-Aware RLHF and Diverse Dialogue Benchmarking further incorporate task relevance and dialogic flow into scoring systems [11,17]. In parallel, TimeCHARA [3] and RoleLLM [20] have been introduced in the role-playing domain to assess LLMs' adherence to predefined characters or roles in character-based, scene-based, and temporal setups—broadening the scope of behavioral evaluation beyond generic instruction-following.

Feedback Signals and Optimization Methods: A major innovation in LLM alignment has been the use of reinforcement learning from human feedback (RLHF), where models are fine-tuned using reward signals derived from user preferences. Traditional RLHF assumes a single reward model, but recent studies suggest modeling heterogeneity using personalized reward learners [13]. Techniques like DPO and KL-regularized reinforcement learning [10] offer alternatives that enhance optimization stability. Furthermore, coactive learning represents an important direction in using weak but implicit feedback—such as user edits—to iteratively refine models without needing explicit preference labeling [18]. Complementarily, active learning approaches using expected entropy reduction let models infer user preferences through strategic questioning, facilitating efficient adaptation [14].

2.3 Preference Optimization and Feedback-Based Learning

The field of dialogue generation has increasingly embraced preference optimization and feedback-based learning to achieve fine-grained behavioral alignment and personalization [1]. These paradigms aim to improve response quality by aligning model outputs with desirable traits such as coherence, persona consistency, and instruction compliance, often without explicit supervised labels.

Preference optimization has evolved significantly, with methods like Direct DPO and RLHF gaining traction. While RLHF relies on costly human annotations, DPO offers a more efficient alternative by directly optimizing models using comparative preference data. Notably, DPOC [6] leverages user feedback across turns to build models that improve interaction-level coherence and personalization, highlighting the role of implicit feedback as a rich optimization signal. This aligns with the broader shift towards implicit reward modeling and scalable feedback mechanisms explored in other works [5].

Behavioral alignment presents challenges, as models often appear fluent while lacking persona fidelity or intent understanding. Knowledge-grounded systems now leverage contrastive preference learning to distinguish between high- and low-value responses, enhancing informativeness without compromising personalization [19].

Recent work in preference-based learning emphasizes automatic construction of preference pairs as a scalable alternative to manual labels. Instead of annotations, models infer preferences using learned rewards, heuristics, or implicit signals. Multi-dimensional evaluation criteria—such as coherence, user alignment, and formatting—enable more precise control over generation and reduce supervision needs [6,13].

3 Methodology

Problem Statement. Starting with a formal task definition, we follow the formulation introduced in prior work [4] on personalized dialogue generation. Given a dialogue context $C = \{u_1, \ldots, u_m\}$ and a set of persona descriptions $P = \{p_1, \ldots, p_n\}$, the goal is to generate a response r that is both contextually grounded and aligned with the specified persona. The generation objective is modeled as a conditional language generation task:

$$P(r \mid C, P; \theta) = \prod_{t=1}^{T} P(r_t \mid r_{1:t-1}, C, P; \theta) \quad (1)$$

Here, r_t represents the t-th token of the response, and θ denotes the parameters of the underlying language model.

3.1 PersoDPO

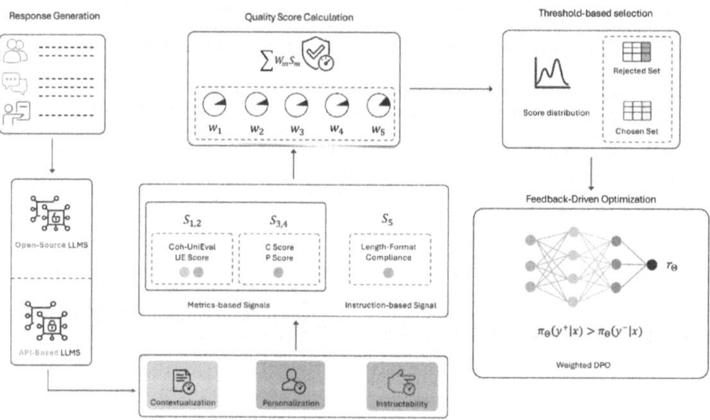

Fig. 1. PersoDPO framework overview.

Figure 1 illustrates the overall pipeline of the PersoDPO framework. The process begins by passing persona-aware dialogues to a diverse set of open- and closed-source LLMs within instruction-augmented prompts. This heterogeneous pool of models is selected to capture complementary strengths, reflecting variations in architecture, training data, and intended use cases. Each model generates a response under the same output format and length constraints. To assess the quality of these outputs, we employ a set of automatic evaluation metrics—previously used in the PersoBench benchmark [8]—that are specifically fine-tuned for evaluating coherence and personalization. The selected metrics offer more targeted insights than general-purpose measures like BERTScore or

ROUGE. Moreover, they enable a structured comparative analysis of our framework against the referenced benchmark. In addition to metric-aligned features for coherence and personalization, we include a length-format compliance signal to capture model instructability. Building on findings from PersoBench that highlight the influence of response failure rates on overall response evaluations, we place greater emphasis on instructability in our quality score computation. Preference pairs are then selected using margin-based sampling over the score distribution and used to fine-tune the model through a weighted preference optimization strategy.

Preference Signals. The quality of feedback used during language model tuning plays a critical role in shaping behavior [15]. Building on this, we compute a quality score for each generated response by combining automated evaluation metrics capturing coherence, personalization, and instruction adherence, as introduced in PersoBench [2]. Samples with clear score margins between accepted and rejected responses are retained, ensuring more focused and reliable fine-tuning. To structure preference signals, we define two complementary types. The first targets response quality and includes four metric-based signals (UE, C, Coh-UniEval, and P), which emphasize coherence and persona alignment under the LLM-as-a-judge paradigm. Formally, the combined signal from this group is computed as: Formally, the combined signal from this group is computed as:

$$S_{\text{Metric-based}} = \frac{1}{|S|} \sum_{s \in S} s$$

where $S = \{\text{C Score}, \text{P Score}, \text{UE Score}, \text{Coh-UniEval Score}\}$ represents the set of metric-based evaluators.

The second signal type addresses instruction adherence, captured through a custom Length-Format Compliance (LFC) signal. LFC provides a bonus reward for outputs that satisfy the instruction constraints on format and response length, encouraging instruction compliance without rigid enforcement. Based on empirical observations, we assign higher weight to length compliance than to format compliance, as strict enforcement of format led to degraded generation quality. The signal is computed as:

$$S_{\text{LFC}} = w_1 \cdot s_{\text{length}} + w_2 \cdot s_{\text{format}}, \quad \text{where } w_1 > w_2$$

Model Training. Training pairs were constructed by computing a total quality score for each response and selecting pairs with a sufficient margin between chosen and rejected candidates, thereby reducing ambiguity and improving supervision reliability. Fine-tuning followed a preference-based objective inspired by DPO, where responses are ranked according to automatically computed quality signals:

$$\mathcal{L}_{\text{PersoDPO}} = \mathbb{E}_{x,y_c,y_r}\Big[\sigma(\Delta S) \cdot \beta \cdot \big(\log p_\theta(y_c \mid x) - \log p_\theta(y_r \mid x)\big)\Big], \qquad (2)$$

where ΔS denotes the score margin between the chosen (y_c) and rejected (y_r) responses, and the total score $S_{\text{total}} = S_{\text{metric}} + S_{\text{LFC}}$. This objective encourages the model to assign higher likelihood to higher-scoring responses.

4 Exprimental Setup

Dataset. We used the FoCus dataset[1], a benchmark for personalized response generation with multi-turn dialogues and persona annotations. Its longer contexts make it well-suited for testing coherence and personalization. Following PersoBench [2], prompts combined persona and dialogue context, with models instructed to generate a personalized response in a JSON format containing a single "response" field, ensuring consistency and enabling analysis of instruction adherence.

Baselines. We selected three open-source instruction-tuned LLMs—Qwen2-7B, Mistral-7B, and LLaMA 3.1-8B—to align with PersoBench [2] and ensure consistent comparison. We also included a vanilla DPO-tuned Qwen2-5B-Instruct as a direct baseline for our custom DPO approach. Only models evaluated with dedicated alignment metrics were considered, discarding BLEU/ROUGE-based methods. The Qwen2-5B variant was chosen due to GPU memory constraints. All baselines were tested on 1,000 FoCus validation records with identical persona-augmented inputs and evaluation metrics.

Evaluation Metrics. Following PersoBench [2], we evaluated response quality with three automatic metrics covering personalization and coherence. Personalization was measured using the Consistency Score (C) and Persona Distance Score (P), while coherence was assessed with the Utterance Entailment Score (UE) and Coh-UniEval. All scores were normalized to [0,1].

4.1 Implementation Setup

Baseline. For initial response generation, we sampled **1,500 records** from the FoCus training set due to API query costs. In a zero-shot setup (`max_tokens = 110`, `temperature = 0`), we prompted six LLMs: three open-source instruction-tuned models (`Qwen2-7B`, `Mistral-7B`, `LLaMA 3.1-8B`) and three API-based models (`GPT-3.5-Turbo`, `GPT-4-Turbo`, `GPT-4o-Mini`). The `max_tokens` limit matched the observed upper bound of FoCus golden responses, ensuring comparable lengths. Deterministic generation was enforced by fixing `temperature = 0`. All models produced responses in a predefined JSON format with persona-augmented prompts. To construct the baseline DPO dataset, outputs were grouped by format validity: each training instance paired a prompt with a "chosen" (valid) and "rejected" (invalid) response.

[1] https://github.com/pkchat-focus/FoCus.

PersoDPO. We created ∼9,000 preference pairs, each with a prompt, "chosen" and "rejected" responses, and quality scores. Final scores combined four metric-based features with an instruction-based feature assessing response length and JSON format compliance; the length component was weighted twice as much due to its stronger impact on generation stability [2]. Fine-tuning was performed on `Qwen2-5B-Instruct` using a score-weighted DPO setup with the `TRL` library[2] and the `ScoreWeightedDPOTrainer` class. Key hyperparameters included batch size = 4, gradient accumulation steps = 4, and 150 warm-up steps. The implementation is available upon request.

5 Results and Discussion

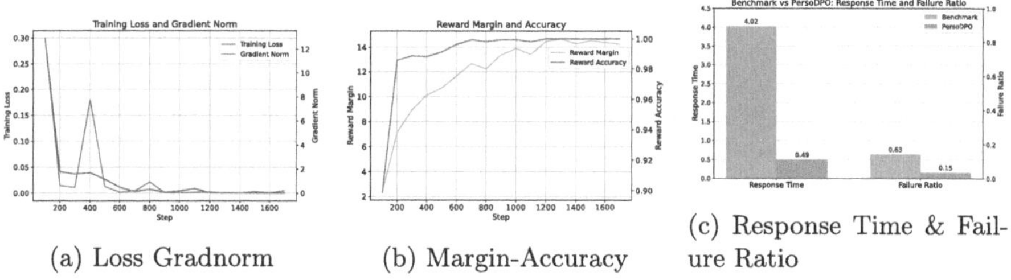

(a) Loss Gradnorm (b) Margin-Accuracy (c) Response Time & Failure Ratio

Fig. 2. Comparison of (a) Loss Gradnorm, (b) Margin-Augmented Accuracy, and (c) Response Time with Failure Ratio.

Figure 2 illustrates the optimization behavior of Qwen2-5B during PersoDPO fine-tuning. The training loss steadily declines with only minor early spikes in gradient norm, indicating smooth and robust convergence under score-guided supervision. Reward accuracy remains near the upper bound, while the reward margin narrows as the model learns to produce more consistent responses. Beyond training stability, PersoDPO achieves lower failure ratios—showing stronger adherence to length and format constraints—and faster response times, enhancing instructability, reliability, and responsiveness for industrial deployment.

The performance of the proposed framework is evaluated using the metrics described in the previous section and compared against the baselines. As shown in Table 1, PersoDPO consistently outperforms all open-source benchmark models across all four evaluation metrics, demonstrating its strength in both response contextualization and personalization. This highlights the effectiveness of training with diverse LLM outputs, enabling PersoDPO to implicitly inherit complementary strengths from multiple pre-trained models. Considering the Coh-UniEval as one of the metrics designed to capture both contextual coherence and persona consistency, a remarkable improvement is observed, indicating

[2] huggingface.co/docs/trl.

Table 1. Result comparison of the proposed framework with the baselines.

Model	Coh-UniEval	C Score	UE Score	P Score
Qwen2 7B Benchmark	0.37 ± 0.48	-0.31 ± 0.84	0.17 ± 0.48	0.29 ± 0.30
Mistral 7B Benchmark	0.53 ± 0.46	-0.23 ± 0.82	0.21 ± 0.52	0.30 ± 0.28
Llama3.1 8B Benchmark	0.55 ± 0.49	-0.22 ± 0.87	0.17 ± 0.48	0.33 ± 0.33
Qwen2 5B DPO	0.98 ± 0.49	0.06 ± 0.49	0.21 ± 0.58	0.29 ± 0.26
Qwen2 5B PersoDPO	0.70 ± 0.45	**0.18 ± 0.87**	**0.30 ± 0.62**	**0.44 ± 0.30**

PersoDPO's strong capability in generating well-grounded and persona-aligned responses. Additionally, there is a tangible improvement in the UE Score as another metric evaluating the same aspects. These gains suggest an enhanced ability to generate responses that are contextually appropriate while remaining aligned with persona traits. A consistent performance boost is also observed on C Score and P Score, which focus more directly on personalization, further confirming the benefit of multi-LLM preference modeling in capturing nuanced persona-driven behavior. When compared to the vanilla DPO variant fine-tuned on Qwen2 5B, PersoDPO demonstrates clear improvements in three out of four evaluation metrics. It outperforms the baseline in both personalization-specific metrics—C Score and P Score—highlighting the effectiveness of multi-LLM preference modeling in capturing persona-aligned behavior. Notably, the P Score achieved by the vanilla DPO model not only fails to surpass any of the benchmarked LLMs but also matches the lowest among them, indicating its limited ability to model semantic alignment with persona traits. Although PersoDPO's Coh-UniEval score is slightly lower than that of the DPO baseline, this is mitigated by its higher UE Score, which evaluates similar coherence and persona consistency dimensions. This balance suggests that PersoDPO maintains strong contextual grounding while offering significantly better personalization quality overall. Among these metrics, C Score remains one of the most challenging for language models to perform well on, as it penalizes persona inconsistencies more severely than other evaluators, often assigning negative scores to misaligned responses. Nonetheless, PersoDPO achieves a substantial improvement over all baselines in this dimension, indicating its enhanced ability to maintain persona alignment even under stricter evaluative conditions. The raw responses generated by the proposed method, along with those from the baseline, are available in the GitHub repository for further analysis [3]

6 Conclusion

This study introduced PersoDPO, a preference optimization framework designed to improve both personalization and contextual coherence in persona-grounded dialogue systems. By leveraging outputs from diverse open- and closed-source

[3] https://github.com/salehafzoon/PersoDPO/tree/main/Raw20Responses/FoCus.

LLMs, PersoDPO constructs high-quality preference pairs based on automatic evaluation signals without requiring manual annotation. The framework integrates coherence- and persona-driven metrics alongside a novel Length-Format Compliance feature, enabling more instructable and structurally consistent responses. Empirical results on a personalized dialogue benchmark demonstrate that PersoDPO consistently outperforms strong open-source baselines and a vanilla DPO model across personalization and coherence metrics. Moreover, it shows clear advantages in industrially relevant aspects such as response time and instruction adherence, indicating its practical suitability for real-world deployment.

Acknowledgments. We acknowledge the Center for Applied Artificial Intelligence at Macquarie University (Sydney, NSW, Australia) for supporting and funding this research.

References

1. Afzoon, S., Jahanandish, Z., Huynh, P.T., Beheshti, A., Naseem, U.: Modeling and optimizing user preferences in AI copilots: a comprehensive survey and taxonomy. arXiv preprint arXiv:2505.21907 (2025)
2. Afzoon, S., Naseem, U., Beheshti, A., Jamali, Z.: Persobench: benchmarking personalized response generation in large language models. arXiv preprint arXiv:2410.03198 (2024)
3. Ahn, J., et al.: Timechara: Evaluating point-in-time character hallucination of role-playing large language models. arXiv preprint arXiv:2405.18027 (2024)
4. Chen, L., Wang, H., Deng, Y., Kwan, W.C., Wang, Z., Wong, K.F.: Towards robust personalized dialogue generation via order-insensitive representation regularization. In: Findings of the Association for Computational Linguistics: ACL 2023, pp. 7337–7345. Association for Computational Linguistics, Toronto, Canada (2023)
5. Chen, Y.P., Nishida, N., Nakayama, H., Matsumoto, Y.: Recent trends in personalized dialogue generation: A review of datasets, methodologies, and evaluations. arXiv preprint arXiv:2405.17974 (2024)
6. Cheng, C., et al.: In-dialogues we learn: Towards personalized dialogue without pre-defined profiles through in-dialogue learning. In: Al-Onaizan, Y., Bansal, M., Chen, Y.N. (eds.) Proceedings of the 2024 Conference on Empirical Methods in Natural Language Processing. pp. 10408–10422. Association for Computational Linguistics, Miami, Florida, USA (2024). https://aclanthology.org/2024.emnlp-main.581/
7. Chiang, W.L., et al.: Chatbot arena: An open platform for evaluating llms by human preference. In: Forty-first International Conference on Machine Learning (2024)
8. Cho, I., Wang, D., Takahashi, R., Saito, H.: A personalized dialogue generator with implicit user persona detection. In: Proceedings of the 29th International Conference on Computational Linguistics, pp. 367–377. International Committee on Computational Linguistics, Gyeongju, Republic of Korea (2022)
9. Hao, J., Kong, F.: Enhancing emotional support conversations: a framework for dynamic knowledge filtering and persona extraction. In: Proceedings of the 31st International Conference on Computational Linguistics, pp. 3193–3202 (2025)

10. Huang, Y., Zhang, Q., Sun, L., et al.: Trustgpt: a benchmark for trustworthy and responsible large language models. arXiv preprint arXiv:2306.11507 (2023)
11. Lee, J.Y., Lee, K.A., Gan, W.S.: Improving contextual coherence in variational personalized and empathetic dialogue agents. In: ICASSP 2022-2022 IEEE International Conference on Acoustics, Speech and Signal Processing (ICASSP), pp. 7052–7056. IEEE (2022)
12. Liu, Z., Salleh, S., Krishnaswamy, P., Chen, N.: Context aggregation with topic-focused summarization for personalized medical dialogue generation. In: Proceedings of the 6th Clinical Natural Language Processing Workshop, pp. 310–321 (2024)
13. Park, C., Liu, M., Kong, D., Zhang, K., Ozdaglar, A.: RLHF from heterogeneous feedback via personalization and preference aggregation. arXiv preprint arXiv:2405.00254 (2024)
14. Piriyakulkij, W.T., Kuleshov, V., Ellis, K.: Active preference inference using language models and probabilistic reasoning. arXiv preprint arXiv:2312.12009 (2023)
15. Rafailov, R., Sharma, A., Mitchell, E., Manning, C.D., Ermon, S., Finn, C.: Direct preference optimization: your language model is secretly a reward model. Adv. Neural. Inf. Process. Syst. **36**, 53728–53741 (2023)
16. Serramia, M., Criado, N., Luck, M.: Collaborative filtering to capture ai user's preferences as norms. In: International Conference on Principles and Practice of Multi-Agent Systems, pp. 669–678. Springer (2022)
17. Sun, W., Wang, J., Guo, Q., Li, Z., Wang, W., Hai, R.: Cebench: a benchmarking toolkit for the cost-effectiveness of llm pipelines. arXiv preprint arXiv:2407.12797 (2024)
18. Tucker, A.D., Brantley, K., Cahall, A., Joachims, T.: Coactive learning for large language models using implicit user feedback. In: Forty-first International Conference on Machine Learning (2024)
19. Wang, B., Xu, F., Zhu, Z., Liu, P.: Knowledge-grounded dialogue generation with contrastive knowledge selection. In: International Conference on Web Information Systems Engineering, pp. 710–719. Springer (2023)
20. Wang, Z.M., et al.: Rolellm: Benchmarking, eliciting, and enhancing role-playing abilities of large language models. arXiv preprint arXiv:2310.00746 (2023)
21. Wolf, T., Sanh, V., Chaumond, J., Delangue, C.: Transfertransfo: a transfer learning approach for neural network based conversational agents. arXiv preprint arXiv:1901.08149 (2019)
22. Yoon, S.e., He, Z., Echterhoff, J.M., McAuley, J.: Evaluating large language models as generative user simulators for conversational recommendation. In: Proceedings of the 2024 Conference of the North American Chapter of the Association for Computational Linguistics: Human Language Technologies, Volume 1 (Long Papers), pp. 1490–1504. Association for Computational Linguistics, Mexico City, Mexico (2024). https://doi.org/10.18653/v1/2024.naacl-long.83
23. Zhang, S., Dinan, E., Urbanek, J., Szlam, A., Kiela, D., Weston, J.: Personalizing dialogue agents: i have a dog, do you have pets too? In: Gurevych, I., Miyao, Y. (eds.) Proceedings of the 56th Annual Meeting of the Association for Computational Linguistics (Volume 1: Long Papers). pp. 2204–2213. Association for Computational Linguistics, Melbourne, Australia (2018). https://aclanthology.org/P18-1205/
24. Zhu, L., Li, W., Mao, R., Pandelea, V., Cambria, E.: Paed: zero-shot persona attribute extraction in dialogues. In: Proceedings of the 61st Annual Meeting of the Association for Computational Linguistics (Volume 1: Long Papers), pp. 9771–9787 (2023)

Distributed Data and Code Generation

Controllable Structured Data Generation and Augmentation Mechanism for Power Grid Applications

Yuteng Huang[1], Yuqing Xie[1], Xiaoke Xu[1], Huihang Lai[2], Enquan Ge[2](✉), and Peng Lu[2]

[1] Information and Communication Branch of State Grid Zhejiang Electric Power Co., Ltd., Hangzhou, China
{huang_yuteng,xie_yuqing,xu_xiaoke}@zj.sgcc.com.cn
[2] Institute of Computer Innovation, Zhejiang University, Hangzhou, China
{hylai,geq,lupeng}@zjuici.com

Abstract. Structured data is widely used in domains such as industry, finance, and healthcare. However, real-world datasets often suffer from issues such as data sparsity, distribution imbalance, and missing features, which significantly hinder the generalization performance of machine learning models. To address these challenges, this paper proposes a structured data augmentation method based on high-entropy sample masking and large language model-assisted completion. The method first employs a lightweight RandomForest classifier to estimate the prediction entropy of each sample, identifying high-uncertainty instances. For these samples, only key features—selected based on feature importance—are masked, and the masked inputs are then completed using DeepSeek-R1. To ensure the consistency of generated samples with the original data distribution, Kullback-Leibler (KL) divergence is introduced as a filtering criterion to retain only the most distribution-aligned samples. Furthermore, an iterative enhancement framework is established, which terminates automatically when the average KL divergence between generated datasets across two consecutive iterations falls below a defined threshold (0.01). Experimental results on multiple classification tasks demonstrate that the proposed method achieves superior performance in terms of accuracy, stability, and generation efficiency compared to conventional augmentation methods and full-field LLM generation. This work offers an efficient, controllable, and trustworthy solution for structured data augmentation.

Keywords: Structured Data · Data Augmentation · Entropy Sampling · Large Language Model · KL Divergence

1 Introduction

In modern power systems, structured tabular data—collected from smart meters, SCADA logs, and dispatch records—serves as a critical foundation for intelligent

I. Awan et al. (Eds.): WISE 2025, LNCS 16368, pp. 489–504, 2026.
https://doi.org/10.1007/978-981-95-7251-9_33

applications such as load forecasting, fault detection, and dispatch decision-making. These tasks rely on data with consistent schema and strict feature-label dependencies. However, practical power grid datasets are often plagued by four key issues: (1) severe class imbalance and rarity of critical events (e.g., transformer faults, peak loads); (2) missing or noisy records caused by sensor failures or transmission errors; (3) high labeling costs under complex operational conditions; and (4) limited accessibility due to regulatory and commercial restrictions. Such challenges are further amplified in domains like energy systems, where temporal continuity and device-level causality are essential. Traditional augmentation techniques—such as SMOTE or GAN-based generation—fail to account for these domain-specific constraints, often yielding semantically invalid or distributionally skewed samples.

To mitigate these limitations, recent efforts have turned to large language models (LLMs) for generating privacy-preserving synthetic data [3,6]. While LLMs offer flexibility and scalability, they often underperform when applied to structured data with non-textual semantics [5,15]. Full-table completion without explicit control may lead to semantic drift, invalid numerical values, or inconsistent dependencies among fields. These deficiencies compromise the reliability and usability of synthetic records in high-stakes domains like power grids.

To address these challenges, we propose a lightweight and controllable data augmentation pipeline tailored for structured tabular domains. As illustrated in Fig. 1, the framework integrates five key stages: entropy-guided sample selection, SHAP-based feature masking, prompt-driven LLM completion, KL divergence filtering, and iterative refinement. This design enables targeted augmentation of high-uncertainty samples while maintaining semantic consistency and statistical alignment with the original dataset.

First, a predictive model (e.g., RandomForest) is used to estimate the entropy of each sample's output probability, identifying ambiguous or underrepresented instances. Next, only a few high-importance features are masked—based on SHAP attribution scores—while preserving most contextual fields to guide coherent generation. These masked samples are then converted into prompt templates and completed using a pretrained DeepSeek-R1 model. By focusing generation on top-m key fields and leveraging contextual constraints, the method avoids full-record regeneration, reduces hallucination risk, and preserves structural fidelity. To guarantee distributional alignment, a KL divergence filter compares marginal field distributions before and after augmentation; only samples below a specified divergence threshold are retained.

This process is executed iteratively until inter-round divergence stabilizes, yielding a high-quality augmented dataset that expands coverage of rare or noisy regions without incurring excessive computational cost or semantic degradation. While this study evaluates the method on power grid fault data, the proposed framework is model-agnostic and generalizable to other structured domains such as healthcare or finance. Furthermore, the modular design allows for future integration of task-specific entropy estimators and adaptive masking strategies, supporting broader applications in data-scarce environments.

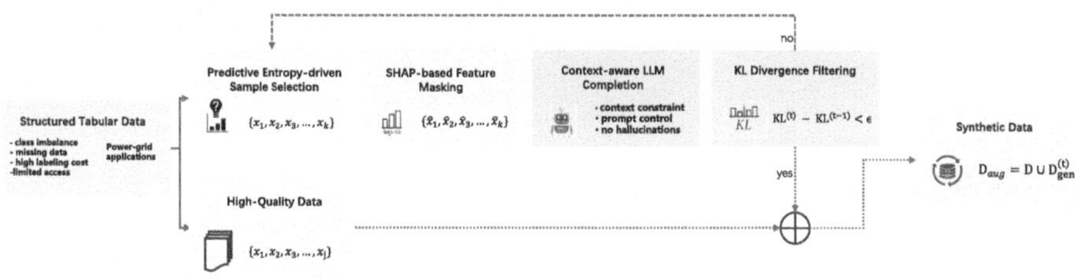

Fig. 1. Overview of the proposed structured data augmentation framework. Each module addresses a core challenge in structured data generation.

2 Related Work

Large language models (LLMs) have shown increasing potential in generating synthetic data for various domains, such as healthcare [11], governance [3], and energy systems [4]. These pretrained models are capable of producing privacy-preserving and diverse samples [6,13], offering valuable substitutes for sensitive or scarce real-world datasets. However, their applications to structured tabular data remain challenging due to the semantic misalignment, statistical inconsistency, and loss of field dependencies [2,8].

To address these limitations, several studies have explored prompt engineering and controllability strategies. Notably, class-conditional and attributed prompting methods [14] can improve both the diversity and reliability of generated samples. Frameworks such as Mixture of Soft Prompts (MSP) [5], REGEN [15], and Chain-of-Thought prompting [9] guide the generation process by injecting structured control signals. While these approaches improve alignment and reasoning in unstructured text domains, their adaptation to structured data with strict feature-label dependencies is still underdeveloped. Knowledge-infused strategies [11] and structured masking [12] offer further avenues for enhancing generation quality under schema constraints.

Despite these advancements, two key challenges remain: limited field-level controllability and the lack of mechanisms to ensure distributional fidelity. This is especially problematic in domains like power systems, where semantic correctness and numerical plausibility are critical. Safety concerns, including bias and hallucinations [7,16], have also been raised when deploying LLM-generated data in sensitive applications.

In contrast, traditional data augmentation techniques such as SMOTE and k-means-based synthesis [10] offer more predictable and computationally efficient solutions, though they often fall short in semantic richness and adaptability to complex data patterns. Emerging hybrid approaches suggest that integrating classical model outputs (e.g., entropy or clustering) with LLM-driven completion and filtering [2,5,15] can yield improved quality and controllability.

In summary, existing augmentation methods either lack semantic control or fail to maintain statistical fidelity. Our proposed method combines entropy-aware selection, attribution-based masking, controlled prompt completion, and

KL-divergence filtering to address these limitations in structured data domains such as power grids.

3 Proposed Methodology

To address the challenge of class imbalance and label scarcity in structured data for power systems, we propose a structured data augmentation method based on high-entropy sample selection, field-level masking, LLM-based completion, and KL-divergence-based filtering. The proposed method produces semantically coherent and statistically aligned data, and iteratively updates the training set until distribution convergence is achieved.

3.1 Notations

(see Table 1).

Table 1. Summary of Notations

Notation	Description
$\mathbb{R}^d$	d-dimensional real-valued feature space
D	Original labeled dataset
D_{aug}	Final augmented dataset including generated samples
x	Feature vector of a sample
y	Ground truth label
M_{rfc}	Lightweight classifier (e.g., RandomForest)
$H(x)$	Entropy of prediction for sample x
S	Set of high-entropy samples
$F(x)$	Set of fields in sample x
f_i	The i-th field in x
$I(f_i)$	Importance score of field f_i
$\mathcal{M}(x)$	Masked version of sample x
$\hat{x}_j$	LLM-generated completion candidate
$P(f), Q(f)$	Field-wise distributions in original and generated datasets
D_{gen}^t	Generated samples at iteration t
δ	KL divergence filtering threshold
ϵ	Iteration convergence threshold
$\mathrm{Acc}(D)$	Test accuracy using dataset D
$\mathrm{Acc}(D_{\mathrm{aug}})$	Test accuracy using augmented dataset

We consider a supervised classification task based on a structured dataset $D = \{(x_i, y_i)\}_{i=1}^N$, where $x_i \in \mathbb{R}^d$ is a feature vector and y_i is the associated label. The goal is to construct an augmented dataset $D_{\text{aug}} = D \cup D_{\text{gen}}$ that, when used to train a classifier (e.g., RandomForest), yields better predictive performance on a held-out test set compared to using the original dataset alone.

Formally, let $\text{Acc}(D)$ denote the test accuracy of a classifier trained on D, and $\text{Acc}(D_{\text{aug}})$ the accuracy after augmentation. The primary objective of the proposed framework is:

$$\text{Acc}(D_{\text{aug}}) > \text{Acc}(D)$$

under a consistent training setup.

To achieve this, the generated samples must not only be label-consistent but also helpful for enhancing model generalization. In addition to accuracy improvement, we impose the following secondary constraints to ensure data quality and efficiency:

- **Semantic Consistency**: Generated records should preserve valid feature-label semantics.
- **Distributional Alignment**: The augmented data should maintain field-wise statistical similarity to the original dataset to avoid artificial distribution shift.
- **Efficiency and Controllability**: The augmentation pipeline should selectively target uncertain or underrepresented samples while minimizing unnecessary computation or redundant generation.

We implement this goal using an entropy-guided sample selection, field-level masking based on feature importance, LLM-based completion, and KL divergence filtering, forming a controllable and iterative augmentation framework.

3.2 Algorithm Overview

To address the challenges outlined in Sect. 3.1, we propose an iterative structured data augmentation framework that integrates sample selection, feature masking, controlled completion, and quality filtering. The method is designed to generate semantically coherent and statistically consistent tabular data, thereby improving the robustness of downstream machine learning models.

The overall pipeline is illustrated in Algorithm 1. At each iteration, the algorithm begins by computing predictive uncertainty scores over the original dataset using an entropy-based metric derived from a pretrained classifier. Samples with the highest uncertainty are selected for augmentation, as they are more likely to benefit from additional synthetic data.

Next, we apply feature-level masking guided by attribution scores (e.g., SHAP values), where only the top-m most influential fields are masked. This masking strategy ensures that the masked input retains contextual integrity and that generation focuses on the most informative attributes.

The masked records are then passed to a pretrained large language model (LLM), which fills in the missing fields based on the surrounding context.

To enhance the reliability of generation, we formulate prompts that preserve domain-specific field semantics and constraints.

Finally, a KL divergence-based filter is applied to each generated sample by comparing the marginal distributions of selected fields to those of the original dataset. Only samples whose average KL score falls below a predefined threshold are retained. The process repeats until the augmentation converges based on distributional stability.

This modular algorithm supports flexible configuration of uncertainty metrics, masking strategies, and prompt formats. It is compatible with various tabular datasets and LLM architectures, making it broadly applicable across structured domains.

Algorithm 1. Structured Data Augmentation with Entropy and KL Filtering

Require: Original dataset D, classification model M_{rfc}, DeepSeek-R1 generator $\mathcal{G}_{\text{deepseek}}$, KL threshold δ, convergence threshold ϵ

Ensure: Final augmented dataset D_{aug}

Initialize: $D^0_{\text{train}} \leftarrow D$, $t \leftarrow 0$, $\Delta \leftarrow \infty$
while $\Delta > \epsilon$ and $t < T_{\max}$ **do**
  Train M_{rfc} on D^t_{train}
  for each $x \in D$ **do**
    Compute entropy: $H(x) = -\sum p_i(x) \log p_i(x)$
  end for
  Select top-K high-entropy samples: $S = \text{TopK}_{x \in D}(H(x))$
  for each $x \in S$ **do**
    Compute importance scores $I(f_i)$ for all fields
    Mask top-m important fields: $\mathcal{M}(x) = x \setminus \{f_i \mid I(f_i) \in \text{Top-m}(I(F(x)))\}$
    Generate completions: $\{\hat{x}_j\}_{j=1}^{k} = \mathcal{G}_{\text{deepseek}}(\mathcal{M}(x))$
    for each $\hat{x}_j$ **do**
      Compute average KL divergence:

$$\text{KL}_{\text{avg}}(\hat{x}_j) = \frac{1}{m} \sum_{f} \text{KL}(P(f) \parallel Q_{\hat{x}_j}(f))$$

      if $\text{KL}_{\text{avg}}(\hat{x}_j) < \delta$ **then**
        Add $\hat{x}_j$ to D^{t+1}_{gen}
      end if
    end for
  end for
  Compute divergence gap: $\Delta \leftarrow |\text{KL}_{t+1} - \text{KL}_t|$
  Update training set: $D^{t+1}_{\text{train}} = D \cup D^{t+1}_{\text{gen}}$
  $t \leftarrow t + 1$
end while
return $D_{\text{aug}} = D^t_{\text{train}}$

3.3 Step-by-Step Explanation

Step 1: Entropy-Based Sample Selection
To focus the augmentation process on samples with high uncertainty, we compute the entropy of each sample's predicted label distribution from a trained classifier:

$$H(x) = -\sum_{i=1}^{C} p_i(x) \log p_i(x) \tag{1}$$

Here, $p_i(x)$ denotes the probability of assigning sample x to class i, and C is the number of classes. Entropy measures the uncertainty in prediction; a higher entropy indicates that the model is less confident in its classification decision. By selecting the top-K samples with the highest entropy values, we prioritize regions of the feature space that are underrepresented or ambiguous. This strategy helps to improve model generalization by generating new samples in decision-boundary regions where errors are more likely.

$$S = \text{TopK}_{x \in D}(H(x)) \tag{2}$$

This filtering results in a subset S of uncertain samples that serve as candidates for augmentation.

Step 2: Field-Level Masking
For each selected sample $x \in S$, we identify and mask only the most influential features rather than masking the entire input. Feature importance scores $I(f_i)$ can be obtained using SHAP values or gradient-based attribution from the RandomForest model. The masked sample $\mathcal{M}(x)$ is defined as:

$$\mathcal{M}(x) = x \setminus \{f_i \mid I(f_i) \in \text{Top-m}(I(F(x)))\} \tag{3}$$

This step is motivated by the need to preserve most of the sample's structural context while still introducing controlled uncertainty. By masking only a small number m of highly informative fields, we avoid semantic drift and allow the language model to focus on plausible completions for these key features. This selective perturbation enhances diversity without corrupting the original data structure.

Step 3: LLM Completion
The masked sample $\mathcal{M}(x)$ is passed to a pretrained large language model (e.g., DeepSeek-R1), which fills in the masked fields to produce k alternative versions $\hat{x}_j$ of the original sample:

$$\hat{x}_j = \mathcal{G}_{\text{deepseek}}(\mathcal{M}(x)), \quad j = 1, \ldots, k \tag{4}$$

This step leverages the generative capability and contextual reasoning of the LLM to synthesize realistic values for missing fields. By prompting the LLM with partially structured data, we constrain its generation scope and improve consistency with the domain. Multiple completions allow us to sample diverse interpretations of each uncertain input, increasing the variability of the augmented data.

Step 4: KL Divergence Filtering
Each generated candidate $\hat{x}_j$ is evaluated to ensure its compatibility with the original data distribution. Specifically, for each masked field f, we compute the Kullback-Leibler (KL) divergence between the empirical distribution $P(f)$ from the original dataset and the field-wise distribution $Q_{\hat{x}_j}(f)$ from the generated sample:

$$\mathrm{KL}(P(f) \parallel Q(f)) = \sum_{v} P(f = v) \log \left(\frac{P(f = v)}{Q(f = v)} \right) \tag{5}$$

To obtain a single metric for filtering, we compute the average KL divergence over all masked fields:

$$\mathrm{KL}_{\mathrm{avg}}(\hat{x}_j) = \frac{1}{m} \sum_{f \in F_{\mathrm{mask}}} \mathrm{KL}(P(f) \parallel Q_{\hat{x}_j}(f)) \tag{6}$$

This divergence score quantifies the statistical shift between the generated sample and the original data distribution. A low $\mathrm{KL}_{\mathrm{avg}}$ indicates that the synthetic data is well-aligned and unlikely to introduce noise. We discard generated samples whose average divergence exceeds a predefined threshold δ to ensure the statistical fidelity of augmented data.

Step 5: Iterative Refinement
The above process is repeated across multiple iterations. At each iteration t, we monitor the average KL divergence gap between consecutive steps:

$$|\mathrm{KL}_t - \mathrm{KL}_{t-1}| < \epsilon \tag{7}$$

When the divergence stabilizes—i.e., changes across iterations fall below the convergence threshold ϵ—we terminate the augmentation loop. The final output is the union of original and high-quality generated samples:

$$D_{\mathrm{aug}} = D \cup \bigcup_{t=1}^{T} D_{\mathrm{gen}}^{t} \tag{8}$$

This iterative enhancement ensures that the augmentation process converges and does not overfit or oversample low-quality data. It also provides a self-regulating mechanism to balance generation quality and volume.

3.4 Complexity Analysis

We analyze the computational complexity of the proposed augmentation framework with respect to both time and space, focusing on one iteration of the generation-refinement loop.

Time Complexity. The time cost of each iteration mainly comes from four stages:

- **Entropy Computation**: For a dataset of size N and C classes, entropy is computed for each sample based on its predicted class distribution. This requires $\mathcal{O}(N \cdot C)$ time.
- **Field Ranking and Masking**: For the top-K high-entropy samples, field importance scores are computed and sorted (e.g., via SHAP or RandomForest gain), yielding a complexity of $\mathcal{O}(K \cdot d \log d)$, where d is the number of features.
- **LLM-Based Completion**: Each masked sample is submitted to an LLM k times for generation, each with time T_g (dependent on prompt length). This step takes $\mathcal{O}(K \cdot T_g)$.
- **KL Filtering**: For each candidate, KL divergence is calculated across m fields compared with reference distributions. This requires $\mathcal{O}(K \cdot d)$ assuming $m \leq d$.

The overall per-iteration time complexity is:

$$\mathcal{O}(N \cdot C + K \cdot d \log d + K \cdot T_g + K \cdot d), \quad \text{where } K \ll N \tag{9}$$

This ensures that the dominant overhead remains sublinear with respect to dataset size N, due to the focused entropy-based sampling.

Space Complexity. The storage requirement is modest because:

- Only the generated samples $\hat{x}_j$ for the selected K high-entropy samples are retained;
- The model M_{rfc} and feature statistics can be discarded between iterations;
- LLMs are accessed externally (e.g., via API) and do not consume local memory.

Thus, the space complexity is:

$$\mathcal{O}(K \cdot d) \tag{10}$$

Comparison with Baselines. Compared to full-record generation approaches (e.g., DeepSeek-only), which require $\mathcal{O}(N \cdot T_g)$ calls to the LLM and store N full synthetic records, our method is significantly more efficient. Specifically:

- **Selective generation**: Only K samples are augmented per iteration ($K \ll N$), reducing LLM calls by over 90%;
- **Partial completion**: Only m fields per sample are generated, further decreasing generation time;
- **Filtered output**: The KL divergence screening removes low-quality generations early, avoiding unnecessary model retraining.

Summary. In summary, the proposed method achieves high-quality augmentation with:

- Sublinear time complexity per iteration;
- Minimal memory footprint;
- Strong scalability due to its selective, partial, and filtered generation design.

These properties make the framework well-suited for deployment in real-world data-constrained scenarios, especially in critical domains like power systems.

4 Experimental Setup

Hardware Configuration: We utilize an Intel(R) Xeon(R) Gold 6240 CPU @ 2.60 GHz with 16 threads and 32 GB of memory as the CPU server to evaluate efficiency and performance using the CPU.

Dataset: We employ Electrical Fault detection and classification dataset to benchmark the performance of algorithm. This dataset describes the collection of line current and voltage under different fault conditions, with 6 input columns and 4 output columns [1]. This dataset has 7861 rows, and the training set and test set are divided in a 8:2 ratio, ensuring that the evaluation indicators are the same for each experiment.

To comprehensively evaluate the effectiveness of our proposed augmentation strategy, we design a series of comparative experiments covering multiple methods and varying data scales. The experimental goals are two-fold: first, to validate the superiority of our KL-guided augmentation pipeline; second, to assess its efficiency and scalability on datasets of different sizes.

We compare the following methods:

- **BaseLine**: Only use the original dataset.
- **DeepSeek-Only**: Directly generates full structured records using DeepSeek-R1 based on prompt templates without any field masking, sampling, or filtering.
- **RandMask+DeepSeek**: Randomly masks fields before DeepSeek-R1 generation but does not perform entropy sampling or KL filtering.
- **NoKL (Ours w/o KL)**: Uses our entropy-based selection and field masking, but skips KL-divergence filtering.
- **REaLTabFormer**: Generate tabular data using the autoregressive (GPT-2) and sequence-to-sequence (Seq2Seq) Transformer models.
- **Ours (KL-Guided)**: The full proposed pipeline including entropy-based sampling, field-level masking, LLM generation, KL filtering, and iterative refinement.

All methods are evaluated using an RandomForest classifier trained on the augmented dataset. The generation ratio is 1:1 (i.e., the number of generated samples equals the original training data). We test each method on datasets of size 1000, 2000, and 3000. Four metrics are used for evaluation:

- **Accuracy**: The classification accuracy on the test set.
- **F1-Score (Macro)**: The macro-averaged F1 score across all classes.
- **Average KL Divergence**: Mean KL divergence over generated fields.

Table 2 reports the performance on the 6287-sample dataset.

Table 2. Comparison on 6287-sample dataset

Method	Accuracy (%)	F1 (Macro)	Avg KL
BaseLine	76.11	69.56	0
DeepSeek-Only	75.03	67.77	5.89934
RandMask+DeepSeek	81.39	77.35	0.05018
NoKL (Ours w/o KL)	81.45	77.6	0.05579
REaLTabFormer	82.15	76.56	0.01958
Ours (KL-Guided)	**83.42**	**80.04**	**0.00028**

Our method achieves the best classification performance while maintaining the lowest divergence. This confirms that entropy-based focus and KL filtering contribute significantly to both effectiveness and efficiency.

Table 3 shows results across datasets of increasing size, demonstrating scalability and consistency.

Table 3. Scalability comparison across data sizes

Size	Method	Accuracy (%)	F1 (Macro)	Avg KL
1000	DeepSeek-Only	56.99	50.77	6.21438
	Ours (KL-Guided)	**70.58**	**66.61**	**0.00027**
2000	DeepSeek-Only	73.06	65.66	5.96512
	Ours (KL-Guided)	**81.51**	**78.27**	**0.00029**
3000	DeepSeek-Only	73.95	66.19	5.65321
	Ours (KL-Guided)	**81.64**	**77.91**	**0.00028**

From these results, we observe that our method consistently outperforms DeepSeek-only generation across all dataset scales. Particularly, the margin of improvement increases with larger datasets, indicating enhanced generalization and exhibits better distribution alignment.

These experiments validate that our KL-guided augmentation framework achieves a better tradeoff between semantic control, statistical fidelity, and computational cost, making it well-suited for structured data modeling in domains like smart grid forecasting.

Implementation Details

All experiments were implemented in Python using the `scikit-learn` library. For all baseline and augmented datasets, a Random Forest classifier was employed as the downstream model. The classifier was configured with a fixed number of estimators, a maximum tree depth to control model complexity, a fixed random seed to ensure reproducibility, and a balanced class weighting scheme to mitigate the effect of class imbalance.

The classifier was retrained in each iteration of the augmentation process to dynamically re-evaluate sample uncertainty based on prediction entropy. All computations were executed on an Intel Xeon Gold 6240 CPU with 16 threads and 32GB RAM. The source code used for training and evaluation is available at: https://github.com/Laihuihang/Structured-Data-Generation.

5 Results and Discussion

In this section, we analyze the effectiveness of core components in our KL-guided data augmentation framework. Specifically, we perform ablation studies and sensitivity analysis to understand the contribution of each module, including entropy sampling, field masking, KL divergence filtering, and iterative training.

5.1 Ablation Study

To isolate the impact of each component, we design the following ablation variants:

- **NoEntropy**: Removes entropy-based sample selection; samples for augmentation are chosen randomly.
- **NoMask**: Generates completions using full-record prompts without any field masking.
- **NoKL**: Does not perform KL divergence filtering after LLM generation.
- **NoIter**: Executes only one augmentation cycle without iterative refinement.

Table 4 summarizes the impact of these ablations on the 6287-sample dataset.

Table 4. Ablation results on 6287-sample dataset

Variant	Accuracy (%)	F1 (Macro)	Avg KL
Full Model (Ours)	**83.42**	**80.04**	**0.00028**
NoEntropy	75.22	68.05	5.91108
NoMask	75.03	67.77	5.89934
NoKL	81.45	77.60	0.05579
NoIter	81.7	77.93	0.05257
REaLTabFormer	82.15	76.56	0.01958

The results show that removing KL filtering results in the largest degradation in distribution alignment (KL increases from 0.037 to 0.084), while entropy sampling and masking both significantly impact downstream model performance. The absence of iterative updates also leads to reduced effectiveness, confirming the benefit of convergence-based refinement.

5.2 Sensitivity Analysis

We further examine how model performance varies under different values of key hyperparameters: the number of masked fields m and the KL divergence threshold δ.

Effect of Masked Field Count. Figure 2 shows the accuracy curve as we increase m from 1 to 4. Moderate masking ($m = 2$) yields the best results, balancing context retention and novelty injection. Too few masked fields provide limited variation, while excessive masking leads to noisy completions.

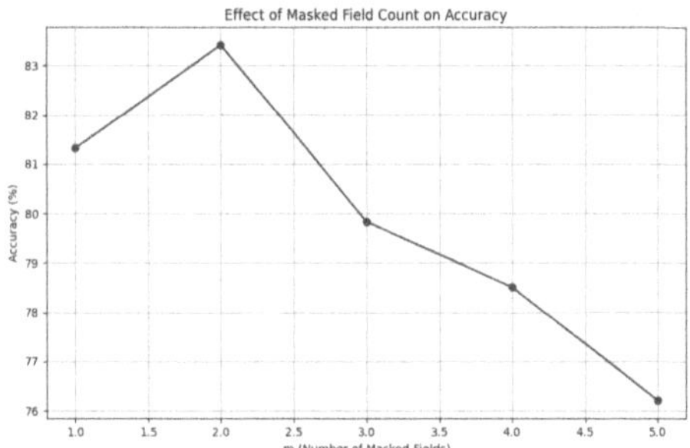

Fig. 2. Accuracy vs. number of masked fields.

Effect of KL Filtering Threshold. We also vary the KL filtering threshold δ in the range $[0.0001, 0.01]$. As shown in Fig. 3, overly strict filtering ($\delta < 0.0002$) eliminates too many useful samples, making convergence difficult, while loose filtering ($\delta > 0.005$) introduces drift. A threshold around $\delta = 0.0003$ achieves optimal trade-off.

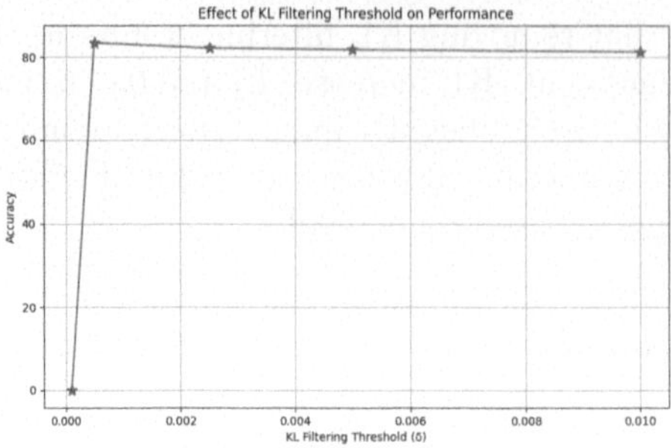

Fig. 3. Accuracy vs. KL filtering threshold.

5.3 Discussion

The ablation results highlight that each component in the pipeline is essential for performance. The KL divergence constraint is particularly crucial for statistical fidelity. Sensitivity analysis also reveals that the system is stable across reasonable parameter ranges, with optimal performance achieved using selective masking and moderate KL control.

In practical deployments, the proposed method provides a configurable and robust solution for structured data augmentation. It avoids over-generation, maintains semantic consistency, and adapts well to limited supervision scenarios often found in power grid data modeling.

6 Conclusion and Future Work

This paper proposes a structured data augmentation framework that integrates high-entropy sampling, field-level masking, large language model (LLM) completion, and KL-divergence filtering. By controlling sample uncertainty, applying semantic-aware masking, and filtering low-fidelity generations, the method improves downstream model performance while preserving distributional consistency. Extensive experiments on various dataset sizes confirm that the proposed method significantly outperforms baseline generation strategies in terms of accuracy, F1-score, and efficiency.

Positioned within the current shift from template-based to model-driven data generation, this work represents a step toward more controlled and distribution-aware structured data synthesis. Unlike traditional methods relying on random perturbations or handcrafted templates, our approach leverages uncertainty cues and LLM semantic priors to produce samples aligned with task-relevant regions.

Looking ahead, the proposed method shows strong potential for extension. One direction is to expand from structured tabular data to semi-structured or unstructured contexts, where structural priors can be imposed on free-form generation. Another direction is to integrate knowledge graphs or GNN-based schema modeling, allowing domain-specific logic to guide field-level dependencies and value consistency.

In summary, our work delivers a practical and generalizable method for controllable structured data augmentation. Beyond the empirical improvements demonstrated, it lays the groundwork for future intelligent data generation systems capable of handling heterogeneous inputs and evolving domain requirements. The approach holds promise for adoption in domains like smart grid analytics, where reliable and cost-effective synthetic data is essential for robust AI systems.

Acknowledgements. This work was supported by the Information and Communication Branch of State Grid Zhejiang Electric Power Co. (Grant No. B311XT25003A).

References

1. Electrical fault detection and classification (2021). https://www.kaggle.com/datasets/esathyaprakash/electrical-fault-detection-and-classification
2. Borji, A.: A categorical archive of chatgpt failures. arXiv preprint arXiv:2302.03494 (2023)
3. Busker, T., Choenni, S., Bargh, M.S.: Stereotypes in chatgpt: an empirical study. In: Proceedings of the 16th International Conference on Theory and Practice of Electronic Governance, pp. 24–32 (2023)
4. Cegin, J., Pecher, B., Simko, J., Srba, I., Bielikova, M., Brusilovsky, P.: Effects of diversity incentives on sample diversity and downstream model performance in LLM-based text augmentation. arXiv preprint arXiv:2401.06643 (2024)
5. Chen, D., Lee, C., Lu, Y., Rosati, D., Yu, Z.: Mixture of soft prompts for controllable data generation. arXiv preprint arXiv:2303.01580 (2023)
6. Choenni, S., Busker, T., Bargh, M.S.: Generating synthetic data from large language models. In: 2023 15th International Conference on Innovations in Information Technology (IIT), pp. 73–78. IEEE (2023)
7. Ferrara, E.: Should chatgpt be biased? Challenges and risks of bias in large language models. arXiv preprint arXiv:2304.03738 (2023)
8. Liu, R., et al.: Best practices and lessons learned on synthetic data. arXiv preprint arXiv:2404.07503 (2024)
9. Wei, J., et al.: Chain-of-thought prompting elicits reasoning in large language models. Adv. Neural. Inf. Process. Syst. **35**, 24824–24837 (2022)
10. Wilkin, G.A., Huang, X.: K-means clustering algorithms: implementation and comparison. In: Second International Multi-Symposiums on Computer and Computational Sciences (IMSCCS), pp. 133–136. IEEE (2007)
11. Xu, R., et al.: Knowledge-infused prompting: assessing and advancing clinical text data generation with large language models. arXiv preprint arXiv:2311.00287 (2023)
12. Ye, J., et al.: Zerogen: efficient zero-shot learning via dataset generation. arXiv preprint arXiv:2202.07922 (2022)
13. Yoo, K.M., Park, D., Kang, J., Lee, S.W., Park, W.: Gpt3mix: leveraging large-scale language models for text augmentation. arXiv preprint arXiv:2104.08826 (2021)
14. Yu, Y., et al.: Large language model as attributed training data generator: a tale of diversity and bias. Adv. Neural. Inf. Process. Syst. **36**, 55734–55784 (2023)

15. Yu, Y., Zhuang, Y., Zhang, R., Meng, Y., Shen, J., Zhang, C.: Regen: zero-shot text classification via training data generation with progressive dense retrieval. arXiv preprint arXiv:2305.10703 (2023)
16. Zhuo, T., Huang, Y., Chen, C., Xing, Z.: Red teaming chatgpt via jailbreaking: bias, robustness, reliability and toxicity. arXiv preprint arXiv:2301.12867 (2023)

A Distributed Sharing Model for EMRs Based on Hybrid Consortium Chain and Stackelberg Game

Rong Jiang[1,2,3,4], Wenlu Lou[1,2,4](✉), Jinpeng Zhang[1,2,3], Hejiao Zhang[1,2,4], and Haiyang Wang[1,2,3]

[1] Yunnan Key Laboratory of Service Computing, Kunming 650221, Yunnan, People's Republic of China
wenlu_lou@163.com

[2] Institute of Intelligence Application Research, Yunnan University of Finance and Economics, Kunming 650224, Yunnan, People's Republic of China

[3] School of Information, Yunnan University of Finance and Economics, Kunming 650224, Yunnan, People's Republic of China

[4] School of Business, Yunnan University of Finance and Economics, Kunming 650221, Yunnan, People's Republic of China

Abstract. The sharing of electronic medical records (EMRs) can significantly improve the quality of medical services and is crucial for disease research and the diagnostic process of doctors. However, due to insufficient trust and concerns over data security, data holders often refuse to share EMRs data with data users. On the premise of ensuring data security, how to motivate data holders to conduct trusted sharing is a major challenge currently faced by the academic community. To address this challenge, this paper proposes a distributed sharing model based on hybrid consortium chains and Stackelberg games. This model integrates the decentralized feature of the consortium chain with the game strategy optimization method to construct a trusted and secure shared framework. By analyzing the decision-making conflicts of the participants and designing the incentive mechanism to ensure reasonable returns, the ADMM (Alternating Direction Method of Multipliers) is utilized to achieve the dual maximization of the profits of data providers and the utility of consumers. The AHC (Agglomerative hierarchical clustering) algorithm was adopted to cluster consensus nodes to improve the traditional PBFT (Practical Byzantine Fault Tolerance) consensus algorithm, enhancing the efficiency of EMRs data sharing. And it has reduced the phenomenon of data silos. The simulation experiments show that the medical consortium chain system constructed in this paper can provide secure EMRs management and transactions, reduce the communication overhead and delay of medical nodes when sharing EMRs data, increase the throughput, and promote the interoperability among medical institutions and relevant departments.

I. Awan et al. (Eds.): WISE 2025, LNCS 16368, pp. 505–520, 2026.
https://doi.org/10.1007/978-981-95-7251-9_34

Keywords: Stackelberg games · EMRs sharing · Hybrid consortium chain · ADMM · AHC-PBFT

1 Introduction

Medical digitalization plays a crucial role in advancing the modernization and efficiency of the healthcare sector. Through the integration of cutting-edge information technologies like artificial intelligence, cloud computing, and big data, it becomes feasible to digitize medical records and enhance the connectivity of information, ultimately enhancing the quality and effectiveness of medical services [20]. The continuous advancement of medical digitization has led to increased interest in EMRs, which are widely utilized for their ability to offer convenient and superior electronic medical services.

However, the dispersion of electronic medical records across different medical institutions not only hinders data sharing but also increases the risk of patient privacy breaches [9,10,18]. Therefore, designing an open and shared medical and health service system to improve diagnostic capabilities and medical quality is a huge challenge [15]. Currently, many domestic hospitals or individual institutions still use traditional databases to store patient information. When a doctor needs to view a patient's medical records, the system extracts the required data from the database. However, this method cannot achieve data sharing with other medical institutions, resulting in the problem of information islands.

In order to overcome the constraints of data sharing within the current medical system, there is a critical requirement for technology that can facilitate collaboration among various medical institutions and foster strong mutual trust. Blockchain is a promising approach to securely and efficiently manage and share EMRs between different HIS (Healthcare Information Systems) [2]. Blockchain technology addresses the issue of data islands by facilitating secure and efficient exchange of EMRs information among different medical institutions through distributed ledger technology [4,16,17,23]. In response to the risk of privacy leakage, blockchain leverages encryption technology and access control strategies to safeguard medical record data. However, the delay time of blockchain-based transaction confirmation is long and is not suitable for sharing a large number of EMRs in HIS. At the same time, there is currently a large amount of health and medical data, but due to the lack of clear principles of benefit distribution, managers are faced with the dilemma of being afraid or unwilling to share.

This article proposes a distributed security management and transaction mechanism for EMRs based on Stackelberg Game, promotes the sharing of EMRs through transactions based on Stackelberg Game, and introduces blockchain technology to ensure distributed security management of EMRs. This article regards ordinary nodes in the blockchain network as followers in the Stackelberg game model, and the duty nodes as leaders in the Stackelberg game model. The transaction of EMRs between leaders and followers in Stackelberg game model can promote the data sharing of EMRs in the whole blockchain network and the interoperability of medical systems and related institutions, improve the circulation efficiency of EMRs, alleviate the problem of information islands and ensure the security of data. The main contributions of this work are summarized as follows.

- Using blockchain technology, the EMRs in the medical health data management system are managed, and the mathematical planning model of interaction between ordinary nodes and duty nodes is established.
- In order to promote the execution of the EMRs sharing process, a pricing mechanism is introduced to charge for the sharing process, a secure transaction and sharing model between ordinary nodes and duty nodes is constructed, and multi-leader multi-follower Stackelberg game theory is used to balance the supply and demand relationship of EMRs.
- Considering that the strategy space of each ordinary node (follower) is highly multi-dimensional and the Nash equilibrium solution cannot be obtained using the traditional backward induction method, the ADMM algorithm is used to implement the optimal strategy of EMRs secure transactions and shared models.
- Since the research scenario of this article involves multiple heterogeneous networks, the network scale is large and the number of nodes is large. Therefore, this article uses agglomerative hierarchical clustering (AHC) to improve the PBFT consensus algorithm to boost the efficiency of the consensus algorithm.

The rest of this paper is arranged as follows: Sect. 2 reviews the relevant work; In Sect. 3, the system scenario and model are described, and the multi-leader and multi-follower Stackelberg game is proposed. In Sect. 4, experimental analysis and verification of the proposed model method are carried out. Section 5 conducts the full text summary and outlook.

2 Related Works

Hospital Information System (HIS) is a centralized system that provides comprehensive automated management and various services for the overall operation of the hospital. EMRs are the core component of HISs. They replace traditional paper medical records and record patients' medical information in digital form. With the explosive growth of EMRs data, some new methods based on IoT technology have been proposed to improve the robustness and security of the system. [5] put forward a novel multi-cloud-based architecture designed to facilitate secure and collaborative sharing of EMRs within a semi-trusted cloud computing environment. [19] proposed a HIS for medical big data storage based on the Internet of Things (IoTs), and proposed a new dual adaptive access control system for EMRs sharing. [13] proposed an agent-based access control scheme for selective EMRs sharing among different healthcare providers in cloud computing. In order to maintain the identity authentication of medical users and EMRs sharing the system, [8] uses Public Key Infrastructure (PKI) on the cloud to ensure the security standards of electronic medical systems. In addition, the authors in [21] use attribute permissions to grant keys to data consumers in an attribute-based encryption prototype to enable fine-grained access control for

EMRs sharing on the cloud. However, IoT-based HISs are centralized and may not fully address the increasing demands for security and efficiency. At the same time, due to privacy considerations and competitive pressure, different medical institutions are reluctant to share their own data [6], and the consistency and interoperability of different data types from different medical institutions are also important issues in data sharing [7].

With the development of blockchain technology, its decentralization, traceability, anonymity and other characteristics have received widespread attention in the application of the medical industry. Currently, many scholars are paying attention to the issue of EMRs sharing based on blockchain technology. Mukkamala et al. proposed a conceptual design for personal continuous dynamic health data sharing based on blockchain technology, supplemented by cloud storage to share personal health-related information in a safe and transparent manner [24]. Cao et al. proposed a cloud-assisted secure e-health system that uses blockchain technology to protect outsourced EMRs in the cloud from illegal modifications [1]. The key idea of this system is that EMRs can only be outsourced by certified participants, and each operation of outsourced EMRs is integrated into the public blockchain as a transaction, resulting in higher security performance compared to [24]. On the basis of [1], Liu et al. proposed a blockchain-based privacy-preserving data sharing scheme, namely BPDS. In BPDS, the cloud is used to securely store original EMRs, and a tamper-proof consortium blockchain is designed to share the EMRs index [12]. Chen et al. proposed a blockchain-based searchable encryption scheme for EMRs sharing to improve the searchability of data [14]. In this case, the construction of indexes of EMRs stored in the blockchain are complex logical expressions that data users can use to search the index. In order to further improve the security of EMRs sharing, Ding proposed a storage solution and service framework for medical data storage, sharing and use based on blockchain and cloud. In this scheme, blockchain-based personal medical data applications can provide patient EMRs sharing services without violating privacy [3].

The above work puts forward various EMRs sharing schemes from different aspects, but there is no detailed solution for specific application scenarios. In particular, in the process of EMRs cross-domain sharing, how to ensure the mutual trust between different organizations in different scenarios and ensure the security of data sharing is an urgent problem to be solved. In addition, the traditional consensus algorithm based on blockchain has a large communication overhead and cannot meet the scalability requirements of large-scale networks. Meanwhile, for single-chain networks, large-scale user accesses will cause huge pressure on the blockchain network, thus affecting the operational efficiency of the system. Therefore, this paper designed a multi-scenario medical health data management system based on the consortium chain, modeled the interaction between ordinary nodes and duty nodes using Stackelberg game theory, and used AHC to group consensus nodes in the blockchain network to improve consensus efficiency, and finally realized the purpose of promoting EMRs sharing,as shown in Fig. 1.

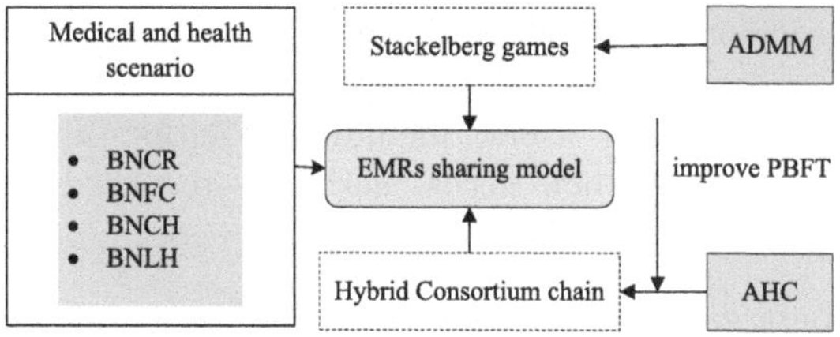

Fig. 1. Technical architecture.

3 System Model

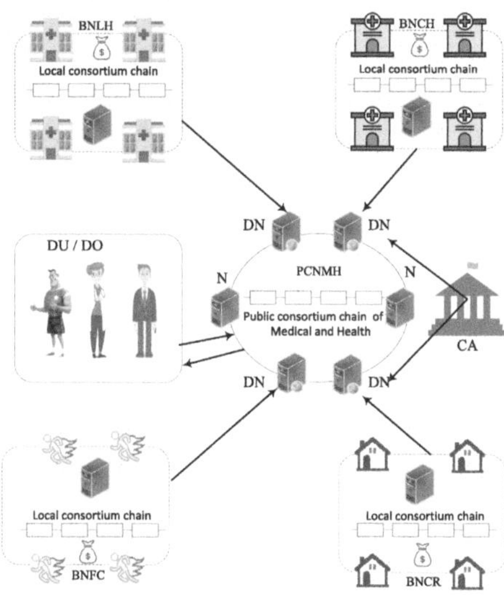

Fig. 2. Medical and health data management scenario based on Hybrid consortium chain.

The healthcare scenario involves four heterogeneous Blockchain networks, the Blockchain network of large hospitals (BNLH), Blockchain network of community hospitals (BNCH), Blockchain network of fitness clubs(BNFC), Blockchain network of Community residents(BNCR), these four heterogeneous networks together form the Public consortium-chain network of medical and health (PCNMH). Furthermore, each local consortium chain and the public consortium chain together constitute a hybrid consortium chain. The two main interacting roles in the medical and health scenario based on the hybrid consortium chain include: duty nodes (DN) and data users (DU).

1. **Duty Node (DN):** As a node manager in a single network, the duty node is trusted by the nodes in the network and is responsible for communication

between heterogeneous networks and processing internal and external access requests.

2. **Data User (DU):** Data users, including doctors, fitness trainers, and other data visitors, have their access activities recorded and stored in the blockchain.

In the Stackelberg game, there are two types of participants, namely leaders and followers. The game is divided into two stages. In the first stage, the leader takes action first, makes decisions and makes them public. In the second stage, after observing the leader's decisions, the followers make their own decisions accordingly. The DNs and DUs in the blockchain have role logic similarities with the leaders and followers in the Stackelberg game. Therefore, this paper considers the DUs(ordinary nodes) in the blockchain network as followers and the DNs as leaders. By facilitating the transaction of EMRs resources between leaders and followers in the Stackelberg game model, the paper aims to promote the sharing of EMRs across the blockchain network and enhance interoperability among medical systems and related institutions. This will ultimately improve information flow efficiency and mitigate issues related to information islands, as shown in Fig. 2.

3.1 Parameters and Definitions

There are data users (DUs) as ordinary nodes in the whole healthcare public consortium chain network, where ordinary nodes $i \in \mathcal{N} = \{1, 2, ..., N\}$. There is one Duty Node (DN) in each local consortium chain network, and there are M Duty Nodes in the whole healthcare public consortium chain network, $N > M$, where DNs $j \in \mathcal{M} = \{1, 2, ..., M\}$. Each DU is both the creator of EMRs data in the local blockchain network and the user of EMRs data in the heterogeneous blockchain network. However, each DU can only share access to the local electronic medical record (L-EMRs) within its own blockchain network. In order to access EMRs in heterogeneous blockchain network across domains, the DN will charge a certain price to the ordinary node, and then the DN will share the EMRs in its medical and health public consortium chain with the corresponding ordinary node. It is worth noting that: when the ordinary node/data user (DU) and the DN belong to the same LAN, the DN cannot share the global electronic medical record (G-EMRs) to the ordinary node/ DU freely, even if it owns the G-EMRs in the entire medical public alliance chain network. They can only share local electronic medical records (L-EMRs) on the LAN.

In the first stage of the Stackelberg game, the DN, aiming at profit maximization, acts as a leader to set the unit price p_j of G-EMRs in the entire healthcare public consortium chain network; In the second stage of the Stackelberg game, the ordinary nodes/DUs, based on the price of the EMR data resources, act as followers to determine the price of the demand of their data resources d_{ij}. When $d_{ij} = 0$, $p_{ij} = 0$. Therefore, the demand matrix of all ordinary nodes/ DUs is D:

The corresponding payment matrix for all ordinary nodes/ DU is P:

Since all DNs have the same data, which are real and trustworthy G-EMRs data on the healthcare public consortium chain after PBFT consensus, Moreover, since ordinary nodes/DUs are rational and their demands are atomic, they will make data requests to the DN with the lowest price to achieve the goal of data sharing. Therefore, the sharing request matrix between an ordinary nodes/DUs and DNs is X:

$$\mathbf{D} = \begin{bmatrix} d_{11} & d_{12} & \cdots & d_{1M} \\ d_{21} & d_{22} & \cdots & d_{2M} \\ \vdots & \vdots & \ddots & \vdots \\ d_{N1} & d_{N2} & \cdots & d_{NM} \end{bmatrix} \qquad \mathbf{P} = \begin{bmatrix} p_{11} & p_{12} & \cdots & p_{1M} \\ p_{21} & p_{22} & \cdots & p_{2M} \\ \vdots & \vdots & \ddots & \vdots \\ p_{N1} & p_{N2} & \cdots & p_{NM} \end{bmatrix} \qquad \mathbf{X} = \begin{bmatrix} x_{11} & x_{12} & \cdots & x_{1M} \\ x_{21} & x_{22} & \cdots & x_{2M} \\ \vdots & \vdots & \ddots & \vdots \\ x_{N1} & x_{N2} & \cdots & x_{NM} \end{bmatrix}$$

Where $\sum_{k \in \mathcal{M}} x_{ik} = 1$, when $x_{ij} = 1$, ordinary node i makes a sharing request d_{ij} to current node j and pays the price p_{ij}; when $x_{ij} = 0$, $d_{ij} = 0$, and $p_{ij} = 0$ accordingly.

3.2 Stackelberg Game Model

This paper refers to [22] to model the interactions between DNs and ordinary nodes, which sets the probability for each ordinary node i to choose DN j:

$$\omega_{ij} = \frac{b_{ij} x_{ij}}{\sum_{k \in \mathcal{M}} b_{ik}} \tag{1}$$

where b_{ij} is the difference value between the largest unit price $\hat{p}$ and the unit price p_{ij} paid by ordinary node i. Similarly, b_{ik} is the motivation of unit price reduction of DN, when DN provides G-EMRs data sharing for ordinary nodes.

$$b_{ik} = \hat{p} - p_{ik}, \quad i \in \mathcal{N}, k \in \mathcal{M} \tag{2}$$

Proposition 1: According to (1) and (2), when the pricing of EMRs data of other DN is constant, the value of ω_{ij} is negatively correlated with the price p_{ij} paid by ordinary node i to DN j. Moreover, ω_{ij} is strictly concave.

Proof. First, according to (1) and (2), ω_{ij} can be converted to the following form:

$$\begin{aligned} \omega_{ij}(p_{ij}) &= \frac{\hat{p} - p_{ij}}{\sum_{k \in \mathcal{M}} (\hat{p} - p_{ik})} x_{ij} \\ &= \frac{\hat{p} - p_{ij}}{\left[\hat{p} + \sum_{k \in \mathcal{M}, k \neq j} (\hat{p} - p_{ik})\right] - p_{ij}} x_{ij} \\ &= \frac{A - p_{ij}}{B - p_{ij}} x_{ij} \end{aligned} \tag{3}$$

Then, when $x_{ij} = 1$, we can get the first and second derivatives of $\omega_{ij}(p_{ij})$ based on the formula (3):

$$\frac{\partial \omega_{ij}}{\partial p_{ij}} = \frac{A - B}{(B - p_{ij})^2} < 0 \tag{4}$$

$$\frac{\partial^2 \omega_{ij}}{\partial p_{ij}^2} = \frac{2(A - B)}{(B - p_{ij})^3} < 0 \tag{5}$$

Thus the ω_{ij} is a concave function, $\omega_{ij}(p_{ij}) \in [0, 1]$, when $x_{ij} = 0$, $\omega_{ij}(p_{ij}) = 0$, $B = \hat{p} + \sum_{k \in \mathcal{M}, k \neq j} (\hat{p} - p_{ik})$, $A = \hat{p}$, $B \geq A \geq p_{ij} \geq 0$. The fact that ω_{ij} is a convex function indicates that there exists an optimal solution in the solution space of the DN that the ordinary node DU selects for data sharing. The selection process can be modeled as an optimization problem. Based on the Stackelberg game model, each DN tends to offer a lower price to DU, which leads to price competition among DNs.

The EMRs data resource requests from DUs to DNs are regarded as the data sharing and access capabilities of DUs. Before the DU makes a data sharing request to the DN, the ordinary node i has the initial data sharing and accessing capability l_i. Therefore, the total sharing and accessing capability of the ordinary node i after purchasing the EMRs data resource d_{ij} from the DN j is:

$$l_i^{total} = l_i + \sum_{j \in \mathcal{M}} \omega_{ij} d_{ij} \tag{6}$$

The data sharing and access capability of ordinary node i can affect its decision and behavior in the process of purchasing EMRs data resources of DN j, thus affecting the satisfaction S_i^{sat} of ordinary node i:

$$S_i^{sat} = \lambda_i \ln l_i^{total} \tag{7}$$

Since satisfaction is generally regarded as a positive feedback process, we set $\lambda_i > 0$ as the impact factor of the sharing and access ability of ordinary node i, and use the impact factor λ_i and the total sharing and access ability of ordinary node i to describe the satisfaction S_i^{sat} of ordinary node i. For each ordinary node/DU as follower, he determines the EMRs data resource demand $d_i = \{d_{i1}, d_{i2}, \ldots, d_{iM}\}$ based on the price set by DN (leader). Each ordinary node/DU i aims for maximizing its expected utility, which is given as follows:

$$\begin{aligned} u_i &= \sum_{j \in \mathcal{M}} (S_i^{sat} - p_{ij}\omega_{ij}d_{ij}) \\ &= \sum_{j \in \mathcal{M}} \left[\lambda_i \ln \left(l_i + \sum_{j \in \mathcal{M}} \omega_{ij} d_{ij} \right) - p_{ij}\omega_{ij}d_{ij} \right] \end{aligned} \tag{8}$$

In addition to the revenue from charging the ordinary nodes/DUs for EMRs data resource, the DNs have the service cost of operation and maintenance. The cost of DNs is related to the electricity consumption or hardware loss denote by cd_{ij}, where c represent the cost coefficient, $0 < c < p_{ij}$. Therefore, each DN j determines the pricing within the strategy space $\{p_j = [p_{ij}]_{i \in \mathcal{N}} : 0 \leq p_{ij} \leq \hat{p}\}$ to maximize its profit, which is formulated as follows:

$$\begin{aligned}\prod_j &= \sum_{i\in\mathcal{N}} \left[\omega_{ij}\left(\sum_{i\in\mathcal{N}} p_{ij}d_{ij} - \sum_{i\in\mathcal{N}} cd_{ij}\right)\right] \\ &= \sum_{i\in\mathcal{N}} \left[\frac{(\hat{p}-p_{ij})x_{ij}}{\sum_{k\in\mathcal{M}}(\hat{p}-p_{ik})}\left(\sum_{i\in\mathcal{N}} p_{ij}d_{ij} - \sum_{i\in\mathcal{N}} cd_{ij}\right)\right]\end{aligned} \tag{9}$$

This paper examines the two stages of the Stackelberg game: in the first stage, DN (the leader) sets the price p_{ij} of EMRs data resources to maximize profit $\prod_j$, while in the second stage, DU (followers) determine their demand d_{ij} for EMRs data resources to maximize utility u_i based on the price set by DN.

A1: EMRs data resource demand of the ordinary nodes/DUs in Stage II

The demand d_{ij} for EMRs data resources of ordinary nodes/DUs is influenced by externalities, such as the price $P = \{p_1, p_2, \ldots, p_M\}$ of DN j and the demand D_{-i} of other DUs. Each DU determines its own EMRs data resource demand d_{ij} by solving the following utility maximization problem:

$$\begin{aligned}u_i(d_i, D_{-i}, P) &= \sum_{j\in\mathcal{M}} (S_i^{sat} - p_{ij}\omega_{ij}d_{ij}) \\ &= \sum_{j\in\mathcal{M}} \left[\lambda_i \ln\left(l_i + \sum_{j\in\mathcal{M}} \omega_{ij}d_{ij}\right) - p_{ij}\omega_{ij}d_{ij}\right]\end{aligned} \tag{10}$$

The ordinary node/DU i sub-game problem can be written as follows:

$$\begin{aligned}&\underset{d_i}{maximize} : u_i(d_i, D_{-i}, P) \\ &\text{subject to} : d_{ij} \geq 0 \\ &\qquad \sum_{j\in\mathcal{M}} d_{ij} \leq D_{\max} \\ &\qquad \sum_{j\in\mathcal{M}} x_{ij} = 1\end{aligned} \tag{11}$$

D_{max} in the second constraint denotes the maximum EMRs data resource demand of one ordinary node/DU due to its limited total budget. Note that each ordinary node/DU has no incentive to unboundedly increase its EMRs data resource demand due to financial burden.

B1: DNs' pricing in Stage I
The pricing of DN's EMRs data resource will be influenced by the prices P_{-j} of other DNs and the demand D for DUs. Each DN establishes its own EMRs data resource price p_{ij} by solving the following profit maximization problem:

$$\begin{aligned}\prod_j(p_j, P_{-j}, D) &= \sum_{i\in\mathcal{N}}\left[\omega_{ij}\left(\sum_{i\in\mathcal{N}} p_{ij}d_{ij} - \sum_{i\in\mathcal{N}} cd_{ij}\right)\right] \\ &= \sum_{i\in\mathcal{N}}\left[\frac{(\hat{p}-p_{ij})x_{ij}}{\sum_{k\in\mathcal{M}}(\hat{p}-p_{ik})}\left(\sum_{i\in\mathcal{N}} p_{ij}d_{ij} - \sum_{i\in\mathcal{N}} cd_{ij}\right)\right]\end{aligned} \tag{12}$$

The DN j sub-game problem can be written as follows:

$$\begin{aligned}&\underset{d_i}{\text{maximize}} : \Pi_j(p_j, P_{-j}, D) \\ &\text{subject to} : 0 \le p_j \le \hat{p}\end{aligned} \tag{13}$$

$$\left\|\sum_{j\in\mathcal{M}} \Pi_j(p_j^{(q)}) - \sum_{j\in\mathcal{M}} \Pi_j(p_j^{(q-1)})\right\| \le \sigma \tag{14}$$

Algorithm 1 Stackelberg game based on ADMM algorithm

1: **Initialization:**
Select initial input $p_{ij} \in [0, \hat{p}], \forall i \in \mathcal{N}, \forall j \in \mathcal{M}$, precision threshold $\sigma, q = 1$;
2: **Repeat**
3: (Inner Loop) Utility optimization for ordinary nodes through ADMM:Ordinary nodes observe the set prices p_{ij}, to determine their EMRs data resource demand $d_{ij}^{(q)}$ by evaluating their resulting utilities, $u_i(d_i)$;
4: (Outer Loop) Profit optimization for DNs through ADMM: DNs predict the ordinary node behaviors d_{ij}, employ ADMM to perform maximization for their individual profit Π_j. The optimal price $p_{ij}^{(q)}$ is obtained such that their profits are maximized;
5: $q = q + 1$
6: **Until** $\left\|\sum_{j\in\mathcal{M}} \Pi_j(p_j^{(q)}) - \sum_{j\in\mathcal{M}} \Pi_j(p_j^{(q-1)})\right\| \le \sigma$
Output: The optimal EMRs data resource demand $d_i^* = d_i^{(q)}, \forall i \in \mathcal{N}$, and the optimal pricing profile $p_j^* = p_j^{(q)}, \forall j \in \mathcal{M}$

The traditional Stackelberg game problem has only one leader and multiple followers. The key challenge of the multi-leader multi-follower Stackelberg game model proposed in this paper lies in the high dimensionality of the strategy space of each ordinary node (follower), which makes it impossible to obtain the Nash equilibrium solution using traditional backward induction. This is the motivation behind our use of the ADMM algorithm to implement the optimal strategy for EMRs sharing models. The basic framework of the ADMM algorithm is shown in Algorithm 1.

4 Experimental Analysis

4.1 Experimental Setting

The experimental data used in this study was provided by the hospital and consists of 1200G of data stored in 5 databases, comprising a total of 1360 data tables with 2139373 records. In order to evaluate the performance and effectiveness of the proposed EMRs distributed sharing model, this study constructs a blockchain platform using Hyperledger Fabric and Docker containers. The Caliper testing tool is utilized to collect relevant data on model performance. As referenced [11], the PBFT consensus algorithm is employed, the block size is set to 32MB, block generation time to 2 s. It is assumed that the initial computing power of ordinary nodes follows a normal distribution $\mathcal{N}(\mu_{\updownarrow}, \sigma_{\updownarrow}^{\in})$, $\mu_l = 10$, $\sigma_l^2 = 5$.

4.2 Competitive and Cooperative Game of ADMM

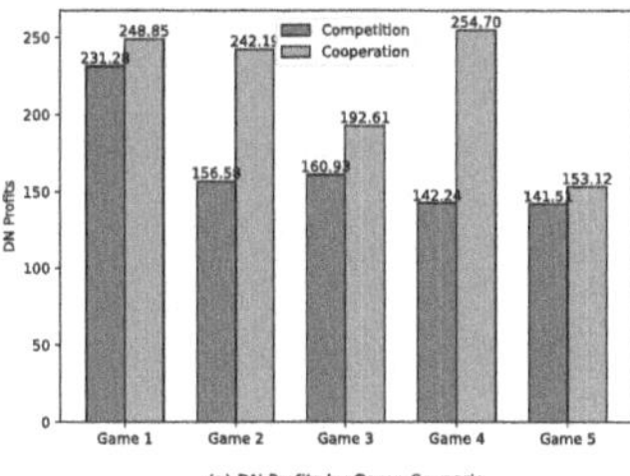

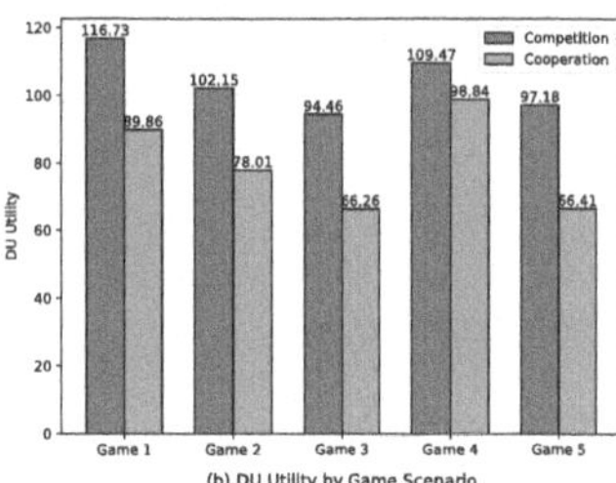

Fig. 3. Performance comparison under ADMM-based competition and cooperation scenarios.

The study compared system performance in ADMM-based competition and cooperation scenarios, as illustrated in Fig. 2. In the cooperation scenario, DNs collaborate to maximize their collective profit. Results indicate that the total profit of duty nodes in the ADMM-based cooperation scenario surpasses that in the ADMM-based competition scenario. This suggests that in a cooperative setting, DNs work together to optimize their total profits, rather than engaging in competitive pricing strategies to attract ordinary nodes. Instead, DNs can cooperate to incentivize ordinary nodes to request more EMRs data sharing services. In this case, the DNs can extract more surplus from the ordinary nodes, leading to a decrease in the total utility of the ordinary nodes. As the demand for EMRs data sharing services by ordinary nodes rises, the total profit of DNs also increases. Future research could explore collusive pricing among cloud/edge DNs. However, in real transactions of EMRs data sharing services, DNs tend to act selfishly, making cooperative scenarios rare. In addition, since the DN is priced based on EMRs data and the demand for EMRs data from ordinary nodes has a certain degree of randomness, the profit of the DN and the utility of ordinary nodes have a certain degree of fluctuation.

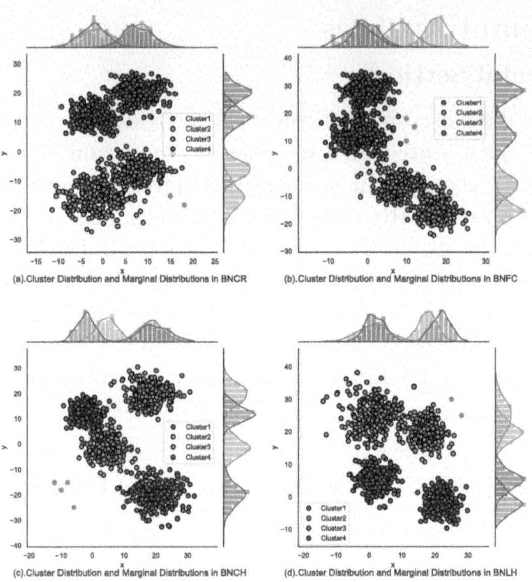

Fig. 4. Cluster results in different local consortium chain networks.

4.3 Data Clustering

In the AHC algorithm simulation experiment, it is assumed that in the entire medical and health public consortium chain, a part of network consensus nodes are artificially and randomly generated. Each consensus node/ordinary node $i \in \mathcal{N} = \{\infty, \in, ..., \mathcal{N}\}$ has EMRs transaction request information, such as blood pressure, blood sugar, heartbeat and other physical indicators. By standardizing indicators and similarity measurement criteria, any number M of clusters that is satisfactory to the user's specification can be obtained cross-cutting. Figure 4 illustrates that the AHC algorithm successfully categorizes consensus nodes within local consortium chain networks into 4 groups,as shown in Fig. 3 with the nodes in each sub-cluster following a normal distribution. Malicious nodes are represented by gray points, and the PBFT consensus algorithm has the capability to withstand a certain number of malicious nodes. Therefore, when the AHC algorithm is used to improve the traditional PBFT consensus algorithm, the classification effect of the AHC algorithm is not affected by malicious nodes in the blockchain network.

4.4 Delay and Throughput

This section verifies the improvement effect of AHC on the traditional PBFT consensus algorithm. Consensus delay refers to the time elapsed from submission to completion of transactions between blockchain nodes. It is an important indicator to measure blockchain performance. The shorter the delay, the faster the transaction confirmation and the higher the efficiency of the consensus. This article compares the consensus efficiency of AHC-PBFT and PBFT based on the consensus delay. It discusses the delay when the number of clusters is M = 4, M = 8 and M = 10, and when the data set size is different, as shown in Fig. 5(a)(b).

The delay of the traditional PBFT consensus algorithm increases sharply with the number of nodes in the public consortium-chain network of medical and health, as it is determined by the complexity of $O(N)^2$. During the Prepare and Commit stages, all nodes broadcast messages to the entire network, leading to significant time consumption. In contrast, the AHC-PBFT consensus algorithm divides consensus nodes into sub-clusters across the network, reducing the number of communications between nodes. This results in a communication complexity of $O(\zeta^2)$, where $\zeta = \max\left\{\frac{N}{\sqrt{M}}, M\right\}$. Consequently, the AHC-PBFT consensus algorithm experiences a slower increase in delay with a growing number of nodes in the public consortium-chain network of medical and health.

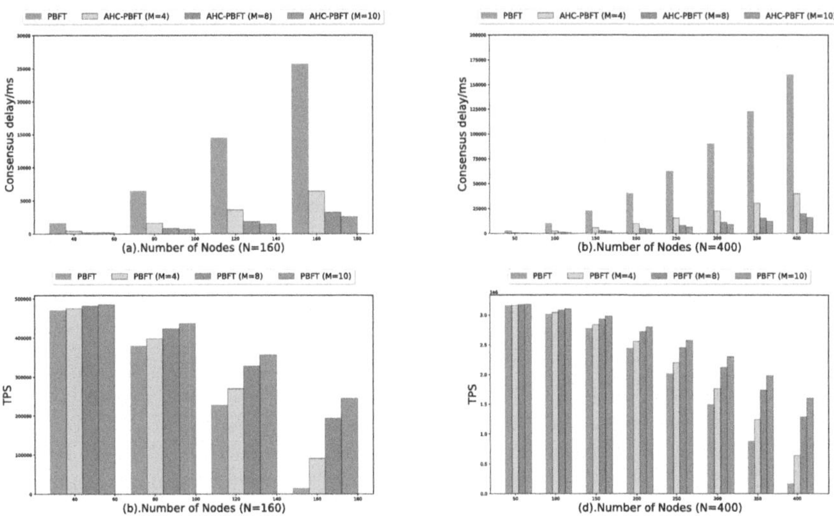

Fig. 5. Comparison of delay and throughput.

Throughput refers to the number of transactions processed per unit time, reflecting the performance of the blockchain system. It is calculated using the following formula:

$$TPS = \frac{Transactions_{\triangle t}}{\triangle\, t}$$

In the formula, $Transactions_{\triangle t}$ represents the number of transactions processed by the blockchain system per unit of time, while $\triangle\ t$ represents the time spent processing transactions. The AHC-PBFT consensus algorithm is a PBFT consensus algorithm obtained through the clustering optimization of the

AHC algorithm. This algorithm initially achieves consensus on a small scale within each sub-cluster, and subsequently reaches consensus among a relatively small number of DNs, thus significantly reducing communication overhead. This enables the system to process transactions quickly even when faced with a large number of network nodes, ensuring high throughput of transaction processing. This paper compares the consensus efficiency of AHC-PBFT and PBFT based on throughput, and discusses the throughput when the number of clusters is M = 4, M = 8 and M = 10 with different dataset sizes, respectively, as shown in Fig. 5(c)(d). When the number of nodes N in the public consortium-chain network of medical and health remains constant, M = 4, M = 8 and M = 10, the throughput of the AHC-PBFT consensus algorithm increases progressively.

5 Conclusion

To address the distributed sharing of EMRs, this paper innovatively integrates Stackelberg game theory and blockchain technologies. The EMRs sharing model, built on consortium chains and Stackelberg games to maximize the interests of both supply and demand sides, verifies convergence via the ADMM algorithm. The PBFT consensus algorithm is enhanced with AHC to boost sharing efficiency, promote interoperability in the medical system, and break down data silos. The organic combination of the Stackelberg game (where participant role logic mirrors blockchain node types) and blockchain effectively tackles EMRs distributed sharing. Game theory compensates for blockchain's shortcomings in resource allocation and user motivation, while the improved PBFT caters to large - scale medical institutions' EMRs sharing needs. Future work will explore the model's application in data sharing scenarios like cross - border digital business and multi - departmental urban management.

Acknowledgement. This work was supported by the National Natural Science Foundation of China (Nos. 72471206, 71972165, 61763048, 72164037, 62202415), the Yunnan Fundamental Research Projects (Nos. 202201AU070115, 202401AT070279, 202501AT070455), Scientific Research Foundation of Yunnan Education Department (Grant No. 2024J0643).

References

1. Cao, S., Zhang, G., Liu, P., Zhang, X., Neri, F.: Cloud-assisted secure ehealth systems for tamper-proofing EHR via blockchain. Inf. Sci. **485**, 427–440 (2019)
2. Chen, L., Lee, W.K., Chang, C.C., Choo, K.K.R., Zhang, N.: Blockchain based searchable encryption for electronic health record sharing. Futur. Gener. Comput. Syst. **95**, 420–429 (2019)
3. Chen, Y., Ding, S., Xu, Z., Zheng, H., Yang, S.: Blockchain-based medical records secure storage and medical service framework. J. Med. Syst. **43**(1) (2019). https://doi.org/10.1007/s10916-018-1121-4

4. Dai, W., Dai, C., Choo, K.K.R., Cui, C., Zou, D., Jin, H.: SDTE: a secure blockchain-based data trading ecosystem. IEEE Trans. Inf. Forensics Secur. **15**, 725–737 (2019)
5. Fabian, B., Ermakova, T., Junghanns, P.: Collaborative and secure sharing of healthcare data in multi-clouds. Inf. Syst. **48**, 132–150 (2015)
6. Ge, Y., Ahn, D.K., Unde, B., Gage, H.D., Carr, J.J.: Patient-controlled sharing of medical imaging data across unaffiliated healthcare organizations. J. Am. Med. Inform. Assoc. **20**(1), 157–163 (2013)
7. Gordon, W.J., Catalini, C.: Blockchain technology for healthcare: facilitating the transition to patient-driven interoperability. Comput. Struct. Biotechnol. J. **16**, 224–230 (2018)
8. Ibrahim, A., Mahmood, B., Singhal, M.: A secure framework for sharing electronic health records over clouds. In: 2016 IEEE International Conference on Serious Games and Applications for Health (SeGAH), pp. 1–8. IEEE (2016)
9. Jiang, R., Chen, X., Yu, Y., Zhang, Y., Ding, W.: Risk and ucon-based access control model for healthcare big data. J. Big Data **10**(1), 104 (2023)
10. Jiang, R., Liu, R., Zhang, T., Ding, W., Tian, S.: An electronic medical record access control model based on intuitionistic fuzzy trust. Inf. Sci. **658**, 120054 (2024)
11. Jiao, Y., Wang, P., Niyato, D., Suankaewmanee, K.: Auction mechanisms in cloud/fog computing resource allocation for public blockchain networks. IEEE Trans. Parallel Distrib. Syst. **30**(9), 1975–1989 (2019)
12. Liu, J., Li, X., Ye, L., Zhang, H., Du, X., Guizani, M.: BPDS: a blockchain based privacy-preserving data sharing for electronic medical records. In: 2018 IEEE Global Communications Conference (GLOBECOM), pp. 1–6. IEEE (2018)
13. Manoj, R., Alsadoon, A., Prasad, P.W.C., Costadopoulos, N., Ali, S.: Hybrid secure and scalable electronic health record sharing in hybrid cloud. In: 2017 5th IEEE International Conference on Mobile Cloud Computing, Services, and Engineering (MobileCloud), pp. 185–190 (2017)
14. Niu, S., Chen, L., Wang, J., Yu, F.: Electronic health record sharing scheme with searchable attribute-based encryption on blockchain. IEEE Access **8**, 7195–7204 (2019)
15. Qiu, H., Qiu, M., Liu, M., Memmi, G.: Secure health data sharing for medical cyber-physical systems for the healthcare 4.0. IEEE J. Biomed. Health Inform. **24**(9), 2499–2505 (2020)
16. Wang, M., Han, S., Chen, G., Yin, J., Cao, J.: Blockchain-empowered resource allocation and data security for efficient vehicular edge computing. In: International Conference on Web Information Systems Engineering, pp. 205–219. Springer, Cham (2023)
17. Xiong, W., Xiong, L.: Smart contract based data trading mode using blockchain and machine learning. IEEE Access **7**, 102331–102344 (2019)
18. Xu, G., et al.: A privacy-preserving medical data sharing scheme based on blockchain. IEEE J. Biomed. Health Inform. **27**(2), 698–709 (2022)
19. Yang, Y., Zheng, X., Guo, W., Liu, X., Chang, V.: Privacy-preserving smart IoT-based healthcare big data storage and self-adaptive access control system. Inf. Sci. **479**, 567–592 (2019)
20. Yao, Y., Cen, X., Liu, Y., Yuan, J., Ye, Y.: Blockchain-based electronic medical record security sharing scheme. In: 2023 45th Annual International Conference of the IEEE Engineering in Medicine & Biology Society (EMBC), pp. 1–4. IEEE (2023)
21. Ying, Z., Wei, L., Li, Q., Liu, X., Cui, J.: A lightweight policy preserving EHR sharing scheme in the cloud. IEEE Access **6**, 53698–53708 (2018)

22. Zhang, H., Xiao, Y., Bu, S., Yu, F.R., Niyato, D., Han, Z.: Distributed resource allocation for data center networks: a hierarchical game approach. IEEE Trans. Cloud Comput. **8**(3), 778–789 (2018)
23. Zhao, Y., Yu, Y., Li, Y., Han, G., Du, X.: Machine learning based privacy-preserving fair data trading in big data market. Inf. Sci. **478**, 449–460 (2019)
24. Zheng, X., Mukkamala, R.R., Vatrapu, R., Ordieres-Mere, J.: Blockchain-based personal health data sharing system using cloud storage. In: 2018 IEEE 20th International Conference on e-Health Networking, Applications and Services (Healthcom), pp. 1–6. IEEE (2018)

CODE ACROSTIC: Robust Watermarking for Code Generation

Li Lin[1(✉)], Siyuan Xin[2], Yang Cao[3], and Xiaochun Cao[4]

[1] Institude of Science Tokyo, Tokyo, Japan
lin.l.ac@m.titech.ac.jp

[2] Shanghai University, Shanghai, China
zeshixing@shu.edu.cn

[3] Institude of Science Tokyo, Tokyo, Japan
cao@c.titech.ac.jp

[4] Sun Yat-sen University, Guangzhou, China
caoxiaochun@mail.sysu.edu.cn

Abstract. Watermarking large language models (LLMs) is vital for preventing their misuse, including the fabrication of fake news, plagiarism, and spam. It is especially important to watermark LLM-generated code, as it often contains intellectual property. However, we found that existing methods for watermarking LLM-generated code fail to address *comment removal attack*. In such cases, an attacker can simply remove the comments from the generated code without affecting its functionality, significantly reducing the effectiveness of current code-watermarking techniques. On the other hand, injecting a watermark into code is challenging because, as previous works have noted, most code represents a low-entropy scenario compared to natural language. Our approach to addressing this issue involves leveraging prior knowledge to distinguish between low-entropy and high-entropy parts of the code, as indicated by a *Cue List* of words. We then inject the watermark guided by this Cue List, achieving higher detectability and usability than existing methods. We evaluated our proposed method on *HumanEval* and compared our method with three state-of-the-art code watermarking techniques. The results demonstrate the effectiveness of our approach.

Keywords: Watermark for LLM · Data Protection · Ownership for AI

1 Introduction

The rapid proliferation of Large Language Models (LLMs) has revolutionized various fields, showcasing their potential in automating tasks [1], generating creative content [2], and solving complex problems [3]. However, the growing reliance on LLMs has also raised significant concerns, particularly regarding the potential for plagiarism and dishonesty [4], especially in contexts where the originality of content is crucial, such as homework programming [5] or open-source activities. Furthermore, AI hallucination would lead to misinformation

I. Awan et al. (Eds.): WISE 2025, LNCS 16368, pp. 521–531, 2026.
https://doi.org/10.1007/978-981-95-7251-9_35

and degradation of future language models [6]. This issue of ownership and accountability remains an open problem. Tools are formulated to counteract the plagiarism associated with LLMs, part of them are the Post-hoc detection approaches [7,8] (i.e. without changing the text generation process), which analyze the features of generated context and judge the genuineness across different samples. However, after the machine-originated text turned out to be flawlessly close to the human-written one, as *the first sentence is generated by one of the LLMs*, the Post-hoc fashion approaches are expected to struggle. Watermark-based methods have been developed as a potential solution to address challenges in tracking and verifying content, especially in programming languages.

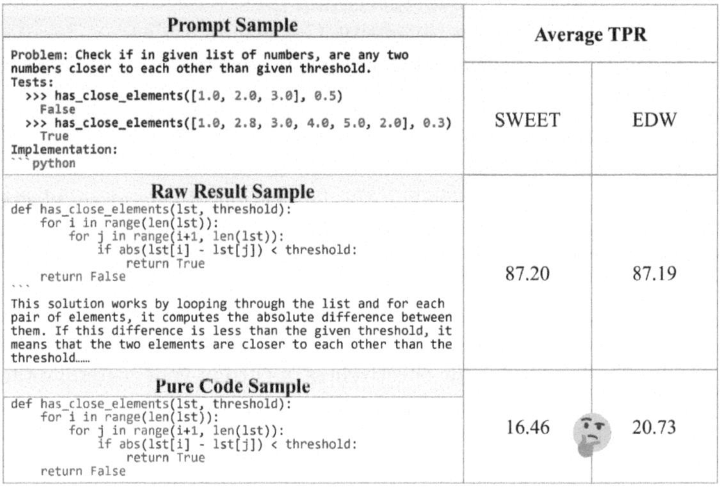

Sample	Average TPR	

Prompt Sample
Problem: Check if in given list of numbers, are any two numbers closer to each other than given threshold.
Tests:
  >>> has_close_elements([1.0, 2.0, 3.0], 0.5)
    False
  >>> has_close_elements([1.0, 2.8, 3.0, 4.0, 5.0, 2.0], 0.3)
    True
Implementation:
``python
	SWEET	EDW

Raw Result Sample
def has_close_elements(lst, threshold):
    for i in range(len(lst)):
        for j in range(i+1, len(lst)):
            if abs(lst[i] - lst[j]) < threshold:
                return True
    return False
``
This solution works by looping through the list and for each pair of elements, it computes the absolute difference between them. If this difference is less than the given threshold, it means that the two elements are closer to each other than the threshold......
	87.20	87.19

Pure Code Sample
def has_close_elements(lst, threshold):
    for i in range(len(lst)):
        for j in range(i+1, len(lst)):
            if abs(lst[i] - lst[j]) < threshold:
                return True
    return False
	16.46	20.73

Fig. 1. *Comment Removal Attack* that simply removes the comments from the generated code without affecting its functionality(True Positive Rate on HumanEval Dataset here), can significantly reduce the effectiveness of the state-of-the-art code-watermarking techniques **EWD** and **SWEET**.

Watermarking techniques have evolved significantly in recent years, beginning with the approach introduced by Kirchenbauer(**KGW**) [9], where service providers embed identifiable marks or patterns into content generated by LLMs for future tracking and origin verification. Building on this, **SWEET** [10] enhances watermarking by applying an entropy threshold, selectively injecting watermarks into high-entropy regions while clamping low-entropy tokens during the detection phase. This architecture results in a more robust watermarking scheme. Later, **EWD** [11] further refines this by incorporating entropy into the weighting of the detection process, producing a "soft" detector.

However, existing watermarking methods [9–11] for code generation neglect *robustness* the watermark against attacks. As illustrated in Fig. 1, a simple but effective comment removal attack can degrade the detectability of the watermark to a level that is unacceptable.

To tackle the challenges of watermarking in code generation, we introduce a novel approach called **Code Acrostic**, to improve robustness and detectability. The key insight behind Code Acrostic is that some segments of the code can tolerate modifications without affecting functionality. Leveraging this, Code Acrostic selectively injects watermarks into areas resilient to changes and minimally disruptive to the code's correctness. The core of this method is the use of high-entropy tokens, which are less predictable and more adaptable to modifications, making them ideal for watermarking. By pre-calculating a **Cue List**, which identifies the tokens immediately **preceding** these high-entropy tokens, Code Acrostic inserts watermark tokens only **after** the cue tokens. This creates a sparse watermark that enhances detectability and robustness while minimizing the impact on the usability of the code, ensuring it remains fully functional.

Summary of Our Technical Contributions. For the first time, we identify that comment removal attacks present an overlooked challenge for existing code watermarking methods. Second, we introduce Code Acrostics, a novel watermarking technique for LLM-generated code that maintains high detectability, even against comment removal attacks. Finally, we experimentally evaluated the robustness, detectability, and usability of code watermarking methods, confirming the effectiveness and superiority of our proposed approach.

2 Related Work

2.1 Watermark-Based Methods

Watermark techniques are considered to be important to counter the abuse of LLM [12], and it is also a tool with abundant research history [13], focused on embedding identifiers in natural language for tracking and attribution purposes.

Kirchenbauer et al. [9] formulate the framework for watermarking in LLM-generated text, introducing a groundwork that integrates watermarking directly into the generation process. Christ et al. [14] introduced advanced cryptographic techniques to enhance watermark security, making detection more robust under attack or modification. Fairoze et al. [15] introduce the important idea of public-key cryptography to the scheme of watermark, which is able to be used at the proof of the possession of a LLM or detection when it is required. Furthermore, Fu et al. [16] refined the watermark injection process using the Gumbel-max trick, improving both the imperceptibility and detectability of watermarks. Furthermore, SynthID [17] presents a random mechanism called tournament sampling for the watermark injection, which alleviates the destruction to the generation quality. For the situation that the model cannot be modified, Yang et al. [18] explored injecting watermarks via bi-directional models in a black-box setting, addressing scenarios where the generation pipeline is inaccessible.

2.2 Watermarking for Code Generation

The application of watermarking in code generation presents unique challenges, as the structure and functionality of code must remain untouched. Li et al.

[19] introduced ACW, which uses a set of predefined transformations to inject watermarks without compromising code correctness. By modifying the training dataset, Sun et al. [20] proposed injecting watermarks effectively, biasing the model to generate watermarked code. Guan et al. [21] leveraged code syntax engines and type predictors to embed watermarks in a way that aligns with the syntactical and semantic properties of the code. Likely, Kim et al. [22] present a framework called STONE, which selectively inject watermark to non-syntax tokens. Lee et al. [10] utilized selective entropy thresholds to embed watermarks in high-entropy regions, while Lu et al. [11] incorporated entropy as part of the detection weight. Furthermore, Suresh et al. [23] evaluate the robustness of existing methods on watermarking code and point out that vulnerability to attack is a common issue for the current methods.

Despite these advancements, a critical issue remains unsolved: the entropy of LLM-generated code often differs significantly from that of real-world code. This mismatch renders many existing methods vulnerable to attacks, such as comment removal attack, where low-entropy regions like comments are stripped away without affecting functionality. Addressing this vulnerability requires techniques that adaptively identify and watermark high-entropy regions, ensuring robustness even under adversarial conditions.

3 Preliminaries

3.1 Watermark for LLMs

The watermark technique for LLM can be viewed as two split processes, watermark injection and watermark detection. A typical scenario is that the LLM provider injects the watermark into the text which they provide to the customer, and provides the detection toolkit for the customer if needed.

Watermark Injection Watermarking techniques require a fundamental hash function that splits the token space into a green list and a red list [9]. In natural language, the green-to-red list ratio is expected to be balanced as long as the hash is random. The goal of watermarking methods is to alter this balance by introducing a bias to the green list. To enhance a specific green list token's likelihood by a magnitude δ,

$$l'_{wt} = l_{wt} + \delta F_{hash}(w_t, w_p, \gamma, \theta_{key}). \tag{1}$$

Watermark Detection For detection, the text is first tokenized using the same tokenizer, and the length of the sequence is denoted as T, while the hit rate of the green list is calculated as $|s|_G$, as

$$|s|_G = \sum_{i=0}^{t} w_i \in V_G(w_p, \gamma, \theta). \tag{2}$$

Then, a z-statistic under null-hypothesis is applied to evaluate how far this ratio deviates from the expected natural ratio:

$$z = \frac{|S|_G - \gamma T}{\sqrt{T\gamma(1-\gamma)}}. \tag{3}$$

If the z-score exceeds a predetermined threshold, known as the z-threshold, it indicates with high confidence that the text was generated by an LLM.

4 Our Method

The proposed method, **Code Acrostic**, employs a three-step approach: the construction of a **Cue List**, the selective watermark injection through **Cue Sampling**, and the final identification using **Cue Detection**.

4.1 Cue List

The **Cue List** is a central element of Code Acrostic, serving as a filter to determine high-entropy regions suitable for watermark injection. By focusing on tokens with high entropy, this method avoids disrupting low-entropy sections, such as comments or predictable code patterns, which are more vulnerable to removal or modification. Importantly, the Cue List must remain confidential to ensure robustness against adversarial attacks.

To compute the Cue List, Code Acrostic uses a 1-gram model, which calculates the conditional probability of the next token based on a single preceding token. By introducing a third-party corpus, such as [24], denoted as $C = (t_1, t_2, \ldots, t_N)$ with size N, we calculate the 1-gram probabilities. The corpus C is arbitrarily chosen, and any alternative can be used without restriction. The function $k_{t_a}(t_b)$ represents the number of times the pair (t_a, t_b) appears consecutively in a sequence of pairs (t_i, t_{i+1}), where i ranges from 0 to $N-1$. For any token pair (t_a, t_b), the co-occurrence frequency $k_{t_a}(t_b)$ is defined as:

$$k_{t_a}(t_b) = \sum_{i=0}^{N-1} (\{t_a, t_b\} = \{t_i, t_{i+1}\}). \tag{4}$$

Using these frequencies, a list of probabilities for token pairs is

$$K = \{k_{t_0}(T), k_{t_1}(T), \cdots, k_{t_N}(T)\}. \tag{5}$$

It gets the Cue List $\hat{K}$, by:

$$\forall k \in \hat{K}, k \in K \ \ \& \ \ k' = \frac{k}{\sum k} \tag{6}$$

And formulate the cue poll with a threshold β, as :

$$F_{\text{cue}}(k) = \begin{cases} 1 : -\sum k' * \log k' < \beta \\ 0 : \text{else} \end{cases} \tag{7}$$

This thresholding ensures that only high-entropy tokens, which are tokens with greater unpredictability, are included in the Cue List. Such tokens are more robust against modifications and less likely to affect code correctness.

Algorithm 1 Code Acrostics watermarks generation

function GENERATE_WATERMARK(w_{prompt})
    $t_{\text{previous}} \leftarrow w_{prompt}[-1]$
    while $t_{\text{previous}} \neq t_{EOS}$ **do**
        $l \leftarrow F_{llm}(w_{prompt})$
        $hash \leftarrow \delta * H(\gamma, w_{prompt}[-N : -1])$
        $Cue \leftarrow F_{\text{cue}}(t_{\text{previous}})$
        $w_{prompt} \leftarrow w_{prompt} + Sampler(Cue * hash)$
    end while
    return w_{prompt}
end function

4.2 Cue Sample

Cue Sampling leverages the Cue List to selectively inject watermarks into sequences during code generation. By focusing on regions identified as high-entropy, the watermarking process minimizes its impact on usability while maximizing robustness and detectability. With the Cue List, we can sample the original watermark function, as

$$w'_t = F_{\text{cue}} \circ F_{\text{sample}} \circ F_{llm}(w_{1:t-1}). \tag{8}$$

This cue function is a component of the watermark function, and can be viewed as a high-order sampler over the F_{sample}. The algorithm 1 showcases the pseudo-code of watermark injection.

4.3 Cue Detection

Code Acrostic exclusively detect tokens next to the token from Cue List by adopting the Cue List as a token filter. Given a sequence to be detect denoted as $W' = (w'_0, w'_1, \cdots, w'_t)$, the counted token number T and green list token $|S|_G$ should be calculated as:

$$|S|_G = \sum_{i=1}^{t} F_{cue}(w'_{i-1}) F_{hash}(w'_i, w'_{i-N:i-1}, \gamma, \theta_{key}) \tag{9}$$

As the process described with Eq. 3, final z-score can be calculated and apply to a comparison with the z-threshold. The algorithm 2 showcases this process. The detection phase involves verifying the presence of watermarks by analyzing tokens adjacent to those in the Cue List. By using the same threshold and hash function as in the sampling phase, the detection process ensures consistency and accuracy.

Algorithm 2 Code Acrostic Watermarks Detection

function DETECT_WATERMARKS(w_{test})
  $S \leftarrow 0$ & $T \leftarrow 0$
  for all $i = 2, 3, \cdots, |w_{test}|$ **do**
    $t_{\text{previous}} \leftarrow w_{test}[i-1]$
    if $F_{\text{cue}}(t_{\text{previous}})$ **then**
      $T \leftarrow T + 1$
      $G \leftarrow H(\gamma, w_{test}[i-N : i-1])$
      if $G[W_{test}[i]]$ **then** ▷ if the token is green
        $S \leftarrow S + 1$
      end if
    end if
  end for
  $z_{score} = \frac{S - \gamma T}{\sqrt{T\gamma(1-\gamma)}}$
  return $z_{score} > z_{\text{threshold}}$
end function

Table 1. Detectability and usability on Human Eval Dataset comparing to other major approaches. "Raw" represents the original output of LLM without any watermark technique. Improvements in AUROC are calculated relative to KGW. Green indicates positive improvement.

Methods	Human Eval		
	Pass@1 ↑	AUROC ↑	Δ AUROC (%) over KGW
Raw	53.05	-	-
Code Acrostic (Ours)	51.20	**0.772**	**+12.70%**
KGW [9]	54.27	0.685	-
SWEET [10]	**54.88**	0.692	+1.02%
EWD [11]	**54.88**	0.750	+9.49%

5 Experiments and Benchmarks

5.1 Setups

We evaluates the **robustness,detectability and usability** of the proposed method.

Implementaion. For a fair comparison, the experiments leverage the *MarkLLM* framework [25], implemented with the DeepSeek-Coder-1.3b model [26]. Code Acrostic and other competing approaches were integrated into this infrastructure. The source code for this study is publicly available at https://github.com/xhaughearl/code_acrostic, ensuring reproducibility and transparency.

Dataset. The *HumanEval* benchmark [27], designed to evaluate code generation models, was used for assessing the performance of watermarking techniques. This benchmark consists of 164 coding problems, each accompanied by test cases to evaluate code correctness.

Metrics. To evaluate the proposed method, we assess performance using **Pass@1**, which measures whether the generated code passes all test cases (total 164 problems for *HumanEval* [27]) on the first attempt. For watermarking, we evaluate the **True Positive Rate (TPR)**, which reflects the accuracy of detecting watermarked code,While the False Positive Rate(FPR) is similar metric on Non-marked code, as:

$$\mathrm{TPR} = \frac{\text{Marked Code Detected}}{\text{All Marked Code}}; \tag{10}$$

while False Positive Rate (FPR) evaluates the proportion of raw (non-marked) code that is mistakenly classified as watermarked as

$$\mathrm{FPR} = \frac{\text{Raw Code Detected}}{\text{All Raw Code}}. \tag{11}$$

We also use the **Area Under the Receiver Operating Characteristic Curve (AUROC)** to gauge the detector's ability to distinguish between watermarked and non-watermarked code across varying thresholds t, as:

$$\mathrm{AUROC} = \int_{-\infty}^{\infty} \mathrm{TPR}(t), d(\mathrm{FPR}(t)). \tag{12}$$

These metrics provide a holistic view of both the functionality of the watermarked code and the effectiveness of the watermark detection process.

Table 2. Comparison of detectability and parameter ablation results.

Natural	Code	CA	KGW	SWEET	EWD
✓	✓	85.37	24.39	**87.20**	87.19
	✓	**34.76**	17.07	16.46	20.73

(a) **Detectability**. TPR of each approach w/ or w/o natural language (comments) mixed, with a uniform z-threshold.

δ	0	8	12	40
Pass@1	**53.05**	50.00	37.80	15.85
TPR		37.20	**59.15**	20.73

(b) Parameters Ablation. Different Îť with Pass@1 and TPR metrics.

5.2 Robustness

It compares the results before and after filtering out the natural language portion from the detection scope. It shows that all methods exhibit higher detectability when natural language is included in the scope. However, once the natural language is filtered out, **the proposed method stands out with the highest detectability**. This suggests that the proposed method effectively embeds the watermark directly into the code itself, rather than relying on the presence of natural language. It is also notable that SWEET and EWD require longer runtimes compared to CA and KGW when detecting watermark with LLMs.

5.3 Detectability and Usability

Detectability and usability are discussed in this section, and the proposed method achieves superior detectability with acceptable usability.

usability. Maintaining an acceptable level of code accuracy is essential for watermarked code. Table 1 shows how various watermarking methods impact accuracy. While our method experiences a slight degradation in Pass@1, others increase Pass@1 by about 1%. This improvement is likely due to the watermark acting as a random sampler, introducing beneficial variability in the generated content. As noted by Kirchenbauer et al. [9], mild watermarking schemes can enhance content quality. However, Code Acrostic does not exhibit this effect, likely due to its strict Cue List, which prioritizes robustness and detectability, limiting flexibility in watermark placement.

Detectability. Table 1 showcases the results, highlighting that the proposed method achieves superior detectability on the HumanEval benchmark. The AUROC shows that Code Acrostic excels in detectability, thereby outperforming other methods. As for why the other approaches are significantly struggling, part of the reason is that the watermark is injected into the natural language part of the content.

5.4 Ablation Experiments

Different magnitudes of the watermark were tested, with the results for Pass@1 and TPR presented in Table 2b. As expected, increasing the watermark's magnitude tends to trade off some accuracy, reflected in a decrease in Pass@1. As [28] pointed out, there is a trade-off between the detectability and the usability for the series of watermark methods. Interestingly, we observed that the TPR initially increases as the watermark magnitude grows, but it starts to decline when the magnitude becomes too large. This pattern highlights the importance of carefully balancing watermark magnitude to optimize both accuracy and detectability.

6 Conclusion

In this paper, we presented Code Acrostic, a novel approach to watermarking in programming languages. With the aid of a list of high-entropy token cues, Code Acrostic embedded watermarks in resilient, high-entropy code regions, and ensured minimal disruption to code **usability** while maintaining high **detectability**. Furthermore, we introduced a code-only measurement technique that eliminates the influence of natural language elements, thereby measuring the **robustness** of the watermark. The proposed method has demonstrated superior performance, and we hope this method offers new insights for further research in this field.

Acknowledgement. This work is supported by JSPS KAKENHI JP23K24851, JST PRESTO JP MJPR23P5, JSTCRESTJPMJCR21M2, JSPSJPJSBP120247401,

JSTNEXUS JPMJNX25C4. We also thank the anonymous reviewers and all who contributed to improving the quality of this paper.

References

1. Boiko, D.A., MacKnight, R., Kline, B., Gomes, G.: Autonomous chemical research with large language models. Nature, **624**(7992), 570–578 (2023)
2. Zhao, W.X., et al.: A survey of large language models. arXiv preprint arXiv:2303.18223 (2023)
3. Li, R., et al.: Starcoder: may the source be with you! arXiv preprint arXiv:2305.06161 (2023)
4. Kasneci, E., Sessler, K., K üchemann, S., Bannert, M., et al.: Chatgpt for good? On opportunities and challenges of large language models for education. Learn. Individual Diff. (2023)
5. Ghimire, A., Edwards, J.: Coding with AI: how are tools like ChatGpt being used by students in foundational programming courses. In: International Conference on Artificial Intelligence in Education, pages 259–267. Springer (2024)
6. Ji, Z., et al.: Survey of hallucination in natural language generation. ACM Comput. Surv. (2023)
7. Zhong, W., Tang, D., Xu, Z., Wang, R., et al.: Neural deepfake detection with factual structure of text. In: Proceedings of the 2020 Conference on Empirical Methods in Natural Language Processing (EMNLP), pp. 2461–2470. Association for Computational Linguistics (2020)
8. Koike, R., Kaneko, M., Okazaki, N.: Outfox: LLM-generated essay detection through in-context learning with adversarially generated examples. In: Proceedings of the AAAI Conference on Artificial Intelligence, pp. 21258–21266 (2024)
9. Kirchenbauer, J., Geiping, J., Wen, Y., Katz, J., Miers, I., Goldstein, T.: A watermark for large language models. In: Proceedings of the 40th International Conference on Machine Learning, Proceedings of Machine Learning Research, pp. 17061–17084. PMLR (2023)
10. Taehyun et al.: Lee. Who wrote this code? watermarking for code generation. In *Proceedings of the 62nd Annual Meeting of the Association for Computational Linguistics (Volume 1: Long Papers)*, pages 4890–4911. Association for Computational Linguistics (2024)
11. Lu, Y., Liu, A., Yu, D., Li, J., King, I.: An entropy-based text watermarking detection method. arXiv preprint arXiv:2403.13485 (2024)
12. Liu, A., et al.: A survey of text watermarking in the era of large language models. ACM Comput. Surv. **57**(2), 1–36 (2024)
13. Atallah, M.J., et al.: Natural language watermarking: Design, analysis, and a proof-of-concept implementation. In: Ira S. Moskowitz, editor, Information Hiding, Lecture Notes in Computer Science, pages 185–200. Springer (2001)
14. Christ, M., Gunn, S., Zamir,O.: Undetectable watermarks for language models. In: The Thirty Seventh Annual Conference on Learning Theory, pp. 1125–1139. PMLR (2024)
15. Fairoze, J., Garg, S., Jha, S., Mahloujifar, S., Mahmoody, M., Wang, M.: Publicly detectable watermarking for language models. arXiv preprint arXiv:2310.18491, 2023
16. Fu, J., Zhao, X., Yang, R., Zhang, Y., et al.: Gumbelsoft: diversified language model watermarking via the gumbelmax-trick. arXiv preprint arXiv:2402.12948 2024

17. Dathathri, S., et al.: Scalable watermarking for identifying large language model outputs. Nature **634**(8035), 818–823 (2024)
18. Yang, X., et al.: Watermarking text generated by black-box language models. arXiv preprint arXiv:2305.08883 (2023)
19. Boquan Li, Mengdi Zhang, Peixin Zhang, Jun Sun, and Xingmei Wang. Resilient watermarking for llm-generated codes. arXiv preprint arXiv:2402.07518 2024
20. Sun, Z., Du, X., Song, F., Li, L.: Codemark: imperceptible watermarking for code datasets against neural code completion models. In: Proceedings of the 31st ACM Joint European Software Engineering Conference and Symposium on the Foundations of Software Engineering, pp. 1561–1572 (2023)
21. BGuan, L., Wan, Y., Bi, Z., Wang, Z., et al.: Codeip: a grammar-guided multi-bit watermark for large language models of code. arXiv preprint arXiv:2404.15639 (2024)
22. Kim, J., Park, S., Han, Y.-S.: Marking code without breaking it: code watermarking for detecting LLM-generated code. arXiv preprint arXiv:2502.18851 (2025)
23. Suresh, T., Ugare, S., Singh, G., Misailovic, S.: Is watermarking LLM-generated code robust? In: The Second Tiny Papers Track at ICLR 2024 (2024)
24. Lutellier, T., Pham, H.V., Pang, L., Li, Y., et al.: CoCoNuT: combining context-aware neural translation models using ensemble for program repair. In: Proceedings of the 29th ACM SIGSOFT International Symposium on Software Testing and Analysis, ISSTA 2020, pp. 101–114. Association for Computing Machinery (2020)
25. Pan, L., Liu, A., He, Z., Gao, Z., et al.: Markllm: an open-source toolkit for LLM watermarking. arXiv preprint arXiv:2405.10051 (2024)
26. Guo, D., et al.: Deepseek-coder: when the large language model meets programming–the rise of code intelligence. arXiv preprint arXiv:2401.14196 (2024)
27. Chen, M., Tworek, J., Jun, H., et al.: Evaluating large language models trained on code. arXiv preprint arXiv:2107.03374 (2021)
28. Hu, Z., Huang, H.: Inevitable trade-off between watermark strength and speculative sampling efficiency for language models. In: The Thirty-eighth Annual Conference on Neural Information Processing Systems (2024)

Reimagining Attentional Copulas: A Transformer-Based Approach with Proportional Dependency Learning

Yankin Chi(✉) and Raymond Wong

The University of New South Wales, Sydney, NSW 2033, Australia
{yan_kin.chi,ray.wong}@unsw.edu.au

Abstract. Multivariate probabilistic time series forecasting is crucial for decision-making tasks that rely on future values, uncertainty quantification, and inter-variable dependencies. Recently, attentional copulas have gained popularity for successfully combining the expressiveness of deep learning with the modular structure of copula models, which separate the modeling of marginals from that of the joint distribution. Despite their promise, existing methods such as TACTiS face challenges related to convergence stability and the accurate calibration of dependencies. We propose T-PAKC, a Transformer-based Proportional Attentional Kernelized Copula model to address these challenges through: (1) replacing discrete copula binning with a Gaussian kernelized estimator for smooth gradients and expressive density modeling, and (2) adding a Proportional Absolute Error (PAE) regularizer to improve joint calibration without harming marginals. Experiments on five real-world datasets show T-PAKC consistently outperforming strong baselines in CRPS and Energy Scores, with more stable convergence. This work offers a robust, domain-agnostic framework that combines statistical rigor with deep learning flexibility, advancing scalable, uncertainty-aware probablistic multivariate forecasting.

Keywords: Probablistic Time Series Modeling · Attentional Copula · Transformers

1 Introduction

Forecasting future outcomes under uncertainty is crucial in many real-world applications such as managing electrical grids, pricing insurance, anticipating supply chain disruptions, and monitoring patient health. These contexts requires capturing the range of outcomes instead of point estimates. This involves multivariate probabilistic forecasting where better decisions can be attributed to the proper modeling of tail risks and temporal or non-linear dependencies. For example, an electricity provider forecasting consumption across substations must understand not only individual demands but also their co-variation, especially during extreme events.

I. Awan et al. (Eds.): WISE 2025, LNCS 16368, pp. 532–547, 2026.
https://doi.org/10.1007/978-981-95-7251-9_36

Over the years, many machine learning methods for time series forecasting—especially Transformer-based architectures—have been proposed. These models have significantly advanced the field by modeling complex temporal patterns using parallelizable self-attention mechanisms. However, most Transformers are still limited to point estimation and lack the ability to quantify uncertainty or model joint distributions [9,17,18]. Probabilistic models aim to bridge this gap by estimating conditional distributions. Among them, copula-based approaches are particularly powerful due to their ability to separately model marginal distributions and joint dependency structures—an advantage when dealing with heterogeneous multivariate data.

Recently, a promising direction in this space is the class of attentional copula models, with notable examples such as TACTiS (Transformer-Attentional Copulas for Time Series) [3]. These models combine the representational power of Transformers with the flexibility of nonparametric copula modeling. Specifically, attention mechanisms are used to adaptively capture joint dependencies among variables, independently of their marginal behaviors, which are modeled separately via flow-based transformations. Despite their innovation, attentional copula models suffer from practical limitations, particularly in large-scale or time-constrained settings. One known issue is convergence failure, where the model overfits the marginals while failing to meaningfully update trivial copula parameters [3]. As we will demonstrate, another source of training instability stems from its discrete piecewise constant copula density likelihood objective, which introduces discontinuous gradients and sparse bin statistics. These problems limit the model's usability in real-world settings where training time is finite and interpretability or calibration of joint dependencies is crucial.

In this paper, we introduce **Transformer-based Proportional Attentional Kernelized Copula (T-PAKC)**, a new probabilistic forecasting architecture that addresses the aforementioned limitations while retaining the strengths of attentional copula modeling. T-PAKC introduces two key enhancements. The first one is a Gaussian kernelized copula estimator that replaces discrete copula binning, yielding smoother gradients, reduced bin sparsity, and more expressive density modeling. The second one is a Proportional Absolute Error (PAE) term that penalizes inaccuracies in the relative scale and dependency structure between variables, thus guiding the model to optimize both marginal and joint fidelity. Our experiments show that these innovations result in a more stable and efficient training process, improving the likelihood landscape and accelerating convergence, especially in complex or high-dimensional datasets. Overall, this work contributes a robust and generalizable framework for probabilistic multivariate forecasting, particularly suited for applications that require calibrated risk assessments under complex, dynamic inter-dependencies.

2 Problem Statement

Given a multivariate time series setting with the goal of modeling the joint distribution of unobserved values at particular time points conditioned on other observed values. Let $\mathbf{X}$ be a set of s possibly related univariate time series where each $\mathbf{X_i}$ is a random vector containing d_i observations such that $\mathbf{X_i} \stackrel{\text{def}}{=} [X_{i1}, \ldots, X_{i,d_i}]$. For each realisation $\mathbf{x_i} \stackrel{\text{def}}{=} [x_{i1}, \ldots, x_{i,d_i}]$, there exists:

1. A Boolean value m_{ij} where $m_{ij} = 1$ if x_{ij} is observed or else $m_{ij} = 0$.
2. An associated set containing p dimension time varying covariates or additionally available information (such as weather indicators) at each time step represented as $\mathbf{C_i} \stackrel{\text{def}}{=} [c_{i,1}, \ldots, c_{i,d_i}] \in \mathbb{R}^{p \times d_i}$.
3. $\mathbf{t_i} \stackrel{\text{def}}{=} [t_{i,1}, \ldots, t_{i,d_i}] \in \mathbb{R}^{d_i}$ being a vector of time stamps such that $t_{ij} < t_{i,j+1}$.

Then, if $\mathbf{X_i^{(m)}} = [X_{i,1}^{(m)}, \ldots, X_{i,d_i}^{(m)} \mid m_{i,j} = 0]$ and $\mathbf{X_i^{(o)}} = [X_{i,1}^{(o)}, \ldots, X_{i,d_i}^{(o)} \mid m_{i,j} = 1]$ represent the missing and observed components of $\mathbf{X_i}$, the problem of modeling the joint distribution can be written to be conditioned on all known information as the following:

$$P(\{\mathbf{X_i^{(m)}}\}_{i=1}^{s} | \{\mathbf{X_i^o}, \mathbf{C_i}, \mathbf{t_i}\}_{i=1}^{s}) \tag{1}$$

2.1 Copulas

Copulas are statistical constructs whose aim is to model the joint distribution of a given set of random variables independently to their respective marginal distributions. Let n be the total number of random variables modelled within the joint distribution, and $\mathbf{X} = [X_1, \ldots, X_n]$ as a vector of n random variables. With reference to the work in TACTiS [1,3], the joint multivariate CDF of any n-dimensional random vector on the unit cube $[U_1, \ldots, U_n]$ can be modelled using a copula $C : [0,1]^n \rightarrow [0,1]$ and each random variable's marginal univariate CDF $F_i(x_i)$. Note that $F_i(x_i) = u_i$ represents the probability integral transform of x_i. And the CDF of $\mathbf{X}$ can be expressed as:

$$P(X_1 \leq x_1, \ldots, X_n \leq x_n) = C(F_1(x_1), F_2(x_2), \ldots, F_n(x_n)) \tag{2}$$

with C representing the n dimensional joint CDF on the unit cube with uniform distributed marginals on [0, 1]. Specifically,

$$C(u_1, u_2, \ldots, u_n) \stackrel{\text{def}}{=} P(U_1 \leq u_1, U_2 \leq u_2, \ldots, U_n \leq u_n) \tag{3}$$

where $U_i \sim U_{[0,1]}$. We then construct the copula-based density function $g_\phi(x_1, \ldots, x_n)$ with parameters ϕ conditioned on observed variables:

$$g_\phi(x_1, \ldots, x_n) \stackrel{\text{def}}{=} c_{\phi_c}(F_{\phi_1}(x_1), \ldots, F_{\phi_n}(x_n)) \cdot \prod_{i=1}^{n} f_{\phi_i}(x_i) \tag{4}$$

f_i represents the marginal PDF of X_i while ϕ_i and ϕ_c represent the marginal and copula distributional parameters respectively.

Ultimately, this results in a standard copula likelihood optimization problem defined as the following:

$$\underset{\phi}{\text{argmin}} \underset{\mathbf{x} \sim \mathbf{X}}{\mathbb{E}} - \log g_\phi(x_1^m, \ldots, x_{s_m}^{(m)}) \tag{5}$$

3 Related Work

Multivariate time series forecasting models capture dependencies but struggle with nonlinearity and missing data. Though interpretable and low-cost, these methods are limited for complex modern datasets. Deep learning methods model temporal patterns directly. RNNs [14], LSTMs [6], and GRUs [2] use feedback loops, and attention mechanisms like DA-RNN [11] highlight key inputs. Transformers improved efficiency and captured global dependencies, with variants such as Informer [18], Autoformer [17], and iTransformer [9] enhancing long-horizon forecasting. Yet, these mostly produce **point forecasts** lacking uncertainty and dependency modeling. Distributional models like DeepAR [16], TimeGrad [12], and TempFlow [13] estimate full predictive distributions via autoregressive, diffusion, or flow-based methods. While flexible, they often assume parametric noise and may not fully capture high-dimensional dependencies. Copula-based methods separate marginals from joint dependencies, accommodating heteroskedasticity and complex relationships. TACTiS [3] introduced Transformer-based attentional copulas with nonparametric density estimation. TACTiS-2 [1] added curriculum training; PRACTiS [8] improved efficiency through localized attention. Still, these approaches face challenges: unstable training from piecewise-constant binning, premature marginal convergence with trivial copulas, and sensitivity to binning and sparsity—especially in high dimensions.

4 T-PAKC

We propose a novel model, Transformer-based Proportional Attentional Kernelized Copula (T-PAKC), to address the challenges outlined in the previous section. T-PAKC follows an encoder-decoder architecture, as shown in Fig. 1.

Encoder
The encoder in T-PAKC builds upon the standard Transformer architecture. Inputs, including both observed and missing values, are first vectorized by passing the covariates, Boolean mask, and masked values through a neural network:

$$\boldsymbol{e}_{ij} = \text{Embed}_{\theta_{emb}}(x_{ij} \cdot m_{ij}, \mathbf{c}_{ij}, m_{ij}) \tag{6}$$

where $\boldsymbol{e}_{ij} \in \mathbb{R}^{d_{emb}}$. Next, positional encodings $\boldsymbol{pos}_{ij} \in \mathbb{R}^{d_{emb}}$, generated using the timestamp $\mathbf{t}_{ij}$ is added:

$$\boldsymbol{e}'_{ij} = \boldsymbol{e}_{ij}\sqrt{d_{emb}} + \boldsymbol{pos}_{ij} \tag{7}$$

Finally, multi-head self-attention layers adaptively capture the relevance across variables and encode temporal dependencies within each variable's token:

$$\boldsymbol{z}_{ij} = \text{self\_attention}(\boldsymbol{e}'_{ij}) \tag{8}$$

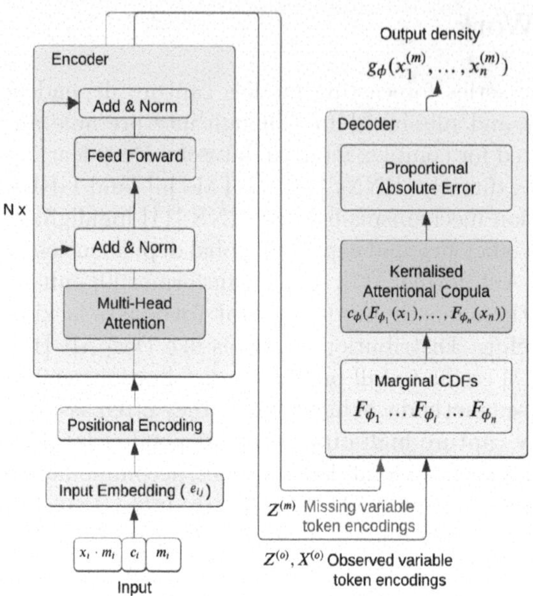

Fig. 1. T-PAKC Architecture.

Decoder

Let $Z^{(m)} \stackrel{\text{def}}{=} \{\boldsymbol{z}_1^{(m)}, \ldots, \boldsymbol{z}_{n_m}^{(m)}\}$, $Z^{(o)} \stackrel{\text{def}}{=} \{\boldsymbol{z}_1^{(o)}, \ldots, \boldsymbol{z}_{n_o}^{(o)}\}$, $X^{(m)} \stackrel{\text{def}}{=} \{x_1^{(m)}, \ldots, x_{n_m}^{(m)}\}$ and $X^{(o)} \stackrel{\text{def}}{=} \{x_1^{(o)}, \ldots, x_{n_o}^{(o)}\}$ represent the encodings and values of unobserved and observed variables. The goal is to estimate the joint distribution:

$$g_\phi(x_1^{(m)}, \ldots, x_{n_m}^{(m)}) \stackrel{\text{def}}{=} c_{\phi_c}(F_{\phi_1}(x_1^{(m)}), \ldots, F_{\phi_{n_m}}(x_{n_m}^{(m)})) \cdot \prod_{i=1}^{n_m} f_{\phi_i}(x_i^{(m)}) \tag{9}$$

This approach entails modeling the marginal and copula densities separately. Since the parameter set ϕ is derived from the decoder using $X^{(o)}, Z^{(o)}, Z^{(m)}$ as input, the resulting joint density is conditioned on the observed variables.

4.1 Marginal Distributions

T-PAKC models the marginals using a normalizing flow approach. Specifically, each marginal transformation F_{ϕ_i} is computed via Deep Sigmoidal Flows (DSF) [7], which employs a hypernetwork HN_{θ_F}) to generate flow parameters:

$$\phi_i = HN_{\theta_F}(\boldsymbol{z}_i^{(m)}), \quad u_i = DSF_{\phi_i}(x_i) \tag{10}$$

Here, u_i is the probability integral transform of x_i, and each x_i receives unique flow paramters. Note that DSF is preferred for its flexibility in modeling a wide range of univariate distributions [1,7].

4.2 Copula Distribution

Let $\boldsymbol{\pi} = [\pi_1, \ldots, \pi_{n_m}]$ denote a permutation of $\{1, 2, \ldots, n_m\}$. The copula c_{ϕ_c} can be factorized as:

$$c_{\phi_c^\pi}(u_1, \ldots, u_{n_m}) = c_{\phi_{c1}^\pi}(u_{\pi_1}) \times c_{\phi_{c2}^\pi}(u_{\pi_2}|u_{\pi_1}) \times \ldots \times c_{\phi_{cn_m}^\pi}(u_{\pi_{n_m}}|u_{\pi_1}, \ldots, u_{\pi_{n_m-1}}) \quad (11)$$

Assuming $c_{\phi_{c1}}(u_{\pi_1}) = U_{[0,1]}$, the remaining conditional copulas are estimated via attention-based mechanisms. This marks a major departure from TACTiS, which uses a non-parametric piecewise-constant approximation. TACTiS has three drawbacks: (i) difficulty overwriting trivial copulas without extensive training data, (ii) bin sparsity due to hard discretization, and (iii) discontinuities in the gradient. We resolve these by adopting a non-parametric Gaussian kernel estimator. Let $\{c_1, c_2, \ldots, c_\delta\}$ be the kernel centers and δ the bandwidth. We compute weights as:

$$w_{\pi_i j} = \exp\left(-\frac{(u_{\pi_i} - c_j)^2}{2\sigma^2}\right) \quad (12)$$

and

$$\hat{w}_{\pi_i j} = \frac{w_{\pi_i j}}{\sum_{k=1}^{\delta} w_{\pi_i k}} \quad (13)$$

Then, the conditional copula is estimated via a weighted sum:

$$c_{\phi_{c\pi_{n_m}}^\pi}(u_{\pi_{n_m}}|u_{\pi_1}, \ldots, u_{\pi_{n_m-1}}) = \sum_{j=1}^{\delta} \hat{w}_{\pi_{n_m} j} \cdot L_{c_j}(u_{\pi_{n_m}}|u_{\pi_1}, u_{\pi_2}, \ldots, u_{\pi_{n_m-1}}; c_{\phi_{c\pi_{n_m}}, j}) \quad (14)$$

The attention-based transformation to compute these parameters is summarized in Algorithm 1.

4.3 Permutation Invariant Copula Training Objective

Define $\Theta \stackrel{\text{def}}{=} \{\theta_{enc}, \theta_{dec}\}$ as all learnable parameters. Training minimizes the negative log-likelihood over data samples and random permutations $\pi \in \Pi$:

$$\underset{\Theta}{\operatorname{argmin}} \underset{\substack{\mathbf{x}\sim\mathbf{X} \\ \pi\sim\Pi}}{\mathbb{E}} - \log g_{\phi^\pi}(x_1^{(m)}, \ldots, x_{n_m}^{(m)}) \quad (15)$$

To ensure permutation invariance, we apply Jensen's inequality:

$$\begin{aligned} \underset{\substack{\mathbf{x}\sim\mathbf{X} \\ \pi\sim\Pi}}{\mathbb{E}} - \log g_{\phi^\pi}(x_1^{(m)}, \ldots, x_{n_m}^{(m)}) &= \underset{\mathbf{x}\sim\mathbf{X}}{\mathbb{E}} - \frac{1}{|\Pi|}\sum_{\pi\in\Pi} \log g_{\phi^\pi}(x_1^{(m)}, \ldots, x_{n_m}^{(m)}) \\ &\geq \underset{\mathbf{x}\sim\mathbf{X}}{\mathbb{E}} - \log\left[\frac{1}{|\Pi|}\sum_{\pi\in\Pi} g_{\phi^\pi}(x_1^{(m)}, \ldots, x_{n_m}^{(m)})\right] \end{aligned} \quad (16)$$

Equality is achieved only if all $g_{\phi^\pi}(x_1^{(m)}, \ldots, x_{n_m}^{(m)}) = g_\phi(x_1^{(m)}, \ldots, x_{n_m}^{(m)}), \forall \pi \in \Pi$, i.e., when the model is permutation-invariant. Because the first marginal copula is fixed to $U_{[0,1]}$, the full joint copula is valid.

Algorithm 1. Attention Transformation of $z_{\pi_i}^{(m)}$ to z'' conditioned on all predecessor variables in the permutation

Input: $\{z_1^{(o)}, \ldots, z_{n_o}^{(o)}, z_1^{(m)}, \ldots, z_{\pi_{i-1}}^{(m)}\}$, $\{u_1^{(o)}, \ldots, u_{n_o}^{(o)}, u_{\pi_1}^{(m)}, \ldots, u_{\pi_{i-1}}^{(m)}\}$, Multilayer Perceptrons (MLP) Key_{θ_k}, Value_{θ_v}, and Query_{θ_q} parameterised by θ_k, θ_v, and θ_q.

Output: $z'' \in \mathbb{R}^{d_{attn}}$

```
for each attention layer do
    Calculate keys k ∈ R^{d_attn}, values v ∈ R^{d_attn} using k = Key_{θ_k}(z, u), v = Value_{θ_v}(z, u) for all element pairs (z, u). Concatenate to form matrices K, V.
    Calculate q ∈ R^{d_attn} using q = Query_{θ_q}(z_{π_i}^{(m)})
    z' = LayerNorm(V^T Softmax(Kq) + z_{π_i}^{(m)})
    z'' = LayerNorm(FeedForward_{θ_ff}(z') + z'
    z_{π_i}^{(m)} = z''
end for
return z_{π_i}^{(m)}
```

4.4 Proportional Absolute Error (PAE)

After resolving bin-related instabilities, we address convergence slowdown due to flat likelihood regions. In this paper, we introduce Proportional Absolute Error (PAE) to penalize mismatch in dependency structure.

Let the output logits O of the final attention layer be a vector of $[b \times n_m \times \delta]$, where b is the batch number, and δ is the bin resolution. The prediction of the trained joint distribution can be computed as a weighted sum of the bin centers with each weight obtained by normalizing the logits using softmax. Let p_{ij} be the prediction for the k-th batch and j-th variable and c_i is the center of the i-th bin:

$$p_{kj} = \sum_{i=1}^{\delta} \text{Softmax}(O_{kji}) \cdot c_i \tag{17}$$

For both the predictions p and the probability integral transformed true values $u \stackrel{\text{def}}{=} \{u_{\pi_1}, \ldots, u_{\pi_n}\}$, the batch specific proportions can be calculated as follows:

$$\text{prop}(p_{k\pi_j}) = \frac{p_{k\pi_j}}{\sum_{s=1}^{n_m} p_{k\pi_s}} \tag{18}$$

Assuming non-trival dependencies, as the number of modelled variables n_m increases, the probability of exact proportional equality across all variables approaches zero **while the values are not the same**:

$$\lim_{n_m \to \infty} P\left(\frac{p_{k\pi_j}}{\sum_{i=1}^{n_m} p_{k\pi_i}} = \frac{u_{k\pi_j}}{\sum_{i=1}^{n_m} u_{k\pi_i}}, \forall j \text{ while } p_{k\pi_j} \neq u_{k\pi_j}\right) = 0 \tag{19}$$

This is a reasonable assumption since PAE is a proxy estimating the difference in dependency structures modelled by the underlying joint distributions of the predictions and true values. Next, upon obtaining the element-wise absolute difference between the predictions and true values,

$$\mathrm{D}_{k\pi_j} = |\mathrm{prop}(p_{k\pi_j}) - \mathrm{prop}(u_{k\pi_j})| \tag{20}$$

The proportional error can be calculated as the sum of each element's absolute difference passed through a penalty function $y(x)$ with the penalty constant α being a learnable hyperparameter that adjusts the sensitivity to deviations:

$$PAE_k = \sum_{j=1}^{n_m} y(D_{k\pi_j}) \qquad y(D_{kj}) = \frac{\alpha \cdot D_{kj}}{\sqrt{1 - {D_{kj}}^2}} \tag{21}$$

Note that by construction, $\sum_{j=1}^{n_m} y(D_{k\pi_j}) = \sum_{j=1}^{n_m} y(D_{kæ}), \forall \pi \in \Pi$. This means that PAE_k itself is permutation invariant, preserving the validity of the proof and thus the copula. Finally, we look at the choice of $y(x)$. For the domain $0 < D_{kj} \leq 1$ representing valid absolute values for ratio differences, PAE asymptotes to positive infinity as D_{kj} approaches 1 while having a single minimum at $D_{kj} = 0$. This satisfies our requirement to increasingly punish the model when forecasts' ratio deviates too much while minimizing the penalty for small deviations.

$$y'(D_{kj}) = \frac{\alpha}{(1 - {D_{kj}}^2)^{3/2}}, \quad y''(D_{kj}) = \frac{3\alpha \cdot D_{kj}}{(1 - {D_{kj}}^2)^{5/2}} \tag{22}$$

We further look at the first and second derivatives of the penalty function. Specifically, for the range $[0, 1)$ the second derivative is always positive, showing that PAE introduces a convex curvature to the loss landscape. Incorporating the assumption in Eq. 19, previously flat regions with small gradients is now likely to possess steeper gradients. This completes the final optimization objective:

$$\underset{\Theta}{\operatorname{argmin}} \underset{\mathbf{x} \sim \mathbf{X}}{\mathbb{E}} \left[-\log\left(g_\phi(x_1, \ldots, x_{n_m})\right) + \sum_{j=1}^{n_m} y(D_{k\pi_j}) \right] \tag{23}$$

To obtain the best results, α should be scaled appropriately to prevent it overpowering the likelihood loss. We examine the sensitivity of α in detail in Sect. 7.

5 Experimental Setting

In our experimental evaluation, the primary objective is to assess whether the proposed training enhancements in T-PAKC—namely the kernelized copula estimator and the proportional absolute error (PAE) regularizer—lead to better model performance, convergence, and generalization across diverse real-world forecasting tasks. We evaluate this along three axes: (i) forecast accuracy under uncertainty, using standard probabilistic metrics; (ii) training dynamics, i.e., convergence speed and stability of optimization; and (iii) robustness and scalability across datasets of varying size, resolution, and complexity.

5.1 Datasets

We evaluate our models on five real-world datasets from the Monash Time Series Forecasting Repository [5], chosen to represent diverse domains and temporal characteristics shown in Table 1. These datasets were also used in prior work on probablistic multivariate time series modeling: [1,3,12,13]. Importantly, the datasets span different levels of temporal resolution, forecast horizons, and degrees of dependency, providing a comprehensive testbed for evaluating multivariate uncertainty modeling.

Table 1. Dataset Specification

Abbreviation	Monash Dataset Code Name	Frequency	Number of Series	Prediction Length
Electricity	electricity_hourly	hour	321	24
FredMD	fred_md	month	107	12
KDD	kdd_cup_2018_without_missing	hour	270	48
Solar	solar_10min	10 min	137	72
Traffic	traffic	hour	862	24

5.2 Baseline Models

We compare our T-PAKC and its curriculum-trained variant T-PAKC-2 against the following six baselines with a diverse set of modeling strategies on autoregressive, flow-based, attention-based, and copula-based: (i) TACTiS [3] - Transformer-attentional copula model; our main reference point, (ii) TACTiS-2 [1] - An enhanced variant using curriculum training that reduces computational cost, (iii) TempFlow [13] - Probabilistic model using invertible normalizing flows, (iv) TimeGrad [12] - Autoregressive diffusion model for probabilistic forecasting, (v) GPVar [15] - Gaussian process-based copula model with low-rank approximation, and (vi) iTransformer [9] - Deterministic Transformer adapted to probabilistic forecasts via Monte Carlo sampling.

5.3 Evaluation Metrics

We use two standard distributional scoring rules to assess model quality:

- Continuous Ranked Probability Score (CRPS) [3]: Measures the accuracy of the predicted cumulative distribution function (CDF) against the empirical CDF for each individual time series. Lower CRPS indicates sharper and better calibrated forecasts. For random variable X_{ij} with series number i and time stamp j:

$$CRPS(X_{ij}, x_{ij}) = \underset{X_{ij}}{\mathrm{E}} \left[|X_{ij} - x_{ij}|\right] - \frac{1}{2} \underset{X_{ij}, x'_{ij}}{\mathrm{E}} \left[|X_{ij} - x'_{ij}|\right] \tag{24}$$

  In our multivariate setting, variable X_{ij} is replaced by S_j which is the summation across all series' dimensions. This sum is denoted CRPS-Sum.

– Energy Score (ES) [4]: Measures the accuracy of the joint distribution by comparing predicted samples to observed values in multivariate space, β set to 1 and $||.||_F$ being the Frobenius matrix norm.

$$ES(X, \mathbf{x}) = \mathop{\mathrm{E}}_{\mathbf{X}}\left[||\mathbf{X} - \mathbf{y}||_F^{\beta}\right] - \frac{1}{2}\mathop{\mathrm{E}}_{\mathbf{X},\mathbf{X}'}\left[||\mathbf{X} - \mathbf{X}'||_F^{\beta}\right] \tag{25}$$

CRPS-Sum emphasizes marginal calibration, while ES captures joint dependency accuracy—making them complementary for evaluating multivariate copula models. Standard errors are estimated using the Newey-West estimator [10].

5.4 Training Protocol and Implementation

The evaluation process consists of training, validation, and test windows. In our experiments, we train all models exclusively on the backtest ID 0 training split and evaluate them on the test windows of all six backtests, thereby preserving temporal integrity and testing generalization across unseen windows. Importantly, we remove early stopping mechanisms used in earlier work to avoid skewing convergence behavior due to arbitrary stopping criteria. Instead, we allocate a fixed training budget of 50 epochs, with the number of batches per epoch fixed at 512 for all models. This decision is critical, as one of the main objectives of our study is to evaluate training dynamics and convergence behavior under realistic computational constraints. By standardizing the number of updates, we isolate the effect of model architecture and training objectives, particularly the effect of the kernelized copula and PAE loss components. Model hyperparameters are tuned via random search based on prior configurations used in TACTiS [9] and held fixed across datasets to avoid overfitting to any particular benchmark. For T-PAKC, we set the Gaussian kernel bandwidth σ to 3 and the proportional absolute error (PAE) penalty constant α to 0.03 across all datasets. These values are later examined in detail in the ablation study.

6 Result

We evaluate the proposed Transformer-based Proportional Attentional Kernelized Copula (T-PAKC) in two complementary stages: a controlled synthetic experiment to examine its ability to recover known dependency structures, and an extensive evaluation across five real-world multivariate time series datasets.

6.1 Synthetic Case Study: Recovering Ground-Truth Copulas

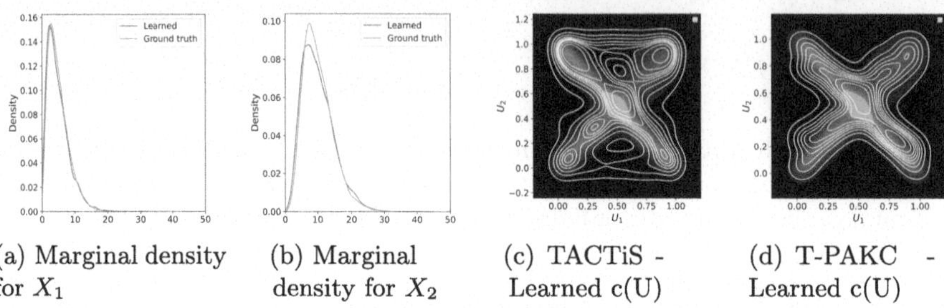

(a) Marginal density for X_1 (b) Marginal density for X_2 (c) TACTiS - Learned c(U) (d) T-PAKC - Learned c(U)

Fig. 2. Density Plots for Marginal Distributions and Copula Structure.

We begin with the ground-truth recovery experiment, where samples are generated from a bivariate distribution with known marginals $X_1 \sim \chi^2(5)$ and $X_2 \sim \chi^2(10)$, and a joint copula defined as a uniform mixture of two Clayton copulas with parameters θ set to 9.75 and -0.99 respectively. However, we differ from [3] by constraining each model's loss objective to train for a maximum of 8000 iterations. To ensure fairness, the seed and all shared hyper-parameters were identical between TACTiS and T-PAKC, except that T-PAKC replaces the discrete piecewise constant copula representation with a continuous Gaussian kernel estimator. The proportional absolute error term is disabled in this test to isolate the effect of the kernelized copula on convergence. As shown in Fig. 2, T-PAKC succeeds in recovering the underlying copula structure, with the learned density contours (white lines) closely matching the ground-truth (colored heatmap). In contrast, TACTiS fails to refine the initial trivial copula, showing sparse and inconsistent contours. This validates T-PAKC's ability to learn complex dependency patterns more efficiently. Despite the concern that smoothing via the Gaussian kernel might dilute expressive power, the results show that expressiveness is preserved, and convergence is substantially improved.

Table 2. CRPS-Sum Results with Std Errors (Newey-West Estimator)

Method	Electricity	KDD	Traffic	Solar-10min	Fred-md
GPVar	$0.2866_{\pm 0.0098}$	$0.3542_{\pm 0.0070}$	$0.6681_{\pm 0.0021}$	$1.1139_{\pm 0.0050}$	$0.0505_{\pm 0.0114}$
TimeGrad	$0.1618_{\pm 0.0061}$	$0.4672_{\pm 0.0722}$	$0.3780_{\pm 0.0031}$	$0.4935_{\pm 0.0217}$	$0.0375_{\pm 0.0076}$
TempFlow	$0.0745_{\pm 0.0173}$	-	$0.4398_{\pm 0.0072}$	$81.5761_{\pm 0.5903}$	$0.1000_{\pm 0.0092}$
iTransformer	$0.0483_{\pm 0.0217}$	$0.2981_{\pm 0.0319}$	$0.2945_{\pm 0.0108}$	$0.6708_{\pm 0.0013}$	$\mathbf{0.0357}_{\pm 0.0095}$
TACiS	$0.0274_{\pm 0.0127}$	$0.3088_{\pm 0.0246}$	$\mathbf{0.0936}_{\pm 0.0070}$	$0.3425_{\pm 0.0997}$	$0.0653_{\pm 0.0173}$
TACiS-2	$0.0567_{\pm 0.0185}$	$0.3208_{\pm 0.0135}$	$0.2167_{\pm 0.0063}$	$0.3609_{\pm 0.0366}$	$0.0389_{\pm 0.0066}$
T-PAKC	$\mathbf{0.0254}_{\pm 0.0119}$	$\mathbf{0.2937}_{\pm 0.0064}$	$0.0950_{\pm 0.0091}$	$\mathbf{0.3357}_{\pm 0.0856}$	$0.0521_{\pm 0.0064}$
T-PAKC-2	$0.0525_{\pm 0.0148}$	$0.2951_{\pm 0.0176}$	$0.1845_{\pm 0.0070}$	$0.4866_{\pm 0.1134}$	$0.0361_{\pm 0.0068}$

Table 3. Energy Score with Std Errors (Newey-West Estimator)

	Electricity	KDD	Traffic	Solar-10min	Fred-md
GPVar	$312791_{\pm 7746}$	$3153.37_{\pm 316.87}$	$6.96_{\pm 0.12}$	$787.93_{\pm 71.48}$	$969396_{\pm 197160}$
TimeGrad	$175289_{\pm 9453}$	$5144.53_{\pm 1072.65}$	$6.07_{\pm 0.13}$	$463.90_{\pm 27.85}$	$824245_{\pm 177287}$
TempFlow	$119482_{\pm 10617}$	-	$6.30_{\pm 0.09}$	$178554_{\pm 18348}$	$1853906_{\pm 134833}$
iTransformer	$101613_{\pm 13116}$	$3027.45_{\pm 281.91}$	$5.13_{\pm 0.08}$	$639.19_{\pm 51.77}$	$\mathbf{734679}_{\pm 175443}$
TACiS	$55851_{\pm 10232}$	$3109.30_{\pm 348.77}$	$3.89_{\pm 0.40}$	$314.07_{\pm 37.58}$	$1215861_{\pm 231335}$
TACiS-2	$104269_{\pm 12296}$	$3049.43_{\pm 359.07}$	$4.10_{\pm 0.05}$	$311.69_{\pm 4.73}$	$887010_{\pm 168166}$
T-PAKC	$\mathbf{53688}_{\pm 9501}$	$3062.44_{\pm 348.93}$	$\mathbf{3.39}_{\pm 0.25}$	$\mathbf{305.36}_{\pm 20.88}$	$996184_{\pm 93835}$
T-PAKC-2	$84729_{\pm 8951}$	$\mathbf{3012.29}_{\pm 367.72}$	$3.96_{\pm 0.03}$	$331.23_{\pm 23.26}$	$767496_{\pm 157387}$

6.2 Overall Results from Eight Models

Tables 2 and 3 summarize the performance of T-PAKC and its curriculum-based variant, T-PAKC-2, across five diverse real-world datasets varying in temporal resolution, forecasting horizon, and scale. Evaluation metrics include CRPS-Sum for marginal accuracy and Energy Score for joint distribution quality. Overall, T-PAKC and T-PAKC-2 consistently achieve superior or competitive results over the six baseline models on four out of five datasets. T-PAKC alone reduces CRPS-Sum by an average of 8.6%, with improvements reaching up to 20%, while its Energy Score drops by 7.8% on average and up to 18%. Similarly, T-PAKC-2 reduces CRPS-Sum by an average of 9.4% (up to 15%) and the Energy Score by 9.2% (up to 19%) compared to TACTiS-2.

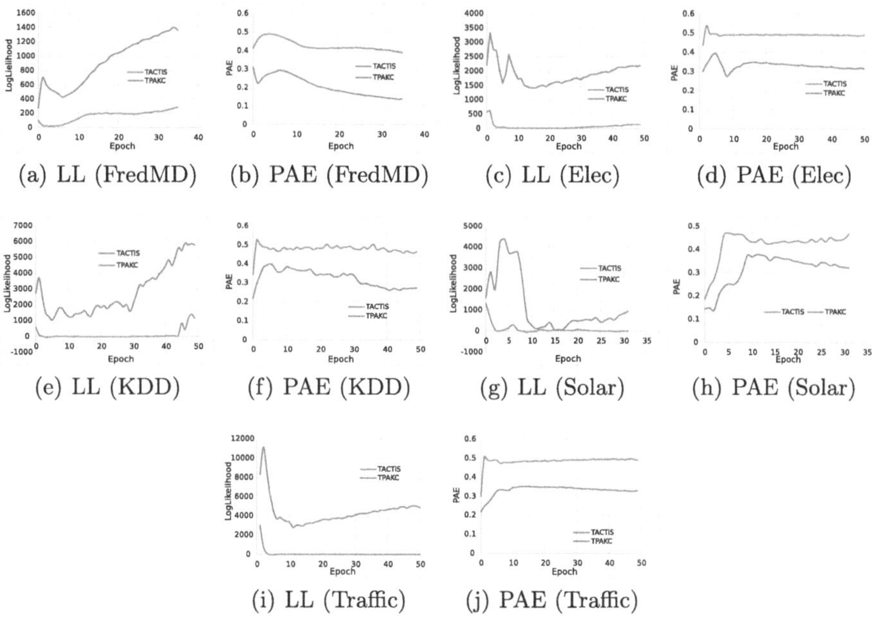

(a) LL (FredMD) (b) PAE (FredMD) (c) LL (Elec) (d) PAE (Elec)
(e) LL (KDD) (f) PAE (KDD) (g) LL (Solar) (h) PAE (Solar)
(i) LL (Traffic) (j) PAE (Traffic)

Fig. 3. Training Dynamics for T-PAKC and TACTiS.

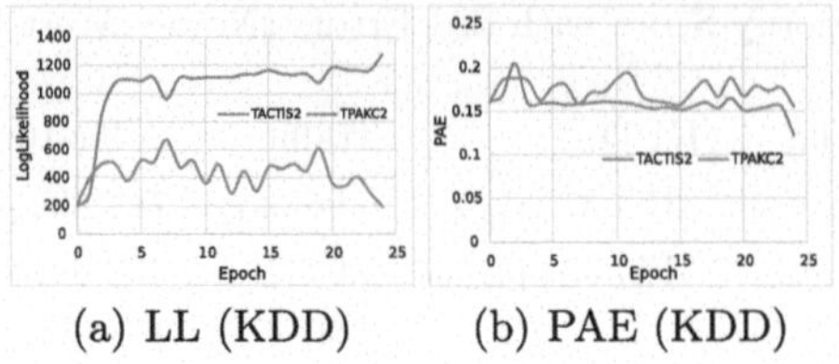

(a) LL (KDD) (b) PAE (KDD)

Fig. 4. Training Dynamics for T-PAKC 2 and TACTiS 2.

To better understand these performance gains, we analyze the training dynamics of TACTiS and T-PAKC by tracking average log-likelihood (LL) and Proportional Absolute Error (PAE) over training epochs (Fig. 3). The results reveal that T-PAKC significantly enhances optimization behavior. It can be seen that TACTiS's LL plateaues early in training, supports the claim that the original loss objective often prioritizes fitting marginal distributions over the joint distribution's likelihood. Unlike TACTiS, T-PAKC exhibits a clear upward trajectory with consistently higher LL values throughout training. At the same time, T-PAKC maintains lower PAE across epochs, with a more stable and monotonic decrease. These show the effectiveness of the revised training objective in leveraging optimization steps more effectively to navigate the loss landscape. The progressive decline in PAE values shown in the figure further supports its utility. This downward trend is noteworthy because it suggests that minimizing PAE aligns well with the optimization of the log-likelihood objective. Therefore, incorporating PAE into the loss function not only does not cause conflict with the primary objective but also addresses the issue of early convergence and training stagnation, reinforcing its role as a complementary and stabilizing regularizer.

We further examine the impact of our improvements on TACTiS-2, a variant of TACTiS that separates marginal and copula training phases via curriculum learning. As shown in Figs. 4a and 4b (KDD dataset), T-PAKC-2 avoids the high-variance spikes in log-likelihood observed in TACTiS-2, rising smoothly to 1400, while TACTiS-2 fluctuates between 0 and 1000. The corresponding PAE values for T-PAKC-2 steadily drop to 0.1, whereas TACTiS-2 exhibits noisy behavior, failing to fall below 0.2. This further illustrates that the kernelized copula and PAE regularization stabilize training even in curriculum-based frameworks.

7 Ablation Study

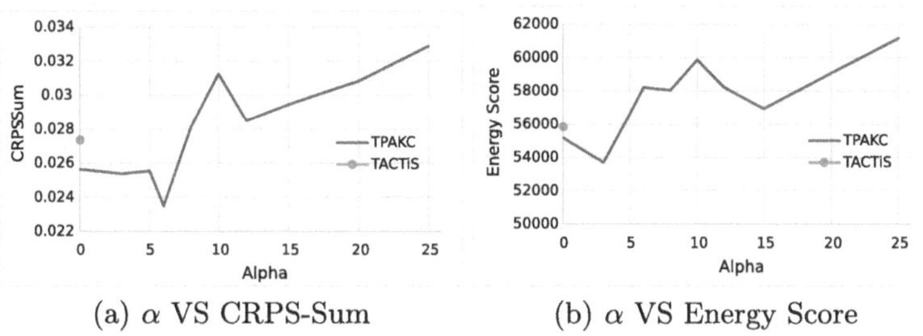

(a) α VS CRPS-Sum (b) α VS Energy Score

Fig. 5. Effects of varying Penalty Constant α on Electric.

To examine the behavior of T-PAKC's training objective, we analyze the sensitivity of the penalty constant α using the `electricity_hourly` dataset, where T-PAKC shows initially unstable but eventually stable likelihood curves (Fig. 3c). Figures 5a and 5b illustrate how CRPS-Sum and Energy scores vary with α. Even at $\alpha = 0$, where the PAE regularizer is inactive, the Gaussian kernel estimator alone improves performance. Two key trends emerge: (1) high values of α ($\gtrsim 8$) degrade both metrics, often surpassing TACTiS's errors, suggesting that α should be introduced conservatively; and (2) while CRPS-Sum and Energy are correlated, optimizing one does not always improve the other. For $\alpha \leq 5$, both metrics benefit, but in the range of 5–8, the model prioritizes marginal accuracy (CRPS) at the cost of capturing inter-series dependencies (Energy), likely due to gradient instability. This highlights the trade-off inherent in copula-based models between fitting marginals and modeling joint structure. T-PAKC offers a tunable mechanism to improve model robustness and convergence.

8 Discussion on Interpretability and Transparency

T-PAKC enables interpretability and transparency through two complementary mechanisms: attention-based dependency modeling and proportional structure regularization. The attention-based copula module allows each predicted variable to condition its joint distribution on selected context variables via learnable attention weights. These weights are not only central to the model's probabilistic reasoning but also offer a direct window into which observed variables most influence each prediction. By visualizing them as attention heatmaps, we can uncover structured patterns in the data—for example, cross-series influences in electricity demand across substations or lead-lag effects in economic indicators. These visual cues allow practitioners to validate whether the model is learning plausible dependencies or spurious correlations.

The Proportional Absolute Error (PAE) regularizer adds another layer of interpretability by encouraging forecasts to maintain realistic inter-variable proportionality—that is, preserving dominant-minor relationships across dimensions. We illustrate this using proportionality plots, which compare the predicted and actual ratio structures across variables at each time step. These plots reveal that T-PAKC better preserves underlying relationships, even under volatile or shifted distributions where other models degrade. This form of structural interpretability is particularly useful in regulated domains where not only prediction accuracy but also relational consistency matters.

Together, these interpretability tools enhance transparency, support human validation, and increase the model's trustworthiness—especially in high-stakes applications like healthcare, energy, or finance, where understanding how a model arrives at a forecast is often as critical as the forecast itself.

9 Conclusion

This paper presents T-PAKC, a Transformer-based model for multivariate probabilistic time series forecasting that integrates a kernelized copula density estimator with a proportional absolute error (PAE) regularizer. These components address key limitations in copula-based models, including training instability, sparse gradients, and weak dependency modeling. Evaluated on five real-world datasets, T-PAKC consistently surpasses baselines like TACTiS in both marginal and joint forecasting accuracy, while achieving faster and more stable convergence—making it suitable for resource-limited settings. The Gaussian kernel estimator enhances gradient smoothness for better optimization, while the PAE regularizer promotes consistency in inter-variable dependencies critical to downstream performance. Together, the resulting model is both expressive and robust.

References

1. Ashok, A., Marcotte, É., Zantedeschi, V., Chapados, N., Drouin, A.: Tactis-2: better, faster, simpler attentional copulas for multivariate time series. In: Proceedings of the Twelfth International Conference on Learning Representations (2024)
2. Cho, K., et al.: Learning phrase representations using RNN encoder-decoder for statistical machine translation. In: Proceedings of the 2014 Conference on Empirical Methods in Natural Language Processing (EMNLP), pp. 1724–1734 (2014)
3. Drouin, A., Marcotte, É., Chapados, N.: Tactis: transformer-attentional copulas for time series. In: Proceedings of the International Conference on Machine Learning, pp. 5447–5493 (2022)
4. Gneiting, T., Raftery, A.E.: Strictly proper scoring rules, prediction, and estimation. J. Am. Stat. Assoc. **102**(477), 359–378 (2007)
5. Godahewa, R.W., Bergmeir, C., Webb, G.I., Hyndman, R., Montero-Manso, P.: Monash time series forecasting archive. In: Proceedings of the Neural Information Processing Systems Track on Datasets and Benchmarks (2021)
6. Hochreiter, S., Schmidhuber, J.: Long short-term memory. Neural Comput. **9**(8), 1735–1780 (1997)

7. Huang, C.W., Krueger, D., Lacoste, A., Courville, A.: Neural autoregressive flows. In: Proceedings of the 35th International Conference on Machine Learning, vol. 80, pp. 2078–2087. PMLR (2018)
8. Le, C.P., Cannella, C., Hasan, A., Ng, Y., Tarokh, V.: Perceiving copulas for multimodal time series forecasting. In: Proceedings of the Winter Simulation Conference, WSC 2024, pp. 690–701. IEEE Press (2025)
9. Liu, Y., et al.: iTransformer: inverted transformers are effective for time series forecasting. In: Proceedings of The Twelfth International Conference on Learning Representations (2024)
10. Newey, W.K., West, K.D.: Automatic lag selection in covariance matrix estimation. Rev. Econ. Stud. **61**(4), 631–653 (1994)
11. Qin, Y., Song, D., Cheng, H., Cheng, W., Jiang, G., Cottrell, G.W.: A dual-stage attention-based recurrent neural network for time series prediction. In: Proceedings of the 26th International Joint Conference on Artificial Intelligence, pp. 2627–2633. AAAI Press (2017)
12. Rasul, K., Seward, C., Schuster, I., Vollgraf, R.: Autoregressive denoising diffusion models for multivariate probabilistic time series forecasting. In: Proceedings of the International Conference on Machine Learning, pp. 8857–8868. PMLR (2021)
13. Rasul, K., Sheikh, A.S., Schuster, I., Bergmann, U.M., Vollgraf, R.: Multivariate probabilistic time series forecasting via conditioned normalizing flows. In: Proceedings of the International Conference on Learning Representations (2021)
14. Rumelhart, D.E., Hinton, G.E., Williams, R.J.: Learning representations by back-propagating errors. Nature **323**(6088), 533–536 (1986)
15. Salinas, D., Bohlke-Schneider, M., Callot, L., Medico, R., Gasthaus, J.: High-dimensional multivariate forecasting with low-rank gaussian copula processes, vol. 32, pp. 6824–6834. Curran Associates, Inc., Red Hook, NY, USA (2019)
16. Salinas, D., Flunkert, V., Gasthaus, J., Januschowski, T.: Deepar: probabilistic forecasting with autoregressive recurrent networks. Int. J. Forecast. **36**(3), 1181–1191 (2020)
17. Wu, H., Xu, J., Wang, J., Long, M.: Autoformer: decomposition transformers with auto-correlation for long-term series forecasting. Adv. Neural. Inf. Process. Syst. **34**, 22419–22430 (2021)
18. Zhou, H., et al.: Informer: beyond efficient transformer for long sequence time-series forecasting. In: Proceedings of the AAAI Conference on Artificial Intelligence, vol. 35, pp. 11106–11115 (2021)

Author Index

I. Awan et al. (Eds.): WISE 2025, LNCS 16368, pp. 549–551, 2026.
https://doi.org/10.1007/978-981-95-7251-9

The manufacturer's authorised representative in the EU is Springer Nature Customer Service Centre GmbH, Europaplatz 3, 69115 Heidelberg, Germany. If you have any concerns regarding our products, please contact ProductSafety@springernature.com

Printed and bound by CPI Group (UK) Ltd, Croydon, CR0 4YY
07/07/2026
02160917-0017